AMSCO® ADVANCED PLACEMENT®
UNITED STATES HISTORY

John J. Newman, Ed.D., served for many years as an Advanced Placement® U.S. History teacher and the Department Coordinator of Art, Foreign Language, and Social Studies at Naperville North High School, Naperville, Illinois. He continued his career as Adjunct Professor of History at the College of DuPage and Adjunct Assistant Professor of History Education at Illinois State University.

John M. Schmalbach, Ed.D., taught Advanced Placement® U.S. History and was Social Studies Department head at Abraham Lincoln High School, Philadelphia, Pennsylvania. He continued his career as Adjunct Assistant Professor at Temple University.

AMSCO® ADVANCED PLACEMENT®
UNITED STATES HISTORY

Third Edition

John J. Newman
John M. Schmalbach

Perfection Learning®

This book is dedicated to our wives,
Anne Newman and Rosemarie Schmalbach;
our children, Louise Newman,
and John, Suzanne, and Robert Schmalbach;
and our students, who share our study of America's past.

Reviewers

William McKee
Former Chairperson, Social Studies,
Brockport High School, Brockport, New York

Stephen A. Shultz
Former Social Studies Coordinator,
Rocky Point Public Schools, New York

Acknowledgments

"First Fig" by Edna St. Vincent Millay. First published in *First Figs from Thistles* (Harper & Bros., 1922).

© 2020 Perfection Learning®

Please visit our websites at:
www.amscopub.com and *www.perfectionlearning.com*

When ordering this book, please specify:
Softcover: ISBN 978-1-5311-2912-5 or **R742201**
Hardcover: ISBN 978-1-5311-2913-2 or **R742206**
eBook: ISBN 978-1-5311-2914-9 or **R7422D**

1 2 3 4 5 6 SBI 24 23 22 21 20 19

Printed in the United States of America

Contents

Preface

This update of *AMSCO® Advanced Placement® United States History* revises the recommendations in the Introduction for answering long essay questions and document-based questions, the practice short-answer questions in each chapter, and the content in Chapter 31 for events since 2016. It maintains the concise and accessible chapter content and other instructional content. The pagination remains compatible with all editions since 2014–2015.

Since 1998, this textbook has been used by hundreds of thousands of students in various ways. Many teachers have successfully used it as a core textbook in conjunction with college-level resources and supplemental materials. Others have used it as a supplemental text to bridge the gap between a college-level textbook and the needs of their AP® high school students. In addition, students have effectively used it on their own to support their study of the content. Given the diverse instructional settings across the nation, the most effective use of this textbook is an instructional decision best made by the educators responsible for their students' performance.

We are committed to an ongoing process to keep this textbook current and plan to incorporate any future changes as released by the College Board. It is good to remember that, as the College Board fine-tunes the curriculum and exam rubrics, the effective study of AP® U.S. History has not fundamentally changed for teachers and students. During this period of change, we are mindful of the issues associated with repeated updates of the text and the Answer Key. We encourage teachers to check the College Board website for the latest updates: AP® Central site (apcentral.collegeboard.com) and the Advances in AP® section (advancesinap.collegeboard.org).

The authors want to thank the staff of Perfection Learning Corporation for their support and the tireless effort they have put into the revision and updates of this text. We also appreciate the continued opportunity to support the efforts of high school students and teachers as they strive to meet the challenges of the Advanced Placement® U.S. History examination.

John Newman and John Schmalbach, March 2019

INTRODUCTION

Studying Advanced Placement®
United States History

Since 1998, the number of high school students taking the Advanced Placement® Exam in United States History has tripled. Students enroll in AP® U.S. History classes for many reasons:

- to demonstrate one's ability to succeed as a college undergraduate
- to become eligible for scholarships
- to save on college expenses by earning college credit
- to test out of introductory college courses
- to enrich one's high school experience

The placement and credit offered varies from college to college. The College Board's website provides a list of colleges and universities that normally use AP® examination grades for determining placement and credits.

Most students who have taken AP® courses report that they are more difficult than regular classes but are more interesting and worth the extra effort. The rewards of these challenging classes go beyond the placement and grades to include the development of lifelong reading, thinking, and writing skills and, for many students, an increased interest in and enjoyment of history.

Overview of the AP® U. S. History Exam

This edition of this textbook was revised to address the most recent changes to the *AP® United States History Course and Exam Description.* The revision places a greater focus on the history practices and reasoning skills used by historians and on historical themes and related concepts in order to deepen a student's understanding of U.S. history. Compared to previous exams, the 3-hour-and-15-minute exam includes more excerpts, images, and other data sources.

The AP® exam includes the following components, along with the amount of time allotted for each and the percentage each is weighted in the final grade:

- 55 Multiple-Choice Questions (MCQs)   55 minutes   40%
- 3 Short-Answer Questions (SAQs)   40 minutes   20%
- 1 Document-Based Question (DBQ)   60 minutes   25%
- 1 Long Essay Question (LEQ)   40 minutes   15%

The multiple-choice section still has the greatest weight in a student's final grade, but students' performance on recent exams suggests that working on writing skills may offer the greatest opportunity for improvement. Each of these components, along with a guide to sequential skill development, will be explained in this Introduction.

The College Board grades student performance on Advanced Placement® examinations, including the U.S. History exam, on a five-point scale:

- 5: Extremely well qualified
- 4: Well qualified
- 3: Qualified
- 2: Possibly qualified
- 1: No recommendation

An AP® grade of 3 or higher is usually considered evidence of mastery of course content similar to that demonstrated in a college-level introductory course in the same subject area. However, since the requirements of introductory courses may vary from college to college, some colleges may accept a 2 on the AP® History exam, while others may require a score of 4.

Unlike most classroom tests designed to measure mastery of a lesson or unit in which 90 percent or more correct may receive an "A," the AP® exams are deliberately constructed to provide a wider distribution of scores and higher reliability (the likelihood that test takers repeating the same exam will receive the same scores). AP® exams, while more difficult than most testing in high school, are also scored differently. The cutoff for a "qualified," or level 3, grade may range between 50 and 60 percent of the possible points. Only a small percentage of students will gain more than 80 percent of the possible points. Students who are having difficulty with a third or more of the questions on the practice AP® exams should not be discouraged. The exam is challenging, but like any challenge, if it is broken down into manageable steps it can be mastered.

How This Book Can Help

The goal of this textbook is to provide U.S. history students with the essential content and instructional materials to develop the knowledge, the history practices and reasoning skills, and the writing skills needed to understand U.S. history and to approach the past as historians do. These resources are found in the following sections of the book:

Introduction This section introduces students to the history practices and reasoning skills, course themes, and nine periods of the AP® U.S. History program. A step-by-step skill development guide explains how to answer the four types of questions found on the exam: (1) multiple choice, (2) short answer, (3) long essay, and (4) document-based.

Concise History The 31 chapters of essential historical content and accessible explanations of events form the heart of this textbook. The content reflects the revised AP® U.S. History curriculum. Each of the nine periods is introduced with a summary along with the AP® key concepts for that period.

Maps and Graphics Maps, charts, graphs, cartoons, photographs, and other visual materials are integrated into the text to help students practice their analytical skills.

Historical Perspectives At the end of the text of each chapter is a section that introduces conflicting interpretations about significant historical issues.

Key Terms by Themes In each chapter, a list of key names, places, and words, organized by theme, is included to aid in review.

Multiple-Choice Questions Each chapter contains three sets of source-based, multiple-choice questions to evaluate students' historical knowledge and skills using sources.

Short-Answer Questions Each chapter contains four sets of short-answer questions for review of the chapter and opportunities to apply AP® history practices and reasoning skills.

Long Essay Questions Periods 2 through 9 conclude with a review section that includes four or more long essay questions, depending on the number of chapters in the period. The long essay questions prompt students to deal with significant themes and to apply course reasoning and writing skills.

Document-Based Questions The reviews for periods 2 through 8 include one or two DBQs.

Practice Examination Following the final chapter is a complete practice examination using the current format.

Index The index is included to help locate key terms for review.

Answer Key A separate Answer Key is available from the publisher for teachers and other authorized users of the book.

The Study of AP® U.S. History

Historians attempt to give meaning to the past by collecting historical evidence and then explaining how these "facts" are connected. Historians interpret and organize a wide variety of evidence from both primary and secondary sources in order to understand the past. Students should develop their ability to analyze and use historical sources, to answer probing questions about past events, and to to demonstrate these abilities in their writing. There is no one "answer" for many historical questions, nor can one find all of the answers in any one historical source. AP® teachers and exam readers are looking for a student's ability to think about history and to support ideas with evidence.

AP® students should appreciate how both participants and historians differ in their interpretations of critical questions in U.S. history. The Historical

Perspectives feature in each chapter introduces readers to some of the issues raised by historians over time. AP® U.S. History does not require an advanced knowledge of historiography or, one might say, "the history of history." Nevertheless, prior knowledge of the richness of historical thought can add depth to a student's analysis of historical questions.

The study of AP® U.S. History includes three basic components that shape the course: (1) the practices and skills of history, (2) thematic analysis, and (3) the concepts and understandings of the nine periods that organize the content. These three components are explained below for orientation and future reference.

These components may strike some students as overwhelming at first. Mastering them takes time. Working on the skills and the understandings needs to be an ongoing part of the study of AP® U.S. History. The introduction provided here will become more helpful as a reference as the course proceeds.

How Historians Think

The Advanced Placement® History courses encourage students to think like historians. The practices and skills that historians use in researching and writing about historical events and developments are the foundation of the AP® U.S. History course and exam. Learning these skills and reasoning processes can be developed over a course of study, but an introduction to them is a good place to start.

- Historians need to be able to **analyze historical evidence** found in a wide variety of **primary sources** from written records to historical images and artifacts. Historians also need to explain and evaluate the evidence from **secondary sources,** especially the work of other historians with differing points of view.

- As historians research the evidence, they look for **connections** and patterns among historical events and developments. They use reasoning processes, such as making **comparisons**, studying **causation**, and analyzing **continuity and change** to find and test possible connections.

- Most historians communicate their findings through publications and presentations. This creative process takes the additional practice of **argument development,** which includes making a defensible claim and marshaling relevant and persuasive evidence to support an argument. Writing about history also challenges one to clarify and refine one's thinking about the subject or the question under study.

Historical Thinking Skills

The study of history includes the use of many thinking skills. Of these, AP® courses focus on six.

1. Developments and Processes The ability to identify and explain historical concepts, developments, and processes is fundamental to the analysis of historical evidence. For example, "salutary neglect" has proved a useful concept to describe and explain British behavior toward the American colonies before the 1750s. During that period colonists were relatively autonomous. That is, the British allowed colonies to govern themselves with minimal interference. Students need to be able to explain the historical concepts and developments, and provide specific historical evidence to illustrate or support such a historical concept or development. For example, a multiple-choice question on the AP® exam might ask, "Which of the following is the best example of British salutary neglect in the American colonies before 1750?"

2. Sourcing and Situations The use of historical evidence involves the ability to explain and evaluate diverse kinds of primary and secondary sources, including written works, data, images, and artifacts. Students need to be able to explain (1) the historical setting of the source, (2) its intended audience, (3) its purpose, and (4) the point of view of the original writer or creator. For example, an AP® exam question might ask, "Which of the following best reflects the point of view expressed by the author?" Another possible question is, "Briefly explain ONE characteristic of the intended audience for this image."

For secondary sources, this skill also involves understanding how particular circumstances might influence authors. Historians can "rewrite" history because their personal perspective or society's perspective changes, or because they discover new sources and information, and, above all, because they ask new questions.

3. Source Claims and Evidence The analysis of either primary or secondary sources also includes the ability to identify the author's argument and the evidence used to support it. For example, an AP® question might provide short quotations from two secondary sources about the causes of the American Revolution. The reading might be evaluated by a multiple-choice question such as, "Which of the following would best support the argument of historian A?" A short-answer question might ask, "Briefly explain ONE major difference between historian A's and historian B's historical interpretations." Questions can also ask students to discover patterns or trends in quantitative data found in charts and graphs.

4. Contextualization The skill of contextualization involves the ability to accurately and explicitly explain how a historical event, policy, or source fits into the broader historical picture, often on the regional, national, or global level. Placing the specifics of history into their larger context gives them additional usefulness and significance as historical evidence. Contextualization is evaluated through questions such as: "(The excerpt) best reflects which of the following developments in U.S. foreign policy?" or "The conditions shown in the image depict which of the following trends in the late 19th century?"

5. Making Connections This skill involves identifying and analyzing patterns and connections between and among historical developments and processes, and how one development or process relates to another. Making connections on the AP exam will used the three "reasoning processes" of comparisons, causation, and continuity and change (see below). For example, the developments of large-scale industrial production, concentration of wealth, and the labor movement, were taking place during the same period from 1865 to 1900. Are any patterns and connection common among these developments? The exam could ask in an essay question, "To what extent was the rise of labor unions related to the development of large corporations during the period from 1865 to 1900?"

6. Argumentation Argument development also includes the skill of using evidence effectively to support an argument. Students need to recognize that not all evidence has equal value in support of an argument. Writers need to select examples that are accurate and relevant to an argument. Making judgments about the use of relevant historical evidence is an essential skill in free-response questions on the AP® exam.

Again, the focus will be not on the simple recall of facts, but on a conceptual understanding of the evidence and the ability to link that understanding to the argument. For example, to support the argument about the impact of technology from 1865 to 1900, it is not enough to describe the technologies of the period. In addition, one should explain the connection of specific new technologies, such as railroads or electric power, to the changes in the economy. The AP exam also values the use of diverse and alternative evidence to qualify or modify an argument in order to develop a more complex insight into history.

Reasoning Processes

The study of history includes the use of several reasoning processes. Of these, AP® courses focus on three very important ones.

1. Comparison Thinking about comparison involves the ability to describe and evaluate similarities and differences between two or more historical developments in the same era or from different periods. This process also asks one to explain the relative significant of similarities and differences between historical developments. It also involves the ability to study a given historical event or development from multiple perspectives. Comparison is evaluated in questions such as, "The ideas expressed in the excerpt were most similar to those of which of the following?" or "Compare and contrast views of the United States' overseas expansion in the late 19th century." Expect AP® questions to test similarities and differences of conceptual understandings rather than simple recall.

2. Causation The study of causation is the primary tool of historians to explore the connections—both causes and effects—among events. Historians are often challenged to make judgments between primary and secondary causes and between short-term and long-term effects for developments such as the American Civil War. Students will need to not only identify causes or effects but also to explain the relationship. For example, it will not be enough to argue that slavery or states' rights was the primary cause of the Civil War; one must be able to explain the connections of specific evidence to one's position. At the AP® level, a causation question might ask, "Which of the following most strongly influenced A?" or "B contributed most directly to which of the following trends?" The use of causation as a reasoning skill is used with all historical thinking skills.

3. Continuity and Change over Time The study of history also involves the ability to describe and explain patterns that reveal both continuity and change over time. The study of themes especially lends itself to discovering continuity and change in varying lengths of time from a few decades to hundreds of years. For example, one might argue that President Washington's foreign policy from the 1790s continued as the standard for American foreign policy into the mid-20th century. The AP® exam might evaluate the understanding of continuity and change by asking, "Which of the following developments best represented the continuation of A?" or "Which of the following best represents a later example of the change B?" A more complex essay question can ask, "Evaluate the extent to which C contributed to maintaining continuity as well as fostering change in D." Responding to this item involves not only understanding an event but also its significance in longer trends in United States history.

Thematic Learning Objectives

Just as historians combine the use of multiple historical thinking skills and reasoning processes, they address multiple themes in their work. Questions on the AP® exam will focus on one or more of eight themes that recur thoughout U.S. history. Following are an analysis of each of the eight. The quotations are from the *AP® U.S. History Course and Exam Description.*

1. American and National Identity (NAT) "This theme focuses on how and why definitions of American and national identity and values have developed among the diverse and changing population of North America as well as on related topics, such as citizenship, constitutionalism, foreign policy, assimilation, and American exceptionalism." Students should be able to explain how identities related to American values and institutions, regions, and societal groups developed in response to events and have affected political debates. For example, the American Revolution changed the identity of Americans from British colonial subjects to citizens of a free and independent republic.

2. Work, Exchange, and Technology (WXT) "This theme focuses on the factors behind the development of systems of economic exchange, particularly the role of technology, economic markets, and government." Students should also understand how the economy in turn shaped society, labor systems, government policy and innovation. For example, the transportation revolution in the 19th century transformed the market economy and the lives of farmers, workers, and consumers.

3. Geography and the Environment (GEO) "This theme focuses on the role of geography and both the natural and human-made environments in the social and political developments in what would become the United States." Students need to examine how geography and climate contributed to regional differences and how debates over the use and control of natural resources have impacted different groups and government policies. For example, how did the frontier experience shape early settlers' attitudes toward the natural environment?

4. Migration and Settlement (MIG) "This theme focuses on why and how the various people who moved to and within the United States both adapted to and transformed their new social and physical environments." Students should be able to answer questions about the peoples who have moved to and lived in the United States. For example, they should be able to explain how Irish and German Catholics in the 19th century, southern and eastern Europeans in the early 20th century, and Hispanics and Asians in recent decades have each affected U.S. society.

5. Politics and Power (POL) "This theme focuses on how different social and political groups have influenced society and government in the United States, as well as how political beliefs and institutions have changed over time." Students need to understand the debates over power between branches of government, between the national and state governments, and among voters and special interest groups. For example, the debate over government policies in Congress during the 1790s led to the development of political parties in the United States.

6. America in the World (WOR) "This theme focuses on the interactions between nations that affected North American history in the colonial period and on the influence of the United States on world affairs." Students need to understand key developments in foreign policy, as well as domestic debates over these policies. For example, they need to understand how the French Revolution and the Napoleonic Wars challenged U.S. efforts to remain neutral and ultimately contributed to U.S. involvement in the War of 1812.

7. American and Regional Culture (ARC) "This theme focuses on the how and why national, regional, and group cultures developed and changed as well as how culture has shaped government policy and the economy." It also addresses how various identities, cultures, and values have shaped lives of citizens, politics, and the economy. Students should be able to explain why and how cultural components both hold constant and change over time, as well as the conflicts between traditional and modern values. For example, "In what ways did artistic expression change in response to war and to the growth of industry and cities from 1865 to 1898?"

8. Social Structures (SOC) "This theme focuses on how and why systems of social organization develop and change as well as the impact that these systems have on the broader society." It involves the study of the roles of men, women, and other categories of family and civic units, and how they have been maintained, challenged, and transformed throughout American history. This theme could be evaluated with questions, such as, "To what extent were the roles of women in the United States transformed during the period from 1890 to 1945?" "In what ways did the government policies change the role of children in American society during the Progressive Era?"

Using the Themes The tracing of multiple themes through each period of U.S. history is an effective way to study and review content throughout the course. A thematic approach encourages one to think about specific events in a larger framework and to make judgments about comparison, causation, and continuity and change over time.

Historical Periods

The content of AP® U.S. History is also organized by a framework of the nine chronological periods. The periods include the following chapters and content:

Period 1 (Chapter 1), 1491–1607 The period from pre-Columbian Indian cultures to the founding of Jamestown covers the interaction of cultures and how Europeans, Native Americans, and Africans created a "new" world.

Period 2 (Chapters 2–3), 1607–1754 Various mixtures of American Indians, Europeans, and African Americans created colonies with distinctive cultures, economies, and populations.

Period 3 (Chapters 4–6), 1754–1800 Wars over empires provided the context for the American Revolution and the founding of the United States, including the political struggles to form a "more perfect union."

Period 4 (Chapters 7–11), 1800–1848 The promise of the new republic played out during a period of rapid economic, territorial, and population growth, which tested the political institutions that held the nation together.

Period 5 (Chapters 12–15), 1844–1877 A war with Mexico intensified the conflict over slavery and states' rights, which led to the Civil War and then to struggles to reconstruct the Union and address the legacy of slavery.

Period 6 (Chapters 16–19), 1865–1898 Industrialization, the rapid growth of cities, and a large new wave of immigration transformed the American economy, society, culture, and regional identities.

Period 7 (Chapters 20–25), 1890–1945 While the United States responded to the impact of industrialization during the Progressive Era and New Deal years, it also became deeply involved in world affairs during World Wars I and II.

Period 8 (Chapters 26–29), 1945–1980 The United States assumed a world leadership role during the Cold War while society became more divided over issues of economic and social justice, especially for minorities and women.

Period 9 (Chapters 30–31), 1980–Present A renewed conservative movement challenged the efficacy of government at home while the end of the Cold War, the spread of globalization, and the increase in terrorism forced the federal government to redefine its policies.

The text begins each period with a one-page introduction that provides an overview of the content and alternative views about the period. The text does not attempt to cover every historical fact, but it includes all of the essential evidence and understandings needed to address the challenges of the AP® History exam.

The College Board provides a key to the amount of emphasis to be put on each period of history, but recognizes the amount of emphasis on each period will vary in diverse instruction settings.

- Period 1, 1491–1607: from 4 to 6 percent

- Period 2, 1607–1754: from 6 to 8 percent

- Periods 3 to 8, 1754 to 1980: from 10 to 17 percent each

- Period 9, 1980–Present: from 4 to 6 percent

In the AP® U.S. History exam, some multiple-choice and short-answer questions will be based on periods 1 and 9, and content from these periods may be used in the long essays and DBQs. However, no long essay or DBQ will focus exclusively on these two periods of history.

History, like any other field of study, is a combination of subject matter and methodology. The practices, skills, and themes are methods or tools to explore the subject matter of history. One cannot practice these skills without knowledge of the historical context and understanding of specific historical evidence. The following section provides suggestions for development of another set of skills useful for answering the questions on the exam. Again, the "mastery" of these skills, particularly writing answers to AP® questions, takes practice.

To the Student: The Course and Exam Description

The Course and Exam Description describes the four types of questions on the AP® U.S. History exam: (1) multiple choice, (2) short answer, (3) long essay, and (4) document-based. On the exam, the long essay questions are last. Once you have developed the long essay writing skills, you are more than halfway to writing a competent answer to the DBQ. For this reason, in the following section, the long essay is presented before the DBQ.

Answering the Multiple-Choice Questions

The AP® exam asks 55 multiple-choice questions (MCQ), and you will have 55 minutes to answer them. The value of the MCQs is 40 percent of your score. Each question is related to the analysis of a primary or secondary source, such as a written text, image, chart, graph, or map. From two to five questions will be asked about each source. Each MCQ assesses one or more history skills but also requires historical knowledge you have learned studying U.S. history. Each question will have one BEST answer and three distractors. Compared to most history tests, the AP® exam will place less emphasis on simple recall and more emphasis on your ability to analyze primary and secondary sources and to use history reasoning skills.

At the end of each chapter, this textbook assists content review with a list of Key Terms by Theme and provides practice analyzing sources with three sets of multiple-choice questions. In addition to the MCQs in the chapters, the practice AP® exam includes 55 multiple-choice questions. The MCQs in the chapters are similar to ones on the AP® exam but are also designed to review the content and understanding of the chapter.

Analyzing Historical Evidence On the AP® exam, all multiple-choice questions will be introduced by a primary or secondary source. Below is one example of a primary source, a political cartoon from 1934. Your first step in analyzing this kind of evidence, whether an image or a reading, is to ask these questions: What was the historical context in which it was created? Who was the intended audience? What was the point of view of the author? What was the author's purpose? The development of these four skill-building questions is part of the foundation of studying U.S. history at the AP® level.

You might recognize the patient in the cartoon as Uncle Sam, a characterization used by political cartoonists since the early 19th century as a stand-in for the United States. The doctor (President Franklin D. Roosevelt) is clearly under pressure from "old lady" Congress to cure the ills of the nation. However, in order to interpret and use the evidence in this cartoon, you need knowledge of the 1930s Great Depression and Roosevelt's New Deal program (Chapter 24). A source by itself will not reveal the answers to the MCQs: You will also need to call upon your knowledge and skills to effectively unlock and use the evidence.

Source: C. K. Berryman, *Washington Star,* 1934. Library of Congress

Below are examples of the kind of MCQs that might be asked on the AP® exam about a source and the skills being accessed:

- *Analyzing Historical Evidence:* Which of the following most directly supports the argument in the cartoon?

- *Causation:* Which of the following most directly states the cause of the point of view of the cartoon?

- *Comparison:* Which of the following most closely resembles the point of view of the cartoon?

- *Contextualization:* Which of the following developments best reflects the point of view of the cartoon?

- *Continuity and Change over Time:* Which of the following was a continuation of the ideas in the source?

Making a Choice Read the stem of the question and all four choices carefully before you record your answer. A number of choices may appear to be correct, but you must select the BEST answer. Choices that reflect absolute positions, such as "always," "never," and "exclusively," are seldom correct because historical evidence rarely offers such absolute certainty. Keep in mind the need to make judgments about the significance of a variety of causes and effects.

Should you guess on the AP® exam? The current format does not penalize guessing. Obviously, the process of first eliminating a wrong answer or two increases your chances of guessing correctly.

Budgeting Your Time The AP® History exam gives you 55 minutes to answer 55 questions. You will not have enough time to spend two or three minutes on difficult questions. Follow a relaxed but reasonable pace rather than rushing through the exam and then going back and second-guessing your decisions. Avoid skipping questions and be careful changing answers.

Recommended Activity Become familar with the type of multiple-choice questions on the exam before taking it. This will reduce the chance of surprises over the format of the questions.

However, for many students, the review of content through multiple-choice questions is not the most productive way to absorb the information. The purpose of the chapter content in this textbook is to provide a useful and concise presentation of the essential concepts and evidence needed for the exam. By reviewing the essential facts in their historical context, you will better recall and understand the connections between events—so important for applying the history reasoning skills.

Answering the Short-Answer Questions

The short-answer questions (SAQ) section of the AP® U.S. History exam will have three sets of questions and allow you 40 minutes to answer them. They will count for 20 percent of one's final score. The first two sets of questions are **required,** but in the third set, you can **choose** between question 3 from periods 1–5 and question 4 from periods 6–9. This option gives students an opportunity to write in an area of their strength. Each question consists of three tasks, and you receive one point for a successful response to each task, so each question is worth three points.

In the format for the current exam, question 1 will involve the skill of analyzing a secondary source. Question 2 will involve a primary source and the skill of either causation or comparison. Questions 3 and 4 will involve the skill of either causation or comparison without a reference to a source.

Below is an example of how an SAQ is structured. It consists of three tasks, labeled (A), (B), and (C).

1. Answer (A), (B), and (C).

   (A) Briefly explain ONE important similarity between the British colonies in the Chesapeake region and the British colonies in New England in the period from 1607 to 1754.

   (B) Briefly explain ONE important difference between the British colonies in the Chesapeake region and the British colonies in New England in the period from 1607 to 1754.

   (C) Briefly explain ONE factor that accounts for the difference that you indicated in (B).

All tasks will involve the practice of at least one history skill. For example, the above sample directs students to use the skill of comparison.

Writing Short Answers

Short-answer questions, unlike essay questions, do not require the development of a thesis statement. However, they do need to be answered in complete sentences. An outline or bulleted list alone is not acceptable. Students have a total of 40 minutes to answer three questions, each of which consists of three tasks. "Briefly" is the key direction in most short-answer questions. The number of sentences that it will take to answer the question will depend on the task in the question. As you write responses to short-answer questions, work on your ability to write clear and complete sentences supported with specific and accurate evidence. Use the proper names of persons, places, and events as proof that you know the evidence. While the College Board does not give specific directions, most exam readers recommend labeling the three tasks in your answer A, B, and C. You will have one page in the exam booklet that includes approximately 23 lines on which to write your answers to each short-answer question of three tasks.

Recommended Activity At the end of each chapter, this textbook contains four short-answer questions based on the models provided by the College Board. Some questions may have more options than one might find on the AP® exam. The purpose was not to make them easier but to broaden the review. Of course, students who want to be as prepared as possible should be able to explain each option clearly.

As you answer the short-answer questions at the end of each chapter, first try to identify the history skill(s) used in the question. This will help you become more oriented to the purpose of the question, whether it involves analyzing the evidence, causation, comparison, or another skill. To evaluate your progress in answering these short-answer questions, use this simple scoring standard:

- 1 point for accomplishing the task identified in the prompt

- 0 points for each task that is not accomplished or completed

You might need to answer many short-answer questions over several weeks to learn how to budget the 12 to 14 minutes available to answer each of the three-point questions.

Answering the Long Essay Question

In the current format of the AP® U.S. History exam, students choose ONE long essay question (LEQ) from among THREE options. Each option will focus on the same theme and same reasoning skill, but the options will be about different sets of periods. This means that students choose to answer a question from periods 1–3, or from periods 4–6, or from periods 7–9. The suggested writing time is 40 minutes. The long essay represents 15 percent of the final grade on the exam. An edited copy of the current format released by the College Board is reproduced below:

Students will choose one of the three long essay questions to answer. The long essay requires students to demonstrate their ability to use historical evidence in crafting a thoughtful historical argument.

Question from periods 1–3: Evaluate the extent to which trans-Atlantic interactions fostered change in the labor systems in British North American colonies from 1600 to 1763.

Question from periods 4–6: Evaluate the extent to which new technology fostered change in the United States economy from 1865 to 1900.

Question from periods 7–9: Evaluate the extent to which globalization fostered change in the United States economy from 1945 to 2000.

In the sample above, all three essays are based on the same theme—Work, Exchange, and Technology (WXT)—and the same reasoning skill, "Continuity and Change over Time." Much like the SAQ format, the LEQ format gives students the choice to answer a question from a period that best reflects their understanding of the relevant examples from that period.

Requirements of the Long Essay Question The AP® exam is very specific in what is expected in answering an LEQ. The grading rubric is based on a six-point scale, which is worth 15 percent of one's final grade. While the traditional model of writing an essay with an introduction, body, and conclusion is still useful in the overall organization of your essay, the AP® U.S. History exam rubrics for the LEQ clearly define what you need to do to gain each point.

- **Point 1: Thesis** Make a historically defensible thesis or claim that establishes a line of reasoning and how it will be argued. This thesis must do more than restate the question. It must create an argument. The thesis must consist of one or more sentences in either the introduction or the conclusion.

- **Point 2: Contextualization** Describe a broader historical context, relevant to the question, such as events or development before, during, or after the time frame of the question. This requires more elaboration than a mere reference.

- **Points 3 and 4: Evidence** Earn one point for describing at least two specific examples that are relevant to the question. For two points, you must explain how the specific examples support your arguments established in the thesis.

- **Points 5 and 6: Historical Reasoning and Complexity** Earn one point for using the historical reasoning skill in the question (comparison, causation, or change over time) to frame your arguments that address the question. To gain a second point one must demonstrate a complex understanding that uses evidence to corroborate, qualify, or modify your argument, such as using an additional historical reasoning skill.

The next section on writing long essay question answers explains how to achieve each of these points.

Practice Writing Long Essay Question Answers The long essay question (LEQ), along with the document-based question (DBQ), have proven to be the two parts of the exam on which students need to improve the most. Although the DBQ is worth more than the LEQ, it is better to start with learning how to master the LEQ skills, because they include the fundamental skills for writing the DBQ and also have fewer elements to handle. For many students, writing an AP® history essay is much different than writing an essay for an English or literature class.

The skills you need to write AP® history essays take time and practice to master, so you will benefit from starting to work on them as early as possible.Instead of writing and rewriting complete essays until all elements are mastered, break down the essay writing into sequential steps to develop the skills needed for each point. The following steps have proven useful in developing the skills needed to answer the AP® long essay question:

1. Analyze the Question

2. Organize the Evidence

3. Write the Thesis Paragraph

4. Provide Context

5. Use Evidence

6. Address Historical Reasoning and Complexity

7. Evaluate a Long Essay Answer

Let's look at the sequential steps that you can use to develop your skill at writing long essays.

1. Analyze the Question Taking the time to consider what the question really asks is often overlooked in the rush to start writing. Take time to fully understand the question and avoid the mistake of writing an essay that receives little or no credit because it answered a question that was not asked. Consider this sample long essay question:

> Evaluate the extent to which trans-Atlantic interactions fostered change in the labor systems in British North American colonies from 1600 to 1763.

Stop and ask yourself, "What are the key words in the question? What is the targeted history reasoning skill in the question?" Underline words related to the reasoning skill and the time frame, such as "evaluate the extent," "change," and "from 1600 to 1763." Next, circle the content words, such as "trans-Atlantic interactions" and "labor systems" and "British North American colonies." During this step, identify all parts of the question. In the above essay question, the history skill of continuity and change over time needs to be addressed.

It is not enough to simply describe trans-Atlantic interactions and labor systems in the colonies. You must explain and evaluate how interactions, such as trade and migration, contributed to continuity and change in labor systems, such as free labor, indentured servitude, and slavery.

Recommended Activity As an initial skill-building activity, analyze the LEQs in the period review sections. *Underline* the key words that indicate what the writer should do and the targeted reasoning skill. *Circle* the words that indicate the specific aspects of the content that need to be addressed.

2. Organize the Evidence Many students start writing their answers to an essay question without first thinking through what they know, and they often write themselves into a corner. Directions for the AP® History exam suggest you spend some time reading and planning before starting to write. Take a few minutes to identify what you know about the question and organize your information by making a rough outline in the test booklet, using abbreviations and other memory aids. This outline is not graded. Taking a few minutes to organize your knowledge can help you answer an important question: Do you have enough evidence to select a certain essay or to support your argument?

Below is a sample list of items that could be used in answering the long essay question about the impact of trans-Atlantic interactions on the continuity and changes in the labor systems in the North American British colonies.

Trans-Atlantic Interactions	Labor Systems	North American British Colonies
Migration over time	Adventurers	Plantation system
Mercantilism	Free labor	Raw materials for export
Triangular trade	Family units	New England
Navigation Acts	Indentured servants	Middle Colonies
Slave trade	Headright system	Chesapeake region
Racial prejudices	Slavery	Carolina and Georgia
Cash crops, tobacco	Native Americans	
	Labor shortages	

However, the key to writing an effective long essay answer is that your thesis and arguments drive your writing so that you do not simply list facts.

Recommended Activity Create a list of the kinds of relevant information that could be incorporated into the responses to the long essay questions found in the period reviews. Organize the information under headings that reflect the major parts of the question. This activity parallels the lists developed by AP® consultants before readers start scoring essays. It is a very useful prewriting activity.

3. Write the Thesis Paragraph The development of a strong claim or thesis is an essential part of every AP® History essay answer. Some students seem to have difficulty taking a position. Some are afraid of making a mistake. Remember, different interpretations of events is part of the study of history. AP® readers are looking not for the "right answer" but for a writer's ability to interpret the historical evidence and marshal it into a persuasive argument.

A thesis must be more than a restatement of the question. The AP® scoring guide also adds this requirement: "The thesis must consist of one or more sentences located in one place, either in the introduction or the conclusion." It also requires that the thesis address the history reasoning skill in the question, such as causation, comparison, or continuity and change over time. The following thesis is one effort to address the long essay question presented earlier:

Trans-Atlantic interactions fostered continuity in the demand for labor in the British North American colonies from 1600 to 1783 but also fostered change in the kinds of labor systems in use.

This statement is straightforward and it takes a position on the question and the reasoning skill of continuity and change, but does it provide a well-developed a line of reasoning? Below is an example of how to extend and develop the short thesis statement from the question about labor systems:

Not surprisingly, the colonies from New England to Georgia tried different labor systems, such as indentured servitude, slavery, and free labor. Changes in these labor systems were affected by changes in trade and migrations, but the racial attitudes of the period also hardened the institution of slavery against change, especially in the Southern colonies.

By developing and extending a thesis statement, one both clarifies the thesis and provides the organizing ideas and arguments that will guide the development of the essay. An effective introductory paragraph should introduce the main arguments of the essay. The above example of an extended thesis does that by identifying three labor systems, which will be evaluated for continuity and change. This second feature of the introduction is sometimes called the essay's "blueprint" or "organizing ideas." By the end of the first paragraph, the reader should not only know your thesis but also have a clear idea of the main arguments to be developed in support of the thesis.

The AP® exam rubric states that the thesis must be "located in one place, either in the introduction or in the conclusion." Based on experience, most teachers and readers of the exam recommend putting your thesis in the introductory paragraph. While it might seem to create more drama to reveal the thesis in the last paragraph, you are not writing a who-done-it mystery.

Recommended Activity Practice writing an introductory paragraph with a thesis statement and introduction of main arguments to support it. Use LEQs from this text and from prior AP® exams. Use the following criteria to assess your work:

- Does the thesis consist of one or more sentences?

- Does the thesis make a historically defensible claim?

- Does the thesis address the history reasoning skill and all parts of the question?

- Does the introduction provide a framework for understanding the main arguments to be used to support the thesis?

- How could the thesis and supporting arguments be improved?

4. Provide Context The AP® program describes the context requirement as "describe a broader historical context relevant to the prompt." For the above essay question about continuity and change in the "labor systems," an explanation of the competition among European powers, such as Britain, France, and Spain could provide context for "trans-Atlantic interactions" and what was happening in the colonies. Explaining the growing political conflicts over slavery after independence could also provide the context for the significance of this question.

Context could become the separate second introductory paragraph, since the AP® exam expects "more than a mere phrase or reference." However, the placement for the contextualization point should be determined by the logical flow of the essay. Explaining the context from after the time frame of the question may make more sense at the end of the essay than the beginning.

Recommended Activity The first step is to think about the possible historical context that you can provide for the question. It can be historical events or developments before, during, or after the time frame of the question. Next write a separate paragraph for the context point. For practice use LEQs from this text and from prior AP® exams. Use these criteria to assess your work:

- Is the context more than a phrase or reference?

- Is the context passage or paragraph relevant to the topic of the question?

- Does the response explain broader historical events, developments, or processes that occur before, during, or after the time frame of the question?

- How can the explanation of context for the question be improved?

5. Use Evidence As explained above, to receive at least one point for use of evidence, one must describe at least two specific examples of evidence (proper nouns, historical terms, and developments) relevant to the topic of the question. However, two examples are the minimum. Most teachers and graders recommend more. What if one example is wrong? For the above LEQ about impact of trade on labor systems in the colonies, one may gain one point for describing the three labor systems of free labor, indenture servitude, and slavery in the colonies supported with specific historical facts.

Recommended Activity Before your first efforts to write paragraphs for the evidence points, practice outlining three paragraphs of evidence to back up your thesis and arguments. Incorporate historical terms, such as proper names or terms in each paragraph. Once you understand the thinking skills involved, practice writing complete paragraphs. Use the following criteria to assess your work:

- Does the response earn one point by providing at least two specific examples of historical evidence relevant to the question?

- Does the response earn two points by using examples of specific historical evidence to support the arguments made to support the thesis?

- How effectively is the evidence linked to the arguments?

- How can the variety, depth, and analysis of the evidence be improved?

6. Address Historical Reasoning and Complexity To receive one point for historical reasoning, one must use the appropriate reasoning process (causation, comparison, or continuity and change over time) to structure the argument used to address the question. In the question above on changes in colonial labor systems, the essay must use continuity and change over time to frame its arguments. For example, one argument might explain how the growing demand for cash crops from the British-American colonies promoted the growth of the plantation system, which needed a cheap and permanent labor supply that at that time was satisfied by slavery. This requirement does not demand writing a separate paragraph for the point, but the historical reasoning process can and should be integrated into your use of evidence.

The second point for complexity has been the hardest point for students to earn in recent years. It is not given out just for good essays that are clearly written and organized with no historical errors. The response needs to show a deeper, more complex understanding of the question. The AP® exam rubrics from the College Board state the following ways to demonstrate a complex understanding:

- Explaining nuance of an issue by analyzing multiple variables

- Explaining both similarities and differences, or explaining both continuity and change, or explaining multiple causes, or explaining both causes and effects

- Explaining relevant and insightful connections within and across periods

- Confirming the validity of an argument by corroborating multiple perspectives across themes

- Qualifying or modifying an argument by considering diverse or alternative views or evidence

For example, a point for a complex understanding of historical developments for this LEQ could be gained by explaining both change and continuity. As another example of complexity, one could explain that the institution of slavery developed in the colonies not only for economic causes, but also for social or racial reasons.

However, to receive two points one must explain the relationship of evidence to the arguments used to support the thesis. For example, it is not enough to simply describe the labor systems used in the colonies. You must explain and evaluate, for example, how changes in voluntary and involuntary migration were linked to the growth of free labor and slavery and the decline of indenture servitude. Linking the evidence to your arguments also helps one to avoid writing out a "laundry list" of unrelated facts.

Recommended Activity The demonstration of the targeted reasoning process (causation, comparison, or change and continuity over time) and the complex understanding can be integrated into paragraphs using evidence to support one's arguments. However, for initial practice write a separate paragraph for each process that demonstrates the use of it to frame the argument and a complex understanding of the question using one of the various ways outlined above. Use the following criteria to assess your work:

- Does the essay use historical reasoning to frame or structure the argument made?

- How could the targeted reasoning process be better analyzed in the arguments?

- Does the response demonstrate a complex understanding of the question using evidence to corroborate, qualify, or modify an argument that addressed the question?

- How could a complex understanding of the question be better demonstrated?

7. Evaluate a Long Essay Answer The feedback from your practice essays—whether from teachers, peers, or self-evaluation—is essential for making the practice produce progress and for learning to master the exam requirements. You might find teacher evaluation and self-evaluation of essays less threatening than peer evaluation. However, once you establish more confidence, peer evaluation is a useful form of feedback. The comments you receive from your peers, as well as the comments you make on their essays, will help you become a better writer.

Recommended Activity Before writing out your first practice essay, it helps to first organize your arguments by outlining each paragraph for the essay. The first effort for writing a complete AP® History essay will be a more positive experience if it is an untimed assignment. After some confidence is gained in writing the long essay, you should apply these skills in a timed test, similar to that of the AP® exam (e.g., 40 minutes for the long essay). The purpose of this practice is to become familiar with the time restraints of the AP® exam. Use the following practice scoring guide for the LEQ or the most recent rubric released by the College Board to evaluate your own work and to help you internalize the grading standards used on the AP® exam. While the AP® exam booklet will list what needs to be done to gain each point, with effective practice you should know going into the exam what you need to write before opening the booklet.

Practice Scoring Guide for a Long Essay

A. Thesis: 0–1 Point

❑ 1 point for a historically defensible thesis/claim that establishes a line of reasoning to address the question and not merely restate it. The thesis must be at least one sentence and located in one place, either in the introduction or in the conclusion.

B. Contextualization: 0–1 Point

❑ 1 point to describe the broader historical context of the question, such as developments either before, during, or after its time frame. Describing the context requires more than a mere phrase or reference.

C. Evidence: 0–2 Points

❑ 1 point for identifying specific historical examples of evidence relevant to the question.

OR (Either the 1 point above or the 2 points below, but not both.)

❑ 2 points for using specific and relevant historical examples of evidence that **support the arguments** used to address the question.

D. Analysis and Reasoning: 0–2 Points

❑ 1 point for using **historical reasoning** to frame or structure the arguments that address the question, such as causation, comparison, or continuity and change over time. Reasoning may be uneven or not as complex as needed to gain 2 points.

OR (Either the 1 point above or the 2 points below, but not both.)

❑ 2 points for using historical reasoning and demonstrating a **complex understanding** of the historical developments by analyzing the multiple variables in the evidence. This can include analyzing more than one cause, both similarities and differences, both continuity and change, and/or the diversity of evidence that corroborates, qualifies, or modifies an argument used to address the question.

Other Suggestions for Writing Essay Questions

The following suggestions, while not part of the formal rubrics for grading essays, can help or detract from the impact of your essay writing in AP history:

Be accurate and clear. AP® readers realize that students are writing a first draft under pressure. However, accuracy and clarity are problems when they detract from the overall quality of the work. Does the historical content of the essay demonstrate accurate content knowledge? Does grammar obscure the successful demonstration of the content knowledge and skills in the essay? The AP® scoring guidelines allow for some errors in content and grammar, unless they detract from or obscure the students' overall demonstration of knowledge and thinking skills.

Follow the writing style used by historians. Avoid use of the first person ("I," "we"). Rather, use the third person ("he," "she," "they"). Write in the past tense, except when referring to documents or sources that currently exist (e.g., "the document implies"). Use the active voice rather than the passive voice because it states cause and effect more strongly (e.g., "Edison created" is in the active voice; "was created by Edison" is in the passive voice). The AP® long essays do not call for a narrative style of historical writing or "stories." Rather, they should be analytical essays that support the writer's argument with specific knowledge and historical reasoning.

Remain objective. Avoid emotional appeals, especially on social issues. The AP® test is not the place to argue that a group was racist or that some people were the "good guys" and others the "bad guys." Avoid absolutes, such as "all" and "none." Rarely in history is the evidence so conclusive that you can prove that there were no exceptions. Do not use slang terms!

Communicate awareness of the complexity of history. Distinguish between primary and secondary causes, between long-term and short-term effects, and between the more and less significant events. Use verbs that communicate judgment and analysis (e.g., "reveal," "exemplify," "demonstrate," "imply," "symbolize").

Communicate the organization and logical development of your argument. Each paragraph should develop a main point that is clearly stated in the topic sentence. Provide a few words or a phrase of transition to connect one paragraph to another. While length is no guarantee of a top grade, depth of analysis and use of evidence does require space. Hence, good essays are often longer than weak ones. However, a concise essay in which every word has a purpose is better than an essay bloated with filler and flowery language.

Use specific words. Clearly identify persons, factors, and judgments. Replace vague verbs such as "felt" and "says" with more precise ones. Do not use words such as "they" and "others say" as vague references to unidentified groups or events.

Define or explain key terms. If the question deals with terms (such as "liberal," "conservative," or "manifest destiny"), an essential part of your analysis should include an explanation of these terms.

Anticipate counterarguments. Consider arguments that are against your thesis, not to prove them but to show that you are aware of opposing points of view. The strongest essays confront conflicting evidence.

Recognize the role of a conclusion. An effective conclusion should focus on the thesis. One can restate the thesis in a fresh and meaningful manner that supports its significance. The conclusion should not try to summarize all the evidence or introduce new evidence. If you are running out of time, consider omitting a conclusion. If you have written a well-organized essay with a clear thesis that is stated in the introduction and developed in the supporting paragraphs, no conclusion is better than a meaningless effort.

Model for Organizing Answers to Essay Questions This model for a five-paragraph expository essay illustrates how an introductory paragraph relates to a well-organized essay. An essay should not always consist of five paragraphs. The total number of paragraphs is for the writer to determine. What the model does suggest is that the introductory paragraph is crucial because it should shape the full essay. An effective introduction tells the reader the arguments you will develop in the body of the essay and then explains how you will develop that view, identifying the main points you will be making in the body of your essay. If your introductory paragraph is properly written, the rest of the essay will be relatively easy to write, especially if you have already organized your information.

Paragraph 1: Introduction Background and context to the question

_____ Thesis

statement _____ Development

of the thesis with preview of main arguments _____

_____

Paragraph 2: First Argument Topic sentence explaining first argument

related to the thesis _____ Evidence

to support argument using the targeted reasoning skill _____

_____

Paragraph 3: Second Argument Topic sentence explaining

second argument related to the thesis _____

_____ Evidence to support argument using the targeted reasoning

skill _____

_____

Paragraph 4: Third Argument Topic sentence explaining third argument related to the thesis _____

_____ Evidence to support argument using the targeted reasoning skill

_____

Paragraph 5: Conclusion _____

_____

_____

Answering the Document-Based Question

This part of the AP® exam comes closest to the challenges and work of practicing historians. The AP® exam's document-based question (DBQ) will be drawn from the concepts and content of periods 3 through 8. Students have no choice of questions, but they are given 60 minutes to write their answer. Directions suggest that students spend the first 15 minutes to read and study the seven primary documents because they are the essential focus for this kind of question. These documents include mostly texts, but they will usually include one or more images, such as cartoons, maps, or graphs. These sources will include differing points of view and often contradictory evidence.

Requirements of the Document-Based Question There are seven possible points in the rubric used to grade the DBQ, and the question counts for 25 percent of one's overall exam grade. Many of the DBQ requirements are the same or similar to ones for the LEQ. However, in addition students need to be able to analyze at least six of the seven historical documents provided and use them to support the arguments of the essay.

- **Point 1: Thesis** Respond to the prompt with a historically defensible thesis or claim that establishes a line of reasoning.

- **Point 2: Contextualization** Describe a broader historical context relevant to the prompt.

- **Points 3 and 4: Evidence from the Documents** Earn one point for using the content of at least three documents to address the question. For two points you must use at least six documents and must also explain how the documents are related to the thesis arguments.

- **Point 5: Evidence Beyond the Documents** Use at least one additional piece of specific historical evidence, beyond that found in the documents, relevant to one's arguments.

- **Point 6: Analysis of the Sources** For at least three documents, one must explain how or why the document's point of view, purpose, historical situation, or audience (or more than one of these) is relevant to one's argument.

- **Point 7: Complexity** Demonstrate a complex understanding of the question by using the evidence to corroborate, qualify, or modify an argument that addresses the question.

Practice Writing the Document-Based Question Keep in mind that writing a DBQ answer is similar to writing an effective long essay and that many of the same skills apply. As with an LEQ, a DBQ answer needs an effective thesis that addresses all parts of the question and uses a historical reasoning skill, usually causation. As in a long essay, you need to make persuasive arguments supported by evidence.

However, in a DBQ much of the evidence can be drawn from the seven documents. You must still utilize your knowledge of history to help you analyze the documents. The better you understand the concepts and evidence from the historical periods used in the question, the greater understanding you are likely to gain from the documents and the less likely you are to misinterpret them.

This next section recommends steps to develop the skills for writing an effective response to the DBQ. The sample DBQ below will be used in the explanation and practice of each skill.

> Analyze major changes and continuities in the social and economic experiences of African Americans who migrated from the rural South to urban areas in the North in the period 1910 to 1930.

1. Analyze the Question and the Documents Besides analyzing the question, as explained under the LEQ section, the preparation for answering a DBQ must include analyzing the seven documents. This is why the directions for the DBQ on the exam recommend taking 15 minutes to read the documents before you begin writing. Use the first 15 minutes not only to read the documents, but also to underline and make notes on them in the margin. While reading the documents, note what side of possible arguments the document could be used to support. Also identify at least three documents that you could use to explain the relevance of the source's point of view, purpose, historical situation, or audience to your arguments.

2. Organize the Evidence Unlike the LEQ, the DBQ gives one much of the evidence to support a thesis and arguments. The poorest approach to answering a DBQ is to write about just the seven documents from 1 to 7 and hope for the best. Instead, much like with LEQ, take time during the reading of the documents to organize them into categories such as northern experience versus southern experiences. You might create a chart or matrix that uses a combination of rows and columns to organize information. For example, you might have one row for each region and one column for each type of information, such as economic conditions (jobs) and social conditions (prejudice and segregation). If time allows, add short notes about relevant knowledge from outside the documents to support your arguments.

3. Write a Thesis Paragraph The requirement for gaining the one point for a thesis or claim is the same as the LEQ. The thesis must be historically defensible and establish a line of reasoning. (See LEQ section for details.)

4. Provide Context As with the LEQ, the DBQ essay also requires one to describe a broader historical context for the question. This involves explaining a relevant historical development not found in the documents. For example, in the response to the sample DBQ, one could broaden the discussion of the

African American migrant experience by explaining a context not found in the documents, such as the race riots in northern cities like Chicago during and after World War I. This contextualization point also requires an explanation of multiple sentences or a full paragraph.

5. Use Evidence from the Documents You must use six of the seven documents in writing the essay to gain two points for use of evidence. Think of the seven documents in terms of evidence to be linked to your arguments. Your thesis and arguments, not the arrangement of the documents in the exam booklet, should control the organization of the essay. To receive two points, it is not enough to accurately explain the content from six documents. You also need to integrate the content into a persuasive argument to support your thesis.

In use of documents as evidence, you must do more than just quote or paraphrase the document. The readers already know the content of the documents, so there is no need to quote them. Another novice mistake is to write no more than a description of each document. "Document 1 says . . . Document 2 says . . . ." At best this approch will gain you one point.

Below is a sample document for the above AP® sample DBQ. It is just one of seven documents that a DBQ would include.

Document 2. Letter from a prospective African American migrant, April 27, 1917, New Orleans, Louisiana.

"Dear Sirs:

Being desirous of leaving the South for the betterment of my condition generally and seeking a Home Somewhere in Ill' Chicago or some other prosperous town, I am at sea about the best place to locate having a family dependent upon me for support. I am informed by the *Chicago Defender* a very valuable paper which has for its purpose the Uplifting of my race, and of which I am a constant reader and real lover, that you were in position to show some light to one in my condition.

Seeking a Northern Home. If this is true, Kindly inform me by next mail the next best thing to do. Being a poor man with a family to care for, I am not coming to live on flowery Beds of ease for I am a man who works and wish to make the best I can out of life. I do not wish to come there hoodwinked not know, where to go or what to do, so I Solicit your help in this matter and thanking you in advance for what advice you may be pleased to Give. I am yours for success."

The sample below illustrates a couple of ways to integrate documents in support of an argument and how to reference them in an essay. Documents 3 and 7 (not included in this book) describe discrimination in employment and housing:

The southern reader of the northern African American newspaper, *Chicago Defender,* (Doc. 2) had cause for being suspicious that moving his family North would not be an easy escape from conditions in the South. During this period, black migrants to the North faced racial barriers in finding a place to live in segregated cities like Chicago (Doc. 7) and discrimination on the job in northern industries (Doc. 3).

The documents should influence your arguments to the extent that you will have to deal with the complexity, contradictions, and limitations found in them. Realize that not all documents will have equal weight. Communicate to the reader your awareness of the contradictions or limitations of a document, or how a document may not support your thesis but fits into the context relevant to the question.

6. Use Evidence Beyond the Documents Much like the LEQ, the DBQ does require at least one example of historical evidence to support your arguments, but it should not duplicate the evidence in the documents or their analysis. For example, the documents provide for the sample DBQ might not explicitly address the impact of African American music during the Harlem Renaissance in the North. Explaining how African American music enhanced the image of black artists and changed their experience in northern cities after migration would be going beyond the documents.

You could establish that you understand the era by setting the historical scene early in the essay using "outside" information. However, do not "double-dip" by using the same example from your outside information in the explanation of context. If you do, you will not receive credit for both.

7. Source the Documents One additional point is gained for analyzing at least three of the documents in one or more of the following aspects: a) historical situation for the document, b) intended audience for the document, c) purpose of the document, or d) point of view of the author. Identifying one of the sourcing elements, such as historical situation, to get over the threshold for sourcing, one must also explain how or why this element of the source is relevant to an argument. In the example, for the 1917 letter from a reader of the *Chicago Defender,* one could explain the historical situation of the letter, that it was written during World War I. This was significant because labor shortages in the North encouraged employers to recruit workers from the South, which contributed to the great migration of African Americans.

In this text, you will find dozens of excerpts, cartoons, or other kinds of documents for practicing the sourcing of documents as a prewriting activity. In writing the DBQ, the "sourcing a document" requirement can be accomplished in the same paragraph as where the document was used as evidence. To explain the historical situation for a document you need not take more than one sentence or modifying phrase in the paragraph that uses the document as evidence. The readers are looking for the sourcing of **three** documents for the one point.

8. Provide Complexity As explained before, an essay needs to show a deeper, more complex understanding of the question to gain this point. Refer back to the AP® Guidelines for complexity under "Writing the LEQ" for the many ways to demonstrate a complex understanding. The options are the same for both the LEQ and the DBQ. In recent exams, few students have received the complexity point for their DBQ answer. In one recent year, the average score for a DBQ was 2.42 out of a possible 7 points. This suggests that most students should focus on linking the document evidence to their arguments and to achieving both the contextualization and outside evidence points before tackling complexity.

9. Evaluate a DBQ Answer At this point, some students may ask, how can one possibly juggle all the requirements to write a strong DBQ essay? First remember that in writing a DBQ, you apply many of the same skills you

Source: GettyImages.

learned in writing a strong LEQ answer, such as writing an effective thesis, providing context for the question, and using outside knowledge to support your arguments. As recommended for development of LEQ writing, use a step-by-step skill development approach to the DBQ. It will take time to master each new skill, such as the use of documents as evidence. Only practice can prepare you to answer a challenging DBQ successfully.

After writing your first untimed and timed DBQ essays, use the DBQ practice scoring guide, or the rubrics released by the College Board, to evaluate your essays. Using the scoring guide will help you to internalize the criteria for writing an effective DBQ. Samples of recent DBQ rubrics, scoring guidelines, and graded essays can be found at https://apcentral.collegeboard.org/pdf/ap-us-history-dbq-2018.pdf?course=ap-united-states-history.

Finally, AP readers counsel students to "take ownership of the question." This means to address the LEQ and DBQ directly and commit your writing to supporting your arguments, rather than just describing documents and other evidence like isolated bits of information. Again, the time you spend on the front end thinking about the question and organizing the documents and other evidence into categories can give your essay purpose, direction, and clarity while you write.

Most AP® teachers recommend that contextualization should be addressed in the essay's introduction or second paragraph as part of the background to the question. Contextualization usually requires an explanation that is multiple sentences or a full paragraph long.

Other suggestions for writing an effective DBQ answer include the following:

- Use the first 15 minutes to read the documents and make marginal notes on them. If time allows, organize your notes and the relevant "outside" knowledge to support your main arguments.

- Brief references to the documents are enough. The readers already know the content of the documents, so do not quote them.

Recommended Activity In this textbook, you will have dealt with more than a dozen excerpts, cartoons, or other forms of a source before practicing the first DBQ. There are ten DBQs in the reviews at the ends of period 2 through period 8 and in the practice exam. As a prewriting activity, identify and discuss each document's point of view, historical situation or context, intended audience, and purpose.

In writing a DBQ answer, apply the same skills you use in writing a strong long essay answer. In addition, use the documents to support your thesis. After writing your first DBQ answers, use the scoring guide that follows or the DBQ exam rubrics released by the College Board to help you internalize the criteria for writing a strong DBQ answer.

Scoring Guide for a
Document-Based Question Answer

A. Thesis: 0–1 Point

❑ 1 point for a historically defensible thesis/claim that establishes a line of reasoning to address the question and does not merely restate it. The thesis must be at least one sentence and located in one place, either in the introduction or in the conclusion.

B. Contextualization: 0–1 Point

❑ 1 point to describe the broader historical context of the question, such as developments either before, during, or after its time frame. Describing the context requires more than a mere phrase or reference.

C. Evidence: 0–3 Points

Evidence from the Documents: 0–2 Points

❑ 1 point for accurately describing the content of **three documents** that address the question.

OR (Either the 1 point above or the 2 points below, but not both)

❑ 2 points for accurately describing the content of **six documents** and using them to **support the arguments** used in response to the question. Using the documents requires more than simply quoting them.

Evidence Beyond the Documents: 0–1 Point

❑ 1 point for using at least one additional piece of specific historical evidence **beyond** those found in the documents that is relevant to the arguments for the question. The evidence must be different from evidence used for the contextualization point and more than a mere phrase.

D. Analysis and Reasoning: 0–2 Points (Unlike the LEQ scoring, both points can be gained)

❑ 1 point for using at least **three documents** to explain **how or why** the document's point of view, purpose, historical situation, and/or audience is relevant to an argument used to address the question.

❑ 1 point for demonstrating a **complex understanding** of the historical developments by analyzing the multiple variables in the evidence. This can include analyzing more than one cause, both similarities and differences, both continuity and change, and/or the diversity of evidence that corroborates, qualifies, or modifies an argument used to address the question.

Review Schedule

Under the best conditions, preparation for the AP® U.S. History exam takes place within the context of an Advanced Placement® or Honors course. However, whether this text is used in conjunction with the course or as a review book before the exam, the teacher or students will benefit from organizing a review schedule before the exam. Many AP® candidates find that study groups are helpful, especially if the students bring to the group a variety of strengths.

Following is a sample of a six-week review schedule using this text that either teachers or students might construct to organize their preparation.

Proposed Review Schedule		
Week	Time Period	Content
1	1491 to 1800	Chapters 1–6
2	1800 to 1861	Chapters 7–13
3	1861 to 1898	Chapters 14–19
4	1890 to 1945	Chapters 20–25
5	1945 to the present	Chapters 26–31
6	All	Practice Exam

Staying with such a schedule requires discipline. This discipline is greatly strengthened if a study group chooses a specific time and place to meet and sets specific objectives for each meeting. For example, students might divide the material by chapters and prepare outline responses to key terms and review questions. Some individuals may find it more productive to review on their own. Either way, the essential content presented and the reasoning skills developed in this book should make it a convenient and efficient tool for understanding U.S. history.

UNIT 1: Period 1, 1491–1607

Chapter 1 *A New World of Many Cultures, 1491–1607*

Today, the United States is a synthesis, or combination, of people from around the world. The first people arrived in the Americas at least 10,000 years ago. Chapter 1 begins with a survey of how these people lived in 1491, the year before the arrival of European Christopher Columbus in the Americas. His arrival was a turning point in world history. It initiated lasting contact between people on opposite sides of the Atlantic Ocean. The chapter and the period end in 1607, with the founding of the first permanent English settlement at Jamestown, Virginia. The Jamestown settlement marked the beginning of the framework of a new nation.

Overview Contact between Europeans and the natives of America touched off a trans-Atlantic trade in animals, plants, and germs known as the Columbian Exchange. This trade altered the way people around the globe lived and thought.

Within a century of the arrival of Columbus, Spanish and Portuguese explorers and settlers developed colonies using natives and enslaved Africans for labor in agriculture and mining precious metals. In particular, mines in Mexico and South America produced vast amounts of silver that made Spain a wealthy empire. Natives and Africans resisted oppression by maintaining elements of their cultures.

The Spanish and the Portuguese were quickly followed to the Americas by the French and the Dutch. Later, the English joined in the competition to claim land in the Americas and establish colonies. A combination of religious and economic motives drove Europeans to colonize the Americas. The religious motive was to spread Christianity. The economic motives included finding an all-water route to Asia, to establish fur trading posts, and to take control of natural resources.

Alternate Views Until the mid-20th century, most historians viewed Columbus and European explorers and settlers as great adventurers who founded colonies that developed into modern democracies. However, in recent years, historians have highlighted the vibrant and diverse native cultures that existed in the Americas before the arrival of Columbus, and how European diseases and violence destroyed so much of these cultures. The native population declined by 90 percent after the arrival of Europeans. To demonstrate this greater appreciation of the importance of native cultures, historians often begin this period in 1491 rather than 1492.

A NEW WORLD OF MANY CULTURES, 1491–1607

Thirty-three days after my departure from [the Canary Islands] I reached the Indian Sea, where I discovered many islands, thickly peopled, of which I took possession without resistance in the name of our most illustrious monarch, by public proclamation and with unfurled banners.

Christopher Columbus, *Select Letters,* 1493.

The original discovery, exploration, and settlement of North and South America occurred at least 10,000 years before Christopher Columbus was born. Some archeologists estimate that the first people settled in North America 40,000 years ago. Migrants from Asia may have crossed a land bridge that once connected Siberia and Alaska (land now submerged under the Bering Sea). Over time, people migrated southward from near the Arctic Circle to the southern tip of South America. The first Americans adapted to the varied environments of the regions that they found. They evolved into hundreds of tribes, spoke different languages, and practiced different cultures. Estimates of the native population in the Americas in the 1490s vary from 50 million to 100 million people.

Cultures of Central and South America

The native population was concentrated in three highly developed civilizations. Between A.D. 300 and 800, the Mayas built remarkable cities in the rain forests of the Yucatán Peninsula (present-day Guatemala, Belize, and southern Mexico). Several centuries after the decline of the Mayas, the Aztecs from central Mexico developed a powerful empire. The Aztec capital, Tenochtitlán, had a population of about 200,000, equivalent in population to the largest cities of Europe. While the Aztecs were dominating Mexico and Central America, the Incas based in Peru developed a vast empire in South America. All three civilizations developed highly organized societies, carried on an extensive trade, and created calendars that were based on accurate scientific observations. All three cultivated crops that provided a stable food supply, particularly corn (maize) for the Mayas and Aztecs and potatoes for the Incas.

Cultures of North America

The population in the region north of Mexico (present-day United States and Canada) in the 1490s may have been anywhere from under 1 million to more than 10 million. In general, the native societies in this region were smaller and less sophisticated than those in Mexico and South America. One reason for this was how slowly the cultivation of corn (maize) spread northward from Mexico.

Some of the most populous and complex societies in North America had disappeared by the 15th century, for reasons not well understood. By the time of Columbus, most people in the Americas in what is now the United States and Canada lived in semipermanent settlements in groups seldom exceeding 300 people. The men made tools and hunted for game, while the women gathered plants and nuts or grew crops such as corn (maize), beans, and tobacco.

NATIVE PEOPLES OF THE AMERICAS, 1491

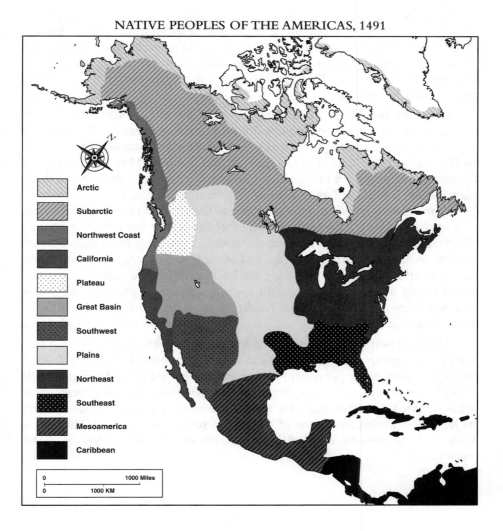

Language Beyond these similarities, the cultures of American Indians were very diverse. For example, while English, Spanish, and almost all other European languages were part of just one language family (Indo-European), American Indian languages constituted more than 20 language families. Among the largest of these were Algonquian in the Northeast, Siouan on the Great Plains, and Athabaskan in the Southwest. Together, these 20 families included more than 400 distinct languages.

Southwest Settlements In the dry region that now includes New Mexico and Arizona, groups such as the Hokokam, Anasazi, and Pueblos evolved multifaceted societies supported by farming with irrigation systems. In large numbers they lived in caves, under cliffs, and in multistoried buildings. By the time Europeans arrived, extreme drought and other hostile natives had taken their toll on these groups. However, much of their way of life was preserved in the arid land and their stone and masonry dwellings.

Northwest Settlements Along the Pacific coast from what is today Alaska to northern California, people lived in permanent longhouses or plank houses. They had a rich diet based on hunting, fishing, and gathering nuts, berries, and roots. To save stories, legends, and myths, they carved large totem poles. The high mountain ranges in this region isolated tribes from one another, creating barriers to development.

Great Plains Most people who lived on the Great Plains were either nomadic hunters or sedentary people who farmed and traded. The nomadic tribes survived on hunting, principally the buffalo, which supplied their food as well as decorations, crafting tools, knives, and clothing. They lived in tepees, frames of poles covered in animal skins, which were easily disassembled and transported. While the farming tribes also hunted buffalo, they lived permanently in earthen lodges often along rivers. They raised corn (maize), beans, and squash while actively trading with other tribes. Not until the 17th century did American Indians acquire horses by trading or stealing them from Spanish settlers. With horses, tribes such as the Lakota Sioux moved away from farming to hunting and easily following the buffalo across the plains. The plains tribes would at times merge or split apart as conditions changed. Migration also was common. For example, the Apaches gradually migrated southward from Canada to Texas.

Midwest Settlements East of the Mississippi River, the Woodland American Indians prospered with a rich food supply. Supported by hunting, fishing, and agriculture, many permanent settlements developed in the Mississippi and Ohio River valleys and elsewhere. The Adena-Hopewell culture, centered in what is now Ohio, is famous for the large earthen mounds it created, some as large as 300 feet long. One of the largest settlements in the Midwest was Cahokia (near present-day East St. Louis, Illinois), with as many as 30,000 inhabitants.

Northeast Settlements Some descendants of the Adena-Hopewell culture spread from the Ohio Valley into New York. Their culture combined hunting and farming. However, their farming techniques exhausted the soil quickly, so people had to move to fresh land frequently. Among the most famous groups of American Indians in this region was the Iroquois Confederation, a political union of five independent tribes who lived in the Mohawk Valley of New York. The five tribes were the Seneca, Cayuga, Onondaga, Oneida, and Mohawk. Multiple families related through a mother lived in longhouses, up to 200 feet long. From the 16th century through the American Revolution, the Iroquois were a powerful force, battling rival American Indians as well as Europeans.

Atlantic Seaboard Settlements In the area from New Jersey south to Florida lived the people of the Coastal Plains. Many were descendants of the Woodland mound builders and built timber and bark lodgings along rivers. The rivers and the Atlantic Ocean provided a rich source of food.

Europe Moves Toward Exploration

Until the late 1400s, Americans and the people of Europe, Africa, and Asia had no knowledge of the people on the other side of the Atlantic Ocean. While Vikings from Scandinavia had visited Greenland and North America around the year 1000, these voyages had no lasting impact. Columbus's voyages of exploration finally brought people into contact across the Atlantic. Several factors made an oceanic crossing and exploration possible in the late 15th century.

Improvements in Technology In Europe, a rebirth of classical learning prompted an outburst of artistic and scientific activity in the 15th and 16th centuries known as the Renaissance. Several of the technological advances during the Renaissance resulted from Europeans making improvements in the inventions of others. For example, they began to use gunpowder (invented by the Chinese) and the sailing compass (adopted from Arab merchants who learned about it from the Chinese). Europeans also made major improvements in shipbuilding and mapmaking. In addition, the invention of the printing press in the 1450s aided the spread of knowledge across Europe.

Religious Conflict

The later years of the Renaissance were a time of intense religious zeal and conflict. The Roman Catholic Church that had once dominated Western Europe was threatened from without by Ottoman Turks who were followers of Islam and from within by a revolt against the pope's authority.

Catholic Victory in Spain In the 8th century, Islamic invaders from North Africa, known as Moors, rapidly conquered most of what is now Spain. Over the next several centuries, Spanish Christians reconquered much of the land and set up several independent kingdoms. Two of the largest of these kingdoms united when Isabella, queen of Castile, and Ferdinand, king of Aragon, married in 1469. In 1492, under the leadership of Isabella and Ferdinand, the Spanish conquered the last Moorish stronghold in Spain, the city of Granada. In that year, the monarchs also funded Christopher Columbus on his historic first voyage. The uniting of Spain under Isabella and Ferdinand, the conquest of Granada, and the launching of Columbus signaled new leadership, hope, and power for Europeans who followed the Roman Catholic faith.

Protestant Revolt in Northern Europe In the early 1500s, certain Christians in Germany, England, France, Holland, and other northern European countries revolted against the authority of the pope in Rome. Their revolt was known as the Protestant Reformation. Conflict between Catholics and Protestants led to a series of religious wars. The conflict also caused the Catholics of Spain and Portugal and the Protestants of England and Holland to want to spread their own versions of Christianity to people in Africa, Asia, and the Americas. Thus, a religious motive for exploration and colonization was added to political and economic motives.

Expanding Trade

Economic motives for exploration grew out of a fierce competition among European kingdoms for increased trade with Africa, India, and China. In the past, merchants had traveled from the Italian city-state of Venice and the Byzantine city of Constantinople on a long, slow, expensive overland route that reached all the way to the capital of the Chinese empire. This land route to Asia had become blocked in 1453 when the Ottoman Turks seized control of Constantinople.

New Routes So the challenge to finding a new way to the rich Asian trade appeared to be by sailing either south along the West African coast east to China, or sailing west across the Atlantic Ocean. The Portuguese, who realized the route south and east was the shortest path, thought this option seemed more promising. Voyages of exploration sponsored by Portugal's Prince Henry the Navigator eventually succeeded in opening up a long sea route around South Africa's Cape of Good Hope. In 1498, the Portuguese sea captain Vasco da Gama was the first European to reach India via this route. By this time, Columbus had attempted what he mistakenly believed would be a shorter route to Asia.

Slave Trading Since ancient times people in Europe, Africa, and Asia had enslaved people captured in wars. In the 15th century, the Portuguese began trading for slaves from West Africa. They used the slaves to work newly established sugar plantations on the Madeira and Azores islands off the African coast. Producing sugar with slave labor was so profitable that when Europeans later established colonies in the Americas, they used the slave system there.

African Resistance Enslaved Africans resisted slavery in whatever ways they could. Though transported thousands of miles from their homelands and brutally repressed, they often ran away, sabotaged work, or revolted. And for generations they maintained aspects of their African culture, particularly in music, religion, and folkways.

Developing Nation-States

Europe was also changing politically in the 15th century. Small kingdoms, such as Castile and Aragon, were uniting into larger ones. Enormous multiethnic empires, such as the sprawling Holy Roman Empire in central Europe, were breaking up. Replacing the small kingdoms and the multiethnic empires were nation-states, countries in which the majority of people shared both a common culture and common loyalty toward a central government. The monarchs of the emerging nation-states, such as Isabella and Ferdinand of Spain; Prince Henry the Navigator of Portugal; and similar monarchs of France, England, and the Netherlands; depended on trade to bring in needed revenues and on the church to justify their right to rule. They used their power to search for riches abroad and to spread the influence of their version of Christianity to new overseas dominions.

Early Explorations

Changing economic, political, and social conditions in Europe shaped the ambitions of the Italian-born Christopher Columbus.

Christopher Columbus

Columbus spent eight years seeking financial support for his plan to sail west from Europe to the "Indies." Finally, in 1492, he succeeded in winning the backing of Isabella and Ferdinand. The two Spanish monarchs were then at the height of their power, having just defeated the Moors in Granada. They agreed to outfit three ships and to make Columbus governor, admiral, and viceroy of all the lands that he would claim for Spain.

After sailing from the Canary Islands on September 6, Columbus landed on an island in the Bahamas on October 12. His success in reaching lands on the other side of the ocean brought him a burst of glory in Spain. But three subsequent voyages across the Atlantic were disappointing—he found little gold, few spices, and no simple path to China and India.

Columbus's Legacy Columbus died in 1506, still believing that he had found a western route to Asia. However, many Spaniards viewed Columbus as a failure because they suspected that he had found not a valuable trade route, but a "New World." Today, some people scoff at Columbus for having erroneously giving the people he encountered the name "Indians." Even the land that he had explored was named for someone else, Amerigo Vespucci, another Italian sailor. Columbus's critics also point out the many problems and injustices suffered by the natives of the Americas after Europeans arrived and took over their land.

Nevertheless, most historians agree on Columbus's importance. Modern scholars have recognized his great skills as a navigator and his daring commitment in going forth where nobody else had ever dared to venture. Furthermore, Columbus's voyages brought about, for the first time in history, permanent interaction between people from all over the globe. He changed the world forever.

Exchanges Europeans and the original inhabitants of the Americas had developed vastly different cultures over the millennia. The contact between them resulted in the Columbian Exchange, a transfer of plants, animals, and germs from one side of the Atlantic to the other for the first time. Europeans learned about many new plants and foods, including beans, corn, sweet and white potatoes, tomatoes, and tobacco. They also contracted a new disease, syphilis. Europeans introduced to the Americas sugar cane, bluegrasses, pigs, and horses, as well as the wheel, iron implements, and guns. Deadlier than all the guns was the European importation of germs and diseases, such as small-pox and measles, to which the natives had no immunity. Millions died (there was a mortality rate of more than 90 percent), including entire tribal communities. These exchanges, biological and cultural, would permanently change the entire world.

Dividing the Americas

Spain and Portugal were the first European kingdoms to claim territories in the Americas. Their claims overlapped, leading to disputes. The Catholic monarchs of the two countries turned to the pope in Rome to resolve their differences. In 1493, the pope drew a vertical, north-south line on a world map, called the *line of demarcation.* The pope granted Spain all lands to the west of the line and Portugal all lands to the east.

In 1494, Spain and Portugal moved the pope's line a few degrees to the west and signed an agreement called the Treaty of Tordesillas. The line passed through what is now the country of Brazil. This treaty, together with Portuguese explorations, established Portugal's claim to Brazil. Spain claimed the rest of the Americas. However, other European countries soon challenged these claims.

Spanish Exploration and Conquest

Spanish dominance in the Americas was based on more than a papal ruling and a treaty. Spain owed its expanding power to its explorers and conquerors (called *conquistadores*). Feats such as the journey across the Isthmus of Panama to the Pacific Ocean by Vasco Núñez de Balboa, the circumnavigation of the world by one of Ferdinand Magellan's ships (Magellan died before completing the trip), the conquests of the Aztecs in Mexico by Hernan Cortés, and the conquest of the Incas in Peru by Francisco Pizzaro secured Spain's initial supremacy in the Americas.

The conquistadores sent ships loaded with gold and silver back to Spain from Mexico and Peru. They increased the gold supply by more than 500 percent, making Spain the richest and most powerful nation in Europe. Spain's success encouraged other nations to turn to the Americas in search of gold and power. After seizing the wealth of the Indian empires, the Spanish instituted an *encomienda* system, with the king of Spain giving grants of land and natives to individual Spaniards. These Indians had to farm or work in the mines. The fruits of their labors went to their Spanish masters, who in turn had to "care" for them. As Europeans' diseases and brutality reduced the native population, the Spanish brought enslaved people from West Africa under the *asiento* system. This required the Spanish to pay a tax to their king on each slave they imported to the Americas.

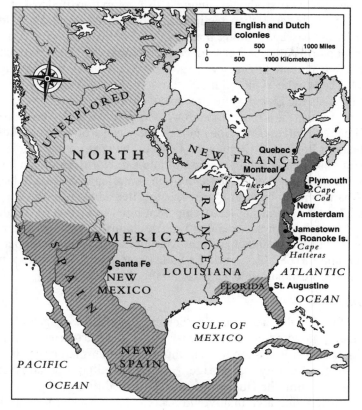

English Claims

England's earliest claims to territory in the Americas rested on the voyages of John Cabot, an Italian sea captain who sailed under contract to England's King Henry VII. Cabot explored the coast of Newfoundland in 1497.

England, however, did not follow up Cabot's discoveries with other expeditions of exploration and settlement. Other issues preoccupied England's monarchy in the 1500s, including Henry VIII's break with the Roman Catholic Church. In the 1570s and 1580s, under Queen Elizabeth I, England challenged Spanish shipping in both the Atlantic and Pacific Oceans. Sir Francis Drake, for example, attacked Spanish ships, seized the gold and silver that they carried, and even attacked Spanish settlements on the coast of Peru. Another English adventurer, Sir Walter Raleigh, attempted to establish a settlement at Roanoke Island off the North Carolina coast in 1587, but the venture failed.

French Claims

The French monarchy first showed interest in exploration in 1524 when it sponsored a voyage by an Italian navigator, Giovanni da Verrazano. Hoping to find a northwest passage leading through the Americas to Asia, Verrazano explored part of North America's eastern coast, including the New York harbor. French claims to American territory were also based on the voyages of Jacques Cartier (1534–1542), who explored the St. Lawrence River extensively.

Like the English, the French were slow to develop colonies across the Atlantic. During the 1500s, the French monarchy was preoccupied with European wars as well as with internal religious conflict between Roman Catholics and French Protestants known as Huguenots. Only in the next century did France develop a strong interest in following up its claims to North American land.

The first permanent French settlement in America was established by Samuel de Champlain in 1608 at Quebec, a fortified village on the St. Lawrence River. Champlain's strong leadership won him the nickname "Father of New France." Other explorers extended French claims across a vast territory. In 1673, Louis Jolliet and Father Jacques Marquette explored the upper Mississippi River, and in 1682, Robert de La Salle explored the Mississippi basin, which he named Louisiana (after the French king, Louis XIV).

Dutch Claims

During the 1600s, the Netherlands also began to sponsor voyages of exploration. The Dutch government hired Henry Hudson, an experienced English sailor, to seek westward passage to Asia through northern America. In 1609, while searching for a northwest passage, Hudson sailed up a broad river that was later named for him, the Hudson River. This expedition established Dutch claims to the surrounding area that would become New Amsterdam (and later New York). The Dutch government granted a private company, the Dutch West India Company, the right to control the region for economic gain.

Spanish Settlements in North America

Spanish settlements developed slowly in North America, as a result of limited mineral resources and strong opposition from American Indians.

Florida After a number of failed attempts and against the strong resistance of American Indians in the region, the Spanish established a permanent settlement at St. Augustine in 1565. Today, St. Augustine is the oldest city in North America founded by Europeans.

New Mexico Santa Fe was established as the capital of New Mexico in 1610. Harsh efforts to Christianize the American Indians caused the Pueblo people to revolt in 1680. The Spanish were driven from the area until 1692.

Texas In between Florida and New Mexico, the Spanish established settlements in Texas. These communities grew in the early 1700s as Spain attempted to resist French efforts to explore the lower Mississippi River.

California In response to Russian exploration from Alaska, the Spanish established permanent settlements at San Diego in 1769 and San Francisco in 1776. By 1784, a series of missions or settlements had been established along the California coast by members of the Franciscan order. Father Junípero Serra founded nine of these missions.

European Treatment of Native Americans

Most Europeans looked down upon Native Americans. The Europeans who colonized North and South America generally viewed Native Americans as inferior people who could be exploited for economic gain, converted to Christianity, and used as military allies. However, Europeans used various approaches for controlling Native Americans and operating their colonies.

Spanish Policy

The Spanish who settled in Mexico and Peru encountered the highly organized Aztec and Inca empires. Even after diseases killed most natives, millions remained in these empires that the Spanish could incorporate as laborers in their own empire. Many natives who did not die from disease died from forced labor. Because few families came from Spain to settle the empire, the explorers and soldiers intermarried with natives as well as with Africans. The latter were captured in Africa and forced to travel across the ocean to provide slave labor for the Spanish colonists. A rigid class system developed in the Spanish colonies, one dominated by pure-blooded Spaniards.

Bartolomé de Las Casas One European who dissented from the views of most Europeans toward Native Americans was a Spanish priest named Bartolomé de Las Casas. Though he had owned land and slaves in the West Indies and had fought in wars against the Indians, he eventually became an advocate for better treatment for Indians. He persuaded the king to institute the New Laws of 1542. These laws ended Indian slavery, halted forced Indian labor, and began to end the encomienda system which kept the Indians in serfdom. Conservative Spaniards, eager to keep the encomienda system, responded and successfully pushed the king to repeal parts of the New Laws.

Valladolid Debate The debate over the role for Indians in the Spanish colonies came to a head in a formal debate in 1550–1551 in Valladolid, Spain. On one side, Las Casas argued that the Indians were completely human and morally equal to Europeans, so enslaving them was not justified. On the other side, another priest, Juan Ginés de Sepúlveda, argued that Indians were less than human. Hence, they benefited from serving the Spaniards in the econmienda system. Neither side clearly won the debate. Though Las Casas was unable to gain equal treatment for Native Americans, he established the basic arguments on behalf of justice for Indians.

English Policy

Unlike the Spanish, the English settled in areas without large native empires that could be controlled as a workforce. In addition, many English colonists came in families rather than as single young men, so marriage with natives was less common. Initially, at least in Massachusetts, the English and the American Indians coexisted, traded, and shared ideas. American Indians taught the settlers how to grow new crops such as corn (maize) and showed them how to hunt in the forests. They traded various furs for an array of English manufactured goods, including iron tools and weapons. But peaceful relations soon gave way to conflict and open warfare. The English had no respect for American Indian cultures, which they viewed as primitive or "savage." For their part, American Indians saw their way of life threatened as the English began to take more land to support their ever-increasing population. The English occupied the land and forced the small, scattered tribes they encountered to move away from the coast to inland territories. They expelled the natives rather than subjugating them.

French Policy

The French, looking for furs and converts to Catholicism, viewed American Indians as potential economic and military allies. Compared to the Spaniards and the English, the French maintained good relations with the tribes they encountered. Seeking to control the fur trade, the French built trading posts throughout the St. Lawrence Valley, the Great Lakes region, and along the Mississippi River. At these posts, they exchanged French goods for beaver pelts and other furs collected by American Indians. Because the French had few colonists, farms, or towns, they posed less threat to the native population than did other Europeans. In addition, French soldiers assisted the Huron people in fighting their traditional enemy, the Iroquois.

Native American Reaction

North American tribes saw themselves as groups distinct from each other, not as part of a larger body of Native Americans. As a result, European settlers rarely had to be concerned with a unified response from the Native Americans. Initially the European goods such as copper pots and guns had motivated the natives to interact with the strangers. After the decimation of their peoples from the violence and disease of the Europeans, the Native Americans had to adopt new ways to survive. Upon observing the Europeans fighting each other, some tribes allied themselves with one European power or another in hopes of gaining support in order to survive. A number of tribes simply migrated to new land to get away from the slowly encroaching settlers. Regardless of how they dealt with the European invasion, Native Americans would never be able to return to the life they had known prior to 1492.

HISTORICAL PERSPECTIVES: WAS COLUMBUS A GREAT HERO?

Over the centuries, Columbus has received both praise for his role as a "discoverer" and blame for his actions as a "conqueror." In the United States, he has traditionally been viewed as a hero. As early as 1828, Washington Irving wrote a popular biography extolling the explorer's virtues. The apex of Columbus's heroic reputation was reached in 1934 when President Franklin Roosevelt declared October 12 a national holiday.

Since the 1990s, however, revisionist histories and biographies have been highly critical of Columbus. His detractors argue that Columbus was simply at the right place at the right time. Europe at the end of the 15th century was ready to expand. If Columbus had not crossed the Atlantic in 1492, some other explorer—perhaps Vespucci or Cabot—would have done so a few years later. According to this interpretation, Columbus was little more than a good navigator and a self-promoter who exploited an opportunity.

Some revisionists take a harsh view of Columbus and regard him not as the first discoverer of America but rather as its first conqueror. They portray him as a religious fanatic in the European Christian tradition who sought to convert the American natives to Christianity and liquidated those who resisted.

The revisionist argument has not gone unanswered. For example, historian Arthur M. Schlesinger Jr. has argued that the chief motivation for Columbus's deeds was neither greed for gold nor ambition for conquest. What drove him, in Schlesinger's view, was the challenge of the unknown. Columbus's apologists admit that millions of Native Americans died as a result of European exploration in the Americas, but they point out that an unknown number had suffered horrible deaths in Aztec sacrifices. Moreover, the mistreatment of Native Americans was perhaps partially offset by such positive results as the gradual development of democratic institutions in the colonies and later the United States.

Historians will continue to debate the nature of Columbus's achievement. As with other historical questions, distinguishing between fact and fiction and separating a writer's personal biases from objective reality is difficult. One conclusion is inescapable: As a result of Columbus's voyages, world history took a sharp turn in a new direction. His explorations established a permanent point of contact between Europeans and the first Americans, and soon between both groups and Africans. People are still living with the consequences of this interaction.

KEY TERMS BY THEME

Exchange and Interaction (WXT, GEO)
corn (maize)
horses
disease

Labor Systems (WXT)
encomienda system
asiento system
slavery

Migration (MIG, ARC)
land bridge
Adena-Hopewell
Hokokam, Anasazi, and Pueblos
Woodland mound builders
Lakota Sioux

Identity and Politics (NAT, POL)
Mayas
Incas
Aztecs
conquistadores
Hernan Cortés
Francisco Pizarro
New Laws of 1542
Roanoke Island

Atlantic Trade (WOR)
compass
printing press
Ferdinand and Isabella
Protestant Reformation
Henry the Navigator
Christopher Columbus
Treaty of Tordesillas
slave trade
nation-state

American Indians (MIG, POL, ARC)
Algonquian
Siouan
Iroquois Confederation
longhouses

Search for Resources (GEO)
John Cabot
Jacques Cartier
Samuel de Champlain
Henry Hudson

Values and Attitudes (SOC)
Bartolomé de Las Casas
Valladolid Debate
Juan Ginés de Sepúlveda

MULTIPLE-CHOICE QUESTIONS

Questions 1–2 refer to the excerpt below.

"To oppose those hordes of northern tribes, singly and alone, would prove certain destruction. We can make no progress in that way. We unite ourselves into one common band of brothers. We must have but one voice. Many voices makes confusion. We must have one fire, one pipe and one war club. This will give us strength. If our warriors are united they can defeat the enemy and drive them from our land; If we do this, we are safe . . . .

"And you of the different nations of the south, and you of the west, may place yourselves under our protection, and we will protect you. We earnestly desire the alliance and friendship of you all . . . ."

—Chief Elias Johnson, *Legends, Traditions, and Laws of the Iroquois, or Six Nations, and History of the Tuscarora Indians,* 1881

1. Which of these was a common reaction by Indians to Europeans and represented a rejection of Chief Johnson's suggestions?

   (A) Converting to Christianity

   (B) Migrating westward

   (C) Selling their land

   (D) Accepting European leadership

2. Which of the following factors best explains why Native American efforts to unite were rare?

   (A) Most tribes were isolated from each other

   (B) Europeans discouraged tribes from uniting

   (C) People had different foods and cultures

   (D) Tribes had traditions of independence

Questions 3–5 refer to the excerpt below.

"Concerning the treatment of Native American workers:
When they were allowed to go home, they often found it deserted and had no other recourse than to go out into the woods to find food and to die. When they fell ill, which was very frequently because they are a delicate people unaccustomed to such work, the Spaniards did not believe them and pitilessly called them lazy dogs, and kicked and beat them; and when illness was apparent they sent them home as useless, giving them some cassava for the twenty- to eighty-league journey. They would go then, falling into the first stream and dying there in desperation; others would hold on longer, but very few ever made it home. I sometimes came upon dead bodies on my way, and upon others who were gasping and moaning in their death agony, repeating 'Hungry, hungry.'"

—Bartolomé de Las Casas, priest and social reformer,
In Defense of the Indian, c. 1550

3. Which of the following best explains the underlying cause of the Spanish actions described by Las Casas?

(A) Racism

(B) Religion

(C) Desire for wealth

(D) Fear of native power

4. The primary audience that Las Casas hoped to influence by his writing was

(A) the monarchs of Spain

(B) the Roman Catholic Church

(C) the conquistadores

(D) the Native Americans

5. Which of the following factors that affected Native Americans is directly implied but not stated in this excerpt?

(A) Many Spaniards were sympathetic to the Native Americans

(B) The Catholic Church was trying to help the Native Americans

(C) European diseases were killing millions of Native Americans

(D) The Spanish faced strong resistance from Native Americans

Questions 6–7 refer to the excerpt below.

"Apart from his navigational skills, what most set Columbus apart from other Europeans of his day were not the things that he believed, but the intensity with which he believed in them and the determination with which he acted upon those beliefs. . . .

"Columbus was, in most respects, merely an especially active and dramatic embodiment of the European—and especially the Mediterranean—mind and soul of his time: a religious fanatic obsessed with the conversion, conquest, or liquidation of all non-Christians; a latter-day Crusader in search of personal wealth and fame, who expected the enormous and mysterious world he had found to be filled with monstrous races inhabiting wild forests, and with golden people living in Eden."

—David E. Stannard, historian, *American Holocaust: Columbus and the Conquest of the New World,* 1992

6. Which of the following European nations would be the least likely to share the characteristics Stannard uses in describing Columbus?

   (A) England

   (B) Italy

   (C) Portugal

   (D) Spain

7. Which of the following is a reason historians are most likely to criticize the view of Columbus expressed in this excerpt?

   (A) It ignores the period in which Columbus lived

   (B) It displays a bias against Christians

   (C) It skips over the progress brought by Columbus

   (D) It uses highly charged language

Questions 8–9 refer to the excerpt below.

"The province of Quivira is 950 leagues from Mexico. Where I reached it, it is in the fortieth degree [of latitude]. . . . I have treated the natives of this province, and all the others whom I found wherever I went, as well as was possible, agreeably to what Your Majesty had commanded, and they have received no harm in any way from me or from those who went in my company. I remained twenty- five days in this province of Quivira, so as to see and explore the country and also to find out whether there was anything beyond which could be of service to Your Majesty, because the guides who had brought me had given me an account of other provinces beyond this. And what I am sure of is that there is not any gold nor any other metal in all that country."

—Francisco Coronado, Spanish conquistador, *Travels in Quivira,*
c. 1542

8. Based on Coronado's observations, which of the following best describes Spanish efforts in Mexico in the mid-16th century?

   (A) Exploring lands new to them

   (B) Establishing colonies

   (C) Warring with Native Americans

   (D) Spreading the Christian faith

9. The activities of Coronado and other Spanish and Portuguese explorers in the Americas in the 16th century primarily depended on the support of

   (A) merchants and fur traders

   (B) the Catholic Church

   (C) the monarchs

   (D) enslaved Europeans

10. The activities of Coronado and other Spanish and Portuguese explorers in the Americas in the 16th century primarily depended on the support of

   (A) merchants and fur traders

   (B) the Catholic Church

   (C) the monarchs

   (D) enslaved Europeans

SHORT-ANSWER QUESTIONS

Use complete sentences; an outline or bulleted list alone is not acceptable.

Question 1. Answer (A), (B), and (C).

(A) Briefly explain ONE specific example of how religion in Europe during the early 16th century helped bring about the exploration and colonization of lands across the seas.

(B) Briefly explain ONE specific example of how trade in Europe during the early 16th century helped bring about the exploration and colonization of lands across the seas.

(C) Briefly explain ONE specific example of how technology in Europe during the early 16th century helped bring about the exploration and colonization of lands across the seas.

Question 2 is based on the following excerpt.

"I marvel not a little, right worshipful, that since the first discovery of America (which is now full four score and ten years), after so great conquests and plannings of the Spaniards and Portuguese there, that we of England could never have the grace to set fast footing in such fertile and temperate places as are left as yet unpossessed of them. But . . . I conceive great hope that the time approacheth and now is that we of England may share and part stakes . . . in part of America and other regions as yet undiscovered. . . .

"Yea, if we would behold with the eye of pity how all our prisons are pestered and filled with able men to serve their country, which for small robberies are daily hanged up in great numbers, . . . we would hasten . . . the deducting [conveying] of some colonies of our superfluous people into these temperate and fertile parts of America, which being within six weeks' sailing of England, are yet unpossessed by any Christians, and seem to offer themselves unto us, stretching nearer unto Her Majesty's dominions than to other parts of Europe."

—Richard Hakluyt, English writer, *Divers Voyages Touching the Discovery of America and the Islands Adjacent,* 1582

2. Using the excerpt, answer (A), (B), and (C).

(A) Briefly explain ONE reason not in this passage why England was so far behind Spain and Portugal in colonization.

(B) Briefly explain ONE place where the author believes England could find a supply of potential colonists for the Americas.

(C) Briefly explain ONE development of the late 16th century that challenges or supports the point of view expressed by the writer.

Question 3 is based on the following excerpt.

"I want the natives to develop a friendly attitude toward us because I know that they are a people who can be made free and converted to our Holy Faith more by love than by force. I therefore gave red caps to some and glass beads to others. They hung the beads around their necks, along with some other things of slight value that I gave them. . . . I warned my men to take nothing from the people without giving something in exchange."

—Christopher Columbus, *Log,* October 12, 1492

3. Using the excerpt, answer (A), (B), and (C).
   (A) Briefly explain the point of view expressed by Columbus in the excerpt.
   (B) Briefly explain what ONE powerful group in Spain, other than the monarchy, Columbus would be appealing to in the above passage.
   (C) Briefly explain ONE example of contact between Europeans and the first inhabitants of America that is not consistent with the above passage.

Question 4. Answer (A), (B), and (C).
   (A) Briefly explain ONE specific policy of England toward Native Americans during the period 1492 to 1607.
   (B) Briefly explain ONE specific policy of Spain toward Native Americans during the period 1492 to 1607.
   (C) Briefly explain ONE specific reaction of Native Americans to European policies during the period 1492 to 1607.

THINK AS A HISTORIAN: QUESTIONS ABOUT CAUSATION

Tests often ask students to explain why one event or trait happened after or resulted from another. Which THREE prompts below would best be answered with an essay that emphasizes causation?

1. Explain why American Indians were so diverse in 1491.
2. How did Spanish colonies differ from English colonies?
3. How did religious beliefs influence American colonization?
4. Did Columbus reflect the values of the late 15th-century Europe?
5. Analyze the impact of colonization on Spain.

Unit 1: Period 1 Review, Analyzing Evidence

Below are a primary source and a secondary source provided to help you develop the skill of analyzing evidence. The italicized questions provide a suggested sequential step-by-step development process to analyze a document. As you study the questions and answers, consider alternate answers based on your own knowledge and understanding as a historical thinker.

Analyzing a Primary Source

"Being earnestly requested by a dear friend to put down in writing some true relation of our late performed voyage to the north parts of Virginia [Massachusetts] I resolved to satisfy his request. . . .

"Coming ashore, we stood awhile like men ravished at the beauty and delicacy of this sweet soil. For besides diverse clear lakes of fresh water . . . meadows very large and full of green grass. . . .

"[This climate so agreed with us] that we found our health and strength all the while we remained there so to renew and increase as, notwithstanding our diet and lodging was none of the best, yet not one of our company (God be thanked) felt the least grudging or inclination to any disease or sickness but were much fatter and in better health than when we went out of England."

—John Brereton, *The Discovery of the North Part of Virginia*, 1602

Content

- *What is the key point?* New England has a healthy environment.
- *What content is useful?* It provides early impressions of New England.

The Author's Point of View

- *Who was the author?* John Brereton, an Englishman
- *How reliable is the author?* Answering this requires additional research.
- *What was the author's point of view?* New England is a wonderful place.
- *What other beliefs might the author hold?* He believes in God.

The Author's Purpose

- *Why did the author create this document at this time?* Others expressed interest in his experiences in land that was new to them.
- *How does the document's purpose reflect its reliability?* The author could be biased to encourage investment in colonization.

Audience

- *Who was this document created for?* for people in England
- *How might the audience affect the document's content?* The audience was looking for opportunities for success in the Americas.
- *How might the audience affect the document's reliability?* The document might emphasize positive information.

Historical Context

- *When and where was this produced?* England in the early 17th century
- *What concurrent events might have affected the author?* the desire of many to encourage and profit from the new colonies

Format/Medium

- *What is the format?* a first-person narrative

Limitations

- *What is one limitation of the excerpt or the author's view?* The document says nothing about the indigenous people living in the region.

Analyzing a Second Source

"Why did the English found colonies and make them stick? For most the goal was material. . . . For some the goal was spiritual. . . . But all the colonists who suffered perilous voyages and risked early death in America were either hustlers or hustled. That is, they knew the hardships beforehand and were courageous, desperate, or faithful enough to face them, or else they did not know what lay ahead but were taken in by the propaganda of sponsors. . . . In every case colonists left a swarming competitive country that heralded self-improvement but offered limited opportunities for it."

—Walter A. McDougall, *Freedom Just Around the Corner,* 2004

Content and Argument

- *What is the main idea of the excerpt?* English settlers came to America for diverse reasons.
- *What information supports this historian?* the examples of both the religious Puritans and adventurers at Jamestown
- *What information challenges this historian?* Many people were forced to settle America as slaves or convicts.
- *What is the interpretation of events argued for in this excerpt?* The opportunities for prosperity and religious freedom were far greater in the colonies than those they left behind in Europe.

Author's Point of View

- *How could the author's perspective have been shaped by the times in which he wrote?* The belief in American exceptionalism at the beginning of the 21st century could have shaped his view of the colonial era.
- *Why might a different historian have a different view of the same events?* Another historian might emphasize that one factor, such as the search for wealth, was much more important than any combination of factors.

UNIT 2: Period 2, 1607–1754

Chapter 2 *The Thirteen Colonies and the British Empire, 1607–1754*

Chapter 3 *Colonial Society in the 18th Century*

In a period of almost 150 years during the 17th and 18th centuries, the British established 13 colonies along the Atlantic coast of North America. These colonies provided a profitable trade and a home to a diverse group of American Indians, Europeans, and Africans.

Overview From the establishment of the first permanent English settlement in North America in 1607 to the start of a decisive war for European control of the continent in 1756, the colonies evolved. At first, they struggled for survival. Over time, they became a society of permanent farms, plantations, towns, and cities. European settlers brought various cultures, economic plans, and ideas for governing to the Americas. In particular, with varying approaches, they all sought to dominate the native inhabitants.

The British took pride in their tradition of free farmers working the land. The various colonies developed regional or sectional differences based on many influences including topography, natural resources, climate, and the background of their settlers. In general, British colonists largely viewed the American Indian as an obstacle to colonial growth. Those who survived contact with European diseases were pushed westward off of their land.

With the settlers' emphasis on agriculture came a demand for labor. This led to a growing dependence on the labor of enslaved Africans, especially in the southern colonies. The Atlantic slave trade was important to the economy, and much of the trade was financed or conducted by people in northern colonies.

During the colonial period, the British and the French fought a series of wars for power in both Europe and the Americas. The last of these, the Seven Years' War, began in North America in 1756. The British victory freed the colonists from concerns about attacks by the French. In addition, the contributions by the colonies also signified their political maturity. They began to think of themselves and their ability to stand up for their interests with more confidence.

Alternate Views Historians disagree on what date best marks the end of the colonial era. Some identify the conclusion of the Seven Years' War in 1763 or the start of the American Revolution in 1775 or the signing of a peace treaty in 1783. Historians who focus on cultural rather than political and military events might choose other dates for both the start and end of the period that emphasized the role of non-English residents, such as the Scotch-Irish, Germans, and enslaved Africans, in the colonies.

2

THE THIRTEEN COLONIES AND THE BRITISH EMPIRE, 1607–1754

If they desire that Piety and godliness should prosper; accompanied with sobriety, justice and love, let them choose a Country such as this is; even like France, or England, which may yield sufficiency with hard labour and industry. . . .

Reverend John White, *The Planter's Plea,* 1630

Starting with Jamestown (Virginia) in 1607 and ending with Georgia in 1733, a total of 13 distinct English colonies developed along the Atlantic Coast of North America. Every colony received its identity and its authority to operate by means of a charter (a document granting special privileges) from the English monarch. Each charter described in general terms the relationship that was supposed to exist between the colony and the crown. Over time, three types of charters—and three types of colonies—developed:

- Corporate colonies, such as Jamestown, were operated by joint-stock companies, at least during these colonies' early years.
- Royal colonies, such as Virginia after 1624, were to be under the direct authority and rule of the king's government.
- Proprietary colonies, such as Maryland and Pennsylvania, were under the authority of individuals granted charters of ownership by the king.

Unlike the French and Spanish colonists, the English brought a tradition of representative government. They were accustomed to holding elections for representatives who would speak for property owners and decide important measures, such as taxes, proposed by the king's government. While political and religious conflicts dominated England, feelings for independence grew in the colonies. Eventually, tensions emerged between the king and his colonial subjects. This chapter summarizes the development of the English colonies.

Early English Settlements

In the early 1600s, England was finally in a position to colonize the lands explored more than a century earlier by John Cabot. By defeating a large Spanish fleet—the Spanish Armada—in 1588, England had gained a reputation as a major naval power. Also in this period, England's population was growing rapidly while its economy was depressed. The number of poor and landless people increased, people who were attracted to opportunities in the Americas. The English devised a practical method for financing the costly and risky enterprise of founding colonies. A joint-stock company pooled the savings of many investors, thereby spreading the risk. Thus, colonies on the North Atlantic Coast were able to attract large numbers of English settlers.

Jamestown

England's King James I chartered the Virginia Company, a joint-stock company that founded the first permanent English colony in America at Jamestown in 1607.

Early Problems The first settlers of Jamestown suffered greatly, mostly from their own mistakes. The settlement's location in a swampy area along the James River resulted in fatal outbreaks of dysentery and malaria. Moreover, many of the settlers were gentlemen unaccustomed to physical work. Others were gold-seeking adventurers who refused to hunt or farm. One key source of goods was from trade with American Indians—but when conflicts erupted between settlers and the natives, trade would stop and settlers went hungry. Starvation was a persistent issue in Jamestown.

Through the forceful leadership of Captain John Smith, Jamestown survived its first five years, but barely. Then, through the efforts of John Rolfe and his Indian wife, Pocahontas, the colony developed a new variety of tobacco that would become popular in Europe and become a profitable crop.

Transition to a Royal Colony Despite tobacco, by 1624 the Virginia colony remained near collapse. More than 6,000 people had settled there, but only 2,000 remained alive. Further, the Virginia Company made unwise decisions that placed it heavily in debt. King James I had seen enough. He revoked the charter of the bankrupt company and took direct control of the colony. Now known as Virginia, the colony became England's first royal colony.

Plymouth and Massachusetts Bay

Religious motivation, not the search for wealth, was the principal force behind the settlement of two other English colonies, Plymouth and Massachusetts Bay. Both were settled by English Protestants who dissented from the official government-supported Church of England, also known as the Anglican Church. The leader of the Church of England was the monarch of England. The Church of England had broken away from the control of the pope in Rome, so it was no longer part of the Roman Catholic Church. However, it had kept most of the Catholic rituals and governing structure. The dissenters, influenced by the teachings of Swiss theologian John Calvin, charged that the Church of England should break more completely with Rome. In addition, the dissenters adopted Calvin's doctrine of predestination, the belief that God guides those he has selected for salvation even before their birth. England's King James I, who reigned from 1603 to 1625, viewed the religious dissenters as a threat to his religious and political authority and ordered them arrested and jailed.

The Plymouth Colony

Radical dissenters to the Church of England were known as the Separatists because they wanted to organize a completely separate church that was independent of royal control. Several hundred Separatists left England for Holland in search of religious freedom. Because of their travels, they became known as Pilgrims. Economic hardship and cultural differences with the Dutch led many of the Pilgrims to seek another haven for their religion. They chose the new colony in America, then operated by the Virginia Company of London. In 1620, a small group of Pilgrims set sail for Virginia aboard the *Mayflower.* Fewer than half of the 100 passengers on this ship were Separatists; the rest were people who had economic motives for making the voyage.

After a hard and stormy voyage of 65 days, the *Mayflower* dropped anchor off the Massachusetts coast, a few hundred miles to the north of the intended destination in Virginia. Rather than going on to Jamestown as planned, the Pilgrims decided to establish a new colony at Plymouth.

Early Hardships After a first winter that saw half their number perish, the settlers at Plymouth were helped to adapt to the land by friendly American Indians. They celebrated a good harvest at a thanksgiving feast (the first Thanksgiving) in 1621. Under strong leaders, including Captain Miles Standish and Governor William Bradford, the Plymouth colony grew slowly but remained small. Fish, furs, and lumber became the mainstays of the economy.

Massachusetts Bay Colony

A group of more moderate dissenters believed that the Church of England could be reformed. Because they wanted to purify the church, they became known as Puritans. The persecution of Puritans increased when a new king, Charles I, took the throne in 1625. Seeking religious freedom, a group of Puritans gained a royal charter for the Massachusetts Bay Company (1629).

In 1630, about a thousand Puritans led by John Winthrop sailed for the Massachusetts shore and founded Boston and several other towns. A civil war in England in the 1630s drove some 15,000 more settlers to the Massachusetts Bay Colony—a movement known as the Great Migration.

Early Political Institutions

From their very beginning, the American colonies began taking steps toward self-rule.

Representative Assembly in Virginia The Virginia Company encouraged settlement in Jamestown by guaranteeing colonists the same rights as residents of England, including representation in the lawmaking process. In 1619, just 12 years after the founding of Jamestown, Virginia's colonists organized the first representative assembly in America, the House of Burgesses.

Representative Government in New England Aboard the *Mayflower* in 1620, the Pilgrims drew up and signed a document that pledged them to make decisions by the will of the majority. This document, known as the Mayflower Compact, was an early form of colonial self-government and a rudimentary written constitution.

In the Massachusetts Bay Colony, all freemen—male members of the Puritan Church—had the right to participate in yearly elections of the colony's governor, his assistants, and a representative assembly.

Limits to Colonial Democracy Despite these steps, most colonists were excluded from the political process. Only male property owners could vote for representatives. Those who were either female or landless had few rights; slaves and indentured servants had practically none at all. Also, many colonial governors ruled with autocratic or unlimited powers, answering only to the king or others in England who provided the colonies' financial support. Thus, the gradual development of democratic ideas in the colonies coexisted with antidemocratic practices such as slavery and the widespread mistreatment of American Indians.

The Chesapeake Colonies

In 1632, King Charles I subdivided the Virginia colony. He chartered a new colony on either side of Chesapeake Bay and granted control of it to George Calvert (Lord Baltimore), as a reward for this Catholic nobleman's service to the crown. The new colony of Maryland thus became the first proprietary colony.

Religious Issues in Maryland

The king expected proprietors to carry out his wishes faithfully, thus giving him control over a colony. The first Lord Baltimore died before he could achieve great wealth in his colony while also providing a haven for his fellow Catholics. The Maryland proprietorship passed to his son, Cecil Calvert—the second Lord Baltimore—who set about implementing his father's plan in 1634.

Act of Toleration To avoid persecution in England, several wealthy English Catholics emigrated to Maryland and established large colonial plantations. They were quickly outnumbered, however, by Protestant farmers. Protestants therefore held a majority in Maryland's assembly. In 1649, Calvert persuaded the assembly to adopt the Act of Toleration, the first colonial statute granting religious freedom to all Christians. However, the statute also called for the death of anyone who denied the divinity of Jesus.

Protestant Revolt In the late 1600s, Protestant resentment against a Catholic proprietor erupted into a brief civil war. The Protestants triumphed, and the Act of Toleration was repealed. Catholics lost their right to vote in elections for the Maryland assembly. In the 18th century, Maryland's economy and society was much like that of neighboring Virginia, except that in Maryland there was greater tolerance of religious diversity among different Protestant sects.

Labor Shortages

In both Maryland and Virginia, landowners saw great opportunities. They could get land, either by taking it from or trading for it with American Indians, and Europeans had a growing demand for tobacco. However, they could not find enough laborers. For example, in Virginia, the high death rate from disease, food shortages, and battles with American Indians meant that the population grew slowly. Landowners tried several ways to find the workers they wanted.

Indentured Servants At first, the Virginia Company hoped to meet the need for labor using indentured servants. Under contract with a master or landowner who paid for their passage, young people from the British Isles agreed to work for a specified period—usually between four to seven years—in return for room and board. In effect, indentured servants were under the absolute rule of their masters until the end of their work period. At the expiration of that period, they gained their freedom and either worked for wages or obtained land of their own to farm. For landowners, the system provided laborers, but only temporarily.

Headright System Virginia attempted to attract immigrants through offers of land. The colony offered 50 acres of land to (1) each immigrant who paid for his own passage and (2) any plantation owner who paid for an immigrant's passage.

Slavery In 1619, a Dutch ship brought an unusual group of indentured servants to Virginia: they were black Africans. Because English law at that time did not recognize hereditary slavery, the first Africans in Virginia were not in bondage for life, and any children born to them were free. Moreover, the early colonists were struggling to survive and too poor to purchase the Africans who were being imported as slaves for sugar plantations in the West Indies. By 1650, there were only about 400 African laborers in Virginia. However, by the end of the 1660s, the Virginia House of Burgesses had enacted laws that discriminated between blacks and whites. Africans and their offspring were to be kept in permanent bondage. They were slaves.

Economic Problems Beginning in the 1660s, low tobacco prices, due largely to overproduction, brought hard times to the Chesapeake colonies Maryland and Virginia. When Virginia's House of Burgesses attempted to raise tobacco prices, the merchants of London retaliated by raising their own prices on goods exported to Virginia.

Conflict in Virginia

Sir William Berkeley, the royal governor of Virginia (1641–1652; 1660–1677), used dictatorial powers to govern on behalf of the large planters. He antagonized small farmers on Virginia's western frontier because he failed to protect them from Indian attacks.

Bacon's Rebellion Nathaniel Bacon, an impoverished gentleman farmer, seized upon the grievances of the western farmers to lead a rebellion against Berkeley's government. Bacon and others resented the economic and political control exercised by a few large planters in the Chesapeake area. He raised an army of volunteers and, in 1676, conducted a series of raids and massacres against American Indian villages on the Virginia frontier. Berkeley's government in Jamestown accused Bacon of rebelling against royal authority. Bacon's army succeeded in defeating the governor's forces and even burned the Jamestown settlement. Soon afterward, Bacon died of dysentery and the rebel army collapsed. Governor Berkeley brutally suppressed the remnants of the insurrection, executing 23 rebels.

Lasting Problems Although it was short-lived, Bacon's Rebellion, or the Chesapeake Revolution, highlighted two long-lasting disputes in colonial Virginia: (1) sharp class differences between wealthy planters and landless or poor farmers, and (2) colonial resistance to royal control. These problems would continue into the next century, even after the general conditions of life in the Chesapeake colonies became more stable and prosperous.

Development of New England

Strong religious convictions helped sustain settlers in their struggle to establish the Plymouth and Massachusetts Bay colonies. However, Puritan leaders showed intolerance of anyone who questioned their religious teachings. The Puritans often banished dissidents from the Bay colony. These banished dissidents formed settlements that would develop into Rhode Island and Connecticut.

Rhode Island Roger Williams went to Boston in 1631 as a respected Puritan minister. He believed, however, that the individual's conscience was beyond the control of any civil or church authority. His teachings on this point placed him in conflict with other Puritan leaders, who ordered his banishment from the Bay colony. Leaving Boston, Williams fled southward to Narragansett Bay, where he and a few followers founded the settlement of Providence in 1636. The new colony was unique in two respects. First, it recognized the rights of American Indians and paid them for the use of their land. Second, Williams' government allowed Catholics, Quakers, and Jews to worship freely. Williams also founded one of the first Baptist churches in America.

Another dissident who questioned the doctrines of the Puritan authorities was Anne Hutchinson. She believed in *antinomianism*—the idea that faith alone, not deeds, is necessary for salvation. Banished from the Bay colony, Hutchinson and a group of followers founded the colony of Portsmouth in 1638, not far from Williams' colony of Providence. A few years later, Hutchinson migrated to Long Island and was killed in an American Indian uprising.

In 1644, Roger Williams was granted a charter from the Parliament that joined Providence and Portsmouth into a single colony, Rhode Island. Because this colony tolerated diverse beliefs, it served as a refuge for many.

Connecticut To the west of Rhode Island, the fertile Connecticut River Valley attracted other settlers who were unhappy with the Massachusetts authorities. The Reverend Thomas Hooker led a large group of Boston Puritans into the valley and founded the colony of Hartford in 1636. The Hartford settlers then drew up the first written constitution in American history, the *Fundamental Orders of Connecticut* (1639). It established a representative government consisting of a legislature elected by popular vote and a governor chosen by that legislature. South of Hartford, a second settlement in the Connecticut Valley was started by John Davenport in 1637 and given the name New Haven.

In 1665, New Haven joined with the more democratic Hartford settlers to form the colony of Connecticut. The royal charter for Connecticut granted it a limited degree of self-government, including election of the governor.

NEW ENGLAND AND ATLANTIC COLONIES
1600s

New Hampshire The last colony to be founded in New England was New Hampshire. Originally part of Massachusetts Bay, it consisted of a few settlements north of Boston. Hoping to increase royal control over the colonies, King Charles II separated New Hampshire from the Bay colony in 1679 and made it a royal colony, subject to the authority of an appointed governor.

Halfway Covenant In the 1660s, a generation had passed since the founding of the first Puritan colonies in New England. To be a full member of a Puritan congregation, an individual needed to have felt a profound religious experience known as a conversion. However, fewer members of the new native-born generation were having such experiences. In an effort to maintain the church's influence and membership, a *halfway covenant* was offered by some clergy. Under this, people could become partial church members even if they had not had felt a conversion.

Other ministers rejected the halfway covenant and denounced it from the pulpit. Nevertheless, as the years passed, strict Puritan practices weakened in most New England communities in order to maintain church membership.

New England Confederation In the 1640s, the New England colonies faced the constant threat of attack from American Indians, the Dutch, and the French. Because England was in the midst of a civil war, the colonists could expect little assistance. Therefore in 1643, four New England colonies (Plymouth, Massachusetts Bay, Connecticut, and New Haven) formed a military alliance known as the New England Confederation. The confederation was directed by a board composed of two representatives from each colony. It had limited powers to act on boundary disputes, the return of runaway servants, and dealings with American Indians.

The confederation lasted until 1684, when colonial rivalries and renewed control by the English monarch brought this first experiment in colonial cooperation to an end. It was important because it established a precedent for colonies taking unified action toward a common purpose.

King Philip's War Only a few years before the confederation's demise, it helped the New England colonists cope successfully with a dire threat. A chief of the Wampanoags named Metacom—known to the colonists as King Philip—united many tribes in southern New England against the English settlers, who were constantly encroaching on the American Indians' lands. In a vicious war (1675–1676), thousands on both sides were killed, and dozens of towns and villages were burned. Eventually, the colonial forces prevailed, killing King Philip and ending most American Indian resistance in New England.

Restoration Colonies

New American colonies were founded in the late 17th century during a period in English history known as the Restoration. (The name refers to the restoration to power of an English monarch, Charles II, in 1660 following a brief period of Puritan rule under Oliver Cromwell.)

The Carolinas

As a reward for helping him gain the throne, Charles II granted a huge tract of land between Virginia and Spanish Florida to eight nobles, who in 1663 became the lord proprietors of the Carolinas. In 1729, two royal colonies, South Carolina and North Carolina, were formed from the original grant.

THE THIRTEEN ENGLISH COLONIES AROUND 1750

South Carolina In 1670, in the southern Carolinas, a few colonists from England and some planters from the island of Barbados founded a town named for their king. Initially, the southern economy was based on trading furs and providing food for the West Indies. By the middle of the 18th century, South Carolina's large rice-growing plantations worked by enslaved Africans resembled the economy and culture of the West Indies.

North Carolina The northern part of the Carolinas developed differently. There, farmers from Virginia and New England established small, self-sufficient tobacco farms. The region had few good harbors and poor transportation; therefore, compared to South Carolina, there were fewer large plantations and less reliance on slavery. North Carolina in the 18th century earned a reputation for democratic views and autonomy from British control.

New York

Charles II wished to consolidate the crown's holdings along the Atlantic Coast and close the gap between the New England and the Chesapeake colonies. This required compelling the Dutch to give up their colony of New Amsterdam centered on Manhattan Island and the Hudson River Valley.

In 1664, the king granted his brother, the Duke of York (the future James II), the lands lying between Connecticut and Delaware Bay. As the lord high admiral of the navy, James dispatched a force that easily took control of the Dutch colony from its governor, Peter Stuyvesant. James ordered his agents in the renamed colony of New York to treat the Dutch settlers well and to allow them freedom to worship as they pleased and speak their own language.

James also ordered new taxes, duties, and rents without seeking the consent of a representative assembly. In fact, he insisted that no assembly should be allowed to form in his colony. But taxation without representation met strong opposition from New York's English-speaking settlers, most of whom were Puritans from New England. Finally, in 1683, James yielded by allowing New York's governor to grant broad civil and political rights, including a representative assembly.

New Jersey

Believing that the territory of New York was too large to administer, James split it in 1664. He gave the section of the colony located between the Hudson River and Delaware Bay to Lord John Berkeley and Sir George Carteret. In 1674, one proprietor received West New Jersey and the other East New Jersey. To attract settlers, both proprietors made generous land offers and allowed religious freedom and an assembly. Eventually, they sold their proprietary interests to various groups of Quakers. Land titles in the Jerseys changed hands repeatedly, and inaccurate property lines added to the general confusion. To settle matters, the crown decided in 1702 to combine the two Jerseys into a single royal colony: New Jersey.

Pennsylvania and Delaware

To the west of New Jersey lay a broad expanse of forested land that was originally settled by a peace-loving Christian sect, the Quakers.

Quakers Members of the Religious Society of Friends—commonly known as Quakers—believed in the equality of all men and women, nonviolence, and resistance to military service. They further believed that religious authority was found within each person's soul and not in the Bible and not in any outside source. Such views posed a radical challenge to established authority. Therefore, the Quakers of England were persecuted and jailed for their beliefs.

William Penn William Penn was a young convert to the Quaker faith. His father had served the king as a victorious admiral. Although the elder Penn opposed his son's religious beliefs, he respected William's sincerity and bequeathed him considerable wealth. In addition, the royal family owed the father a large debt, which they paid to William in 1681 in the form of a grant of American land for a colony that he called Pennsylvania, or Penn's woods.

"The Holy Experiment" Penn put his Quaker beliefs to the test in his colony. He wanted his new colony to provide a religious refuge for Quakers and other persecuted people, to enact liberal ideas in government, and generate income and profits for himself. He provided the colony with a Frame of Government (1682–1683), which guaranteed a representative assembly elected by landowners, and a written constitution, the Charter of Liberties (1701), which guaranteed freedom of worship for all and unrestricted immigration.

Unlike other colonial proprietors, who governed from afar in England, Penn crossed the ocean to supervise the founding of a new town on the Delaware River named Philadelphia. He brought with him a plan for a grid pattern of streets, which was later imitated by other American cities. Also unusual was Penn's attempt to treat the American Indians fairly and not to cheat them when purchasing their land.

To attract settlers to his new land, Penn hired agents and published notices throughout Europe, which promised political and religious freedom and generous land terms. Penn's lands along the Delaware River had previously been settled by several thousand Dutch and Swedish colonists, who eased the arrival of the newcomers attracted by Penn's promotion.

Delaware In 1702, Penn granted the lower three counties of Pennsylvania their own assembly. In effect, Delaware became a separate colony, even though its governor was the same as Pennsylvania's until the American Revolution.

Georgia: The Last Colony

In 1732, a thirteenth colony, Georgia, was chartered. It was the last of the British colonies and the only one to receive direct financial support from the government in London. There were two reasons for British interest in starting a new southern colony. First, Britain wanted to create a defensive buffer to protect the prosperous South Carolina plantations from the threat of Spanish Florida. Second, thousands of people in England were being imprisoned for debt. Wealthy philanthropists thought it would relieve the overcrowded jails if debtors were shipped to an American colony to start life over.

Special Regulations Given a royal charter for a proprietary colony, a group of philanthropists led by James Oglethorpe founded Georgia's first settlement, Savannah, in 1733. Oglethorpe acted as the colony's first governor and put into effect an elaborate plan for making the colony thrive. There were strict regulations, including bans on drinking rum and slavery. Nevertheless, partly because of the constant threat of Spanish attack, the colony did not prosper.

Royal Colony By 1752, Oglethorpe and his group gave up their plan. Taken over by the British government, Georgia became a royal colony. Restrictions on rum and slavery were dropped. The colony grew slowly by adopting the plantation system of South Carolina. Even so, at the time of the American Revolution, Georgia was the smallest and poorest of the 13 colonies.

Mercantilism and the Empire

Most European kingdoms in the 17th century adopted the economic policy of *mercantilism*, which looked upon trade, colonies, and the accumulation of wealth as the basis for a country's military and political strength. According to mercantilist doctrine, a government should regulate trade and production to enable it to become self-sufficient. Colonies were to provide raw materials to the parent country for the growth and profit of that country's industries. Colonies existed for one purpose only: to enrich the parent country.

Mercantilist policies had guided both the Spanish and the French colonies from their inception. Mercantilism began to be applied to the English colonies, however, only after the turmoil of England's civil war had subsided.

Acts of Trade and Navigation England's government implemented a mercantilist policy with a series of Navigation Acts between 1650 and 1673, which established three rules for colonial trade:

1. Trade to and from the colonies could be carried only by English or colonial-built ships, which could be operated only by English or colonial crews.

2. All goods imported into the colonies, except for some perishables, had to pass through ports in England.

3. Specified or "enumerated" goods from the colonies could be exported to England only. Tobacco was the original "enumerated" good, but over the years, the list was greatly expanded.

Impact on the Colonies The Navigation Acts had mixed effects on the colonies. The acts caused New England shipbuilding to prosper, provided Chesapeake tobacco with a monopoly in England, and provided English military forces to protect the colonies from potential attacks by the French and Spanish. However, the acts also severely limited the development of colonial manufacturing, forced Chesapeake farmers to accept low prices for their crops, and caused colonists to pay high prices for manufactured goods from England.

In many respects, mercantilist regulations were unnecessary, since England would have been the colonies' primary trading partner in any case. Furthermore, the economic advantages from the Navigation Acts were offset by their negative political effects on British-colonial relations. Colonists resented the regulatory laws imposed by the distant government in London. Especially in New England, colonists defied the acts by smuggling in French, Dutch, and other goods.

Enforcement of the Acts The British government was often lax in enforcing the acts, and its agents in the colonies were known for their corruption. Occasionally, however, the crown would attempt to overcome colonial resistance to its trade laws. In 1684, it revoked the charter of Massachusetts Bay because that colony had been the center of smuggling activity.

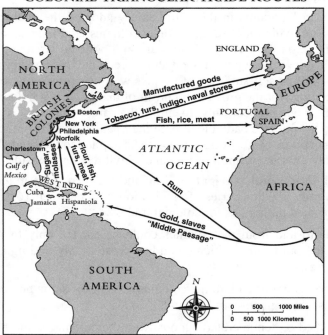

COLONIAL TRIANGULAR TRADE ROUTES

The Dominion of New England A new king, James II, succeeded to the throne in 1685. He was determined to increase royal control over the colonies by combining them into larger administrative units and doing away with their representative assemblies. In 1686, he combined New York, New Jersey, and the various New England colonies into a single unit called the Dominion of New England. Sir Edmund Andros was sent from England to serve as governor of the dominion. The new governor made himself instantly unpopular by levying taxes, limiting town meetings, and revoking land titles.

James II did not remain in power for long. His attempts at asserting his royal powers led to an uprising against him. The Glorious Revolution of 1688 succeeded in deposing James and replacing him with two new sovereigns, William and Mary. James's fall from power brought the Dominion of New England to an end and the colonies again operated under separate charters.

Permanent Restrictions Despite the Glorious Revolution, mercantilist policies remained in force. In the 18th century, there were more English officials in the colonies than in any earlier era. Restrictions on colonial trade, though poorly enforced, were widely resented and resisted.

The Institution of Slavery

More important than mercantilism in the early 18th century was the growth of slavery. By 1750, half of Virginia's population and two-thirds of South Carolina's population were enslaved.

Increased Demand for Slaves The following factors explain why slavery became increasingly important, especially in the southern colonies:

1. *Reduced migration:* Increases in wages in England reduced the supply of immigrants to the colonies.

2. *Dependable workforce:* Large plantation owners were disturbed by the political demands of small farmers and indentured servants and by the disorders of Bacon's Rebellion (see page 29). They thought that slavery would provide a stable labor force totally under their control.

3. *Cheap labor:* As tobacco prices fell, rice and indigo became the most profitable crops. To grow such crops required a large land area and many inexpensive, relatively unskilled field hands.

Slave Laws As the number of slaves increased, white colonists adopted laws to ensure that African Americans would be held in bondage for life and that slave status would be inherited. In 1641, Massachusetts became the first colony to recognize the enslavement of "lawful" captives. Virginia in 1661 enacted legislation stating that children automatically inherited their mother's enslaved status for life. By 1664, Maryland declared that baptism did not affect the enslaved person's status, and that white women could not marry African American men. It became customary for whites to regard all blacks as social inferiors. Racism and slavery soon became integral to colonial society.

Triangular Trade In the 17th century, English trade in enslaved Africans had been monopolized by a single company, the Royal African Company. But after this monopoly expired, many New England merchants entered the lucrative slave trade. Merchant ships would regularly follow a triangular, or three-part, trade route. First, a ship starting from a New England port such as Boston would carry rum across the Atlantic to West Africa. There the rum would be traded for hundreds of captive Africans. Next, the ship would set out on the horrendous

Middle Passage. Those Africans who survived the frightful voyage would be traded as slaves in the West Indies for a cargo of sugarcane. Third, completing the last side of the triangle, the ship would return to a New England port where the sugar would be sold to be used in making rum. Every time one type of cargo was traded for another, the slave-trading entrepreneur usually succeeded in making a substantial profit.

HISTORICAL PERSPECTIVES: HOW INFLUENTIAL WERE THE PURITANS?

To what extent did the Puritan founders of Massachusetts shape the development of an American culture? Although some early historians such as James Truslow Adams have minimized the Puritan role, more recent scholars generally agree that the Puritans made significant cultural and intellectual contributions. There is continuing disagreement, however, about whether the Puritan influence encouraged an individualistic spirit or just the opposite.

Some historians have concentrated their study on the writings and sermons of the Puritan clergy and other leaders. They have concluded that the leaders stressed conformity to a strict moral code and exhorted people to sacrifice their individuality for the common good. According to these historians, in other words, the Puritan influence tended to suppress the individualism that later came to characterize American culture.

Other historians believe that the opposite is true. They raise objections to the method of studying only sermons and the journals of leading Puritans such as John Winthrop. If one examines the writings and actions of ordinary colonists in Massachusetts society, say these historians, then one observes many instances of independent thought and action by individuals in Puritan society. According to their argument, American individualism began with the Puritan colonists.

KEY TERMS BY THEME

Religion (SOC)
Cecil Calvert, Lord
  Baltimore
Act of Toleration
Roger Williams
Providence
Anne Hutchinson
antinomianism
Rhode Island
Halfway covenant
Quakers
William Penn
Holy Experiment
Charter of Liberties
  (1701)

Crops (GEO)
rice plantations
tobacco farms

Settlements (ARC)
John Cabot
Jamestown
Captain John Smith
John Rolfe
Pocahontas
Jamestown
Puritans
Separatists
Pilgrims
Mayflower
Plymouth Colony

Massachusetts Bay
  Colony
John Winthrop
Great Migration
Virginia
Thomas Hooker
John Davenport
Connecticut
New Hampshire
The Carolinas
New York
New Jersey
Pennsylvania
Delaware
Georgia
James Oglethorpe

Conflict (MIG)
Wampanoags
Metacom
King Philip's War

Self-Rule (POL)
Mayflower Compact
Virginia House of
  Burgesses
Sir William Berkeley
Bacon's Rebellion
Fundamental Orders of
  Connecticut (1639)
New England
  Confederation
Frame of Government
  (1682)

Authority (WOR)
corporate colonies
royal colonies
proprietary colonies
Chesapeake colonies
joint-stock company
Virginia Company

Royal Authority (WOR)
mercantilism
Navigation Acts
Dominion of New
  England
Sir Edmund Andros
Glorious Revolution

Labor (WXT)
indentured servants
headright system
slavery
triangular trade
Middle Passage

Questions 1–2 refer to the excerpt below.

"Be it therefore ordered and enacted. . . . That whatsoever person or persons within this Province...shall henceforth blaspheme God, that is, curse Him or shall deny our Savior Jesus Christ to be the Son of God, or shall deny the Holy Trinity . . . or the Godhead of any of the said Three persons of the Trinity or the Unity of the Godhead . . . shall be punished with death and confiscation or forfeiture of all his or her lands. . . . And whereas . . . that no person or persons whatsoever within this province, or the islands, ports, harbors, creeks, or havens thereunto belonging professing to believe in Jesus Christ, shall from henceforth be any way troubled, molested or discountenanced for or in respect of his or her religion nor in free exercise thereof within this province or the islands thereunto belonging nor any way compelled to the belief or exercise of any other Religion against his or her consent."

—The Maryland Act of Toleration, 1649

1. Which of the following religious groups were the authors of the Maryland Act of Toleration trying to protect?

   (A) Jews

   (B) Puritans

   (C) Quakers

   (D) Roman Catholics

2. Which of the following best summarizes the attitude toward religious beliefs expressed in this document?

   (A) All individuals should be free to believe or not believe in God as they wished

   (B) Religion was a personal matter that the government should not try to influence

   (C) Christians should be able to practice their faith without fear of persecution

   (D) The colony should be reserved for the one specific type of Christianity approved by the local government officials

Questions 3–5 refer to the excerpt below.

"These at the heads of James and York rivers . . . grew impatient at the many slaughters of their neighbors and rose for own defense, who choosing Mr. Bacon for their leader, sent oftentimes to the Governor, . . . beseeching a commission to go against the Indians at their own charge; which His Honor as often promised, but did not send. . . .

"During these protractions and people often slain, most or all the officers, civil and military, . . . met and concerted together, the danger of going without a commission on the one part and the continual murders of their neighbors on the other part. . . . This day lapsing and no commission come, they marched into the wilderness in quest of these Indians, after whom the Governor sent his proclamation, denouncing all rebels who should not return within a limited day; whereupon those of estates obeyed. But Mr. Bacon, with fifty-seven men, proceeded. . . . They fired and . . . slew 150 Indians."

—Samuel Kercheval, Virginia author and lawyer, "On Bacon's Rebellion in Virginia," 1833

3. Based on the information in this excerpt, what is Samuel Kercheval's point of view toward Bacon and his followers?
   (A) They were dangerous men who threatened colonial stability and prosperity
   (B) They were frustrated men who were taking action because the government did not
   (C) They were allies of the governor who carried out actions that he supported
   (D) They were a primarily political movement that wanted Bacon to become governor

4. Bacon's Rebellion was initiated by a group of farmers who felt most directly threatened by
   (A) an increase in royal taxes
   (B) the power of large planters
   (C) conflicts with American Indians
   (D) the growth of the slave trade

5. Which of the following led the opposition to Bacon's Rebellion?
   (A) leaders of the Church of England
   (B) members of the Virginia House of Burgesses
   (C) soldiers from the British army
   (D) the colonial governor

Questions 6–8 refer to the excerpt below.

"As touching the quality of this country, three thinges there bee, which in fewe yeares may bring this Colony to perfection; the English plough, Vineyards, & Cattle. . . .

"All our riches for the present doe consiste in Tobacco, wherein one man by his owne laboour hath in one yeare, raised to himself to the value of 200 sterling; and another by the means of six seruants hath cleared at one crop a thousand pound english. These be true, yet indeed rare examples, yet possible to be done by others. Our principall wealth (I should haue said) consisteth in servants: but they are chargeable to be furnished with armes, apparel, & bedding, and for their transportation, and casuall both at sea, & for their first yeare commonly at lande also: but if they escape, they proove very hardy, and sound able men."

—John Pory, Secretary of Virginia, Letter to Sir Dudley Carlton, 1619

6. Despite the success of tobacco in Virginia, the colony still faced problems and eventually became a

   (A) royal colony

   (B) corporate charter settlement

   (C) proprietorship

   (D) joint-stock company

7. Which of the following groups made up most of the servants referred to in the passage?

   (A) American Indians

   (B) Indentured servants from Europe

   (C) Enslaved Africans

   (D) Women whose husbands had escaped

8. The primary market for the Virginia tobacco crop during this period was

   (A) Virginia

   (B) England

   (C) New England

   (D) Africa

SHORT-ANSWER QUESTIONS

Use complete sentences; an outline or bulleted list alone is not acceptable.

Question 1. Answer (A), (B), and (C).

(A) Briefly explain ONE specific new colony that developed because of religious differences in New England during the period 1630 to 1680.

(B) Briefly explain ONE specific individual who played a leading role in founding a new colony in New England during the period 1630 to 1680.

(C) Briefly explain ONE specific reason for the New England Confederation during the period 1640 to 1684.

Question 2 is based on the following excerpt.

"[This colony] was for the most part at first peopled by persons of low circumstances. . . . Nor was it hardly possible it should be otherwise; for 'tis not likely that any man of a plentiful estate should voluntarily abandon a happy certainty to roam after imaginary advantages in a New World. Besides which uncertainty, must have proposed to himself to encounter the infinite difficulties and dangers that attend a new settlement. These discouragements were sufficient to terrify any man that could live easy in England from going to . . . a strange land."

—Robert Beverly, historian, *The History and Present State of Virginia,* 1705

2. Using the excerpt, answer (A), (B), and (C).

(A) Briefly explain Robert Beverly's main point in the excerpt.

(B) Briefly explain ONE example of historical evidence that supports Beverly's position.

(C) Briefly explain ONE example of historical evidence that challenges Beverly's position.

Question 3. Answer (A), (B), and (C).

(A) Briefly explain ONE specific historical aspect of William Penn's unique approach in founding the colony of Pennsylvania.

(B) Briefly explain ONE specific colony of the 13 original ones that came close to Penn's approach to religious toleration.

(C) Briefly explain ONE specific historical event or development associated with the founding of the colony of Georgia.

Question 4 is based on the following excerpts.

"As to the natives of this country, I find them entirely savage and wild, strangers to all decency, yea, uncivil and stupid as garden stakes, proficient in all wickedness and ungodliness, devilish men who serve nobody but the devil. . . . They have so much witchcraft, divination, sorcery, and wicked arts that they can hardly be held in by any bands or locks. They are as thievish and treacherous as they are tall, and in cruelty they are altogether inhuman."

—Jonas Michaelius, pastor, Dutch Reformed Church, Letter to Reverend Andrianus Smoutius, 1628

"I confess I think no great good will be done till they [Indians] be more civilized. But why may not God begin with some few to awaken others by degrees? Nor do I expect any great good will be wrought by the English . . . because God is wont ordinarily to convert nations and peoples by some of their own countrymen who are nearest to them and can best speak, and, most of all, pity their brethren."

—John Eliot, Puritan, "The Day-Breaking of the Gospel with the Indians," 1646

4. Using the excerpts, answer (A), (B), and (C).

(A) Briefly explain ONE major difference between Michaelius's and Eliot's views of the Native Americans.

(B) Briefly explain how ONE historical event or development in the period 1607 to 1754 that is not explicitly mentioned in the excerpts could be used to support Michaelius's interpretation.

(C) Briefly explain how ONE historical event or development in the period 1607 to 1754 that is not explicitly mentioned in the excerpts could be used to support Eliot's interpretation.

THINK AS A HISTORIAN: QUESTIONS ABOUT CONTINUITY

Essay questions often ask students to focus on how a society has stayed the same or evolved over time. Which THREE of the questions or statements below would best be answered with an essay that emphasizes historical continuity and change over time?

1. How did the Massachusetts and the Chesapeake colonies differ?

2. Use examples from both New England and Virginia to show the development in colonial America of a pattern of resistance to authority.

3. Describe how attitudes toward equality evolved during the colonial era.

4. Between 1607 and 1754, did England's colonies become more or less like it?

5. What caused the colonial economy to prosper?

3

COLONIAL SOCIETY IN THE 18TH CENTURY

The American is a new man, who acts upon new principles; he must therefore entertain new ideas, and form new opinions. From involuntary idleness, servile dependence, and useless labor, he has passed to toils of a very different nature, rewarded by ample subsistence. This is an American.

J. Hector St. John Crèvecoeur, *Letters from an American Farmer*, 1782

The Frenchman who wrote the above description of Americans in 1782 observed a very different society from the struggling colonial villages that had existed in the 17th century. The British colonies had grown, and their inhabitants had evolved a culture distinct from any in Europe. This chapter describes the mature colonies and asks: If Americans in the 1760s constituted a new kind of society, what were its characteristics and what forces shaped its "new people"?

Population Growth

At the start of the new century, in 1701, the English colonies on the Atlantic Coast had a population of barely 250,000 Europeans and Africans. By 1775, the figure had jumped to 2,500,000, a tenfold increase within the span of a single lifetime. Among African Americans, the population increase was even more dramatic: from about 28,000 in 1701 to 500,000 in 1775.

The spectacular gains in population during this period resulted from two factors: immigration of almost a million people and a sharp natural increase, caused chiefly by a high birthrate among colonial families. An abundance of fertile American land and a dependable food supply attracted thousands of European settlers each year and also supported the raising of large families.

European Immigrants

Newcomers to the British colonies came not only from England, Scotland, Wales, and Ireland, but also from other parts of Western and Central Europe. Many immigrants, most of whom were Protestants, came from France and German-speaking kingdoms and principalities. Their motives for leaving Europe were many. Some came to escape religious persecution and wars. Others sought economic opportunity either by farming new land or setting up shop in a colonial town as an artisan or a merchant. Most immigrants settled in the middle colonies (Pennsylvania, New York, New Jersey, Maryland, and Delaware) and on the western frontier of the southern colonies (Virginia, the Carolinas, and Georgia). In the 18th century, few immigrants headed for New England, where land was both limited in extent and under Puritan control.

English Settlers from England continued to come to the American colonies. However, with fewer problems at home, their numbers were relatively small compared to others, especially the Germans and Scotch-Irish.

Germans This group of non-English immigrants settled chiefly on the rich farmlands west of Philadelphia, an area that became known as Pennsylvania Dutch country. They maintained their German language, customs, and religion (Lutheran, Amish, Brethren, Mennonite, or one of several smaller groups) and, while obeying colonial laws, showed little interest in English politics. By 1775, people of German stock comprised 6 percent of the colonial population.

Scotch-Irish These English-speaking people emigrated from northern Ireland. Since their ancestors had moved to Ireland from Scotland, they were commonly known as the Scotch-Irish or Scots-Irish. They had little respect for the British government, which had pressured them into leaving Ireland. Most settled along the frontier in the western parts of Pennsylvania, Virginia, the Carolinas, and Georgia. By 1775, they comprised 7 percent of the population.

Other Europeans Other immigrant groups included French Protestants (called Huguenots), the Dutch, and the Swedes. These groups made up 5 percent of the population of all the colonies in 1775.

Africans

The largest single group of non-English immigrants did not come to America by choice. They were Africans—or the descendants of Africans—who had been taken captive, forced into European ships, and sold as enslaved laborers to southern plantation owners and other colonists. Some Africans were granted their freedom after years of forced labor. Outside the South, thousands of African Americans worked at a broad range of occupations, such as being a laborer, bricklayer, or blacksmith. Some of these workers were enslaved and others were free wage earners and property owners. Every colony, from New Hampshire to Georgia, passed laws that discriminated against African Americans and limited their rights and opportunities.

By 1775, the African American population (both enslaved and free) made up 20 percent of the colonial population. About 90 percent lived in the southern colonies in lifelong bondage. African Americans formed a majority of the population in South Carolina and Georgia.

The Structure of Colonial Society

Each of the thirteen British colonies developed distinct patterns of life. However, they all also shared a number of characteristics.

General Characteristics

Most of the population was English in origin, language, and tradition. However, both Africans and non-English immigrants brought diverse influences that would modify the culture of the majority in significant ways.

Self-government The government of each colony had a representative assembly that was elected by eligible voters (limited to white male property owners). In only two colonies, Rhode Island and Connecticut, was the governor also elected by the people. The governors of the other colonies were either appointed by the crown (for example, New York and Virginia) or by a proprietor (Pennsylvania and Maryland).

Religious Toleration All of the colonies permitted the practice of different religions, but with varying degrees of freedom. Massachusetts, the most conservative, accepted several types of Protestants, but it excluded non-Christians and Catholics. Rhode Island and Pennsylvania were the most liberal.

No Hereditary Aristocracy The social extremes of Europe, with a nobility that inherited special privileges and masses of hungry poor, were missing in the colonies. A narrower class system, based on economics, was developing. Wealthy landowners were at the top; craft workers and small farmers made up the majority of the common people.

Social Mobility With the major exception of the African Americans, all people in colonial society had an opportunity to improve their standard of living and social status by hard work.

The Family

The family was the economic and social center of colonial life. With an expanding economy and ample food supply, people married at a younger age and reared more children than in Europe. More than 90 percent of the people lived on farms. While life in the coastal communities and on the frontier was hard, most colonists had a higher standard of living than did most Europeans.

Men While wealth was increasingly being concentrated in the hands of a few, most men did work. Landowning was primarily reserved to men, who also dominated politics. English law gave the husband almost unlimited power in the home, including the right to beat his wife.

Women The average colonial wife bore eight children and performed a wide range of tasks. Household work included cooking, cleaning, making clothes, and providing medical care. Women also educated the children. A woman usually worked next to her husband in the shop, on the plantation, or on the farm. Divorce was legal but rare, and women had limited legal and political rights. Yet the shared labors and mutual dependence with their husbands gave most women protection from abuse and an active role in decision-making.

The Economy

By the 1760s, almost half of Britain's world trade was with its American colonies. The British government permitted limited kinds of colonial manufacturing, such as making flour or rum. It restricted efforts that would compete with English industries, such as textiles. The richness of the American land and British mercantile policy produced colonies almost entirely engaged in agriculture.

As the people prospered and communities grew, increasing numbers became ministers, lawyers, doctors, and teachers. The quickest route to wealth was through the land, although regional geography often provided distinct opportunities for hardworking colonists.

New England With rocky soil and long winters, farming was limited to subsistence levels that provided just enough for the farm family. Most farms were small—under 100 acres—and most work was done by family members and an occasional hired laborer. The industrious descendants of the Puritans profited from logging, shipbuilding, fishing, trading, and rum-distilling.

Middle Colonies Rich soil produced an abundance of wheat and corn for export to Europe and the West Indies. Farms of up to 200 acres were common. Often, indentured servants and hired laborers worked with the farm family. A variety of small manufacturing efforts developed, including iron-making. Trading led to the growth of such cities as Philadelphia and New York.

Southern Colonies Because of the diverse geography and climate of the southern colonies, agriculture varied greatly. Most people lived on small subsistence family farms with no slaves. A few lived on large plantations of over 2,000 acres and relied on slave labor. Plantations were self-sufficient—they grew their own food and had their own slave craftworkers. Products were mainly tobacco in the Chesapeake and North Carolina colonies, timber and naval stores (tar and pitch) in the Carolinas, and rice and indigo in South Carolina and Georgia. Most plantations were located on rivers so they could ship exports directly to Europe.

Monetary System One way the British controlled the colonial economy was to limit the use of money. The growing colonies were forced to use much of the limited hard currency—gold and silver—to pay for the imports from Britain that increasingly exceeded colonial exports. To provide currency for domestic trade, many colonies issued paper money, but this often led to inflation. The British government also vetoed colonial laws that might harm British merchants.

Transportation Transporting goods by water was much easier than attempting to carry them over land on rough and narrow roads or trails. Therefore, trading centers such as Boston, New York, Philadelphia, and Charleston were located on the sites of good harbors and navigable rivers. Despite the difficulty and expense of maintaining roads and bridges, overland travel by horse and stage became more common in the 18th century. Taverns not only provided food and lodging for travelers, but also served as social centers where news was exchanged and politics discussed. A postal system using horses on overland routes and small ships on water routes was operating both within and between the colonies by the mid-18th century.

Religion

Although Maryland was founded by a Catholic proprietor, and larger towns such as New York and Boston attracted some Jewish settlers, the overwhelming majority of colonists belonged to various Protestant denominations. In New England, Congregationalists (the successors to the Puritans) and Presbyterians were most common. In New York, people of Dutch descent often attended services of the Reformed Church, while many merchants belonged to the Church of England, also known as Anglicans (and later, Episcopalians). In Pennsylvania, Lutherans, Mennonites, and Quakers were the most common groups. Anglicans were dominant in Virginia and some of the other southern colonies.

Challenges Each religious group, even the Protestants who dominated the colonies, faced problems. Jews, Catholics, and Quakers suffered from the most serious discrimination and even persecution. Congregationalist ministers were criticized by other Protestants as domineering and for preaching an overly complex doctrine. Because the Church of England was headed by the king, it was viewed as a symbol of English control in the colonies. In addition, there was no Church of England bishop in America to ordain ministers. The absence of such leadership hampered the church's development.

Established Churches In the 17th century, most colonial governments taxed the people to support one particular Protestant denomination. Churches financed through the government are known as established churches. For example, in Virginia, the established church was the Church of England. In Massachusetts Bay it was the Congregational Church. As various immigrant groups increased the religious diversity of the colonies, governments gradually reduced their support of churches. In Virginia, all tax support for the Anglican Church ended shortly after the Revolution. In Massachusetts by the time of the Revolution, members of other denominations were exempt from supporting the Congregational Church. However, some direct tax support of the denomination remained until the 1830s.

The Great Awakening

In the first decades of the 18th century, sermons in Protestant churches tended to be long intellectual discourses and portrayed God as a benign creator of a perfectly ordered universe. Ministers gave less emphasis than in Puritan times on human sinfulness and the perils of damnation. In the 1730s, however, a dramatic change occurred that swept through the colonies with the force of a hurricane. This was the Great Awakening, a movement characterized by fervent expressions of religious feeling among masses of people. The movement was at its strongest during the 1730s and 1740s.

Jonathan Edwards In a Congregational church at Northampton, Massachusetts, Reverend Jonathan Edwards expressed the Great Awakening ideas in a series of sermons, notably one called "Sinners in the Hands of an Angry God"

(1741). Invoking the Old Testament scriptures, Edwards argued that God was rightfully angry with human sinfulness. Each individual who expressed deep penitence could be saved by God's grace, but the souls who paid no heed to God's commandments would suffer eternal damnation.

George Whitefield While Edwards mostly influenced New England, George Whitefield, who came from England in 1739, spread the Great Awakening throughout the colonies, sometimes attracting audiences of 10,000 people. In barns, tents, and fields, he delivered rousing sermons that stressed that God was all-powerful and would save only those who openly professed belief in Jesus Christ. Those who did not would be damned into hell and face eternal torments. Whitefield taught that ordinary people with faith and sincerity could understand the gospels without depending on ministers to lead them.

Religious Impact The Great Awakening had a profound effect on religious practice in the colonies. As sinners tearfully confessed their guilt and then joyously exulted in being "saved," emotionalism became a common part of Protestant services. Ministers lost some of their former authority among those who now studied the Bible in their own homes.

The Great Awakening also caused divisions within churches, such as the Congregational and Presbyterian, between those supporting its teachings ("New Lights") and those condemning them ("Old Lights"). More evangelical sects such as the Baptists and Methodists attracted large numbers. As denominations competed for followers, they also called for separation of church and state.

Political Influence A movement as powerful as the Great Awakening affected all areas of life, including politics. For the first time, the colonists—regardless of their national origins or their social class—shared in a common experience as Americans. The Great Awakening also had a democratizing effect by changing the way people viewed authority. If common people could make their own religious decisions without relying on the "higher" authority of ministers, then might they also make their own political decisions without deferring to the authority of the great landowners and merchants? This revolutionary idea was not expressed in the 1740s, but 30 years later, it would challenge the authority of a king and his royal governors.

Cultural Life

In the early 1600s, the chief concern of most colonists was economic survival. People had neither the time nor the resources to pursue leisure activities or create works of art and literature. One hundred years later, however, the colonial population had grown and matured enough that the arts could flourish, at least among the well-to-do southern planters and northern merchants.

Achievements in the Arts and Sciences

In the coastal areas, as fear of American Indians faded, people displayed their prosperity by adopting architectural and decorative styles from England.

Architecture In the 1740s and 1750s, the Georgian style of London was widely imitated in colonial houses, churches, and public buildings. Brick and stucco homes built in this style were characterized by a symmetrical placement of windows and dormers and a spacious center hall flanked by two fireplaces. Such homes were found only on or near the eastern seaboard. On the frontier, a one-room log cabin was the common shelter.

Painting Many colonial painters were itinerant artists who wandered the countryside in search of families who wanted their portraits painted. Shortly before the Revolution, two American artists, Benjamin West and John Copley, went to England where they acquired the necessary training and financial support to establish themselves as prominent artists.

Literature With limited resources available, most authors wrote on serious subjects, chiefly religion and politics. There were, for example, widely read religious tracts by two Massachusetts ministers, Cotton Mather and Jonathan Edwards. In the years preceding the American Revolution, writers including John Adams, James Otis, John Dickinson, Thomas Paine, and Thomas Jefferson issued political essays and treatises highlighting the conflict between American rights and English authority. The lack of support for literature did not stop everyone. The poetry of Phillis Wheatley is noteworthy both for her triumph over slavery and the quality of her verse.

By far the most popular and successful American writer of the 18th century was that remarkable jack-of-all-trades, Benjamin Franklin. His witty aphorisms and advice were collected in *Poor Richard's Almanack,* a best-selling book that was annually revised from 1732 to 1757.

Science Most scientists, such as the botanist John Bartram of Philadelphia, were self-taught. Benjamin Franklin won fame for his work with electricity and his developments of bifocal eyeglasses and the Franklin stove.

Education

Basic education was limited and varied among the colonies. Formal efforts were directed to males, since females were trained only for household work.

Elementary Education In New England, the Puritans' emphasis on learning the Bible led them to create the first tax-supported schools. A Massachusetts law in 1647 required towns with more than fifty families to establish primary schools for boys, and towns with more than a hundred families to establish grammar schools to prepare boys for college. In the middle colonies, schools were either church-sponsored or private. Often, teachers lived with the families of their students. In the southern colonies, parents gave their children whatever education they could. On plantations, tutors provided instruction for the owners' children.

Higher Education The first colonial colleges were sectarian, meaning that they promoted the doctrines of a particular religious group. The Puritans founded Harvard in Cambridge, Massachusetts, in 1636 in order to give candidates for the ministry a proper theological and scholarly education. The

Anglicans opened William and Mary in Virginia in 1694, and the Congregationalists started Yale in Connecticut in 1701. The Great Awakening prompted the creation of five new colleges between 1746 and 1769:

- College of New Jersey (Princeton), 1746, Presbyterian
- King's College (Columbia), 1754, Anglican
- Rhode Island College (Brown), 1764, Baptist
- Queens College (Rutgers), 1766, Reformed
- Dartmouth College, 1769, Congregationalist

Only one nonsectarian college was founded during this period. The College of Philadelphia, which later became the University of Pennsylvania, had no religious sponsors. On hand for the opening ceremonies in 1765 were the college's civic-minded founders, chief among them Benjamin Franklin.

Ministry During the 17th century, the Christian ministry was the only profession to enjoy widespread respect among the common people. Ministers were often the only well-educated person in a small community.

Physicians Colonists who fell prey to epidemics of smallpox and diphtheria were often treated by "cures" that only made them worse. One common practice was to bleed the sick, often by employing leeches or bloodsuckers. A beginning doctor received little formal medical training other than acting as an apprentice to an experienced physician. The first medical college in the colonies was begun in 1765 as part of Franklin's idea for the College of Philadelphia.

Lawyers Often viewed as talkative troublemakers, lawyers were not common in the 1600s. In that period, individuals would argue their own cases before a colonial magistrate. During the 1700s, however, as trade expanded and legal problems became more complex, people felt a need for expert assistance in court. The most able lawyers formed a bar (committee or board), which set rules and standards for aspiring young lawyers. Lawyers gained further respect in the 1760s and 1770s when they argued for colonial rights. John Adams, James Otis, and Patrick Henry were three such lawyers whose legal arguments would ultimately provide the intellectual underpinnings of the American Revolution.

The Press

News and ideas circulated in the colonies principally by means of a postal system and local printing presses.

Newspapers In 1725, only five newspapers existed in the colonies, but by 1776 the number had grown to more than 40. Issued weekly, each newspaper consisted of a single sheet folded once to make four pages. It contained such items as month-old news from Europe, ads for goods and services and for the return of runaway indentured servants and slaves, and pious essays giving advice for better living. Illustrations were few or nonexistent. The first cartoon appeared in the Philadelphia *Gazette*, placed there by, of course, Ben Franklin.

The Zenger Case Newspaper printers in colonial days ran the risk of being jailed for libel if any article offended the political authorities. In 1735, John Peter Zenger, a New York editor and publisher, was brought to trial on a charge of libelously criticizing New York's royal governor. Zenger's lawyer, Andrew Hamilton, argued that his client had printed the truth about the governor. According to English common law at the time, injuring a governor's reputation was considered a criminal act, no matter whether a printed statement was true or false. Ignoring the English law, the jury voted to acquit Zenger. While this case did not guarantee complete freedom of the press, it encouraged newspapers to take greater risks in criticizing a colony's government.

Rural Folkways

The majority of colonists rarely saw a newspaper or read any book other than the Bible. As farmers on the frontier or even within a few miles of the coast, they worked from first daylight to sundown. The farmer's year was divided into four ever-recurring seasons: spring planting, summer growing, fall harvesting, and winter preparations for the next cycle. Food was usually plentiful, but light and heat in the colonial farmhouse were limited to the kitchen fireplace and a few well-placed candles. Entertainment for the well-to-do consisted chiefly of card playing and horse-racing in the southern colonies, theater-going in the middle colonies, and attending religious lectures in Puritan New England.

The Enlightenment

In the 18th century, some educated Americans felt attracted to a European movement in literature and philosophy that is known as the Enlightenment. The leaders of this movement believed that the "darkness" of past ages could be corrected by the use of human reason in solving most of humanity's problems.

A major influence on the Enlightenment and on American thinking was the work of John Locke, a 17th-century English philosopher and political theorist. Locke, in his *Two Treatises of Government,* reasoned that while the state (the government) is supreme, it is bound to follow "natural laws" based on the rights that people have simply because they are human. He argued that sovereignty ultimately resides with the people rather than with the state. Furthermore, said Locke, citizens had a right and an obligation to revolt against whatever government failed to protect their rights.

Other Enlightenment philosophers adopted and expounded on Locke's ideas. His stress on natural rights would provide a rationale for the American Revolution and later for the basic principles of the U.S. Constitution.

Emergence of a National Character

The colonists' motivations for leaving Europe, the political heritage of the English majority, and the influence of the American natural environment combined to bring about a distinctly American viewpoint and way of life. Especially among white male property owners, the colonists exercised the rights of free speech and a free press, became accustomed to electing representatives to colonial assemblies, and tolerated a variety of religions. English travelers in the colonies remarked that Americans were restless, enterprising, practical, and forever seeking to improve their circumstances.

Politics

By 1750, the 13 colonies had similar systems of government, with a governor acting as chief executive and a separate legislature voting either to adopt or reject the governor's proposed laws.

Structure of Government

There were eight royal colonies with governors appointed by the king (New Hampshire, Massachusetts, New York, New Jersey, Virginia, North Carolina, South Carolina, and Georgia). In the three proprietary colonies (Maryland, Pennsylvania, and Delaware), governors were appointed by the proprietors. The governors in only two of the colonies, Connecticut and Rhode Island, were elected by popular vote.

In every colony, the legislature consisted of two houses. The lower house, or assembly, elected by the eligible voters, voted for or against new taxes. Colonists thus became accustomed to paying taxes only if their chosen representatives approved. (Their unwillingness to surrender any part of this privilege would become a cause for revolt in the 1770s.) In the royal and proprietary colonies, members of the legislature's upper house—or council—were appointed by the king or the proprietor. In the two self-governing colonies, both the upper and lower houses were elective bodies.

Local Government From the earliest period of settlement, colonists in New England established towns and villages, clustering their small homes around an open space known as a green. In the southern colonies, on the other hand, towns were much less common, and farms and plantations were widely separated. Thus, the dominant form of local government in New England was the town meeting, in which people of the town would regularly come together, often in a church, to vote directly on public issues. In the southern colonies, local government was carried on by a law-enforcing sheriff and other officials who served a large territorial unit called a *county*.

Voting

If democracy is defined as the participation of all the people in the making of government policy, then colonial democracy was at best limited and partial. Those barred from voting—white women, poor white men, slaves of both sexes, and most free blacks—constituted a sizable majority of the colonial population. Nevertheless, the barriers to voting that existed in the 17th century were beginning to be removed in the 18th. Religious restrictions, for example, were removed in Massachusetts and other colonies. On the other hand, voters in all colonies were still required to own at least a small amount of property.

Another factor to consider is the degree to which members of the colonial assemblies and governors' councils represented either a privileged elite or the larger society of plain citizens. The situation varied from one colony to the next. In Virginia, membership in the House of Burgesses was tightly restricted to certain families of wealthy landowners. In Massachusetts, the legislature was more open to small farmers, although there, too, an educated, propertied elite held power for generations. The common people everywhere tended to defer to their "betters" and to depend upon the privileged few to make decisions for them.

Without question, colonial politics was restricted to participation by white males only. Even so, compared with other parts of the world, the English colonies showed tendencies toward democracy and self-government that made their political system unusual for the time.

HISTORICAL PERSPECTIVES: WAS COLONIAL SOCIETY DEMOCRATIC?

Was colonial America "democratic" or not? The question is important for its own sake and also because it affects one's perspective on the American Revolution and on the subsequent evolution of democratic politics in the United States. Many historians have focused on the politics of colonial Massachusetts. Some have concluded that colonial Massachusetts was indeed democratic, at least for the times. By studying voting records and statistics, they determined that the vast majority of white male citizens could vote and were not restricted by property qualifications. According to these historians, class differences between an elite and the masses of people did not prevent the latter from participating fully in colonial politics.

Other historians question whether broad voting rights by themselves demonstrate the existence of real democracy. The true test of democratic practice, they argue, would be whether different groups in a colonial town felt free to debate political questions in a town meeting. In the records of such meetings, they found little evidence of true political conflict and debate. Instead, they found that the purpose of town meetings in colonial days was to reach a consensus and to avoid conflict and real choices. These historians believe that the nature of consensus-forming limited the degree of democracy.

A third historical perspective is based on studies of economic change in colonial Boston. According to this view, a fundamental shift from an agrarian to a maritime economy occurred in the 18th century. In the process, a new elite emerged to dominate Boston's finances, society, and politics. The power of this elite prevented colonial Massachusetts from being considered a true democracy.

The question remains: To what extent were Massachusetts and the other colonies democratic? Much of the answer depends on the definition of democracy.

KEY TERMS BY THEME

Arts & Science (SOC)
English cultural
  domination
Benjamin West
John Copley
Benjamin Franklin
*Poor Richard's
  Almanack*
Phillis Wheatley
John Bartram
professions: religion,
  medicine, law

Religion (SOC)
religious toleration
established church
Great Awakening

Jonathan Edwards
George Whitefield
Cotton Mather
sectarian
nonsectarian

The Land (GEO)
subsistence farming

Ethnicity (NAT)
J. Hector St. John
  Crevecoeur
colonial families
Germans
Scotch-Irish
Huguenots
Dutch
Swedes
Africans

People (MIG)
immigrants
social mobility

Government (POL)
hereditary aristocracy
John Peter Zenger
Andrew Hamilton
Enlightenment
colonial governors
colonial legislatures
town meetings
county government
limited democracy

Questions 1–3 refer to the excerpt below.

"To understand political power . . . we must consider what estate all men are naturally in, and that it is a state of perfect freedom to order their actions and dispose of their possessions . . . within the bounds of the law of nature, without asking leave, or depending upon the will of any other man. . . .

"Whosoever therefore out of a state of nature unite into a community must be understood to give up all the power necessary to the ends for which they unite into society, to the majority of the community . . . And this is done by barely agreeing to unite into one political society. . . . And thus that which begins and actually constitutes any political society is nothing but the consent of any number of freemen capable of a majority to unite. . . . And this is that . . . which did or could give beginning to any lawful government in the world."

—John Locke, *Second Treatise of Government,* 1690

1. How is the topic of Locke's writing similar to most writing in the colonies in the 18th century?

   (A) He wrote about nature, and most writing was about nature or agriculture

   (B) He wrote about the rights of the majority, and most writing was about rights and liberties

   (C) He wrote about freemen, and most writing was about freedom and slavery

   (D) He wrote about politics, and most writing was about politics or religion

2. Locke's writings had the most direct influence on the

   (A) American Revolution

   (B) Great Awakening

   (C) Mayflower Compact

   (D) Zenger case

3. Which of the following groups in the colonies in the late 17th century would be most critical of Locke's ideas?

   (A) Slave owners

   (B) Church leaders

   (C) Merchants

   (D) Women

Questions 4–6 refer to the excerpt below.

"[Lawyer for the prosecution:] Gentlemen of the jury; the information now before the Court, and to which the Defendant Zenger has pleaded not guilty, is an information for printing and publishing a false, scandalous, and seditious libel, in which His Excellency the Governor of this Province . . . is greatly and unjustly scandalized as a person that has no regard to law nor justice. . . . Indeed Sir, as Mr. Hamilton [Zenger's attorney] has confessed the printing and publishing these libels, I think the jury must find a verdict for the King; for supposing they were true, the law says that they are not the less libelous for that; nay, indeed the law says their being true is an aggravation of the crime.

"[Mr. Hamilton:] Not so . . . I hope it is not our bare printing and publishing a paper that will make it libel. You will have something more to do before you make my client a libeler; for the words themselves must be libelous, that is false . . . or else we are not guilty."

—James Alexander, lawyer for J. Peter Zenger,
The Trial of John Peter Zenger, 1736

4. Which of the following had an effect on attitudes toward traditional authority similar to the effect of the Zenger case?

   (A) The arrival of new immigrants in the British colonies

   (B) The growth of the legal profession

   (C) The spread of the Great Awakening

   (D) The westward movement of settlers

5. Which group would most strongly support Zenger's position on the press?

   (A) Farmers in New England

   (B) Southern planters

   (C) Settlers on the frontier

   (D) Residents of cities

6. Which of the following was a long-term effect of the jury's decision in the Zenger case?

   (A) Zenger became a colonial leader

   (B) The colonial press became more willing to criticize the British

   (C) Restrictions on the press increased

   (D) New York became the center of anti-British sentiments

Questions 7–10 refer to the excerpt below.

"For a nation thus abused to arise unanimously and to resist their prince, even to dethroning him, is not criminal but a reasonable way of vindicating their liberties and just rights; it is making use of the means, and the only means, which God has put into their power for mutual and self-defense. . . .

"To conclude, let us all learn to be free and to be loyal. . . . But let us remember . . . government is sacred and not to be trifled with. It is our happiness to live under the government of a prince who is satisfied with ruling according to law. . . . Let us prize our freedom but not use our liberty for a cloak of maliciousness. There are men who strike at liberty under the term licentiousness. There are others who aim at popularity under the disguise of patriotism. Be aware of both. Extremes are dangerous."

—Jonathan Mayhew, church minister,"On Unlimited
Submission to Rulers," 1750

7. According to Mayhew, the people should be willing to challenge abuses by the
   (A) royal governors
   (B) church ministers
   (C) slave owners
   (D) king

8. Which of the following possible influences on Mayhew is most clearly reflected in his statement?
   (A) The Great Awakening
   (B) The teachings in the colonial colleges
   (C) The ideas of the Enlightenment
   (D) The rulings by royal governors

9. Mayhew would probably apply his warning, "not use our liberty for a cloak of maliciousness" to
   (A) the Mayflower Compact
   (B) the Act of Toleration
   (C) Bacon's Rebellion
   (D) the Zenger case

10. What was the context in which Mayhew was writing?
    (A) democratic practices were slowly increasing
    (B) opposition to British rule of the colonies was increasing
    (C) the Great Awakening was making authorities stronger
    (D) restrictions on voting were becoming tighter

SHORT-ANSWER QUESTIONS

Use complete sentences; an outline or bulleted list alone is not acceptable.

Question 1 is based on the following graph.

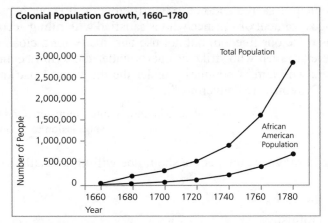

Colonial Population Growth, 1660–1780

Source: U.S. Bureau of the Census. *Historical Statistics of the United States, Colonial Times to 1970*

1. Using the graph, answer (A), (B), and (C).

   (A) Briefly explain the role slavery played in the population growth of the 18th century.

   (B) Briefly describe ONE place other than Africa from which people came to the British colonies in the 18th century.

   (C) Briefly explain the impact of voluntary immigration on ONE specific section of the British colonies in the 18th century.

Question 2. Answer (A), (B), and (C).

(A) Briefly explain ONE specific effect of geography on the economy of the New England colonies in the 18th century.

(B) Briefly explain ONE specific effect of geography on the economy of the Southern colonies in the 18th century.

(C) Briefly explain ONE specific influence on the colonial economy by British government policy in the 18th century.

Question 3 is based on the excerpts below.

"The design of erecting a college in this province is a matter of such grand and general importance that I have frequently made it the topic of my serious meditation. . . .

"It is, in the first place, observable that, unless its constitution and government be such as will admit persons of all Protestant denominations upon a perfect parity as to privileges, it will itself be greatly prejudiced and prove a nursery of animosity, dissension and disorder . . .

"Should our college, therefore, unhappily through our own bad policy fall into the hands of any one religious sect in the province; establish its religion in the college . . . it is easy to see that Christians of all other denominations among us, will, from the same principles, rather conspire to oppose and oppress it."

—William Livingston, Presbyterian, 1753

"Colleges are religious societies of a superior nature to all others. . . . colleges are societies of ministers for training up persons for the work of the ministry . . . all their religious instruction, worship, and ordinances are carried on within their own jurisdiction by their own officers and under their own regulations . . . And we know that religion, and the religion of these churches in particular, both as to doctrine and discipline, was the main design of the founders of this college, . . . and this design their successors are bound in duty to pursue. And, indeed, religion is a matter of so great consequences and importance that the knowledge of the arts and sciences, how excellent soever in themselves, are comparatively worth but little without it."

—Thomas Clap, president of Yale University, 1754

3. Using the excerpts, answer (A), (B), and (C).

(A) Briefly explain ONE major difference between Livingston's and Clap's views of the role of religion in colleges.

(B) Briefly explain how ONE historical event or development in the mid-18th century that is not explicitly mentioned in the excerpts could influence the authors' interpretations.

(C) Briefly explain ONE other implication of this debate beyond the question of college governance in the mid-18th century colonies.

Question 4. Answer (A), (B), and (C).

(A) Briefly explain ONE specific advance made in cultural areas in the mid-18th century in the colonies.

(B) Briefly explain ONE specific role of formal education in the mid-18th century in the cultural development of the colonies.

(C) Briefly explain why ONE specific group in the colonies was generally unable to share in the growing pursuit of the arts and sciences in the 18th century.

THINK AS A HISTORIAN: QUESTIONS ABOUT CHANGE OVER TIME

Historical changes often occur gradually over years or decades or centuries. To recognize the beginning or the end of a change over time, historians often identify key events that mark the beginning or end of the change. The choice of key events reflects a historian's point of view. Which THREE of the following prompts most clearly ask for an essay that focuses on change over time?

1. Compare and contrast the ideas and influence of Jonathan Edwards and George Whitefield.

2. How did the 1730s mark an important shift in colonial religious history?

3. Some people call the years from 1607 to 1733 the Era of English Settlement. Explain whether you think this label accurately distinguishes these years from the years before 1607 or after 1733.

4. Describe the ethnic diversity of the English colonies in 1775.

5. The Massachusetts school law of 1647 marked the beginning of a new era in American education.

Unit 2: Period 2 Review, 1607–1754

Directions: The suggested writing time for each question is 40 minutes. In your response you **should** do the following:

- **Thesis:** Make a defensible claim that establishes a line of reasoning and consists of one or more sentences found in one place.
- **Contextualization:** Relate the argument to a broader historical context.
- **Evidence:** Support an argument with specific and relevant historical evidence.
- **Reasoning:** Organize an argument using the skill in the question.
- **Analysis:** Demonstrate a complex understanding of the question using historical evidence to support, qualify, or modify an argument.

1. Compare and contrast the role of religion in the founding of the Spanish colonies in the 16th century with that of the English colonies in the 17th century.

2. Analyze why freedom of religion was important in the founding of some of the English colonies while being denied in others.

3. Analyze the impact of geography and the environment on the development of at least two different regions of the English colonies along the Atlantic coast in the 17th and 18th centuries.

4. Analyze the influence of TWO of the following on the development of a democratic society in the English colonies during the period from 1607 to 1745.
   - Bacon's Rebellion
   - Enlightenment
   - Great Awakening
   - Zenger case

DOCUMENT-BASED QUESTION

Directions: Question 1 is based on the accompanying documents. The documents have been edited for the purpose of this exercise. You are advised to spend 15 minutes planning and 45 minutes writing your answer. In your response you should do the following:

- **Thesis:** Make a defensible claim that establishes a line of reasoning and consists of one or more sentences found in one place.
- **Contextualization:** Relate the argument to a broader historical context.
- **Document Evidence:** Use content from at least six documents.
- **Outside Evidence:** Use one piece of evidence not in the documents.
- **Document Sourcing:** Explain how or why the point of view, purpose, situation, or intended audience is relevant for at least three documents.
- **Analysis:** Show the relationships among pieces of historical evidence and use them to support, qualify, or modify an argument.

1. Analyze the similarities and differences in the various influences and approaches toward unity in the English colonies in the period of the 17th and early 18th centuries.

Document 1

Source: The Mayflower Compact, 1620

This day before we came to harbor, observing some not well affected to unity and concord, but gave some appearance of faction, it was thought good there should be an association and agreement that we should combine together in one body, and to submit to such government and governors as we should be common consent agree to make and choose, and set out hands to this that follows word for word. . . . [We] do by these present, solemnly and mutually, in the presence of God and one another, covenant and combine ourselves together into a civil body politic, for our better ordering and preservation and furtherance of the ends aforesaid; and by virtue hereof to enact, constitute, and frame such just and equal laws, ordinances, acts, constitutions, offices from time to time as shall be thought most meet and convenient for the general good of the colony.

Document 2

Source: Fundamental Orders of Connecticut, 1639

As it has pleased the Almighty God . . . we, the inhabitants and residents of Windsor, Hartford, and Wethersfield are now cohabiting and dwelling in and upon the river of Conectecotte [Connecticut] and the lands thereunto adjoining; and well knowing where a people are gathered together the Word of God requires that, to maintain the peace and union of such a people, there should be an orderly and decent government established according to God, to order and dispose of the affairs of the people at all seasons as occasion shall require; do therefore associate and conjoin ourselves to be as one public state or commonwealth, and do, for ourselves and our successors and such as shall be adjoined to us at any time hereafter, enter into combination and confederation together, to maintain and preserve the liberty and purity of the Gospel of our Lord Jesus which we now profess.

Document 3

Source: The New England Confederation, 1643

The Articles of confederation between the Plantations under the Government of the Massachusetts . . . New Plymouth . . . Connecticut and . . . New Haven with the Plantations in Combination therewith. . . .

The said United Colonies . . . hereby enter into a firm and perpetual league of friendship and amity for offence and defence, mutual advice . . . upon all just occasions . . . and for their own mutual safety and welfare. . . .

It is by these Confederates agreed that the charge of all just wars, whether offensive or defensive, upon what part or member of this Confederation soever they fall . . . be borne by all the parts of this Confederation . . .

It is further agreed that if any of these Jurisdictions or any Plantation under or in combination with them, be invaded by any enemy whatsoever, upon notice and request of any three magistrates of that Jurisdiction so invaded, the rest of the Confederates without any further meeting or expostulation shall forthwith send aid to the Confederate in danger.

Document 4

Source: William Penn, Plan of Union, 1697

A brief and plain scheme how the English colonies in the North parts of America... Boston, Connecticut, Rhode Island, New York, New Jerseys, Pennsylvania, Maryland, Virginia, and Carolinas—may be made more useful to the crown and one another's peace and safety. . . .

1. That the several colonies before mentioned do meet . . . at least once intwo years in times of peace . . . to debate and resolve of such measures as are most advisable for their better understanding and the public tranquillity and safety.

2. That, in order to it, two persons . . . be appointed by each province as their representatives or deputies, which in the whole make the congress. . . .

6. That their business shall be to hear and adjust all matters of complaint or difference between province and province . . . to consider the ways and means to support the union and safety of these provinces against the public enemies.

Document 5

Source: The Albany Plan of Union, 1754

It is proposed that humble application be made for an act of Parliament of Great Britain, by virtue of which one general government may be formed in America, including all the said colonies, within and under which government each colony may retain its present constitution, except in the particulars wherein a change may be directed by the said act, as hereafter follows:

1. That the said general government be administered by a President-General, to be appointed and supported by the crown; and a Grand Council, to be chosen by the representatives of the people of the several Colonies met in their respective assemblies. . . .

15. That they raise and pay soldiers and build forts for the defense of any of the colonies. . . .

16. That for these purposes they have power to make laws, and lay and levy such general duties, imposts, or taxes, as to them shall appear most equal and just.

Document 6

Source: Pennsylvania *Gazette,* 1754. Library of Congress

Document 7

Source: Ben Franklin, "The Problem of Colonial Union," 1754

[On] the subject of uniting the colonies more intimately with Great Britain by allowing them representatives in Parliament, I have something further considered that matter and am of opinion that such a union would be very acceptable to the colonies, provided they had a reasonable number of representatives allowed them; and that all the old acts Parliament restraining the trade or cramping the manufacturers of the colonies be at the same time repealed. . . .

I should hope, too, that by such a union the people of Great Britain and the people of the colonies would learn to consider themselves as not belonging to different community with different interests but to one community with one interest, which I imagine, would contribute to strengthen the whole and greatly lessen the danger of future separations.

UNIT 3: Period 3, 1754–1800

In 1763, the British defeated the French and seemed to have consolidated their control along the Atlantic coast of North America. However, within two decades, they saw 13 of their colonies unite in revolt and establish an independent nation.

Overview After the Seven Years' War ended in 1763, the British desired more revenue from the colonies they were protecting in North America. In contrast, many American colonists saw themselves as self-sufficient. These clashing views resulted in the colonies declaring independence, winning a war, and founding a new nation.

The new United States of America was initially governed by Articles of Confederation. The national government was so weak that people soon replaced it with a new constitution, the document that still provides the basis of the government of the United States today. That document created a federal government that was stronger than the one under the Articles of Confederation, but still one with limited powers.

Debates over the new constitution and over policies under the first president, George Washington, revealed contrasting views of government. By the end of Washington's eight years in office, two political parties had emerged. One key difference between the parties was how to balance power between the federal and state governments. The Federalists argued for a stronger federal government. The Democratic-Republicans argued for stronger state governments. The test of the stability of the American system came in 1800, when the Federalists peacefully transferred power to the Democratic-Republicans.

Throughout the last half of the 18th century, colonists continued to migrate westward. They were in search of fresh land and economic opportunities. As they moved, they caused increased conflicts with the American Indians who already lived on those lands and other European nations that had claims on territories.

Alternate Views Some historians start the story of the birth of the United States in 1763, at the end of the Seven Years' War. Starting in 1754 emphasizes that fighting the war drove the colonies and the British apart. While the United States declared independence in 1776 and ratified the Constitution in 1788, not until 1800 had it clearly survived the divisions of the early years.

4

IMPERIAL WARS AND COLONIAL PROTEST, 1754–1774

The people, even to the lowest ranks, have become more attentive to their liberties, more inquisitive about them, and more determined to defend them than they were ever before known or had occasion to be.

John Adams, 1765

What caused American colonists in the 1760s to become, as John Adams expressed it, "more attentive to their liberties"? The chief reason for their discontent in these years was a dramatic change in Britain's colonial policy. Britain began to assert its power in the colonies and to collect taxes and enforce trade laws much more aggressively than in the past. To explain why Britain took this fateful step, we must study the effects of its various wars for empire.

Empires at War

Late in the 17th century, war broke out involving Great Britain, France, and Spain. This was the first of a series of four wars that were worldwide in scope, with battles in Europe, India, and North America. These wars occurred intermittently over a 74-year period from 1689 to 1763. The stakes were high, since the winner of the struggle stood to gain supremacy in the West Indies and Canada and to dominate the lucrative colonial trade.

The First Three Wars

The first three wars were named after the British king or queen under whose reign they occurred. In both King William's War (1689–1697) and Queen Anne's War (1702–1713), the British launched expeditions to capture Quebec, but their efforts failed. American Indians supported by the French burned British frontier settlements. Ultimately, the British forces prevailed in Queen Anne's War and gained both Nova Scotia from France and trading rights in Spanish America.

A third war was fought during the reign of George II: King George's War (1744–1748). Once again, the British colonies were under attack from their perennial rivals, the French and the Spanish. In Georgia, James Oglethorpe led a colonial army that managed to repulse Spanish attacks. To the north, a force of New Englanders captured Louisbourg, a major French fortress, on Cape Breton Island, controlling access to the St. Lawrence River. In the peace treaty ending the war, however, Britain agreed to give Louisbourg back to the French in exchange for political and economic gains in India. New Englanders were furious about the loss of a fort that they had fought so hard to win.

The Seven Years' War (French and Indian War)

The first three wars between Britain and France focused primarily on battles in Europe and only secondarily on conflict in the colonies. The European powers saw little value in committing regular troops to America. However, in the fourth and final war in the series, the fighting began in the colonies and then spread to Europe. Moreover, Britain and France now recognized the full importance of their colonies and shipped large numbers of troops overseas to North America rather than rely on "amateur" colonial forces. This fourth and most decisive war was known in Europe as the Seven Years' War. The North American phase of this war is often called the French and Indian War.

Beginning of the War From the British point of view, the French provoked the war by building a chain of forts in the Ohio River Valley. One of the reasons the French did so was to halt the westward growth of the British colonies. Hoping to stop the French from completing work on Fort Duquesne (Pittsburgh) and thereby win control of the Ohio River Valley, the governor of Virginia sent a small militia (armed force) under the command of a young colonel named George Washington. After gaining a small initial victory, Washington's troops surrendered to a superior force of Frenchmen and their American Indian allies on July 3, 1754. With this military encounter in the wilderness, the final war for empire began.

At first the war went badly for the British. In 1755, another expedition from Virginia, led by General Edward Braddock, ended in a disastrous defeat, as more than 2,000 British regulars and colonial troops were routed by a smaller force of French and American Indians near Ft. Duquesne. The Algonquin allies of the French ravaged the frontier from western Pennsylvania to North Carolina. The French repulsed a British invasion of French Canada that began in 1756.

The Albany Plan of Union Recognizing the need for coordinating colonial defense, the British government called for representatives from several colonies to meet in a congress at Albany, New York, in 1754. The delegates from seven colonies adopted a plan—the Albany Plan of Union—developed by Benjamin Franklin that provided for an intercolonial government and a system for recruiting troops and collecting taxes from the various colonies for their common defense. Each colony was too jealous of its own taxation powers to accept the plan, however, and it never took effect. The Albany congress was significant, however, because it set a precedent for later, more revolutionary congresses in the 1770s.

British Victory The British prime minister, William Pitt, concentrated the government's military strategy on conquering Canada. This objective was accomplished with the retaking of Louisbourg in 1758, the surrender of Quebec to General James Wolfe in 1759, and the taking of Montreal in 1760. After these British victories, the European powers negotiated a peace treaty (the Peace of Paris) in 1763. Great Britain acquired both French Canada and Spanish Florida. France ceded (gave up) to Spain its huge western territory, Louisiana, and claims west of the Mississippi River in compensation for Spain's loss of Florida. With this treaty, the British extended their control of North America, and French power on the continent virtually ended.

Immediate Effects of the War Britain's victory in the Seven Years' War gave them unchallenged supremacy in North America and also established them as the dominant naval power in the world. No longer did the American colonies face the threat of concerted attacks from the French, the Spanish, and their American Indian allies. More important to the colonies, though, was a change in how the British and the colonists viewed each other.

The British View The British came away from the war with a low opinion of the colonial military abilities. They held the American militia in contempt as a poorly trained, disorderly rabble. Furthermore, they noted that some of the colonies had refused to contribute either troops or money to the war effort. Most British were convinced that the colonists were both unable and unwilling to defend the new frontiers of the vastly expanded British empire.

The Colonial View The colonists took an opposite view of their military performance. They were proud of their record in all four wars and developed confidence that they could successfully provide for their own defense. They were not impressed with British troops or their leadership, whose methods of warfare seemed badly suited to the densely wooded terrain of eastern America.

Reorganization of the British Empire

More serious than the resentful feelings stirred by the war experience was the British government's shift in its colonial policies. Previously, Britain had exercised little direct control over the colonies and had generally allowed its navigation laws regulating colonial trade to go unenforced. This earlier policy of salutary neglect was abandoned as the British adopted more forceful policies for taking control of their expanded North American dominions.

All four wars—and the last one in particular—had been extremely costly. In addition, Britain now felt the need to maintain a large British military force to guard its American frontiers. Among British landowners, pressure was building to reduce the heavy taxes that the colonial wars had laid upon them. To pay for troops to guard the frontier without increasing taxes at home, King George III and the dominant political party in Parliament (the Whigs) wanted the American colonies to bear more of the cost of maintaining the British empire.

Pontiac's Rebellion The first major test of the new British imperial policy came in 1763 when Chief Pontiac led a major attack against colonial settlements on the western frontier. The American Indians were angered by the growing westward movement of European settlers onto their land and by the British refusal to offer gifts as the French had done. Pontiac's alliance of American Indians in the Ohio Valley destroyed forts and settlements from New York to Virginia. Rather than relying on colonial forces to retaliate, the British sent regular British troops to put down the uprising.

Proclamation of 1763 In an effort to stabilize the western frontier, the British government issued a proclamation that prohibited colonists from settling west of the Appalachian Mountains. The British hoped that limiting settlements would prevent future hostilities between colonists and American Indians. But the colonists reacted to the proclamation with anger and defiance. After their victory in the Seven Years' War, colonists hoped to reap benefits in the form of access to western lands. For the British to deny such benefits was infuriating. Defying the prohibition, thousands streamed westward beyond the imaginary boundary line drawn by the British. (See map, page 76.)

British Actions and Colonial Reactions

The Proclamation of 1763 was the first of a series of acts by the British government that angered colonists. From the British point of view, each act was justified as a proper method for protecting its colonial empire and making the colonies pay their share of costs for such protection. From the colonists' point of view, each act represented an alarming threat to their cherished liberties and long-established practice of representative government.

New Revenues and Regulations

In the first two years of peace, King George III's chancellor of the exchequer (treasury) and prime minister, Lord George Grenville, successfully pushed through Parliament three measures that aroused colonial suspicions of a British plot to subvert their liberties.

Sugar Act (1764) This act (also known as the Revenue Act of 1764) placed duties on foreign sugar and certain luxuries. Its chief purpose was to raise money for the crown, and a companion law also provided for stricter enforcement of the Navigation Acts to stop smuggling. Those accused of smuggling were to be tried in admiralty courts by crown-appointed judges without juries.

Quartering Act (1765) This act required the colonists to provide food and living quarters for British soldiers stationed in the colonies.

Stamp Act In an effort to raise funds to support British military forces in the colonies, Lord Grenville turned to a tax long in use in Britain. The Stamp Act, enacted by Parliament in 1765, required that revenue stamps be placed on most printed paper in the colonies, including all legal documents, newspapers, pamphlets, and advertisements. This was the first direct tax—collected from those who used the goods—paid by the people in the colonies, as opposed to the taxes on imported goods, which were paid by merchants.

People in every colony reacted with indignation to news of the Stamp Act. A young Virginia lawyer named Patrick Henry spoke for many when he stood up in the House of Burgesses to demand that the king's government recognize the rights of all citizens—including the right not to be taxed without representation. In Massachusetts, James Otis initiated a call for cooperative action among the colonies to protest the Stamp Act. Representatives from nine colonies met in New York in 1765 to form the so-called Stamp Act Congress. They resolved that only their own elected representatives had the legal authority to approve taxes.

The protest against the stamp tax took a violent turn with the formation of the Sons and Daughters of Liberty, a secret society organized for the purpose of intimidating tax agents. Members of this society sometimes destroyed revenue stamps and tarred and feathered revenue officials.

Boycotts against British imports were the most effective form of protest. It became fashionable in the colonies in 1765 and 1766 for people not to purchase any article of British origin. Faced with a sharp drop in trade, London merchants put pressure on Parliament to repeal the controversial Stamp Act.

Declaratory Act In 1766, Grenville was replaced by another prime minister, and Parliament voted to repeal the Stamp Act. When news of the repeal reached the colonies, people rejoiced. Few colonists at the time noted that Parliament had also enacted a face-saving measure known as the Declaratory Act (1766). This act asserted that Parliament had the right to tax and make laws for the colonies "in all cases whatsoever." This declaration of policy would soon lead to renewed conflict between the colonists and the British government.

Second Phase of the Crisis, 1767–1773

Because the British government still needed new revenues, the newly appointed chancellor of the exchequer, Charles Townshend, proposed another tax measure.

The Townshend Acts Adopting Townshend's program in 1767, Parliament enacted new duties to be collected on colonial imports of tea, glass, and paper. The law required that the revenues raised be used to pay crown officials in the colonies, thus making them independent of the colonial assemblies that had previously paid their salaries. The Townshend Acts also provided for the search of private homes for smuggled goods. All that an official needed to conduct such a search would be a *writ of assistance* (a general license to search anywhere) rather than a judge's warrant permitting a search only of a specifically named property. Another of the Townshend Acts suspended New York's assembly for that colony's defiance of the Quartering Act.

At first, most colonists accepted the taxes under the Townshend Acts because they were indirect taxes paid by merchants (not direct taxes on consumer goods). However, soon leaders began protesting the new duties. In 1767 and 1768, John Dickinson of Pennsylvania in his *Letters From a Farmer in Pennsylvania* wrote that Parliament could regulate commerce but argued that because duties were a form of taxation, they could not be levied on the colonies without the consent of their representative assemblies. Dickinson argued that the idea of no taxation without representation was an essential principle of English law.

In 1768, James Otis and Samuel Adams jointly wrote the Massachusetts Circular Letter and sent copies to every colonial legislature. It urged the various colonies to petition Parliament to repeal the Townshend Acts. British officials in Boston ordered the letter retracted, threatened to dissolve the legislature, and increased the number of British troops in Boston. Responding to the circular letter, the colonists again conducted boycotts of British goods. Merchants increased their smuggling activities to avoid the offensive Townshend duties.

Repeal of the Townshend Acts Meanwhile, in London, there was another change in the king's ministers. Lord Frederick North became the new prime minister. He urged Parliament to repeal the Townshend Acts because they damaged trade and generated a disappointingly small amount of revenue. The repeal of the Townshend Acts in 1770 ended the colonial boycott and, except for an incident in Boston (the "massacre" described below), there was a three-year respite from political troubles as the colonies entered into a period of economic prosperity. However, Parliament retained a small tax on tea as a symbol of its right to tax the colonies.

Boston Massacre Most Bostonians resented the British troops who had been quartered in their city to protect customs officials from being attacked by the Sons of Liberty. On a snowy day in March 1770, a crowd of colonists harassed the guards near the customs house. The guards fired into the crowd, killing five people including an African American, Crispus Attucks. At their trial for murder, the soldiers were defended by colonial lawyer John Adams and acquitted. Adams' more radical cousin, Samuel Adams, angrily denounced the shooting incident as a "massacre" and used it to inflame anti-British feeling.

Renewal of the Conflict

Even during the relatively quiet years of 1770–1772, Samuel Adams and a few other Americans kept alive the view that British officials were undermining colonial liberties. A principal device for spreading this idea was by means of the Committees of Correspondence initiated by Samuel Adams in 1772. In Boston and other Massachusetts towns, Adams began the practice of organizing committees that would regularly exchange letters about suspicious or potentially threatening British activities. The Virginia House of Burgesses took the concept a step further when it organized intercolonial committees in 1773.

The *Gaspee* One incident frequently discussed in the committees' letters was that of the *Gaspee,* a British customs ship that had caught several smugglers. In 1772, it ran aground off the shore of Rhode Island. Seizing their opportunity to destroy the hated vessel, a group of colonists disguised as American Indians ordered the British crew ashore and then set fire to the ship. The British ordered a commission to investigate and bring guilty individuals to Britain for trial.

Boston Tea Party The colonists continued their refusal to buy British tea because the British insisted on their right to collect the tax. Hoping to help the British East India Company out of its financial problems, Parliament passed the Tea Act in 1773, which made the price of the company's tea—even with the tax included—cheaper than that of smuggled Dutch tea.

Many Americans refused to buy the cheaper tea because to do so would, in effect, recognize Parliament's right to tax the colonies. A shipment of the East India Company's tea arrived in Boston harbor, but there were no buyers. Before the royal governor could arrange to bring the tea ashore, a group of Bostonians disguised themselves as American Indians, boarded the British ships, and dumped 342 chests of tea into the harbor. Colonial reaction to this incident (December 1773) was mixed. While many applauded the Boston Tea Party as a justifiable defense of liberty, others thought the destruction of private property was far too radical.

Intolerable Acts

In Great Britain, news of the Boston Tea Party angered the king, Lord North, and members of Parliament. In retaliation, the British government enacted a series of punitive acts (the Coercive Acts), together with a separate act dealing with French Canada (the Quebec Act). The colonists were outraged by these various laws, which were given the epithet "Intolerable Acts."

The Coercive Acts (1774) There were four Coercive Acts, directed mainly at punishing the people of Boston and Massachusetts and bringing the dissidents under control.

1. The Port Act closed the port of Boston, prohibiting trade in and out of the harbor until the destroyed tea was paid for.

2. The Massachusetts Government Act reduced the power of the Massachusetts legislature while increasing the power of the royal governor.

3. The Administration of Justice Act allowed royal officials accused of crimes to be tried in Great Britain instead of in the colonies.

4. A fourth law expanded the Quartering Act to enable British troops to be quartered in private homes. It applied to all colonies.

Quebec Act (1774) When it passed the Coercive Acts, the British government also passed a law organizing the Canadian lands gained from France. This plan was accepted by most French Canadians, but it was resented by many in the 13 colonies. The Quebec Act established Roman Catholicism as the official religion of Quebec, set up a government without a representative assembly, and extended Quebec's boundary to the Ohio River.

The colonists viewed the Quebec Act as a direct attack on the American colonies because it took away lands that they claimed along the Ohio River. They also feared that the British would attempt to enact similar laws in America to take away their representative government. The predominantly Protestant Americans also resented the recognition given to Catholicism.

BRITISH COLONIES: PROCLAMATION LINE
OF 1763 AND QUEBEC ACT OF 1774

Philosophical Foundations of the American Revolution

For Americans, especially those who were in positions of leadership, there was a long tradition of loyalty to the king and Great Britain. As the differences between them grew, many Americans tried to justify this changing relationship. As discussed in Chapter 3, the Enlightenment, particularly the writings of John Locke, had a profound influence on the colonies.

Enlightenment Ideas The era of the Enlightenment (see Chapter 3) was at its peak in the mid-18th century—the very years that future leaders of the American Revolution (Washington, Jefferson, Franklin, and Adams) were coming to maturity. Many Enlightenment thinkers in Europe and America were Deists, who believed that God had established natural laws in creating the universe, but that the role of divine intervention in human affairs was minimal. They believed in rationalism and trusted human reason to solve the many problems of life and society, and emphasized reason, science, and respect for humanity. Their political philosophy, derived from Locke and developed further by the French philosopher Jean-Jacques Rousseau, had a profound influence on educated Americans in the 1760s and 1770s—the decades of revolutionary thought and action that finally culminated in the American Revolution.

HISTORICAL PERSPECTIVES: WHY DID THE COLONIES REBEL?

Did America's break with Great Britain in the 18th century signify a true revolution with radical change, or was it simply the culmination of evolutionary changes in American life? For many years, the traditional view of the founding of America was that a revolution based on the ideas of the Enlightenment had fundamentally altered society.

During the 20th century, historians continued to debate whether American independence from Great Britain was revolutionary or evolutionary. At the start of the century, Progressive historians believed that the movement to end British dominance had provided an opportunity to radically change American society. A new nation was formed with a republican government based on federalism and stressing equality and the rights of the individual. The revolution was social as well as political.

During the second half of the 20th century, a different interpretation argued that American society had been more democratic and changed long before the war with Great Britain. Historian Bernard Bailyn has suggested that the changes that are viewed as revolutionary—representative government, expansion of the right to vote, and written constitutions— had all developed earlier, during the colonial period. According to this perspective, what was revolutionary or significant about the break from Great Britain was the recognition of an American philosophy based on liberty and democracy that would guide the nation.

KEY TERMS BY THEME

Colonial Unrest (NAT, POL)
Patrick Henry
Stamp Act Congress
Sons and Daughters of Liberty
John Dickinson; "Letters From . . ."
Samuel Adams
James Otis
Massachusetts Circular Letter
Committees of Correspondence
Intolerable Acts

Rulers & Policies (WXT)
George III
Whigs
Parliament
salutary neglect
Lord Frederick North

American Indians (MIG)
Pontiac's Rebellion
Proclamation of 1763

Empire (POL, GEO)
Seven Years' War (French and Indian War)
Albany Plan of Union (1754)
Edward Braddock
George Washington
Peace of Paris (1763)

Economic Policies (WOR)
Sugar Act (1764)
Quartering Act (1765)
Stamp Act (1765)
Declaratory Act (1766)
Townshend Acts (1767)
Writs of Assistance
Tea Act (1773)
Coercive Acts (1774)
—Port Act
—Massachusetts Government Act
—Administration of Justice Act
Quebec Act (1774)

Philosophy (SOC)
Enlightenment
Deism
Rationalism
John Locke
Jean-Jacques Rousseau

MULTIPLE-CHOICE QUESTIONS

Questions 1–3 refer to the excerpt below.

"We apprehend that as freemen and English subjects, we have an indisputable title to the same privileges and immunities with His Majesty's other subjects who reside in the interior counties . . . , and therefore ought not to be excluded from an equal share with them in the very important privilege of legislation. . . . We cannot but observe with sorrow and indignation that some persons in this province are at pains to extenuate the barbarous cruelties practised by these savages on our murdered brethren and relatives . . . by this means the Indians have been taught to despise us as a weak and disunited people, and from this fatal source have arisen many of our calamities. . . . We humbly pray therefore that this grievance may be redressed."

—The Paxton Boys, to the Pennsylvania Assembly, "A Remonstrance of Distressed and Bleeding Frontier Inhabitants," 1764

1. The protests by the Paxton Boys occurred during a period when many colonists were objecting to British policies that were a result of the

   (A) Albany Plan of Union

   (B) Great Awakening

   (C) Seven Years' War

   (D) Enlightenment

2. The concern expressed in this excerpt helps explain why the British passed the

   (A) Peace of Paris

   (B) Proclamation of 1763

   (C) Quartering Act

   (D) Port Act

3. Which of the following leaders from an earlier period represented a group in a similar situation as cited in this excerpt?

   (A) Edmond Andros

   (B) Nathaniel Bacon

   (C) John Smith

   (D) Roger Williams

Questions 4–6 refer to the excerpt below.

"It is inseparably essential to the freedom of a People, and the undoubted Right of Englishmen, that no taxes be imposed on them, but with their own Consent, given personally, or by their representatives. . . . That it is the indispensable duty of these colonies, to the best of sovereigns . . . to procure the repeal of the act for granting and applying certain stamp duties, of all clauses of any other acts of Parliament . . . for the restriction of American commerce."

—Resolutions of the Stamp Act Congress, 1765

4. The resolution of the Stamp Act Congress expressed respect for which person or group?
   (A) Colonial merchants
   (B) The king
   (C) Leaders in Parliament
   (D) Residents of England

5. For the first time, the Stamp Act placed on the colonies a tax that was
   (A) indirect
   (B) direct
   (C) to regulate trade
   (D) to support a church

6. Which of the following was a direct British response to the colonial views expressed by the Stamp Act Congress?
   (A) Quartering Act for British soldiers
   (B) Sugar Act taxing luxuries
   (C) Coercive Act closing the port of Boston
   (D) Declaratory Act stating the right to tax

Questions 7–8 refer to the excerpt below.

"The unhappy disputes between Great Britain and her American colonies . . . have proceeded to lengths so dangerous and alarming as to excite just apprehensions in the minds of His Majesty's faithful subjects of this colony. . . .

"It cannot admit of a doubt but that British subjects in America are entitled to the same rights and privileges as their fellow subjects possess in Britain; and therefore, that the power assumed by the British Parliament to bind America by their statutes in all cases whatsoever is unconstitutional, and the source of these unhappy differences. . . .

"To obtain a redress of these grievances, without which the people of America can neither be safe, free, nor happy, they are willing to undergo the great inconvenience that will be derived to them from stopping all imports whatsoever from Great Britain."

—Instructions to the Virginia Delegates to the First Continental
Congress, Williamsburg, 1774

7. Which of the following actions by the colonists is most similar to the one recommended in the excerpt above?

(A) The Boston Massacre

(B) The Boston Tea Party

(C) The formation of the Committees of Correspondence

(D) The distribution of the Massachusetts Circular Letter

8. Which of the following is the underlying goal of the colonists in the excerpt?

(A) Win political representation

(B) Declare independence

(C) Promote free trade

(D) Reduce the overall level of taxes

SHORT-ANSWER QUESTIONS

Use complete sentences; an outline or bulleted list alone is not acceptable.

Question 1 is based on the excerpts below.

"The colonists believed they saw . . . what appeared to be evidence of nothing less than a deliberated assault launched surreptitiously by plotters against liberty both in England and in America. The danger to America, it was believed, was in fact only the small immediately visible part of the greater whole whose ultimate manifestation would be the destruction of the English constitution with all the rights and privileges embedded in it...

It was this—the overwhelming evidence, as they saw it, that they were faced with conspirators against liberty determined at all costs to gain ends which their words dissembled [portrayed falsely]—that was signaled to the colonists after 1763, and it was this above all else that in the end propelled them into Revolution."

—Bernard Bailyn, historian, *The Logic of Rebellion,* 1967

"The Americans, 'born the heirs of freedom,' revolted not to create but to maintain their freedom. American society had developed differently from that of the Old World. . . . While the speculative philosophers of Europe were laboriously searching their minds in an effort to decide the first principles of liberty, the Americans had come to experience vividly that liberty in their everyday lives. . . . The Revolution was thus essentially intellectual and declaratory: it 'explained the business to the world, and served to confirm what nature and society had before produced.' 'All was the result of reason. . . .' The Revolution had taken place not in a succession of eruptions that had crumbled the existing social structure, but in a succession of new thoughts and new ideas that had vindicated that social structure. . . . The Americans revolted not out of actual suffering but out of reasoned principle."

—Gordon S. Wood, historian, *The Idea of America,* 2011

1. Using the excerpts, answer (A), (B), and (C).

   (A) Briefly explain ONE major difference between Wood's and Bailyn's historical interpretations of why the American colonies rebelled against the British.

   (B) Briefly explain how ONE historical event or development in the period 1754 to 1776 that is not explicitly mentioned in the excerpts could be used to support Bailyn's interpretation.

   (C) Briefly explain how ONE historical event or development in the period 1754 to 1776 that is not explicitly mentioned in the excerpts could be used to support Wood's interpretation.

Question 2. Answer (A), (B), and (C).

(A) Briefly explain how ONE historical event or development during the Seven Years' War supported a fundamental change in the British view of its relationship with its American colonies.

(B) Briefly explain ONE historical event or development that supported the colonial view that resulted from the war.

(C) Briefly describe ONE historical event or development resulting from the changing views by either the British or the colonists.

Question 3 is based on the cartoon below.

Source: *Political Register,* London, 1767. Library of Congress

3. Using the cartoon, answer (A), (B), and (C). In the cartoon, the labels on the limbs are "Virg," "Pensyl," "New York," and "New Eng."

(A) Briefly describe ONE perspective about colonial unity expressed in the image.

(B) Briefly explain ONE specific way that British Colonial policies changed based on their experiences with the colonies in the Seven Years' War.

(C) Briefly explain ONE specific way that the lack of colonial unity depicted in the image was challenged in the period 1754 to 1774.

Question 4. Answer (A), (B), and (C).

(A) ONE specific reason in the period 1754 to 1776 that resulted in the British issuing the Proclamation of 1763.

(B) Briefly explain ONE specific reaction of the colonists in the period 1754 to 1776 to the Proclamation of 1763.

(C) Briefly explain how effective the Proclamation of 1763 was.

THINK AS A HISTORIAN: QUESTIONS ABOUT COMPARISONS

Historians often compare events to highlight similarities and differences. They might compare two contempory developments or two developments in different time periods. Which THREE of the questions or statements below would best be answered with an essay that emphasizes comparison?

1. How did Pontiac's Rebellion support the British argument for the Proclamation of 1763?

2. Explain how the Declaratory Act was a cause of the Boston Tea Party.

3. Describe the similarities between Patrick Henry and James Otis.

4. How was the relationship between the colonies and Great Britain before and after the Seven Years' War different?

5. Analyze differences between Bacon's Rebellion and the Stamp Act Congress.

5

THE AMERICAN REVOLUTION AND CONFEDERATION, 1774–1787

*O! ye that love mankind! Ye that dare oppose not only the tyranny but
the tyrant, stand forth! Every spot of the Old World is overrun with
oppression. Freedom hath been hunted round the globe. . . . O! receive
the fugitive and prepare in time an asylum for mankind.*
Thomas Paine, *Common Sense*, 1776

Parliament's passage of the Intolerable Acts in 1774 intensified the conflict between the colonies and Great Britain. In the next two years, many Americans reached the conclusion—unthinkable only a few years earlier—that the only solution to their quarrel with the British government was to sever all ties with it. How did events from 1774 to 1776 lead ultimately to this revolutionary outcome?

The First Continental Congress

The punitive Intolerable Acts drove all the colonies except Georgia to send delegates to a convention in Philadelphia in September 1774. The purpose of the convention—later known as the First Continental Congress—was to respond to what the delegates viewed as Britain's alarming threats to their liberties. However, most Americans had no desire for independence. They simply wanted to protest parliamentary infringements of their rights and restore the relationship with the crown that had existed before the Seven Years' War.

The Delegates

The delegates were a diverse group, whose views about the crisis ranged from radical to conservative. Leading the radical faction—those demanding the greatest concessions from Britain—were Patrick Henry of Virginia and Samuel Adams and John Adams of Massachusetts. The moderates included George Washington of Virginia and John Dickinson of Pennsylvania. The conservative delegates—those who favored a mild statement of protest—included John Jay of New York and Joseph Galloway of Pennsylvania. Unrepresented were the loyal colonists, who would not challenge the king's government in any way.

Actions of the Congress

The delegates voted on a series of proposed measures, each of which was intended to change British policy without offending moderate and conservative colonists. Joseph Galloway proposed a plan, similar to the Albany Plan of 1754, that would have reordered relations with Parliament and formed a union of the colonies within the British empire. By only one vote, Galloway's plan failed to pass. Instead, the convention adopted these measures:

1. It endorsed the Suffolk Resolves, a statement originally issued by Massachusetts. The Resolves called for the immediate repeal of the Intolerable Acts and for colonies to resist them by making military preparations and boycotting British goods.

2. It passed the Declaration and Resolves. Backed by moderate delegates, this petition urged the king to redress (make right) colonial grievances and restore colonial rights. In a conciliatory gesture, it recognized Parliament's authority to regulate commerce.

3. It created the Continental Association (or just Association), a network of committees to enforce the economic sanctions of the Suffolk Resolves.

4. It declared that if colonial rights were not recognized, delegates would meet again in May 1775.

Fighting Begins

Angrily dismissing the petition of the First Continental Congress, the king's government declared Massachusetts to be in a state of rebellion and sent additional troops to put down any further disorders there. The combination of colonial defiance and British determination to suppress it led to violent clashes in Massachusetts—what would prove to be the first battles of the American Revolution.

Lexington and Concord

On April 18, 1775, General Thomas Gage, the commander of British troops in Boston, sent a large force to seize colonial military supplies in the town of Concord. Warned of the British march by two riders, Paul Revere and William Dawes, the militia (or Minutemen) of Lexington assembled on the village green to face the British. The Americans were forced to retreat under heavy British fire; eight of their number were killed in the brief encounter. Who fired the first shot of this first skirmish of the American Revolution? The evidence is ambiguous, and the answer will probably never be known.

Continuing their march, the British entered Concord, where they destroyed some military supplies. On the return march to Boston, the long column of British soldiers was attacked by hundreds of militiamen firing at them from behind stone walls. The British suffered 250 casualties—and also considerable humiliation at being so badly mauled by "amateur" fighters.

Bunker Hill

Two months later, on June 17, 1775, a true battle was fought between opposing armies on the outskirts of Boston. A colonial militia of Massachusetts farmers fortified Breed's Hill, next to Bunker Hill, for which the ensuing battle was wrongly named. A British force attacked the colonists' position and managed to take the hill, suffering over a thousand casualties. Americans claimed a victory of sorts, having succeeded in inflicting heavy losses on the attacking British army.

The Second Continental Congress

Soon after the fighting broke out in Massachusetts, delegates to the Second Continental Congress met in Philadelphia in May 1775. The congress was divided. One group of delegates, mainly from New England, thought the colonies should declare their independence. Another group, mainly from the middle colonies, hoped the conflict could be resolved by negotiating a new relationship with Great Britain.

Military Actions

The congress adopted a Declaration of the Causes and Necessities for Taking Up Arms and called on the colonies to provide troops. George Washington was appointed the commander-in-chief of a new colonial army and sent to Boston to lead the Massachusetts militia and volunteer units from other colonies. Congress also authorized a force under Benedict Arnold to raid Quebec in order to draw Canada away from the British empire. An American navy and marine corps was organized in the fall of 1775 for the purpose of attacking British shipping.

Peace Efforts

At first the congress adopted a contradictory policy of waging war while at the same time seeking a peaceful settlement. Many in the colonies did not want independence, for they valued their heritage and Britain's protection, but they did want a change in their relationship with Britain. In July 1775, the delegates voted to send an "Olive Branch Petition" to King George III, in which they pledged their loyalty and asked the king to intercede with Parliament to secure peace and the protection of colonial rights.

King George angrily dismissed the congress' plea and agreed instead to Parliament's Prohibitory Act (August 1775), which declared the colonies in rebellion. A few months later, Parliament forbade all trade and shipping between Britain and the colonies.

Thomas Paine's Argument for Independence

In January 1776, a pamphlet was published that quickly had a profound impact on public opinion and the future course of events. The pamphlet, written by

Thomas Paine, a recent English immigrant to the colonies, argued strongly for what until then had been considered a radical idea. Entitled Common Sense, Paine's essay argued in clear and forceful language for the colonies becoming independent states and breaking all political ties with the British monarchy. Paine argued that it was contrary to common sense for a large continent to be ruled by a small and distant island and for people to pledge allegiance to a king whose government was corrupt and whose laws were unreasonable.

The Declaration of Independence

After meeting for more than a year, the congress gradually and somewhat reluctantly began to favor independence rather than reconciliation. On June 7, 1776, Richard Henry Lee of Virginia introduced a resolution declaring the colonies to be independent. Five delegates including Thomas Jefferson formed a committee to write a statement in support of Lee's resolution. The declaration drafted by Jefferson listed specific grievances against George III's government and also expressed the basic principles that justified revolution: "We hold these truths to be self-evident: That all men are created equal; that they are endowed by their Creator with certain unalienable rights; that among these are Life, Liberty, and the pursuit of Happiness."

The congress adopted Lee's resolution calling for independence on July 2; Jefferson's work, the Declaration of Independence, was adopted on July 4, 1776.

The Revolutionary War

From the first shots fired on Lexington green in 1775 to the final signing of a peace treaty in 1783, the American War for Independence, or Revolutionary War, was a long and bitter struggle. As Americans fought they also forged a new national identity, as the former colonies became the United States of America.

About 2.6 million people lived in the 13 colonies at the time of the war. Maybe 40 percent of the population actively participated in the struggle against Britain. They called themselves American Patriots. Around 20 to 30 percent sided with the British as Loyalists. Everyone else tried to remain neutral and uninvolved.

Patriots

The largest number of Patriots were from the New England states and Virginia. Most of the soldiers were reluctant to travel outside their own region. They would serve in local militia units for short periods, leave to work their farms, and then return to duty. Thus, even though several hundred thousand people fought on the Patriot side in the war, General Washington never had more than 20,000 regular troops under his command at one time. His army was chronically short of supplies, poorly equipped, and rarely paid.

African Americans Initially, George Washington rejected the idea of African Americans serving in the Patriot army. However, when the British promised freedom to enslaved people who joined their side, Washington and the congress quickly made the same offer. Approximately 5,000 African Americans fought as Patriots. Most of them were free citizens from the North, who fought in mixed racial forces, although there were some all-African-American units. African Americans took part in most of the military actions of the war, and a number, including Peter Salem, were recognized for their bravery.

Loyalists

Tories The Revolutionary War was in some respects a civil war in which anti-British Patriots fought pro-British Loyalists. Those who maintained their allegiance to the king were also called Tories (after the majority party in Parliament). Almost 60,000 American Tories fought next to British soldiers, supplied them with arms and food, and joined in raiding parties that pillaged Patriot homes and farms. Members of the same family sometimes joined opposite sides. For example, while Benjamin Franklin was a leading patriot, his son William joined the Tories and served as the last royal governor of New Jersey.

How many American Tories were there? Estimates range from 520,000 to 780,000 people—roughly 20 to 30 percent of the population. In New York, New Jersey, and Georgia, they were probably in the majority. Toward the end of the war, about 80,000 Loyalists emigrated from the states to settle in Canada or Britain rather than face persecution at the hands of the victorious Patriots.

Although Loyalists came from all groups and classes, they tended to be wealthier and more conservative than the Patriots. Most government officials and Anglican clergy in America remained loyal to the crown.

American Indians At first, American Indians tried to stay out of the war. Eventually, however, attacks by colonists prompted many American Indians to support the British, who promised to limit colonial settlements in the West.

Initial American Losses and Hardships

The first three years of the war, 1775 to 1777, went badly for Washington's poorly trained and equipped revolutionary army. It barely escaped complete disaster in a battle for New York City in 1776, in which Washington's forces were routed by the British. By the end of 1777, the British occupied both New York and Philadelphia. After losing Philadelphia, Washington's demoralized troops suffered through the severe winter of 1777–1778 camped at Valley Forge in Pennsylvania.

Economic troubles added to the Patriots' bleak prospects. British occupation of American ports resulted in a 95 percent decline in trade between 1775 and 1777. Goods were scarce and inflation was rampant. The paper money issued by Congress, known as continentals, became almost worthless.

Alliance with France

The turning point for the American revolutionaries came with a victory at Saratoga in upstate New York in October 1777. British forces under General John Burgoyne had marched from Canada in an ambitious effort to link up with other forces marching from the west and south. Their objective was to cut off New England from the rest of the colonies (or states). But Burgoyne's troops were attacked at Saratoga by troops commanded by American generals Horatio Gates and Benedict Arnold. The British army was forced to surrender.

The diplomatic outcome of the Battle of Saratoga was even more important than the military result. News of the surprising American victory persuaded France to join in the war against Britain. France's king, Louis XVI, was an absolute monarch who had no interest in aiding a revolutionary movement. Nevertheless, he saw a chance to weaken his country's traditional foe, Great Britain, by helping to undermine its colonial empire. France had secretly extended aid to the American revolutionaries as early as 1775, giving both money and supplies. After Saratoga, in 1778, France openly allied itself with the Americans. (A year later, Spain and Holland also entered the war against Britain.) The French alliance proved a decisive factor in the American struggle for independence because it widened the war and forced the British to divert military resources away from America.

Victory

Faced with a larger war, Britain decided to consolidate its forces in America. British troops were pulled out of Philadelphia, and New York became the chief base of British operations. In a campaign through 1778–1779, the Patriots, led by George Rogers Clark, captured a series of British forts in the Illinois country to gain control of parts of the vast Ohio territory. In 1780, the British army adopted a southern strategy, concentrating its military campaigns in Virginia and the Carolinas where Loyalists were especially numerous and active.

Yorktown In 1781, the last major battle of the Revolutionary War was fought near Yorktown, Virginia, on the shores of Chesapeake Bay. Strongly supported by French naval and military forces, Washington's army forced the surrender of a large British army commanded by General Charles Cornwallis.

Treaty of Paris News of Cornwallis's defeat at Yorktown was a heavy blow to the Tory party in Parliament that was conducting the war. The war had become unpopular in Britain, partly because it placed a heavy strain on the economy and the government's finances. Lord North and other Tory ministers resigned and were replaced by Whig leaders who wanted to end the war.

In Paris, in 1783, a treaty of peace was finally signed by the various belligerents. The Treaty of Paris provided for the following: (1) Britain would recognize the existence of the United States as an independent nation. (2) The Mississippi River would be the western boundary of that nation. (3) Americans would have fishing rights off the coast of Canada. (4) Americans would pay debts owed to British merchants and honor Loyalist claims for property confiscated during the war.

Organization of New Governments

While the Revolutionary War was being fought, leaders of the 13 colonies worked to change them into independently governed states, each with its own constitution (written plan of government). At the same time, the revolutionary Congress that originally met in Philadelphia tried to define the powers of a new central government for the nation that was coming into being.

State Governments

By 1777, ten of the former colonies had written new constitutions. Most of these documents were both written and adopted by the states' legislatures. In a few of the states (Maryland, Pennsylvania, and North Carolina), a proposed constitution was submitted to a vote of the people for ratification (approval).

Each state constitution was the subject of heated debate between conservatives, who stressed the need for law and order, and liberals, who were most concerned about protecting individual rights and preventing future tyrannies. Although the various constitutions differed on specific points, they had the following features in common:

List of Rights Each state constitution began with a "bill" or "declaration" listing the basic rights and freedoms, such as a jury trial and freedom of religion, that belonged to all citizens by right and that state officials could not infringe (encroach on).

Separation of Powers With a few exceptions, the powers of state government were given to three separate branches: (1) legislative powers to an elected two-house legislature, (2) executive powers to an elected governor, and (3) judicial powers to a system of courts. The principle of separation of powers was intended to be a safeguard against tyranny—especially against the tyranny of a too-powerful executive.

Voting The right to vote was extended to all white males who owned some property. The property requirement, usually for a minimal amount of land or money, was based on the assumption that propertyowners had a larger stake in government than did the poor and propertyless.

Office-Holding Those seeking elected office were usually held to a higher property qualification than the voters.

The Articles of Confederation

At Philadelphia in 1776, as Jefferson was writing the Declaration of Independence, John Dickinson drafted the first constitution for the United States as a nation. Congress modified Dickinson's plan to protect the powers of the individual states. The Articles of Confederation, as the document was called, was adopted by Congress in 1777 and submitted to the states for ratification.

Ratification Ratification of the Articles was delayed by a dispute over the vast American Indian lands west of the Alleghenies. Seaboard states such as Rhode Island and Maryland insisted that these lands be under the jurisdiction of the new central government. When Virginia and New York finally agreed to cede their claims to western lands, the Articles were ratified in March 1781.

Structure of Government The Articles established a central government that consisted of just one body, a congress. In this unicameral (one-house) legislature, each state was given one vote, with at least 9 votes out of 13 required to pass important laws. Amending the Articles required a unanimous vote. A Committee of States, with one representative from each state, could make minor decisions when the full congress was not in session.

THE UNITED STATES IN 1783

Powers The Articles gave the congress the power to wage war, make treaties, send diplomatic representatives, and borrow money. However, Congress did not have the power to regulate commerce or to collect taxes. To finance any of its decisions, the congress had to rely upon taxes voted by each state. Neither did the government have executive power to enforce its laws.

Accomplishments Despite its weaknesses, the congress under the Articles did succeed in accomplishing the following:

1. Winning the war. The U.S. government could claim some credit for the ultimate victory of Washington's army and for negotiating favorable terms in the treaty of peace with Britain.

2. Land Ordinance of 1785. Congress established a policy for surveying and selling the western lands. The policy provided for setting aside one section of land in each township for public education.

3. Northwest Ordinance of 1787. For the large territory lying between the Great Lakes and the Ohio River, the congress passed an ordinance (law) that set the rules for creating new states. The Northwest Ordinance granted limited self-government to the developing territory and prohibited slavery in the region.

Problems with the Articles The 13 states intended the central government to be weak—and it was. The government faced three kinds of problems:

1. Financial Most war debts were unpaid. Individual states as well as the congress issued worthless paper money. The underlying problem was that the congress had no taxing power and could only request that the states donate money for national needs.

2. Foreign. European nations had little respect for a new nation that could neither pay its debts nor take effective and united action in a crisis. Britain and Spain threatened to take advantage of U.S. weakness by expanding their interests in the western lands soon after the war ended.

3. Domestic. In the summer of 1786, Captain Daniel Shays, a Massachusetts farmer and Revolutionary War veteran, led other farmers in an uprising against high state taxes, imprisonment for debt, and lack of paper money. The rebel farmers stopped the collection of taxes and forced the closing of debtors' courts. In January 1787, when Shays and his followers attempted to seize weapons from the Springfield armory, the state militia of Massachusetts broke Shays's Rebellion.

Social Change

In addition to revolutionizing the politics of the 13 states, the War for Independence also profoundly changed American society. Some changes occurred immediately before the war ended, while others evolved gradually as the ideas of the Revolution began to filter into the attitudes of the common people.

Abolition of Aristocratic Titles

State constitutions and laws abolished old institutions that had originated in medieval Europe. No legislature could grant titles of nobility, nor could any court recognize the feudal practice of primogeniture (the first born son's right to inherit his family's property). Whatever aristocracy existed in colonial America was further weakened by the confiscation of large estates owned by Loyalists. Many such estates were subdivided and sold to raise money for the war.

Separation of Church and State

Most states adopted the principle of separation of church and state; in other words, they refused to give financial support to any religious group. The Anglican Church, which formerly had been closely tied to the king's government, was disestablished (lost state support) in the South. Only in three New England states—New Hampshire, Connecticut, and Massachusetts—did the Congregational Church continue to receive state support in the form of a religious tax. This practice was finally discontinued in New England early in the 1830s.

Women

During the war, both the Patriots and Loyalists depended on the active support of women. Some women followed their men into the armed camps and worked as cooks and nurses. In a few instances, women actually fought in battle, either taking their husband's place, as Mary McCauley (Molly Pitcher) did at the Battle of Monmouth, or passing as a man and serving as a soldier, as Deborah Sampson did for a year.

The most important contribution of women during the war was in maintaining the colonial economy. While fathers, husbands, and sons were away fighting, women ran the family farms and businesses. They provided much of the food and clothing necessary for the war effort.

Despite their contributions, women remained in a second-class status. Unanswered went pleas such of those of Abigail Adams to her husband, John Adams: "I desire you would remember the ladies and be more generous and favorable to them than your ancestors."

Slavery

The institution of slavery contradicted the spirit of the Revolution and the idea that "all men are created equal." For a time, the leaders of the Revolution recognized this and took some corrective steps. The Continental Congress abolished the importation of enslaved people, and most states went along with the prohibition. Most northern states ended slavery, while in the South, some owners voluntarily freed their slaves.

However, in the decades following the Revolutionary War, more and more slaveowners came to believe that enslaved labor was essential to their economy. As explained in later chapters, they developed a rationale for slavery that found religious and political justification for continuing to hold human beings in lifelong bondage.

Was the American Revolution (1) a radical break with the past or (2) a conservative attempt simply to safeguard traditional British liberties? One approach to this question is to compare the American Revolution with other revolutions in world history.

In his *Anatomy of a Revolution* (1965), historian Crane Brinton found striking similarities between the American Revolution and two later revolutions—the French Revolution (1789–1794) and the Russian Revolution (1917–1922). He observed that each revolution passed through similar stages and became increasingly radical from one year to the next.

Other historians have been more impressed with the differences between the American experience and the revolutions in Europe. They argue that the French and Russian revolutionaries reacted to conditions of feudalism and aristocratic privilege that did not exist in the American colonies. In their view, Americans did not revolt against outmoded institutions but, in their quest for independence, merely carried to maturity a liberal, democratic movement that had been gaining force for years.

In comparing the three revolutions, a few historians have concentrated on the actions of revolutionary groups of citizens, such as the American Sons of Liberty. Again there are two divergent interpretations: (1) the groups in all three countries engaged in the same radical activities, and (2) the Americans had a much easier time of it than the French and Russians, who encountered ruthless repression by military authorities.

Another interpretation of the American Revolution likens it to the colonial rebellions that erupted in Africa and Asia after World War II. According to this view, the colonial experience in America caused a gradual movement away from Britain that culminated in demands for independence. Other studies of the military aspects of the Revolution have pointed out similarities between American guerrilla forces in the 1770s and the guerrilla bands that fought in such countries as Cuba in the 1950s and Vietnam in the 1960s. Recall that the British controlled the cities while the American revolutionaries controlled the countryside—a pattern that in the 20th century was often repeated in revolutionary struggles throughout the world. Typically, as in the case of the American Revolution, insurgent forces were weak in the cities, but strong in the surrounding territory.

Since the American Revolution pre-dated the other modern revolutions it is compared to, its influence on them is a topic of study. Seeing the American Revolution in the context of other uprisings provides insights to help understand it better.

KEY TERMS BY THEME

Separation (NAT)
Intolerable Acts
Patrick Henry
Samuel Adams
John Adams
John Dickinson
John Jay
First Continental
   Congress (1774)
Joseph Galloway
Suffolk Resolves
economic sanctions
Declaration of Rights
   and Grievances
Second Continental
   Congress (1775)
Olive Branch Petition
Declaration of the
   Causes and Neces-
   sities for Taking Up
   Arms
Thomas Jefferson
Declaration of
   Independence
George Washington

Expansion (MIG, POL)
Land Ordinance of 1785
Northwest Ordinance
   of 1787

War (POL)
Paul Revere
William Dawes
Lexington
Concord
Battle of Bunker Hill
Battle of Saratoga
George Rogers Clark
Battle of Yorktown
Articles of
   Confederation
unicameral legislature

Final Break (WOR)
absolute monarch
Prohibitory Act (1775)
Treaty of Paris (1783)

A New Nation (SOC)
Thomas Paine;
   Common Sense
Patriots
Loyalists (Tories)
Minutemen
Continentals
Valley Forge
Abigail Adams
Deborah Sampson
Mary McCauley (Molly
   Pitcher)
Shays's Rebellion

Questions 1–3 refer to the excerpt below.

"The authors and promoters of this desperate conspiracy have . . . meant only to amuse, by vague expressions of attachment to the parent state, and the strongest protestations of loyalty to me, whilst they were preparing for a general revolt. . . . The resolutions of Parliament breathed a spirit of moderation and forbearance; conciliatory propositions accompanied the measures taken to enforce authority. . . . I have acted with the same temper, anxious to prevent, if it had been possible . . . the calamities which are inseparable from a state of war; still hoping that my people in America would have discerned the traitorous views of their leaders, and have been convinced, that to be a subject of Great Britain, with all its consequences, is to be the freest member of any civil society in the known world."

—King George III, Speech to Parliament, October 27, 1775

1. King George's rejection of the Olive Branch Petition demonstrates that he believed that most colonists
   (A) were personally loyal to him
   (B) blamed Parliament for their problems
   (C) had always planned to revolt
   (D) failed to understand his policies

2. Which of the following documents most forcefully disagreed with the views King George expressed in this excerpt?
   (A) Galloway's plan for a union of colonies
   (B) Declaration and Resolves
   (C) Olive Branch Petition
   (D) *Common Sense* by Thomas Paine

3. Which of the following groups or individuals would have been most likely to agree with King George?
   (A) Continentals
   (B) Loyalists
   (C) John Dickenson
   (D) Thomas Paine

Questions 4–6 refer to the excerpt below.

"A Declaration of Rights made by the representatives of the good people of Virginia . . .

Section 1.   That all men are by nature equally free and independent and have certain inherent rights. . . .

Section 2.   That all power is vested in and consequently derived from, the people. . . .

Section 4.   That no man, or set of men, is entitled to exclusive or separate . . . privileges from the community. . . .

Section 5.   That the legislative and executive powers of the state should be separate and distinct from the judiciary. . . .

Section 6.   That elections of members . . . as representatives of the people, in assembly, ought to be free; and that all men, having sufficient evidence of permanent common interest with and attachment to the community, have the right of suffrage. . . .

Section 12. That freedom of the press is one of the great bulwarks of liberty. . . .

Section 16. All men are equally entitled to the free exercise of religion."

—Virginia Declaration of Rights, 1776

4. In the context of the various disputes between the colonists and Britain, which of the following would be the most important right cited?

   (A) Section 1: all people are by nature free

   (B) Section 2: all power comes from the people

   (C) Section 4: no person has special privileges

   (D) Section 16: people should be able to worship freely

5. Which of the rights in the excerpt is expressed in a way that would today be considered a limitation of individual rights?

   (A) Section 5: separation of government powers

   (B) Section 2: origins of governmental power

   (C) Section 6: right to vote

   (D) Section 12: freedom of the press

6. The group most likely to oppose the ideas expressed in this excerpt would have been

   (A) the Minutemen of Lexington

   (B) advocates of a unicameral legislature

   (C) Tories such as William Franklin

   (D) supporters of Shays's Rebellion

Questions 7–8 refer to the excerpt below.

"I have not the least doubt that the Negroes will make very excellent soldiers, with proper management. . . .

"I foresee that this project will have to combat much opposition from prejudice and self-interest. The contempt we have been taught to entertain for the black makes us fancy many things that are founded neither in reason nor experience; and an unwillingness to part with property of so valuable a kind will furnish a thousand arguments to show the impracticability or pernicious tendency of a scheme which requires such a sacrifice. But it should be considered that if we do not make use of them in this way, the enemy probably will. . . . An essential part of the plan is to give them their freedom with their muskets."

—Alexander Hamilton, "A Proposal to Arm and Then Free the Negroes," 1779

7. For some the Revolutionary War was also a civil war because of the role played in the war by the

   (A) American Indians

   (B) African Americans

   (C) Quakers

   (D) Tories

8. Which of the following was the primary reason for Hamilton's call for African American soldiers?

   (A) The New York militia was short of troops

   (B) The British were recruiting African Americans

   (C) The Declaration of Independence called for equal rights

   (D) General Washington trusted that blacks would make good soldiers

SHORT-ANSWER QUESTIONS

Question 1 is based on the excerpts below.

"In the decades following the Revolution, American society was transformed. . . . The Revolution resembled the breaking of a dam, releasing thousands upon thousands of pent-up pressures. . . . It was as if the whole traditional structure, enfeebled and brittle to begin with, broke apart, and the people and their energies were set loose in an unprecedented outburst.

Nothing contributed more to this explosion of energy than did the idea of equality. Equality was in fact the most radical and most powerful ideological force let loose in the Revolution. Its appeal was far more potent than any of the revolutionaries realized. Once invoked, the idea of equality could not be stopped, and it tore through American society and culture with awesome power. . . . Within decades following the Declaration of Independence, the United States became the most egalitarian nation in the history of the world, and it remains so today, regardless of its great disparities of wealth."

—Gordon S. Wood, *Radicalism of the American Revolution*, 1993

"Today, 'equality' is generally interpreted to include protection for the rights of minorities; during the Revolution, 'the body of the people' referred exclusively to the majority...

It is one of the supreme ironies of the American revolution that the assumption of authority by "the body of the people"—probably its most radical feature —served to oppress as well as to liberate. This was a real revolution: the people did seize power, but they exercised that power at the expense of others—loyalists, pacifists, merchants, Indians, slaves—who, although certainly people, were not perceived to be part of the whole. This was, after all, a war. It would not be the last time Americans sacrificed notions of liberty and equality in the name of the general good.

Our Revolutionary heritage works both ways. 'The body of the people,' the dominant force during the 1770s, has empowered and deprived."

—Ray Raphael, *A People's History of the American Revolution,* 2001

1. Using the excerpts, answer (A), (B), and (C).

    (A) Briefly explain ONE major difference between Wood's and Raphael's historical interpretations of how radical the American Revolution was.

    (B) Briefly explain how ONE historical event or development in the period 1774 to 1787 that is not explicitly mentioned in the excerpts could be used to support Wood's interpretation.

    (C) Briefly explain how ONE historical event or development in the period 1774 to 1787 that is not explicitly mentioned in the excerpts could be used to support Raphael's interpretation.

Question 2. Answer (A), (B), and (C).

   (A) Briefly explain ONE specific role that African Americans played in the American Revolution in the period 1774 to 1783.

   (B) Briefly explain ONE specific way that France influenced the American Revolution in the period 1774 to 1783.

   (C) Briefly explain ONE specific role that Native Americans played in the American Revolution in the period 1774 to 1783.

Question 3 is based on the cartoon below.

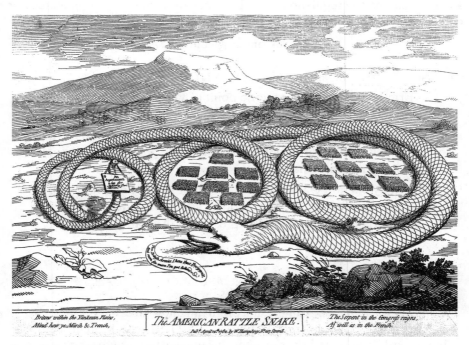

Source: James Gillray, London, 1782. Library of Congress

3. Using the cartoon, answer (A), (B), and (C). The title of the cartoon is "The American Rattle Snake." The squares surrounded by the snake's coils represent British soldiers.

   (A) Briefly explain ONE historical event or development that resulted in the degree of American unity portrayed in this cartoon.

   (B) Briefly explain ONE historical impact on the British public's view of the American Revolution based on this cartoon.

   (C) Briefly explain how ONE specific historical event or development from 1776 to 1783 could support the French view of the cartoon.

Question 4 is based on the excerpt below.

"I wish I knew what mighty things were fabricating. If a form of government is to be established here, what one will be assumed? Will it be left to our assemblies to choose one? And will not many men have many minds? And shall we not run into dissensions among ourselves?

"I am more and more convinced that man is a dangerous creature; and that power, whether vested in many or a few, is ever grasping. . . .

"How shall we be governed so as to retain our liberties? Who shall frame these laws? Who will give them force and energy. . . .

"When I consider these things, and the prejudices of people in favor of ancient customs and regulations, I feel anxious for the fate of our monarchy or democracy, or whatever is to take place."

—Abigail Adams, Letter to John Adams, November 27, 1775

4. Using the excerpt, answer (A), (B), and (C).

   (A) Briefly explain ONE specific point of view expressed by Abigail Adams in the excerpt above.

   (B) Briefly explain ONE historical event or development in the period leading up to independence that led to the point of view expressed here by Abigail Adams.

   (C) Briefly explain ONE historical event or development in the period immediately after the Revolutionary War that challenges or supports the point of view expressed by Abigail Adams.

THINK AS A HISTORIAN: QUESTIONS ABOUT CONTEXTUALIZATION

Contextualization is explaining and evaluating how an event is shaped by broader trends or its historical setting. Which THREE of the items below would best be answered with an essay that emphasizes contextualization?

1. Explain how geography shaped the conflict between Great Britain and its American colonies.

2. How did the Enlightenment influence the American Revolution?

3. Explain why the ideas expressed in the Articles of Confederation would make conducting a war difficult.

4. What caused the American Revolution?

5. How did the American and French revolutions differ?

6

THE CONSTITUTION AND THE NEW REPUBLIC, 1787–1800

Thus I consent, sir, to this Constitution, because I expect no better, and because I am not sure that it is not the best. The opinions I have had of its errors I sacrifice to the public good. . . .

Benjamin Franklin, 1787

With these words, Benjamin Franklin, the oldest delegate at the Constitutional Convention in Philadelphia, attempted to overcome the skepticism of other delegates about the document that they had created. Would the new document, the Constitution, establish a central government strong enough to hold 13 states together in a union that could prosper and endure?

In September 1787, when Franklin, Washington, and other delegates signed the Constitution that they had drafted, their young country was in a troubled condition. This chapter will summarize the problems leading to the Constitutional Convention, the debates in the various states on whether to ratify the new plan of government, and the struggles of two presidents, Washington and Adams, to meet the domestic and international challenges of the 1790s.

The United States Under the Articles, 1781–1787

Four years separated the signing of the Treaty of Paris of 1783 and the meeting of the Constitutional Convention in Philadelphia. During that time, the government operated under the Articles of Confederation, which consisted of a one-house congress, no separate executive, and no separate judiciary (court system). The country faced several major problems.

Foreign Problems

Relations between the United States and the major powers of Europe were troubled from the start. States failed to adhere to the Treaty of Paris, which required that they restore property to Loyalists and repay debts to foreigners. In addition, the U.S. government under the Articles was too weak to stop Britain from maintaining military outposts on the western frontier and restricting trade.

Economic Weakness and Interstate Quarrels

Reduced foreign trade and limited credit because states had not fully repaid war debts contributed to widespread economic depression. The inability to levy national taxes and the printing of worthless paper money by many states added to the problems. In addition, the 13 states treated one another with suspicion and competed for economic advantage. They placed tariffs and other restrictions on the movement of goods across state lines. A number of states faced boundary disputes with neighbors that increased interstate rivalry and tension.

The Annapolis Convention

To review what could be done about the country's inability to overcome critical problems, George Washington hosted a conference at his home in Mt. Vernon, Virginia (1785). Representatives from Virginia, Maryland, Delaware, and Pennsylvania agreed that the problems were serious enough to hold further discussions at a later meeting at Annapolis, Maryland, at which all the states might be represented. However, only five states sent delegates to the Annapolis Convention in 1786. After discussing ways to improve commercial relations among the states, James Madison and Alexander Hamilton persuaded the others that another convention should be held in Philadelphia for the purpose of revising the Articles of Confederation.

Drafting the Constitution at Philadelphia

After a number of states elected delegates to the proposed Philadelphia convention, congress consented to give its approval to the meeting. It called upon all 13 states to send delegates to Philadelphia "for the sole and express purpose of revising the Articles of Confederation." Only Rhode Island, not trusting the other states, refused to send delegates.

The Delegates

Of the 55 delegates who went to Philadelphia for the convention in the summer of 1787, all were white, all were male, and most were college-educated. As a group, they were relatively young (averaging in their early forties). With few exceptions, they were far wealthier than the average American of their day. They were well acquainted with issues of law and politics. A number of them were practicing lawyers, and many had helped to write their state constitutions.

The first order of business was to elect a presiding officer and decide whether or not to communicate with the public at large. The delegates voted to conduct their meetings in secret and say nothing to the public about their discussions until their work was completed. George Washington was unanimously elected chairperson. Benjamin Franklin, the elder statesman at age 81, provided a calming and unifying influence. The work in fashioning specific articles of the Constitution was directed by James Madison (who came to be known as the Father of the Constitution), Alexander Hamilton, Gouverneur

Morris, and John Dickinson. While they represented different states, these convention leaders shared the common goal of wanting to strengthen the young nation.

Several major leaders of the American Revolution were not at the convention. John Jay, Thomas Jefferson, John Adams, and Thomas Paine were on diplomatic business abroad. Samuel Adams and John Hancock were not chosen as delegates. Patrick Henry, who opposed any growth in federal power, refused to take part in the convention.

Key Issues

The convention opened with the delegates disagreeing sharply on its fundamental purpose. Some wanted to simply revise the Articles. Strong nationalists, such as Madison and Hamilton, wanted to draft an entirely new document. The nationalists quickly took control of the convention.

Americans in the 1780s generally distrusted government and feared that officials would seize every opportunity to abuse their powers, even if they were popularly elected. Therefore, Madison and other delegates wanted the new constitution to be based on a system of checks and balances so that the power of each branch would be limited by the powers of the others.

Representation Especially divisive was the issue of whether the larger states such as Virginia and Pennsylvania should have proportionally more representatives in Congress than the smaller states such as New Jersey and Delaware. Madison's proposal—the Virginia Plan—favored the large states; it was countered by the New Jersey Plan, which favored the small states. The issue was finally resolved by a compromise solution. Roger Sherman of Connecticut proposed what was called the Connecticut Plan or the Great Compromise. It provided for a two-house Congress. In the Senate, states would have equal representation, but in the House of Representatives, each state would be represented according to the size of its population.

Slavery Two of the most contentious issues grew out of slavery. Should enslaved people be counted in the state populations? The delegates agreed to the Three-Fifths Compromise, which counted each enslaved individual as three-fifths of a person for the purposes of determining a state's level of taxation and representation. Should the slave trade be allowed? The delegates decided to guarantee that slaves could be imported for at least 20 years longer, until 1808. Congress could vote to abolish the practice after that date if it wished.

Trade The northern states wanted the central government to regulate interstate commerce and foreign trade. The South was afraid that export taxes would be placed on its agricultural products such as tobacco and rice. The Commercial Compromise allowed Congress to regulate interstate and foreign commerce, including placing tariffs (taxes) on foreign imports, but it prohibited placing taxes on any exports.

The Presidency The delegates debated over the president's term of office—some argued that the chief executive should hold office for life. The delegates limited the president's term to four years but with no limit on the number of terms. They also debated the method for electing a president. Rather than having voters elect a president directly, the delegates decided to assign to each state a number of electors equal to the total of that state's representatives and senators. This electoral college system was instituted because the delegates feared that too much democracy might lead to mob rule. Finally, the delegates debated what powers to give the president. They finally decided to grant the president considerable power, including the power to veto acts of Congress.

Ratification On September 17, 1787, after 17 weeks of debate, the Philadelphia convention approved a draft of the Constitution to submit to the states for ratification. Anticipating opposition to the document, the Framers (delegates) specified that a favorable vote of only nine states out of 13 would be required for ratification. Each state would hold popularly elected conventions to debate and vote on the proposed Constitution.

Federalists and Anti-Federalists

Ratification was fiercely debated for almost a year, from September 1787 until June 1788. Supporters of the Constitution and its strong federal government were known as Federalists. Opponents were known as Anti-Federalists. Federalists were most common along the Atlantic Coast and in the large cities while Anti-Federalists tended to be small farmers and settlers on the western frontier. (See table on the next page for more on the two groups.)

The Federalist Papers

A key element in the Federalist campaign for the Constitution was a series of highly persuasive essays written for a New York newspaper by James Madison, Alexander Hamilton, and John Jay. The 85 essays, later published in book form as *The Federalist Papers,* presented cogent reasons for believing in the practicality of each major provision of the Constitution.

Outcome

The Federalists won early victories in the state conventions in Delaware, New Jersey, and Pennsylvania—the first three states to ratify. By promising to add a bill of rights to the Constitution, they successfully addressed the Anti-Federalists' most telling objection. With New Hampshire voting yes in June 1788, the Federalists won the necessary nine states to achieve ratification of the Constitution. Even so, the larger states of Virginia and New York had not yet acted. If they failed to ratify, any chance for national unity and strength would be in dire jeopardy.

Debating the Constitution		
	Federalists	**Anti-Federalists**
Leaders	George Washington, Benjamin Franklin, James Madison, Alexander Hamilton	From Virginia: George Mason and Patrick Henry; From Massachusetts: James Winthrop and John Hancock; From New York: George Clinton
Arguments	Stronger central government was needed to maintain order and preserve the Union	Stronger central government would destroy the work of the Revolution, limit democracy, and restrict states' rights
Strategy	Emphasized the weaknesses of the Articles of Confederation; showed their opponents as merely negative opponents with no solutions	Argued that the proposed Constitution contained no protection of individual rights, that it gave the central government more power than the British ever had
Advantages	Strong leaders; well organized	Appealed to popular distrust of government based on colonial experiences
Disadvantages	Constitution was new and untried; as originally written, it lacked a bill of rights	Poorly organized; slow to respond to Federalist challenge

Virginia In 1788, Virginia was by far the most populous of the original 13 states. There, the Anti-Federalists rallied behind two strong leaders, George Mason and Patrick Henry, who viewed the Constitution and a strong central government as threats to Americans' hard-won liberty. Virginia's Federalists, led by Washington, Madison, and John Marshall, managed to prevail by a close vote only after promising a bill of rights.

Final States News of Virginia's vote had enough influence on New York's ratifying convention (combined with Alexander Hamilton's efforts) to win the day for the Constitution in that state. North Carolina in November 1789 and Rhode Island in May 1790 reversed their earlier rejections and thus became the last two states to ratify the Constitution as the new "supreme law of the land."

Adding the Bill of Rights

Did the Constitution need to list the rights of individuals? Anti-Federalists argued vehemently that it did, while Federalists argued that it was unnecessary.

Arguments for a Bill of Rights

Anti-Federalists argued that Americans had fought the Revolutionary War to escape a tyrannical government in Britain. What was to stop a strong central government under the Constitution from acting similarly? Only by adding a bill of rights could Americans be protected against such a possibility.

Arguments Against a Bill of Rights

Federalists argued that since members of Congress would be elected by the people, they did not need to be protected against themselves. Furthermore, people should assume that all rights were protected rather than create a limited list of rights that might allow unscrupulous officials to assert that unlisted rights could be violated at will.

In order to win adoption of the Constitution in the ratifying conventions, the Federalists finally backed off their position and promised to add a bill of rights to the Constitution as the first order of business for a newly elected Congress.

The First Ten Amendments

In 1789, the first Congress elected under the Constitution acted quickly to adopt a number of amendments listing people's rights. Drafted largely by James Madison, the amendments were submitted to the states for ratification. The ten that were adopted in 1791 have been known ever since as the U.S. Bill of Rights. Originally, they provided protection against abuses of power by the central (or federal) government. Since the ratification of the 14th Amendment in 1868, most of the protections have been extended to apply to abuses by state governments as well. Below is the text of the Bill of Rights.

First Amendment "Congress shall make no law respecting an establishment of religion, or prohibiting the free exercise thereof; or abridging the freedom of speech, or of the press, or the right of the people peaceably to assemble, and to petition the Government for a redress of grievances."

Second Amendment "A well regulated Militia, being necessary to the security of a free State, the right of the people to keep and bear Arms, shall not be infringed."

Third Amendment "No Soldier shall, in time of peace be quartered in any house, without the consent of the Owner, nor in time of war, but in a manner prescribed by law."

Fourth Amendment "The right of the people to be secure in their persons, houses, papers, and effects, against unreasonable searches and seizures shall not be violated, and no Warrants shall issue, but upon probable cause, supported by Oath or affirmation, and particularly describing the place to be searched, and the persons or things to be seized."

Fifth Amendment "No person shall be held to answer for a capital, or otherwise infamous crime, unless on a presentment or indictment of a Grand Jury, except in cases arising in the land or naval forces, or in the Militia, when in actual service in time of War or public danger; nor shall any person be subject for the same offence to be twice put in jeopardy of life or limb; nor shall be compelled in any criminal case to be a witness against himself, nor be deprived of life, liberty, or property, without due process of law; nor shall private property be taken for public use without just compensation."

Sixth Amendment "In all criminal prosecutions, the accused shall enjoy the right to a speedy and public trial, by an impartial jury of the State and district wherein the crime shall have been committed; which district shall have been previously ascertained by law, and to be informed of the nature and cause of the accusation; to be confronted with the witnesses against him; to have compulsory process for obtaining witnesses in his favor, and to have the assistance of counsel for his defense."

Seventh Amendment "In suits of common law, where the value in controversy shall exceed twenty dollars, the right of trial by jury shall be preserved, and no fact tried by a jury shall be otherwise re-examined in any Court of the United States, than according to the rules of the common law."

Eighth Amendment "Excessive bail shall not be required, nor excessive fines imposed, nor cruel and unusual punishments inflicted."

Ninth Amendment "The enumeration in the Constitution of certain rights shall not be construed to deny or disparage others retained by the people."

Tenth Amendment "The powers not delegated to the United States by the Constitution, nor prohibited by it to the States, are reserved to the States respectively, or to the people."

Washington's Presidency

Members of the first Congress under the Constitution were elected in 1788 and began their first session in March 1789 in New York City (then the nation's temporary capital). People assumed that George Washington would be the electoral college's unanimous choice for president, and indeed he was.

Organizing the Federal Government

Washington took the oath of office as the first U.S. president on April 30, 1789. From then on, what the Constitution and its system of checks and balances actually meant in practice would be determined from day to day by the decisions of Congress as the legislative branch, the president as the head of the executive branch, and the Supreme Court as the top federal court in the judicial branch.

Executive Departments As chief executive, Washington's first task was to organize new departments of the executive (law-enforcing) branch. The Constitution authorizes the president to appoint chiefs of departments, although they must be confirmed, or approved, by the Senate. Washington appointed four heads of departments: Thomas Jefferson as secretary of state, Alexander Hamilton as secretary of the treasury, Henry Knox as secretary of war, and Edmund Randolph as attorney general. These four men formed a cabinet of advisers with whom President Washington met regularly to discuss major policy issues. Today, presidents still meet with their cabinets to obtain advice and information.

Federal Court System The only federal court mentioned in the Constitution is the Supreme Court. Congress, however, was given the power to create other federal courts with lesser powers and to determine the number of justices making up the Supreme Court. One of Congress' first laws was the Judiciary Act of 1789, which established a Supreme Court with one chief justice and five associate justices. This highest court was empowered to rule on the constitutionality of decisions made by state courts. The act also provided for a system of 13 district courts and three circuit courts of appeals.

Hamilton's Financial Program

One of the most pressing problems faced by Congress under the Articles had been the government's financial difficulties. Alexander Hamilton, secretary of the treasury, presented to Congress a plan for putting U.S. finances on a stable foundation. Hamilton's plan included three main actions. (1) Pay off the national debt at face value and have the federal government assume the war debts of the states. (2) Protect the young nation's "infant" (new and developing) industries and collect adequate revenues at the same time by imposing high tariffs on imported goods. (3) Create a national bank for depositing government funds and printing banknotes that would provide the basis for a stable U.S. currency. Support for this program came chiefly from northern merchants, who would gain directly from high tariffs and a stabilized currency.

Opponents of Hamilton's financial plan included the Anti-Federalists, who feared that the states would lose power to the extent that the central government gained it. Thomas Jefferson led a faction of southern Anti-Federalists who viewed Hamilton's program as benefiting only the rich at the expense of indebted farmers. After much political wrangling and bargaining, Congress finally adopted Hamilton's plan in slightly modified form. For example, the tariffs were not as high as Hamilton wanted.

Debt Jefferson and his supporters agreed to Hamilton's urgent insistence that the U.S. government pay off the national debt at face value and also assume payment of the war debts of the states. In return for Jefferson's support on this vital aspect of his plan, Hamilton agreed to Jefferson's idea to establish the nation's capital in the South along the Potomac River (an area that, after Washington's death, would be named Washington, D.C.).

National Bank Jefferson argued that the Constitution did not give Congress the power to create a bank. But Hamilton took a broader view of the Constitution, arguing that the document's "necessary and proper" clause authorized Congress to do whatever was necessary to carry out its enumerated powers. Washington supported Hamilton on the issue, and the proposed bank was voted into law. Although chartered by the federal government, the Bank of the United States was privately owned. As a major shareholder of the bank, the federal government could print paper currency and use federal deposits to stimulate business.

Foreign Affairs

Washington's first term as president (1789–1793) coincided with the outbreak of revolution in France, a cataclysmic event that was to touch off a series of wars between the new French Republic and the monarchies of Europe. Washington's entire eight years as president, as well as the four years of his successor, John Adams, were taken up with the question of whether to give U.S. support to France, France's enemies, or neither side.

The French Revolution Americans generally supported the French people's aspiration to establish a republic, but many were also horrified by reports of mob hysteria and mass executions. To complicate matters, the U.S.– French alliance remained in effect, although it was an alliance with the French monarchy, not with the revolutionary republic. Jefferson and his supporters sympathized with the revolutionary cause. They also argued that, because Britain was seizing American merchant ships bound for French ports, the United States should join France in its defensive war against Britain.

Proclamation of Neutrality (1793) Washington, however, believed that the young nation was not strong enough to engage in a European war. Resisting popular clamor, in 1793 he issued a proclamation of U.S. neutrality in the conflict. Jefferson resigned from the cabinet in disagreement with Washington's policy.

"Citizen" Genêt Objecting to Washington's policy, "Citizen" Edmond Genêt, the French minister to the United States, broke all the normal rules of diplomacy by appealing directly to the American people to support the French cause. So outrageous was his conduct that even Jefferson approved of Washington's request to the French government that they remove the offending diplomat. Recalled by his government, Genêt chose to remain in the United States, where he married and became a U.S. citizen.

The Jay Treaty (1794) Washington sent Chief Justice John Jay on a special mission to Britain to talk that country out of its offensive practice of searching and seizing American ships and impressing seamen into the British navy. After a year of negotiations, Jay brought back a treaty in which Britain agreed to evacuate its posts on the U.S. western frontier. But the treaty said nothing about British seizures of American merchant ships. Narrowly ratified by the Senate, the unpopular Jay Treaty angered American supporters of France, but it did maintain Washington's policy of neutrality, which kept the United States at peace.

The Pinckney Treaty (1795) Totally unexpected was the effect that the Jay Treaty had on Spain's policy toward its territories in the Americas. Seeing the treaty as a sign that the United States might be drawing closer to Spain's longtime foe Britain, Spain decided to consolidate its holdings in North America. The Spanish influence in the Far West had been strengthened by a series of Catholic missions along the California coast but they were concerned about their colonies in the Southeast. Thomas Pinckney, the U.S. minister to Spain, negotiated a treaty in which Spain agreed to open the lower Mississippi River and New Orleans to American trade. The right of deposit was granted to Americans so that they could transfer cargoes in New Orleans without paying duties to the Spanish government. Spain further agreed to accept the U.S. claim that Florida's northern boundary should be at the 31st parallel (not north of that line, as Spain had formerly insisted).

Domestic Concerns

In addition to coping with foreign challenges, stabilizing the nation's credit, and organizing the new government, Washington faced a number of domestic problems and crises.

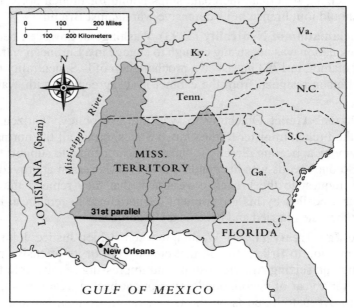

PINCKNEY'S TREATY, 1795

American Indians Through the final decades of the 18th century, settlers crossed the Alleghenies and moved the frontier steadily westward into the Ohio Valley and beyond. In an effort to resist the settlers' encroachment on their lands, a number of the tribes formed the Northwest (or Western) Confederacy. Initially the tribes, including the Shawnee, Delaware, Iroquois, and others under the Miami war chief Little Turtle, won a series of bloody victories over the local militia. Americans on the frontier were incensed by evidence that the British were supplying the American Indians with arms and encouraging them to attack the "intruding" Americans. In 1794 the U.S. army led by General Anthony Wayne defeated the Confederacy tribes at the Battle of Fallen Timbers in northwestern Ohio. The next year, the chiefs of the defeated peoples agreed to the Treaty of Greenville, in which they surrendered claims to the Ohio Territory and promised to open it up to settlement.

The Whiskey Rebellion (1794) Hamilton, to make up the revenue lost because the tariffs were lower than he wanted, persuaded Congress to pass excise taxes, particularly on the sale of whiskey. In western Pennsylvania, the refusal of a group of farmers to pay the federal excise tax on whiskey seemed to pose a major challenge to the viability of the U.S. government under the Constitution. The rebelling farmers could ill afford to pay a tax on the whiskey that they distilled from surplus corn. Rather than pay the tax, they defended their "liberties" by attacking the revenue collectors.

Washington responded to this crisis by federalizing 15,000 state militiamen and placing them under the command of Alexander Hamilton. The show of force had its intended effect, causing the Whiskey Rebellion to collapse with almost no bloodshed. Some Americans applauded Washington's action, contrasting it with the previous government's helplessness to do anything about Shays's Rebellion. Among westerners, however, the military action was widely resented and condemned as an unwarranted use of force against the common people. The government's chief critic, Thomas Jefferson, gained in popularity as a champion of the western farmer.

Western Lands In the 1790s, the Jay Treaty and the victory at the Battle of Fallen Timbers gave the federal government control of vast tracts of land. Congress encouraged the rapid settlement of these lands by passing the Public Land Act in 1796, which established orderly procedures for dividing and selling federal lands at reasonable prices. The process for adding new states to the Union, as set forth in the Constitution, went smoothly. In 1791 Vermont became the first new state, followed by Kentucky in 1792 and Tennessee in 1796.

Political Parties

Washington's election by unanimous vote of the Electoral College in 1789 underscored the popular belief that political parties were not needed. The Constitution itself did not mention political parties, and the Framers assumed none would arise. They were soon proven wrong. The debates between Federalists and Anti-Federalists in 1787 and 1788 were the first indication that a two-party system would emerge as a core feature of American politics.

Origins

In colonial times, groups of legislators commonly formed temporary factions and voted together either for or against a specific policy. When an issue was settled, the factions would dissolve. The dispute between Federalists and Anti-Federalists over the ratification of the Constitution closely resembled the factional disputes of an earlier period. What was unusual about this conflict was that it was organized—at least by the Federalists—across state lines and in that sense prefigured the national parties that emerged soon afterward.

In the 1790s, sometimes called the Federalist era because it was dominated largely by Federalist policies, political parties began to form around two leading figures, Hamilton and Jefferson. The Federalist party supported Hamilton and his financial program. An opposition party known as the Democratic-Republican party supported Jefferson and tried to elect candidates in different states who opposed Hamilton's program. The French Revolution further solidified the formation of national political parties. Americans divided sharply over whether to support France. A large number of them followed Jefferson's lead in openly challenging President Washington's neutrality policy.

NEW STATES IN THE UNION, 1791–1796

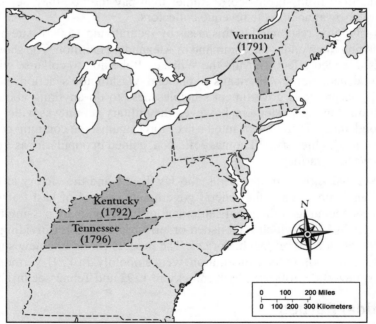

Differences Between the Parties

The Federalists were strongest in the northeastern states and advocated the growth of federal power. The Democratic-Republicans were strongest in the southern states and on the western frontier and argued for states' rights. (See the table on the next page for additional differences between the parties.) By 1796, the two major political parties were already taking shape and becoming better organized. In that year, President Washington announced that he intended to retire to private life at the end of his second term.

Washington's Farewell Address

Assisted by Alexander Hamilton, the retiring president wrote a farewell address for publication in the newspapers in late 1796. In this message, which had enormous influence because of Washington's prestige, the president spoke about policies and practices that he considered unwise. He warned Americans

- not to get involved in European affairs
- not to make "permanent alliances" in foreign affairs
- not to form political parties
- not to fall into sectionalism

For the next century, future presidents would heed as gospel Washington's warning against "permanent alliances." However, in the case of political parties, Washington was already behind the times, since political parties were well on their way to becoming a vital part of the American political system.

One long-range consequence of Washington's decision to leave office after two terms was that later presidents followed his example. Presidents elected to two terms (including Jefferson, Madison, Monroe, and Jackson) would voluntarily retire even though the Constitution placed no limit on a president's tenure in office. The two-term tradition continued unbroken until 1940 when Franklin Roosevelt won election to a third term. Then, the 22nd Amendment, ratified in 1951, made the two-term limit a part of the Constitution.

John Adams' Presidency

Even as Washington was writing his Farewell Address, political parties were working to gain majorities in the two houses of Congress and to line up enough electors from the various states to elect the next president. The vice president, John Adams, was the Federalists' candidate, while former secretary of state Thomas Jefferson was the choice of the Democratic-Republicans.

Adams won by three electoral votes. Jefferson became vice-president, since the original Constitution gave that office to the candidate receiving the second highest number of electoral votes. (Since the ratification of the 12th Amendment in 1804, the president and vice-president have run as a team.)

Comparison of Federalist and Democratic-Republican Parties		
	Federalists	**Democratic-Republicans**
Leaders	John Adams Alexander Hamilton	Thomas Jefferson James Madison
View of the Constitution	Interpret loosely Create strong central government	Interpret strictly Create weak central government
Foreign Policy	Pro-British	Pro-French
Military Policy	Develop large peacetime army and navy	Develop small peacetime army and navy
Economic Policy	Aid business Create a national bank Support high tariffs	Favor agriculture Oppose a national bank Oppose tariffs
Chief Supporters	Northern business owners Large landowners	Skilled workers Small farmers Plantation owners

The XYZ Affair

Troubles abroad related to the French Revolution presented Adams with the first major challenge of his presidency. Americans were angered by reports that U.S. merchant ships were being seized by French warships and privateers. Seeking a peaceful settlement, Adams sent a delegation to Paris to negotiate with the French government. Certain French ministers, known only as X, Y, and Z because their names were never revealed, requested bribes as the basis for entering into negotiations. The American delegates indignantly refused. Newspaper reports of the demands made by X, Y, and Z infuriated many Americans, who now clamored for war against France. "Millions for defense, but not one cent for tribute" became the slogan of the hour. One faction of the Federalist party, led by Alexander Hamilton, hoped that by going to war the United States could gain French and Spanish lands in North America.

President Adams, on the other hand, resisted the popular sentiment for war. Recognizing that the U.S. Army and Navy were not yet strong enough to fight a major power, the president avoided war and sent new ministers to Paris.

The Alien and Sedition Acts

Anger against France strengthened the Federalists in the congressional elections of 1798 enough to win a majority in both houses. The Federalists took advantage of their victory by enacting laws to restrict their political opponents, the Democratic-Republicans. For example, since most immigrants voted Democratic-Republican, the Federalists passed the Naturalization Act, which increased from 5 to 14 the years required for immigrants to qualify for U.S. citizenship. They also passed the Alien Acts, which authorized the president to deport aliens considered dangerous and to detain enemy aliens in time of war. Most seriously, they passed the Sedition Act, which made it illegal for newspaper editors to criticize either the president or Congress and imposed fines or imprisonment for editors who violated the law.

The Kentucky and Virginia Resolutions

Democratic-Republicans argued that the Alien and Sedition Acts violated rights guaranteed by the 1st Amendment of the Constitution. In 1799, however, the Supreme Court had not yet established the principle of judicial review (see Chapter 7). Democratic-Republican leaders challenged the legislation of the Federalist Congress by enacting nullifying laws of their own in the state legislatures. The Kentucky legislature adopted a resolution that had been written by Thomas Jefferson, and the Virginia legislature adopted a resolution introduced by James Madison. Both resolutions declared that the states had entered into a "compact" in forming the national government, and, therefore, if any act of the federal government broke the compact, a state could nullify the federal law. Although only Kentucky and Virginia adopted nullifying resolutions in 1799, they set forth an argument and rationale that would be widely used in the nullification controversy of the 1830s (see Chapter 10).

The immediate crisis over the Alien and Sedition Acts faded when the Federalists lost their majority in Congress after the election of 1800, and the new Democratic-Republican majority allowed the acts to expire or repealed them. In addition, the Supreme Court under John Marshall asserted its power in deciding whether a certain federal law was constitutional.

The Election of 1800

During Adams' presidency, the Federalists rapidly lost popularity. People disliked the Alien and Sedition Acts and complained about the new taxes imposed by the Federalists to pay the costs of preparing for a war against France. Though Adams avoided war, he had persuaded Congress that building up the U.S. Navy was necessary for the nation's defense.

Election Results

The election of 1800 swept the Federalists from power in both the executive and legislative branches of the U.S. government. A majority of the presidential electors cast their ballots for two Democratic-Republicans: Thomas Jefferson and Aaron Burr. Because both these candidates received the same number of electoral ballots, it was necessary (according to the rules in the original Constitution) to hold a special election in the House of Representatives to break the tie. In December 1800 the Federalists still controlled the House. They debated and voted for days before they finally gave a majority to Jefferson. (Alexander Hamilton had urged his followers to vote for Jefferson, whom he considered less dangerous and of higher character than Burr.)

Democratic-Republican lawmakers elected in 1800 took control of both the House and the Senate when a new Congress met in March 1801.

A Peaceful Revolution

The passing of power in 1801 from one political party to another was accomplished without violence. This was a rare event for the times and a major indication that the U.S. constitutional system would endure the various strains that were placed upon it. The Federalists quietly accepted their defeat in the election of 1800 and peacefully relinquished control of the federal government to Jefferson's party, the Democratic-Republicans. The change from Federalist to Democratic-Republican control is known as the Revolution of 1800.

HISTORICAL PERSPECTIVES: WHAT DOES THE CONSTITUTION MEAN?

From the moment it was drafted in 1787, the U.S. Constitution has been a continuing subject of controversy. As political issues changed from one era to the next, Americans changed their views of how the Constitution should be interpreted. The dispute between the Federalists and the Anti-Federalists over the proper powers of the central government has never been completely resolved and, to a certain extent, continues to be debated by modern-day Republicans and Democrats.

In the decades preceding the Civil War (1790–1860), the chief constitutional issue concerned the nature of the federal union and whether the states could nullify acts of the federal government. The North's triumph in the Civil War settled the issue in favor of centralized power and against southern champions of states' rights. In the post-Civil War era, northerners regarded Hamilton and other Federalist Framers of the Constitution as heroes. At the same time, states'-rights advocates were portrayed as demagogues and traitors.

In the early 20th century, a change in politics again brought a change in scholars' views toward the Framers of the Constitution. Reacting to the excesses of big business, certain historians identified economic factors and class conflict as the primary force behind the Constitutional

Convention of 1787. Published in 1913, at the height of the Progressive era, Charles Beard's *An Economic Interpretation of the Constitution* argued that, in writing the Constitution, the Framers were chiefly motivated by their own economic interests in preserving their wealth and property. Beard's controversial thesis dominated historical scholarship on the Constitution for almost 50 years. Expanding on Beard's thesis, some historians have argued that even the sectional differences between northern Framers and southern Framers were chiefly economic in nature.

In recent years, many historians have concluded that the economic interpretation of the Framers' motives, while valid up to a point, oversimplifies the issues of the 1780s. Historians place greater stress on the philosophical and intellectual backgrounds of the delegates at Philadelphia and explain how they shared similar 18th-century views of liberty, government, and society.

KEY TERMS BY THEME

Founders (NAT, SOC)
James Madison
Alexander Hamilton
Framers of the
 Constitution
Gouverneur Morris
John Dickinson
Federalists
Anti-Federalists
The Federalist Papers
Bill of Rights;
 amendments
Washington's Farewell
 Address
"permanent alliances"
Alien and Sedition Acts
Kentucky and Virginia
 Resolutions

Disputes (WXT)
slave trade
infant industries
national bank
tariffs; excise taxes

Expansion (MIG, POL)
Battle of Fallen Timbers
Treaty of Greenville
Public Land Act (1796)

A Constitution (POL, ARC)
Mt. Vernon Conference
Annapolis Convention
Constitutional
 Convention
checks and balances
Virginia Plan
New Jersey Plan
Connecticut Plan; Great
 Compromise
House of
 Representatives
Senate
Three-Fifths
 Compromise
Commercial
 Compromise
electoral college system
legislative branch
Congress

A New Republic (POL)
executive depart-
 ments; cabinet
Henry Knox
Edmund Randolph
Judiciary Act (1789)
federal courts
Supreme Court
national debt
Whiskey Rebellion
Federalist era
Democratic-Republi-
 can party
political parties
two-term tradition
John Adams
Revolution of 1800

Foreign Affairs (WOR)
French Revolution
Proclamation of Neu-
 trality (1793)
"Citizen" Genêt
Jay Treaty (1794)
Pinckney Treaty (1795)
right of deposit
XYZ Affair

Questions 1–3 refer to the excerpt below.

"It is not denied that there are implied as well as express powers, and that the former are as effectually delegated as the latter.

"It is conceded that implied powers are to be considered as delegated equally with express ones. Then it follows, that as a power of erecting a corporation [such as a bank] may as well be implied as any other thing, it may as well be employed as an instrument or means of carrying into execution any of the specified powers. . . . But one may be erected in relation to the trade with foreign countries, or to the trade between the States . . . because it is the province of the federal government to regulate those objects, and because it is incident to a general sovereign or legislative power to regulate a thing, to employ all the means which relate to its regulation to the best and greatest advantage."

—Alexander Hamilton, Constitutionality of the Bank
of the United States, 1791

1. Hamilton's constitutional argument was based on which of the following types of powers?
   (A) Employed
   (B) Expressed
   (C) Implied
   (D) Regulated

2. Which of the following benefited most directly from the bank that Hamilton strongly supported?
   (A) Manufacturers
   (B) Farmers
   (C) State governments
   (D) Slaveowners

3. Who of the following would be most critical of Hamilton's position on the bank?
   (A) George Washington
   (B) John Adams
   (C) Thomas Jefferson
   (D) Henry Knox

Questions 4–5 refer to the excerpt below.

"Friends and Fellow Citizens: I should now apprise you of the resolution I have formed to decline being considered among the number of those out of whom a choice is to be made. . . .

"I have already intimated to you the danger of parties . . . with particular reference to . . . geographical discriminations. . . .

"Let it simply be asked—where is the security for property, for reputation, for life, if the sense of religious obligation desert the oaths. . . .

"As a very important source of strength and security, cherish public credit . . . avoiding likewise the accumulation of debt . . . which unavoidable wars may have occasioned . . . in mind that toward the payment of debt there must be . . . taxes. . . .

"By interweaving our destiny with that of any part of Europe, [we] entangle our peace and prosperity in the toils of European ambition, rivalship, interest, humor, or caprice. . . . It is our true policy to steer clear of permanent alliances with any portion of the foreign world."

—George Washington, Farewell Address, 1796

4. One of the strong reasons Washington and others warned against political parties was concern about

(A) damages to the national reputation

(B) divisive sectionalism

(C) rights of property owners

(D) unavoidable wars

5. In addition to his Farewell Address, part of Washington's legacy was that he

(A) started the two-party system

(B) established the precedent of a two-term limit

(C) created the first presidential library

(D) advocated for greater involvement overseas

Questions 6–8 refer to the excerpt below.

"Resolved, that the several States composing the United States of America are not united on the principle of unlimited submission to their general government; but that by compact under the style and title of a Constitution for the United States and of amendments thereto, they constituted a general government for specific purposes, delegated to that government certain definite powers, reserving, each State to itself, the residuary mass of right to their own self-government; and that whensoever the general government assumes undelegated powers, its acts are unauthoritative, void, and of no force. . . .

"That this would be to surrender the form of government we have chosen, and to live under one deriving its powers from its own will, and not from our authority; and that the co-States, recurring to their natural right in cases not made Federal, will concur in declaring these acts void and of no force."

—Thomas Jefferson (anonymously), Kentucky Resolutions,
November 16, 1798

6. The Kentucky and Virginia Resolutions were issued in reaction to the

(A) ratification of the Bill of Rights

(B) passage of the Alien and Sedition Acts

(C) the revelations about the XYZ Affair

(D) the declaration of the Proclamation of Neutrality

7. The dispute involving the Kentucky Resolutions demonstrated that some people had rejected George Washington's warning against

(A) creating a national bank

(B) forming permanent foreign alliances

(C) getting involved in European affairs

(D) encouraging sectional differences

8. Which individual or group among the following would be the strongest supporter of the Kentucky Resolution?

(A) John Adams

(B) Democratic-Republicans

(C) Federalists

(D) Alexander Hamilton

SHORT-ANSWER QUESTIONS

Use complete sentences; an outline or bulleted list alone is not acceptable.

Question 1 is based on the excerpts below.

"To speak more precisely, the contest over the Constitution was not primarily a war over abstract political ideals, such as states' rights and centralization, but over concrete economic issues, and the political division which accompanied it was substantially along the lines of the interests affected—the financiers, public creditors, traders, commercial men, manufacturers, and allied groups, centering mainly in the larger seaboard towns, being chief among the advocates of the Constitution, and the farmers, particularly in the inland regions, and the debtors being chief among its opponents. That other considerations, such as the necessity for stronger national defense, entered into the campaign is, of course, admitted, but with all due allowances, it may be truly said that the Constitution was a product of a struggle between capitalistic and agrarian interests."

—Charles A. Beard, historian, *Economic Origins of Jeffersonian Democracy,* 1915

"It is easy to accept the general proposition that ideas and interests are somehow associated. . . . But there are some dangers in working with any such formula. The first is that ideas—or all those intangible emotional, moral, and intellectual forces that may roughly be combined under the rubric of ideas — will somehow be dissolved and that we will be left only with interests on our hands. . . Then there is the danger that interests will be too narrowly construed: that we will put too much emphasis on the motives and purposes of individuals and groups, not enough on the structural requirements of a social system or on the limitations imposed on men by particular historical situations . . . that the way in which men perceive and define their interests is in some good part a reflex of the ideas they have inherited and the experiences they have undergone. . .

For the generation of the Founding Fathers, the central, formative, shattering, and then reintegrating experience of civic life was the Revolution, which recast the pattern of their interests and galvanized their inherited store of ideas."

—Richard Hofstadter, historian, *The Progressive Historians,* 1968

1. Using the excerpts, answer (A), (B), and (C).

    (A) Briefly explain ONE major difference between Beard's and Hofstadter's interpretations of the influences on the Constitution.

    (B) Briefly explain how ONE historical event or development in the period 1776 to 1789 that is not explicitly mentioned in the excerpts could be used to support Beard's interpretation.

    (C) Briefly explain how ONE historical event or development in the period 1776 to 1789 that is not explicitly mentioned in the excerpts could be used to support Hofstadter's interpretation.

Question 2. Answer (A), (B), and (C).

(A) Briefly explain ONE compromise of the Constitutional Convention in response to the question of slavery.

(B) Briefly explain ONE specific criticism of a Constitutional compromise.

(C) Briefly explain the role of ONE person or group in bringing about a compromise made at the Constitutional Convention.

Question 3 is based on the excerpt below.

"Sir, suffer me to recall to your mind that time, in which the arms and tyranny of the British crown were exerted. . . .

"This, Sir, was a time when you clearly saw into the injustice of a State of slavery . . . that you publicly held forth this true and invaluable doctrine. . . . 'We hold these truths to be self-evident, that all men are created equal; that they are endowed by their Creator with certain inalienable rights. . . .'

"But, Sir, how pitiable is it to reflect, that although you were so fully convinced of the benevolence of the Father of Mankind, and of his equal and impartial distribution of these rights and privileges, which he hath conferred upon them, that you should at the same time counteract his mercies, in detaining by fraud and violence so numerous a part of my brethren, under groaning captivity, and cruel oppression."

—Benjamin Banneker, African American scientist and surveyor, letter to Secretary of State Thomas Jefferson, 1792

3. Using the excerpt, answer (A), (B), and (C).

(A) Briefly explain ONE specific reason for Banneker questioning Jefferson's actions on slavery.

(B) Briefly explain how ONE historic contemporary of Banneker would either support or question this letter to Jefferson.

(C) Briefly explain ONE specific way Thomas Jefferson might have responded to Banneker's questions about slavery.

Question 4. Answer (A), (B), and (C).

(A) Briefly explain ONE historical event or development in the period 1789 to 1800 that is an example of the American foreign policy of avoiding war.

(B) Briefly explain ONE historical event or development in the period 1789 to 1800 that remained unresolved while following the American foreign policy of avoiding war.

(C) Briefly explain ONE person or group in the U.S. in the period 1789 to 1800 that challenged the United States government's foreign policy.

THINK AS A HISTORIAN: QUESTIONS ABOUT ARGUMENTATION

A historical argument is a carefully written chain of thoughts that includes a clear thesis and analysis supported with evidence. Which THREE of the following prompts would be best answered with an essay that makes a historical argument?

1. Summarize the differences between the Federalists and the Anti-Federalists.

2. Using more than one type of evidence, support or oppose this statement: "The Founders failed to see fundamental developments in American politics."

3. Explain whether you agree or disagree that differences in foreign policy in the 1700s were rooted in economic interests.

4. Explain whether you think the information in this chapter supports or opposes the idea that compromise has been an essential part of American government since the founding of the country.

5. Explain the main points of Hamilton's financial plan.

Unit 3: Period 3 Review, 1754–1800

LONG ESSAY QUESTIONS

Directions: The suggested writing time for each question is 40 minutes. In your response you should do the following:

- **Thesis:** Make a defensible claim that establishes a line of reasoning and consists of one or more sentences found in one place.
- **Contextualization:** Relate the argument to a broader historical context.
- **Evidence:** Support an argument with specific and relevant historical evidence.
- **Reasoning:** Organize an argument using the skill in the question.
- **Analysis:** Demonstrate a complex understanding of the question using historical evidence to support, qualify, or modify an argument.

1. It has been argued that the American Revolution came about primarily through an evolving series of meetings, conventions, and congresses. Support, modify, or refute this contention using specific evidence.

2. It has been argued that the U.S. Constitution came about primarily through an evolving series of meetings, conventions, and congresses. Support, modify, or refute this contention using specific evidence.

3. For some historians, the leadership provided by the Founders during events leading up to the Revolutionary War was the key to the successful developments. Support, modify, or refute this contention using specific evidence.

4. For some historians, the leadership provided by the Founders during events leading up to the writing of the Constitution was the key to the successful developments. Support, modify, or refute this contention using specific evidence.

5. For some, enslaved African Americans and American Indians significantly influenced events before and during the Revolutionary War. Support, modify, or refute this contention using specific evidence.

6. For some, enslaved African Americans and American Indians significantly influenced events before and during the writing of the Constitution. Support, modify, or refute this contention using specific evidence.

DOCUMENT-BASED QUESTION

Directions: Question 1 is based on the accompanying documents. The documents have been edited for the purpose of this exercise. You are advised to spend 15 minutes planning and 45 minutes writing your answer. In your response you should do the following:

- **Thesis:** Make a defensible claim that establishes a line of reasoning and consists of one or more sentences found in one place.
- **Contextualization:** Relate the argument to a broader historical context.
- **Document Evidence:** Use content from at least six documents.
- **Outside Evidence:** Use one piece of evidence not in the documents.
- **Document Sourcing:** Explain how or why the point of view, purpose, situation, or intended audience is relevant for at least three documents.
- **Analysis:** Show the relationships among pieces of historical evidence and use them to support, qualify, or modify an argument.

1. To what extent was the demand for no taxation without representation both the primary force motivating the American revolutionary movement and a symbol for democracy?

Document 1

Source: Resolution of the Virginia House of Burgesses, 1764

Resolved, That a most humble and dutiful Address be presented to his Majesty, imploring his Royal Protection of his faithful Subjects, the People of this Colony, in the Enjoyment of all their natural and civil Rights, as Men, and as Descendents of Britons; which rights must be violated, if Laws respecting the internal Government, and Taxation of themselves, are imposed upon them by any other Power than that derived from their own Consent, by and with the Approbation of their Sovereign, or his Substitute.

Document 2

Source: Resolutions of the Stamp Act Congress, 1765

Section 4. That the people of these colonies are not, and from their local circumstances cannot be, represented in the House of Commons in Great-Britain.
Section 5. That the only representatives of the people of these colonies, are persons chosen therein by themselves, and that no taxes ever have been, or can be constitutionally imposed on them, but by their respective legislatures.

Document 3

Source: Daniel Dulany, Maryland lawyer, "Considerations on the Propriety of Imposing Taxes in the British Colonies," 1765

A right to impose an internal tax on the colonies, without their consent for the single purpose of revenue, is denied, a right to regulate their trade without their consent is admitted.

Document 4

Source: Joseph Warren, Boston patriot, speech in Boston, March 5, 1772

And as it was soon found that this taxation could not be supported by reason and argument, it seemed necessary that one act of oppression should be enforced by another, and therefore—contrary to our just rights as possessing, or at least having a just title to possess, all the liberties and immunities of British subjects, a standing army was established among us in time of peace; and evidently for the purpose of effecting that which it was one principal design of the founders of the constitution to prevent (when they declared a standing army in a time of peace to be against law), namely, for the enforcement of obedience to acts which, upon fair examination, appeared to be unjust and unconstitutional.

Document 5

Source: Second Continental Congress, Declaration of the Causes and Necessity of Taking Up Arms, July 6, 1775

They [Parliament] have undertaken to give and grant our money without our consent, though we have ever exercised an exclusive right to dispose of our own property; statutes have been passed for extending the jurisdiction of courts of Admiralty and Vice-Admiralty beyond their ancient limits; for deprivinus of the accustomed and inestimable privilege of trial by jury, in cases affecting both life and property; for suspending the legislature of one of the colonies; for interdicting all commerce to the capital of another; and for altering fundamentally the form of government established by charter, and secured by acts of its own legislature solemnly confirmed by the crown; for exempting the "murderers" of colonists from legal trial.

Document 6

Source: Thomas Paine, *Common Sense,* 1776

Small islands not capable of protecting themselves are the proper objects for kingdoms to take under their care; but there is something very absurd in supposing a continent to be perpetually governed by an island. In no instance hath nature made the satellite larger than its primary planet; and as England and America, with respect to each other, reverse the common order of nature, it is evident that they belong to different systems. England to Europe: America to itself.

Document 7

Source: Petition of Seven Free Negroes to the Massachusetts Legislature in Protest of Taxation Without the Right to Vote, February 10, 1780

Petitioners farther sheweth that we apprehand ourselves to be Aggreeved, in that while we are not allowed the Privilage of freemen of the State having no vote or influence in the Election of those that Tax us yet many of our Colour (as is well known) have cheerfully Entered the field of Battle in the defence of the Common Cause and that (as we conceive) against a similar Exertion of Power (in Regard to taxation).

UNIT 4: Period 4, 1800–1848

In 1826, in the midst of the years covered in this period, the young nation of the United States celebrated its 50th birthday with great optimism. The founders of the country were passing on, and a new generation was taking over leadership.

Overview The new republic worked to define itself during a time of rapid demographic, economic, and territorial growth. In response to this growth, the country reformed several institutions and practices. It expanded the right to vote, allowing more men who did not own property to cast ballots. It opened new schools to improve the education of children. It reformed its prisons and asylums to make them more humane. It developed its own art, literature, and philosophy that reflected its sense of itself as independent from Europe, one with its own distinctive culture.

These changes took place as a market economy emerged. People became less dependent on what they raised or made for themselves and more involved in buying and selling goods. The country benefited from the addition of fertile land farther west and advances in industry and transportation everywhere. Agriculture and manufacturing grew together.

Politically, the country focused on expanding its borders and trade. As part of this, it avoided getting entangled in European diplomatic affairs and wars.

Alternate Views While this period saw growth, it also had increased conflict with American Indians and its neighbors. Many of the immigrants attracted by new opportunities also found prejudice and discrimination. Rights for the common man excluded American Indians, African Americans, and women. Efforts to improve life succeeded for many but not those enslaved. Landmarks in the institution of slavery came earlier, with the development of the cotton gin in 1793 and the end of the importation of enslaved Africans in 1808. Others came later, such as the Compromise of 1850.

7

THE AGE OF JEFFERSON, 1800–1816

Let us then, fellow-citizens, unite with one heart and one mind. Let us restore to social intercourse that harmony and affection without which liberty and even life itself are but dreary things. . . . But every difference of opinion is not a difference of principle. We have called by different names brethren of the same principle. We are all Republicans, we are all Federalists.

Thomas Jefferson, First Inaugural Address, 1801

In the election of 1800, there had been much animosity and bitter partisan feeling between the two national political parties. Following this Revolution of 1800, Thomas Jefferson, the new president, recognized the need for a smooth and peaceful transition of power from the Federalists to the Democratic-Republicans. That is why, in his inaugural address of 1801, Jefferson stressed the popular acceptance of the basic principles of constitutional government when he stated: "We are all Republicans, we are all Federalists."

By 1816, Jefferson's call for unity seems to have been realized. The Federalists had nearly disappeared, but the Democratic-Republicans had adopted many of their positions. Under Jefferson and his close friend James Madison, the nation experienced peaceful political change, expanded territorially, survived another war, and strengthened its democratic and nationalistic spirit. It was thriving, even as it faced significant problems—including slavery, the treatment of American Indians, and loyalty to local interests.

Jefferson's Presidency

During his first term, Jefferson attempted to win the allegiance and trust of Federalist opponents by maintaining the national bank and debt-repayment plan of Hamilton. In foreign policy, he carried on the neutrality policies of Washington and Adams. At the same time, Jefferson retained the loyalty of Democratic-Republican supporters by adhering to his party's guiding principle of limited central government. He reduced the size of the military, eliminated a number of federal jobs, repealed the excise taxes—including those on whiskey— and lowered the national debt. Only Republicans were named to his cabinet, as he sought to avoid the internal divisions that distracted Washington.

Compared to Adams' troubled administration, Jefferson's first four years in office were relatively free of discord. The single most important achievement of these years was the acquisition by purchase of vast western lands known as the Louisiana Territory.

The Louisiana Purchase

The Louisiana Territory encompassed a large and largely unexplored tract of western land through which the Mississippi and Missouri rivers flowed. At the mouth of the Mississippi lay the territory's most valuable property in terms of commerce—the port of New Orleans. For many years, Louisiana and New Orleans had been claimed by Spain. But in 1800, the French military and political leader Napoleon Bonaparte secretly forced Spain to give the Louisiana Territory back to its former owner, France. Napoleon hoped to restore the French empire in the Americas. By 1803, however, Napoleon had lost interest in this plan for two reasons: (1) he needed to concentrate French resources on fighting England and (2) a rebellion led by Toussaint l'Ouverture against French rule on the island of Santo Domingo had resulted in heavy French losses.

U.S. Interest in the Mississippi River During Jefferson's presidency, the western frontier extended beyond Ohio and Kentucky into the Indiana Territory. Settlers in this region depended for their economic existence on transporting goods on rivers that flowed westward into the Mississippi and southward as far as New Orleans. They were greatly alarmed therefore when in 1802 Spanish officials, who were still in charge of New Orleans, closed the port to Americans. They revoked the *right of deposit* granted in the Pinckney Treaty of 1795, which had allowed American farmers tax-free use of the port. People on the frontier clamored for government action. In addition to being concerned about the economic impact of the closing of New Orleans, President Jefferson was troubled by its consequences on foreign policy. He feared that, so long as a foreign power controlled the river at New Orleans, the United States risked entanglement in European affairs.

Negotiations Jefferson sent ministers to France with instructions to offer up to $10 million for both New Orleans and a strip of land extending from that port eastward to Florida. If the American ministers failed in their negotiations with the French, they were instructed to begin discussions with Britain for a U.S.-British alliance. Napoleon's ministers, seeking funds for a war against Britain, offered to sell not only New Orleans but also the entire Louisiana Territory for $15 million. The surprised American ministers quickly went beyond their instructions and accepted.

Constitutional Predicament Jefferson and most Americans strongly approved of the Louisiana Purchase. Nevertheless, a constitutional problem troubled the president. Jefferson was committed to a strict interpretation of the Constitution and rejected Hamilton's argument that certain powers were implied. No clause in the Constitution explicitly stated that a president could purchase foreign land. In this case, Jefferson determined to set aside his idealism for the country's good. He submitted the purchase agreement to the Senate, arguing that lands could be added to the United States as an application of the president's power to make treaties. Casting aside the criticisms of Federalist senators, the Republican majority in the Senate quickly ratified the purchase.

Consequences The Louisiana Purchase more than doubled the size of the United States, removed a European presence from the nation's borders, and extended the western frontier to lands beyond the Mississippi. Furthermore, the acquisition of millions of acres of land strengthened Jefferson's hopes that his country's future would be based on an agrarian society of independent farmers rather than Hamilton's vision of an urban and industrial society. In political terms, the Louisiana Purchase increased Jefferson's popularity and showed the Federalists to be a weak, sectionalist (New England-based) party that could do little more than complain about Democratic-Republican policies.

THE LOUISIANA PURCHASE, 1803

Lewis and Clark Expedition Even before Louisiana was purchased, Jefferson had persuaded Congress to fund a scientific exploration of the trans-Mississippi West to be led by Captain Meriwether Lewis and Lieutenant William Clark. The Louisiana Purchase greatly increased the importance of the expedition. Lewis and Clark set out from St. Louis in 1804, crossed the Rockies, reached the Oregon coast on the Pacific Ocean, then turned back and completed the return journey in 1806. The benefits of the expedition were many: greater geographic and scientific knowledge of the region, stronger U.S. claims to the Oregon Territory, better relations with American Indians, and more accurate maps and land routes for fur trappers and future settlers.

John Marshall and the Supreme Court

After the sweeping Democratic-Republican victory of 1800, the only power remaining to the Federalists was their control of the federal courts. The Federalist appointments to the courts, previously made by Washington and Adams, were not subject to recall or removal except by impeachment. Federalist judges therefore continued in office, much to the annoyance of the Democratic-Republican president, Jefferson.

John Marshall Ironically, the Federalist judge who caused Jefferson the most grief was one of his own cousins from Virginia, John Marshall. Marshall had been appointed Chief Justice of the Supreme Court during the final months of John Adams' presidency. He held his post for 34 years, in which time he exerted as strong an influence on the Supreme Court as Washington had exerted on the presidency. Marshall's decisions in many landmark cases generally strengthened the central government, often at the expense of states' rights.

Case of Marbury v. Madison (1803) The first major case decided by Marshall put him in direct conflict with President Jefferson. Upon taking office, Jefferson wanted to block the Federalist judges appointed by his predecessor, President John Adams. He ordered Secretary of State James Madison not to deliver the commissions to those Federalists judges. One of Adams' "midnight appointments," William Marbury, sued for his commission. The case of *Marbury v. Madison* went to the Supreme Court in 1803. Marshall ruled that Marbury had a right to his commission according to the Judiciary Act passed by Congress in 1789. However, Marshall said the Judiciary Act of 1789 had given to the Court greater power than the Constitution allowed. Therefore, the law was unconstitutional, and Marbury would not receive his commission.

In effect, Marshall sacrificed what would have been a small Federalist gain (the appointment of Marbury) for a much larger, long-term judicial victory. By ruling a law of Congress to be unconstitutional, Marshall established the doctrine of *judicial review*. From this point on, the Supreme Court would exercise the power to decide whether an act of Congress or of the president was allowed by the Constitution. The Supreme Court could now overrule actions of the other two branches of the federal government.

Judicial Impeachments Jefferson tried other methods for overturning past Federalist measures and appointments. Soon after entering office, he suspended the Alien and Sedition Acts and released those jailed under them. Hoping to remove partisan Federalist judges, Jefferson supported a campaign of impeachment. The judge of one federal district was found to be mentally unbalanced. The House voted his impeachment and the Senate then voted to remove him. The House also impeached a Supreme Court justice, Samuel Chase, but the Senate acquitted him after finding no evidence of "high crimes." Except for these two cases, the impeachment campaign was largely a failure, as almost all the Federalist judges remained in office. Even so, the threat of impeachment caused the judges to be more cautious and less partisan in their decisions.

Jefferson's Reelection

In 1804 Jefferson won reelection by an overwhelming margin, receiving all but 14 of the 176 electoral votes. His second term was marked by growing difficulties. There were plots by his former vice president, Aaron Burr; opposition by a faction of his own party (the "Quids"), who accused him of abandoning Democratic-Republican principles; and foreign troubles from the Napoleonic wars in Europe.

Aaron Burr

A Democratic-Republican caucus (closed meeting) in 1804 decided not to nominate Aaron Burr for a second term as vice president. Burr then embarked on a series of ventures, one of which threatened to break up the Union and another of which resulted in the death of Alexander Hamilton.

Federalist Conspiracy Secretly forming a political pact with some radical New England Federalists, Burr planned to win the governorship of New York in 1804, unite that state with the New England states, and then lead this group of states to secede from the nation. Most Federalists followed Alexander Hamilton in opposing Burr, who was defeated in the New York election. The conspiracy then disintegrated.

Duel with Hamilton Angered by an insulting remark attributed to Hamilton, Burr challenged the Federalist leader to a duel and fatally shot him. Hamilton's death in 1804 deprived the Federalists of their last great leader and earned Burr the enmity of many.

Trial for Treason By 1806, Burr's intrigues had turned westward with a plan to take Mexico from Spain and possibly unite it with Louisiana under his rule. Learning of the conspiracy, Jefferson ordered Burr's arrest and trial for treason. Presiding at the trial was Chief Justice of the Supreme Court John Marshall, a long-time adversary of Jefferson. A jury acquitted Burr, basing its decision on Marshall's narrow definition of treason and the lack of witnesses to any "overt act" by Burr.

Difficulties Abroad

As a matter of policy and principle, Jefferson tried to avoid war. Rejecting permanent alliances, he sought to maintain U.S. neutrality despite increasing provocations from both France and Britain during the Napoleonic wars.

Barbary Pirates The first major challenge to Jefferson's foreign policy came not from a major European power, but from the piracy practiced by the Barbary states on the North African coast. To protect U.S. merchant ships from being seized by Barbary pirates, Presidents Washington and Adams had reluctantly agreed to pay tribute to the Barbary governments. The ruler of Tripoli demanded a higher sum in tribute from Jefferson. Refusing to pay, Jefferson sent a small fleet of the U.S. Navy to the Mediterranean. Sporadic fighting with Tripoli lasted for four years (1801–1805). Although the American navy did not achieve a decisive victory, it did gain some respect and also offered a measure of protection to U.S. vessels trading in Mediterranean waters.

Challenges to U.S. Neutrality Meanwhile, the Napoleonic wars continued to dominate the politics of Europe—and to shape the commercial economy of the United States. The two principal belligerents, France and Britain, attempted naval blockades of enemy ports. They regularly seized the ships of neutral nations and confiscated their cargoes. The chief offender from the U.S. point of view was Britain, since its navy dominated the Atlantic. Most infuriating was the British practice of capturing U.S. sailors who it claimed were British citizens and impressing (forcing) them to serve in the British navy.

Chesapeake-Leopard Affair One incident at sea especially aroused American anger and almost led to war. In 1807, only a few miles off the coast of Virginia, the British warship *Leopard* fired on the U.S. warship *Chesapeake*. Three Americans were killed and four others were taken captive and impressed into the British navy. Anti-British feeling ran high, and many Americans demanded war. Jefferson, however, resorted to diplomacy and economic pressure as his response to the crisis.

Embargo Act (1807) As an alternative to war, Jefferson persuaded the Democratic-Republican majority in Congress to pass the Embargo Act in 1807. This measure prohibited American merchant ships from sailing to any foreign port. Since the United States was Britain's largest trading partner, Jefferson hoped that the British would stop violating the rights of neutral nations rather than lose U.S. trade. The embargo, however, backfired and brought greater economic hardship to the United States than to Britain. The British were determined to control the seas at all costs, and they had little difficulty substituting supplies from South America for U.S. goods. The embargo's effect on the U.S. economy, however, was devastating, especially for the merchant marine and shipbuilders of New England. So bad was the depression that a movement developed in the New England states to secede from the Union.

Recognizing that the Embargo Act had failed, Jefferson called for its repeal in 1809 during the final days of his presidency. Even after repeal, however, U.S. ships could trade legally with all nations except Britain and France.

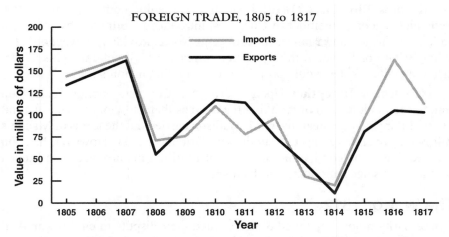

FOREIGN TRADE, 1805 to 1817

Source: U.S. Bureau of the Census. *Historical Statistics of the United States, Colonial Times to 1970*

Madison's Presidency

Jefferson believed strongly in the precedent set by Washington of voluntarily retiring from the presidency after a second term. For his party's nomination for president, he supported his close friend, Secretary of State James Madison.

The Election of 1808

Ever since leading the effort to write and ratify the Constitution, Madison was widely viewed as a brilliant thinker. He had worked tirelessly with Jefferson in developing the Democratic-Republican party. On the other hand, he was a weak public speaker, possessed a stubborn temperament, and lacked Jefferson's political skills. With Jefferson's backing, Madison was nominated for president by a caucus of congressional Democratic-Republicans. Other factions of the Democratic-Republican party nominated two other candidates. Even so, Madison was able to win a majority of electoral votes and to defeat both his Democratic-Republican opponents and the Federalist candidate, Charles Pinckney. Nevertheless, the Federalists managed to gain seats in Congress as a result of the widespread unhappiness with the effects of the embargo.

Commercial Warfare

Madison's presidency was dominated by the same European problems that had plagued Jefferson's second term. Like Jefferson, he attempted a combination of diplomacy and economic pressure to deal with the Napoleonic wars. Unlike Jefferson, he finally consented to take the United States to war.

Nonintercourse Act of 1809 After the repeal of Jefferson's disastrous embargo act, Madison hoped to end economic hardship while maintaining his country's rights as a neutral nation. The Nonintercourse Act of 1809 provided that Americans could now trade with all nations except Britain and France.

Macon's Bill No. 2 (1810) Economic hardships continued into 1810. Nathaniel Macon, a member of Congress, introduced a bill that restored U.S. trade with Britain and France. Macon's Bill No. 2 provided, however, that if either Britain or France formally agreed to respect U.S. neutral rights at sea, then the United States would prohibit trade with that nation's foe.

Napoleon's Deception Upon hearing of Congress' action, Napoleon announced his intention of revoking the decrees that had violated U.S. neutral rights. Taking Napoleon at his word, Madison carried out the terms of Macon's Bill No. 2 by embargoing U.S. trade with Britain in 1811. However, he soon realized that Napoleon had no intention of fulfilling his promise. The French continued to seize American merchant ships.

The War of 1812

Neither Britain nor the United States wanted their dispute to end in war. And yet war between them did break out in 1812.

Causes of the War

From the U.S. point of view, the pressures leading to war came from two directions: the continued violation of U.S. neutral rights at sea and troubles with the British on the western frontier.

Free Seas and Trade As a trading nation, the United States depended upon the free flow of shipping across the Atlantic. Yet the chief belligerents in Europe, Britain, and France, had no interest in respecting neutral rights so long as they were locked in a life-and-death struggle with each other. They well remembered that Britain had seemed a cruel enemy during the American Revolution, and the French had supported the colonists. In addition, Jeffersonian Democratic-Republicans applauded the French for having overthrown their monarchy in their own revolution. Moreover, even though both the French and the British violated U.S. neutral rights, the British violations were worse because of the British navy's practice of impressing American sailors.

Frontier Pressures Added to long-standing grievances over British actions at sea were the ambitions of western Americans for more open land. Americans on the frontier longed for the lands of British Canada and Spanish Florida. Standing in the way were the British and their Indian and Spanish allies.

Conflict with the American Indians was a perennial problem for the restless westerners. For decades, settlers had been gradually pushing the American Indians farther and farther westward. In an effort to defend their lands from further encroachment, Shawnee brothers—Tecumseh, a warrior, and Prophet, a religious leader—attempted to unite all of the tribes east of the Mississippi River. White settlers became suspicious of Tecumseh and persuaded the governor of the Indiana Territory, General William Henry Harrison, to take aggressive action. In the Battle of Tippecanoe, in 1811, Harrison destroyed the Shawnee headquarters and put an end to Tecumseh's efforts to form an Indian confederacy. The British had provided only limited aid to Tecumseh.

Nevertheless, Americans on the frontier blamed the British for instigating the rebellion.

War Hawks A congressional election in 1810 had brought a group of new, young Democratic-Republicans to Congress, many of them from frontier states (Kentucky, Tennessee, and Ohio). Known as war hawks because of their eagerness for war with Britain, they quickly gained significant influence in the House of Representatives. Led by Henry Clay of Kentucky and John C. Calhoun of South Carolina, the war-hawk members of Congress argued that war with Britain would be the only way to defend American honor, gain Canada, and destroy American Indian resistance on the frontier.

Declaration of War British delays in meeting U.S. demands over neutral rights combined with political pressures from the war hawks finally persuaded Madison to seek a declaration of war against Britain. Ironically, the British government had by this time (June 1812) agreed to suspend its naval blockade. News of its decision reached the White House after Congress had declared war.

A Divided Nation

Neither Congress nor the American people were united in support of the war. In Congress, Pennsylvania and Vermont joined the southern and western states to provide a slight majority for the war declaration. Voting against the war were most representatives from New York, New Jersey, and the rest of the states in New England.

VOTE ON DECLARING WAR IN 1812

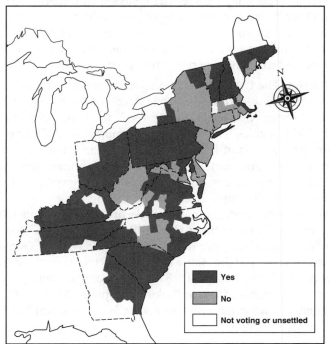

Election of 1812 A similar division of opinion was seen in the presidential election of 1812, in which Democratic-Republican strength in the South and West overcame Federalist and antiwar Democratic-Republican opposition to war in the North. Madison won reelection, defeating De Witt Clinton of New York, the candidate of the Federalists and antiwar Democratic-Republicans.

Opposition to the War Americans who opposed the war viewed it as "Mr. Madison's War" and the work of the war hawks in Congress. Most outspoken in their criticism of the war were New England merchants, Federalist politicians, and "Quids," or "Old" Democratic-Republicans. New England merchants were opposed because, after the repeal of the Embargo Act, they were making sizable profits from the European war and viewed impressment as merely a minor inconvenience. Both commercial interests and religious ties to Protestantism made them more sympathetic to the Protestant British than to the Catholic French. Federalist politicians viewed the war as a Democratic-Republican scheme to conquer Canada and Florida, with the ultimate aim of increasing Democratic-Republican voting strength. For their part, the "Quids" criticized the war because it violated the classic Democratic-Republican commitment to limited federal power and to the maintenance of peace.

Military Defeats and Naval Victories

Facing Britain's overwhelming naval power, Madison's military strategists based their hope for victory on (1) Napoleon's continued success in Europe and (2) a U.S. land campaign against Canada.

Invasion of Canada A poorly equipped American army initiated military action in 1812 by launching a three-part invasion of Canada, one force starting out from Detroit, another from Niagara, and a third from Lake Champlain. These and later forays into Canada were easily repulsed by the British defenders. An American raid and burning of government buildings in York (Toronto) in 1813 only served to encourage retaliation by the British.

Naval Battles The U.S. navy achieved some notable victories, due largely to superior shipbuilding and the valorous deeds of American sailors, including many free African Americans. In late 1812, the U.S. warship Constitution (nicknamed "Old Ironsides") raised American morale by defeating and sinking a British ship off the coast of Nova Scotia. American privateers, motivated by both patriotism and profit, captured numerous British merchant ships. Offsetting these gains was the success of the British navy in establishing a blockade of the U.S. coast, which crippled trading and fishing.

Probably the most important naval battle of the war was in 1813 on Lake Erie with American Captain Oliver Hazard Perry, declaring victory with, "We have met the enemy and they are ours." This led the way for General William Henry Harrison's victory at the Battle of Thames River (near Detroit), in which Tecumseh was killed. The next year, 1814, ships commanded by Thomas Macdonough defeated a British fleet on Lake Champlain. As a result, the British had to retreat and abandon their plan to invade New York and New England.

Chesapeake Campaign By the spring of 1814, the defeat of Napoleon in Europe enabled the British to increase their forces in North America. In the summer of that year, a British army marched through the nation's capital, Washington, D.C., and set fire to the White House, the Capitol, and other government buildings. The British also attempted to take Baltimore, but Fort McHenry held out after a night's bombardment—an event immortalized by Francis Scott Key in the words of "The Star-Spangled Banner."

Southern Campaign Meanwhile, U.S. troops in the South were ably commanded by General Andrew Jackson. In March 1814, at the Battle of Horseshoe Bend in present-day Alabama, Jackson ended the power of an important British ally, the Creek nation. The victory eliminated the Indians and opened new lands to white settlers. A British effort to control the Mississippi River was halted at New Orleans by Jackson leading a force of frontier soldiers, free African Americans, and Creoles. The victory was impressive—but also meaningless. The Battle of New Orleans was fought on January 8, 1815, two weeks after a treaty ending the war had been signed in Ghent, Belgium.

The Treaty of Ghent

By 1814, the British were weary of war. Having fought Napoleon for more than a decade, they now faced the prospect of maintaining the peace in Europe. At the same time, Madison's government recognized that the Americans would be unable to win a decisive victory. American peace commissioners traveled to Ghent, Belgium, to discuss terms of peace with British diplomats. On Christmas Eve 1814, an agreement was reached. The terms halted fighting, returned all conquered territory to the prewar claimant, and recognized the prewar boundary between Canada and the United States.

The Treaty of Ghent, promptly ratified by the Senate in 1815, said nothing at all about the grievances that led to war. Britain made no concessions concerning impressment, blockades, or other maritime differences. Thus, the war ended in stalemate with no gain for either side.

The Hartford Convention

Just before the war ended, the New England states threatened to secede from the Union. Bitterly opposed to both the war and the Democratic-Republican government in Washington, radical Federalists in New England urged that the Constitution be amended and that, as a last resort, secession be voted upon. To consider these matters, a special convention was held at Hartford, Connecticut, in December 1814. Delegates from the New England states rejected the radical calls for secession. But to limit the growing power of the Democratic-Republicans in the South and West, they adopted a number of proposals. One of them called for a two-thirds vote of both houses for any future declaration of war.

Shortly after the convention dissolved, news came of both Jackson's victory at New Orleans and the Treaty of Ghent. These events ended criticism of the war and further weakened the Federalists by stamping them as unpatriotic.

The War's Legacy

From Madison's point of view, the war achieved none of its original aims. Nevertheless, it had a number of important consequences for the future development of the American republic, including the following:

1. Having survived two wars with Britain, the United States gained the respect of other nations.

2. The United States accepted Canada as a part of the British Empire.

3. Denounced for its talk of secession, the Federalist party came to an end as a national force and declined even in New England.

4. Talk of nullification and secession in New England set a precedent that would later be used by the South.

5. Abandoned by the British, American Indians were forced to surrender land to white settlement.

6. With the British naval blockade limiting European goods, U.S. factories were built and Americans moved toward industrial self-sufficiency.

7. War heroes such as Andrew Jackson and William Henry Harrison would soon be in the forefront of a new generation of political leaders.

8. The feeling of nationalism grew stronger as did a belief that the future for the United States lay in the West and away from Europe.

HISTORICAL PERSPECTIVES: WHAT CAUSED POLITICAL PARTIES?

Thomas Jefferson's election to the presidency was popularly known as the Revolution of 1800. The real revolution in 1800 was the complete absence of violence in the transition of power. While the Framers of the Constitution had opposed political parties, parties were accepted as an essential element of the U.S. political system.

Historians have identified various stages in the emergence of two major parties. At first (1787–1789), Federalist and Anti-Federalist factions arose in the various state ratifying conventions as people debated the merits and pitfalls of the proposed Constitution. The second stage was the initial years of the new federal government (1789–1800). Especially during Adams' controversial presidency, the Anti-Federalists became a true political party—Jefferson's Democratic-Republican party. In 1800, for the first time, a party actively recruited members (both voters and candidates for office) and forged alliances with politicians in every state. As a result of their organized efforts, the Democratic-Republicans took power in 1800.

Over time, historians' interpretations of the early parties have changed. In the early 20th century, historians described the partisan struggles of the 1790s as a conflict between the undemocratic, elitist

Hamiltonian Federalists and the democratic, egalitarian Jeffersonian Democratic-Republicans. Charles Beard's *Economic Origins of Jeffersonian Democracy* interpreted the struggle as one between Hamilton's capitalist class and Jefferson's agrarian class. More recently, historians have focused more on personalities in defining the two parties. Finding general agreement in the practices of the opposing parties, these historians emphasize the differing characters of Jefferson and Hamilton and the significance of Washington's friendship with Hamilton and of Jefferson's friendship with Madison.

Richard Hofstadter, a leading historian of the 1950s and 1960s, observed both the differences and the shared ideas of the Democratic-Republicans and Federalists. He saw the parties maturing in 1800, moving past excessive rhetoric to accommodation, as both came to terms with the same political realities.

KEY TERMS BY THEME

Decisions (NAT, POL)
Thomas Jefferson
Louisiana Purchase
war hawks
Henry Clay
John C. Calhoun

The West (MIG, ARC)
Tecumseh
Prophet
William Henry Harrison
Battle of Tippecanoe

Supreme Court (POL)
strict interpretation
John Marshall
judicial review
Marbury v. Madison
Aaron Burr
"Quids"
Hartford Convention
(1814)

War (WOR)
Napoleon Bonaparte
Toussaint l'Ouverture
Barbary pirates
neutrality
impressment
Chesapeake-Leopard
  affair
Embargo Act (1807)
James Madison
Nonintercourse Act
  (1809)
Macon's Bill No. 2 (1810)
War of 1812
"Old Ironsides"
Battle of Lake Erie
Oliver Hazard Perry
Battle of the Thames
  River

Thomas Macdonough
Battle of Lake
  Champlain
Andrew Jackson
Battle of Horseshoe
  Bend
Creek nation
Battle of New Orleans
Treaty of Ghent (1814)

Exploration (GEO)
Lewis and Clark
  expedition

The Anthem (SOC)
Francis Scott Key
"The Star-Spangled
  Banner"

Questions 1–3 refer to the excerpt below.

"I am ready to allow, Mr. President, that both Great Britain and France have given us abundant cause for war. . . . My plan would be, and my first wish is, to prepare for it—to put the country in complete armor—in the attitude imperiously demanded in a crisis of war, and to which it must be brought before any war can be effective. . . . I must call on every member of this Senate to pause before he leaps into or crosses the Rubicon—declaring war is passing the Rubicon in reality."

—Senator Obadiah German of New York, speech in the Senate,
June 1812

1. In the United States, support for the War of 1812 was the strongest from
   (A) frontier settlers who wanted land and protection from American Indians
   (B) New England merchants who feared impressment
   (C) Protestants who had religious sympathies with Great Britain
   (D) "Quids" who held classic Democratic-Republican beliefs

2. Who of the following would be most likely to agree with German's position on the war?
   (A) John Calhoun and other politicians from the South
   (B) Henry Clay and other politicians from the West
   (C) James Madison and other politicians from the executive branch
   (D) Merchants from New England

3. Which of the following is the best support for German's claim that the United States has "abundant cause for war"?
   (A) the impressment of U.S. sailors
   (B) the controversy over the Louisiana Purchase
   (C) the actions by the Barbary pirates
   (D) the findings of the Lewis and Clark expedition

Questions 4–6 refer to the excerpt below.

"All, too, will bear in mind this sacred principle, that though the will of the majority is in all cases to prevail, that will to be rightful must be reasonable; that the minority possess their equal rights, which equal law must protect, and to violate would be oppression.

"We have called by different names brethren of the same principle. We are all Republicans, we are all Federalists. If there be any among us who would wish to dissolve this Union or to change its republican form, let them stand undisturbed as monuments of the safety with which error of opinion may be tolerated where reason is left free to combat it. . . .

"Equal and exact justice to all men, of whatever state or persuasion, religious or political; peace, commerce, and honest friendship with all nations, entangling alliances with none."

—Thomas Jefferson, First Inaugural Address, 1801

4. Which of the following describes a policy of Jefferson's that reflects the attitude toward Federalists expressed in this speech?

(A) He adopted a Federalist plan for increasing the size of the military.

(B) He appealed to Federalists by increasing taxes to pay for new roads.

(C) He attempted to gain the trust of Federalists by continuing the national bank.

(D) He showed that party was unimportant by appointing some Federalists to his cabinet.

5. Jefferson's statement "that the minority possesses their equal rights, which equal law must protect" was supported by his actions with regard to

(A) the case of *Marbury v. Madison*

(B) the Alien and Sedition Acts

(C) the Louisiana Purchase

(D) the Federalist Conspiracy

6. Jefferson's call to avoid entangling alliances is similar to advice found in

(A) the Declaration of Independence

(B) *The Federalist Papers*

(C) the Kentucky Resolutions

(D) Washington's Farewell Address

Questions 7–8 refer to the excerpt below.

"It is true I am a Shawnee. My forefathers were warriors. Their son is a warrior. From them I take only my existence; from my tribe I take nothing. . . . [I] come to Governor Harrison to ask him to tear the treaty . . . but I would say to him:
    "'Sir, you have liberty to return to your own country.'
    "Once, nor until lately, there was no white man on this continent. . . . It then all belonged to red men. . . . Once a happy race, since made miserable by the white people, who are never contented but always encroaching. The way, and the only way, to check and to stop this evil, is for all the red men to unite in claiming a common and equal right in the land. . . . For it never was divided, but belongs to all for the use of each. For no part has a right to sell."

—Tecumseh, Letter to Governor William Henry Harrison, August 1810

7. Tecumseh believed that which of the following would be the best way for the American Indians to respond to the desire of white settlers for land?

    (A) Signing a treaty with the United States

    (B) Joining the British in order to stop westward expansion

    (C) Moving westward to lands unoccupied by American Indians

    (D) Forming a confederacy among all American Indians

8. Based on this excerpt, which of the following would Tecumseh most likely have objected to?

    (A) The War of 1812

    (B) The Alien and Sedition Acts

    (C) British actions on the western frontier

    (D) The Louisiana Purchase

SHORT-ANSWER QUESTIONS

Use complete sentences; an outline or bulleted list alone is not acceptable.

Question 1 is based on the following excerpts.

"The issue, then, is not whether Jefferson's policies toward Louisiana were right or wrong but rather how he managed to implement decisions that defied in so many ways his long-standing commitment to limitations on executive power and the near-sacred character of republican principles. . . . Jefferson was not simply sized by power-hungry impulses once he assumed the presidency, since in a broad range of other policy areas he exhibited considerable discipline over the executive branch and habitual deference to the Congress; . . . he did not suddenly discover a pragmatic streak in his political philosophy, . . . he clung tenaciously to Jeffersonian principles despite massive evidence that they were at odds with reality. . . . The answer would seem to be the special, indeed almost mystical place the West had in his thinking. . . . For Jefferson more than any other major figure in the revolutionary generation, the West was America's future."

—Joseph J. Ellis, historian, *American Sphinx,* 1997

"The story of the Louisiana Purchase is one of strength, of Jefferson's adaptability and, most important, his determination to secure the territory from France, . . . A slower or less courageous politician might have bungled the acquisition; an overly idealistic one might have lost it by insisting on strict constitutional scruples. . . . The philosophical Jefferson had believed an amendment necessary. The political Jefferson, however, was not going to allow theory to get in the way of reality. . . . [He] expanded the powers of the executive in ways that would have likely driven Jefferson to distraction had another man been president. Much of his political life, though, had been devoted to the study and the wise exercise of power. He did what had to be done to preserve the possibility of republicanism and progress. Things were neat only in theory. And despite his love of ideas and image of himself, Thomas Jefferson was as much a man of action as he was of theory."

—Jon Meacham, historian, *Thomas Jefferson: The Art of Power,* 2012

1. Using the excerpts, answer (A), (B), and (C).

   (A) Briefly explain ONE major difference between Ellis's and Meacham's historical interpretations of how Thomas Jefferson came to approve the Louisiana Purchase.

   (B) Briefly explain how ONE historical event or development in the period 1787 to 1803 that is not explicitly mentioned in the excerpts could be used to support Ellis's interpretation.

   (C) Briefly explain how ONE historical event or development in the period 1787 to 1803 that is not explicitly mentioned in the excerpts could be used to support Meacham's interpretation.

Question 2. Answer (A), (B), and (C).

(A) Briefly explain ONE specific reason given by those in the United States who opposed the War of 1812.

(B) Briefly explain ONE specific reason given by those in the United States who supported the War of 1812.

(C) Briefly explain how ONE of the reasons for or against the War of 1812 would continue after the war to play a major role in the politics and policies of the United States.

Question 3. Answer (A), (B), and (C).

(A) Briefly explain ONE historical event or development during the period 1800 to 1816 that demonstrates Presidents Jefferson's and Madison's reliance on economic policies to carry out foreign policies.

(B) Briefly explain ONE historical event or development during the period 1800 to 1816 that demonstrates the failure of Presidents Jefferson's and Madison's reliance on economic policies to carry out foreign policies.

(C) Briefly explain ONE historical event or development during the period 1800 to 1816 that demonstrates the use of the military by either Presidents Jefferson and Madison to carry out foreign policies.

Question 4 is based on the following excerpt.

"And if this court is not authorized to issue a writ of mandamus. . . . It must be because the law is unconstitutional and therefore absolutely incapable of conferring the authority. . . .

"Certainly, all those who have framed written constitutions contemplate them as forming the fundamental and paramount law . . . and consequently . . . an act of the legislature repugnant to the constitution is void. . . .

"If, then, the courts are to regard the Constitution, and the Constitution is superior to any ordinary act of the legislature, the Constitution, and not such ordinary act must govern the case to which they both apply.

"The judicial power of the United States is extended to all cases arising under the Constitution. . . .

"Thus, the particular phraseology of the Constitution . . . confirms and strengthens the principle . . . that a law repugnant to the Constitution is void and that courts, as well as other departments, are bound by that instrument."

—John Marshall, *Marbury v. Madison,* 1803

4. Using the excerpt, answer (A), (B), and (C).
   (A) Briefly explain ONE specific historical element of Marshall's opinion in the *Marbury v. Madison* decision.
   (B) Briefly explain ONE specific reaction Thomas Jefferson would have toward the *Marbury v. Madison* decision.
   (C) Briefly explain ONE specific reaction John Adams would have toward the *Marbury v. Madison* decision.

THINK AS A HISTORIAN: USES OF HISTORICAL EVIDENCE

A key skill of historians is the ability to use evidence accurately. Describe the kind of evidence that should be included in essays responding to each of these prompts.

1. If the Supreme Court was asked to decide the constitutionality of the Louisiana Purchase, how would you expect John Marshall to have ruled?
2. How important was the War of 1812 to the development of the United States?
3. Explain whether you think westward expansion was the most important issue for the new country.

NATIONALISM AND ECONOMIC DEVELOPMENT, 1816–1848

A high and honorable feeling generally prevails, and the people begin to assume, more and more, a national character; and to look at home for the only means, under divine goodness, of preserving their religion and liberty.

Hezekiah Niles, *Niles' Weekly Register,* September 2, 1815

The election of James Monroe as president in 1816 (less than two years after the last battle of the War of 1812) inaugurated what one newspaper editorial characterized as an "Era of Good Feelings." The term gained wide currency and was later adopted by historians to describe Monroe's two terms in office.

The Era of Good Feelings

The period's nickname suggests the Monroe years were marked by a spirit of nationalism, optimism, and goodwill. In some ways, they were. One party, the Federalists, faded into oblivion and Monroe's party, the Democratic-Republicans, adopted some of their policies and dominated politics.

This perception of unity and harmony, however, can be misleading and oversimplified. Throughout the era people had heated debates over tariffs, the national bank, internal improvements, and public land sales. Sectionalist tensions over slavery were becoming ever more apparent. Moreover, a sense of political unity was illusory, since antagonistic factions within the Democratic-Republican party would soon split it in two. The actual period of "good feelings" may have lasted only from the election of 1816 to the Panic of 1819.

James Monroe

As a young man, James Monroe had fought in the Revolutionary War and suffered through the Valley Forge winter. He had become prominent in Virginia politics and had served as Jefferson's minister to Great Britain and as Madison's secretary of state. He continued the Virginia dynasty: of the first five presidents, four were from Virginia. The other, John Adams, was from Massachusetts.

In the election of 1816, Monroe defeated the Federalist, Rufus King, overwhelmingly—183 electoral votes to 34. By 1820, the Federalist party had practically vanished and Monroe received every electoral vote except one. With no organized political opposition, Monroe represented the growing nationalism of the American people. Under Monroe, the country acquired Florida, agreed on the Missouri Compromise, and adopted the Monroe Doctrine.

Cultural Nationalism

The popular votes for James Monroe were cast by a younger generation of Americans whose concerns differed from those of the nation's founders. The young were excited about the prospects of the new nation expanding westward and had little interest in European politics now that the Napoleonic wars (as well as the War of 1812) were in the past. As fervent nationalists, they believed their young country was entering an era of unlimited prosperity.

Patriotic themes infused every aspect of American society, from art to schoolbooks. Heroes of the Revolution were enshrined in the paintings by Gilbert Stuart, Charles Willson Peale, and John Trumbull. A fictionalized biography extolling the virtues of George Washington, written by Parson Mason Weems, was widely read. The expanding public schools embraced Noah Webster's blue-backed speller, which promoted patriotism long before his famous dictionary was published. The basic ideas and ideals of nationalism and patriotism would dominate most of the 19th century.

Economic Nationalism

Parallel with cultural nationalism was a political movement to support the growth of the nation's economy. Subsidizing internal improvements (the building of roads and canals) was one aspect of the movement. Protecting budding U.S. industries from European competition was a second aspect.

Tariff of 1816 Before the War of 1812, Congress had levied low tariffs on imports as a method for raising government revenue. Then, during the war, manufacturers erected many factories to supply goods that previously had been imported from Britain. Now in peacetime, these American manufacturers feared that British goods would be dumped on American markets and take away much of their business. Congress raised tariffs for the express purpose of protecting U.S. manufacturers from competition. This was the first protective tariff in U.S. history—the first of many to come.

New England, which had little manufacturing at the time, was the only section to oppose the higher tariffs. Even the South and West, which had opposed tariffs in the past and would oppose them in the future, generally supported the 1816 tariff, believing that it was needed for national prosperity.

Henry Clay's American System Henry Clay of Kentucky, a leader in the House of Representatives, proposed a comprehensive method for advancing the nation's economic growth. His plan, which he called the American System, consisted of three parts: (1) protective tariffs, (2) a national bank, and (3) internal improvements. Clay argued that protective tariffs would promote American manufacturing and also raise revenue with which to build a national transportation system of federally constructed roads and canals. A national bank would keep the system running smoothly by providing a national currency. The tariffs would chiefly benefit the East, internal improvements would promote growth in the West and the South, and the bank would aid the economies of all sections.

Two parts of Clay's system were already in place in 1816, the last year of James Madison's presidency. Congress in that year adopted a protective tariff and also chartered the Second Bank of the United States. (The charter of the First Bank—Hamilton's brainchild—had been allowed to expire in 1811.)

On the matter of internal improvements, however, both Madison and Monroe objected that the Constitution did not explicitly provide for the spending of federal money on roads and canals. Throughout his presidency, Monroe consistently vetoed acts of Congress providing funds for road-building and canal-building projects. Thus, the individual states were left to make internal improvements on their own.

CANAL BUILDING, 1820 to 1840

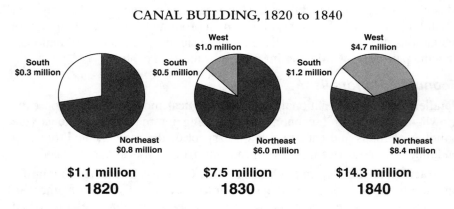

$1.1 million
1820

$7.5 million
1830

$14.3 million
1840

Source: Bureau of the Census, *Historical Statistics of the United States, Colonial Times to 1970*

The Panic of 1819

The Era of Good Feelings was fractured in 1819 by the first major financial panic since the Constitution had been ratified. The economic disaster was largely the fault of the Second Bank of the United States, which had tightened credit in a belated effort to control inflation. Many state banks closed and unemployment, bankruptcies, and imprisonment for debt increased sharply. The depression was most severe in the West, where many people were in debt because they speculated on land during the postwar euphoria. In 1819, the Bank of the United States foreclosed on large amounts of western farmland.

As a result of the bank panic and depression, nationalistic beliefs were shaken. In the West, the economic crisis changed many voters' political outlook. Westerners began calling for land reform and expressing strong opposition to both the national bank and debtors' prisons.

Political Changes

A principal reason for the rapid decline of the Federalist party was its failure to adapt to the changing needs of a growing nation. Having opposed the War of 1812 and presided over a secessionist convention at Hartford, the party seemed completely out of step with the nationalistic temper of the times. After its crushing defeat in the election of 1816, it ceased to be a national party and failed to nominate a presidential candidate in 1820.

Changes in the Democratic-Republican Party Meanwhile, the Democratic-Republican party, as the only remaining national party, underwent serious internal strains as it adjusted to changing times. Members such as John Randolph clung to the old party ideals of limited government and a strict interpretation of the Constitution. Most members, however, adopted what had once been Federalist ideas, such as the need for maintaining of a large army and navy and support for a national bank. Some members reversed their views from one decade to the next. For example, Daniel Webster of Massachusetts, strongly opposed both the tariffs of 1816 and 1824 but then supported even higher tariff rates in 1828. John C. Calhoun of South Carolina was another Democratic-Republican leader who reversed positions. An outspoken war hawk and nationalist in 1812, Calhoun championed states' rights after 1828.

Political factions and sectional differences became more intense during Monroe's second term. When Monroe, honoring the two-term tradition, declined to be a candidate again, four other Republicans sought election as president in 1824. How this election split of the Democratic-Republican party and led to the emergence of two rival parties is explained in Chapter 10.

Marshall's Supreme Court and Central Government Powers

One Federalist official continued to have major influence throughout the years of Democratic-Republican ascendancy: John Marshall. He had been appointed to the Supreme Court in 1800 by Federalist President John Adams and was still leading the Court as its chief justice. His decisions consistently favored the central government and the rights of property against the advocates of states' rights. Even when justices appointed by Democratic-Republican presidents formed a majority on the Court, they often sided with Marshall because they were persuaded that the U.S. Constitution had created a federal government with strong and flexible powers. Several of Marshall's decisions became landmark rulings that defined the relationship between the central government and the states. The first of these cases, *Marbury v. Madison* (1803), established the principle of judicial review. It was described in Chapter 7. Six others influential cases are described below.

Fletcher v. Peck (1810) In a case involving land fraud in Georgia, Marshall concluded that a state could not pass legislation invalidating a contract. This was the first time that the Supreme Court declared a state law to be unconstitutional and invalid. (In *Marbury v. Madison,* the Court ruled a federal law unconstitutional.)

Martin v. Hunter's Lease (1816) The Supreme Court established that it had jurisdiction over state courts in cases involving constitutional rights.

Dartmouth College v. Woodward (1819) This case involved a law of New Hampshire that changed Dartmouth College from a privately chartered college into a public institution. The Marshall Court struck down the state law as unconstitutional, arguing that a contract for a private corporation could not be altered by the state.

McCulloch v. Maryland (1819) Maryland attempted to tax the Second Bank of the United States located in Maryland. Marshall ruled that a state could not tax a federal institution because "the power to tax is the power to destroy," and federal laws are supreme over state laws. In addition, Marshall settled the long-running debate over constitutionality of the national bank. Using a loose interpretation of the Constitution, Marshall ruled that, even though no clause in the Constitution specifically mentions a national bank, the Constitution gave the federal government the *implied power* to create one.

Cohens v. Virginia (1821) A pair of brothers named Cohens were convicted in Virginia of illegally selling lottery tickets for a lottery authorized by Congress for Washington, D.C. While Marshall and the Court upheld the conviction, they established the principle that the Supreme Court could review a state court's decision involving any of the powers of the federal government.

Gibbons v. Ogden (1821) Could the state of New York grant a monopoly to a steamboat company if that action conflicted with a charter authorized by Congress? In ruling that the New York monopoly was unconstitutional, Marshall established the federal government's broad control of interstate commerce.

Western Settlement and the Missouri Compromise

Less than ten years after the start of the War of 1812, the population west of the Appalachian Mountains had doubled. Much of the nationalistic and economic interest in the country was centered on the West, which presented both opportunities and new questions.

Reasons for Westward Movement

Several factors combined to stimulate rapid growth along the western frontier during the presidencies of Madison and Monroe.

Acquisition of American Indians' Lands Large areas were open for settlement after American Indians were driven from their lands by the victories of Generals William Henry Harrison in the Indiana Territory and Andrew Jackson in Florida and the South.

Economic Pressures The economic difficulties in the Northeast from the embargo and the war caused people from this region to seek a new future across the Appalachians. In the South, tobacco planters needed new land to replace the soil exhausted by years of poor farming methods. They found good land for planting cotton in Alabama, Mississippi, and Arkansas.

Improved Transportation Pioneers had an easier time reaching the frontier as a result of the building of roads and canals, steamboats, and railroads.

Immigrants More Europeans were being attracted to America by speculators offering cheap land in the Great Lakes region and in the valleys of the Ohio, Cumberland, and Mississippi rivers.

New Questions and Issues

Despite their rapid growth, the new states of the West had small populations relative to those of the other two sections. To enhance their limited political influence in Congress, western representatives bargained with politicians from other sections to obtain their objectives. Of greatest importance to the western states were: (1) "cheap money" (easy credit) from state banks rather than from the Bank of the United States, (2) low prices for land sold by the federal government, and (3) improved transportation.

However, on the critical issue of slavery, westerners could not agree whether to permit it or to exclude it. Those settling territory to the south wanted slavery for economic reasons (labor for the cotton fields), while those settling to the north had no use for slavery. In 1819, when the Missouri Territory applied to Congress for statehood, the slavery issue became a subject of angry debate.

The Missouri Compromise

Ever since 1791–1792, when Vermont entered the Union as a free state and Kentucky entered as a slave state, politicians in Congress had attempted to preserve a sectional balance between the North and the South. Keeping a balance in the House of Representatives was difficult because population in the North was growing more rapidly than in the South. By 1818 the northern states held a majority of 105 to 81 in the House. However, in the Senate, the votes remained divided evenly: 11 slave and 11 free states. As long as this balance was preserved, southern senators could block legislation that they believed threatened the interests of their section.

Missouri's bid for statehood alarmed the North because slavery was well established there. If Missouri came in as a slave state, it would tip the political balance in the South's favor. Furthermore, Missouri was the first part of the Louisiana Purchase to apply for statehood. Southerners and northerners alike worried about the future status of other new territories applying for statehood from the rest of the vast Louisiana Purchase.

Tallmadge Amendment Representative James Tallmadge from New York ignited the debate about the Missouri question by proposing an amendment to the bill for Missouri's admission. The amendment called for (1) prohibiting the further introduction of slaves into Missouri and (2) requiring the children of Missouri slaves to be emancipated at the age of 25. If adopted, the Tallmadge Amendment would have led to the gradual elimination of slavery in Missouri. The amendment was defeated in the Senate as enraged southerners saw it as the first step in a northern effort to abolish slavery in all states.

THE UNITED STATES IN 1821
AFTER THE MISSOURI COMPROMISE

Clay's Proposals After months of heated debate in Congress and throughout the nation, Henry Clay won majority support for three bills that, taken together, represented a compromise:

1. Admit Missouri as a slave-holding state.

2. Admit Maine as a free state.

3. Prohibit slavery in the rest of the Louisiana Territory north of latitude 36° 30'.

Both houses passed the bills, and President Monroe added his signature in March 1820 to what became known as the Missouri Compromise.

Aftermath Sectional feelings on the slavery issue subsided after 1820. The Missouri Compromise preserved sectional balance for more than 30 years and provided time for the nation to mature. Nevertheless, if an era of good feelings existed, it was badly damaged by the storm of sectional controversy over Missouri. After this political crisis, Americans were torn between feelings of nationalism (loyalty to the Union) on the one hand and feelings of sectionalism (loyalty to one's own region) on the other.

Foreign Affairs

Following the War of 1812, the United States adopted a more aggressive, nationalistic approach it its relations with other nations. During Madison's presidency, when problems with the Barbary pirates again developed, a fleet under Stephen Decatur was sent in 1815 to force the rulers of North Africa to allow American shipping the free use of the Mediterranean. President Monroe and Secretary of State John Quincy Adams continued to follow a nationalistic policy that actively advanced American interests while maintaining peace.

Canada

Although the Treaty of Ghent of 1814 had ended the war between Britain and the United States, it left unresolved most of their diplomatic differences, including many involving Canada.

Rush-Bagot Agreement (1817) During Monroe's first year as president, British and American negotiators agreed to a major disarmament pact. The Rush-Bagot Agreement strictly limited naval armament on the Great Lakes. In time the agreement was extended to place limits on border fortifications as well. Ultimately, the border between the United States and Canada was to become the longest unfortified border in the world.

Treaty of 1818 Improved relations between the United States and Britain continued in a treaty that provided for (1) shared fishing rights off the coast of Newfoundland; (2) joint occupation of the Oregon Territory for ten years; and (3) the setting of the northern limits of the Louisiana Territory at the 49th parallel, thus establishing the western U.S.-Canada boundary line.

Florida

During the War of 1812, U.S. troops had occupied western Florida, a strip of land on the Gulf of Mexico extending all the way to the Mississippi delta. Previously, this land had been held by Spain, Britain's ally. After the war, Spain had difficulty governing the rest of Florida (the peninsula itself) because its troops had been removed from Florida to battle revolts in the South American colonies. The chaotic conditions permitted groups of Seminoles, runaway slaves, and white outlaws to conduct raids into U.S. territory and retreat to safety across the Florida border. These disorders gave Monroe and General Andrew Jackson an opportunity to take military action in Spanish Florida, a territory long coveted by American expansionists.

Jackson's Military Campaign In late 1817, the president commissioned General Jackson to stop the raiders and, if necessary, pursue them across the border into Spanish west Florida. Jackson carried out his orders with a vengeance and probably went beyond his instructions. In 1818, he led a force of militia into Florida, destroyed Seminole villages, and hanged two Seminole chiefs. Capturing Pensacola, Jackson drove out the Spanish governor, and hanged two British traders accused of aiding the Seminoles.

Many members of Congress feared that Jackson's overzealousness would precipitate a war with both Spain and Britain. However, Secretary of State John Quincy Adams persuaded Monroe to support Jackson, and the British decided not to intervene.

Florida Purchase Treaty (1819) Spain, worried that the United States would seize Florida and preoccupied with troubles in Latin America, decided to get the best possible terms for Florida. By treaty in 1819, Spain turned over all of its possessions in Florida and its own claims in the Oregon Territory to the United States. In exchange, the United States agreed to assume $5 million in claims against Spain and give up any U.S. territorial claims to the Spanish province of Texas. The agreement is also called the Adams-Onís Treaty.

The Monroe Doctrine

Although focused on its own growth, the United States did not ignore the ambitions of Europe in the Western Hemisphere. The restoration of a number of monarchies in Europe after the fall of Napoleon in 1815 produced a backlash against republican movements. Restored monarchies in France, Austria, and Prussia, together with Russia, worked together to suppress liberal elements in Italy and Spain. They also considered helping Spain to return to power in South America, where a number of republics had recently declared their independence. In addition, Russia's presence in Alaska worried both Britain and the United States. Using their trading posts in Alaska as a base, Russian seal hunters had spread southward and established a trading post at San Francisco Bay. British and U.S. leaders decided they had a common interest in protecting North and South America from possible aggression by a European power.

British Initiative British naval power deterred the Spanish from attempting a comeback in Latin America. But to maintain British trade with the Latin American republics required diplomacy. British Foreign Secretary George Canning proposed to Richard Rush, the U.S. minister in London, a joint Anglo-American warning to the European powers not to intervene in South America.

American Response Monroe and most of his advisers thought Canning's idea of a joint declaration made sense. However, Secretary of State John Quincy Adams disagreed. He believed that joint action with Britain would restrict U.S. opportunities for further expansion in the hemisphere. Adams reasoned as follows: (1) If the United States acted alone, Britain could be counted upon to stand behind the U.S. policy. (2) No European power would risk going to war in South America, and if it did, the British navy would surely defeat the aggressor. President Monroe decided to act as Adams advised—to issue a statement to the world that did not have Britain as a coauthor.

The Doctrine On December 2, 1823, President Monroe inserted into his annual message to Congress a declaration of U.S. policy toward Europe and Latin America. The Monroe Doctrine, as it came to be called, asserted

> as a principle in which the rights and interests of the United States are involved, that the American continents, by the free and independent condition which they have assumed and maintain, are henceforth not to be considered as subjects for future colonization by any European powers.

Monroe declared further that the United States opposed attempts by a European power to interfere in the affairs of any republic in the Western Hemisphere.

Impact Monroe's bold words of nationalistic purpose were applauded by the American public but soon forgotten, as most citizens were more concerned with domestic issues. In Britain, Canning was annoyed by the doctrine because he recognized that it applied, not just to the other European powers, but to his country as well. The British too were warned not to intervene and not to seek new territory in the Western Hemisphere. The European monarchs reacted angrily to Monroe's message. Still, they recognized that their purposes were thwarted, not by his words, but by the might of the British navy.

The Monroe Doctrine had less significance at the time than in later decades, when it would be hailed by politicians and citizens alike as the cornerstone of U.S. foreign policy toward Latin America. In the 1840s, President James Polk was the first of many presidents to justify his foreign policy by referring to Monroe's warning words.

A National Economy

In the early 1800s, the Jeffersonian dream of a nation of independent farmers remained strong in rural areas. As the century progressed, however, an increasing percentage of the American people were swept up in the dynamic economic changes of the Industrial Revolution. Political conflicts over tariffs, internal improvements, and the Bank of the United States reflected the importance to people's lives of a national economy that was rapidly growing.

Population Growth

Population growth provided both the laborers and the consumers required for industrial development. Between 1800 and 1825, the U.S. population doubled; in the following 25 years it doubled again. A high birthrate accounted for most of this growth, but it was strongly supplemented after 1830 by immigrants arriving from Europe, particularly from Great Britain and Germany. The nonwhite population—African Americans and American Indians—grew despite the ban on the importation of slaves after 1808. However, as a percentage of the total population, nonwhites declined from almost 20 percent in 1790 to 15 percent in the 1850s.

By the 1830s, almost one-third of the population lived west of the Alleghenies. At the same time, both old and new urban areas were growing rapidly.

UNITED STATES POPULATION, 1790 to 1860

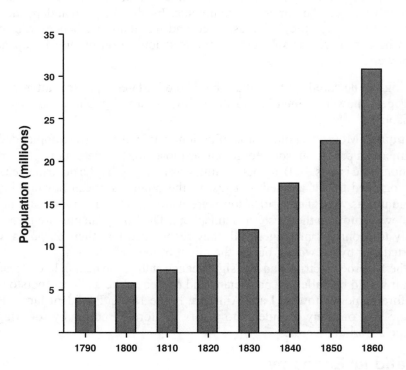

Source: U.S. Bureau of the Census. *Historical Statistics of the United States, Colonial Times to 1970*

Transportation

Vital to the development of both a national and an industrial economy was an efficient network of interconnecting roads and canals for moving people, raw materials, and manufactured goods.

Roads Pennsylvania's Lancaster Turnpike, built in the 1790s, connected Philadelphia with the rich farmlands around Lancaster. Its success stimulated the construction of other privately built and relatively short toll roads that, by the mid-1820s, connected most of the country's major cities.

Despite the need for interstate roads, states' righters blocked the spending of federal funds on internal improvements. Construction of highways that crossed state lines was therefore unusual. One notable exception was the National, or Cumberland Road, a paved highway and major route to the west extending more than a thousand miles from Maryland to Illinois. It was begun in 1811 and completed in the 1850s, using both federal and state money, with the different states receiving ownership of segments of the highway.

Canals The completion of the Erie Canal in New York State in 1825 was a major event in linking the economies of western farms and eastern cities. The success of this canal in stimulating economic growth touched off a frenzy of canal-building in other states. In little more than a decade, canals joined together all of the major lakes and rivers east of the Mississippi. Improved transportation meant lower food prices in the East, more immigrants settling in the West, and stronger economic ties between the two sections.

Steamboats The age of mechanized, steam-powered travel began in 1807 with the successful voyage up the Hudson River of the *Clermont,* a steamboat developed by Robert Fulton. Commercially operated steamboat lines soon made round-trip shipping on the nation's great rivers both faster and cheaper.

Railroads Even more rapid and reliable links between cities became possible with the building of the first U.S. railroad lines in the late 1820s. The early railroads were hampered at first by safety problems, but by the 1830s they were competing directly with canals as an alternative method for carrying passengers and freight. The combination of railroads with the other major improvements in transportation rapidly changed small western towns such as Cleveland, Cincinnati, Detroit, and Chicago into booming commercial centers of the expanding national economy.

Growth of Industry

At the start of the 19th century, a manufacturing economy had barely begun in the United States. By midcentury, however, U.S. manufacturing surpassed agriculture in value, and by century's end, it was the world's leader. This rapid industrial growth was the result of a unique combination of factors.

Mechanical Inventions Protected by patent laws, inventors looked forward to handsome rewards if their ideas for new tools or machines proved practical. Eli Whitney was only the most famous of hundreds of Americans whose long hours of tinkering in their workshops resulted in improved technology. Besides inventing the cotton gin in 1793, Whitney devised a system for making rifles out of interchangeable parts during the War of 1812. Interchangeable parts then became the basis for mass production methods in the new northern factories.

Corporations for Raising Capital In 1811, New York passed a law that made it easier for a business to incorporate and raise capital (money) by selling shares of stock. Other states soon imitated New York's example. Owners of a corporation risked only the amount of money that they invested in a venture. Changes in state corporation laws facilitated the raising of the large sums of capital necessary for building factories, canals, and railroads.

Factory System When Samuel Slater emigrated from Britain, he took with him the British secrets for building cotton-spinning machines, and he put this knowledge to work by helping establish the first U.S. factory in 1791. Early in the next century, the embargo and the War of 1812 stimulated domestic manufacturing, and the protective tariffs enacted by Congress helped the new factories prosper.

MAJOR CANALS, ROADS, AND RAILROADS 1820–1850

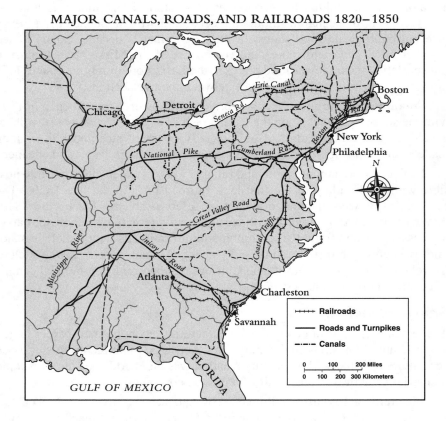

In the 1820s, New England emerged as the country's leading manufacturing center as a result of the region's abundant waterpower for driving the new machinery and excellent seaports for shipping goods. Also, the decline of New England's maritime industry made capital available for manufacturing, while the decline of farming in the region yielded a ready labor supply. Other northern states with similar resources and problems—New York, New Jersey, and Pennsylvania—followed New England's lead. As the factory system expanded, it encouraged the growth of financial businesses such as banking and insurance.

Labor At first, factory owners had difficulty finding workers for their mills. Factory life could not compete with the lure of cheap land in the West. In response to this difficulty, textile mills in Lowell, Massachusetts, recruited young farm women and housed them in company dormitories. In the 1830s, other factories imitated the Lowell System. Many factories also made extensive use of child labor. (Children as young as seven left home to work in the new factories.) Toward the middle of the century northern manufacturers began to employ immigrants in large numbers.

Unions Trade (or craft) unions were organized in major cities as early as the 1790s and increased in number as the factory system took hold. Many skilled workers (shoemakers and weavers, for example) had to seek employment in factories because their earlier practice of working in their own shops (the crafts system) could no longer compete with lower-priced, mass-produced goods. Long hours, low pay, and poor working conditions led to widespread discontent among factory workers. A prime goal of the early unions was to reduce the workday to ten hours. The obstacles to union success, however, were many: (1) immigrant replacement workers, (2) state laws outlawing unions, and (3) frequent economic depressions with high unemployment.

Commercial Agriculture

In the early 1800s, farming became more of a commercial enterprise and less a means of providing subsistence for the family. This change to cash crops was brought about by a blend of factors.

Cheap Land and Easy Credit Large areas of western land were made available at low prices by the federal government. State banks also made it easy to acquire land by providing farmers with loans at low interest rates.

Markets Initially, western farmers were limited to sending their products down the Ohio and Mississippi rivers to southern markets. The advent of canals and railroads opened new markets in the growing factory cities in the East.

Cotton and the South

Throughout the 19th century, the principal cash crop in the South was cotton. Eli Whitney's invention of the cotton gin in 1793 transformed the agriculture of an entire region. Now that they could easily separate the cotton fiber from the seeds, southern planters found cotton more profitable than tobacco and indigo, the leading crops of the colonial period. They invested their capital in the purchase of slaves and new land in Alabama and Mississippi and shipped most of their cotton crop overseas for sale to British textile factories.

Effects of the Market Revolution

Specialization on the farm, the growth of cities, industrialization, and the development of modern capitalism meant the end of self-sufficient households and a growing interdependence among people. These changes combined to bring about a revolution in the marketplace. The farmers fed the workers in the cities, who in turn provided farm families with an array of mass-produced goods. For most Americans, the standard of living increased. At the same time, however, adapting to an impersonal, fast-changing economy presented challenges and problems.

Women As American society became more urban and industrialized, the nature of work and family life changed for women, many of whom no longer worked next to their husbands on family farms. Women seeking employment in a city were usually limited to two choices: domestic service or teaching. Factory jobs, as in the Lowell System, were not common. The overwhelming majority of working women were single. If they married, they left their jobs and took up duties in the home.

In both urban and rural settings, women were gaining relatively more control over their lives. Marriages arranged by one's parents were less common, and some women elected to have fewer children. Nevertheless, legal restrictions on women remained. For example, they could not vote.

Economic and Social Mobility Real wages improved for most urban workers in the early 1800s, but the gap between the very wealthy and the very poor increased. Social mobility (moving upward in income level and social status) did occur from one generation to the next, and economic opportunities in the United States were greater than in Europe. Extreme examples of poor, hard-working people becoming millionaires, however, were rare.

Slavery At the outset of the 19th century, many people throughout the nation believed and hoped that slavery would gradually disappear. They thought that the exhaustion of soil in the coastal lands of Virginia and the Carolinas and the constitutional ban on the importation of slaves after 1808 would make slavery economically unfeasible. However, the rapid growth of the cotton industry and the expansion of slavery into new states such as Alabama and Mississippi ended hopes for a quiet end to slavery. As the arguments over the Missouri Compromise suggested, the slavery issue defied easy answers.

Population of Enslaved African Americans			
	1800	1830	1860
New York	20,613	75	0
Maryland	106,635	102,994	87,189
Virginia	346,671	469,767	490,865
Georgia	59,699	217,531	462,198
Alabama	-----	117,549	435,080
Mississippi	-----	65,659	436,631
Arkansas	-----	4,576	111,115
All States	893,605	2,009,043	3,953,760

Source: State-level data from Historical Census Browser from the University of Virginia, Geospatial and Statistical Data Center. Data drawn from the U.S. Census

---

HISTORICAL PERSPECTIVES: WHAT LED TO THE MONROE DOCTRINE?

The Monroe Doctrine is an example of where historians agree on the basic facts—the words of the document and the events that led up to it—but disagree on the interpretation of them. They disagree on (1) who was chiefly responsible for the Monroe Doctrine, (2) what its primary purpose was, and (3) the extent to which it was influenced by British diplomacy.

Some historians argue that the original inspiration for the doctrine came from Thomas Jefferson, while others attribute the astute thinking of Secretary of State John Quincy Adams. Those crediting Jefferson with the policy of nonintervention in the Western Hemisphere point to his idea of the political world falling into "two spheres," one European and the other American. Those stressing the key role played by John Quincy Adams argue that Adams (1) had consistently opposed further colonization by a European power and (2) had written the original draft of Monroe's message to Congress containing the doctrine. Other historians say that, regardless of the roots of the doctrine, Monroe himself deserves the real credit for having made the policy choice and issuing the doctrine.

A second area of contention concerns the real purpose behind the doctrine. Was it aimed primarily, as some historians argue, at stopping the territorial ambitions of Spain, France, and Russia? In the early 1820s, France was threatening to reconquer Spanish colonies in South America, and Russia was advancing southward from Alaska toward the California coast. A contrary view is that Monroe and Adams were chiefly concerned

continued

about sending a message to Great Britain. Not only was Britain the dominant seapower in 1823, but it was also regarded with suspicion as a traditional foe of American liberty.

A third question revolves around the role of British Foreign Secretary George Canning, whose suggestion for a joint Anglo-U.S. communiqué against the restoration of the Spanish colonies precipitated President Monroe's declaration. Historians disagree about Canning's motivation for suggesting the communiqué. Was he more concerned with protecting British political interests by attempting to block a European alliance? Or was he chiefly concerned with cultivating U.S.-British economic cooperation so as to lower U.S. tariff barriers and promote British trading interests?

Historians also disagree on the impact of the Monroe Doctrine. They take conflicting positions on Latin Americans' perception of U.S. policy and on the influence of the doctrine on U.S. policy in the second half of the 20th century. Amassing facts is just the start of a historian's task. Equally important is applying critical thought and analysis.

KEY TERMS BY THEME

Public Confidence (NAT)
Era of Good Feelings
sectionalism
James Monroe
cultural nationalism
economic nationalism

Industry (WXT)
Tariff of 1816
protective tariff
Henry Clay; American System
Second Bank of the United States
Panic of 1819
Lancaster Turnpike
National (Cumberland) Road

Erie Canal
Robert Fulton; steamboats
railroads
Eli Whitney; interchangeable parts
corporations
Samuel Slater
factory system
Lowell System; textile mills
industrialization
specialization
unions
cotton gin
market revolution

Making the Law (POL)
John Marshall
Fletcher v. Peck
McCulloch v. Maryland
Dartmouth College v. Woodward
Gibbons v. Ogden
implied powers
Tallmadge Amendment
Missouri Compromise (1820)

Foreign Affairs (WOR)
Stephen Decatur
Rush-Bagot Agreement (1817)
Treaty of 1818
Andrew Jackson
Florida Purchase Treaty (1819)
Monroe Doctrine (1823)

MULTIPLE-CHOICE QUESTIONS

Questions 1–3 refer to the excerpt below.

"The only encouragements we hold out to strangers are a good climate, fertile soil, wholesome air and water, plenty of provisions, good pay for labor, kind neighbors, good laws, a free government, and a hearty welcome. The rest depends on a man's own industry and virtue."

"If a European has previously resolved to go to the western country near the Allegheny or Ohio rivers, . . . a few day journey will bring him to Cumberland . . . from whence the public road begun by the United States, crosses the mountains. . . .

"You will, however, observe that the privilege of citizenship is not granted without proper precautions; to secure that, while the worthy are admitted, the unworthy should, if practicable, be rejected. You will from hence deduce the importance of good moral habits, even to the acquisition of political rights."

—Clements Burleigh, Shamrock Society of New York,
"Advice to Emigrants to America," 1817

1. Which phrase by Burleigh best addresses the motives of the largest number of immigrants coming to the United States during the years from 1816 to 1848?

   (A) "a good climate"

   (B) "good pay for labor"

   (C) "kind neighbors"

   (D) "a hearty welcome"

2. In the two decades following Burleigh's comments, the portions of the United States most affected by immigration were the

   (A) rural areas in the Northeast

   (B) states with large plantations

   (C) lands west of the Appalachian Mountains

   (D) cities in territories that were not yet states

3. Which of the following reinforced the message that Burleigh was sending to people who wanted to move to America?

   (A) American System

   (B) Industrialization

   (C) Protective tariff

   (D) Rush-Bagot Agreement

Questions 4–6 refer to the excerpt below.

"With the existing colonies or dependencies of any European power we have not interfered and shall not interfere. But with the governments who have declared their independence and maintained it, and whose independence we have acknowledged, we could not view any interposition for the purpose of oppressing them, or controlling . . . by any European power in any other light than as the manifestation of an unfriendly disposition toward the United States. . . .

"Our policy in regard to Europe . . . which is not to interfere in the internal concerns of any of its powers . . . but in regard to those continents [the Americas], circumstances are eminently and conspicuously different. It is impossible that the allied powers should extend their political system to any portion of either continent without endangering our peace and happiness; nor can anyone believe that our southern brethren if left to themselves, would adopt it of their own accord."

—James Monroe, The Monroe Doctrine, 1823

4. Who of the following provided the strongest influence on President Monroe in the writing of the Monroe Doctrine?

   (A) George Washington

   (B) John Adams

   (C) Thomas Jefferson

   (D) John Quincy Adams

5. Monroe counted on which of the following European nations to be an ally if any nation challenged the Monroe Doctrine?

   (A) Britain, because it opposed the strengthening of its European rivals

   (B) France, because it was frequently an ally of the United States

   (C) Russia, because it feared the resurgence of a powerful France

   (D) Spain, because it had long-standing claims in the Americas

6. Which best explains why the American people were so supportive of the Monroe Doctrine?

   (A) Nationalism

   (B) Sectionalism

   (C) States' rights

   (D) Dislike of Britain

Questions 7–8 refer to the chart below.

Vote in the U.S. House of Representatives on a Bill to Fund Internal Improvements, 1824		
Region	**For**	**Against**
New England	12	26
Middle States	37	26
West	43	0
South	23	34
Total	115	86

Source: Jeffrey B. Morris and Richard B. Morris, editors. *Encyclopedia of American History*

7. Based on the voting patterns shown in the chart, support for federal funding for internal improvements was strongest in

    (A) agricultural regions

    (B) undeveloped regions

    (C) regions where slavery was strong

    (D) regions where the Federalist party had been strong

8. Support for the bill would have been consistent with support for which of the following?

    (A) American System

    (B) Cultural nationalism

    (C) Specialization

    (D) Factory system

Use complete sentences; an outline or bulleted list alone is not acceptable.

Question 1 is based on the following excerpts.

"Whatever its [the Monroe Doctrine] reception, neither Monroe nor Adams could claim full credit for a policy that had been evolving for some years. . . . Both Jefferson and Madison advised fuller cooperation with Great Britain than Monroe may have implied when he told them he was inclined 'to meet' Canning's proposal. From the outset Monroe made clear his opposition to any course that had the appearance of subordination to Great Britain. . . .

"That Monroe proceeded cautiously to his final decision is evident from the prolonged cabinet meetings... The influence of the secretary of state on the final outcome was significant, but it was Monroe who conducted the unrestrained cabinet deliberations and drafted—and redrafted—his message to Congress until he found a policy that he and his cabinet could support. While Adams influenced the content, it was Monroe who decided to announce the policy in his message to Congress, thus proclaiming it to the world."

—Noble E. Cunningham, historian, *The Presidency of James Monroe,* 1996

"He [Adams] long imagined a United States someday coterminous with the continent. . . . 'And is it not time,' he told a congressman, 'for the American Nations to inform the sovereigns of Europe, that the American continents are no longer open to the settlement of new European colonies?' That was the first formulation of what later became known as the Monroe Doctrine. . . .

"In heated cabinet discussions Adams persuaded Monroe to make a declaration along Canning's lines, but to do so unilaterally. Monroe missed the point. His draft declaration condemning European intervention in the Americas included rebukes. . . . Adams patiently explained the United States might persuade European courts not to interfere in the New World only by assuring them the United States would not interfere in the Old World. Any American crusade against monarchy and imperialism, even if confined to rhetoric, would place U.S. national interests in gratuitous peril. . . When Monroe made Adams' text the highlight of his December 2, 1823, message to Congress, Americans cheered as one."

— Walter A. McDougall, historian, *Freedom Just Around the Corner,* 2004

1. Using the excerpts, answer (A), (B), and (C).

   (A) Briefly explain ONE major difference between Cunningham's and McDougall's historical interpretations of how the Monroe Doctrine was developed.

   (B) Briefly explain how ONE historical event or development in the period 1800 to 1823 that is not explicitly mentioned in the excerpts could be used to support Cunningham's interpretation.

   (C) Briefly explain how ONE historical event or development in the period 1800 to 1823 that is not explicitly mentioned in the excerpts could be used to support McDougall's interpretation.

Question 2. Answer (A), (B), and (C).

   (A) Briefly explain ONE of the specific parts of Henry Clay's proposed American System, a comprehensive plan to bring about economic improvement.

   (B) Briefly explain the specific support by ONE individual or group that favored Henry Clay's plan for an American System.

   (C) Briefly explain the specific criticism by ONE individual or group that opposed Henry Clay's plan for an American System.

Question 3. Answer (A), (B), and (C).

   (A) Briefly explain ONE historical event or development that had an impact on the growth of manufacturing in the period 1790 to 1848.

   (B) Briefly explain ONE historical event or development in transportation that had an impact on the industrial growth in the period 1790 to 1848.

   (C) Briefly explain how ONE section of the country experienced industrial growth different from other sections of the country in the period 1790 to 1848.

Question 4 is based on the following excerpt.

"The Accounts . . . given . . . of the depredations committed by bankers will make you suppose that affairs are much deranged here. . . .

"The money in circulation is puzzling to traders, and more particularly to strangers; for besides the multiplicity of banks, and the diversity in supposed value, fluctuations are so frequent and so great that no man who holds it in his possession can be safe for a day. . . . "Trade is stagnated, produce cheap, and merchants find it difficult to lay in assortments of foreign manufactures. . . . Agriculture languishes—farmers cannot find profit in hiring laborers. . . . Laborers and mechanics are in want of employment. . . . The operations of bankers and the recent decline in trade have been effective causes of poverty."

—James Flint, visitor from Scotland, *Flint's Letters from America,*
May 4, 1820

4. Using the excerpt, answer (A), (B), and (C).

   (A) Briefly explain ONE specific impact felt by people during the Panic described in the excerpt.

   (B) Briefly explain ONE historical event or development that was a primary cause of the Panic described in the excerpt.

   (C) Briefly explain ONE specific action recommended in response to the causes of the Panic.

THINK AS A HISTORIAN: QUESTIONS ABOUT INTERPRETATION

Which TWO of these prompts asks for an essay that emphasizes the forces shaping how historians interpret the past?

1. Explain why two historians might disagree about the federal government's role in economic changes between 1816 and 1824.

2. Describe two ways historians have viewed the Monroe Doctrine's purpose.

3. Analyze why the Era of Good Feelings ended so quickly.

9

SECTIONALISM, 1820–1860

The East, the West, the North, and the stormy South all combine to throw the whole ocean into commotion, to toss its billows to the skies, and to disclose its profoundest depths.

Daniel Webster, March 7, 1850

In 1826, Americans took great pride in celebrating 50 years of independence. A unique political system based on a written Constitution had proven practical and flexible enough to permit territorial growth and industrial change. The United States had both a central government and a collection of self-governing states. However, many citizens resisted giving up powers to a national government and the first two political parties, the Federalists and the Democratic-Republicans, had expressed strong regional differences. In short, although the United States was young and vibrant in the 1820s, it was still a fragile union.

The previous chapter treated the nation as a whole in the early 1800s; this chapter looks at the differences among the three sections—North, South, and West. Daniel Webster, in the opening quotation of this chapter, rhetorically refers to these three sections in terms of the four main points of the compass as he attempts to portray the dangers these divisions hold for the nation. By examining sectional differences, we can better understand the sectionalism (loyalty to a particular region) that ultimately led to the Union's worst crisis: civil war between the North and the South in the early 1860s.

The North

The northern portion of the country in the early 19th century contained two parts: (1) the Northeast, which included New England and the Middle Atlantic states, and (2) the Old Northwest, which stretched from Ohio to Minnesota. The northern states were bound together by transportation routes and rapid economic growth based on commercial farming and industrial innovation. While manufacturing was expanding, the vast majority of northerners were still involved in agriculture. The North was the most populous section in the country as a result of both a high birthrate and increased immigration.

The Industrial Northeast

Originally, the Industrial Revolution centered in the textile industry, but by the 1830s, northern factories were producing a wide range of goods—everything from farm implements to clocks and shoes.

Organized Labor Industrial development meant that large numbers of people who had once earned their living as independent farmers and artisans became dependent on wages earned in a factory. With the common problems of low pay, long hours, and unsafe working conditions, urban workers in different cities organized both unions and local political parties to protect their interests. The first U.S. labor party, founded in Philadelphia in 1828, succeeded in electing a few members of the city council. For a brief period in the 1830s, an increasing number of urban workers joined unions and participated in strikes.

Organized labor achieved one notable victory in 1842 when the Massachusetts Supreme Court ruled in *Commonwealth v. Hunt* that "peaceful unions" had the right to negotiate labor contracts with employers. During the 1840s and 1850s, most state legislatures in the North passed laws establishing a ten-hour workday for industrial workers. Improvement for workers, however, continued to be limited by (1) periodic depressions, (2) employers and courts that were hostile to unions, and (3) an abundant supply of cheap immigrant labor.

Urban Life The North's urban population grew from approximately 5 percent of the population in 1800 to 15 percent by 1850. As a result of such rapid growth in cities from Boston to Baltimore, slums also expanded. Crowded housing, poor sanitation, infectious diseases, and high rates of crime soon became characteristic of large working-class neighborhoods. Nevertheless, the new opportunities in cities offered by the Industrial Revolution continued to attract both native-born Americans from farms and immigrants from Europe.

U.S. Manufacturing by Region, 1860			
Region	Number of Establishments	Number of Employees	Value of Product
North Atlantic	69,831	900,107	$1,213,897,518
Old Northwest	33,335	188,651	$346,675,290
South	27,779	166,803	$248,090,580
West	8,777	50,204	$71,229,989

Source: U.S. Bureau of the Census. *Manufactures of the United States in 1860*

African Americans The 250,000 African Americans who lived in the North in 1860 constituted only 1 percent of northerners. However, they represented 50 percent of all free African Americans. Freedom may have meant they could maintain a family and in some instances own land, but it did not mean economic or political equality, since strong racial prejudices kept them from voting and holding jobs in most skilled professions and crafts. In the mid-1800s, immigrants displaced them from occupations and jobs that they had held since the time of the Revolution. Denied membership in unions, African Americans were often hired as strikebreakers—and often dismissed after the strike ended.

The Agricultural Northwest

The Old Northwest consisted of six states west of the Alleghenies that were admitted to the Union before 1860: Ohio (1803), Indiana (1816), Illinois (1818), Michigan (1837), Wisconsin (1848), and Minnesota (1858). These states came from territories formed out of land ceded to the national government in the 1780s by one of the original 13 states. The procedure for turning these territories into states was part of the Northwest Ordinance, passed by Congress in 1787.

In the early years of the 19th century, much of the Old Northwest was unsettled frontier, and the part of it that was settled relied upon the Mississippi to transport grain to southern markets via New Orleans. By mid-century, however, this region became closely tied to the other northern states by two factors: (1) military campaigns by federal troops that drove American Indians from the land and (2) the building of canals and railroads that established common markets between the Great Lakes and the East Coast.

Agriculture In the states of the Old Northwest, crops of corn and wheat were very profitable. Using the newly invented steel plow (by John Deere) and mechanical reaper (by Cyrus McCormick), a farm family was more efficient and could plant more acres, needing to supplement its labor only with a few hired workers at harvest time. Part of the crop was used to feed cattle and hogs and also to supply distillers and brewers with grain for making whiskey and beer. Farmers shipped grain quickly to cities to avoid spoilage.

New Cities At key transportation points, small villages and towns grew into thriving cities after 1820: Buffalo, Cleveland, Detroit, and Chicago on the Great Lakes, Cincinnati on the Ohio River, and St. Louis on the Mississippi River. The cities served as transfer points, processing farm products for shipment to the East, and distributing manufactured goods from the East to their region.

Immigration

In 1820, about 8,000 immigrants arrived from Europe, but beginning in 1832, there was a sudden increase. After that year, the number of new arrivals never fell below 50,000 a year and in one year, 1854, climbed as high as 428,000. From the 1830s through the 1850s, nearly 4 million people from northern Europe crossed the Atlantic to seek a new life in the United States. Arriving by ship in the northern seacoast cities of Boston, New York, and Philadelphia, many immigrants remained where they landed, while others traveled to farms and cities of the Old Northwest. Few journeyed to the South, where the plantation economy and slavery limited the opportunities for free labor.

The surge in immigration between 1830 and 1860 was chiefly the result of: (1) the development of inexpensive and relatively rapid ocean transportation, (2) famines and revolutions in Europe that drove people from their homelands, and (3) the growing reputation of the United States as a country offering economic opportunities and political freedom. The immigrants strengthened the U.S. economy by providing both a steady stream of inexpensive labor and an increased demand for mass-produced consumer goods.

Irish During this period, half of all the immigrants—almost 2 million— came from Ireland. These Irish immigrants were mostly tenant farmers driven from their homeland by potato crop failures and a devastating famine in the 1840s. They arrived with limited interest in farming, few special skills, and little money. They faced strong discrimination because of their Roman Catholic religion. The Irish worked hard at whatever employment they could find, usually competing with African Americans for domestic work and unskilled laborer jobs. Faced with limited opportunities, they congregated for mutual support in the northern cities (Boston, Philadelphia, and New York) where they had first landed. Many Irish entered local politics. They organized their fellow immigrants and joined the Democratic party, which had long traditions of anti-British feelings and support for workers. Their progress was difficult but steady. For example, the Irish were initially excluded from joining New York City's Democratic organization, Tammany Hall. But by the 1850s they had secured jobs and influence, and by the 1880s they controlled this party organization.

Germans Both economic hardships and the failure of democratic revolutions in 1848 caused more than 1 million Germans to seek refuge in the United States in the late 1840s and the 1850s. Most German immigrants had at least modest means as well as considerable skills as farmers and artisans. Moving westward in search of cheap, fertile farmland, they established homesteads throughout the Old Northwest and generally prospered. At first their political influence was limited. As they became more active in public life, many strongly supported public education and staunchly opposed slavery.

Nativists Many native-born Americans were alarmed by the influx of immigrants, fearing that the newcomers would take their jobs and also subvert (weaken) the culture of the Anglo majority. The nativists (those reacting most strongly against the foreigners) were Protestants who distrusted the Roman Catholicism practiced by the Irish and many of the Germans. In the 1840s, opposition to immigrants led to sporadic rioting in the big cities and the organization of a secret antiforeign society, the Supreme Order of the Star-Spangled Banner. This society turned to politics in the early 1850s, nominating candidates for office as the American party, or Know-Nothing party (see Chapter 13).

Antiforeign feeling faded in importance as North and South divided over slavery prior to the Civil War. However, nativism would periodically return when enough native-born citizens felt threatened by a sudden increase in immigration.

The South

The states that permitted slavery formed a distinctive region, the South. By 1861, the region included 15 states, all but four of which (Delaware, Maryland, Kentucky, and Missouri) seceded and joined the Confederacy.

Agriculture and King Cotton

Agriculture was the foundation of the South's economy, even though by the 1850s small factories in the region were producing approximately 15 percent of the nation's manufactured goods. Tobacco, rice, and sugarcane were important cash crops, but these were far exceeded by the South's chief economic activity: the production and sale of cotton.

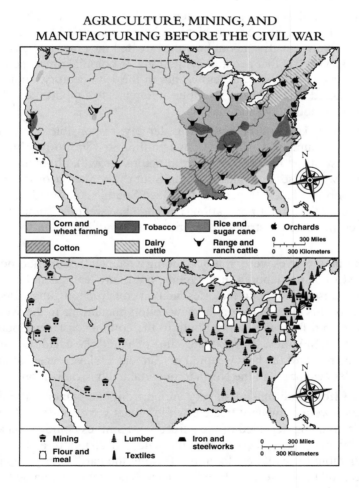

AGRICULTURE, MINING, AND
MANUFACTURING BEFORE THE CIVIL WAR

The development of mechanized textile mills in England, coupled with Eli Whitney's cotton gin, made cotton cloth affordable, not just in Europe and the United States, but throughout the world. Before 1860, the world depended chiefly on Britain's mills for its supply of cloth, and Britain in turn depended chiefly on the American South for its supply of cotton fiber. Originally, the cotton was grown almost entirely in two states, South Carolina and Georgia, but as demand and profits increased, planters moved westward into Alabama, Mississippi, Louisiana, and Texas. New land was constantly needed, for the high cotton yields required for profits quickly depleted the soil. By the 1850s, cotton provided two-thirds of all U.S. exports and linked the South and Great Britain. "Cotton is king," said one southerner of his region's greatest asset.

Slavery, the "Peculiar Institution"

Wealth in the South was measured in terms of land and slaves. The latter were treated as a form of property, subject to being bought and sold. However, some whites were sensitive about how they treated the other humans that they referred to slavery as "that peculiar institution." In colonial times, people justified slavery as an economic necessity, but in the 19th century, apologists for slavery mustered historical and religious arguments to support their claim that it was good for both slave and master.

Population The cotton boom was largely responsible for a fourfold increase in the number of slaves, from 1 million in 1800 to nearly 4 million in 1860. Most of the increase came from natural growth, although thousands of Africans were also smuggled into the South in violation of the 1808 law against importing slaves. In parts of the Deep South, slaves made up as much as 75 percent of the total population. Fearing slave revolts, southern legislatures added increased restrictions on movement and education to their slave codes.

Economics Slaves were employed doing whatever their owners demanded of them. Most slaves labored in the fields, but many learned skilled crafts or worked as house servants, in factories, and on construction gangs. Because of the greater profits to be made on the new cotton plantations in the West, many slaves were sold from the Upper South to the cotton-rich Deep South of the lower Mississippi Valley. By 1860, the value of a field slave had risen to almost $2,000. One result of the heavy capital investment in slaves was that the South had much less capital than the North to undertake industrialization.

Slave Life Conditions of slavery varied from one plantation to the next. Some slaves were humanely treated, while others were routinely beaten. All suffered from being deprived of their freedom. Families could be separated at any time by an owner's decision to sell a wife, a husband, or a child. Women were vulnerable to sexual exploitation. Despite the hard, nearly hopeless circumstances of their lives, enslaved African Americans maintained a strong sense of family and of religious faith.

United States Labor Force, 1800–1860 (in millions)			
Year	Free	Slave	Total
1800	1.4	0.5	1.9
1810	1.6	0.7	2.3
1820	2.1	1.0	3.1
1830	3.0	1.2	4.2
1840	4.2	1.5	5.7
1850	6.3	2.0	8.3
1860	8.8	2.3	11.1

Source: U.S. Bureau of the Census. *Historical Statistics of the United States, Colonial Times to 1970*

Resistance Slaves contested their status through a range of actions, primarily work slowdowns, sabotage, and escape. In addition, there were a few major slave uprisings. One was led by Denmark Vesey in 1822 and another by Nat Turner in 1831. The revolts were quickly and violently suppressed, but even so, they had a lasting impact. They gave hope to enslaved African Americans, drove southern states to tighten already strict slave codes, and demonstrated to many the evils of slavery. Revolts polarized the country by making slaveholders more defensive about slavery and nonslaveholders more critical of the institution.

Free African Americans

By 1860, as many as 250,000 African Americans in the South were not slaves. They were free citizens (even though, as in the North, racial prejudice restricted their liberties). A number of slaves had been emancipated during the American Revolution. Some were mulatto children whose white fathers had decided to liberate them. Others achieved freedom on their own, when permitted, through self-purchase—if they were fortunate enough to have been paid wages for extra work, usually as skilled craftspeople.

Most of the free southern blacks lived in cities where they could own property. By state law, they were not equal with whites, were not permitted to vote, and were barred from entering certain occupations. Constantly in danger of being kidnapped by slave traders, they had to show legal papers proving their free status. They remained in the South for various reasons. Some wanted to be near family members who were still in bondage; others believed the South to be home and the North to offer no greater opportunities.

White Society

Southern whites observed a rigid hierarchy among themselves. Aristocratic planters lived comfortably at the top of society while poor farmers and mountain people struggled at the bottom.

Aristocracy Members of the South's small elite of wealthy planters owned at least 100 slaves and at least 1,000 acres. The planter aristocracy maintained its power by dominating the state legislatures of the South and enacting laws that favored the large landholders' economic interests.

Farmers The vast majority of slaveholders owned fewer than 20 slaves and worked only several hundred acres. Southern white farmers produced the bulk of the cotton crop, worked in the fields with their slaves, and lived as modestly as farmers of the North.

Poor Whites Three-fourths of the South's white population owned no slaves. They could not afford the rich river-bottom farmland controlled by the planters, and many lived in the hills as subsistence farmers. These "hillbillies" or "poor white trash," as they were derisively called by the planters, defended the slave system, thinking that some day they too could own slaves and that at least they were superior on the social scale to someone (slaves).

Mountain People A number of small farmers lived in frontier conditions in isolation from the rest of the South, along the slopes and valleys of the Appalachian and Ozark mountains. The mountain people disliked the planters and their slaves. During the Civil War, many (including a future president, Andrew Johnson of Tennessee) would remain loyal to the Union.

Cities Because the South was primarily an agricultural region, there was only a limited need for major cities. New Orleans was the only southern city among the nation's 15 largest in 1860 (it was fifth, after New York, Philadelphia, Baltimore, and Boston). Cities such as Atlanta, Charleston, Chattanooga, and Richmond were important trading centers, but had relatively small populations in comparison to those of the North.

Southern Thought

The South developed a unique culture and outlook on life. As cotton became the basis of its economy, slavery became the focus of its political thought. White southerners felt increasingly isolated and defensive about slavery, as northerners grew hostile toward it, and as Great Britain, France, and other European nations outlawed it altogether.

Code of Chivalry Dominated by the aristocratic planter class, the agricultural South was largely a feudal society. Southern gentlemen ascribed to a code of chivalrous conduct, which included a strong sense of personal honor, the defense of womanhood, and paternalistic attitudes toward all who were deemed inferior, especially slaves.

Education The upper class valued a college education for their children. Acceptable professions for gentlemen were limited to farming, law, the ministry, and the military. For the lower classes, schooling beyond the early elementary grades was generally not available. To reduce the risk of slave revolts, slaves were strictly prohibited by law from receiving any instruction in reading and writing.

Religion The slavery question affected church membership. Partly because they preached biblical support for slavery, both Methodist and Baptist churches gained in membership in the South while splitting in the 1840s with their northern brethren. The Unitarians, who challenged slavery, faced declining membership and hostility. Catholics and Episcopalians took a neutral stand on slavery, and their numbers declined in the South.

The West

As the United States expanded westward, the definition of the "West" kept changing. In the 1600s, the West referred to all the lands not along the Atlantic Coast. In the 1700s, the West meant lands on the other side of the Appalachian Mountains. By the mid-1800s, the West lay beyond the Mississippi River and reached to California and the Oregon Territory on the Pacific Coast.

American Indians

The original settlers of the West—and the entire North American continent—were various groups of American Indians. However, from the time of Columbus, American Indians were cajoled, pushed, or driven westward as white settlers encroached on their original homelands.

Exodus By 1850, the vast majority of American Indians were living west of the Mississippi River. Those to the east had either been killed by disease, died in battles, emigrated reluctantly, or been forced to leave their land by treaty or military action. The Great Plains, however, would provide only a temporary respite from conflict with white settlers.

Life on the Plains Horses, brought to America by the Spanish in the 1500s, revolutionized life for American Indians on the Great Plains. Some tribes continued to live in villages and farm, but the horse allowed tribes such as the Cheyenne and the Sioux to become nomadic hunters following the buffalo. Those living a nomadic way of life could more easily move away from advancing settlers or oppose their encroachments by force.

The Frontier

Although the location of the western frontier constantly shifted, the *concept* of the frontier remained the same from generation to generation. The same forces that had brought the original colonists to the Americas motivated their descendants and new immigrants to move westward. In the public imagination, the West represented the possibility of a fresh start for those willing to venture there. If not in fact, at least in theory and myth, the West beckoned as a place promising greater freedom for all ethnic groups: American Indians, African Americans, European Americans, and eventually Asian Americans as well.

Mountain Men From the point of view of white Americans, the Rocky Mountains in the 1820s were a far-distant frontier—a total wilderness except for American Indian villages. The earliest whites in the area had followed Lewis and Clark and explored American Indian trails as they trapped for furs.

These mountain men, as they were called, served as the guides and pathfinders for settlers crossing the mountains into California and Oregon in the 1840s. (See Chapter 12.)

White Settlers on the Western Frontier

Whether the frontier lay in Minnesota or Oregon or California in the 1840s and 1850s, daily life for white settlers was similar to that of the early colonists. They worked hard from sunrise to sunset and lived in log cabins, sod huts, or other improvised shelters. Disease and malnutrition were far greater dangers than attacks by American Indians.

Women Often living many miles from the nearest neighbor, pioneer women performed myriad daily tasks, including those of doctor, teacher, seamstress, and cook—as well as chief assistant in the fields to their farmer-husbands. The isolation, endless work, and rigors of childbirth resulted in a short lifespan for frontier women.

Environmental Damage Settlers had little understanding of the fragile nature of land and wildlife. As settlers moved into an area, they would clear entire forests and after only two generations exhaust the soil with poor farming methods. At the same time, trappers and hunters brought the beaver and the buffalo to the brink of extinction.

Population by Region, 1820 to 1860			
Region	1820	1840	1860
Northeast: Maine, New Hampshire, Vermont, Massachusetts, Rhode Island, Connecticut, New York, New Jersey, Pennsylvania	4,360,000	6,761,000	10,594,000
North Central: Ohio, Indiana, Illinois, Michigan, Wisconsin, Minnesota, Iowa, Missouri, North Dakota, South Dakota, Nebraska, Kansas	859,000	3,352,000	9,097,000
South: Delaware, Maryland, Washington DC, Virginia, North Carolina, South Carolina, Georgia, Florida, Kentucky, Tennessee, Alabama, Mississippi, Arkansas, Louisiana, Oklahoma, Texas	4,419,000	6,951,000	11,133,000
West: Colorado, New Mexico, Nevada, Utah, Washington, Oregon, California	-----	-----	619,000
All States	9,618,000	17,120,000	31,513,000

Source: U.S. Bureau of the Census. *Historical Statistics of the United States, Colonial Times to 1970.* All figures rounded to the nearest thousand.

Slavery was of fundamental importance in defining both the character of the South and its differences with the North. Until about 1950, the prevailing scholarship on slavery followed Ulrich Phillips' *American Negro Slavery* (1918). Phillips portrayed slavery as an economically failing institution in which the paternalistic owners were civilizing the inferior but contented African Americans. Later historians challenged Phillips' thesis by showing slaves and owners to be in continual conflict. Today the older view of slavery as a paternalistic and even benign institution has been discredited.

The newer views were summarized by Kenneth Stampp in *The Peculiar Institution: Slavery in the Ante-Bellum South* (1956). Stampp acknowledged that the civil rights movement of the 1950s and 1960s stimulated many of the new interpretations: "There is a strange paradox in the historian's involvement with both present and past, for his knowledge of the present is clearly a key to his understanding of the past."

Historians continue to debate how destructive slavery was. Some have argued that the oppressive and racist nature of slavery destroyed the culture and self-respect of the slaves and their descendants. In contrast, others have concluded that slaves managed to adapt and to overcome their hardships by developing a unique African American culture focused around religion and extended families.

Economics has also provided a focus for viewing the nature of slavery. Historians have debated whether slave labor was profitable to southern planters, as compared to using free labor. Unlike Phillips, many historians have demonstrated that slavery was generally profitable. A more complex analysis of the economics, social, and cultural nature of slavery is found in Eugene Genovese's *Roll, Jordan, Roll: The World the Slaves Made.* In this work, southern society is shown centered on a paternalism that gave rise to a unique social system with a clear hierarchy, in which people were classified according to their ability or their economic and social standing. For whites this paternalism meant control, while for slaves it provided the opportunity to develop and maintain their own culture, including family life, tradition, and religion.

Recently, historians have focused more on regional variations in slavery. For example, compared to slaves on South Carolina rice plantations, slaves on Virginia tobacco planations lived longer lives, worked in smaller groups, and had more contact with whites. In South Carolina, slaves kept stronger ties to their African heritage.

The changing interpretations of slavery since the early 1900s reflect changing attitudes toward race and culture. While all interpretations do not seem equally accurate today, each provides readers a perspective to consider as they develop their own views.

KEY TERMS BY THEME

Identities & Conflict (ARC)
Northeast
Old Northwest
sectionalism
Free African Americans
planters
Codes of Chivalry
poor whites
hillbillies
mountain men
the West
the frontier

Conflict (NAT)
Nativists
AmericaSupreme Order
   of the Star-Spangled
   Banner
Know-Nothing Party
n party

Migration (NAT, MIG)
Deep South
American Indian removal
Great Plains
white settlers

Urban Growth (MIG)
urbanization
urban life
new cities
Irish; potato famine
Roman Catholic
Tammany Hall
Germans
Old Northwest
immigration

The Slave Industry (MIG, WXT)
King Cotton
Eli Whitney
"peculiar institution"
Denmark Vesey
Nat Turner
slave codes
Code of Chivalry

Industry & Problems (WXT)
Industrial Revolution
unions
Commonwealth v. Hunt
ten-hour workday
Cyrus McCormick
John Deere

Changing Politics (POL)
Daniel Webster
Tammany Hall

Ignorance (GEO)
environmental damage
extinction

Questions 1–3 refer to the excerpt below.

"We, the journeyman mechanics of the city and county of Philadelphia . . . are serious of forming an association which shall avert as much as possible those evils which poverty and incessant toil have already inflicted. . . .

"If the masses of the people were enabled by their labor to procure for themselves and families a full and abundant supply of the comforts and conveniences of life, the consumption . . . would amount to at least twice the quantity it does at present, and of course the demand, by which alone employers are enabled either to subsist or accumulate, would likewise be increased in an equal proportion.

"The real object, therefore, of this association is to avert, if possible, the desolating evils which must inevitably arise from a depreciation of the intrinsic value of human labor; to raise the mechanical and productive classes to that condition of true independence and equality."

—Philadelphia Mechanics' Union of Trade Associations, 1828

1. One of the primary reasons to form a union during this period was to
   (A) improve working conditions
   (B) win a shorter work week
   (C) prevent immigration
   (D) show racial solidarity

2. Workers in the 1820s faced difficulty because of problems with
   (A) transportation
   (B) ethnic rivalries
   (C) federal laws
   (D) inventions

3. Urban workers such as the Philadelphia Mechanics' Union of Trade Associations believed they could improve their conditions through labor unions and
   (A) churches
   (B) political parties
   (C) ethnic societies
   (D) courts

Questions 4–6 refer to the excerpt below.

"The gentleman . . . has been anxious to proclaim the death of native Americanism. Sir, it is a principle that can never die . . . Native Americanism seeks to defend every institution that exists under that glorious Constitution. . . .

"But we have been told that we belong to a party of "one idea." . . . Our great object is to attain to unity of national character; and as necessary to that end, we embrace every measure and policy decidedly American . . . we go for everything American in contradistinction to everything foreign. That . . . may be called "one idea"; but it is a glorious idea. . . .

"No alien has a right to naturalization . . . To prevent this universal admission to citizenship, we frame naturalization laws, and prescribe forms that operate as a check upon the interference of foreigners in our institutions . . .

"We are now struggling for national character and national identity . . . We stand now on the very verge of overthrow by the impetuous force of invading foreigners."

—Rep. Lewis C. Levin, Speech in Congress, December 18, 1845

4. Which of the following caused the movement described in the excerpt?
   (A) War of 1812
   (B) Immigration
   (C) Importation of slaves
   (D) Naturalization laws

5. The opposition to foreigners is most similar to the view that many had toward which of the following in America at this time?
   (A) Free African Americans
   (B) Southerners
   (C) Unions
   (D) Women

6. The development of which of the following best demonstrates the growing power of the nativist movement in the mid-19th century?
   (A) A belief in nationalism
   (B) A series of restrictive laws
   (C) A secret society
   (D) A political party

Questions 7–8 refer to the excerpt below.

"At home the people are the sovereign power . . . the industrial classes are the true sovereigns. Idleness is a condition so unrecognized and unrespected with us that the few professing it find themselves immediately thrown out of the great machine of active life which constitutes American society.

"The CULTIVATORS OF THE SOIL constitute the great industrial class in this country . . . for, at this moment, they do not only feed all other classes but also no insignificant portion of needy Europe, furnish the raw material for manufactures, and raise the great staples which figure so largely in the accounts of the merchants, the shipowner and manufacturer, in every village, town, and seaport in the Union . . .

"The system of railroads and cheap transportation already begins to supply the seaboard cities with some fair and beautiful fruits of the fertile West."

—A. J. Downing, landscape architect, "In Praise of Farming," 1848

7. The crop that best fits Downing's description as one of "the great staples" in mid-19th century America was

   (A) corn

   (B) tobacco

   (C) sugar

   (D) cotton

8. The development of commercial farming in the Old Northwest by the time this excerpt was written gave support to

   (A) higher crop prices

   (B) (population growth in Eastern cities

   (C) expansion of slavery

   (D) Western settlements

SHORT-ANSWER QUESTIONS

Use complete sentences; an outline or bulleted list alone is not acceptable.

Question 1 is based on the following excerpts.
"Slaves apparently thought of the South's peculiar institution chiefly as a system of labor extortion. Of course they felt its impact in other ways—in their social status, their legal status, and their private lives—but they felt it most acutely in their lack of control of their own time and labor...

In Africa the Negroes had been accustomed to a strictly regulated family life and a rigidly enforced moral code. But in America the disintegration of their social organization removed the traditional sanctions which had encouraged them to respect their old customs. ...Here, as at so many other points, the slaves had lost their native culture without being able to find a workable substitute and therefore lived in a kind of cultural chaos...Marriage, insisted Frederick Douglass, had no existence among slaves. ...His consolation was that at least some slaves "maintained their honor, where all around was corrupt."

—Kenneth M. Stampp, historian, *The Peculiar Institution,* 1956

"We have made a great error in the way in which we have viewed slave life, and this error has been perpetuated by both whites and blacks, racists and antiracists...

"What the sources show...is that the average plantation slave lived in a family setting, developed strong family ties, and held the nuclear family as the proper social norm. ...We do not know just how many slaves lived as a family or were willing and able to maintain a stable family life during slavery. But the number was certainly great, whatever the percentage, and as a result, the social norm that black people carried from slavery to freedom was that of the nuclear family....There are moments in the history of every people–in which they cannot do more than succeed in keeping themselves together and maintaining themselves as human beings with a sense of individual dignity and collective identity. Slavery was such a moment for black people in America."

—Eugene Genovese, historian, *American Slaves and Their History,*
1971

1. Using the excerpts, answer (A), (B), and (C).
    (A) Briefly explain ONE major difference between Stampp's and Genovese's historical interpretations of the nature of slavery.
    (B) Briefly explain how ONE historical event or development in the period 1820 to 1860 that is not explicitly mentioned in the excerpts that could be used to support Stampp's interpretation.
    (C) Briefly explain how ONE historical event or development in the period 1820 to 1860 that is not explicitly mentioned in the excerpts that could be used to support Genovese's interpretation.

Question 2.   Answer (A), (B), and (C).

(A) Briefly explain ONE historical event or development that influenced the westward movement from the original Atlantic colonies.

(B) Briefly explain ONE specific factor in the period 1820 to 1860 that resulted in the rapid development of the Old Northwest.

(C) Briefly explain how ONE specific group of Americans in the period 1820 to 1860 did not benefit from the westward movement.

Question 3.   Answer (A), (B), and (C).

(A) Briefly explain ONE historical event or development in the period 1830 to 1860 that resulted in the rapid increase in immigration.

(B) Briefly explain how ONE specific nationality of immigrants who settled in America in the period 1830 to 1860 lived.

(C) Briefly explain how ONE specific group of Americans reacted negatively to the influx of immigrants.

Question 4 is based on the following excerpt.

"That a country should become eminently prosperous in agriculture, without a high state of perfection in the mechanic arts, is a thing next to impossible . . . that we should follow the footsteps of our forefathers and still further exhaust our soil by the exclusive cultivation of cotton?

"Unless we betake ourselves to some more profitable employment than the planting of cotton, what is to prevent our most enterprising planters from moving with their Negro capital, to the Southwest?

"Cotton . . . has produced us such an abundant supply of all the luxuries and elegancies of life, with so little exertion on our part, that we have become . . . unfitted for other more laborious pursuits, and unprepared to meet the state of things which sooner or later must come about."

—William Gregg, Southern manufacturer,
"Essays on Domestic Industry," 1845

4. Using the excerpt, answer (A), (B), and (C).

(A) Briefly explain ONE specific factor that contributed to the lack of manufacturing in the South during the first half of the 19th century.

(B) Briefly explain ONE specific advantage, if any, the North had over the South in developing manufacturing during the first half of the 19th century.

(C) Briefly explain ONE specific implication for the Southern economy based on Gregg's view presented in the excerpt.

THINK AS A HISTORIAN: QUESTIONS ABOUT RELATIONSHIPS AMONG EVIDENCE

Historians draw up multiple sources of information to answer a question or draw a conclusion. Which TWO of the following prompts most clearly asks for an answer that explains the relationship among different pieces of historical evidence?

1. Use statements, statistics, and an image to explain why the West was more closely tied to the North than to the South by the 1850s.

2. Who are the best examples of modern equivalents of mountain men?

3. Explain why the South was the U.S. region least like Britain but most closely tied to it.

4. Why did Southerners call slavery a "peculiar institution"?

5. What was the key ruling in *Commonwealth v. Hunt*?

10

THE AGE OF JACKSON, 1824–1844

The political activity that pervades the United States must be seen in order to be understood. No sooner do you set foot upon American ground than you are stunned by a kind of tumult.

Alexis de Tocqueville, *Democracy in America,* 1835

The era marked by the emergence of popular politics in the 1820s and the presidency of Andrew Jackson (1829–1837) is often called the Age of the Common Man, or the Era of Jacksonian Democracy. Historians debate whether Jackson was a major molder of events, a political opportunist exploiting the democratic ferment of the times, or merely a symbol of the era. Nevertheless, the era and Jackson's name seem permanently linked.

Jacksonian Democracy

The changing politics of the Jacksonian years paralleled complex social and economic changes.

The Rise of a Democratic Society

Visitors to the United States in the 1830s, such as Alexis de Tocqueville, a young French aristocrat, were amazed by the informal manners and democratic attitudes of Americans. In hotels, under the American Plan, men and women from all classes ate together at common tables. On stagecoaches, steamboats, and later in railroad cars, there was also only one class for passengers, so that the rich and poor alike sat together in the same compartments. European visitors could not distinguish between classes in the United States. Men of all backgrounds wore simple dark trousers and jackets, while less well-to-do women emulated the fanciful and confining styles illustrated in wide-circulation women's magazines like *Godey's Lady's Book.* Equality was becoming the governing principle of American society.

Among the white majority in American society, people shared a belief in the principle of equality—more precisely, equality of opportunity for white males. These beliefs ignored the oppression of enslaved African Americans and discrimination against free blacks. Equality of opportunity would, at least in theory, allow a young man of humble origins to rise as far as his natural talent and industry would take him. The hero of the age was the "self-made man."

There was no equivalent belief in the "self-made woman," but by the end of the 1840s, feminists would take up the theme of equal rights and insist that it should be applied to both women and men (see Chapter 11).

Politics of the Common Man

Between 1824 and 1840, politics moved out of the fine homes of rich southern planters and northern merchants who had dominated government in past eras and into middle- and lower-class homes. Several factors contributed to the spread of democracy, including new suffrage laws, changes in political parties and campaigns, improved education, and increases in newspaper circulation.

Universal Male Suffrage Western states newly admitted to the Union—Indiana (1816), Illinois (1818), and Missouri (1821)—adopted state constitutions that allowed all white males to vote and hold office. These newer constitutions omitted any religious or property qualifications for voting. Most eastern states soon followed suit, eliminating such restrictions. As a result, throughout the country, all white males could vote regardless of their social class or religion. Voting for president rose from about 350,000 in 1824 to more than 2.4 million in 1840, a nearly sevenfold increase in just 16 years, mostly as a result of changes in voting laws. In addition, political offices could be held by people in the lower and middle ranks of society.

Party Nominating Conventions In the past, candidates for office had commonly been nominated either by state legislatures or by "King Caucus"—a closed-door meeting of a political party's leaders in Congress. Common citizens had no opportunity to participate. In the 1830s, however, caucuses were replaced by nominating conventions. Party politicians and voters would gather in a large meeting hall to nominate the party's candidates. The Anti-Masonic party was the first to hold such a nominating convention. This method was more open to popular participation, hence more democratic.

Popular Election of the President In the presidential election of 1832, only South Carolina used the old system in which the state legislature chose the electors for president. All other states had adopted the more democratic method of allowing the voters to choose a state's slate of presidential electors.

Two-party System The popular election of presidential electors—and, in effect, the president—had important consequences for the two-party system. Campaigns for president now had to be conducted on a national scale. To organize these campaigns, candidates needed large political parties.

Rise of Third Parties While only the large national parties (the Democrats and the Whigs in Jackson's day) could hope to win the presidency, other political parties also emerged. The Anti-Masonic party and the Workingmen's party, for example, reached out to groups of people who previously had shown little interest in politics. The Anti-Masons attacked the secret societies of Masons and accused them of belonging to a privileged, antidemocratic elite.

More Elected Offices During the Jacksonian era, a much larger number of state and local officials were elected to office, instead of being appointed, as in the past. This change gave the voters more voice in their government and also tended to increase their interest in participating in elections.

Popular Campaigning Candidates for office directed their campaigns to the interests and prejudices of the common people. Politics also became a form of local entertainment. Campaigns of the 1830s and 1840s featured parades of floats and marching bands and large rallies in which voters were treated to free food and drink. The negative side to the new campaign techniques was that in appealing to the masses, candidates would often resort to personal attacks and ignore the issues. A politician, for example, might attack an opponent's "aristocratic airs" and make him seem unfriendly to "the common man."

Spoils System and Rotation of Officeholders Winning government jobs became the lifeblood of party organizations. At the national level, President Jackson believed in appointing people to federal jobs (as postmasters, for example) strictly according to whether they had actively campaigned for the Democratic party. Any previous holder of the office who was not a Democrat was fired and replaced with a loyal Democrat. This practice of dispensing government jobs in return for party loyalty was called the *spoils system* because of a comment that, in a war, victors seize the spoils, or wealth, of the defeated.

In addition, Jackson believed in a system of rotation in office. By limiting a person to one term in office he could then appoint some other deserving Democrat in his place. Jackson defended the replacement and rotation of officeholders as a democratic reform. "No man," he said, "has any more intrinsic claim to office than another." Both the spoils system and the rotation of officeholders affirmed the democratic ideal that one man was as good as another and that ordinary Americans were capable of holding any government office. These beliefs also helped build a strong two-party system.

Jackson Versus Adams

Political change in the Jacksonian era began several years before Jackson moved into the White House as president. In the controversial election in 1824, Jackson won more popular and electoral votes than any other candidate, but he ended up losing the election.

The Election of 1824

Recall the brief Era of Good Feelings that characterized U.S. politics during the two-term presidency of James Monroe. The era ended in political bad feelings in 1824, the year of a bitterly contested and divisive presidential election. By then, the old congressional caucus system for choosing presidential candidates had broken down. As a result, four candidates of the Democratic-Republican party of Jefferson campaigned for the presidency: John Quincy Adams, Henry Clay, William Crawford, and Andrew Jackson.

Among voters in states that counted popular votes (six did not) Jackson won. But because the vote was split four ways, he lacked a majority in the electoral college as required by the Constitution. Therefore, the House of Representatives had to choose a president from among the top three candidates. Henry Clay used his influence in the House to provide John Quincy Adams of Massachusetts with enough votes to win the election. When President Adams appointed Clay his secretary of state, Jackson and his followers charged that the decision of the voters had been foiled by secret political maneuvers. Angry Jackson supporters accused Adams and Clay of making a "corrupt bargain."

THE ELECTION OF 1824

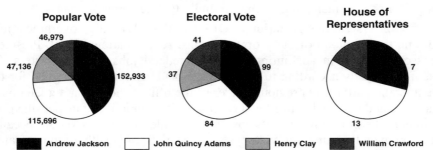

Source: Jeffrey B. Morris and Richard B. Morris, editors. *Encyclopedia of American History*

President John Quincy Adams

Adams further alienated the followers of Jackson when he asked Congress for money for internal improvements, aid to manufacturing, and even a national university and an astronomical observatory. Jacksonians viewed all these measures as a waste of money and a violation of the Constitution. Most significantly, in 1828, Congress patched together a new tariff law, which generally satisfied northern manufacturers but alienated southern planters. Southerners denounced it as a "tariff of abominations."

The Revolution of 1828

Adams sought reelection in 1828. But the Jacksonians were now ready to use the discontent of southerners and westerners and the new campaign tactics of party organization to sweep "Old Hickory" (Jackson) into office. Going beyond parades and barbecues, Jackson's party resorted to smearing the president and accusing Adams' wife of being born out of wedlock. Supporters of Adams retaliated in kind, accusing Jackson's wife of adultery. The mudslinging campaign attracted a lot of interest and voter turnout soared.

Jackson won handily, carrying every state west of the Appalachians. His reputation as a war hero and man of the western frontier accounted for his victory more than the positions he took on issues of the day.

The Presidency of Andrew Jackson

Jackson was a different kind of president from any of his predecessors. A strong leader, he not only dominated politics for eight years but also became a symbol of the emerging working class and middle class (the so-called common man). Born in a frontier cabin, Jackson gained fame as an Indian fighter and as hero of the Battle of New Orleans, and came to live in a fine mansion in Tennessee as a wealthy planter and slaveowner. But he never lost the rough manners of the frontier. He chewed tobacco, fought several duels, and displayed a violent temper. Jackson was the first president since Washington to be without a college education. In a phrase, he could be described as an extraordinary ordinary man. This self-made man and living legend drew support from every social group and every section of the country.

Presidential Power Jackson presented himself as the representative of all the people and the protector of the common man against abuses of power by the rich and the privileged. He was a frugal Jeffersonian, who opposed increasing federal spending and the national debt. Jackson interpreted the powers of Congress narrowly and therefore vetoed more bills—12—than all six preceding presidents combined. For example, he vetoed the use of federal money to construct the Maysville Road, because it was wholly within one state, Kentucky, the home state of Jackson's rival, Henry Clay.

Jackson's closest advisers were a group known as his "kitchen cabinet," who did not belong to his official cabinet. Because of them, the appointed cabinet had less influence on policy than under earlier presidents.

Peggy Eaton Affair The champion of the common man also went to the aid of the common woman, at least in the case of Peggy O'Neale Eaton. The wife of Jackson's secretary of war, she was the target of malicious gossip by other cabinet wives, much as Jackson's recently deceased wife had been in the 1828 campaign. When Jackson tried to force the cabinet wives to accept Peggy Eaton socially, most of the cabinet resigned. This controversy contributed to the resignation of Jackson's vice president, John C. Calhoun, a year later. For remaining loyal during this crisis, Martin Van Buren of New York was chosen as vice president for Jackson's second term.

Indian Removal Act (1830) Jackson's concept of democracy did not extend to American Indians. Jackson sympathized with land-hungry citizens who were impatient to take over lands held by American Indians. Jackson thought the most humane solution was to compel the American Indians to leave their traditional homelands and resettle west of the Mississippi. In 1830, he signed into law the Indian Removal Act, which forced the resettlement of many thousands of American Indians. By 1835 most eastern tribes had reluctantly complied and moved west. The Bureau of Indian Affairs was created in 1836 to assist the resettled tribes.

Most politicians supported a policy of Indian removal. Georgia and other states passed laws requiring the Cherokees to migrate to the West. When the Cherokees challenged Georgia in the courts, the Supreme Court ruled in *Cherokee Nation v. Georgia* (1831) that Cherokees were not a foreign nation with the right to sue in a federal court. But in a second case, *Worcester v. Georgia* (1832), the high court ruled that the laws of Georgia had no force within Cherokee territory. In this clash between a state's laws and the federal courts, Jackson sided with the states. The Court was powerless to enforce its decision without the President's support.

INDIAN REMOVAL IN THE 1830S

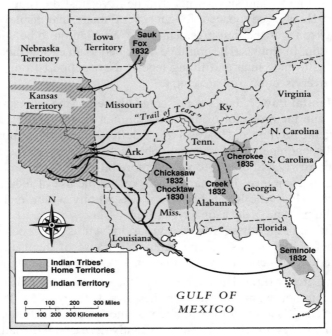

Trail of Tears Most Cherokees repudiated the settlement of 1835, which provided land in the Indian territory. In 1838, after Jackson had left office, the U.S. Army forced 15,000 Cherokees to leave Georgia. The hardships on the "trail of tears" westward caused the deaths of 4,000 Cherokees.

Nullification Crisis Jackson favored states' rights—but not disunion. In 1828, the South Carolina legislature declared the increased tariff of 1828, the so-called Tariff of Abominations, to be unconstitutional. In doing so, it affirmed a theory advanced by Jackson's first vice president, John C. Calhoun. According to this *nullification theory*, each state had the right to decide whether to obey a federal law or to declare it null and void (of no effect).

In 1830, Daniel Webster of Massachusetts debated Robert Hayne of South Carolina on the nature of the federal Union under the Constitution. Webster attacked the idea that any state could defy or leave the Union. Following this famous Webster-Hayne debate, President Jackson declared his own position in a toast he presented at a political dinner. "Our federal Union," he declared, "it must be preserved." Calhoun responded immediately with another toast: "The Union, next to our liberties, most dear!"

In 1832, Calhoun's South Carolina increased tension by holding a special convention to nullify both the hated 1828 tariff and a new tariff of 1832. The convention passed a resolution forbidding the collection of tariffs within the state. Jackson reacted decisively. He told the secretary of war to prepare for military action. He persuaded Congress to pass a Force bill giving him authority to act against South Carolina. Jackson also issued a Proclamation to the People of South Carolina, stating that nullification and disunion were treason.

But federal troops did not march in this crisis. Jackson opened the door for compromise by suggesting that Congress lower the tariff. South Carolina postponed nullification and later formally rescinded it after Congress enacted a new tariff along the lines suggested by the president.

Jackson's strong defense of federal authority forced the militant advocates of states' rights to retreat. On another issue, however, militant southerners had Jackson's support. The president shared southerners' alarm about the growing antislavery movement in the North. He used his executive power to stop antislavery literature from being sent through the U.S. mail. Southern Jacksonians trusted that Jackson would not extend democracy to African Americans.

Bank Veto Another major issue of Jackson's presidency concerned the rechartering of the Bank of the United States. This bank and its branches, although privately owned, received federal deposits and attempted to serve a public purpose by cushioning the ups and downs of the national economy. The bank's president, Nicholas Biddle, managed it effectively. Biddle's arrogance, however, contributed to the suspicion that the bank abused its powers and served the interests of only the wealthy. Jackson shared this suspicion. He believed that the Bank of the United States was unconstitutional.

Henry Clay, Jackson's chief political opponent, favored the bank. In 1832, an election year, Clay challenged Jackson by persuading a majority in Congress to pass a bank-recharter bill. Jackson promptly vetoed it, denouncing the bank as a private monopoly that enriched the wealthy and foreigners at the expense of the common people and a "hydra of corruption." The voters backed Jackson, who won reelection with more than three-fourths of the electoral vote.

The Two-Party System

The one-party system that had characterized Monroe's presidency (the Era of Good Feelings) had given way to a two-party system under Jackson. Supporters of Jackson were now known as Democrats, while supporters of his leading rival, Henry Clay, were called Whigs. The Democratic party harked back to the old Republican party of Jefferson, and the Whig party resembled the defunct Federalist party of Hamilton. At the same time, the new parties reflected the changed conditions of the Jacksonian era. Democrats and Whigs alike were challenged to respond to the relentless westward expansion of the nation and the emergence of an industrial economy.

Democrats and Whigs in the Age of Jackson		
	Democrats	**Whigs**
Issues Supported	• Local rule • Limited government • Free trade • Opportunity for white males	American System: • national bank • Federal funds for internal improvements • A protective tariff
Major Concerns	• Monopolies • National bank • High tariffs • High land prices	• Crime associated with immigrants
Base of Voter Support	• The South and West • Urban workers	• New England and the Mid-Atlantic states • Protestants of English heritage • Urban professionals

Jackson's Second Term

After winning reelection in 1832, Jackson moved to destroy the Bank of the United States.

Pet Banks Jackson attacked the bank by withdrawing all federal funds. Aided by Secretary of the Treasury Roger Taney, he transferred the funds to various state banks, which Jackson's critics called "pet banks."

Species Circular As a result of both Jackson's financial policies and feverish speculation in western lands, prices for land and various goods became badly inflated. Jackson hoped to check the inflationary trend by issuing a presidential order known as the Specie Circular. It required that all future purchases of federal lands be made in specie (gold and silver) rather than in paper banknotes. Soon afterward, banknotes lost their value and land sales plummeted. Right after Jackson left office, a financial crisis—the Panic of 1837—plunged the nation's economy into a depression.

The Election of 1836

Following the two-term tradition set by his predecessors, Jackson did not seek a third term. To make sure his policies were carried out even in his retirement, Jackson persuaded the Democratic party to nominate his loyal vice president, Martin Van Buren, who was a master of practical politics.

Fearing defeat, the Whig party adopted the unusual strategy of nominating three candidates from three different regions. In doing so, the Whigs hoped to throw the election into the House of Representatives, where each state had one vote in the selection of the president. The Whig strategy failed, however, as Van Buren took 58 percent of the electoral vote.

President Van Buren and the Panic of 1837

Just as Van Buren took office, the country suffered a financial panic as one bank after another closed its doors. Jackson's opposition to the rechartering of the Bank of the United States was only one of many causes of the panic and resulting economic depression. But the Whigs were quick to blame the Democrats for their laissez-faire economics, which advocated for little federal involvement in the economy.

The "Log Cabin and Hard Cider" Campaign of 1840

In the election of 1840, the Whigs were in a strong position to defeat Van Buren and the Jacksonian Democrats. Voters were unhappy with the bad state of the economy. In addition, the Whigs were better organized than the Democrats, and had a popular war hero, William Henry "Tippecanoe" Harrison, as their presidential candidate. The Whigs took campaign hoopla to new heights. To symbolize Harrison's humble origins, they put log cabins on wheels and paraded them down the streets of cities and towns. They also passed out hard cider for voters to drink and buttons and hats to wear. Name-calling as a propaganda device also marked the 1840 campaign. The Whigs attacked "Martin Van Ruin" as an aristocrat with a taste for foreign wines.

A remarkable 78 percent of eligible voters (white males) cast their ballots. Old "Tippecanoe" and John Tyler of Virginia, a former states' rights Democrat who joined the Whigs, took 53 percent of the popular vote and most of the electoral votes in all three sections: North, South, and West. This election established the Whigs as a national party.

However, Harrison died of pneumonia less than a month after taking office, and "His Accidency," John Tyler, became the first vice-president to succeed to the presidency. President Tyler was not much of a Whig. He vetoed the Whigs' national bank bills and other legislation, and favored southern and expansionist Democrats during the balance of his term (1841–1845). The Jacksonian era was in its last stage, and came to an end with the Mexican War and the increased focus on the issue of slavery. (See Chapter 12.)

HISTORICAL PERSPECTIVES: WERE THE JACKSONIANS DEMOCRATIC?

Historians debate whether the election of Jackson in 1828 marked a revolutionary and democratic turn in American politics. The traditional view is that Jackson's election began the era of the common man, when the masses of newly enfranchised voters drove out the entrenched ruling class and elected one of their own. The Revolution of 1828 was a victory of the democratic West against the aristocratic East. On the other hand, 19th-century Whig historians viewed Jackson as a despot whose appeal to the uneducated masses and "corrupt" spoils system threatened the republic. *continued*

In the 1940s, the historian Arthur M. Schlesinger Jr. argued that Jacksonian democracy relied as much on the support of eastern urban workers as on western farmers. Jackson's coalition of farmers and workers foreshadowed a similar coalition that elected another Democratic president, Franklin D. Roosevelt, in the 1930s.

Contemporary historians have used quantitative analysis of voting returns to show that increased voter participation was evident in local elections years before 1828 and did not reach a peak until the election of 1840, an election that the Whig party won. Some historians argue that religion and ethnicity were more important than economic class in shaping votes. For example, Catholic immigrants objected to the imposition of the Puritan moral code (e.g., temperance) by the native Protestants.

Recent historians see Jackson's popularity in the 1830s as a reaction of subsistence farmers and urban workers against threatening forces of economic change. A capitalist, or market, economy was taking shape in the early years of the 19th century. This market revolution divided the electorate. Some, including many Whigs, supported the changes giving a greater role for enterprising businessmen. Jackson's veto of the bank captured popular fears about the rise of capitalism.

KEY TERMS BY THEME

Migration (NAT, MIG)
Indian Removal Act (1830)
Cherokee Nation v. Georgia
Worchester v. Georgia
Cherokee trail of tears

Economics (WXT)
Bank of the United States
Nicholas Biddle
Roger Taney
"pet banks"
Specie Circular
Panic of 1837
Martin Van Buren

Common Man (NAT, POL)
common man
universal white male suffrage
party nominating convention
"King Caucus"
popular election of president

Jacksonian Politics (POL)
Anti-Masonic party
Workingmen's party
popular campaigning
spoils system
rotation in office
John Quincy Adams
Henry Clay
"corrupt bargain"

Tariff of 1828; "tariff of abominations"
Revolution of 1828
Andrew Jackson
role of the president
Peggy Eaton affair
states' rights
nullification crisis
Webster-Hayne debate
John C. Calhoun
Proclamation to the People of South Carolina
two-party system
Democrats
Whigs
"log cabin and hard cider" campaign

MULTIPLE-CHOICE QUESTIONS

Questions 1–3 refer to the excerpt below.

"We hold . . . that on their separation from the Crown of Great Britain, the several colonies became free and independent States, each enjoying the separate and independent right of self-government; and that no authority can be exercised over them . . . but by their consent . . . It is equally true, that the Constitution of the United States is a compact formed between the several States . . . that the government created by it is a joint agency of the States, appointed to execute the powers enumerated and granted by that instrument; that all its acts not intentionally authorized are of themselves essentially null and void, and that the States have the right . . . to pronounce, in the last resort, authoritative judgment on the usurpations of the Federal Government . . . Such we deem to be inherent rights of the States."

—John C. Calhoun, statement adopted by a convention
in South Carolina, 1832

1. Which of the following was the immediate cause of the publication of the statement in this excerpt?

   (A) The election of Andrew Jackson

   (B) The decision to halt to slave importation

   (C) A Supreme Court decision on states' rights

   (D) A new tariff

2. While Calhoun and many other Southerners disagreed with President Jackson's opposition to nullification, they agreed with him on

   (A) his support for higher federal spending

   (B) his support for a national bank

   (C) his opposition to the anti-slavery movement

   (D) his opposition to states' rights

3. Which of the following is or are most similar to the statement in the excerpt?

   (A) Kentucky and Virginia Resolutions

   (B) Monroe Doctrine

   (C) Specie Circular

   (D) Tallmadge Amendment

Questions 4–6 refer to the excerpt below.

"It is to be regretted that the rich and powerful too often bend the acts of government to their selfish purposes. Distinctions in society will always exist under every just government . . . In the full enjoyment of the gifts of heaven and the fruits of superior industry, economy, and virtue, every man is equally entitled to protection by law.

"But when the laws undertake to add to these natural and just advantages artificial distinctions . . . to make the rich richer . . . the humble members of society—the farmers, mechanics, and laborers— . . . have a right to complain of the injustices of their government.

"There are no necessary evils in government . . . If it would confine itself to equal protection . . . the rich and the poor, it would be an unqualified blessing. In the act before me there seems to be a wide and unnecessary departure from these just principles."

—President Andrew Jackson, Message vetoing the Bank, July 10, 1832

4. President Jackson's guiding principle to check "the injustices of government" was

   (A) limited government

   (B) the two-party system

   (C) universal suffrage

   (D) civil service system

5. Which of the following groups provided the greatest support for the Jackson's veto of the Bank?

   (A) Manufacturers

   (B) Nativists

   (C) Southerners

   (D) Westerners

6. President Jackson's veto of the Bank bill would contribute most significantly to

   (A) lower interest rates

   (B) a financial panic

   (C) increased land sales

   (D) Clay's political support

Questions 7–8 refer to the excerpt below.

"The framers of our excellent Constitution . . . wisely judged that the less government interferes with private pursuits the better for the general prosperity . . .

"I cannot doubt that on this as on all similar occasions the federal government will find its agency most conducive to the security and happiness of the people when limited to the exercise of its conceded powers . . .

"The difficulties and distresses of the times, though unquestionably great, are limited in their extent, and cannot be regarded as affecting the permanent prosperity of the nation. Arising in a great degree from the transactions of foreign and domestic commerce . . . The great agricultural interest has in many parts of the country suffered comparatively little . . .

"The proceeds of our great staples will soon furnish the means of liquidating debts at home and abroad, and contribute equally to the revival of commercial activity and the restoration of commercial credit."

—Martin Van Buren, "Against Government Aid for
Business Losses," 1837

7. Van Buren believed that the strength of the American economy was based on
   (A) the banking system
   (B) the manufacturing sector
   (C) farmers and planters
   (D) the Specie Circular

8. Which of the following individuals would be most critical of Van Buren's economic policy as presented in this excerpt?
   (A) Andrew Jackson
   (B) Roger Taney
   (C) Robert Hayne
   (D) Henry Clay

SHORT-ANSWER QUESTIONS

Use complete sentences; an outline or bulleted list alone is not acceptable.

Question 1 is based on the following excerpts.

"He [Jackson] believed that removal was the Indians' only salvation against certain extinction . . . Not that the President was motivated by concerns for the Indians. . . . Andrew Jackson was motivated principally by two considerations: First . . . military safety. . . . that Indians must not occupy areas that might jeopardize the defense of this nation; and second . . . the principal that all persons residing within states are subject to the jurisdiction and laws of those states.

"Would it have been worse had the Indians remained in the East? Jackson thought so. He said that they would 'disappear and be forgotten.' One thing does seem certain: the Indians would have been forced to yield to state laws and white society. Indian Nations per se would have been obliterated."

—Robert V. Remini, historian, *Andrew Jackson and the Course of American Freedom,* 1998

"The Georgia legislature passed a law extending the state's jurisdiction . . . over the Cherokees living within the state . . . Georgia's action forced the President's hand. He must see to it that a removal policy long covertly pursued by the White House would now be enacted into law by Congress . . .

"Jackson as usual spoke publicly in a tone of friendship and concern for Indian welfare. . . . He, as President, could be their friend only if they removed beyond the Mississippi, where they should have a "land of their own, which they shall possess as long as grass grows or water runs. . . .

"A harsh policy was nevertheless quickly put in place . . . It is abundantly clear that Jackson and his administration were determined to permit the extension of state sovereignty because it would result in the harassment of Indians, powerless to resist, by speculators and intruders hungry for Indian Land."

—Anthony F. C. Wallace, historian, *The Long, Bitter Trail: Andrew Jackson and the Indians,* 1993

1. Using the excerpts, answer (A), (B), and (C).
   (A) Briefly describe ONE major difference between Remini's and Wallace's historical interpretations of Jackson's Indian removal policies.
   (B) Briefly explain how ONE specific historical event or development in the period 1824 to 1844 that is not explicitly mentioned in the excerpts could be used to support Remini's interpretation.
   (C) Briefly explain how ONE specific historical event or development in the period 1824 to 1844 that is not explicitly mentioned in the excerpts could be used to support Wallace's interpretation.

Question 2 is based on the following cartoon.

Source: "King Andrew the First," 1833.
Library of Congress

2. Using the cartoon, answer (A), (B), and (C).

   (A) Briefly explain ONE historical perspective expressed by the artist about Andrew Jackson's presidency from 1828 to 1836.

   (B) Briefly explain ONE development in the period 1828 to 1836 that supports the perspective of the artist.

   (C) Briefly explain ONE development in the period 1828 to 1836 that challenges the perspective of the artist.

Question 3. Answer (A), (B), and (C).

(A) Briefly explain ONE historical event or development in the period 1824 to 1840 that demonstrated the spread of democracy and the "politics of the Common Man."

(B) Briefly explain how ONE specific group in the period 1824 to 1840 did not share in the spread of democracy and the "politics of the Common Man."

(C) Briefly explain ONE historical event or development in the period 1824 to 1840 that demonstrated the growth of political parties.

Question 4. Answer (A), (B), and (C).

(A) Briefly explain ONE specific historical event or development in the period 1828 to 1836 that demonstrated Andrew Jackson's exercise of presidential powers.

(B) Briefly explain ONE specific historical event or development in the period 1828 to 1836 that challenged an action by President Jackson.

(C) Briefly explain ONE specific example in the period 1824 to 1840 that reveals the growing role of personal attacks in politics.

THINK AS A HISTORIAN: STATEMENTS ABOUT CAUSATION

Statements that express causation often use words such as *cause, effect, because, hence,* and *result*. Which TWO of these statements most clearly express causation?

1. Because of Jackson's Specie Circular, banknotes lost their value.

2. Jackson's threat to use force and his willingness to compromise on the tariff persuaded the states' rights advocates to back down.

3. Jackson charged that Adams and Clay made a "corrupt bargain."

4. The Anti-Masonic party viewed the Masons as a secret elite.

11

SOCIETY, CULTURE, AND REFORM, 1820–1860

We would have every path laid open to Woman as freely as to Man . . . . As the friend of the Negro assumes that one man cannot by right hold another in bondage, so should the friend of Woman assume that Man cannot by right lay even well-meant restrictions on Woman.

Margaret Fuller, 1845

Several historic reform movements began during the Jacksonian era and in the following decades. This period before the Civil War started in 1861 is known as the *antebellum period*. During this time, a diverse mix of reformers dedicated themselves to such causes as establishing free (tax-supported) public schools, improving the treatment of the mentally ill, controlling or abolishing the sale of alcohol, winning equal rights for women, and abolishing slavery. The enthusiasm for reform had many historic sources: the Puritan sense of mission, the Enlightenment belief in human goodness, the politics of Jacksonian democracy, and changing relationships among men and women, among social classes, and among ethnic groups. The most important source may have been religious beliefs.

Religion: The Second Great Awakening

Religious revivals swept through the United States during the early decades of the 19th century. They were partly a reaction against the rationalism (belief in human reason) that had been the fashion during the Enlightenment and the American Revolution. Calvinist (Puritan) teachings of original sin and predestination had been rejected by believers in more liberal and forgiving doctrines, such as those of the Unitarian Church.

Calvinism began a counterattack against these liberal views in the 1790s. The Second Great Awakening began among educated people such as Reverend Timothy Dwight, president of Yale College in Connecticut. Dwight's campus revivals motivated a generation of young men to become evangelical preachers. In the revivals of the early 1800s, successful preachers were audience-centered and easily understood by the uneducated; they spoke about the opportunity for salvation to all. These populist movements seemed attuned to the democratization of American society.

Revivalism on the Frontier In 1823, Presbyterian minister Charles G. Finney started a series of revivals in upstate New York, where many New Englanders had settled. Instead of delivering sermons based on rational argument, Finney appealed to people's emotions and fear of damnation. He prompted thousands to publicly declare their revived faith. He preached that every individual could be saved through faith and hard work—ideas that appealed to the rising middle class. Because of Finney's influence, western New York became known as the "burned-over district" for its "hell-and-brimstone" revivals.

Baptists and Methodists In the South and on the western frontier, Baptist and Methodist circuit preachers, such as Peter Cartwright, would travel from one location to another and attract thousands to hear their dramatic preaching at outdoor revivals, or camp meetings. These preachers activated the faith of many who had never belonged to a church. By 1850, the Baptists and the Methodists were the largest Protestant denominations in the country.

Millennialism Much of the religious enthusiasm of the time was based on the widespread belief that the world was about to end with the second coming of Jesus. One preacher, William Miller, gained tens of thousands of followers by predicting a specific date (October 21, 1844) for the second coming. Nothing happened on the appointed day, but the Millerites continued as a new Christian denomination, the Seventh-Day Adventists.

Church of Jesus Christ of Latter-day Saints The Church of Jesus Christ of Latter-day Saints, formerly called the Mormon Church, was founded by Joseph Smith in 1830 in New York. Smith based his beliefs on a book of Scripture—the Book of Mormon—which traced a connection between American Indians and the lost tribes of Israel. Smith and his followers, facing persecution, moved to Ohio, then Missouri, and then Illinois. There, Smith was murdered by a local mob. To survive, the Church members, led by Brigham Young, migrated west and settled near the Great Salt Lake in Utah. They named their community New Zion. Their cooperative social organization helped them prosper in the wilderness.

One reason many people strongly opposed the Church was that Smith had accepted polygamy, allowing a man to have more than one wife. The Church of Jesus Christ of Latter-day Saints has prohibited polygamy since 1890.

Reforms The Second Great Awakening, like the first, caused divisions between the newer, evangelical sects and the older Protestant churches throughout the country. In the northern states from Massachusetts to Ohio the Great Awakening also touched off social reform. Activist religious groups provided both the leadership and the well-organized voluntary societies that drove many reform movements during the antebellum era.

Culture: Ideas, the Arts, and Literature

In Europe, during the early years of the 19th century, artists and writers shifted away from the Enlightenment emphasis on balance, order, and reason and toward intuition, feelings, individual acts of heroism, and the study of nature. This new movement, known as romanticism, was expressed in the United States by the transcendentalists, a small group of New England thinkers.

The Transcendentalists

Writers such as Ralph Waldo Emerson and Henry David Thoreau questioned the doctrines of established churches and the business practices of the merchant class. They argued for a mystical and intuitive way of thinking as a means for discovering one's inner self and looking for the essence of God in nature. Their views challenged the materialism of American society by suggesting that artistic expression was more important than the pursuit of wealth. Although the transcendentalists valued individualism highly and viewed organized institutions as unimportant, they supported a variety of reforms, especially the antislavery movement.

Ralph Waldo Emerson (1803–1882) The best-known transcendentalist, Ralph Waldo Emerson, was a very popular American speaker. His essays and lectures expressed the individualistic and nationalistic spirit of Americans by urging them not to imitate European culture but to create a distinctive *American* culture. He argued for self-reliance, independent thinking, and the primacy of spiritual matters over material ones. A northerner who lived in Concord, Massachusetts, Emerson became a leading critic of slavery in the 1850s and then an ardent supporter of the Union during the Civil War.

Henry David Thoreau (1817–1862) Also living in Concord and a close friend of Emerson was Henry David Thoreau. To test his transcendentalist philosophy, Thoreau conducted a two-year experiment of living simply in a cabin in the woods outside town. He used observations of nature to discover essential truths about life and the universe. Thoreau's writings from these years were published in the book for which he is best known, *Walden* (1854). Because of this book, Thoreau is remembered today as a pioneer ecologist and conservationist.

Through his essay "On Civil Disobedience," Thoreau established himself as an early advocate of nonviolent protest. The essay presented Thoreau's argument for disobeying unjust laws and accepting the penalty. The philosopher's own act of civil disobedience was to refuse to pay a tax that would support an action he considered immoral—the U.S. war with Mexico (1846–1848). For breaking the tax law, Thoreau spent one night in the Concord jail. In the next century, Thoreau's essay and actions would inspire the nonviolent movements of both Mohandas Gandhi in India and Martin Luther King Jr. in the United States.

Brook Farm Could a community of people live out the transcendentalist ideal? In 1841, George Ripley, a Protestant minister, launched a communal experiment at Brook Farm in Massachusetts. His goal was to achieve "a more natural union between intellectual and manual labor." Living at Brook Farm at times were some of the leading intellectuals of the period. Emerson went, as did Margaret Fuller, a feminist (advocate of women's rights) writer and editor; Theodore Parker, a theologian and radical reformer; and Nathaniel Hawthorne, a novelist. A bad fire and heavy debts forced the end of the experiment in 1849. But Brook Farm was remembered for its atmosphere of artistic creativity, its innovative school, and its appeal to New England's intellectual elite and their children.

Communal Experiments

The idea of withdrawing from conventional society to create an ideal community, or utopia, in a fresh setting was not a new idea. But never before were social experiments so numerous as during the antebellum years. The open lands of the United States proved fertile ground for more than a hundred experimental communities. The Church of Jesus Christ of Latter-day Saints was an example of a religious communal effort. Brook Farm was an example of a humanistic or secular experiment. Although many of the communities were short-lived, these "backwoods utopias" reflected the diversity of the reform ideas of the time.

Shakers One of the earliest religious communal movements, the Shakers had about 6,000 members in various communities by the 1840s. Shakers held property in common and kept women and men strictly separate (forbidding marriage and sexual relations). For lack of new recruits, the Shaker communities virtually died out by the mid-1900s.

The Amana Colonies The settlers of the Amana colonies in Iowa were Germans who belonged to the religious reform movement known as Pietism. Like the Shakers, they emphasized simple, communal living. However, they allowed for marriage, and their communities continue to prosper, although they no longer practice their communal ways of living.

New Harmony The secular (nonreligious) experiment in New Harmony, Indiana, was the work of the Welsh industrialist and reformer Robert Owen. Owen hoped his utopian socialist community would provide an answer to the problems of inequity and alienation caused by the Industrial Revolution. The experiment failed, however, as a result of both financial problems and disagreements among members of the community.

Oneida Community After undergoing a religious conversion, John Humphrey Noyes in 1848 started a cooperative community in Oneida, New York. Dedicated to an ideal of perfect social and economic equality, community members shared property and, later, marriage partners. Critics attacked the Oneida system of planned reproduction and communal child-rearing as a sinful experiment in "free love." Despite the controversy, the community managed to prosper economically by producing and selling silverware of excellent quality.

Fourier Phalanxes In the 1840s, the theories of the French socialist Charles Fourier attracted the interest of many Americans. In response to the problems of a fiercely competitive society, Fourier advocated that people share work and housing in communities known as Fourier Phalanxes. This movement died out quickly as Americans proved too individualistic to live communally.

Arts and Literature

The democratic and reforming impulses of the Age of Jackson expressed themselves in painting, architecture, and literature.

Painting Genre painting—portraying the everyday life of ordinary people such as riding riverboats and voting on election day—became the vogue of artists in the 1830s. For example, George Caleb Bingham depicted common people in various settings and carrying out domestic chores. William S. Mount won popularity for his lively rural compositions. Thomas Cole and Frederick Church emphasized the heroic beauty of American landscapes, especially in dramatic scenes along the Hudson River in New York State and the western frontier wilderness. The Hudson River school, as it was called, expressed the romantic age's fascination with the natural world.

Architecture Inspired by the democracy of classical Athens, American architects adapted Greek styles to glorify the democratic spirit of the republic. Columned facades like those of ancient Greek temples graced the entryways to public buildings, banks, hotels, and even some private homes.

Literature In addition to the transcendentalist authors (notably Emerson and Thoreau), other writers helped to create a literature that was distinctively American. Partly as a result of the War of 1812, the American people became more nationalistic and eager to read the works of American writers about American themes. Washington Irving and James Fenimore Cooper, for example, wrote fiction using American settings. Cooper's *Leatherstocking Tales* were a series of novels written from 1824 to 1841 that glorified the frontiersman as nature's nobleman. *The Scarlet Letter* (1850) and other novels by Nathaniel Hawthorne questioned the intolerance and conformity in American life. Herman Melville's innovative novel *Moby-Dick* (1855) reflected the theological and cultural conflicts of the era as it told the story of Captain Ahab's pursuit of a white whale.

Source: *Fur Traders Descending the Missouri,* by George Caleb Bingham, 1845. Wikimedia Commons/The Yorck Project/Metropolitan Museum of Art, New York City

Reforming Society

Reform movements evolved during the antebellum era. At first, the leaders of reform hoped to improve people's behavior through moral persuasion. However, after they tried sermons and pamphlets, reformers often moved on to political action and to ideas for creating new institutions to replace the old.

Temperance

The high rate of alcohol consumption (five gallons of hard liquor per person in 1820) prompted reformers to target alcohol as the cause of social ills, and explains why temperance became the most popular of the reform movements.

The temperance movement began by using moral exhortation. In 1826, Protestant ministers and others concerned with drinking and its effects founded the American Temperance Society. The society tried to persuade drinkers to take a pledge of total abstinence. In 1840, a group of recovering alcoholics formed the Washingtonians and argued that alcoholism was a disease that needed practical, helpful treatment. By the 1840s, various temperance societies together had more than a million members.

German and Irish immigrants were largely opposed to the temperance campaign. But they lacked the political power to prevent state and city governments from passing reforms. Factory owners and politicians joined with the reformers when it became clear that temperance measures could reduce crime and poverty and increase workers' output on the job. In 1851, the state of Maine went beyond simply placing taxes on the sale of liquor and became the first state to prohibit the manufacture and sale of intoxicating liquors. Twelve states followed before the Civil War. In the 1850s, the issue of slavery came to overshadow the temperance movement. However, the movement would gain strength again in the late 1870s (with strong support from the Women's Christian Temperance Union) and achieve national success with the passage of the 18th Amendment in 1919.

Movement for Public Asylums

Humanitarian reformers of the 1820s and 1830s called attention to the increasing numbers of criminals, emotionally disturbed persons, and paupers. Often these people were forced to live in wretched conditions and were regularly either abused or neglected by their caretakers. To alleviate the suffering of these individuals, reformers proposed setting up new public institutions—state-supported prisons, mental hospitals, and poorhouses. Reformers hoped that inmates would be cured as a result of being withdrawn from squalid surroundings and treated to a disciplined pattern of life in some rural setting.

Mental Hospitals Dorothea Dix, a former schoolteacher from Massachusetts, was horrified to find mentally ill persons locked up with convicted criminals in unsanitary cells. She launched a cross-country crusade, publicizing the awful treatment she had witnessed. In the 1840s one state legislature after another built new mental hospitals or improved existing institutions and mental patients began receiving professional treatment.

Schools for Blind and Deaf Persons Two other reformers founded special institutions to help people with physical disabilities. Thomas Gallaudet opened a school for the deaf, and Dr. Samuel Gridley Howe started a school for the blind. By the 1850s, special schools modeled after the work of these reformers had been established in many states of the Union.

Prisons Pennsylvania took the lead in prison reform, building new prisons called penitentiaries to take the place of crude jails. Reformers placed prisoners in solitary confinement to force them to reflect on their sins and repent. The experiment was dropped because of the high rate of prisoner suicides. These prison reforms reflected a major doctrine of the asylum movement: structure and discipline would bring about moral reform. A similar penal experiment, the Auburn system in New York, enforced rigid rules of discipline while also providing moral instruction and work programs.

Public Education

Another reform movement started in the Jacksonian era focused on the need for establishing free public schools for children of all classes. Middle-class reformers were motivated in part by their fears for the future of the republic posed by growing numbers of the uneducated poor—both immigrant and native-born. Workers' groups in the cities generally supported the reformers' campaign for free (tax-supported) schools.

Free Common Schools Horace Mann was the leading advocate of the common (public) school movement. As secretary of the newly founded Massachusetts Board of Education, Mann worked for compulsory attendance for all children, a longer school year, and increased teacher preparation. In the 1840s, the movement for public schools spread rapidly to other states.

Moral Education Mann and other educational reformers wanted children to learn not only basic literacy, but also moral principles. Toward this end, William Holmes McGuffey, a Pennsylvania teacher, created a series of elementary textbooks that became widely used to teach reading and morality. The McGuffey readers extolled the virtues of hard work, punctuality, and sobriety—the kind of behaviors needed in an emerging industrial society.

Objecting to the Protestant tone of the public schools, Roman Catholics founded private schools for the instruction of Catholic children.

Higher Education The religious enthusiasm of the Second Great Awakening helped fuel the growth of private colleges. Beginning in the 1830s, various Protestant denominations founded small denominational colleges, especially in the newer western states (Ohio, Indiana, Illinois, and Iowa). At the same time, several new colleges, including Mount Holyoke College in Massachusetts (founded by Mary Lyon in 1837) and Oberlin College in Ohio, began to admit women. Adult education was furthered by lyceum lecture societies, which brought speakers such as Ralph Waldo Emerson to small-town audiences.

Changes in Families and Roles for Women

American society was still overwhelmingly rural in the mid-19th century. But in the growing cities, the impact of the Industrial Revolution was redefining the family. Industrialization reduced the economic value of children. In middle-class families, birth control was used to reduce average family size, which declined from 7.04 family members in 1800 to 5.42 in 1830. More affluent women now had the leisure time to devote to religious and moral uplift organizations. The New York Female Moral Reform Society, for example, worked to prevent impoverished young women from being forced into lives of prostitution.

Cult of Domesticity Industrialization also changed roles within families. In traditional farm families, men were the moral leaders. However, when men took jobs outside the home to work for salaries or wages in an office or a factory, they were absent most of the time. As a result, the women in these households who remained at home took charge of the household and children. The idealized view of women as moral leaders in the home is called the cult of domesticity.

Women's Rights Women reformers, especially those involved in the anti-slavery movement, resented the way men relegated them to secondary roles in the movement and prevented them from taking part fully in policy discussions. Two sisters, Sarah and Angelina Grimké, objected to male opposition to their antislavery activities. In protest, Sarah Grimké wrote her *Letter on the Condition of Women and the Equality of the Sexes* (1837). Another pair of reformers, Lucretia Mott and Elizabeth Cady Stanton, began campaigning for women's rights after they had been barred from speaking at an antislavery convention.

Seneca Falls Convention (1848) The leading feminists met at Seneca Falls, New York, in 1848. At the conclusion of their convention—the first women's rights convention in American history—they issued a document closely modeled after the Declaration of Independence. Their "Declaration of Sentiments" declared that "all men and women are created equal" and listed women's grievances against laws and customs that discriminated against them.

Following the Seneca Falls Convention, Elizabeth Cady Stanton and Susan B. Anthony led the campaign for equal voting, legal, and property rights for women. In the 1850s, however, the issue of women's rights was overshadowed by the crisis over slavery.

Antislavery Movement

Opponents of slavery ranged from moderates who proposed gradual abolition to radicals who demanded immediate abolition without compensating their owners. The Second Great Awakening led many Christians to view slavery as a sin. This moral view made compromise with defenders of slavery difficult.

American Colonization Society The idea of transporting freed slaves to an African colony was first tried in 1817 with the founding of the American Colonization Society. This appealed to moderate antislavery reformers and politicians, in part because whites with racist attitudes hoped to remove free blacks from U.S. society. In 1822, the American Colonization Society established an African-American settlement in Monrovia, Liberia. Colonization never proved a practical course. Between 1820 and 1860, only about 12,000 African Americans were settled in Africa, while the slave population grew by 2.5 million.

American Antislavery Society In 1831, William Lloyd Garrison began publication of an abolitionist newspaper, *The Liberator*, an event that marks the beginning of the radical abolitionist movement. The uncompromising Garrison advocated immediate abolition of slavery in every state and territory without compensating the slaveowners. In 1833, Garrison and other abolitionists founded the American Antislavery Society. Garrison stepped up his attacks by condemning and burning the Constitution as a proslavery document. He argued for "no Union with slaveholders" until they repented for their sins by freeing their slaves.

Liberty Party Garrison's radicalism soon led to a split in the abolitionist movement. Believing that political action was a more practical route to reform than Garrison's moral crusade, a group of northerners formed the Liberty party in 1840. They ran James Birney as their candidate for president in 1840 and 1844. The party's one campaign pledge was to bring about the end of slavery by political and legal means.

Black Abolitionists Escaped slaves and free African Americans were among the most outspoken and convincing critics of slavery. A former slave such as Frederick Douglass could speak about the brutality and degradation of slavery from firsthand experience. An early follower of Garrison, Douglass later advocated both political and direct action to end slavery and racial prejudice. In 1847, he started the antislavery journal *The North Star*. Other African American leaders, such as Harriet Tubman, David Ruggles, Sojourner Truth, and William Still, helped organize the effort to assist fugitive slaves escape to free territory in the North or to Canada, where slavery was prohibited.

Violent Abolitionism David Walker and Henry Highland Garnet were two northern African Americans who advocated the most radical solution to the slavery question. They argued that slaves should take action themselves by rising up in revolt against their owners. In 1831, a Virginia slave named Nat Turner led a revolt in which 55 whites were killed. In retaliation, whites killed hundreds of African Americans in brutal fashion and put down the revolt. Before this event, there had been some antislavery sentiment and discussion in the South. After the revolt, fear of future uprisings as well as Garrison's inflamed rhetoric put an end to antislavery talk in the South.

Other Reforms

Efforts to reform individuals and society during the antebellum era also included smaller movements such as:

- the American Peace Society, founded in 1828 with the objective of abolishing war, which actively protested the war with Mexico in 1846
- laws to protect sailors from being flogged
- dietary reforms, such as eating whole wheat bread or Sylvester Graham's crackers, to promote good digestion
- dress reform for women, particularly Amelia Bloomer's efforts to get women to wear pantalettes instead of long skirts
- phrenology, a pseudoscience that studied the bumps on an individual's skull to assess the person's character and ability

Southern Reaction to Reform

The antebellum reform movement was largely found in the northern and western states, with little impact in the South. While "modernizers" worked to perfect society in the North, southerners were more committed to tradition and slow to support public education and humanitarian reforms. They were alarmed to see northern reformers join forces to support the antislavery movement. Increasingly, they viewed social reform as a northern threat against the southern way of life.

HISTORICAL PERSPECTIVES: WHAT MOTIVATED REFORMERS?

In her history of antebellum reform, *Freedom's Ferment* (1944), Alice Tyler portrayed the reformers as idealistic humanitarians whose chief goal was to create a just and equitable society for all. Other historians generally accepted Tyler's interpretation.

However, in recent years, historians have questioned whether reformers were motivated by humanitarian concerns or by a desire of upper- and middle-class citizens to control the masses. According to their argument, the temperance movement was designed to control the drinking of the poor and recent immigrants. The chief purpose of penitentiaries was to control crime, of poorhouses to motivate the lower classes to pursue work, and of public schools to "Americanize" the immigrant population. Schools were supported by the wealthy, because they would teach the working class hard work, punctuality, and obedience. Revisionist historians also have noted that most of the reformers were Whigs, not Jacksonian Democrats.

Some historians have argued that the reformers had multiple motivations for their work. They point out that, although some reasons for reform may have been self-serving and bigoted, most reformers sincerely thought that their ideas for improving society would truly help people. For example, Dorothea Dix won support for increased spending for treatment of the mentally ill by appealing to both self-interest and morality. She argued that reforms would save the public money in the long run and were humane. Historians point out further that the most successful reforms were ones that had broad support across society—often for a mix of reasons.

KEY TERMS BY THEME

Alternative Groups (NAT)
utopian communities
Shakers
Amana Colonies
Robert Owen
New Harmony
Joseph Henry Noyes
Oneida community
Charles Fourier
phalanxes
Horace Mann

Reforming Society (POL)
temperance
American Temperance Society
Washingtonians
Women's Christian Temperance Union
asylum movement
Dorothea Dix
Thomas Gallaudet
Samuel Gridley Howe
penitentiaries
Auburn system
Horace Mann
public school movement
McGuffey readers
American Peace Society

Abolition Efforts (POL)
American Colonization Society

American Antislavery Society
abolitionism William Lloyd Garrison; The Liberator
Liberty party
Frederick Douglass; *The North Star*
Harriet Tubman
David Ruggles
Sojourner Truth
William Still
David Walker
Henry Highland Garnet
Nat Turner

New Ideas (SOC)
antebellum period
romantic movement
transcendentalists
Ralph Waldo Emerson, "The American Scholar"
Henry David Thoreau, *Walden,* "On Civil Disobedience"
Brook Farm
George Ripley
feminists
Margaret Fuller
Theodore Parker
George Caleb Bingham
William S. Mount
Thomas Cole
Frederick Church
Hudson River school

Washington Irving
James Fenimore Cooper
Nathaniel Hawthorne
Sylvester Graham
Amelia Bloomer

Thoughts on Religion (SOC)
Second Great Awakening
Timothy Dwight
revivalism; revival (camp) meetings
millennialism
Church of Jesus Christ of Latter-day Saints
Joseph Smith
Brigham Young
New Zion

Women's Rights (SOC)
women's rights movement
cult of domesticity
Sarah Grimké
Angelina Grimké
Letter on the Condition of Women and the Equality of the Sexes
Lucretia Mott
Elizabeth Cady Stanton
Seneca Falls Convention (1848)
Susan B. Anthony

Questions 1–3 refer to the excerpt below.

"If, then education be of admitted importance to the people, under all forms of government, and of unquestioned necessity when they govern themselves, it follows, of course, that its cultivation and diffusion is a matter of public concern and a duty which every government owes to its people. . . .

"Many complain of this tax, not so much on account of its amount as because it is for the benefit of others and not themselves. This is a mistake; it is for their own benefit, inasmuch as it perpetuates the government. . . .

"He who would oppose it, either through inability to comprehend the advantages of general education, or from unwillingness to bestow them on all his fellow citizens, even to the lowest and the poorest, or from dread of popular vengeance, seems to me to want either the head of the philosopher, the heart of the philanthropist, or the nerve of the hero."

—Representative Thaddeus Stevens, Speech to the Pennsylvania
Legislature, 1835

1. The first free public education system in the United States began in which of the following colonies?

   (A) Massachusetts

   (B) New York

   (C) Pennsylvania

   (D) Virginia

2. Which of these groups would most strongly agree with Stevens on his view of education?

   (A) Transcendentalists

   (B) Business leaders

   (C) Jacksonian Democrats

   (D) Protestant churches

3. Stevens disagrees with those who oppose free public education because

   (A) it is an example of government control

   (B) it will result in increased taxes

   (C) schools lack qualified teachers

   (D) schools are under Protestant influences

Questions 4–6 refer to the excerpt below.

"Unlike those who call themselves no-government men, I ask for, not . . . no-government, but . . . a better government. . . .

"It is not desirable to cultivate a respect for the law so much as for the right. The only obligation which I have a right to assume is to do at any time what I think right. . . .

"There are thousands who are in opinion opposed to slavery and to the war [with Mexico] who yet in effect do nothing to put an end to them. . . .

"Under a government which imprisons any unjustly, the true place for a just man is also a prison . . . If the alternative is to keep all just men in prison or give up war and slavery, the state will not hesitate which to choose. If a thousand men were not to pay their tax bills this year, that would not be a violent and bloody measure . . . This is . . . the definition of a peaceable revolution."

—Henry David Thoreau, lecturer and author, "Resistance to Civil Government," (Civil Disobedience), 1849

4. Thoreau challenged the government because

   (A) he rejected all forms of government

   (B) he opposed war in all cases

   (C) it engaged in a war to take land from Mexico

   (D) it taxed people without representation

5. Thoreau believed that a just man should be prepared to do which of the following?

   (A) Organize opposition

   (B) Run for elected office

   (C) Overthrow the government

   (D) Go to jail for his beliefs

6. Which of the following groups held views most similar to the ideas expressed in this excerpt?

   (A) Revivalists

   (B) Transcendentalists

   (C) Phalanxes

   (D) Millennialists

Questions 7–8 refer to the excerpt below.

"I think that 'twixt the negroes of the South and the women at the North, all talking about rights, the white men will be in a fix pretty soon. But what's all this here talk about?

"That man over there says that women need to be helped . . . Nobody ever helps me. . . . And ain't I a woman?

"Then they talk about this thing in the head . . . intellect . . . What's that got to do with women's rights or negro's rights? If my cup won't hold but a pint, and yours holds a quart, wouldn't you be mean not to let me have my little half-measure full?

"Then that little man in black there, he says women can't have as much rights as men, 'cause Christ wasn't a woman! Where did Christ come from? . . . From God and a woman! Man had nothing to do with Him."

—Sojourner Truth, abolitionist and former slave, speech to a Women's Convention in Ohio, 1851

7. Sojourner Truth strongly rejects criticisms of women that are based on which of the following?

(A) The ideas of transendentalism

(B) The cult of domesticity

(C) The teachings of religion

(D) The working status of women

8. Sojourner Truth saw connection between the women's rights movement and

(A) the Second Great Awakening

(B) the antislavery movement

(C) the cult of domesticity

(D) the Constitution

SHORT-ANSWER QUESTIONS

Use complete sentences; an outline or bulleted list alone is not acceptable.

Question 1 is based on the following excerpts.

"The transformation of American theology in the first quarter of the nineteenth century released the very forces of romantic perfectionism that conservatives most feared. . . . As it spread, perfectionism swept across denominational barriers and penetrated even secular thought. . . .

As the sum of individual sins, social wrong would disappear when enough people had been converted and rededicated to right conduct. Deep and lasting reform, therefore, meant an educational crusade based on the assumption that when a sufficient number of individual Americans had seen the light, they would automatically solve the country's social problems. Thus formulated, perfectionist reform offered a program of mass conversion achieved through educational rather than political means. In the opinion of the romantic reformers the regeneration of American society began, not in legislative enactments or political manipulation, but in [an] . . . appeal to the American urge for individual self-improvement."

—John L. Thomas, historian, *Romantic Reform in America,*
1815–1865, 1965

"In the United States, the public sphere formed itself in a void, growing lush from the fertilization of religious and political controversies as its signature forms spread rapidly from city to town and town to village. In the ensuing decades, the public realm became an arena of initiatives and experiments, religiously-inspired reform movements and heated political contests. . . . In creating vast pools of proselytizers . . . and designating the entire society a missionary field, the evangelical Protestants, particularly in the North, encouraged social activism. . . . The society as a whole had to be redeemed. . . . Once converted, men and women found ways to express their new-found spiritual awakening by getting government policy, public morals, and private lives to conform to biblical prescriptions."

—Joyce Appleby, historian, *Inheriting The Revolution,* 2000

1. Using the excerpts, answer (A), (B), and (C).

   (A) Briefly explain ONE major difference between Thomas's and Appleby's historical interpretations of influences on the Constitution.

   (B) Briefly explain how ONE historical event or development in the period 1820 to 1860 that is not explicitly mentioned in the excerpts could be used to support Thomas's interpretation.

   (C) Briefly explain how ONE historical event or development in the period 1820 to 1860 that is not explicitly mentioned in the excerpts could be used to support Appleby's interpretation.

Question 2 is based on the following cartoon.

Source: *Woman's Holy War.* Library of Congress

2. Using the cartoon, answer (A), (B), and (C).

   (A) Briefly explain ONE topic addressed in the cartoon that was important between 1820 and 1860.

   (B) Briefly explain how ONE element of the cartoon expresses the point of the cartoonist.

   (C) Briefly explain ONE specific action by the U.S. government between 1820 and 1860 that reflected the cartoon's point of view.

Question 3 is based on the following excerpt.

"America is beginning to assert herself to the senses and to the imagination of her children, and Europe is receding in the same degree. . . . Prudent men have begun to see that every American should be educated with a view to the values of land. . . . The land is the appointed remedy for whatever is false, . . . in our culture. . . . Gentlemen, the development of our American internal resources, the extension to the utmost of the commercial system, and the appearance of new moral causes which are to modify the state are giving an aspect of greatness to the future which the imagination fears to open."

—Ralph Waldo Emerson, writer, "The Young American," 1844

3. Using the excerpt, answer (A), (B), and (C).

   (A) Briefly explain ONE perspective expressed by Emerson on the reform movements in the mid-19th century.

   (B) Briefly explain ONE specific way in which developments in the mid-19th century supported Emerson's point of view.

   (C) Briefly explain ONE specific way in which developments in the mid-19th century challenged Emerson's point of view.

Question 4. Answer (A), (B), and (C).

   (A) Briefly explain ONE specific change in education in response to the reform movements in the period 1820 to 1860.

   (B) Briefly explain ONE historical event or development related to women's rights in the period 1820 to 1860.

   (C) Briefly explain ONE specific government response to the reform movements in the period 1820 to 1860.

THINK AS A HISTORIAN: STATEMENTS ABOUT CONTINUITY

Statements about continuity often include phrases such as "similar to" or "following in the path." Statements about change often include phrases such as "unlike" and "unprecedented." Which TWO of the following statements most clearly express continuity?

1. The Second Great Awakening was one of many reform movements that swept the country in the 1800s.

2. The sense of caring for neighbors that existed in frontier settlements in the 1800s can be traced to the Puritans in the 1600s.

3. African American leaders in the first half of the 1800s responded to slavery in diverse ways.

4. Henry David Thoreau's legacy was revived by reformers in both the United States and India in the 20th century.

Unit 4: Period 4 Review, 1800–1848

LONG ESSAY QUESTIONS

Directions: The suggested writing time for each question is 40 minutes. In your response you should do the following:

- **Thesis:** Make a defensible claim that establishes a line of reasoning and consists of one or more sentences found in one place.
- **Contextualization:** Relate the argument to a broader historical context.
- **Evidence:** Support an argument with specific and relevant historical evidence.
- **Reasoning:** Organize an argument using the skill in the question.
- **Analysis:** Demonstrate a complex understanding of the question using historical evidence to support, qualify, or modify an argument.

1. For some the American Revolution was primarily an effort to maintain basic British rights as opposed to establishing a new form of government. Support, modify, or refute this contention using specific evidence.

2. For some the election of Andrew Jackson brought a revolutionary change in politics for the common man as opposed to it being a continuation of the trend toward greater voter participation. Support, modify, or refute this contention using specific evidence.

3. Analyze and evaluate the impact of Alexander Hamilton's views, including on banking, in the formation of economic policies during the early years of the republic.

4. Analyze and evaluate the impact of Andrew Jackson's views, including on banking, in the formation of economic policies during the 1830s.

5. Compare and contrast the characteristics and influences of the three major groups of the British Atlantic colonies by the mid-18th century.

6. Compare and contrast the characteristics and influences of the three major sections of the United States by the mid-19th century.

7. Analyze and evaluate the ways in which ONE of the following areas helped to form United States foreign policy in the late 18th century.
   - French Revolution
   - Washington's Farewell Address
   - XYZ Affair

8. Analyze and evaluate the ways in which ONE of the following areas helped to form United States foreign policy in the early 19th century.
- Florida Purchase
- Monroe Doctrine
- War Hawks

9. Explain and analyze the impact of ONE of the following on the social and political life during much of the 18th century.
- education
- immigration
- religion

10. Explain and analyze the impact of ONE of the following on the social and political life during much of the first half of the 19th century.
- education
- immigration
- religion

DOCUMENT-BASED QUESTION

Directions: Question 1 is based on the accompanying documents. The documents have been edited for the purpose of this exercise. You are advised to spend 15 minutes planning and 45 minutes writing your answer.In your response you should do the following:

- **Thesis:** Make a defensible claim that establishes a line of reasoning and consists of one or more sentences found in one place.
- **Contextualization:** Relate the argument to a broader historical context.
- **Document Evidence:** Use content from at least six documents.
- **Outside Evidence:** Use one piece of evidence not in the documents.
- **Document Sourcing:** Explain how or why the point of view, purpose, situation, or intended audience is relevant for at least three documents.
- **Analysis:** Show the relationships among pieces of historical evidence and use them to support, qualify, or modify an argument.

1. Both nationalism and sectionalism increased during the Era of Good Feelings. How did both of these beliefs develop concurrently, and did one become of greater importance in the economics and politics of the period?

Document 1

Source: Stephen Decatur, naval officer, toast given at Norfolk, Virginia, 1816

Our Country! In her intercourse with foreign nations may she always be in the right; but our country, right or wrong!

Document 2

Source: Joseph Rodman Drake, poet, "The American Flag," 1819

Flag of the free heart's hope and home,
By angel hands to valor given;
Thy stars have lit the welkin dome
And all the hues were born in heaven!
Forever float that standard sheet!
Where breathes the foe but falls before us?
With freedom's soil beneath our feet,
And freedom's banner streaming o'er us?

Document 3

Source: Emma Hart Willard, educator and feminist, address to the New York Legislature, 1819

But where is that wise and heroic country which has considered that our rights [as women] are sacred . . . ? History shows not that country. Yet though history lifts not her finger to such a one, anticipation does. She points to a nation which, having thrown off the shackles of authority and precedent, shrinks not from schemes of improvement because other nations have never attempted them; but which, in its pride of independence, would rather lead than follow in the march of human improvement: a nation, wise and magnanimous to plan, enterprising to undertake, and rich in resources to execute. Does not every American exult that this country is his own?

Document 4

Source: Henry Clay, Speech in Congress, March 31, 1824

Are we doomed to behold our industry languish and decay yet more and more? But there is a remedy, and that remedy consists in modifying our foreign policy, and in adopting a genuine American system. We must naturalize the arts in our country; and we must naturalize them by the only means which the wisdom of nations has yet discovered to be effectual—by adequate protection against the otherwise overwhelming influence of foreigners. This is only to be accomplished by the establishment of a tariff, to the consideration of which I am now brought. . . . The sole object of the tariff is to tax the produce of foreign industry with the view of promoting American industry. The tax is exclusively leveled at foreign industry.

Document 5

Source: John Quincy Adams, *Diary,* March 3, 1820

I have favored this Missouri Compromise, believing it to be all that could be effected under the present Constitution, and from extreme unwillingness to put the Union at hazard. But perhaps it would have been wiser as well as a bolder course to have persisted in the restriction upon Missouri, till it should have terminated in a convention of states to revise and amend the Constitution. This would have produced a new Union of thirteen or fourteen States, unpolluted with slavery, with a great and glorious object to effect; namely that of rallying to their standard the other states by the universal emancipation of their slaves. If the Union must be dissolved, slavery is precisely the question upon which it ought to break. For the present, however, this contest is laid asleep.

Document 6

Source: Thomas Jefferson, Letter to Congressman John Holmes of Massachusetts, April 22, 1820

I thank you, dear sir, for the copy you have been so kind to send me of the letter to your constituents on the Missouri question. It is perfect justification to them. I had for a long time ceased to read newspapers, or pay any attention to public affairs, confident they were in good hands. . . . But this momentous question, like a firebell in the night, awakened and filled me with terror. I considered it at once as the knell of the union. It is hushed, indeed, for the moment. But this is a reprieve only, not a final sentence. A geographical line, coinciding with a marked principle, moral and political, once conceived and held up to the angry passions of men, will never be obliterated; and every new irritation will mark it deeper and deeper.

Document 7

Source: *Congressional Record,* 1816

Vote on the Tariff of 1816 in the U.S. House of Representatives		
Region	**For**	**Against**
New England	17	10
Middle States	44	10
South	23	34
Total	88	54

UNIT 5: Period 5, 1844–1877

As the young nation grew in population and land, it struggled to resolve problems that ultimately lead to a bloody clash. This clash brought "a new birth of freedom" and permanently changed the nature of the government.

Overview Following a philosophy of manifest destiny, the United States expanded westward, adding land through negotiations, purchase, and war. The largest acquisition in this period came from victory in the Mexican War (1846–1848). Through this conflict, the United States secured its southern border and ports on the Pacific Ocean.

Expansion and sectionalism intensified the differences over politics, economics, and slavery. Opposition to slavery ranging from free soilers to abolitionists and an underground railroad grew in spite of fugitive slave laws and the Dred Scott decision. A series of compromises and attempted compromises failed to settle the issue of whether slavery could expand into new territories.

Then, in 1860, the Republicans nominated Abraham Lincoln for president. Though opposed to slavery, Lincoln also opposed immediate abolition. Still, his election frightened slaveholders. They feared that, despite his pledge to allow slavery where it existed, his opposition to expansion would lead to the end of slavery. Eleven states left the Union, and a four-year war ravaged the country.

The Union victory ended the questions of slavery and states' rights. Reconstruction brought confrontations between the executive and legislative branches, and between the federal government and state governments. As the freed African Americans established new lives, Black Codes and sharecropping were established to maintain their subservience.

Alternate Views Views of the Civil War have covered a wide spectrum. Some have argued it was an unavoidable conflict between two very different cultures. Another was that it was avoidable, but weak leaders failed to find a reasonable compromise.

Views of Reconstruction have also varied greatly. In the past, some historians criticized Reconstruction for its attempts to promote racial equality. Most recent historians have seen it as a missed opportunity to do just that. However, some have pointed out that the institutions and amendments from the Reconstruction era provided the foundation for the civil rights movement that emerged nearly a century after the Civil War ended.

12

TERRITORIAL AND ECONOMIC EXPANSION, 1830–1860

Away, away with all these cobweb issues of the rights of discovery, exploration, settlement, . . . [The American claim] is by the right of our manifest destiny to overspread and to possess the whole of the continent which Providence has given us for the development of the great experiment of liberty.

John L. O'Sullivan, *Democratic Review,* 1845

After John O'Sullivan wrote about manifest destiny, supporters of territorial expansion spread the term across the land. In the 1840s and 1850s, expansionists wanted to see the United States extend westward to the Pacific and southward into Mexico, Cuba, and Central America. By the 1890s, expansionists fixed their sights on acquiring islands in the Pacific and the Caribbean.

The phrase *manifest destiny* expressed the popular belief that the United States had a divine mission to extend its power and civilization across the breadth of North America. Enthusiasm for expansion reached a fever pitch in the 1840s. It was driven by a number of forces: nationalism, population increase, rapid economic development, technological advances, and reform ideals. But not all Americans united behind the idea of manifest destiny and expansionism. Northern critics argued vehemently that at the root of the expansionist drive was the Southern ambition to spread slavery into western lands.

Conflicts Over Texas, Maine, and Oregon

U.S. interest in pushing its borders south into Texas (a Mexican province) and west into the Oregon Territory (claimed by Britain) largely resulted from American pioneers migrating into these lands during the 1820s and 1830s.

Texas

In 1823, after having won its national independence from Spain, Mexico hoped to attract settlers—including Anglo settlers—to farm its sparsely populated northern frontier province of Texas. Moses Austin, a Missouri banker, had obtained a large land grant in Texas but died before he could recruit American settlers for the land. His son, Stephen Austin, succeeded in bringing 300 families into Texas and thereby beginning a steady migration of American settlers into the vast frontier territory. By 1830, Americans (both white farmers and enslaved blacks) outnumbered Mexicans in Texas by three to one.

Friction developed between the Americans and the Mexicans when, in 1829, Mexico outlawed slavery and required all immigrants to convert to Roman Catholicism. When many settlers refused to obey these laws, Mexico closed Texas to additional American immigrants. Land-hungry Americans from the Southern states ignored the Mexican prohibition and streamed into Texas by the thousands.

Revolt and Independence A change in Mexico's government intensified the conflict. In 1834, General Antonio López de Santa Anna made himself dictator of Mexico and abolished that nation's federal system of government. When Santa Anna attempted to enforce Mexico's laws in Texas, a group of American settlers led by Sam Houston revolted and declared Texas to be an independent republic (March 1836).

A Mexican army led by Santa Anna captured the town of Goliad and attacked the Alamo in San Antonio, killing every one of its American defenders. Shortly afterward, however, at the Battle of the San Jacinto River, an army under Sam Houston caught the Mexicans by surprise and captured their general, Santa Anna. Under the threat of death, the Mexican leader was forced to sign a treaty that recognized independence for Texas and granted the new republic all territory north of the Rio Grande. However, when the news of San Jacinto reached Mexico City, the Mexican legislature rejected the treaty and insisted that Texas was still part of Mexico.

Annexation Denied As the first president of the Republic of Texas (or Lone Star Republic), Houston applied to the U.S. government for his country to be annexed, or added to, the United States as a new state. However, presidents Jackson and Van Buren both put off the request for annexation primarily because of political opposition among Northerners to the expansion of slavery and the potential addition of up to five new slave states created out of the Texas territories. The threat of a costly war with Mexico also dampened expansionist zeal. The next president, John Tyler (1841–1845), was a Southern Whig who was worried about the growing influence of the British in Texas. He worked to annex Texas, but the U.S. Senate rejected his treaty of annexation in 1844.

Boundary Dispute in Maine

Another diplomatic issue arose in the 1840s over the ill-defined boundary between Maine and the Canadian province of New Brunswick. At this time, Canada was still under British rule, and many Americans regarded Britain as their country's worst enemy—an attitude carried over from two previous wars (the Revolution and the War of 1812). A conflict between rival groups of lumbermen on the Maine-Canadian border erupted into open fighting. Known as the Aroostook War, or "battle of the maps," the conflict was soon resolved in a treaty negotiated by U.S. Secretary of State Daniel Webster and the British ambassador, Lord Alexander Ashburton. In the Webster-Ashburton Treaty of 1842, the disputed territory was split between Maine and British Canada. The treaty also settled the boundary of the Minnesota territory, leaving what proved to be the iron-rich Mesabi range on the U.S. side of the border.

Boundary Dispute in Oregon

A far more serious British-American dispute involved Oregon, a vast territory on the Pacific Coast that originally stretched as far north as the Alaskan border. At one time, this territory was claimed by four different nations: Spain, Russia, Great Britain, and the United States. Spain gave up its claim to Oregon in a treaty with the United States (the Adams-Onís Treaty of 1819).

Britain based its claim to Oregon on the Hudson Fur Company's profitable fur trade with the American Indians of the Pacific Northwest. However, by 1846, fewer than a thousand British settlers lived north of the Columbia River.

The United States based its claim on (1) the discovery of the Columbia River by Captain Robert Gray in 1792, (2) the overland expedition to the Pacific Coast by Meriwether Lewis and William Clark in 1805, and (3) the fur trading post and fort in Astoria, Oregon, established by John Jacob Astor in 1811. Protestant missionaries and farmers from the United States settled in the Willamette Valley in the 1840s. Their success in farming this fertile valley caused 5,000 Americans to catch "Oregon fever" and travel 2,000 miles over the Oregon Trail to settle in the area south of the Columbia River.

By the 1844 election, many Americans believed it to be their country's manifest destiny to take undisputed possession of all of Oregon and to annex the Republic of Texas as well. In addition, expansionists hoped to persuade Mexico to give up its province on the West Coast—the huge land of California. By 1845, Mexican California had a small Spanish-Mexican population of some 7,000 along with a much larger number of American Indians, but American emigrants were arriving in sufficient numbers "to play the Texas game."

The Election of 1844

Because slavery was allowed in Texas, many Northerners were opposed to its annexation. Leading the Northern wing of the Democratic party, former president Martin Van Buren opposed immediate annexation. Challenging him for the Democratic nomination in 1844 was the proslavery, proannexation Southerner, John C. Calhoun. The dispute between these candidates caused the Democratic convention to deadlock. After hours of wrangling, the Democrats finally nominated a *dark horse* (lesser known candidate). The man they chose, James K. Polk of Tennessee, had been a protegé of Andrew Jackson. Firmly committed to expansion and manifest destiny, Polk favored the annexation of Texas, the "reoccupation" of all of Oregon, and the acquisition of California. The Democratic slogan "Fifty-four Forty or Fight!" appealed strongly to American westerners and Southerners who in 1844 were in an expansionist mood. ("Fifty-four forty" referred to the line of latitude, 54° 40', that marked the northern border between the Oregon Territory and Russian Alaska.)

Henry Clay of Kentucky, the Whig nominee, attempted to straddle the controversial issue of Texas annexation, saying at first that he was against it and later that he was for it. This strategy alienated a group of voters in New York State, who abandoned the Whig party to support the antislavery Liberty party (see Chapter 11). In a close election, the Whigs' loss of New York's electoral votes proved decisive, and Polk, the Democratic dark horse, was the victor. The Democrats interpreted the election as a mandate to add Texas to the Union.

Annexing Texas and Dividing Oregon

Outgoing president John Tyler took the election of Polk as a signal to push the annexation of Texas through Congress. Instead of seeking Senate approval of a treaty that would have required a two-thirds vote, Tyler persuaded both houses of Congress to pass a joint resolution for annexation. This procedure required only a simple majority of each house. Tyler left Polk with the problem of dealing with Mexico's reaction to annexation.

On the Oregon question, Polk decided to compromise with Britain and back down from his party's bellicose campaign slogan, "Fifty-four Forty or Fight!" Rather than fighting for all of Oregon, the president was willing to settle for just the southern half of it. British and American negotiators agreed to divide the Oregon territory at the 49th parallel (the parallel that had been established in 1818 for the Louisiana territory). Final settlement of the issue was delayed until the United States agreed to grant Vancouver Island to Britain and guarantee its right to navigate the Columbia River. In June 1846, the treaty was submitted to the Senate for ratification. Some Northerners viewed the treaty as a sellout to Southern interests because it removed British Columbia as a source of potential free states. Nevertheless, by this time war had broken out between the United States and Mexico. Not wanting to fight both Britain and Mexico, Senate opponents of the treaty reluctantly voted for the compromise settlement.

War with Mexico

The U.S. annexation of Texas quickly led to diplomatic trouble with Mexico. Upon taking office in 1845, President Polk dispatched John Slidell as his special envoy to the government in Mexico City. Polk wanted Slidell to (1) persuade Mexico to sell the California and New Mexico territories to the United States and (2) settle the disputed Mexico-Texas border. Slidell's mission failed on both counts. The Mexican government refused to sell California and insisted that Texas's southern border was on the Nueces River. Polk and Slidell asserted that the border lay farther to the south, along the Rio Grande.

Immediate Causes of the War

While Slidell waited for Mexico City's response to the U.S. offer, Polk ordered General Zachary Taylor to move his army toward the Rio Grande across territory claimed by Mexico. On April 24, 1846, a Mexican army crossed the

Rio Grande and captured an American army patrol, killing 11. Polk used the incident to justify sending his already prepared war message to Congress. Northern Whigs (among them a first-term Illinois representative named Abraham Lincoln) opposed going to war over the incident and doubted Polk's claim that American blood had been shed on American soil. Nevertheless, Whig protests were in vain; a large majority in both houses approved the war resolution.

Military Campaigns

Most of the war was fought in Mexican territory by relatively small armies of Americans. Leading a force that never exceeded 1,500, General Stephen Kearney succeeded in taking Santa Fe, the New Mexico territory, and southern California. Backed by only several dozen soldiers, a few navy officers, and American civilians who had recently settled in California, John C. Frémont quickly overthrew Mexican rule in northern California (June 1846) and proclaimed California to be an independent republic with a bear on its flag—the so-called Bear Flag Republic.

Meanwhile, Zachary Taylor's force of 6,000 men drove the Mexican army from Texas, crossed the Rio Grande into northern Mexico, and won a major victory at Buena Vista (February 1847). President Polk then selected General Winfield Scott to invade central Mexico. The army of 14,000 under Scott's command succeeded in taking the coastal city of Vera Cruz and then captured Mexico City in September 1847.

Consequences of the War

For Mexico, the war was a military disaster from the start, but the Mexican government was unwilling to sue for peace and concede the loss of its northern lands. Finally, after the fall of Mexico City, the government had little choice but to agree to U.S. terms.

Treaty of Guadalupe Hidalgo (1848) The treaty negotiated in Mexico by American diplomat Nicholas Trist provided for the following:

1. Mexico recognized the Rio Grande as the southern border of Texas.

2. The United States took possession of the former Mexican provinces of California and New Mexico—the Mexican Cession. For these territories, the United States paid $15 million and assumed responsibility for any claims of American citizens against Mexico.

In the Senate, some Whigs opposed the treaty because they saw the war as an immoral effort to expand slavery. A few Southern Democrats disliked the treaty for opposite reasons; as expansionists, they wanted the United States to take all of Mexico. Nevertheless, the treaty was finally ratified in the Senate by the required two-thirds vote.

Wilmot Proviso U.S. entry into a war with Mexico provoked controversy from start to finish. In 1846, the first year of war, Pennsylvania Congressman David Wilmot proposed that an appropriations bill be amended to forbid slavery in any of the new territories acquired from Mexico. The Wilmot Proviso, as it was called, passed the House twice but was defeated in the Senate.

Prelude to Civil War? By increasing tensions between the North and the South, did the war to acquire territories from Mexico lead inevitably to the American Civil War? Without question, the acquisition of vast western lands did renew the sectional debate over the extension of slavery. Many Northerners viewed the war with Mexico as part of a Southern plot to extend the "slave power." Some historians see the Wilmot Proviso as the first round in an escalating political conflict that led ultimately to civil war.

WESTWARD EXPANSION AND PIONEER TRAILS, 1840s

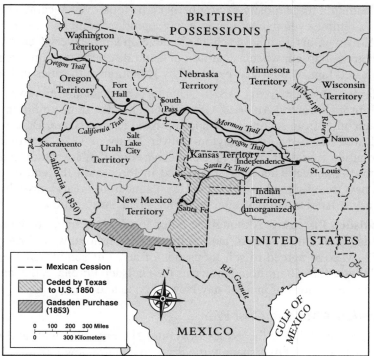

Manifest Destiny to the South

Many Southerners were dissatisfied with the territorial gains from the Mexican War. In the early 1850s, they hoped to acquire new territories, especially in areas of Latin America where they thought plantations worked by slaves were economically feasible. The most tempting, eagerly sought possibility in the eyes of Southern expansionists was the acquisition of Cuba.

Ostend Manifesto President Polk offered to purchase Cuba from Spain for $100 million, but Spain refused to sell the last major remnant of its once glorious empire. Several Southern adventurers led small expeditions to Cuba in an effort to take the island by force of arms. These forays, however, were easily defeated, and those who participated were executed by Spanish firing squads.

Elected to the presidency in 1852, Franklin Pierce adopted pro-Southern policies and dispatched three American diplomats to Ostend, Belgium, where they secretly negotiated to buy Cuba from Spain. The Ostend Manifesto that the diplomats drew up was leaked to the press in the United States and provoked an angry reaction from antislavery members of Congress. President Pierce was forced to drop the scheme.

Walker Expedition Expansionists continued to seek new empires with or without the federal government's support. Southern adventurer William Walker had tried unsuccessfully to take Baja California from Mexico in 1853. Then, leading a force mostly of Southerners, he took over Nicaragua in 1855. Walker's regime even gained temporary recognition from the United States in 1856. However, his grandiose scheme to develop a proslavery Central American empire collapsed, when a coalition of Central American countries invaded and defeated him. Walker was executed by Honduran authorities in 1860.

Clayton-Bulwer Treaty (1850) Another American ambition was to build a canal through Central America. Great Britain had the same ambition. To prevent each other from seizing this opportunity on its own, Great Britain and the United States agreed to the Clayton-Bulwer Treaty of 1850. It provided that neither nation would attempt to take exclusive control of any future canal route in Central America. This treaty continued in force until the end of the century. A new treaty signed in 1901 (the Hay-Pauncefote Treaty) gave the United States a free hand to build a canal without British participation.

Gadsden Purchase Although he failed to acquire Cuba, President Pierce succeeded in adding a strip of land to the American Southwest for a railroad. In 1853, Mexico agreed to sell thousands of acres of semidesert land to the United States for $10 million. Known as the Gadsden Purchase, the land forms the southern sections of present-day New Mexico and Arizona.

Expansion After the Civil War

From 1855 until 1870, the issues of union, slavery, civil war, and postwar reconstruction would overshadow the drive to acquire new territory. Even so, manifest destiny continued to be an important force for shaping U.S. policy. In 1867, for example, Secretary of State William Seward succeeded in purchasing Alaska at a time when the nation was just recovering from the Civil War.

Settlement of the Western Territories

Following the peaceful acquisition of Oregon and the more violent acquisition of California, the migration of Americans into these lands began in earnest. The arid area between the Mississippi Valley and the Pacific Coast was popularly known in the 1850s and 1860s as the Great American Desert. Emigrants passed quickly over this vast, dry region to reach the more inviting lands on the West Coast. Therefore, California and Oregon were settled several decades before people attempted to farm the Great Plains.

Fur Traders' Frontier

Fur traders known as mountain men were the earliest nonnative individuals to open the Far West. In the 1820s, they held yearly rendezvous in the Rockies with American Indians to trade for animal skins. James Beckwourth, Jim Bridger, Kit Carson, and Jedediah Smith were among the hardy band of explorers and trappers who provided much of the early information about trails and frontier conditions to later settlers.

Overland Trails

After the mountain men, a much larger group of pioneers made the hazardous journey west in hopes of clearing the forests and farming the fertile valleys of California and Oregon. By 1860, hundreds of thousands had reached their westward goal by following the Oregon, California, Santa Fe, and Mormon trails. The long and arduous trek usually began in St. Joseph or Independence, Missouri, or in Council Bluffs, Iowa, and followed the river valleys through the Great Plains. Inching along at only 15 miles a day, a wagon train needed months to finally reach the foothills of the Rockies or face the hardships of the southwestern deserts. The final life-or-death challenge was to get through the mountain passes of the Sierras and Cascades before the first heavy snow. While pioneers feared attacks by American Indians, the most common and serious dangers were disease and depression from the harsh everyday conditions on the trail.

Mining Frontier

The discovery of gold in California in 1848 set off the first of many migrations to mineral-rich mountains of the West. Gold or silver rushes occurred in Colorado, Nevada, the Black Hills of the Dakotas, and other western territories. The mining boom brought tens of thousands of men (and afterward women as well) into the western mountains. Mining camps and towns—many of them short-lived—sprang up wherever a strike (discovery) was reported. Largely as a result of the gold rush, California's population soared from a mere 14,000 in 1848 to 380,000 by 1860. Booms attracted miners from around the world. By the 1860s, almost one-third of the miners in the West were Chinese.

Farming Frontier

Most pioneer families moved west to start homesteads and begin farming. Congress' Preemption Acts of the 1830s and 1840s gave squatters the right to settle public lands and purchase them for low prices once the government put them up for sale. In addition, the government made it easier for settlers by offering parcels of land as small as 40 acres for sale.

However, moving west was not for the penniless. A family needed at least $200 to $300 to make the overland trip, which eliminated many of the poor. The trek to California and Oregon was largely a middle-class movement.

The isolation of the frontier made life for pioneers especially difficult during the first years, but rural communities soon developed. The institutions that the people established (schools, churches, clubs, and political parties) were modeled after those that they had known in the East or, for immigrants from abroad, in their native lands.

Urban Frontier

Western cities that arose as a result of railroads, mineral wealth, and farming attracted a number of professionals and business owners. For example, San Francisco and Denver became instant cities created by the gold and silver rushes. Salt Lake City grew because it offered fresh supplies to travelers on overland trails for the balance of their westward journey.

The Expanding Economy

The era of territorial expansion coincided with a period of remarkable economic growth from the 1840s to 1857.

Industrial Technology

Before 1840, factory production had been concentrated mainly in the textile mills of New England. After 1840, industrialization spread rapidly to the other states of the Northeast. The new factories produced shoes, sewing machines, ready-to-wear clothing, firearms, precision tools, and iron products for railroads and other new technologies. The invention of the sewing machine by Elias Howe took much of the production of clothing out of homes into factories. An electric telegraph successfully demonstrated in 1844 by its inventor, Samuel F. B. Morse, went hand in hand with the growth of railroads in enormously speeding up communication and transportation across the country.

Railroads

The canal-building era of the 1820s and 1830s was replaced in the next two decades with the rapid expansion of rail lines, especially across the Northeast and Midwest. The railroads soon emerged as America's largest industry. As such, they required immense amounts of capital and labor and gave rise to complex business organizations. Local merchants and farmers would often buy stocks in the new railroad companies in order to connect their area to the outside world. Local and state governments also helped the railroads grow by granting special loans and tax breaks. In 1850, the U.S. government granted 2.6 million acres of federal land to build the Illinois Central Railroad from Lake Michigan to the Gulf of Mexico, the first such federal land grant.

Cheap and rapid transportation particularly promoted western agriculture. Farmers in Illinois and Iowa were now more closely linked to the Northeast by rail than by the river routes to the South. The railroads not only united the common commercial interests of the Northeast and Midwest, but would also give the North strategic advantages in the Civil War.

Foreign Commerce

The growth in manufactured goods as well as in agricultural products (both Western grains and Southern cotton) caused a large growth of exports and imports. Other factors also played a role in the expansion of U.S. trade in the mid-1800s:

1. Shipping firms encouraged trade and travel across the Atlantic by having their sailing packets depart on a regular schedule (instead of the unscheduled departures that had been customary in the 18th century).

2. The demand for whale oil to light the homes of middle-class Americans caused a whaling boom between 1830 and 1860, in which New England merchants took the lead.

3. Improvements in ship design came just in time to speed goldseekers on their journey to the California gold fields. The development of the American clipper ship cut the six-month trip from New York around the Horn of South America to San Francisco to as little as 89 days.

4. Steamships took the place of clipper ships in the mid-1850s because they had greater storage capacity, could be maintained at lower cost, and could more easily follow a regular schedule.

5. The federal government expanded U.S. trade by sending Commodore Matthew C. Perry and a small fleet of naval ships to Japan, which had been closed to most foreigners for over two centuries. In 1854, Perry pressured Japan's government to sign the Kanagawa Treaty, which allowed U.S. vessels to enter two Japanese ports to take on coal. This treaty soon lead to a commerical agreement on trade.

Panic of 1857 The midcentury economic boom ended in 1857 with a financial panic. Prices, especially for Midwestern farmers, dropped sharply, and unemployment in Northern cities increased. Since cotton prices remained high, the South was less affected. As a result, some Southerners believed that their plantation economy was superior and that continued union with the Northern economy was not needed.

HISTORICAL PERSPECTIVES: WHAT CAUSED MANIFEST DESTINY?

Traditional historians stressed the accomplishments of westward expansion in bringing civilization and democratic institutions to a wilderness area. The heroic efforts of mountain men and pioneering families to overcome a hostile environment have long been celebrated by both historians and the popular media.

As a result of the civil rights movement of the 1950s and 1960s, historians today are more sensitive than earlier historians to racist language and beliefs. They recognized the racial undercurrents in the political speeches of the 1840s that argued for expansion into American Indian, Mexican, and Central American territories. Some historians argue that racist motives might even have prompted the decision to withdraw U.S. troops from Mexico instead of occupying it. They point out that Americans who opposed the idea of keeping Mexico had resorted to racist arguments, asserting that it would be undesirable to incorporate large non-Anglo populations into the republic.

continued

Recent historians have also broadened their research into westward movement. Rather than concentrating on the achievements of Anglo pioneers, they have focused more on these topics: (a) the impact on American Indians whose lands were taken, (b) the influence of Mexican culture on U.S. culture, (c) the contributions of African American and Asian American pioneers, and (d) the role of women in the development of western family and community life.

Mexican historians take a different point of view on the events of the 1840s. As they point out, the Treaty of Guadalupe Hidalgo took half of Mexico's territory. They argue that the war of 1846 gave rise to a number of long-standing economic and political problems that have impeded Mexico's development as a modern nation.

From another perspective, the war with Mexico and especially the taking of California were motivated by imperialism rather than by racism. Historians taking this position argue that the United States was chiefly interested in trade with China and Japan and needed California as a base for U.S. commercial ambitions in the Pacific. U.S. policy makers were afraid that California would fall into the hands of Great Britain or some other European power if the United States did not move in first.

KEY TERMS BY THEME

Belief (NAT)
manifest destiny

Expanding Economy (WXT)
industrial technology
Elias Howe
Samuel F. B. Morse
railroads
Panic of 1857

Westward (MIG, GEO, ARC)
Great American Desert
mountain men
Far West
overland trails
mining frontier
gold rush
silver rush
farming frontier
urban frontier
federal land grants

Expansion Politics (POL)
John Tyler
Oregon territory
"Fifty-four Forty or Fight!"
James K. Polk
Wilmot Proviso
Franklin Pierce
Ostend Manifesto (1852)

Military & Diplomatic Expansion (WOR)
Texas
Stephen Austin
Antonio López de Santa Anna
Sam Houston
Alamo
Aroostook War
Webster-Ashburton Treaty (1842)

Rio Grande; Nueces River
Mexican War (1846–1847)
Zachary Taylor
Stephen Kearney
Winfield Scott
John C. Frémont
California; Bear Flag Republic
Treaty of Guadalupe Hidalgo (1848)
Mexican Cession
Walker Expedition
Clayton-Bulwer Treaty (1850)
Gadsden Purchase (1853)
foreign commerce
exports and imports
Matthew C. Perry
Kanagawa Treaty

Questions 1–3 refer to the excerpt below.

"Where, where was the heroic determination of the executive to vindicate our title to the whole of Oregon—yes sir, 'THE WHOLE OR NONE'[?] . . . It has been openly avowed . . . that Oregon and Texas were born and cradled together in the Baltimore Convention; that they were the twin offspring of that political conclave; and in that avowal may be found the whole explanation of the difficulties and dangers with which the question is now attended. . . . I maintain

"1. That this question . . . is . . . . one for negotiations, compromise, and amicable adjustment.

"2. That satisfactory evidence has not yet been afforded that no compromise which the United States ought to accept can be effected.

"3. That, if no other mode of amicable settlement remains, arbitration ought to be resorted to. . . ."

> —Robert C. Winthrop, speech to the House of Representatives,
> "Arbitration of the Oregon Question," January 3, 1846

1. Winthrop suggests that Polk's slogan of "Fifty-four Forty or Fight!" was based mainly on which of the following attitudes?

    (A) Polk held strong anti-British sentiments

    (B) Polk believed the country needed more free land

    (C) Polk hoped to get political benefit

    (D) Polk felt pressure from Southerners

2. Which of the following served as a major cause of the war with Mexico?

    (A) The annexation of Texas

    (B) The Monroe Doctrine

    (C) The Louisiana Purchase

    (D) The election of 1844

3. President Polk accepted a compromise with Britain on the Oregon dispute because

    (A) the United States was facing problems with Mexico

    (B) the British offered a large payment

    (C) the Russians were becoming involved

    (D) the people who settled in California were successful

Questions 4–6 refer to the map below.

MAJOR LAND ACQUISITIONS OF THE UNITED STATES

4. Which period was the peak of manifest destiny?

(A) 1776 to 1783

(B) 1803 to 1810

(C) 1819 to 1841

(D) 1842 to 1853

5. One attempt to prevent slavery in the territories was the

(A) Webster-Ashburton Agreement

(B) Clayton-Bulwer Treaty

(C) Ostend Manifesto

(D) Wilmot Proviso

6. By going to war, the United States gained the territory labeled as the

(A) Louisiana Purchase

(B) Oregon Country

(C) Annexation of Texas

(D) Mexican Cession

Questions 7–8 refer to the excerpt below.

"I have made known my decision upon the Mexican Treaty. . . . I would submit it [to] the Senate for ratification . . .

"The treaty conformed on the main questions of limits and boundary to the instructions given . . . though, if the treaty was now to be made, I should demand more territory. . . .

"I look, too, to the consequences of its rejection. A [Whig] majority of one branch of Congress [the House] is opposed to my administration. . . . And if I were now to reject a treaty made upon my own terms . . . the probability is that Congress would not grant either men or money to prosecute the war. . . . I might at last be compelled to withdraw them [the army], and thus lose the two provinces of New Mexico and Upper California, which were ceded to the United States by this treaty."

—President James K. Polk, *Diary,* 21st February, 1848

7. The major opposition to the Mexican War was based on the belief that

   (A) Thoreau's ideas about non-violence were correct

   (B) it would expand slavery

   (C) the nation could not pay for a war

   (D) the British would intervene

8. President Polk was motivated to reject the treaty with Mexico because of which of the following?

   (A) Many Southerners wanted the United States to get larger gains in territory

   (B) Many Whigs opposed the treaty and were willing to continue the war

   (C) The United States was in a dispute with Great Britain over the Canadian border

   (D) The treaty called for the United States to give up the territories known as Upper California and New Mexico

SHORT-ANSWER QUESTIONS

Use complete sentences; an outline or bulleted list alone is not acceptable.

Question 1 is based on the following excerpts.

"The Manifest Destiny impulse fed off a mixture of crassness, truculence [hostility], and high idealism. Without question, there were those who proclaimed America's providential mission to expand as a eulogistic [honorary] cover for speculation in land and paper. But those were hardly the motives of John L. O'Sullivan, the writer who coined the term. . . . For O'Sullivan and his allies, the expansionist imperative was essentially democratic . . . in a supercharged moral sense, stressing America's duties to spread democratic values and institutions to a world still dominated by monarchs and deformed superstitions. . . . The mission was even more precise closer to home, where, O'Sullivan claimed six years later, America enjoyed 'the right to our manifest destiny to over-spread and to possess the whole of the continent which Providence has given us for the . . . great experiment of liberty.'"

— Sean Wilentz, *The Rise of American Democracy,* 2005

"O'Sullivan and Young America provided a language and set of aspirations that could be embraced by expansionists with less lofty ambitions because they generally ignored the 'hierarchy' and 'tyranny' of slavery and because their understanding of democratic America was so deeply radicalized and gendered. The 'young American' who would transport 'democracy into new territories was recognizably white, male, probably Protestant, and of martial demeanor— . . . facing, as he saw it, a world beset by economic backwardness, political lethargy, ignorance, superstition, Catholicism, effeminacy, and racial mixing. Expansionism would defeat the institutions that bred these maladies and offer the benefits of 'civilization' for those who wished to seize them. . . . How easy it was for the filibusters, adventurers, and speculators, who set their sights on the main chance in an "ocean-bound republic," to wrap themselves in the garbs of democracy and civilization?"

—Steven Hahn, *A Nation Without Borders,* 2016

1. Using the excerpts, answer (A), (B), and (C).

    (A) Briefly explain ONE major difference between Wilentz's and Hahn's historical interpretations of Manifest Destiny.

    (B) Briefly explain how ONE historical event or development in the period 1830 to 1860 that is not explicitly mentioned in the excerpts could be used to support Wilentz's interpretation.

    (C) Briefly explain how ONE historical event or development in the period 1830 to 1860 that is not explicitly mentioned in the excerpts could be used to support Hahn's interpretation.

Question 2. Answer (A), (B), and (C).

(A) Briefly explain ONE specific military action that added territory to the United States in the period 1840 to 1855.

(B) Briefly explain ONE specific diplomatic action that added territory to the United States in the period 1840 to 1855.

(C) Briefly explain ONE specific criticism of Manifest Destiny in the period 1840 to 1855.

Question 3 is based on the following poem.

Come my tan-faced children
Follow well in order, get your weapons ready,
Have you your pistols? Have you your sharp-edged axes?
Pioneers! O pioneers!

For we cannot tarry here,
We must march my darlings, we must bear the brunt of danger,
We the youthful sinewy races, all the rest on us depend,
Pioneers! O pioneers!

Have the elder races halted?
Do they droop and end their lesson, wearied over there beyond the seas,
We take up the task eternal, and the burden and the lesson.
Pioneers! O pioneers!

We detachments steady throwing,
Down the edges, through the passes, up mountains steep,
Conquering, holding, daring, venturing as we go the unknown ways,
Pioneers! O pioneers!

From Nebraska, from Arkansas,
Central inland race are we, from Missouri, with the continental blood intervein'd,
All the hands of comrades clasping, all the Southern, all the Northern,
Pioneers! O pioneers!

—Walt Whitman, poet, "Pioneers! O Pioneers!" 1865

3. Using the poem, answer (A), (B), and (C).

(A) Briefly explain ONE specific development in the period 1830 to 1860 that led to the point of view expressed by Whitman.

(B) Briefly explain ONE specific development in the period 1830 to 1860 that supported Whitman's point of view.

(C) Briefly explain ONE specific development in the period following 1860 that challenged Whitman's point of view.

Question 4. Answer (A), (B), and (C).

(A) Briefly explain ONE specific force that propelled the development of the territory west of the Mississippi River in the period 1820 to 1860.

(B) Briefly explain ONE specific technological advance that stimulated economic growth in the period 1840 to 1857.

(C) Briefly explain ONE specific factor that stimulated the expansion of U. S. foreign trade in the period 1840 to 1860.

THINK AS A HISTORIAN: SUPPORTING A THESIS ABOUT CONTINUITY

Which TWO of the following statements most clearly supports an argument about continuity and change over time?

1. The Clayton-Bulwer Treaty of 1850 was a defensive measure against the expansion of British influence in Central America.

2. The great era of American expansion began not in 1830, but in 1803 with Jefferson's decision to purchase the Louisiana Territory.

3. In the history of the idea of Manifest Destiny, 1860 is a meaningless date: the national attitude toward expansion was the same before and after that year.

4. The vote on the Wilmot Proviso demonstrated how members of Congress felt about the expansion of slavery in 1846.

5. The controversy over the Ostend Manifesto reflected sharp sectional differences in the United States.

13

THE UNION IN PERIL, 1848–1861

The real issue in this controversy—the one pressing upon every mind—is the sentiment on the part of one class that looks upon the institution of slavery as a wrong, and of another class that does not look upon it as a wrong.

Abraham Lincoln, 1858

Nobody disagrees about the sequence of major events from 1848 to 1861 that led ultimately to the outbreak of the Civil War between the Union and the Confederacy. Facts in themselves, however, do not automatically assemble themselves into a convincing interpretation of *why* war occurred when it did. Historians have identified at least four main causes of the conflict between the North and the South: (1) *slavery*, as a growing moral issue in the North, versus its defense and expansion in the South; (2) *constitutional disputes* over the nature of the federal Union and states' rights; (3) *economic differences* between the industrializing North and the agricultural South over such issues as tariffs, banking, and internal improvements; (4) *political blunders and extremism* on both sides, which some historians conclude resulted in an unnecessary war. This chapter summarizes the events leading up to Lincoln's election and the secession of eleven Southern states from the Union.

Conflict Over Status of Territories

The issue of slavery in the territories gained in the Mexican War became the focus of sectional differences in the late 1840s. The Wilmot Proviso, which excluded slavery from the new territories, would have upset the Compromise of 1820 and the delicate balance of 15 free and 15 slave states. The proviso's defeat only intensified sectional feelings. On the issue of how to deal with these new western territories, there were essentially three conflicting positions.

Free-Soil Movement

Northern Democrats and Whigs supported the Wilmot Proviso and the position that all African Americans—slave and free—should be excluded from the Mexican Cession (territory ceded to the U.S. by Mexico in 1848). While abolitionists advocated eliminating slavery everywhere, many Northerners who opposed the westward expansion of slavery did not oppose slavery in the

South. They sought to keep the West a land of opportunity for whites only so that the white majority would not have to compete with the labor of slaves or free blacks. In 1848, Northerners who opposed allowing slavery in the territories organized the Free-Soil party, which adopted the slogan "free soil, free labor, and free men." In addition to its chief objective—preventing the extension of slavery—the new party also advocated free homesteads (public land grants to small farmers) and internal improvements.

Southern Position

Most whites viewed any attempts to restrict the expansion of slavery as a violation of their constitutional right to take and use their property as they wished. They saw the Free-Soilers—and especially the abolitionists—as intent on the ultimate destruction of slavery. More moderate Southerners favored extending the Missouri Compromise line of 36°30' westward to the Pacific Ocean and permitting territories north of that line to be nonslave.

Popular Sovereignty

Lewis Cass, a Democratic senator from Michigan, proposed a compromise solution that soon won considerable support from both moderate Northerners and moderate Southerners. Instead of Congress determining whether to allow slavery in a new western territory or state, Cass suggested that the matter be determined by a vote of the people who settled the territory. Cass's approach to the problem was known as squatter sovereignty, or popular sovereignty.

The Election of 1848

In 1848, the Democrats nominated Senator Cass and adopted a platform pledged to popular sovereignty. The Whigs nominated Mexican War hero General Zachary Taylor, who had never been involved in politics and took no position on slavery in the territories. A third party, the Free-Soil party, nominated former president Martin Van Buren. It consisted of "conscience" Whigs (who opposed slavery) and antislavery Democrats; the latter group were ridiculed as "barnburners" because their defection threatened to destroy the Democratic party. Taylor narrowly defeated Cass, in part because of the vote given the Free-Soil party in such key Northern states as New York and Pennsylvania.

The Compromise of 1850

The gold rush of 1849 and the influx of about 100,000 settlers into California created the need for law and order in the West. In 1849, Californians drafted a constitution for their new state—a constitution that banned slavery. Even though President Taylor was a Southern slaveholder himself, he supported the immediate admission of both California and New Mexico as free states. (At this time, however, the Mexican population of the New Mexico territory had little interest in applying for statehood.)

Taylor's plan sparked talk of secession among the "fire-eaters" (radicals) in the South. Some Southern extremists even met in Nashville in 1850 to discuss secession. By this time, however, the astute Henry Clay had proposed yet another compromise for solving the political crisis:

- Admit California to the Union as a free state

- Divide the remainder of the Mexican Cession into two territories— Utah and New Mexico—and allow the settlers in these territories to decide the slavery issue by majority vote, or popular sovereignty

- Give the land in dispute between Texas and the New Mexico territory to the new territories in return for the federal government assuming Texas's public debt of $10 million

- Ban the slave trade in the District of Columbia but permit whites to hold slaves as before

- Adopt a new Fugitive Slave Law and enforce it rigorously

In the ensuing Senate debate over the compromise proposal, the three congressional giants of the age—Henry Clay of Kentucky, Daniel Webster of Massachusetts, and John C. Calhoun of South Carolina—delivered the last great speeches of their lives. (Webster and Calhoun, who were both born in 1782, died in 1850; Clay died two years later.) Webster argued for compromise in order to save the Union, and in so doing alienated the Massachusetts abolitionists who formed the base of his support. Calhoun argued against compromise and insisted that the South be given equal rights in the acquired territory.

Northern opposition to compromise came from younger antislavery lawmakers, such as Senator William H. Seward of New York, who argued that a higher law than the Constitution existed. Opponents managed to prevail until the sudden death in 1850 of President Taylor, who had also opposed Clay's plan. Succeeding him was a strong supporter of compromise, Vice President Millard Fillmore. Stephen A. Douglas, a politically astute young senator from Illinois, engineered different coalitions to pass each part of the compromise separately. President Fillmore readily signed the bills into law.

Passage The passage of the Compromise of 1850 bought time for the Union. Because California was admitted as a free state, the compromise added to the North's political power, and the political debate deepened the commitment of many Northerners to saving the Union from secession. On the other hand, parts of the compromise became sources of controversy, especially the new Fugitive Slave Law and the provision for popular sovereignty.

Agitation Over Slavery

For a brief period—the four years between the Compromise of 1850 and the passage of the Kansas-Nebraska Act in 1854—political tensions abated slightly. However, the enforcement of the Fugitive Slave Act and the publication of a best-selling antislavery novel kept the slavery question in the forefront of public attention in both the North and South.

Fugitive Slave Law

The passage of a strict Fugitive Slave Law persuaded many Southerners to accept the loss of California to the abolitionists and Free-Soilers. Yet the enforcement of the new law in the North was bitterly and sometimes forcibly resisted by antislavery Northerners. In effect, therefore, enforcement of the new law drove a wedge between the North and the South.

Enforcement and Opposition The law's chief purpose was to track down runaway (fugitive) slaves who had escaped to a Northern state, capture them, and return them to their Southern owners. The law placed fugitive slave cases under the exclusive jurisdiction of the federal government and authorized special U.S. commissioners to issue warrants to arrest fugitives. Captured persons who claimed to be a free African American and not a runaway slave were denied the right of trial by jury. Citizens who attempted to hide a runaway or obstruct enforcement of the law were subject to heavy penalties.

Underground Railroad

The Underground Railroad, the fabled network of "conductors" and "stations," was a loose network of Northern free blacks and courageous ex-slaves, with the help of some white abolitionists, who helped escaped slaves reach freedom in the North or in Canada. The most famous conductor was an escaped slave woman, Harriet Tubman, who made at least 19 trips into the South to help some 300 slaves escape. Free blacks in the North and abolitionists also organized vigilance committees to protect fugitive slaves from the slave catchers. Once the Civil War broke out, African American leaders such as Frederick Douglass, Harriet Tubman, and Sojourner Truth continued to work for the emancipation of slaves and to support black soldiers in the Union cause.

Books on Slavery—Pro and Con

Popular books as well as unpopular laws stirred the emotions of the people of all regions.

Uncle Tom's Cabin The most influential book of its day was a novel about the conflict between an enslaved man named Tom and the brutal white slave owner Simon Legree. The publication of *Uncle Tom's Cabin* in 1852 by the Northern writer Harriet Beecher Stowe moved a generation of Northerners as well as many Europeans to regard all slave owners as monstrously cruel and inhuman. Southerners condemned the "untruths" in the novel and looked upon it as one more proof of the North's incurable prejudice against the Southern way of life. Later, when President Lincoln met Stowe, he is reported to have said, "So you're the little woman who wrote the book that made this great war."

Impending Crisis of the South. Although it did not appear until 1857, Hinton R. Helper's book of nonfiction, *Impending Crisis of the South*, attacked slavery from another angle. The author, a native of North Carolina, used statistics to demonstrate to fellow Southerners that slavery weakened the South's economy. Southern states acted quickly to ban the book, but it was widely distributed in the North by antislavery and Free-Soil leaders.

Comparing the Free and Slave States in the 1850s			
Category	Free States	Slave States	Slave States as Percentage of Free States
Population	18,484,922	9,612,979	52 percent
Patents for New Inventions	1,929	268	14 percent
Value of Church Buildings	$67,778,477	$21,674,581	32 percent
Newspapers and Periodicals	1,790	740	41 percent
Bank Capital	$230,100,840	$109,078,940	47 percent
Value of Exports	$167,520,098	$107,480,688	64 percent

Source: Hinton R. Helper, *Impending Crisis of the South,* 1857. Data from various years between 1850 and 1856.

Southern Reaction Responding to the Northern literature that condemned slavery as evil, proslavery Southern whites counterattacked by arguing that slavery was just the opposite—a positive good for slave and master alike. They argued that slavery was sanctioned by the Bible and was firmly grounded in philosophy and history. Southern authors contrasted the conditions of Northern wage workers—"wage slaves" forced to work long hours in factories and mines—with the familial bonds that could develop on plantations between slaves and master. George Fitzhugh, the boldest and best known of the proslavery authors, questioned the principle of equal rights for "unequal men" and attacked the capitalist wage system as worse than slavery. Among his works were *Sociology for the South* (1854) and *Cannibals All!* (1857).

Effect of Law and Literature

The Fugitive Slave Law, combined with the antislavery and proslavery literature, polarized the nation even more. Northerners who had earlier scorned abolition became more concerned about slavery as a moral issue. At the same time, a growing number of Southerners became convinced that the North's goal was to destroy the institution of slavery and the way of life based upon it.

National Parties in Crisis

The potency of the slavery controversy increased political instability, as shown in the weakening of the two major parties—the Democrats and the Whigs—and in a disastrous application of popular sovereignty in the territory of Kansas.

The Election of 1852

Signs of trouble for the Whig party were apparent in the 1852 election for president. The Whigs nominated another military hero of the Mexican War, General Winfield Scott. Attempting to ignore the slavery issue, the Whig campaign concentrated on the party's innocuous plans for improving roads and harbors. But Scott quickly discovered that sectional issues could not be held in check. The antislavery and Southern factions of the party fell to quarreling, and the party was on the verge of splitting apart.

The Democrats nominated a safe compromise candidate, Franklin Pierce of New Hampshire. Though a Northerner, Pierce was acceptable to Southern Democrats because he supported the Fugitive Slave Law. In the electoral college vote, Pierce and the Democrats won all but four states in a sweep that suggested the days of the Whig party were numbered.

The Kansas-Nebraska Act (1854)

With the Democrats firmly in control of national policy both in the White House and in Congress, a new law was passed that was to have disastrous consequences. Senator Stephen A. Douglas of Illinois devised a plan for building a railroad and promoting western settlement (while at the same time increasing the value of his own real estate holdings in Chicago). Douglas needed to win Southern approval for his plan to build a transcontinental railroad through the central United States, with a major terminus in Chicago. (Southern Democrats preferred a more southerly route for the railroad.) To obtain Southern approval for his railroad route, Douglas introduced a bill to divide the Nebraska Territory into two parts, the Kansas Territory and Nebraska Territory, and allow settlers in each territory to decide whether to allow slavery or not. Since these territories were located *north* of the 36°30' line, Douglas's bill gave Southern slave owners an opportunity to expand slavery that previously had been closed to them by the Missouri Compromise of 1820. Northern Democrats condemned the bill as a surrender to the "slave power."

After three months of bitter debate, both houses of Congress passed Douglas's bill as the Kansas-Nebraska Act of 1854, and President Pierce signed it into law.

Extremists and Violence

The Kansas-Nebraska Act, in effect, repealed the Missouri Compromise that had kept a lid on regional tensions for more than three decades. After 1854, the conflicts between antislavery and proslavery forces exploded, both in Kansas and on the floor of the United States Senate.

THE UNITED STATES AFTER
THE KANSAS–NEBRASKA ACT OF 1854

"Bleeding Kansas"

Stephen Douglas, the sponsor of the Kansas-Nebraska Act, expected the slavery issue in the territory to be settled peacefully by the antislavery farmers from the Midwest who migrated to Kansas. These settlers did in fact constitute a majority of the population. But slaveholders from the neighboring state of Missouri also set up homesteads in Kansas chiefly as a means of winning control of the territory for the South. Northern abolitionists and Free-Soilers responded by organizing the New England Emigrant Aid Company (1855), which paid for the transportation of antislavery settlers to Kansas. Fighting soon broke out between the proslavery and the antislavery groups, and the territory became known as "bleeding Kansas."

Proslavery Missourians, mockingly called "border ruffians" by their enemies, crossed the border to create a proslavery legislature in Lecompton, Kansas. Antislavery settlers refused to recognize this government and created their own legislature in Topeka. In 1856, proslavery forces attacked the free-soil town of Lawrence, killing two and destroying homes and businesses. Two days later, John Brown, a stern abolitionist who was born in Connecticut and living in New York, retaliated. He and his sons attacked a proslavery farm settlement at Pottawatomie Creek, killing five settlers.

In Washington, the Pierce administration kept aloof from the turmoil in Kansas. It did nothing to keep order in the territory and failed to support honest elections there. As "bleeding Kansas" became bloodier, the Democratic party became ever more divided between its Northern and Southern factions.

Caning of Senator Sumner The violence in Kansas spilled over into the halls of the U.S. Congress. In 1856, Massachusetts Senator Charles Sumner verbally attacked the Democratic administration in a vitriolic speech, "The Crime Against Kansas." His intemperate remarks included personal charges against South Carolina Senator Andrew Butler. Butler's nephew, Congressman Preston Brooks, defended his absent uncle's honor by walking into the Senate chamber and beating Sumner over the head with a cane. (Brooks explained that dueling was too good for Sumner, but a cane was fit for a dog.) Sumner never fully recovered from the attack.

Brooks' action outraged the North, and the House voted to censure him. Southerners, however, applauded Brooks' deed and sent him numerous canes to replace the one he broke beating Sumner. The Sumner-Brooks incident was another sign of growing passions on both sides.

New Parties

The increasing tensions over slavery divided Northern and Southern Democrats, and it completely broke apart the Whig party. In hindsight, it is clear that the breakup of truly national political parties in the mid-1850s paralleled the breakup of the Union. The new parties came into being at this time—one temporary, the other permanent. Both played a role in bringing about the demise of a major national party, the Whigs.

Know-Nothing Party In addition to sectional divisions between North and South, there was also in the mid-1850s growing ethnic tension in the North between native-born Protestant Americans and immigrant Germans and Irish Catholics. Nativist hostility to these newcomers led to the formation of the American party—or the Know-Nothing party, as it was more commonly known (because party members commonly responded "I know nothing" to political questions). The Know-Nothings drew support away from the Whigs at a time when that party was reeling from its defeat in the 1852 election. Their one core issue was opposition to Catholics and immigrants who, in the 1840s and 1850s, were entering Northern cities in large numbers.

Although the Know-Nothings won a few local and state elections in the mid-1850s and helped to weaken the Whigs, they quickly lost influence, as sectional issues again became paramount.

Birth of the Republican Party The Republican party was founded in Wisconsin in 1854 as a direct reaction to the passage of the Kansas-Nebraska Act. Composed of a coalition of Free-Soilers and antislavery Whigs and Democrats, its overriding purpose was to oppose the spread of slavery in the territories—not to end slavery itself. Its first platform of 1854 called for the repeal of both the Kansas-Nebraska Act and the Fugitive Slave Law. As violence increased in Kansas, more and more people, including some abolitionists, joined the Republican party, and it was soon the second largest party in the country. But because it remained in these years strictly a Northern or sectional party, its success alienated and threatened the South.

The Election of 1856

The Republicans' first test of strength came in the presidential election of 1856. Their nominee for president was a senator from California, the young explorer and "Pathfinder," John C. Frémont. The Republican platform called for no expansion of slavery, free homesteads, and a probusiness protective tariff. The Know-Nothings also competed strongly in this election, with their candidate, former President Millard Fillmore, winning 20 percent of the popular vote.

As the one major national party, the Democrats expected to win. They nominated James Buchanan of Pennsylvania, rejecting both President Pierce and Stephen Douglas because they were too closely identified with the controversial Kansas-Nebraska Act. As expected, the Democratic ticket won a majority of both the popular and electoral vote. But the Republicans made a remarkably strong showing for a sectional party. In the electoral college, Frémont carried 11 of the 16 free states. People could predict that the antislavery Republicans might soon win the White House without a single vote from the South.

The election of 1856 foreshadowed the emergence of a powerful political party that would win all but four presidential elections between 1860 and 1932.

Constitutional Issues

Both the Democrats' position of popular sovereignty and the Republicans' stand against the expansion of slavery received serious blows during the Buchanan administration (1857–1861). Republicans attacked Buchanan as a weak president.

Lecompton Constitution

One of Buchanan's first challenges as president in 1857 was to decide whether to accept or reject a proslavery state constitution for Kansas submitted by the Southern legislature at Lecompton. Buchanan knew that the Lecompton constitution, as it was called, did not have the support of the majority of settlers. Even so, he asked Congress to accept the document and admit Kansas as a slave state. Congress did not do so, because many Democrats, including Stephen Douglas, joined with the Republicans in rejecting the Lecompton constitution. The next year, 1858, the proslavery document was overwhelmingly rejected by Kansas settlers, most of whom were antislavery Republicans.

Dred Scott v. Sandford (1857)

Congressional folly and presidential ineptitude contributed to the sectional crisis of the 1850s. Then the Supreme Court worsened the crisis when it infuriated many Northerners with a controversial proslavery decision in the case of a slave named Dred Scott. Scott had been held in slavery in Missouri and then taken to the free territory of Wisconsin where he lived for two years before returning to Missouri. Arguing that his residence on free soil made him a free citizen, Scott sued for his freedom in Missouri in 1846. The case worked its way through the court system. It finally reached the Supreme Court, which rendered its decision in March 1857, only two days after Buchanan was sworn in as president.

Presiding over the Court was Chief Justice Roger Taney, a Southern Democrat. A majority of the Court decided against Scott and gave these reasons:

- Dred Scott had no right to sue in a federal court because the Framers of the Constitution did not intend African Americans to be U.S. citizens.

- Congress did not have the power to deprive any person of property without due process of law; if slaves were a form of property, then Congress could not exclude slavery from any federal territory.

- The Missouri Compromise was unconstitutional because it excluded slavery from Wisconsin and other Northern territories.

The Court's ruling delighted Southern Democrats and infuriated Northern Republicans. In effect, the Supreme Court declared that all parts of the western territories were open to slavery. Republicans denounced the Dred Scott decision as "the greatest crime in the annals of the republic." Because of the timing of the decision, right after Buchanan's inauguration, many Northerners suspected that the Democratic president and the Democratic majority on the Supreme Court, including Taney, had secretly planned the Dred Scott decision, hoping that it would settle the slavery question once and for all. The decision increased Northerners' suspicions of a slave power conspiracy and induced thousands of former Democrats to vote Republican.

Northern Democrats such as Senator Douglas were left with the almost impossible task of supporting popular sovereignty without repudiating the Dred Scott decision. Douglas's hopes for a sectional compromise and his ambitions for the presidency were both in jeopardy.

Lincoln-Douglas Debates

In 1858, the focus of the nation was on Stephen Douglas's campaign for reelection as senator from Illinois. Challenging him for the Senate seat was a successful trial lawyer and former member of the Illinois legislature, Abraham Lincoln. The Republican candidate had served only one two-year term in Congress in the 1840s as a Whig. Nationally, he was an unknown compared to Douglas (the Little Giant), the champion of popular sovereignty and possibly the best hope for holding the nation together if elected president in 1860.

Lincoln was not an abolitionist. Even so, as a moderate who was against the expansion of slavery, he spoke effectively of slavery as a moral issue. ("If slavery is not wrong, nothing is wrong.") Accepting the Illinois Republicans' nomination, the candidate delivered his celebrated "house-divided" speech that won him fame. "This government," said Lincoln, "cannot endure permanently half slave and half free," a statement that made Southerners view Lincoln as a radical. In seven campaign debates held in different Illinois towns, Lincoln shared the platform with his famous opponent, Douglas. The Republican challenger attacked Douglas's seeming indifference to slavery as a moral issue.

In a debate in Freeport, Illinois, Lincoln challenged Douglas to reconcile popular sovereignty with the Dred Scott decision. In what became known as the Freeport Doctrine, Douglas responded that slavery could not exist in a community if the local citizens did not pass laws (slave codes) maintaining it. His views angered Southern Democrats because, from their point of view, Douglas did not go far enough in supporting the implications of the Dred Scott decision.

Douglas won his campaign for reelection to the U.S. Senate. In the long run, however, he lost ground in his own party by alienating Southern Democrats. Lincoln, on the other hand, emerged from the debates as a national figure and a leading contender for the Republican nomination for president in 1860.

The Road to Secession

Outside Illinois, the Republicans did well in the congressional elections of 1858, which alarmed many Southerners. They worried not only about the antislavery plank in the Republicans' program but also about that party's economic program, which favored the interests of Northern industrialists at the expense of the South. The higher tariffs pledged in the Republican platform could only help Northern business and hurt the South's dependence on the export of cotton. Therefore, Southerners feared that a Republican victory in 1860 would spell disaster for their economic interests and also threaten their "constitutional right," as affirmed by the Supreme Court, to hold slaves as property. If this were not enough cause for alarm, Northern radicals provided money to John Brown, the man who had massacred five farmers in Kansas in 1856.

John Brown's Raid at Harpers Ferry

John Brown confirmed the South's worst fears of radical abolitionism when he tried to start a slave uprising in Virginia. In October 1859, he led a small band of followers, including his four sons and some former slaves, in an attack on the federal arsenal at Harpers Ferry. His impractical plan was to use guns from the arsenal to arm Virginia's slaves, whom he expected to rise up in general revolt. Federal troops under the command of Robert E. Lee captured Brown and his band after a two-day siege. Brown and six of his followers were tried for treason, convicted, and hanged by the state of Virginia.

Moderates in the North, including Republican leaders, condemned Brown's use of violence, but Southerners were not convinced by their words. Southern whites saw the raid as final proof of the North's true intentions—to use slave revolts to destroy the South. Because John Brown spoke with simple eloquence at his trial of his humanitarian motives in wanting to free the slaves, he was hailed as a martyr by many antislavery Northerners. (A few years later, when civil war broke out, John Brown was celebrated by advancing Northern armies singing: "Glory, glory, hallelujah! His soul is marching on.")

The Election of 1860

After John Brown's raid, more and more Americans understood that their country was moving to the brink of disintegration. The presidential election of 1860 would be a test if the union could survive.

Breakup of the Democratic Party As 1860 began, the Democratic party represented the last practical hope for coalition and compromise. The Democrats held their national nominating convention in Charleston, South Carolina. Stephen Douglas was the party's leading candidate and the person most capable of winning the presidency. However, his nomination was blocked by a combination of angry Southerners and supporters of President Buchanan.

After deadlocking at Charleston, the Democrats held a second convention in Baltimore. Many delegates from the slave states walked out, enabling the remaining delegates to nominate Douglas on a platform of popular sovereignty and enforcement of the Fugitive Slave Law. Southern Democrats then held their own convention in Baltimore and nominated Vice President John C. Breckinridge of Kentucky as their candidate. The Southern Democratic platform called for the unrestricted extension of slavery in the territories and the annexation of Cuba, a land where slavery was already flourishing.

Republican Nomination of Lincoln When the Republicans met in Chicago, they enjoyed the prospect of an easy win over the divided Democrats. They made the most of their advantage by drafting a platform that appealed strongly to the economic self-interest of Northerners and Westerners. In addition to calling for the exclusion of slavery from the territories, the Republican platform promised a protective tariff for industry, free land for homesteaders, and internal improvements to encourage western settlement, including a railroad to the Pacific. To ensure victory, the Republicans turned away from Senator William H. Seward, a well-known leader but more radical on slavery, to the strong debater from Illinois, Abraham Lincoln—a candidate who could carry the key Midwestern states of Illinois, Indiana, and Ohio.

One cloud on the horizon darkened the Republicans' otherwise bright future. In the South, secessionists warned that if Lincoln was elected president, their states would leave the Union.

A Fourth Political Party Fearing the consequences of a Republican victory, a group of former Whigs, Know-Nothings, and moderate Democrats formed a new party: the Constitutional Union party. For president, they nominated John Bell of Tennessee. The party's platform pledged enforcement of the laws and the Constitution and, above all, preserving the Union.

Election Results While Douglas campaigned across the country, Lincoln confidently remained at home in Springfield, Illinois, meeting with Republican leaders and giving statements to the press. The election results were predictable. Lincoln carried every one of the free states of the North, which represented a solid majority of 59 percent of the electoral votes. He won only 39.8 percent of the popular vote, however, and would therefore be a minority president. Breckinridge, the Southern Democrat, carried the Deep South, leaving Douglas and Bell with just a few electoral votes in the border states.

Together, the two Democrats, Douglas and Breckinridge, received many more *popular* votes than Lincoln, the Republican. Nevertheless, the new political reality was that the populous free states had enough electoral votes to select a president without the need for a single electoral vote from the South.

THE ELECTION OF 1860

	Electoral votes	Popular votes
Lincoln (Rep.)	180	1,866,000
Douglas (No. Dem.)	12	1,375,000
Breckinridge (So. Dem.)	72	848,000
Bell (Const. Union)	39	591,000

Secession of the Deep South

The Republicans controlled neither the Congress nor the Supreme Court. Even so, the election of Lincoln was all that Southern secessionists needed to call for immediate disunion. In December 1860, a special convention in South Carolina voted unanimously to secede. Within the next six weeks, other state conventions in Georgia, Florida, Alabama, Mississippi, Louisiana, and Texas did the same. In February 1861, representatives of the seven states of the Deep South met in Montgomery, Alabama, and created the Confederate States of America. The constitution of this would-be Southern nation was similar to the U.S. Constitution, except that the Confederacy placed limits on the government's power to impose tariffs and restrict slavery. Elected president and vice president of the Confederacy were Senator Jefferson Davis of Mississippi and Alexander Stephens of Georgia.

Crittenden Compromise. A lame-duck president (a leader completing a term after someone else has been elected to his or her office), Buchanan had five months in office before President-elect Lincoln was due to succeed him. Buchanan was a conservative who did nothing to prevent the secession of the seven states. Congress was more active. In a last-ditch effort to appease the South, Senator John Crittenden of Kentucky proposed a constitutional amendment that would guarantee the right to hold slaves in all territories south of 36°30'. Lincoln, however, said that he could not accept this compromise because it violated the Republican position against extension of slavery into the territories.

Southern whites who voted for secession believed they were acting in the tradition of the Revolution of 1776. They argued that they had a right to national independence and to dissolve a constitutional compact that no longer protected them from "tyranny" (the tyranny of Northern rule). Many of them also thought that Lincoln, like Buchanan, might permit secession without a fight. Those who thought this had badly miscalculated.

HISTORICAL PERSPECTIVES: WHAT CAUSED THE CIVIL WAR?

Was slavery the primary cause of the Civil War? In the decades after the war, Northern historians argued emphatically that the South's attachment to slavery was the principal, if not the only, cause. They blamed the war on a conspiracy of slave owners—a small minority of Southerners—who wanted only to expand slavery at the expense of whites and blacks alike.

Southern historians, on the other hand, viewed the conflict between the two sections, North and South, as a dispute over the nature of the Constitution. They argued that Northern abolitionists and Free-Soil politicians attempted to overturn the original compact of the states, and that the Southern states seceded to defend the constitutional rights threatened by Northern aggression.

By the early 20th century, passions had cooled on both sides, and scholars of the Progressive era (1900–1917) thought economic interests were the foundation of all political conflict. Thus, Charles Beard, a leading historian of this era, viewed the sectional conflict of the 1850s as a clash of two opposing economic systems: the industrial North versus the agricultural South. His economic interpretation of the Civil War stressed the importance of the Republicans' commitment to the economic ambitions of Northern industrialists for high tariffs and of western farmers for free land.

American disillusionment with World War I led historians to question whether the Civil War was any more necessary or inevitable than the world war had been. Previously, people had assumed that the Civil War was, in William Seward's words, an "irrepressible conflict between opposing forces." Now, in the 1920s and 1930s, that assumption was challenged by revisionist historians who argued that it was only the blundering of politicians and the rash acts of a few extremists such as John Brown that were chiefly responsible for secession and war. In an essay in 1940, James G. Randall summarized the thinking of the revisionist school: "If one word or phrase were selected to account for the war, that word would not be slavery, or states' rights, or diverse civilizations. It would have to be such a word as fanaticism (on both sides), or misunderstanding, or perhaps politics." Politicians of the 1850s who worked for compromise (Clay, Douglas, and Crittenden) were treated as the revisionists' heroes, whereas Lincoln was criticized for fomenting sectional passions with his house-divided and other speeches.

In the 1950s and 1960s, the civil rights movement provided the backdrop for rethinking the causes of the Civil War. Historians who were sympathetic with African Americans' struggles for civil rights returned to the view that slavery was the chief cause of disunion after all. They argued that moral issues such as slavery are impossible to compromise. Arthur Schlesinger, Jr., a leading historian of the 1950s, wrote: "A society closed in the defense of evil institutions thus creates moral differences far too profound to be solved by compromise." In this view, slavery as an inherently evil institution was at the root of a conflict that was indeed "irrepressible."

KEY TERMS BY THEME

Battle for the Territories (MIG, POL)
free-soil movement
Free-Soil party
conscience Whigs
"barnburners"
New England Emigrant Aid Company
"bleeding Kansas"
Pottawatomie Creek
Lecompton constitution

Compromising (POL)
popular sovereignty
Lewis Cass
Henry Clay
Zachary Taylor
Compromise of 1850
Stephen A. Douglas
Millard Fillmore

Kansas-Nebraska Act (1854)
Crittenden compromise

Politics in Crisis (POL)
Franklin Pierce
Know-Nothing party
Republican party
John C. Frémont
James Buchanan
election of 1860
secession

Slavery (POL, ARC)
Fugitive Slave Law
Underground Railroad
Harriet Tubman
Dred Scott v. Sandford
Roger Taney
Abraham Lincoln

Lincoln-Douglas debates
house-divided speech
Freeport Doctrine

Violent Responses (POL)
Sumner-Brooks incident
John Brown
Harpers Ferry raid

Writing Power (ARC)
Harriet Beecher Stowe, Uncle Tom's Cabin
Hinton R. Helper, Impending Crisis of the South
George Fitzhugh, Sociology of the South

Questions 1–3 refer to the excerpt below.

"It being desirable for the peace, concord, and harmony of the Union of these states to settle and adjust amicably all existing questions of controversy between them arising out of the institution of slavery upon a fair, equitable, and just basis. . . .

"We are told now . . . that the Union is threatened with subversion and destruction . . . If the Union is to be dissolved for any existing causes, it will be dissolved because slavery is interdicted or not allowed to be introduced into the ceded territories, because slavery is threatened to be abolished in the District of Columbia, and because fugitive slaves are not returned . . . to their masters. . . .

"I am for staying within the Union and fighting for my rights."

—Henry Clay, Resolution on the Compromise of 1850, 1850

1. To which politicians is Clay directing the last line of the excerpt?

    (A) Southerners who were threatening to secede

    (B) Senators such as Daniel Webster who rejected any compromise

    (C) Advocates of popular sovereignty

    (D) The president, Zachary Taylor

2. Which of the following parts of the Compromise of 1850 was the most appealing to the South?

    (A) Admitting California as a free state

    (B) Passing a new Fugitive Slave Law

    (C) Ending the slave trade in Washington, D.C.

    (D) Using popular sovereignty in new territories

3. Which of the following parts of the Compromise of 1850 was the most appealing to the North?

    (A) Admitting California as a free state

    (B) Passing a new Fugitive Slave Law

    (C) Ending the slave trade in Washington, D.C.

    (D) Using popular sovereignty in new territories

Questions 4–5 refer to the excerpt below.

"Mr. President . . . I proposed on Tuesday last that the Senate should proceed to the consideration of the bill to organize the territories of Nebraska and Kansas . . . . Now I ask the friends and the opponents of this measure to look at it as it is. Is not the question involved the simple one, whether the people of the territories shall be allowed to do as they please upon the question of slavery, subject only to the limitations of the Constitution? . . .

"If the principle is right, let it be avowed and maintained. If it is wrong, let it be repudiated. Let all this quibbling about the Missouri Compromise, about the territory acquired from France, about the act of 1820, be cast behind you; for the simple question is—Will you allow the people to legislate for themselves upon the subject of slavery? Why should you not?"

—Stephen A. Douglas, Defense of the Kansas-Nebraska Bill, 1854

4. Which of the following ideas is Douglas appealing to when he says, "whether the people of the territories shall be allowed to do as they please upon the question of slavery"?

    (A) The Crittenden Compromise

    (B) Popular sovereignty

    (C) The right of secession

    (D) The distinction between a territory and a state

5. An increase in which of the following was the key part of the Kansas-Nebraska Act to attract Southern support?

    (A) Transportation in the South

    (B) Popular sovereignty

    (C) Fugitive Slave Act

    (D) Representation in Congress

Questions 6–8 refer to the excerpt below.

"And upon full and careful consideration . . . Dred Scott was not a citizen of Missouri within the meaning of the Constitution of the United States and not entitled as such to sue in its courts. . . .

"Upon these considerations it is the opinion of the court that the act of Congress which prohibited a citizen from holding and owning property of this kind in the territory of the United States north of the line therein mentioned is not warranted by the Constitution and is therefore void. . . .

"That it is now firmly settled by the decisions of the highest court in the state that Scott and his family, upon their return, were not free, but were, by the laws of Missouri, the property of the defendant; and that the Circuit Court of the United States has no jurisdiction when by the laws of the state, the plaintiff was a slave and not a citizen."

—Roger B. Taney, *Dred Scott v. Sandford,* 1857

6. Which of the following political groups had its efforts to find a compromise over slavery effectively ended by Taney's decision in the Dred Scott case?

   (A) Whigs

   (B) Free-Soil Party

   (C) Constitution Union Party

   (D) Northern Democrats

7. Northerners were most upset by the Supreme Court's Dred Scott decision because

   (A) the Court included no Republican Justices

   (B) the decision allowed slavery in the territories

   (C) several justices were slave owners

   (D) blacks and whites were not treated equally

8. Which of the following acts of Congress was declared unconstitutional in the Dred Scott decision?

   (A) Missouri Compromise of 1820

   (B) Compromise of 1850

   (C) Kansas-Nebraska Act

   (D) Fugitive Slave Law

SHORT-ANSWER QUESTIONS

Use complete sentences; an outline or bulleted list alone is not acceptable.

Question 1 is based on the following excerpts.

"The country had been founded in compromise, and to compromise it was dedicated. . . . But this conception of compromise was in trouble, and the word would . . . become an epithet.

The underlying issue was the North's increasing power. And that power endangered slavery. Secessionists worried if slavery did not expand into the territories, the black population would stay where it was, bottled up and likely to explode. Fear motivated them. That is to say, racial anxiety was as pervasive as economic anxiety when it came to secession, though it was hard to separate the two, for they were threaded together with the rope that bound secessionists and many Southerners to their land, their way of life, their mint juleps, and their pride of race.

Lincoln's election was thus not so much the cause of secession as its excuse: institutional restraints (read: the federal government) had insulted Southerners, imperiled their way of life, undermined their moral structure, triggered their racial fears."

—Brenda Wineapple, *Ecstatic Nation,* 2013

"During the 1850s, however, the forces that had worked to hold the nation together in the past fell victim to new and much more divisive pressures that were working to split the nation apart. Driving the sectional tensions of the 1850s was a battle over national policy toward the western territories which were clamoring to become states of the Union—and over the place of slavery within them. Should slavery be permitted in the new states? And who should decide whether to permit it or not? . . . Positions on slavery continued to harden in both the North and South until ultimately each region came to consider the other its enemy."

—Alan Brinkley, *American History,* 2003

1. Using the excerpts, answer (A), (B), and (C).

   (A) Briefly explain ONE major difference between Wineapple's and Brinkley's historical interpretations of Manifest Destiny.

   (B) Briefly explain how ONE historical event or development in the period 1848 to 1861 that is not explicitly mentioned in the excerpts could be used to support Wineapple's interpretation.

   (C) Briefly explain how ONE historical event or development in the period 1848 to 1861 that is not explicitly mentioned in the excerpts could be used to support Brinkley's interpretation.

Question 2 is based on the following cartoon.

That's you Dad! more "FREE SOIL." We'll rat 'em out yet. Long life to Davy Wilmot.

SMOKING HIM OUT.

Source: Nathaniel Currier, 1848. Library of Congress

2. Using the cartoon, answer (A), (B), and (C). The figure on the right side of the cartoon is saying, "That's you Dad! more 'Free Soil.' We'll rat 'em out yet. Long life to Davy Wilmot."

(A) Briefly explain ONE historical perspective expressed by the artist about the views of slavery in the territories in the period 1840 to 1854.

(B) Briefly explain ONE development in the period 1840 to 1854 that supported the perspective expressed by the artist.

(C) Briefly explain ONE development in the period 1840 to 1854 that challenged the perspective expressed by the artist.

Question 3. Answer (A), (B), and (C).

(A) Briefly explain ONE specific social or political response to the conflict over slavery in the period 1850 to 1855.

(B) Briefly explain ONE specific social or political response to the conflict over slavery in the period 1855 to 1860.

(C) Briefly explain ONE specific important reason for the change in response from the period 1850 to 1855 to the period 1855 to 1860.

Question 4. Answer (A), (B), and (C).

  (A) Briefly explain ONE specific response in the North to the enforcement of a new Fugitive Slave Law in the 1850s.

  (B) Briefly explain ONE specific response in the South to the Northern actions with regards to slavery in the 1850s.

  (C) Briefly explain how the different responses to the Fugitive Slave Law influenced political parties in the period of the 1850s.

THINK AS A HISTORIAN: STATEMENTS ABOUT COMPARISONS

Which THREE of the following statements most clearly expresses comparisons or contrasts?

1. The reactions to both the Wilmot Proviso and the Ostend Manifesto demonstrated how sensitive the issue of slavery expansion was.

2. Douglas combined a desire to advance his personal interest in railroad expansion with a desire to keep the Union together.

3. Henry Clay was a great legislative leader because he believed in compromise.

4. While Harriet Beecher Stowe's book was fictional and literary, Hinton Rowan Helper's book was nonfiction and statistical.

5. John Brown shared similarities with Anne Hutchinson, Patrick Henry, and Nat Turner.

14

THE CIVIL WAR, 1861–1865

It is enough to make the whole world start to see the awful amount of death and destruction that now stalks abroad. Daily for the past two months has the work progressed and I see no signs of a remission till one or both the armies are destroyed. . . . I begin to regard the death and mangling of a couple of thousand men as a small affair, a kind of morning dash—and it may be well that we become so hardened.

General William T. Sherman, June 30, 1864

The Civil War between the Union and the Confederacy (1861–1865) was the most costly of all American wars in terms of the loss of human life—and also the most destructive war ever fought in the Western Hemisphere. The deaths of 750,000 people, a true national tragedy, constituted only part of the impact of the war on American society. Most important, the Civil War freed 4 million people from slavery, giving the nation what President Lincoln called a "new birth of freedom." The war also transformed American society by accelerating industrialization and modernization in the North and destroying much of the South. These changes were so fundamental and profound that some historians refer to the Civil War as the Second American Revolution. While this chapter summarizes the major military aspects of the Civil War, it, like the AP exam, emphasizes the social, economic, and political changes that took place during the war.

The War Begins

When Lincoln took office as the first Republican president in March 1861, people wondered if he would challenge the secession of South Carolina and other states militarily. In his inaugural address, Lincoln assured Southerners that he would not interfere with slavery. At the same time, he warned, no state had the right to break up the Union. He concluded by appealing for restraint:

> In *your* hands, my dissatisfied fellow-countrymen, and not in *mine,* is the momentous issue of civil war. The government will not assail *you.* You can have no conflict without being yourselves the aggressors.

Fort Sumter

Despite the president's message of both conciliation and warning, the danger of a war breaking out was acute. Most critical was the status of two federal forts in states that had seceded. One of these, Fort Sumter, in the harbor of Charleston, South Carolina, was cut off from vital supplies and reinforcements by Southern control of the harbor. Rather than either giving up Fort Sumter or attempting to defend it, Lincoln announced that he was sending provisions of food to the small federal garrison. He thus gave South Carolina the choice of either permitting the fort to hold out or opening fire with its shore batteries. Carolina's guns thundered their reply and thus, on April 12, 1861, the war began. The attack on Fort Sumter and its capture after two days of incessant pounding united most Northerners behind a patriotic fight to save the Union.

Use of Executive Power More than any previous president, Lincoln acted in unprecedented ways, drawing upon his powers as both chief executive and commander in chief, often without the authorization or approval of Congress. For example, right after the Fort Sumter crisis he (1) called for 75,000 volunteers to put down the "insurrection" in the Confederacy, (2) authorized spending for a war, and (3) suspended the privilege of the writ of habeas corpus. Since Congress was not in session, the president acted completely on his own authority. Lincoln later explained that he had to take strong measures without congressional approval "as indispensable to the public safety."

Secession of the Upper South

Before the attack on Fort Sumter, only seven states of the Deep South had seceded. After it became clear that Lincoln would use troops in the crisis, four states of the Upper South—Virginia, North Carolina, Tennessee, and Arkansas—also seceded and joined the Confederacy. The Confederates then moved their capital to Richmond, Virginia. The people of western Virginia remained loyal to the Union, and the region became a separate state in 1863.

Keeping the Border States in the Union

Four other slaveholding states might have seceded, but instead remained in the Union. The decisions of Delaware, Maryland, Missouri, and Kentucky *not* to join the Confederacy was partly due to Union sentiment in those states and partly the result of shrewd federal policies. In Maryland, pro-secessionists attacked Union troops and threatened the railroad to Washington. The Union army resorted to martial law to keep the state under federal control. In Missouri, the presence of U.S. troops prevented the pro-South elements in the state from gaining control, although guerrilla forces sympathetic to the Confederacy were active throughout the war. In Kentucky, the state legislature voted to remain neutral in the conflict. Lincoln initially respected its neutrality and waited for the South to violate it before moving in federal troops.

Keeping the border states in the Union was a primary military and political goal for Lincoln. Their loss would have increased the Confederate population by more than 50 percent and would have severely weakened the North's strategic position for conducting the war. Partly to avoid alienating Unionists in the border states, Lincoln rejected initial calls for the emancipation of slaves.

Wartime Advantages

The Union and the Confederacy each started the war with some strengths and some weaknesses.

Military The Confederacy entered the war with the advantage of having to fight only a defensive war to win, while the Union had to conquer an area as large as Western Europe. The Confederates had to move troops and supplies shorter distances than the Union. It had a long, indented coastline that was difficult to blockade and, most important, experienced military leaders and high troop morale. The Union hoped that its population of 22 million against the Confederate's population of only 5.5 million free whites would work to its favor in a war of attrition. The North's population advantage was enhanced during the war by 800,000 immigrants. Emancipation also brought 180,000 African Americans into the Union army in the critical final years of the war. The Union could also count on a loyal U.S. Navy, which ultimately gave it command of the rivers and territorial waters.

Economic The Union dominated the nation's economy, controlling most of the banking and capital of the country, more than 85 percent of the factories, more than 70 percent of the railroads, and even 65 percent of the farmland. The skills of Northern clerks and bookkeepers proved valuable in the logistical support of large military operations. Confederates hoped that European demand for its cotton would bring recognition and financial aid. Like other rebel movements in history, the Confederates counted on outside help to be successful.

Political The two sides had distinct goals. The Confederates were struggling for independence while the Union was fighting to preserve the Union. However, the ideology of states' rights proved a serious liability for the new Confederate government. The irony was that in order to win the war, the Confederates needed a strong central government with strong public support. The Confederates had neither, while the Union had a well-established central government, and in Abraham Lincoln and in the Republican and Democratic parties it had experienced politicians with a strong popular base. The ultimate hope of the Confederates was that the people of the Union would turn against Lincoln and the Republicans and quit the war because it was too costly.

The Confederate States of America

The Confederate constitution was modeled after the U.S. Constitution, except that it provided a single six-year term for the president and gave the president an item veto (the power to veto only part of a bill). Its constitution denied the Confederate congress the powers to levy a protective tariff and to appropriate funds for internal improvements, but it did prohibit the foreign slave trade. President Jefferson Davis tried to increase his executive powers during the war, but Southern governors resisted attempts at centralization, some holding back troops and resources to protect their own states. At one point, Vice President

Alexander H. Stephens, in defense of states' rights, even urged the secession of Georgia in response to the "despotic" actions of the Confederate government.

The Confederacy was chronically short of money. It tried loans, income taxes (including a 10 percent tax in-kind on farm produce), and even impressment of private property, but these revenues paid for only a small part of war costs. The government issued more than $1 billion in paper money, so much that it caused severe inflation. By the end of the war, the value of a Confederate dollar was less than two cents. The Confederate congress nationalized the railroads and encouraged industrial development. The Confederacy sustained nearly 1 million troops at its peak, but a war of attrition doomed its efforts.

First Years of a Long War: 1861–1862

People at first expected the war to last no more than a few weeks. Lincoln called up the first volunteers for an enlistment period of only 90 days. "On to Richmond!" was the optimistic cry, but as Americans soon learned, it would take almost four years of ferocious fighting before Union troops finally did march into the Confederate capital.

First Battle of Bull Run In the first major battle of the war (July 1861), 30,000 federal troops marched from Washington, D.C., to attack Confederate forces positioned near Bull Run Creek at Manassas Junction, Virginia. Just as the Union forces seemed close to victory, Confederate reinforcements under General Thomas (Stonewall) Jackson counterattacked and sent the inexperienced Union troops in disorderly and panicky flight back to Washington (together with civilian curiosity-seekers and picnickers). The battle ended the illusion of a short war and also promoted the myth that the Rebels were invincible in battle.

Union Strategy General-in-Chief Winfield Scott, veteran of the 1812 and Mexican wars, devised a three-part strategy for winning a long war:

- Use the U.S. Navy to blockade Southern ports (called the Anaconda Plan), cutting off essential supplies from reaching the Confederacy

- Take control of the Mississippi River, dividing the Confederacy in two

- Raise and train an army 500,000 strong to conquer Richmond

The first two parts of the strategy proved easier to achieve than the third, but ultimately all three were important in achieving Northern victory.

After the Union's defeat at Bull Run, federal armies experienced a succession of crushing defeats as they attempted various campaigns in Virginia. Each was less successful than the one before.

Peninsula Campaign General George B. McClellan, the new commander of the Union army in the East, insisted that his troops be given a long period of training before going into battle. Finally, after many delays that sorely tested Lincoln's patience, McClellan's army invaded Virginia in March 1862. The

Union army was stopped as a result of brilliant tactical moves by Confederate General Robert E. Lee, who emerged as the commander of the South's eastern forces. After five months, McClellan was forced to retreat and was ordered back to the Potomac, where he was replaced by General John Pope.

THE CIVIL WAR:
THE UNION VS. THE CONFEDERACY

Second Battle of Bull Run Lee took advantage of the change in Union generals to strike quickly at Pope's army in Northern Virginia. He drew Pope into a trap, then struck the enemy's flank, and sent the Union army backward to Bull Run. Pope withdrew to the defenses of Washington.

Antietam Following up his victory at Bull Run, Lee led his army across the Potomac into enemy territory in Maryland. In doing so, he hoped that a major Confederate victory in a Union state would convince Britain to give official recognition and support to the Confederacy. By this time (September 1862), Lincoln had restored McClellan to command of the Union army. McClellan had the advantage of knowing Lee's battle plan, because a copy of it had been dropped accidentally by a Confederate officer. The Union army intercepted the invading Confederates at Antietam Creek in the Maryland town of Sharpsburg.

Here the bloodiest single day of combat in the entire war took place, a day in which more than 22,000 soldiers were killed or wounded.

Unable to break through Union lines, Lee's army retreated to Virginia. Disappointed with McClellan for failing to pursue Lee's weakened and retreating army, Lincoln removed him for a final time as the Union commander. The president complained that his general had a "bad case of the slows." While a draw on the battlefield, Antietam proved to be a decisive battle because the Confederates failed to get what they so urgently needed—open recognition and aid from a foreign power. On the other side, Lincoln found enough encouragement in the results of Antietam to claim a Union victory. As explained later in this chapter, Lincoln used the partial triumph of Union arms to announce plans for a direct assault on the institution of slavery.

Fredericksburg Replacing McClellan with the more aggressive General Ambrose Burnside, Lincoln discovered that a strategy of reckless attack could have even worse consequences than McClellan's strategy of caution and inaction. In December 1862, a large Union army under Burnside attacked Lee's army at Fredericksburg, Virginia, and suffered immense losses: 12,000 dead or wounded compared to 5,000 Confederate casualties. Both Union and Confederate generals were slow to learn that improved weaponry, especially the deadly fire from enemy artillery, took the romance out of heroic charges against entrenched positions. By the end of 1862, the awful magnitude of the war was all too clear—with no prospect of military victory for either side.

The second year of war, 1862, was a disastrous one for the Union except for two engagements, one at sea and the other on the rivers of the West.

Monitor **vs.** *Merrimac* The Union's hopes for winning the war depended upon its ability to maximize its economic and naval advantages by an effective blockade of Confederate ports (the Anaconda plan). During McClellan's Peninsula campaign, the Union's blockade strategy was placed in jeopardy by the Confederate ironclad ship the *Merrimac* (a former Union ship, rebuilt and renamed the *Virginia*) that attacked and sunk several Union wooden ships on March 8, 1862, near Hampton Roads, Virginia. The ironclad ship seemed unstoppable. However, on March 9, the Union's own ironclad, the *Monitor,* engaged the *Merrimac* in a five-hour duel. Although the battle ended in a draw, the *Monitor* prevented the Confederate's formidable new weapon from challenging the U.S. naval blockade. More broadly, the *Monitor* and the *Merrimac* marked a turning point in naval warfare, with vulnerable wooden ships being replaced by far more formidable ironclad ones.

Grant in the West The battle of the ironclads occurred at about the same time as a far bloodier encounter in western Tennessee, a Confederate state. The Union's campaign for control of the Mississippi River was partly under the command of a West Point graduate, Ulysses S. Grant, who had joined up for the war after an unsuccessful civilian career. Striking south from Illinois in early 1862, Grant used a combination of gunboats and army maneuvers to capture Fort Henry and Fort Donelson on the Cumberland River (a branch of the Mississippi). These stunning victories, in which 14,000 Confederates were taken prisoner, opened up the state of Mississippi to Union attack. A few weeks later, a Confederate army under Albert Johnston surprised Grant at Shiloh, Tennessee, but the Union army held its ground and finally forced the Confederates to retreat after terrible losses on both sides (more than 23,000 dead and wounded). Grant's drive down the Mississippi was complemented in April 1862 by the capture of New Orleans by the Union navy under David Farragut.

Foreign Affairs and Diplomacy

The Confederate's hopes for securing independence hinged as much on its diplomats as on soldiers. Confederate leaders fully expected that cotton would indeed prove to be "king" and induce Britain or France, or both, to give direct aid to the war effort. Besides depending on cotton for their textile mills, wealthy British industrialists and members of the British aristocracy looked forward with pleasure to the breakup of the American democratic experiment. From the Union's point of view, it was critically important to prevent the Confederacy from gaining the foreign support and recognition that it desperately needed.

Trent Affair

Britain came close to siding with the Confederacy in late 1861 over an incident at sea. Confederate diplomats James Mason and John Slidell were traveling to England on a British steamer, the *Trent,* on a mission to gain recognition for their government. A Union warship stopped the British ship, removed Mason and Slidell, and brought them to the United States as prisoners of war. Britain threatened war over the incident unless the two diplomats were released. Despite intense public criticism, Lincoln gave in to British demands. Mason and Slidell were duly set free, but after again sailing for Europe, they failed to obtain full recognition of the Confederacy from either Britain or France.

Confederate Raiders

The Confederates were able to gain enough recognition as a belligerent to purchase warships from British shipyards. Confederate commerce-raiders did serious harm to U.S. merchant ships. One of them, the *Alabama,* captured more than 60 vessels before being sunk off the coast of France by a Union warship. After the war, Great Britain eventually agreed to pay the United States $15.5 million for damages caused by the South's commerce-raiders.

The U.S. minister to Britain, Charles Francis Adams, prevented a potentially much more serious threat. Learning that the Confederacy had arranged to purchase Laird rams (ships with iron rams) from Britain for use against the Union's naval blockade, Adams persuaded the British government to cancel the sale rather than risk war with the United States.

Failure of Cotton Diplomacy

In the end, the South's hopes for European intervention were disappointed. "King Cotton" did not have the power to dictate another nation's foreign policy, since Europe quickly found ways of obtaining cotton from other sources. By the time shortages of Southern cotton hit the British textile industry, adequate shipments of cotton began arriving from Egypt and India. Also, materials other than cotton could be used for textiles, and the woolen and linen industries were not slow to take advantage of their opportunity.

Two other factors went into Britain's decision not to recognize the Confederacy. First, as mentioned, General Lee's setback at Antietam played a role; without seeing a decisive Confederate military victory, the British government would not risk recognition. Second, Lincoln's Emancipation Proclamation (January 1863) made the end of slavery an objective of the Union, a position that appealed strongly to Britain's working class. While conservative leaders of Britain were sympathetic to the Confederates, they could not defy the pro-Northern, antislavery feelings of the British majority.

The End of Slavery

Even though Lincoln in the 1850s spoke out against slavery as "an unqualified evil," as president he seemed hesitant to take action against slavery as advocated by many of his Republican supporters. Lincoln's concerns included (1) keeping the support of the border states, (2) the constitutional protections of slavery, (3) the racial prejudice of many Northerners, and (4) the fear that premature action could be overturned in the next election. All these concerns made the timing and method of ending slavery fateful decisions. Enslaved individuals were freed during the Civil War as a result of military events, governmental policy, and their own actions.

Confiscation Acts

Early in the war (May 1861), Union General Benjamin Butler refused to return captured slaves to their Confederate owners, arguing that they were "contraband of war." The power to seize enemy property used to wage war against the United States was the legal basis for the first Confiscation Act passed by Congress in August 1861. Soon after the passage of this act, thousands of "contrabands" were using their feet to escape slavery by finding their way into Union camps. In July 1862, Congress passed a second Confiscation Act that freed persons enslaved by anyone engaged in rebellion against the United States. The law also empowered the president to use freed slaves in the Union army in any capacity, including battle.

Emancipation Proclamation

By July 1862, Lincoln had already decided to use his powers as commander in chief of the armed forces to free all enslaved persons in the states then at war with the United States. He justified his policy as a "military necessity." Lincoln delayed announcement of the policy, however, until he could win the support of conservative Northerners. At the same time, he encouraged the border states to come up with plans for emancipation, with compensation to the owners.

After the Battle of Antietam, on September 22, 1862, Lincoln issued a warning that enslaved people in all states still in rebellion on January 1, 1863, would be "then, thenceforward, and forever free." As promised, on the first day of the new year, 1863, the president issued his Emancipation Proclamation. After listing states from Arkansas to Virginia that were in rebellion, the proclamation stated:

> I do order and declare that all persons held as slaves within said designated States and parts of States are, and henceforward shall be, free; and that the Executive Government of the United States, including the military and naval authorities thereof, shall recognize and maintain the freedom of said persons.

Consequences Since the president's proclamation applied only to enslaved people residing in Confederate states *outside* Union control, it immediately freed only about 1 percent of slaves. Slavery in the border states was allowed to continue. Even so, the proclamation was of major importance because it enlarged the purpose of the war. For the first time, Union armies were fighting against slavery, not merely against secession. The proclamation added weight to the Confiscation acts, increasing the number of slaves who sought freedom by fleeing to Union lines. Thus, with each advance of Northern troops into the South, abolition advanced as well. As an added blow to the Confederacy, the proclamation also authorized the use of freed slaves as Union soldiers. Suddenly, the Union army had thousands of dedicated new recruits.

Thirteenth Amendment

Standing in the way of full emancipation were phrases in the U.S. Constitution that had long legitimized slavery. To free all enslaved people in the border states, the country needed to ratify a constitutional amendment. Even the abolitionists gave Lincoln credit for playing an active role in the political struggle to secure enough votes in Congress to pass the 13th Amendment. By December 1865 (months after Lincoln's death), this amendment abolishing slavery was ratified by the required number of states. The language of the amendment could not be simpler or clearer:

> Neither slavery nor involuntary servitude, except as a punishment
> for crime whereof the party shall have been duly convicted, shall exist
> within the United States, or any place subject to their jurisdiction.

Freedmen in the War

After the Emancipation Proclamation (January 1863), hundreds of thousands of Southern blacks—approximately one-quarter of the slave population—walked away from slavery to seek the protection of the approaching Union armies. Almost 200,000 African Americans, most of whom were newly freed slaves, served in the Union army and navy. Segregated into all-black units, such as the Massachusetts 54th Regiment, black troops performed courageously under fire and won the respect of Union white soldiers. More than 37,000 African American soldiers died in what became known as the Army of Freedom.

The Union Triumphs, 1863–1865

By early 1863, the fortunes of war were turning against the Confederates. Although General Lee started the year with another major victory at Chancellorsville, Virginia, the Confederate economy was in desperate shape, as planters and farmers lost control of their slave labor force, and an increasing number of poorly provisioned soldiers were deserting from the Confederate army.

Turning Point

The decisive turning point in the war came in the first week of July when the Confederacy suffered two crushing defeats in the West and the East.

Vicksburg In the West, by the spring of 1863, Union forces controlled New Orleans as well as most of the Mississippi River and surrounding valley. Thus, the Union objective of securing complete control of the Mississippi River was close to an accomplished fact when General Grant began his siege of the heavily fortified city of Vicksburg, Mississippi. Union artillery bombarded Vicksburg for seven weeks before the Confederates finally surrendered the city (and nearly 29,000 soldiers) on July 4. Federal warships now controlled the full length of the Mississippi and cut off Texas, Louisiana, and Arkansas from the rest of the Confederacy.

Gettysburg Meanwhile, in the East, Lee again took the offensive by leading an army into enemy territory: the Union states of Maryland and Pennsylvania. If he could either destroy the Union army or capture a major Northern city, Lee hoped to force the Union to call for peace—or at least to gain foreign intervention on behalf of the Confederacy. On July 1, 1863, the invading Confederate army surprised Union units at Gettysburg in southern Pennsylvania. What followed was the most crucial battle of the war and the bloodiest, with more than 50,000 casualties. Lee's assault on Union lines on the second and third days, including a famous but unsuccessful charge led by George Pickett, proved futile, and destroyed a key part of the Confederate army. What was left of Lee's forces retreated to Virginia, never to regain the offensive.

Grant in Command

Lincoln finally found a general who could fight and win. In early 1864, he brought Grant east to Virginia and made him commander of all the Union armies. Grant settled on a strategy of war by attrition. He aimed to wear down the Confederate's armies and systematically destroy their vital lines of supply. Fighting doggedly for months, Grant's Army of the Potomac suffered heavier casualties than Lee's forces in the battles of the Wilderness, Spotsylvania, and Cold Harbor. But by never letting up, Grant succeeded in reducing Lee's army in each battle and forcing it into a defensive line around Richmond. In this final stage of the Civil War, the fighting foreshadowed the trench warfare that would later characterize World War I. No longer was this a war "between gentlemen" but a modern "total" war against civilians as well as soldiers.

Sherman's March The chief instrument of Grant's aggressive tactics for subduing the South was a hardened veteran, General William Tecumseh Sherman. Leading a force of 100,000 men, Sherman set out from Chattanooga, Tennessee, on a campaign of deliberate destruction that went clear across the state of Georgia and then swept north into South Carolina. Sherman was a pioneer of the tactics of total war. Marching relentlessly through Georgia, his troops destroyed everything in their path, burning cotton fields, barns, and houses—everything the enemy might use to survive. Sherman took Atlanta in September 1864 in time to help Lincoln's prospects for reelection. He marched into Savannah in December and completed his campaign in February 1865 by setting fire to Columbia, the capital of South Carolina and cradle of secession.

Sherman's march had its intended effects: helping to break the spirit of the Confederacy and destroying its will to fight on.

The Election of 1864 The Democrats' nominee for president was the popular General George McClellan, whose platform calling for peace had wide appeal among millions of war-weary voters. The Republicans renamed their party the Unionist party as a way of attracting the votes of "War Democrats" (those who disagreed with the Democratic platform). A brief "ditch-Lincoln" movement fizzled out, and the Republican (Unionist) convention again chose Lincoln as its presidential candidate and a loyal War Democrat from Tennessee, Senator Andrew Johnson, as his running mate. The Lincoln-Johnson ticket won 212 electoral votes to the Democrats' 21. The popular vote, however, was much closer, for McClellan took 45 percent of the total votes cast.

The End of the War

The effects of the Union blockade, combined with Sherman's march of destruction, spread hunger through much of the South in the winter of 1864–1865. On the battlefront in Virginia, Grant continued to outflank Lee's lines until they collapsed around Petersburg, resulting in the fall of Richmond on April 3, 1865. Everyone knew that the end was near.

Surrender at Appomattox The Confederate government tried to negotiate for peace, but Lincoln would accept nothing short of restoration of the Union, and Jefferson Davis still demanded nothing less than independence. Lee retreated from Richmond with an army of less than 30,000 men. He tried to escape to the mountains, only to be cut off and forced to surrender to Grant at Appomattox Court House on April 9, 1865. The Union general treated his longtime enemy with respect and allowed Lee's men to return to their homes with their horses.

Assassination of Lincoln Only a month before Lee's surrender, Lincoln delivered one of his greatest speeches—the second inaugural address. He urged that the defeated South be treated benevolently, "with malice toward none; with charity for all."

On April 14, John Wilkes Booth, an embittered actor and Confederate sympathizer, shot and killed the president while he was attending a performance in Ford's Theater in Washington. On the same night, a co-conspirator attacked but only wounded Secretary of State William Seward. These shocking events aroused the fury of Northerners at the very time that the Confederates most needed a sympathetic hearing. The loss of Lincoln's leadership was widely mourned, but the extent of the loss was not fully appreciated until the two sections of a reunited country had to cope with the overwhelming problems of postwar Reconstruction.

Effects of the War on Civilian Life

Both during the war and in the years that followed, American society underwent deep and sometimes wrenching changes.

Political Change

The electoral process continued during the war with surprisingly few restrictions. Secession of the Southern states had created Republican majorities in both houses of Congress. Within Republican ranks, however, there were sharp differences between the radical faction (those who championed the cause of immediate abolition of slavery) and the moderate faction (Free-Soilers who were chiefly concerned about economic opportunities for whites). Most Democrats supported the war but criticized Lincoln's conduct of it. Peace Democrats and Copperheads opposed the war and wanted a negotiated peace. The most notorious Copperhead, Congressman Clement L. Vallandigham of Ohio, was briefly banished from the United States to the Confederacy for his "treasonable," pro-Confederacy speeches against the war. He then went to Canada.

Civil Liberties Like many leaders in wartime governments, Lincoln focused more on prosecuting the war than with protecting citizens' constitutional rights. Early in the war, Lincoln suspended the writ of habeas corpus in Maryland and other states with strong pro-Confederate sentiment. Suspension of this constitutional right meant that persons could be arrested without being informed of the charges against them. During the war, an estimated 13,000 people were arrested on suspicion of aiding the enemy. Without a right to habeas corpus, many of them were held without trial.

Democrats charged that Lincoln acted no better than a tyrant. However, most historians have been less critical. Especially in the border states, people had difficulty distinguishing between combatants and noncombatants. Moreover, the Constitution does state that the writ of habeas corpus "shall not be suspended, unless when in cases of rebellion or invasion the public safety may require it." After the war, in the case of *Ex Parte Milligan* (1866), the Supreme Court ruled that the government had acted improperly in Indiana where, during the war, certain civilians had been subject to a military trial. The Court declared that such procedures could be used only when regular civilian courts were unavailable.

The Draft When the war begin in 1861, those who fought were volunteers. However, as the need for replacements became acute, both the Union and the Confederacy resorted to laws for conscripting, or drafting, men into service. The Union's first Conscription Act, adopted in March 1863, made all men between the ages of 20 and 45 liable for military service but allowed a draftee to avoid service by either finding a substitute to serve or paying a $300 exemption fee. The law provoked fierce opposition among poorer laborers, who feared that—if and when they returned to civilian life—their jobs would be taken by freed African Americans. In July 1863, riots against the draft erupted in New York City, in which a mostly Irish American mob attacked blacks and wealthy whites. Some 117 people were killed before federal troops and a temporary suspension of the draft restored order.

Political Dominance of the North The suspension of habeas corpus and the operation of the draft were only temporary. Far more important were the long-term effects of the war on the balance of power between two sectional rivals, the North and the South. With the military triumph of the Union came a new definition of the nature of the federal union. Old arguments for nullification and secession ceased to be issues. After the Civil War, the supremacy of the federal government over the states was accepted as an established fact.

Furthermore, the abolition of slavery—in addition to its importance to freed African Americans—gave new meaning and legitimacy to the concept of American democracy. In his famous Gettysburg Address of November 19, 1863, Lincoln rallied Americans to the idea that their nation was "dedicated to the proposition that all men are created equal." Lincoln was probably alluding to the Emancipation Proclamation when he spoke of the war bringing "a new birth of freedom." His words—and even more, the abolition of slavery—advanced the cause of democratic government in the United States and inspired champions of democracy around the world.

Economic Change

The costs of the war in both money and men were staggering and called for extraordinary measures by both the Union and Confederate legislatures.

Financing the War The Union financed the war chiefly by borrowing $2.6 billion, obtained through the sale of government bonds. Even this amount was not enough, so Congress raised tariffs (Morrill Tariff of 1861), added excise taxes, and instituted the first income tax. The U.S. Treasury also issued more than $430 million in a paper currency known as Greenbacks. This paper money could not be redeemed in gold, which contributed to creeping inflation. Prices in the North rose by about 80 percent during the war. To manage the added revenue moving in and out of the Treasury, Congress created a national banking system in 1863. This was the first unified banking network since Andrew Jackson vetoed the recharter of the Bank of the United States in the 1830s.

Modernizing Northern Society The war's impact on the Northern economy was dramatic. Economic historians differ on the question of whether, in the short run, the war promoted or retarded the growth of the Northern economy. On the negative side, workers' wages did not keep pace with inflation. On the other hand, there is little doubt that many aspects of a modern industrial economy were accelerated by the war. Because the war placed a premium on mass production and complex organization, it sped up the consolidation of the North's manufacturing businesses. War profiteers took advantage of the government's urgent needs for military supplies to sell shoddy goods at high prices—a problem that decreased after the federal government took control of the contract process away from the states. Fortunes made during the war produced a concentration of capital in the hands of a new class of millionaires, who would finance the North's industrialization in the postwar years.

Civilians Employed by the Federal Government				
Year	Post Office	Defense	Other	Total
1841	14,290	598	3,150	18,038
1851	21,391	403	4,480	26,274
1861	30,269	946	5,457	36,672
1871	36,696	1,183	13,741	51,020
1881	56,421	16,297	27,302	100,020

Source: U.S. Bureau of the Census. *Historical Statistics of the United States, Colonial Times to 1970*

Republican politics also played a major role in stimulating the economic growth of the North and the West. Taking advantage of their wartime majority in Congress, the Republicans passed an ambitious economic program that included not only a national banking system, but also the following:

- *The Morrill Tariff Act* (1861) raised tariff rates to increase revenue and protect American manufacturers. Its passage initiated a Republican program of high protective tariffs to help industrialists.

- The *Homestead Act* (1862) promoted settlement of the Great Plains by offering parcels of 160 acres of public land free to any person or family that farmed that land for at least five years.

- The *Morrill Land Grant Act* (1862) encouraged states to use the sale of federal land grants to maintain agricultural and technical colleges.

- The *Pacific Railway Act* (1862) authorized the building of a transcontinental railroad over a northern route in order to link the economies of California and the western territories with the eastern states.

Social Change

Although every part of American society away from the battlefield was touched by the war, those most directly affected were women, whose labors became more burdensome, and African Americans, who won emancipation.

Women at Work The absence of millions of men from their normal occupations in fields and factories added to the responsibilities of women in all regions. They stepped into the labor vacuum created by the war, operating farms and plantations and taking factory jobs customarily held by men. In addition, women played a critical role as military nurses and as volunteers in soldiers' aid societies. When the war ended and the war veterans returned home, most urban women vacated their jobs in government and industry, while rural women gladly accepted male assistance on the farm. Of course, for the women whose men never returned—or returned disabled—the economic struggle continued for a lifetime.

The Civil War had at least two permanent effects on American women. First, the field of nursing was now open to women for the first time; previously, hospitals employed only men as doctors and nurses. Second, the enormous responsibilities undertaken by women during the war gave impetus to the movement to obtain equal voting rights for women. (The suffragists' goal would not be achieved until women's efforts in another war—World War I—finally convinced enough male conservatives to adopt the 19th Amendment.)

End of Slavery Both in the short run and the long run, the group in American society whose lives were most profoundly changed by the Civil War were those African Americans who had been born into slavery. After the adoption of the 13th Amendment in 1865, 4 million people (3.5 million in the Confederate states and 500,000 in the border states) were "freed men" and "freed women." For these people and their descendants, economic hardship and political oppression would continue for generations. Even so, the end of slavery represented a momentous step. Suddenly, slaves with no rights were protected by the U.S. Constitution, with open-ended possibilities of freedom.

While four years of nearly total war, the tragic human loss of 750,000 lives, and an estimated $15 billion in war costs and property losses had enormous effects on the nation, far greater changes were set in motion. The Civil War destroyed slavery and devastated the Southern economy, and it also acted as a catalyst to transform America into a complex modern industrial society of capital, technology, national organizations, and large corporations. During the war, the Republicans were able to enact the pro-business Whig program that was designed to stimulate the industrial and commercial growth of the United States. The characteristics of American democracy and its capitalist economy were strengthened by this Second American Revolution.

The Union's victory in the Civil War was by no means inevitable. Why did the Union win and the Confederates lose? To be sure, the Union had the advantage of a larger population and superior wealth, industry, and transportation. On the other hand, the Confederacy's advantages were also formidable. The Confederacy needed merely to fight to a stalemate and hold out long enough to secure foreign recognition or intervention. The Union faced the more daunting challenge of having to conquer an area comparable in size to Western Europe.

Some historians blame the Confederacy's defeat on the overly aggressive military strategy of its generals. For example, Lee's two invasions of the North leading to Antietam and Gettysburg resulted in a much higher loss of his own men, in percentage terms, than of his opponent's forces. If the Confederates had used more defensive and cautious tactics, they might have secured a military stalemate—and political victory (independence).

Other historians blame the Confederacy's loss on its political leadership. They argue that, compared to the Lincoln administration, Jefferson Davis and his cabinet were ineffective. Another weakness was the lack of a strong political party system in the Confederacy. Without a strong party, Davis had trouble developing a base of popular support. Confederates' traditional emphasis on states' rights also worked against a unified war effort. Governors of Confederate states would withhold troops rather than yield to the central government's urgent requests for cooperation. Vital supplies were also held back in state warehouses, where they remained until war's end.

Historian Henry S. Commager argued that slavery may have been responsible for the Confederates' defeat. For one thing, slavery played a role in deterring European powers from intervening in support of the Confederacy and its backward institution. Beyond this, Commager also believed that slavery undermined the region's ability to adapt to new challenges. It fostered an intolerant society, which lacked the "habit of independent inquiry and criticism." Thus, according to Commager, the failure of the Confederacy was not a "failure of resolution or courage or will but of intelligence and morality." If so, then the Confederacy's attachment to an outdated institution—slavery—was what ultimately meant the difference between victory and defeat.

KEY NAMES, EVENTS, AND TERMS

The Break (NAT, POL)
border states
Confederate States of
  America
Jefferson Davis
Alexander H. Stephens
Second American
  Revolution

**Economic Growth
  (WXT)**
greenbacks
Morrill Tariff Act (1861)
Morrill Land Grant Act
  (1862)
Pacific Railway Act
  (1862)

Free Land (MIG)
Homestead Act (1862)

**The Fighting (POL,
  GEO, CUL)**
Fort Sumter
Bull Run
Thomas (Stonewall)
  Jackson

Winfield Scott
Anaconda Plan
George McClellan
Robert E. Lee
Antietam
Fredericksburg
Monitor vs. *Merrimac*
Ulysses S. Grant
Shiloh
David Farragut
Gettysburg
Vicksburg
Sherman's March
Appomattox Court House

War and the Law (POL)
executive power
habeas corpus
insurrection
Confiscation acts
Emancipation Proclama-
  tion
13th Amendment
Ex Parte Milligan
draft riots

Wartime Politics (POL)
Copperheads
election of 1864

War Diplomacy (WOR)
Trent Affair
Alabama
Laird rams

The Final Act (CUL)
John Wilkes Booth

**Social Impact (NAT,
  SOC)**
segregated black troops
Massachusetts 54th
  Regiment
women in the workplace
women in nursing
war's long term effects
4 million freedmen

Questions 1–2 refer to the excerpt below.

"Now, therefore, I, Abraham Lincoln, President of the United States, by virtue of the power in me vested as commander in chief . . . and as a fit and necessary war measure for suppressing said rebellion do . . . order and designate as the states and parts of states wherein the people thereof, respectively, are this day in rebellion against the United States the following . . .

"I do order and declare that all persons held as slaves within said designated states and parts of states are, and henceforward shall be, free. . . .

"And I further declare . . . that such persons of suitable condition will be received into the armed service of the United States . . .

"And upon this act, sincerely believed to be an act of justice, warranted by the Constitution upon military necessity."

—Abraham Lincoln, The Emancipation Proclamation, 1863

1. President Lincoln delayed issuing an Emancipation Proclamation because of his concern that it would

   (A) increase foreign support for the Confederacy

   (B) cause the border states to secede

   (C) decrease power of the cotton industry

   (D) free slaves before they were ready

2. To issue an Emancipation Proclamation, President Lincoln felt that he needed which of the following?

   (A) A Constitutional amendment

   (B) Supreme Court approval

   (C) Republican control of Congress

   (D) A military victory

Questions 3–5 refer to the excerpt below.

"We drift fast toward war with England, but I think we shall not reach that point. The shopkeepers who own England want to do us all harm they can and to give all possible aid and comfort to our slave-breeding and woman-flogging adversary, for England has degenerated into a trader, manufacturer, and banker, and has lost all the instincts and sympathies that her name still suggests . . .

She cannot ally herself with slavery, as she inclines to do, without closing a profitable market, exposing her commerce to [Yankee] privateers, and diminishing the supply of [Northern] breadstuffs on which her operatives depend for life. On the other side, however, is the consideration that by allowing piratical *Alabamas* to be built, armed, and manned in her ports to prey on our commerce, she is making a great deal of money."

—George Templeton Strong, New York lawyer, *Diary,* 1863

3. A major part of the Confederate strategy for winning independence was based on

    (A) building a modern navy to break the Union blockade

    (B) developing factories to manufacture weapons

    (C) encircling the Union capital, Washington, D.C.

    (D) winning recognition and support from Great Britain

4. Which of the following describes a reason not mentioned by Strong in this excerpt that ultimately stopped Britain from recognizing the Confederacy?

    (A) Concern about causing problems in Canada

    (B) Desire for closer ties with Mexico

    (C) Respect for the Monroe Doctrine

    (D) Opposition from the British working class

5. The Union was most disturbed because they believed that Britain was supporting the Confederates by doing which of the following?

    (A) Building warships

    (B) Purchasing cotton

    (C) Loaning money

    (D) Supplying food

Questions 6–8 refer to the map below.

UNITED STATES, JULY 1861

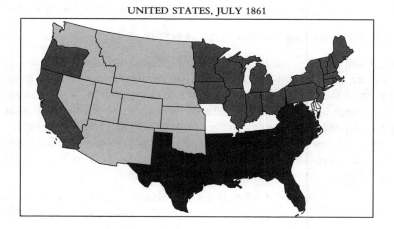

6. In July of 1861, President Lincoln was particularly concerned about how his policies on slavery would affect which areas?

   (A) the states in white because they were slave states that remained in the Union

   (B) the states in medium gray because they were home to most of his political supporters

   (C) the states in dark gray because he thought he could persuade them to rejoin the Union

   (D) the region in light gray because it consisted of territories that had not yet become states

7. Which of the following statements best describes the states in medium gray?

   (A) Most people lived in large cities

   (B) Most people advocated abolition of slavery

   (C) They lacked good river transportation

   (D) They included most of the country's population

8. Which of the following statements best describes the states in dark gray?

   (A) They were economically self-sufficient

   (B) They were well connected by railroads

   (C) They had a strong military tradition

   (D) They had a strong navy

SHORT-ANSWER QUESTIONS

Use complete sentences; an outline or bulleted list alone is not acceptable.

Question 1 is based on the following excerpts.

"[In the Civil War,] great issues were at stake, issues about which Americans were willing to fight and die, issues whose resolution profoundly transformed and redefined the United States. The Civil War was a total war in three senses: It mobilized the total human and material resources of both sides; it ended not in a negotiated peace but in total victory by one side and unconditional surrender by the other; it destroyed the economy and social system of the loser and established those of the winner as the norm for the future . . . The North went to war to preserve the Union; it ended by creating a nation."

—James M. McPherson, historian, "A War That Never Goes Away,"
American Heritage, March 1990

"Should we consecrate a war that killed and maimed over a million Americans? Or should we question . . . whether this was really a war of necessity that justified its appalling costs? . . .

"Very few Northerners went to war seeking or anticipating the destruction of slavery. They fought for the Union, and the Emancipation Proclamation was a means to that end: a desperate measure to undermine the South and save a democratic nation that Lincoln called 'the last best, hope of earth.' . . .

"From the distance of 150 years, Lincoln's transcendent vision at Gettysburg of a 'new birth of freedom' seems premature. . . . Rather than simply consecrate the dead with words, he said, it is for 'us the living' to rededicate ourselves to the unfinished work of the Civil War."

—Tony Horwitz, journalist and writer, "150 Years of Misunderstanding
the Civil War," *The Atlantic,* June 2013

1. Using the excerpts, answer (A), (B), and (C).

   (A) Briefly explain ONE major difference between McPherson's and Horwitz's historical interpretation of the Civil War.

   (B) Briefly explain how ONE historical event or development from the period 1861 to 1865 not directly mentioned in the excerpts supports McPherson's interpretation.

   (C) Briefly explain how ONE historical event or development from the period 1861 to 1865 not directly mentioned in the excerpts supports Horwitz's interpretation.

Question 2. Answer (A), (B), and (C).

(A) Briefly explain ONE specific reason slavery was not ended during the Civil War.

(B) Briefly explain ONE historical event or development that limited slavery during the Civil War.

(C) Briefly describe ONE specific role slaves played in the Civil War.

Question 3 is based on the following cartoon.

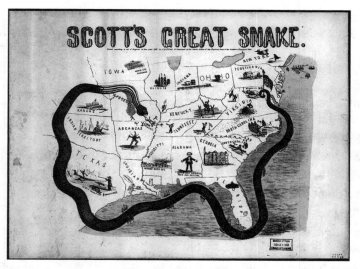

Source: J. B. Elliot, 1861. Library of Congress

3. Using the cartoon, answer (A), (B), and (C).

(A) Briefly explain ONE specific part of the Union strategy for winning the war.

(B) Briefly explain ONE historical event or development in the period 1861 to 1865 that resulted from the Union strategy to win the war.

(C) Briefly explain ONE specific part of the Confederate strategy for winning the war.

Question 4. Answer (A), (B), and (C).

(A) Briefly explain ONE specific action of President Abraham Lincoln during the Civil War that supports the view that he was one of the most democratic presidents.

(B) Briefly explain ONE specific action of President Abraham Lincoln during the Civil War that supports the view that he was one of the most autocratic presidents.

(C) Briefly identify ONE president who came before Lincoln who you believe was both democratic and autocratic.

THINK AS A HISTORIAN: STATEMENTS ABOUT CONTEXTUALIZATION

Which THREE of the following statements best express the idea of contextualization?

1. While slavery ended throughout the Americas in the late 1700s and during the 1800s, the United States and Haiti were the only two places where it ended through large-scale violence.

2. The Republican economic plans carried out the ideas expressed in earlier days by Alexander Hamilton and Henry Clay.

3. The Emancipation Proclamation was written in rather boring language.

4. Considering that Sherman's March was conducted as an act of war, remarkably few people died from it.

5. General Robert E. Lee's decision to join the Confederacy provides a fascinating look into how he thought about the world.

15

RECONSTRUCTION, 1863–1877

Though slavery was abolished, the wrongs of my people were not ended.
Though they were not slaves, they were not yet quite free. No man can be
truly free whose liberty is dependent upon the thought, feeling, and
action of others, and who has no means in his own hands for guarding,
protecting, defending, and maintaining his liberty.

Frederick Douglass, 1882

The silencing of the cannons of war left the victorious United States with immense challenges. How would the South rebuild its shattered society and economy after the damage inflicted by four years of war? What would be the place in that society of 4 million freed African Americans? To what extent, if any, was the federal government responsible for helping ex-slaves adjust to freedom? Should the former states of the Confederacy be treated as states that had never really left the Union (Lincoln's position) or as conquered territory subject to continued military occupation? Under what conditions would the Confederate states be fully accepted as coequal partners in the restored Union? Finally, who had the authority to decide these questions of Reconstruction: the president or the Congress?

The conflicts that existed before and during the Civil War—between regions, political parties, and economic interests—continued after the war. Republicans in the North wanted to continue the economic progress begun during the war. The Southern aristocracy still desired a cheap labor force to work its plantations. The freedmen and women hoped to achieve independence and equal rights. However, traditional beliefs limited the actions of the federal government. Constitutional concepts of limited government and states' rights discouraged national leaders from taking bold action. Little economic help was given to either whites or blacks in the South, because most Americans believed that free people in a free society had both an opportunity and a responsibility to provide for themselves. The physical rebuilding of the South was largely left up to the states and individuals, while the federal government concentrated on political issues.

Reconstruction Plans of Lincoln and Johnson

Throughout his presidency, Abraham Lincoln held firmly to the belief that the Southern states could not constitutionally leave the Union and therefore never did leave. He viewed the Confederates as only a disloyal minority. After Lincoln's assassination, Andrew Johnson attempted to carry out Lincoln's plan for the political Reconstruction of the 11 former states of the Confederacy.

Lincoln's Policies

Because Lincoln thought the Southern states had never left the Union, he hoped they could be reestablished by meeting a minimum test of political loyalty.

Proclamation of Amnesty and Reconstruction (1863) As early as December 1863, Lincoln set up an apparently simple process for political reconstruction—that is, for reconstructing the state governments in the South so that Unionists were in charge rather than secessionists. The president's Proclamation of Amnesty and Reconstruction provided for the following:

- Full presidential pardons would be granted to most Confederates who (1) took an oath of allegiance to the Union and the U.S. Constitution, and (2) accepted the emancipation of slaves.

- A state government could be reestablished and accepted as legitimate by the U.S. president as soon as at least 10 percent of the voters in that state took the loyalty oath.

In practice, Lincoln's proclamation meant that each Southern state would be required to rewrite its state constitution to eliminate the existence of slavery. Lincoln's seemingly lenient policy was designed both to shorten the war and to give added weight to his Emancipation Proclamation. (When Lincoln made this proposal in late 1863, he feared that if the Democrats won the 1864 election, they would overturn the proclamation.)

Wade-Davis Bill (1864) Many Republicans in Congress objected to Lincoln's 10 percent plan, arguing that it would allow a supposedly reconstructed state government to fall under the domination of disloyal secessionists. In 1864, Congress passed the Wade-Davis Bill, which proposed far more demanding and stringent terms for Reconstruction. The bill required 50 percent of the voters of a state to take a loyalty oath and permitted only non-Confederates to vote for a new state constitution. Lincoln refused to sign the bill, pocket-vetoing it after Congress adjourned. How serious was the conflict between President Lincoln and the Republican Congress over Reconstruction policy? Historians still debate this question. In any case, Congress was no doubt ready to reassert its powers in 1865, as Congresses traditionally do after a war.

Freedmen's Bureau In March 1865, Congress created an important new agency: the Bureau of Refugees, Freedmen, and Abandoned Lands, known simply as the Freedmen's Bureau. The bureau acted as an early welfare agency, providing food, shelter, and medical aid for those made destitute by the war—both blacks (chiefly freed slaves) and homeless whites. At first, the Freedmen's Bureau had authority to resettle freed blacks on confiscated farmlands in the South. Its efforts at resettlement, however, were later frustrated when President Johnson pardoned Confederate owners of the confiscated lands, and courts then restored most of the lands to their original owners.

The bureau's greatest success was in education. Under the able leadership of General Oliver O. Howard, it established nearly 3,000 schools for freed blacks, including several colleges. Before federal funding was stopped in 1870, the bureau's schools taught an estimated 200,000 African Americans how to read.

Lincoln's Last Speech In his last public address (April 11, 1865), Lincoln encouraged Northerners to accept Louisiana as a reconstructed state. (Louisiana had already drawn up a new constitution that abolished slavery in the state and provided for African Americans' education.) The president also addressed the question—highly controversial at the time—of whether freedmen should be granted the right to vote. Lincoln said: "I myself prefer that it were *now* conferred on the very intelligent, and on those who serve our cause as soldiers." Three days later, Lincoln's evolving plans for Reconstruction were ended with his assassination. His last speech suggested that, had he lived, he probably would have moved closer to the position taken by the progressive, or Radical, Republicans. In any event, hope for lasting reform was dealt a devastating blow by the sudden removal of Lincoln's skillful leadership.

Johnson and Reconstruction

Andrew Johnson's origins were as humble as Lincoln's. A self-taught tailor, he rose in Tennessee politics by championing the interests of poor whites in their economic conflict with rich planters. Johnson was the only senator from a Confederate state who remained loyal to the Union. After Tennessee was occupied by Union troops, he was appointed that state's war governor. Johnson was a Southern Democrat, but Republicans picked him to be Lincoln's running mate in 1864 in order to encourage pro-Union Democrats to vote for the Union (Republican) party. In one of the accidents of history, Johnson became the wrong man for the job. As a white supremacist, the new president was bound to clash with Republicans in Congress who believed that the war was fought not just to preserve the Union but also to liberate blacks from slavery.

Johnson's Reconstruction Policy At first, many Republicans in Congress welcomed Johnson's presidency because of his animosity for the Southern aristocrats who had led the Confederacy. In May 1865, Johnson issued his own Reconstruction proclamation that was very similar to Lincoln's 10 percent plan. In addition to Lincoln's terms, it provided for the disfranchisement (loss of the right to vote and hold office) of (1) all former leaders and officeholders of the Confederacy and (2) Confederates with more than $20,000 in taxable property. However, the president retained the power to grant individual pardons to "disloyal" Southerners. This was an escape clause for the wealthy planters, and Johnson made frequent use of it. As a result of the president's pardons, many former Confederate leaders were back in office by the fall of 1865.

Southern Governments of 1865 Just eight months after Johnson took office, all 11 of the ex-Confederate states qualified under the president's Reconstruction plan to become functioning parts of the Union. The Southern states drew up constitutions that repudiated secession, negated the debts of the Confederate government, and ratified the 13th Amendment abolishing slavery. On the other hand, none of the new constitutions extended voting rights to blacks. Furthermore, to the dismay of Republicans, former leaders of the Confederacy won seats in Congress. For example, Alexander Stephens, the former Confederate vice president, was elected U.S. senator from Georgia.

Black Codes The Republicans became further disillusioned with Johnson as Southern state legislatures adopted Black Codes that restricted the rights and movements of the former slaves. The codes (1) prohibited blacks from either renting land or borrowing money to buy land; (2) placed freedmen into a form of semibondage by forcing them, as "vagrants" and "apprentices," to sign work contracts; and (3) prohibited blacks from testifying against whites in court. The contract-labor system, in which blacks worked cotton fields under white supervision for deferred wages, seemed little different from slavery.

Appalled by reports of developments in the South, Republicans began to ask, "Who won the war?" In early 1866, unhappiness with Johnson developed into an open rift when the Northern Republicans in Congress challenged the results of elections in the South. They refused to seat Alexander Stephens and other duly elected representatives and senators from ex-Confederate states.

Johnson's Vetoes Johnson alienated even moderate Republicans in early 1866 when he vetoed a bill increasing the services and protection offered by the Freedmen's Bureau and a civil rights bill that nullified the Black Codes and guaranteed full citizenship and equal rights to African Americans. The vetoes marked the end of the first round of Reconstruction. During this round, Presidents Lincoln and Johnson had restored the 11 ex-Confederate states to their former position in the Union, ex-Confederates had returned to high offices, and Southern states began passing Black Codes.

Presidential Vetoes, 1853 to 1880	
President	Vetoes
Franklin Pierce	9
James Buchanan	7
Abraham Lincoln	7
Andrew Johnson	29
Ulysses S. Grant	93
Rutherford B. Hayes	13

Source: "Summary of Bills Vetoed, 1789–Present." United States Senate, www.senate.gov

Congressional Reconstruction

By the spring of 1866, the angry response of many members of Congress to Johnson's policies led to the second round of Reconstruction. This one was dominated by Congress and featured policies that were harsher on Southern whites and more protective of freed African Americans.

Radical Republicans

Republicans had long been divided between (1) moderates, who were chiefly concerned with economic gains for the white middle class, and (2) radicals, who championed civil rights for blacks. Although most Republicans were moderates, several became more radical in 1866 partly out of fear that a reunified Democratic party might again become dominant. After all, now that the federal census counted all people equally (no longer applying the old three-fifths rule for enslaved persons), the South would have more representatives in Congress than before the war and more strength in the electoral college in future presidential elections.

The leading Radical Republican in the Senate was Charles Sumner of Massachusetts (who returned to the Senate three years after his caning by Brooks). In the House, Thaddeus Stevens of Pennsylvania hoped to revolutionize Southern society through an extended period of military rule in which African Americans would be free to exercise their civil rights, would be educated in schools operated by the federal government, and would receive lands confiscated from the planter class. Many Radical Republicans, such as Benjamin Wade of Ohio, endorsed several liberal causes: women's suffrage, rights for labor unions, and civil rights for Northern African Americans. Although their program was never fully implemented, the Radical Republicans struggled to extend equal rights to all Americans.

Civil Rights Act of 1866 Among the first actions in congressional Reconstruction were votes to override, with some modifications, Johnson's vetoes of both the Freedmen's Bureau Act and the first Civil Rights Act. The Civil Rights Act pronounced all African Americans to be U.S. citizens (thereby repudiating the decision in the Dred Scott case) and also attempted to provide a legal shield against the operation of the Southern states' Black Codes. Republicans feared, however, that the law could be repealed if the Democrats ever won control of Congress. They therefore looked for a more permanent solution in the form of a constitutional amendment.

Fourteenth Amendment In June 1866, Congress passed and sent to the states an amendment that, when ratified in 1868, had both immediate and long-term significance for American society. The 14th Amendment

- declared that all persons born or naturalized in the United States were citizens
- obligated the states to respect the rights of U.S. citizens and provide them with "equal protection of the laws" and "due process of law" (clauses full of meaning for future generations)

For the first time, the Constitution required *states* as well as the federal government to uphold the rights of citizens. The amendment's key clauses about citizenship and rights produced mixed results in 19th-century courtrooms. However, in the 1950s and later, the Supreme Court would make "equal protection of the laws" and the "due process" clause the keystone of civil rights for minorities, women, children, disabled persons, and those accused of crimes.

Other parts of the 14th Amendment applied specifically to Congress' plan of Reconstruction. These clauses

- disqualified former Confederate political leaders from holding either state or federal offices
- repudiated the debts of the defeated governments of the Confederacy
- penalized a state if it kept any eligible person from voting by reducing that state's proportional representation in Congress and the electoral college

Report of the Joint Committee In June 1866, a joint committee of the House and the Senate issued a report recommending that the reorganized former states of the Confederacy were not entitled to representation in Congress. Therefore, those elected from the South as senators and representatives should not be permitted to take their seats. The report further asserted that Congress, not the president, had the authority to determine the conditions for allowing reconstructed states to rejoin the Union. By this report, Congress officially rejected the presidential plan of Reconstruction and promised to substitute its own plan, part of which was embodied in the 14th Amendment.

The Election of 1866 Unable to work with Congress, Johnson took to the road in the fall of 1866 in his infamous "swing around the circle" to attack his opponents. His speeches appealed to the racial prejudices of whites by arguing that equal rights for blacks would result in an "Africanized" society. Republicans counterattacked by accusing Johnson of being a drunkard and a traitor. They appealed to anti-Southern prejudices by employing a campaign tactic known as "waving the bloody shirt"—inflaming the anger of Northern voters by reminding them of the hardships of war. Republican propaganda emphasized that Southerners were Democrats and, by a gross jump in logic, branded the entire Democratic party as a party of rebellion and treason.

Election results gave the Republicans an overwhelming victory. After 1866, Johnson's political adversaries—both moderate and Radical Republicans—had more than a two-thirds majority in both the House and the Senate.

Reconstruction Acts of 1867 Over Johnson's vetoes, Congress passed three Reconstruction acts in early 1867, which took the drastic step of placing the South under military occupation. The acts divided the former Confederate states into five military districts, each under the control of the Union army. In addition, the Reconstruction acts increased the requirements for gaining readmission to the Union. To win such readmission, an ex-Confederate state had to ratify the 14th Amendment and place guarantees in its constitution for granting the franchise (right to vote) to all adult males, regardless of race.

Impeachment of Andrew Johnson

Also in 1867, over Johnson's veto, Congress passed the Tenure of Office Act. This law, which may have been an unconstitutional violation of executive authority, prohibited the president from removing a federal official or military commander without the approval of the Senate. The purpose of the law was strictly political. Congress wanted to protect the Radical Republicans in Johnson's cabinet, such as Secretary of War Edwin Stanton, who was in charge of the military governments in the South.

Believing the new law to be unconstitutional, Johnson challenged it by dismissing Stanton on his own authority. The House responded by impeaching Johnson, charging him with 11 "high crimes and misdemeanors." Johnson thus became the first president to be impeached. (Bill Clinton was impeached in 1998.) In 1868, after a three-month trial in the Senate, Johnson's political enemies fell one vote short of the necessary two-thirds vote required to remove a president from office. Seven moderate Republicans joined the Democrats in voting against conviction because they thought it was a bad precedent to remove a president for political reasons.

Reforms After Grant's Election

The impeachment and trial of Andrew Johnson occurred in 1868, a presidential election year. At their convention, the Democrats nominated another candidate, Horatio Seymour, so that Johnson's presidency would have ended soon in any case, with or without impeachment by the Republicans.

The Election of 1868 At their convention, the Republicans turned to a war hero, giving their presidential nomination to General Ulysses S. Grant, even though Grant had no political experience. Despite Grant's popularity in the North, he managed to win only 300,000 more popular votes than his Democratic opponent. The votes of 500,000 blacks gave the Republican ticket its margin of victory. Even the most moderate Republicans began to realize that the voting rights of the freedmen needed federal protection if their party hoped to keep control of the White House in future elections.

Fifteenth Amendment Republican majorities in Congress acted quickly in 1869 to secure the vote for African Americans. Adding one more Reconstruction amendment to those already adopted (the 13th Amendment in 1865 and the 14th Amendment in 1868), Congress passed the 15th Amendment, which prohibited any state from denying or abridging a citizen's right to vote "on account of race, color, or previous condition of servitude." It was ratified in 1870.

Civil Rights Act of 1875 The last civil rights reform enacted by Congress in Reconstruction was the Civil Rights Act of 1875. This law guaranteed equal accommodations in public places (hotels, railroads, and theaters) and prohibited courts from excluding African Americans from juries. However, the law was poorly enforced because moderate and conservative Republicans felt frustrated trying to reform an unwilling South—and feared losing white votes in the North. By 1877, Congress would abandon Reconstruction completely.

Reconstruction in the South

During the second round of Reconstruction, dictated by Congress, the Republican party in the South dominated the governments of the ex-Confederate states. Beginning in 1867, each Republican-controlled government was under the military protection of the U.S. Army until such time as Congress was satisfied that a state had met its Reconstruction requirements. Then the troops were withdrawn. The period of Republican rule in a Southern state lasted from as little as one year (Tennessee) to as much as nine years (Florida), depending on how long it took conservative Democrats to regain control.

Composition of the Reconstruction Governments

In every Radical, or Republican, state government in the South except one, whites were in the majority in both houses of the legislature. The exception was South Carolina, where the freedmen controlled the lower house in 1873. Republican legislators included native-born white Southerners, freedmen, and recently arrived Northerners.

"Scalawags" and "Carpetbaggers" Democratic opponents gave nicknames to their hated Republican rivals. They called Southern Republicans "scalawags" and Northern newcomers "carpetbaggers." Southern whites who supported the Republican governments were usually former Whigs who were interested in economic development for their state and peace between the sections. Northerners went South after the war for various reasons. Some were investors interested in setting up new businesses, while others were ministers and teachers with humanitarian goals. Some went simply to plunder.

African American Legislators Most of the African Americans who held elective office in the reconstructed state governments were educated property holders who took moderate positions on most issues. During the Reconstruction era, Republicans in the South sent two African Americans (Blanche K. Bruce and Hiram Revels) to the Senate and more than a dozen African Americans to the House of Representatives. Revels was elected in 1870 to take the Senate seat from Mississippi once held by Jefferson Davis. Seeing African Americans and former slaves in positions of power caused bitter resentment among disfranchised ex-Confederates.

Evaluating the Republican Record

Much controversy still surrounds the legislative record of the Republicans during their brief control of Southern state politics. Did they abuse their power for selfish ends (plunder and corruption), or did they govern responsibly in the public interest? They did some of each.

Accomplishments On the positive side, Republican legislators liberalized state constitutions in the South by providing for universal male suffrage, property rights for women, debt relief, and modern penal codes. They also promoted the building of roads, bridges, railroads, and other internal improvements. They established such needed state institutions as hospitals, asylums, and homes for the disabled. The reformers established state-supported public school systems in the South, which benefited whites and African Americans alike. They paid for these improvements by overhauling the tax system and selling bonds.

Failures Long after Reconstruction ended, many Southerners and some Northern historians continued to depict Republican rule as utterly wasteful and corrupt. Some instances of graft and wasteful spending did occur, as Republican politicians took advantage of their power to take kickbacks and bribes from contractors who did business with the state. However, corruption occurred throughout the country, Northern states and cities as well. No geographic section, political party, or ethnic group was immune to the general decline in ethics in government that marked the postwar era.

African Americans Adjusting to Freedom

Undoubtedly, the Southerners who had the greatest adjustment to make during the Reconstruction era were the freedmen and freedwomen. Having been so recently emancipated from slavery, they were faced with the challenges of securing their economic survival as well as their political rights as citizens.

Building Black Communities Freedom meant many things to Southern blacks: reuniting families, learning to read and write, migrating to cities where "freedom was free-er." Most of all, ex-slaves viewed emancipation as an opportunity for achieving independence from white control. This drive for autonomy was most evident in the founding of hundreds of independent African American churches after the war. By the hundreds of thousands, African Americans left white-dominated churches for the Negro Baptist and African Methodist Episcopal churches. During Reconstruction, black ministers emerged as leaders in the African American community.

Percentage of School Age Children Enrolled, 1850 to 1880		
Year	White	African American
1850	56	2
1860	60	2
1870	54	10
1880	62	34

Source: U.S. Bureau of the Census. *Historical Statistics of the United States, Colonial Times to 1970*

The desire for education induced large numbers of African Americans to use their scarce resources to establish independent schools for their children and to pay educated African Americans to become their teachers. Black colleges such as Howard, Atlanta, Fisk, and Morehouse were established during Reconstruction to prepare African American black ministers and teachers.

Another aspect of blacks' search for independence and self-sufficiency was the decision of many freedmen to migrate away from the South and establish new black communities in frontier states such as Kansas.

Sharecropping The South's agricultural economy was in turmoil after the war, in part because landowners had lost their compulsory labor force. At first, white landowners attempted to force freed African Americans into signing contracts to work the fields. These contracts set terms that nearly bound the signer to permanent and unrestricted labor—in effect, slavery by a different name. African Americans' insistence on autonomy, however, combined with changes in the postwar economy, led white landowners to adopt a system based on tenancy and sharecropping. Under sharecropping, the landlord provided the seed and other needed farm supplies in return for a share (usually half) of the harvest. While this system gave poor people of the rural South (whites as well as African Americans) the opportunity to work a piece of land for themselves, sharecroppers usually remained either dependent on the landowners or in debt to local merchants. By 1880, no more than 5 percent of Southern African Americans had become independent landowners. Sharecropping had evolved into a new form of servitude.

The North During Reconstruction

The North's economy in the postwar years continued to be driven by the Industrial Revolution and the pro-business policies of the Republicans. As the South struggled to reorganize its labor system, Northerners focused on railroads, steel, labor problems, and money.

Greed and Corruption

During the Grant administration, as the material interests of the age took center stage, the idealism of Lincoln's generation and the Radical Republicans' crusade for civil rights were pushed aside.

Rise of the Spoilsmen In the early 1870s, leadership of the Republican party passed from reformers (Thaddeus Stevens, Charles Sumner, and Benjamin Wade) to political manipulators such as Senators Roscoe Conkling of New York and James Blaine of Maine. These politicians were masters of the game of patronage—giving jobs and government favors (spoils) to their supporters.

Corruption in Business and Government The postwar years were notorious for the corrupt schemes devised by business bosses and political bosses to enrich themselves at the public's expense. For example, in 1869, Wall Street financiers Jay Gould and James Fisk obtained the help of President Grant's brother-in-law in a scheme to corner the gold market. The Treasury Department broke the scheme, but not before Gould had made a huge profit.

In the Crédit Mobilier affair, insiders gave stock to influential members of Congress to avoid investigation of the profits they were making—as high as 348 percent—from government subsidies for building the transcontinental railroad. In the case of the Whiskey Ring, federal revenue agents conspired with the liquor industry to defraud the government of millions in taxes. While Grant himself did not personally profit from the corruption, his loyalty to dishonest men around him badly tarnished his presidency.

Local politics in the Grant years were equally scandalous. In New York City, William Tweed, the boss of the local Democratic party, masterminded dozens of schemes for helping himself and cronies to large chunks of graft. The Tweed Ring virtually stole about $200 million from New York's taxpayers before *The New York Times* and the cartoonist Thomas Nast exposed "Boss" Tweed and brought about his arrest and imprisonment in 1871.

CONGRESSIONAL RECONSTRUCTION 1865–1877

Dates refer to year when a state was readmitted to the Union and ( ) to reestablishment of conservative government.

0   100   200   300 Miles
0 100 200 300 Kilometers

Delaware free 1865
Maryland free 1864
W.Va. 1863 free 1865
Virginia 1870 (1869)
Missouri free 1865
Kentucky free 1865
N. Carolina 1868 (1870)
Tennessee 1866 (1869)
S. Carolina 1868 (1876)
Arkansas 1868 (1874)
Miss. 1870 (1876)
Alabama 1868 (1874)
Georgia 1870 (1872)
Louisiana 1868 (1877)
Texas 1870 (1873)
Florida 1868 (1877)
ATLANTIC OCEAN
N
GULF OF MEXICO

The Election of 1872

The scandals of the Grant administration drove reform-minded Republicans to break with the party in 1872 and select Horace Greeley, editor of the New York *Tribune,* as their presidential candidate. The Liberal Republicans advocated civil service reform, an end to railroad subsidies, withdrawal of troops from the South, reduced tariffs, and free trade. Surprisingly, the Democrats joined them and also nominated Greeley.

The regular Republicans countered by merely "waving the bloody shirt" again—and it worked. Grant was reelected in a landslide. Just days before the counting of the electoral vote, the luckless Horace Greeley died.

The Panic of 1873

Grant's second term began with an economic disaster that rendered thousands of Northern laborers both jobless and homeless. Overspeculation by financiers and overbuilding by industry and railroads led to widespread business failures and depression. Debtors on the farms and in the cities, suffering from the tight money policies, demanded the creation of greenback paper money that was not supported by gold. In 1874, Grant finally decided to side with the hard-money bankers and creditors who wanted a money supply backed by gold and vetoed a bill calling for the release of additional greenbacks.

The End of Reconstruction

During Grant's second term, it was apparent that Reconstruction had entered another phase, which proved to be its third and final round. With Radical Republicanism on the wane, Southern conservatives—known as redeemers—took control of one state government after another. This process was completed by 1877. The redeemers had different social and economic backgrounds, but they agreed on their political program: states' rights, reduced taxes, reduced spending on social programs, and white supremacy.

White Supremacy and the Ku Klux Klan

During the period that Republicans controlled state governments in the South, groups of Southern whites organized secret societies to intimidate blacks and white reformers. The most prominent of these was the Ku Klux Klan, founded in 1867 by an ex-Confederate general, Nathaniel Bedford Forrest. The "invisible empire" burned black-owned buildings and flogged and murdered freedmen to keep them from exercising their voting rights. To give federal authorities the power to stop Ku Klux Klan violence and to protect the civil rights of citizens in the South, Congress passed the Force Acts of 1870 and 1871.

The Amnesty Act of 1872

Seven years after Lee's surrender at Appomattox, many Northerners were ready to put hatred of the Confederacy behind them. As a sign of the changing times, Congress in 1872 passed a general amnesty act that removed the last of the restrictions on ex-Confederates, except for the top leaders. The chief political consequence of the Amnesty Act was that it allowed Southern conservatives to vote for Democrats to retake control of state governments.

The Election of 1876

By 1876, federal troops had been withdrawn from all but three Southern states—South Carolina, Florida, and Louisiana. The Democrats had returned to power in all ex-Confederate states except these. This fact was to play a critical role in the presidential election.

At their convention, the Republicans looked for someone untouched by the corruption of the Grant administration and nominated the governor of Ohio, Rutherford B. Hayes. The Democrats chose New York's reform governor,

Samuel J. Tilden, who had made a name for himself fighting the corrupt Tweed Ring. In the popular votes, the Democrats had won a clear majority and expected to put Tilden in the White House. However, in three Southern states, the returns were contested. To win the election, Tilden needed only one *electoral* vote from the contested returns of South Carolina, Florida, and Louisiana.

A special electoral commission was created to determine who was entitled to the disputed votes of the three states. In a straight party vote of 8–7, the commission gave all the electoral votes to Hayes, the Republican. Outraged Democrats threatened to filibuster the results and send the election to the House of Representatives, which they controlled.

The Compromise of 1877

Leaders of the two parties worked out an informal deal. The Democrats would allow Hayes to become president. In return, he would (1) immediately end federal support for the Republicans in the South, and (2) support the building of a Southern transcontinental railroad. Shortly after his inauguration, President Hayes fulfilled his part in the Compromise of 1877 and promptly withdrew the last of the federal troops protecting African Americans and other Republicans.

The end of a federal military presence in the South was not the only thing that brought Reconstruction to an end. In a series of decisions in the 1880s and 1890s, the Supreme Court struck down one Reconstruction law after another that protected blacks from discrimination. Supporters of the New South promised a future of industrial development, but most Southern African Americans and whites in the decades after the Civil War remained poor farmers, and they fell further behind the rest of the nation.

HISTORICAL PERSPECTIVES: DID RECONSTRUCTION FAIL?

Reconstruction may be the most controversial period in U.S. history. Generations of both northern and southern historians, starting with William Dunning in the early 1900s, portrayed Reconstruction as a failure. According to this traditional interpretation, illiterate African Americans and corrupt Northern carpetbaggers abused the rights of Southern whites and stole vast sums from the state governments. The Radical Republicans brought on these conditions when, in an effort to punish the South, they gave the former slaves too many rights too soon. The Dunning school of historical thought provided a rationale for the racial segregation in the early 20th century. It was given popular expression in a 1915 movie, D. W. Griffith's *The Birth of a Nation,* which pictured the Ku Klux Klanmen as the heroes coming to the rescue of Southern whites oppressed by vindictive Northern radicals and African Americans.

continued

African American historians such as W. E. B. Du Bois and John Hope Franklin countered this interpretation by highlighting the positive achievements of the Reconstruction governments and black leaders. Their view was supported and expanded upon in 1965 with the publication of Kenneth Stampp's *Era of Reconstruction*. Other historians of the 1960s and 1970s followed Stampp's lead in stressing the significance of the civil rights legislation passed by the Radical Republicans and pointing out the humanitarian work performed by Northern reformers.

By the 1980s, some historians criticized Congress' approach to Reconstruction, not for being too radical, but for not being radical enough. They argued that the Radical Republicans neglected to provide land for African Americans, which would have enabled them to achieve economic independence. Furthermore, these historians argued, the military occupation of the South should have lasted longer to protect the freedmen's political rights. Eric Foner's comprehensive *Reconstruction: America's Unfinished Revolution* (1988) acknowledged the limitations of Reconstruction in achieving lasting reforms but also pointed out that, in the post-Civil War years, the freedmen established many of the institutions in the African American community upon which later progress depended. According to Foner, it took a "second Reconstruction" after World War II (the civil rights movement of the 1950s and 1960s) to achieve the promise of the "first Reconstruction."

KEY NAMES, EVENTS, AND TERMS

Equality (NAT, POL)
Civil Rights Act of 1866
14th Amendment
equal protection of the
    laws
due process of law
15th Amendment
Civil Rights Act of 1875

Corruption (WXT, POL)
Jay Gould
Crédit Mobilier
William (Boss) Tweed

Politics (POL)
spoilsmen
patronage
Thomas Nast
Liberal Republicans
Horace Greeley

Panic of 1873
greenbacks
redeemers
Rutherford B. Hayes
Samuel J. Tilden
Compromise of 1877

Reconstruction (POL, SOC, ARC)
presidential
    Reconstruction
Proclamation of Amnesty
    and Reconstruction
    (1863)
Wade-Davis Bill (1864)
Andrew Johnson
Freedmen's Bureau
Black Codes
Congressional
    Reconstruction

Radical Republicans
Charles Sumner
Thaddeus Stephens
Benjamin Wade
Reconstruction Acts
    (1867)
Tenure of Office Act (1867)
Edwin Stanton
impeachment
scalawags
carpetbaggers
Blanche K. Bruce
Hiram Revels
sharecropping
Ku Klux Klan
Force Acts (1870, 1871)
Amnesty Act of 1872

Questions 1–3 refer to the excerpt below.

"Though we have had war, reconstruction, and abolition as a nation, we still linger in the shadow and blight of an extinct institution. Though the colored man is no longer subject to be bought and sold, he is still surrounded by an adverse sentiment . . . In his downward course he meets no resistance, but his course upward is resented and resisted at every step of his progress. . . .

"If liberty, with us, is yet but a name, our citizenship is but a sham, and our suffrage thus far only a cruel mockery, we may yet congratulate ourselves upon the fact that the laws and institutions of the country are sound, just, and liberal. There is hope . . . But until this nation shall make its practice accord with its Constitution and its righteous laws, it will not do to reproach the colored people of this country."

—Frederick Douglass, Speech, September 24, 1883

1. Which of the following would in part cause Douglass's view that for African Americans, "citizenship is but a sham"?

   (A) 14th Amendment

   (B) Black Codes

   (C) Freedmen's Bureau

   (D) Election of Ulysses S. Grant

2. Which best provides an example of how the "Constitution and its righteous laws," according to Douglass, provide hope for the "colored people of this country"?

   (A) Wade-Davis Bill

   (B) Amnesty Act of 1872

   (C) Civil Rights Act of 1866

   (D) 16th Amendment

3. Which of the following developed during Reconstruction to provide direct support and support self-determination for those freed from slavery?

   (A) Crédit Mobilier

   (B) Tenant farming

   (C) Sharecropping

   (D) Black churches

Questions 4–5 refer to the excerpt below.

"1. All persons born or naturalized in the United States . . . are citizens . . . No State shall make or enforce any law which shall abridge the privileges or immunities of citizens . . . nor shall any State deprive any person of life, liberty, or property, without due process; nor deny . . . equal protection of the laws.

"2. Representatives shall be apportioned among the several States . . . counting the whole number of persons in each State, excluding Indians not taxed. But when the right to vote at any election . . . thereof, is denied to any of the male inhabitants . . . being twenty-one years of age, and citizens . . . or in any way abridged, except for . . . crime, . . . the basis of representation therein shall be reduced. . . .

"3. No person shall . . . hold any office . . . who, having previously taken an oath . . . shall have engaged in insurrection or rebellion against the same . . . But Congress may by a vote of two-thirds of each House, remove such disability."

—14th Amendment, Constitution of the United States, July 9, 1868

4. In proclaiming that all persons born in the United States were citizens, the 14th Amendment directly repudiated which of the following?

(A) Compromise of 1850

(B) Dred Scott Decision

(C) Johnson's Reconstruction Plan

(D) Wade-Davis Bill

5. For future Supreme Courts, one of the key points of the 14th Amendment would be which of the following?

(A) "nor deny . . . equal protection of the laws"

(B) "Representatives shall be apportioned"

(C) "the basis of representation therein shall be reduced"

(D) "shall have engaged in insurrection or rebellion"

PRESIDENTIAL ELECTION RESULTS, 1876

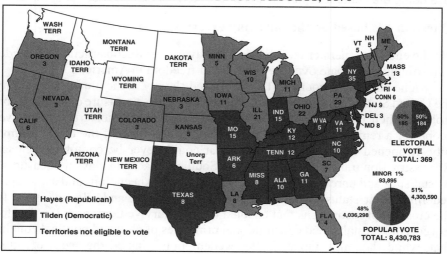

6. Which of the following was most important in enabling the Democratic Party to regain political power in the South?

(A) Limiting education for the freedmen

(B) Limiting the voting rights of the freedmen

(C) The Panic of 1873

(D) The Amnesty Act of 1872

7. The victor in the 1876 presidential election was decided by

(A) a special electoral commission

(B) the House of Representatives

(C) the Senate

(D) the Supreme Court

8. Democrats agreed to accept Rutherford B. Hayes as president in 1876 in part if he agreed to which of the following?

(A) to support a nationwide Black Code

(B) to remove federal troops from the South

(C) to promote Southern industrial development

(D) to support civil service reform

Use complete sentences; an outline or bulleted list alone is not acceptable.

Question 1 is based on the following excerpts.

"In the end, then, neither the abolition of slavery nor Reconstruction succeeded in resolving the debate over the meaning of freedom in American life. . . .

Alone among the societies that abolished slavery in the nineteenth century, the United States, for a moment, offered the freedmen a measure of political control over their own destinies. However brief its sway, Reconstruction allowed scope for a remarkable political and social mobilization of the black community. It opened doors of opportunity that could never be completely closed. Reconstruction transformed the lives of Southern blacks in ways unmeasurable by statistics and unreachable by law. It raised their expectations and aspirations, redefined their status in relation to the larger society, and allowed space for the creation of institutions that enabled them to survive the repression that followed. And it established constitutional principles of civil and political equality that, while flagrantly violated after Redemption, planted the seeds of future struggle."

—Eric Foner, "The New View of Reconstruction," *American Heritage,*
1983

"Reconstruction, which was far from radical, constituted the most democratic decades of the nineteenth century, South or North, so much so that it amounted to the first progressive era in the nation's history. Just ten years after Supreme Court Chief Justice Roger B. Taney endorsed the expansion of slavery into the western territories and announced that black Americans, even if free born, could not be citizens of the republic, blacks were fighting for the franchise in northern states; battling to integrate streetcars in Charleston, New Orleans, and San Francisco; funding integrated public schools; and voting and standing for office in the erstwhile Confederacy. . . . Black veterans, activists, ministers, assemblymen, registrars, poll workers, editors, and a handful of dedicated white allies risked their lives in this cause, nearly brought down a racist president, but ultimately lost their fight because of white violence."

—Douglas R. Egerton, *The Wars of Reconstruction,* 2014

1. Using the excerpts, answer (A), (B), and (C).

   (A) Briefly explain ONE major difference between Foner's and Egerton's historical interpretations of the success or failure of Reconstruction.

   (B) Briefly explain how ONE historical event or development in the period 1863 to 1877 that is not explicitly mentioned in the excerpts could be used to support Foner's interpretation.

   (C) Briefly explain how ONE historical event or development in the period 1863 to 1877 that is not explicitly mentioned in the excerpts could be used to support Egerton's interpretation.

Question 2. Answer (A), (B), and (C).

   (A) Briefly explain how ONE specific group played a significant role in the period of Reconstruction in the South.

   (B) Briefly explain how ONE historical event or development affected African Americans in the period of Reconstruction in the South.

   (C) Briefly explain ONE specific impact of the impeachment of Andrew Johnson in the period of Reconstruction in the South.

Question 3. Answer (A), (B), and (C).

   (A) Briefly explain ONE specific action taken by the Republican Party to maintain power in the period 1863 to 1877.

   (B) Briefly explain ONE historical event or development in the relationship between the government and business in the North in the period 1863 to 1877.

   (C) Briefly explain how ONE specific person or event demonstrated a negative view of President Grant's administration in the period 1869 to 1877.

Question 4 is based on the following cartoon.

Source: Thomas Nast, "Slavery is Dead(?)" *Harper's Weekly,* 1867.
Library of Congress

4. Using the cartoon, answer (A), (B), and (C). The left side shows a scene
   from before the Emancipation Proclamation. The right side shows a
   scene from after the Civil War.

   (A) Briefly explain ONE viewpoint expressed by the artist concerning
   the status of slaves in the period of 1863 to 1866 after the
   Emancipation Proclamation.

   (B) Briefly explain ONE historical event or development during
   President Johnson's administration that contributed to the
   viewpoint of the cartoon.

   (C) Briefly explain ONE specific action by the Radical Republicans in
   the period 1863 to 1866 that could challenge the viewpoint of the
   cartoon.

THINK AS A HISTORIAN: STATEMENTS ABOUT ARGUMENTATION

Which TWO of the following statements most clearly express historical argumentation?

1. Dunning's view of Reconstruction was grounded in racial beliefs
   that almost no one accepts today.

2. I agree with the efforts of Charles Sumner on Reconstruction.

3. The Freedmen's Bureau and Black Codes provide contradictory
   evidence for the conclusion that Reconstruction was a success.

Unit 5: Period 5 Review, 1844–1877

LONG ESSAY QUESTIONS

Directions: The suggested writing time for each question is 40 minutes. In your response you should do the following:

- **Thesis:** Make a defensible claim that establishes a line of reasoning and consists of one or more sentences found in one place.
- **Contextualization:** Relate the argument to a broader historical context.
- **Evidence:** Support an argument with specific and relevant historical evidence.
- **Reasoning:** Organize an argument using the skill in the question.
- **Analysis:** Demonstrate a complex understanding of the question using historical evidence to support, qualify, or modify an argument.

1. Analyze and evaluate the importance and efforts of the Confederate States in gaining international support during the Civil War.

2. Analyze and evaluate the importance and efforts of the Americans in gaining international support during the Revolutionary War.

3. Analyze and evaluate the motivation and rationale behind the Manifest Destiny expansion that began in the United States in the 1840s.

4. Analyze and evaluate the motivation and rationale behind the western expansion through the Louisiana Purchase that took hold in the United States at the start of the 19th century.

5. Compare and contrast the efforts for and against the increasing of guarantees for equal rights for all during Reconstruction.

6. Compare and contrast the efforts for and against the increasing of protections of the rights of individuals during the period of the ratification of the United States Constitution.

7. Analyze and evaluate the arguments presented by the Federalists and the Anti-Federalists during the debate over the ratification of the United States Constitution.

8. Analyze and evaluate the arguments presented by Abraham Lincoln and Stephen A. Douglas in their debates that focused on slavery.

DOCUMENT-BASED QUESTION 1

Directions: Question 1 is based on the accompanying documents. The documents have been edited for the purpose of this exercise. You are advised to spend 15 minutes planning and 45 minutes writing your answer. In your response you should do the following:

- **Thesis:** Make a defensible claim that establishes a line of reasoning and consists of one or more sentences found in one place.
- **Contextualization:** Relate the argument to a broader historical context.
- **Document Evidence:** Use content from at least six documents.
- **Outside Evidence:** Use one piece of evidence not in the documents.
- **Document Sourcing:** Explain how or why the point of view, purpose, situation, or intended audience is relevant for at least three documents.
- **Analysis:** Show the relationships among pieces of historical evidence and use them to support, qualify, or modify an argument.

1. To what extent did Manifest Destiny and territorial expansion unite or divide the United States from 1830 to 1860?

Document 1

Source: Anonymous, "California and the National Interest," *American Review,* a Whig journal, 1846

The natural progress of events will undoubtedly give us that province [California] just as it gave us Texas. Already American emigrants thither are to be numbered by thousands, and we may, at almost any moment, look for a declaration, which shall dissolve the slight bounds that now link the province to Mexico, and prepare the way for its ultimate annexation to the United States. . . .

Here, then, lies the Pacific coast, adjoining our western border . . . which embrace the southern sections of the United States and stretching northward to the southern boundary of Oregon. . . .

California, to become the seat of wealth and power for which nature has marked it, must pass into the hands of another race. And who can conjecture what would now have been its condition, had its first colonists been of the stock which peopled the Atlantic coast?

Document 2

Source: William Ellery Channing, abolitionist and pacifist, statement opposing the annexation of Texas, 1837

Texas is the first step to Mexico. The moment we plant authority on Texas, the boundaries of these two countries will become nominal, will be little more than lines on the sand. . . .

A country has no right to adopt a policy, however gainful, which, as it may foresee, will determine it to a career of war. A nation, like an individual, is bound to seek, even by sacrifices, a position which will favor peace, justice, and the exercise of beneficent influence on the world. A nation provoking war by cupidity, by encroachment, and above all, by efforts to propagate the curse of slavery, is alike false to itself, to God, and to the human race.

Document 3

Source: Editorial, "New Territory versus No Territory," *United States Magazine and Democratic Review,* October 1847

This occupation of territory by the people is the great movement of the age, and until every acre of the North American continent is occupied by citizens of the United States, the foundation of the future empire will not have been laid . . .

When these new states come into the Union, they are controlled by the Constitution only; and as that instrument permits slavery in all the states that are parties to it, how can Congress prevent it? . . .

When through the results of war, territory comes into the possession of the Union, it is equally a violation of the Constitution for Congress to undertake to say that there shall be no slavery then. The people of the United States were nearly unanimous for the admission of Texas into the Union; but probably not an insignificant fraction require its annexation "for the purpose" of extending slavery.

Document 4

Source: John L. O'Sullivan, editor, *Democratic Review,* 1846

California will, probably, next fall away from [Mexico]. . . . The Anglo-Saxon foot is already on its borders. Already the advance guard of the irresistible army of Anglo-Saxon emigration has begun to pour down upon it, armed with the plough and the rifle, and marking its trail with schools and colleges, courts and representative halls, mills and meeting-houses. A population will soon be in actual occupation of California, over which it be idle for Mexico to dream of dominion. They will necessarily become independent. All this without . . . responsibility of our people—in the natural flow of events.

Document 5

Source: Senator Thomas Corwin, Speech, 1847

What is the territory, Mr. President, which you propose to wrest from Mexico? . . .
Sir, look at this pretense of want of room.

There is one topic connected with this subject which I tremble when I approach, and yet I cannot forbear to notice it. It meets you in every step you take; it threatens you which way soever you go in prosecution of this war. I allude to the question of slavery . . . the North and the South are brought together into a collision on a point where neither will yield. Who can foresee or foretell the result . . . why should we participate this fearful struggle, by continuing a war the result of which must be to force us at once upon a civil conflict? . . . Let us wash Mexican blood from our hands, and . . . swear to preserve honorable peace with all the world.

Document 6

Source: President James Polk, Inaugural Address, 1845

None can fail to see the danger to our safety and future peace if Texas remains an independent state, or becomes an ally or dependency of some foreign nation more powerful than herself. Is there one among our citizens who would not prefer perpetual peace with Texas to occasional wars, which often occur between bordering independent nations? Is there one who would not prefer free intercourse with her, to high duties on all our products and manufactures which enter her ports or cross her frontiers? Is there one who would not prefer an unrestricted communication with her citizens, to the frontier obstructions which must occur if she remains out of the Union?

Document 7

Source: Senator Charles Sumner, Massachusetts Legislature, 1847

Resolved, That the present war with Mexico has its primary origin in the unconstitutional annexation to the United States of the foreign state of Texas while the same was still at war with Mexico; that it was unconstitutionally commenced by the order of the President . . . —by a powerful nation against a weak neighbor—unnecessarily and without just cause, at immense cost of a portion of her territory, from which slavery has already been excluded, with the triple object of extending slavery, of strengthening "Slave Power," and of obtaining the control of the Free States, under the Constitution of the United States.

Resolved, That our attention is directed anew to the wrong and "enormity" of slavery, and to the tyranny and usurpation of the "Slave Power," as displayed in the history of our country, particularly in the annexation of Texas and the present war with Mexico.

Directions: See page 312.

2. "The Civil War was not inevitable; it was the result of extremism and failures of leadership on both sides." Assess the validity of this statement, using the following documentation and your knowledge of the period from 1840 to 1861.

Document 1

Source: Daniel Webster, Speech in the Senate, March 7, 1850

Sir, there are those abolition societies, of which I am unwilling to speak, but in regard to which I have very clear notions and opinions. I do not think them useful. I think their operations of the last twenty years have produced nothing good or valuable.

I do not mean to impute gross motives even to the leaders of these societies, but I am not blind to the consequences. I cannot but see what mischiefs their interference with the South has produced. . . . These abolition societies commenced their course of action in 1835. It is said—I do not know how true it may be—that they sent incendiary publications into the slave states. At any event, they attempted to arouse, and did arouse, a very strong feeling. In other words, they created great agitation in the North against . . . slavery.

Document 2

Source: Harriet Beecher Stowe, *Uncle Tom's Cabin,* 1852

Tom spoke in a mild voice . . . Legree shook with anger . . .

"Well, here's a pious dog, at last, let down among us sinners!— a saint, a gentleman, and no less, to talk to us sinners about our sins! Powerful holy crittur, he must be! Here, you rascal, you make to believe to be so pious—didn't you never hear, out of yer Bible, 'Servants, obey yer masters'? An't I yer master? Didn't I pay down twelve hundred dollars, cash, for all there is inside yer old cussed black shell? An't yer mine now body and soul?" . . .

"No! no! no! my soul an't yours, Mas'r! You haven't bought it—ye can't buy it! It's been bought and paid for by One that is able to keep it. No matter, no matter, you can't harm me!"

"I can't!" said Legree, with a sneer, "we'll see—we'll see!"

Document 3

Source: U.S. Bureau of the Census. *Historical Statistics of the United States, Colonial Times to 1970*

Party Control in Congress						
Session	Senate			House		
	Majority Party	Minority Party	Other	Majority Party	Minority Party	Other
1849–51	D: 35	W: 25	2	D: 112	W: 109	9
1851–53	D: 35	W: 24	3	D: 140	W: 88	5
1853–55	D: 40	W: 22	2	D: 159	W: 71	4
1855–57	D: 40	R: 15	5	R: 108	D: 83	43
1857–59	D: 36	R: 20	8	D: 118	R: 92	26
1859–61	D: 36	R: 26	4	R: 114	D: 92	31

D: Democrat   W: Whig   R: Republican

Document 4

Source: Abraham Lincoln, Speech at the Republican state convention, Springfield, Illinois, June 17, 1858

A house divided against itself cannot stand. I believe this Government can not endure permanently half slave and half free. I do not expect the Union to be dissolved—I do not expect the house to fall—but I do expect it will cease to be divided. It will become all one thing, or all the other. Either the opponents of slavery will arrest the further spread of it, and place it where the public mind shall rest in the belief that it is in the course of ultimate extinction; or its advocates will push it forward till it shall become alike lawful in all the States, old as well as new, North as well as South.

Document 5

Source: Stephen Douglas, Speech at Alton, Illinois, October 15, 1858

In my opinion our government can endure forever, divided into free and slave States as our fathers made it,—each State having the right to prohibit, abolish, or sustain slavery, just as it pleases. This government was made upon the great basis of the sovereignty of the states, the right of each State to regulate its own domestic institutions to suit itself; and that right was conferred with the understanding and expectation that, inasmuch as each locality had separate interests, each locality must have different and distinct local and domestic institutions, corresponding to its wants and interests. Our fathers knew, when they made the government, that the laws and institutions which were well adapted to the green mountains of Vermont, were unsuited to the rice plantations of South Carolina.

Document 6

Source: Frederick Douglass, Speech at Storer College, Harpers Ferry, Virginia, May 1882

If John Brown did not end the war that ended slavery, he did, at least, begin the war that ended slavery. . . .

The irrepressible conflict was one of words, votes, and compromises. When John Brown stretched forth his arm the sky was cleared . . . and the clash of arms was at hand.

Document 7

Source: "A Declaration of the Immediate Causes Which Induce and Justify the Secession of South Carolina, from the Federal Union," 1860

We affirm that these ends for which this government was instituted have been defeated and the Government itself has been destructive of them by the action of the nonslaveholding States. Those states have assumed the right of deciding . . . and have denied the rights of property established in fifteen of the states and recognized by the Constitution . . .

A geographical line has been drawn across the Union, and all the States north of that line have united in the election of a man to the high office of President of the United States whose opinions and purposes are hostile to slavery. He is to be entrusted with the administration of the common Government, because he has declared that that "Government cannot endure permanently half slave [and] half free," and that the public mind must rest in the belief that slavery is in the course of ultimate extinction.

UNIT 6: Period 6,1865–1898

The period from the end of Civil War in 1865 to the start of the Spanish-American War in 1898 was one of fast-paced economic change and urban development in the United States. During this period the United States began to fill a new role globally. The country emerged as the largest economy in the world and a potential international power.

Overview Historians have labeled the period in many ways based on what they consider the most important developments that occurred during it. For some, it is the "Second Industrial Revolution," which introduced the wonders of electric-powered technologies, petroleum energy, and the first industrial laboratories. Others called it, the "Railroad Era," which produced a continental network of railroads that could move the products of the new large-scale industries. For some, it is the "Last Frontier," which witnessed the settlement of lands between the Mississippi River and the Pacific Ocean, and the end of the "Indian Wars."

However, the characterization of these years that has most endured is the "Gilded Age," a time during which the "captains of industry" controlled large corporations, created great fortunes, and dominated politics. At the same time, the problems faced by farmers because of low prices and those faced by burgeoning cities festered under the surface.

The period could also be identified by changes in the population. During the late 1800s, large waves of "new" immigrants from southern and eastern Europe moved into the United States. They provided the workforce for factories and mines, and they contributed to the richness and diversity of American culture.

In response to these economic and cultural changes, reform movements arose. Labor unions, farmer organizations, and a growing middle class began to call for changes in economic, political, and cultural institutions.

Alternate Views One limitation to ending the period in 1898 is that it fragments many of the trends that were just beginning in the late 1800s. In particular, some of the reform movements that started in the 1880s and 1890s did not produce results until the first decades of the 1900s. Immigration remained at a high level until 1914. For these reasons, some historians prefer to extend this period to 1914, when World War I began in Europe, or 1920, when the United States elected its first president after that war ended.

16

THE RISE OF INDUSTRIAL AMERICA, 1865–1900

As we view the achievements of aggregated capital,
we discover the existence of trusts, combinations, and monopolies,
while the citizen is struggling far in the rear or is trampled
to death beneath an iron heel. Corporations, which should be
the carefully restrained creatures of the law and servants
of the people, are fast becoming the people's masters.

President Grover Cleveland, 1888

By 1900, the United States was the leading industrial power in the world, manufacturing more than its leading rivals, Great Britain, France, or Germany. Several factors contributed to the rapid growth (about 4 percent a year) of the U.S. economy:

- The country was a treasure-house of raw materials essential to industrialization—coal, iron ore, copper, lead, timber, and oil.

- An abundant labor supply that was, between 1865 and 1900, supplemented yearly by the arrival of hundreds of thousands of immigrants.

- A growing population and an advanced transportation network made the United States the largest market in the world for industrial goods.

- Capital was plentiful, as Europeans with surplus wealth joined well-to-do Americans in investing in the economic expansion.

- The development of labor-saving technologies and an efficient patent system increased productivity. The federal government granted more than 440,000 new patents from 1860 to 1890.

- Businesses benefited from friendly government policies that protected private property, subsidized railroads with land grants and loans, supported U.S. manufacturers with protective tariffs, refrained from regulating business operations, and limited taxes on corporate profits.

- Talented entrepreneurs emerged during this era who were able to build and manage vast industrial and commercial enterprises.

The Business of Railroads

The dynamic combination of business leadership, capital, technology, markets, labor, and government support was especially evident in the development of the nation's first big business—railroads. After the Civil War, railroad mileage increased more than fivefold in a 35-year period (from 35,000 miles in 1865 to 193,000 miles in 1900). Railroads created a market for goods that was national in scale, and by so doing encouraged mass production, mass consumption, and economic specialization. The resources used in railroad-building promoted the growth of other industries, especially coal and steel. Railroads also affected the routines of daily life. Soon after the American Railroad Association divided the country into four time zones in 1883, railroad time became standard time for all Americans. Maybe the most important innovations of the railroads was the creation of the modern stockholder corporation and the development of complex structures in finance, business management, and the regulation of competition.

Eastern Trunk Lines

In the early decades of railroading (1830–1860), the building of dozens of separate local lines had resulted in different gauges (distance between tracks) and incompatible equipment. These inefficiencies were reduced after the Civil War through the consolidation of competing railroads into integrated trunk lines. (A trunk line was the major route between large cities; smaller branch lines connected the trunk line with outlying towns.) "Commodore" Cornelius Vanderbilt used his millions earned from a steamboat business to merge local railroads into the New York Central Railroad (1867), which ran from New York City to Chicago and operated more than 4,500 miles of track. Other trunk lines, such as the Baltimore and Ohio Railroad and the Pennsylvania Railroad, connected eastern seaports with Chicago and other midwestern cities and set standards of excellence and efficiency for the rest of the industry.

Western Railroads

The great age of railroad-building coincided with the settlement of the last frontier. Railroads not only promoted settlement on the Great Plains, but they linked the West with the East to create one great national market.

Federal Land Grants Recognizing that western railroads would lead the way to settlement, the federal government provided railroad companies with huge subsidies in the form of loans and land grants. The government gave 80 railroad companies more than 170 million acres of public land, more than three times the acres given away under the Homestead Act. The land was given in alternate mile-square sections in a checkerboard pattern along the proposed route of the railroad. The government expected that the railroad would sell the land to new settlers to finance construction. Furthermore, the completed railroad might both increase the value of government lands and provide preferred rates for carrying the mail and transporting troops.

The subsidies carried some negative consequences. The land grants and cash loans promoted hasty and poor construction and led to corruption in all levels of government. Insiders used construction companies, like the notorious Crédit Mobilier (see Chapter 15), to bribe government officials and pocket huge profits. Protests against the land grants mounted in the 1880s when citizens discovered that the railroads controlled half of the land in some western states. Transcontinental Railroads During the Civil War, Congress authorized land grants and loans for the building of the first transcontinental railroad to tie California to the rest of the Union. Two newly incorporated railroad companies divided the task. The Union Pacific (UP) started from Omaha, Nebraska, and built westward across the Great Plains. The UP employed thousands of war veterans and Irish immigrants under the direction of General Grenville Dodge. The Central Pacific started from Sacramento, California, and built eastward. Led by Charles Crocker, the workers, including 6,000 Chinese immigrants, took on the great risks of laying track and blasting tunnels through the Sierra Nevada mountains. The two railroads came together on May 10, 1869, at Promontory Point, Utah, where a golden spike was ceremoniously driven into the rail tie to mark the linking of the Atlantic and the Pacific states.

In 1883, three other transcontinental railroads were completed. The Southern Pacific tied New Orleans to Los Angeles. The Atchison, Topeka, and Santa Fe linked Kansas City and Los Angeles. The Northern Pacific connected Duluth, Minnesota, with Seattle, Washington. In 1893, a fifth transcontinental railroad was finished, the Great Northern, which ran from St. Paul, Minnesota, to Seattle. It was built by James Hill. The transcontinental railroads may have helped to settle the West, but many proved failures as businesses. They were built in areas with few customers and with little promise of returning a profit in the near term.

Competition and Consolidation

During speculative bubbles, investors often overbuild new technologies, as did railroads owners in the 1870s and 1880s. Railroads also suffered from mismanagement and outright fraud. Speculators such as Jay Gould entered the railroad business for quick profits and made their millions by selling off assets and watering stock (inflating the value of a corporation's assets and profits before selling its stock to the public). In a ruthless scramble to survive, railroads competed by offering rebates (discounts) and kickbacks to favored shippers while charging exorbitant freight rates to smaller customers such as farmers. They also attempted to increase profits by forming pools, in which competing companies agreed secretly and informally to fix rates and share traffic.

A financial panic in 1893 forced a quarter of all railroads into bankruptcy. J. Pierpont Morgan and other bankers quickly moved in to take control of the bankrupt railroads and consolidate them. With competition eliminated, they could stabilize rates and reduce debts. By 1900, seven giant systems controlled

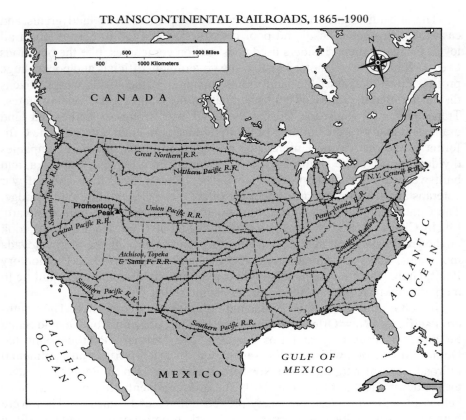

nearly two-thirds of the nation's railroads. The consolidation made the rail system more efficient. However, the system was controlled by a few powerful men such as Morgan, who dominated the boards of competing railroad corporations through interlocking directorates (the same directors ran competing companies). In effect, they created regional railroad monopolies.

Railroads captured the imagination of late-19th century America, as the public, local communities, states, and the federal government invested in their development. At the same time, however, customers and small investors often felt that they were the victims of slick financial schemes and ruthless practices. Early attempts to regulate the railroads by law did little good. The Granger laws passed by midwestern states in the 1870s were overturned by the courts, and the federal Interstate Commerce Act of 1886 was at first ineffective (see Chapter 17). Not until the Progressive era in the early 20th century did Congress expand the powers of Interstate Commerce Commission to protect the public interest.

Industrial Empires

The late 19th century witnessed a major shift in the nature of industrial production. Early factories had concentrated on producing textiles, clothing, and leather products. After the Civil War, a "second Industrial Revolution" resulted in the growth of large-scale industry and the production of steel, petroleum, electric power, and the industrial machinery to produce other goods.

The Steel Industry

The technological breakthrough that launched the rise of heavy industry was the discovery of a new process for making large quantities of steel (a more durable metal than iron). In the 1850s, both Henry Bessemer in England and William Kelly in the United States discovered that blasting air through molten iron produced high-quality steel. The Great Lakes region, from Pennsylvania to Illinois, used its abundant coal reserves and access to the iron ore of Minnesota's Mesabi Range to emerge as the center of steel production.

Andrew Carnegie Leadership of the fast-growing steel industry passed to a shrewd business genius, Andrew Carnegie. Born in 1835 in Scotland, Carnegie immigrated to the United States and worked his way up from poverty to become the superintendent of a Pennsylvania railroad. In the 1870s, he started manufacturing steel in Pittsburgh and soon outdistanced his competitors by a combination of salesmanship and the use of the latest technology. Carnegie employed a business strategy known as vertical integration, by which a company would control every stage of the industrial process, from mining the raw materials to transporting the finished product. By 1900, Carnegie Steel employed 20,000 workers and produced more steel than all the mills in Britain.

U.S. Steel Corporation Deciding to retire from business to devote himself to philanthropy, Carnegie sold his company in 1900 for more than $400 million to a new steel combination headed by J. P. Morgan. The new corporation, United States Steel, was the first billion-dollar company and also the largest enterprise in the world, employing 168,000 people and controlling more than three-fifths of the nation's steel business.

Rockefeller and the Oil Industry

The first U.S. oil well was drilled by Edwin Drake in 1859 in Pennsylvania. Only four years later, in 1863, a young John D. Rockefeller founded a company that would come to control most of the nation's oil refineries by eliminating its competition. Rockefeller took charge of the chaotic oil refinery business by applying the latest technologies and efficient practices. At the same time, as his company grew, he was able to extort rebates from railroad companies and temporarily cut prices for Standard Oil kerosene to force rival companies to sell out. By 1881 his company—by then known as the Standard Oil Trust—controlled 90 percent of the oil refinery business. The trust that Rockefeller put together consisted of the various companies that he had acquired, all managed by a board of trustees that Rockefeller and Standard Oil controlled. Such a combination represented a horizontal integration of an industry, in which former competitors were brought under a single corporate umbrella. By controlling the supply and prices of oil products, Standard Oil's profits soared and so did Rockefeller's fortune, which at the time of his retirement amounted to $900 million. By eliminating waste in the production of kerosene, Standard Oil was also able to keep prices low for consumers. Emulating Rockefeller's success, dominant companies in other industries (sugar, tobacco, leather, meat) also organized trusts.

Antitrust Movement

The trusts came under widespread scrutiny and attack in the 1880s. Middle-class citizens feared the trusts' unchecked power, and urban elites (old wealth) resented the increasing influence of the new rich. After failing to curb trusts on the state level, reformers finally moved Congress to pass the Sherman Antitrust Act in 1890, which prohibited any "contract, combination, in the form of trust or otherwise, or conspiracy in restraint of trade or commerce."

Although a federal law against monopolies was now on the books, it was too vaguely worded to stop the development of trusts in the 1890s. Furthermore, the Supreme Court in *United States* v. *E. C. Knight Co.* (1895) ruled that the Sherman Antitrust Act could be applied only to commerce, not to manufacturing. As a result, the U.S. Department of Justice secured few convictions until the law was strengthened during the Progressive era (see Chapter 21).

Laissez-Faire Capitalism

The idea of government regulation of business was alien to the prevailing economic, scientific, and religious beliefs of the late 19th century. The economic expression of these beliefs was summed up in the phrase "laissez-faire."

Conservative Economic Theories

As early as 1776, the economist Adam Smith had argued in *The Wealth of Nations* that business should be regulated, not by government, but by the "invisible hand" (impersonal economic forces) of the law of supply and demand. If government kept its hands off, so the theory went, businesses would be motivated by their own self-interest to offer improved goods and services at low prices. In the 19th century, American industrialists appealed to laissez-faire theory to justify their methods of doing business—even while they readily accepted the protection of high tariffs and federal subsidies. The rise of monopolistic trusts in the 1880s seemed to undercut the very competition needed for natural regulation. Even so, among conservatives and business leaders, laissez-faire theory was constantly invoked in legislative halls and lobbies to ward off any threat of government regulation.

Social Darwinism Charles Darwin's theory of natural selection in biology offended the beliefs of many religious conservatives, but it bolstered the views of economic conservatives. Led by English social philosopher Herbert Spencer, some people argued for Social Darwinism, the belief that Darwin's ideas of natural selection and survival of the fittest should be applied to the marketplace.

Spencer believed that concentrating wealth in the hands of the "fit" benefited everyone. An American Social Darwinist, Professor William Graham Sumner of Yale University, argued that helping the poor was misguided because it interfered with the laws of nature and would only weaken the evolution of the species by preserving the unfit. Social Darwinism gave some during this period a "scientific" sanction for their racial intolerance. Race theories about the superiority of one group over others would continue to produce in problems in the 20th century.

Gospel of Wealth A number of Americans found religion more convincing than social Darwinism in justifying the wealth of successful industrialists and bankers. Because he diligently applied the Protestant work ethic (that hard work and material success are signs of God's favor) to both his business and personal life, John D. Rockefeller concluded that "God gave me my riches." In a popular lecture, "Acres of Diamonds," the Reverend Russell Conwell preached that everyone had a duty to become rich. Andrew Carnegie's article "Wealth" argued that the wealthy had a God-given responsibility to carry out projects of civic philanthropy for the benefit of society. Practicing what he preached, Carnegie distributed more than $350 million of his fortune to support the building of libraries, universities, and various public institutions.

Technology and Innovations

Vital to industrial progress were new inventions. These led to greater productivity in the workplace and mass-produced goods in the home.

Inventions

The first radical change in the speed of communications was the invention of a workable telegraph by Samuel F. B. Morse, initially demonstrated in 1844. By the time of the Civil War, electronic communication by telegraph and rapid transportation by railroad were already becoming standard parts of modern living, especially in the northern states. After the war, Cyrus W. Field's invention of an improved transatlantic cable in 1866 suddenly made it possible to send messages across the seas in minutes. By 1900, cables linked all continents of the world in an electronic network of nearly instantaneous, global communication. This communication revolution soon internationalized markets and prices for basic commodities, such as grains, coal, and steel, often placing local and smaller producers at the mercy of international forces.

Among the hundreds of noteworthy inventions of the late 19th century were the typewriter (1867), the telephone developed by Alexander Graham Bell (1876), the cash register (1879), the calculating machine (1887), and the adding machine (1888). These new products became essential tools for business. Products for the consumer that were in widespread use by the end of the century were George Eastman's Kodak camera (1888), Lewis E. Waterman's fountain pen (1884), and King Gillette's safety razor and blade (1895).

Edison and Westinghouse

Possibly the greatest inventor of the 19th century, Thomas Edison was a young telegraph operator and patented his first invention, a machine for recording votes in 1869. Income from his early inventions enabled Edison to establish a research laboratory in Menlo Park, New Jersey, in 1876. This was the world's first modern research laboratory. It ranks among Edison's most important contribution to science and industry because it introduced the concept of mechanics and engineers working on a project as a team rather than as lone inventors. Out of Edison's lab came more than a thousand patented inventions, including the phonograph, the improvement of the incandescent lamp in 1879 (the first practical electric lightbulb), the dynamo for generating electric power, the mimeograph machine, and the motion picture camera.

Another remarkable inventor, George Westinghouse, held more than 400 patents and was responsible for developing an air brake for railroads (1869) and a transformer for producing high-voltage alternating current (1885). The latter invention made possible the lighting of cities and the operation of electric streetcars, subways, and electrically powered machinery and appliances.

Marketing Consumer Goods

The increased output of U.S. factories as well as the invention of new consumer products prompted businesses to find ways of selling their merchandise to a large public. R.H. Macy in New York and Marshall Field in Chicago made the large department store the place to shop in urban centers, while Frank Woolworth's Five and Ten Cent Store brought nationwide chain stores to the towns and urban neighborhoods. Two large mail-order companies, Sears, Roebuck and Montgomery Ward, used the improved rail system to ship to rural customers everything from hats to houses ordered from their thick catalogs, which were known to millions of Americans as the "wish book."

Packaged foods under such brand names as Kellogg and Post became common items in American homes. Refrigerated railroad cars and canning enabled Gustavus Swift and other packers to change the eating habits of Americans with mass-produced meat and vegetable products. Advertising and new marketing techniques not only promoted a consumer economy but also created a consumer culture in which shopping became a favorite pastime.

Impact of Industrialization

The growth of American industry raised the standard of living for most people. However, growth also created sharper economic and class divisions among the rich, the middle class, and the poor.

The Concentration of Wealth

By the 1890s, the richest 10 percent of the U.S. population controlled 90 percent of the nation's wealth. Industrialization created a new class of millionaires, some of whom flaunted their wealth by living in ostentatious mansions, sailing enormous yachts, and throwing lavish parties. The Vanderbilts graced the waterfront of Newport, Rhode Island, with summer homes that rivaled the villas of European royalty. Guests at one of their dinner parties were invited to hunt for their party favors by using small silver shovels to seek out the precious gems hidden in sand on long silver trays.

Horatio Alger Myth Many Americans ignored the widening gap between the rich and the poor. They found hope in the examples of "self-made men" in business such as Andrew Carnegie and Thomas Edison and novels by Horatio Alger Jr. Every Alger novel portrayed a young man of modest means who becomes wealthy through honesty, hard work, and a little luck. In reality, opportunities for upward mobility (movement into a higher economic bracket) did exist, but the rags-to-riches career of an Andrew Carnegie was unusual. Statistical studies demonstrate that the typical wealthy businessperson of the day was a white, Anglo-Saxon, Protestant male who came from an upper- or middle-class background and whose father was in business or banking.

The Expanding Middle Class

The growth of large corporations required thousands of white-collar workers (salaried workers whose jobs generally do not involve manual labor) to fill the highly organized administrative structures. Middle management was needed to coordinate the operations between the chief executives and the factories. In addition, industrialization helped expand the middle class by creating jobs for accountants, clerical workers, and salespersons. In turn, these middle-class employees increased the demand for services from other middle-class workers: professionals (doctors and lawyers), public employees, and storekeepers. The increase in the number of good-paying occupations after the Civil War significantly increased the size of the middle class.

Wage Earners

By 1900, two-thirds of all working Americans worked for wages, usually at jobs that required them to work ten hours a day, six days a week. Wages were determined by the laws of supply and demand, and because there was usually a large supply of immigrants competing for factory jobs, wages were barely above the level needed for bare subsistence. Low wages were justified by David Ricardo (1772–1823), whose famous "iron law of wages" argued that raising wages would only increase the working population, and the availability of more workers would in turn cause wages to fall, thus creating a cycle of misery and starvation. Real wages (income adjusted for inflation) rose steadily in the late 19th century, but even so most wage earners could not support a family decently on one income. Therefore, working-class families depended on the income of women and children. In 1890, 11 million of the 12.5 million families in the United States averaged less than $380 a year in income.

Working Women

One adult woman out of every five in 1900 was in the labor force working for wages. Most were young and single—only 5 percent of married women worked outside the home. In 1900, men and women alike believed that, if a family could afford it, a woman's proper role was in the home raising children. Factory work for women was usually in industries that people perceived as an extension of the home: the textile, garment, and food-processing industries, for example. As the demand for clerical workers increased, women moved into formerly male occupations as secretaries, bookkeepers, typists, and telephone operators. Occupations or professions that became feminized (women becoming the majority) usually lost status and received lower wages and salaries.

Labor Discontent

Before the Industrial Revolution, workers labored in small workplaces that valued an artisan's skills. They often felt a sense of accomplishment in creating a product from start to finish. Factory work was radically different. Industrial workers were often assigned just one step in the manufacturing of a product, performing semiskilled tasks monotonously. Both immigrants from abroad and migrants from rural America had to learn to work under the tyranny of the clock. In many industries, such as railroads and mining, working conditions were dangerous. Many workers were exposed to chemicals and pollutants that only later were discovered to cause chronic illness and early death.

Industrial workers rebelled against intolerable working conditions by missing work or quitting. They changed jobs on the average of every three years. About 20 percent of those who worked in factories eventually dropped out of the industrial workplace rather than continuing. This was a far higher percentage than those who protested by joining labor unions.

The American Workforce, 1900–1960				
Year	Farm		Nonfarm	
	Total in millions	Percentage	Total in millions	Percentage
1900	11,050	41	15,906	59
1910	11,260	32	23,299	68
1920	10,440	27	28,768	73
1930	10,340	22	33,843	78
1940	9,540	20	37,980	80
1950	7,160	12	51,760	88
1960	5,458	8	60,318	92

Source: U.S. Bureau of the Census. *Historical Statistics of the United States, Colonial Times to 1970*

The Struggle of Organized Labor

The late 19th century witnessed the most deadly—and frequent—labor conflicts in the nation's history. Many feared the country was heading toward open warfare between capital and labor.

Industrial Warfare

With a surplus of cheap labor, management held most of the power in its struggles with organized labor. Strikers could easily be replaced by bringing in strikebreakers, or scabs—unemployed persons desperate for jobs. Employers also used all of the following tactics for defeating unions:

- *the lockout:* closing the factory to break a labor movement before it could get organized
- *blacklists:* names of pro-union workers circulated among employers
- *yellow-dog contracts:* workers being told, as a condition for employment, that they must sign an agreement not to join a union
- calling in *private guards* and *state militia* to put down strikes
- obtaining *court injunctions* against strikes

Moreover, management fostered public fear of unions as anarchistic and un-American. Before 1900, management won most of its battles with organized labor because, if violence developed, employers could almost always count on the support of the federal and state governments.

Labor itself was often divided on the best methods for fighting management. Some union leaders advocated political action. Others favored direct confrontation: strikes, picketing, boycotts, and slowdowns to achieve union recognition and collective bargaining.

Great Railroad Strike of 1877 One of the worst outbreaks of labor violence in the century erupted in 1877, during an economic depression, when the railroad companies cut wages in order to reduce costs. A strike on the Baltimore and Ohio Railroad quickly spread across 11 states and shut down two-thirds of the country's rail trackage. Railroad workers were joined by 500,000 workers from other industries in an escalating strike that quickly became national in scale. For the first time since the 1830s, a president (Rutherford B. Hayes) used federal troops to end labor violence. The strike and the violence finally ended, but not before more than 100 people had been killed. After the strike, some employers addressed the workers' grievances by improving wages and working conditions, while others took a hard line by busting workers' organizations.

Attempts to Organize National Unions

Before the 1860s, unions had been organized as local associations in one city or region. They usually focused on one craft or type of work.

National Labor Union The first attempt to organize all workers in all states—both skilled and unskilled, both agricultural workers and industrial workers—was the National Labor Union. Founded in 1866, it had some 640,000 members by 1868. Besides championing the goals of higher wages and the eight-hour day, the first national union also had a broad social program: equal rights for women and blacks, monetary reform, and worker cooperatives. Its chief victory was winning the eight-hour day for workers employed by the federal government. It lost support, however, after a depression began in 1873 and after the unsuccessful strikes of 1877.

Knights of Labor A second national labor union, the Knights of Labor, began in 1869 as a secret society in order to avoid detection by employers. Under the leadership of Terence V. Powderly, the union went public in 1881, opening its membership to all workers, including African Americans and women. Powderly advocated a variety of reforms: (1) worker cooperatives "to make each man his own employer," (2) abolition of child labor, and (3) abolition of trusts and monopolies. He favored settling labor disputes by means of arbitration rather than resorting to strikes. Because the Knights were loosely organized, however, he could not control local units that decided to strike. The Knights of Labor grew rapidly and attained a peak membership of 730,000 workers in 1886. It declined just as rapidly, however, after the violence of the Haymarket riot in Chicago in 1886 turned public opinion against the union.

Haymarket Bombing Chicago, with about 80,000 Knights in 1886, was the site of the first May Day labor movement. Also living in Chicago were about 200 anarchists who advocated the violent overthrow of all government. In response to the May Day movement calling for a general strike to achieve an eight-hour day, labor violence broke out at Chicago's McCormick Harvester plant. On May 4, workers held a public meeting in Haymarket Square, and as police attempted to break up the meeting, someone threw a bomb, which killed seven police officers. The bomb thrower was never found. Even so, eight anarchist leaders were tried for the crime and seven were sentenced to death. Horrified by the bomb incident, many Americans concluded that the union movement was radical and violent. The Knights of Labor, as the most visible union at the time, lost popularity and membership.

American Federation of Labor Unlike the reform-minded Knights of Labor, the American Federation of Labor (AF of L) concentrated on attaining narrower economic goals. Founded in 1886 as an association of 25 craft unions, and led by Samuel Gompers until 1924, the AF of L focused on just higher wages and improved working conditions. Gompers directed his local unions of skilled workers to walk out until the employer agreed to negotiate a new contract through collective bargaining. By 1901, the AF of L was by far the nation's largest union, with 1 million members. Even this union, however, would not achieve major successes until the early decades of the 20th century.

Strikebreaking in the 1890s

Two massive strikes in the last decade of the 19th century demonstrated both the growing discontent of labor and the continued power of management to prevail in industrial disputes.

Homestead Strike Henry Clay Frick, the manager of Andrew Carnegie's Homestead Steel plant near Pittsburgh, precipitated a strike in 1892 by cutting wages by nearly 20 percent. Frick used the weapons of the lockout, private guards, and strikebreakers to defeat the steelworkers' walkout after five months. The failure of the Homestead strike set back the union movement in the steel industry until the New Deal in the 1930s.

Pullman Strike Even more alarming to conservatives was a strike of workers living in George Pullman's company town near Chicago. Pullman manufactured the famous railroad sleeping cars known as Pullman cars. In 1894, he announced a general cut in wages and fired the leaders of the workers' delegation who came to bargain with him. The workers at Pullman laid down their tools and appealed for help from the American Railroad Union whose leader, Eugene V. Debs, directed railroad workers not to handle any trains with Pullman cars. The union's boycott tied up rail transportation across the country.

Railroad owners supported Pullman by linking Pullman cars to mail trains. They then appealed to President Grover Cleveland, persuading him to use the army to keep the mail trains running. A federal court issued an injunction forbidding interference with the operation of the mail and ordering railroad workers to abandon the boycott and the strike. For failing to respond to this injunction, Debs and other union leaders were arrested and jailed. The jailing of Debs and others effectively ended the strike. In the case of *In re Debs* (1895), the Supreme Court approved the use of court injunctions against strikes, which gave employers a very powerful weapon to break unions. After serving a six-month jail sentence, Debs concluded that more radical solutions were needed to cure labor's problems. He turned to socialism and the American Socialist party, which he helped to found in 1900.

By 1900, only 3 percent of American workers belonged to unions. Management held the upper hand in labor disputes, with government generally taking its side. However, people were beginning to recognize the need for a better balance between the demands of employers and employees to avoid the numerous strikes and violence that characterized the late 19th century.

Regional Differences During the Gilded Age, industrial growth was concentrated in the Northeast and Midwest regions, the parts of the country with the largest populations, the most capital, and the best transportation. As industry grew, these regions developed more cities, attracted more immigrants and migrants from rural areas, and created more middle-class jobs. The next chapter will analyze the development of the West and South during this period.

Middle-class Americans who enjoyed the benefits of increased industrial production, new consumer goods, and a higher standard of living generally admired the business leaders of the age, viewing them as great industrial statesmen. University professors gave intellectual respectability to this view by drawing upon social Darwinism to argue that business leaders' success was due to their superior intelligence and fitness. Did they not, after all, make the United States the leading economic power in the world?

In the early 20th century, however, a growing number of citizens and historians questioned the methods used by business leaders to build their industrial empires. Charles Beard and other Progressive historians called attention to the oppression of farmers and workers, the corruption of democratic institutions, and the plundering of the nation's resources. Their critical view of 19th-century business leaders received support from historians of the 1930s (the Depression decade). Matthew Josephson, for example, popularized the view that John D. Rockefeller and others like him were robber barons, who took from American workers and small businesses to build personal fortunes. The robber barons were presented as ruthless exploiters who used unethical means to destroy competition, create monopolies, and corrupt the free enterprise system. Any positive contributions that might have been made were merely unplanned by-products of the industrialists' ruthlessness and greed.

The prevailing wisdom of the 1930s shifted in the 1950s, as Allan Nevins urged other historians to right the injustice done to "our business history and our industrial leaders." Nevins and other revisionists argued that the mass production that helped win two world wars and that made the United States an economic superpower far outweighed in significance any self-serving actions by business leaders.

Another approach to the era was taken by historians who analyzed statistical data in an effort to judge the contributions of industrialists and big business. They asked: Were big corporations essential for the economic development of the United States? Did monopolies such as the Standard Oil Trust advance or retard the growth of the U.S. economy? Robert Fogel, for example, used statistical data to prove his startling thesis that railroads were *not* indispensable to the economic growth of the era. The shifting perspectives and criteria of historians from one generation to another may ensure that the question will remain unsettled, yet these perspectives still help to shape economic policy today.

KEY TERMS BY THEME

Transportation (WXT)
nation's first big
  business
Cornelius Vanderbilt
Eastern trunk lines
transcontinental
  railroads
Union and Central
  Pacific
American Railroad
  Association
railroads and time zones
speculation and
  overbuilding
Jay Gould, watering
  stock
rebates and pools
bankruptcy of railroads
Panic of 1893

**Large Scale Industry
  (WXT)**
causes of industrial
  growth
Andrew Carnegie
vertical integration
U.S. Steel
John D. Rockefeller
horizontal integration
Standard Oil Trust
interlocking directorates
J. P. Morgan
leading industrial power

Technology (WXT)
Second Industrial
  Revolution
Bessemer process
transatlantic cable

Alexander Graham Bell
telephone
Thomas Edison
Menlo Park research
  laboratory
electric power; lighting
George Westinghouse
Eastman's Kodak
  camera

Marketing (WXT)
large department stores
R. H. Macy
mail-order companies
Sears, Roebuck
packaged foods
refrigeration; canning
Gustavus Swift
advertising
consumer economy

**Role of Government
  (WXT)**
federal land grants and
  loans
fraud and corruption,
  Crédit Mobilier
Interstate Commerce Act
  of 1886
anti-trust movement
Sherman Antitrust Act of
  1890
federal courts, *U.S. v.
  E. C. Knight*

Organized Labor (WXT)
causes of labor
  discontent
"iron law of wages"
anti-union tactics

railroad strike of 1877
Knights of Labor
Haymarket bombing
American Federation of
  Labor
Samuel Gompers
Pullman Strike
Eugene Debs

**Work and Migration
  (WXT, MIG)**
railroad workers: Chi-
  nese, Irish, veterans
old rich vs. new rich
white-collar workers
expanding middle class
factory wage earners
women and children
  factory workers
women clerical workers

Ideas, Beliefs (CUL)
Protestant work ethic
Adam Smith
laissez-faire capitalism
concentration of wealth
Social Darwinism
William Graham
  Sumner
survival of the fittest
Gospel of Wealth
Horatio Alger stories
"self-made man"

MULTIPLE-CHOICE QUESTIONS

Questions 1–3 refer to the excerpt below.

"Competition therefore is the law of nature. Nature is entirely neutral; she submits to him who most energetically and resolutely assails her. She grants her rewards to the fittest; therefore, without regard to other considerations of any kind. . . . Such is the system of nature. If we do not like it and if we try to amend it, there is one way in which we can do it. We take from the better and give to the worse. . . . Let it be understood that we cannot go outside this alternative: liberty, inequality, survival of the fittest; not-liberty, equality, survival of the unfittest. The former carries society forward and favors all its best members; the latter carries society downward and favors all its worst members."

—William Graham Sumner, social scientist,
The Challenge of Facts, 1882

1. The ideas expressed in this excerpt most clearly show the influence of which of the following?

   (A) John Locke's *Second Treatise of Government*

   (B) Adam Smith's *The Wealth of Nations*

   (C) Thomas Jefferson's Declaration of Independence

   (D) Charles Darwin's *On the Origins of Species*

2. Which idea would Sumner most likely support?

   (A) Socialism

   (B) Laissez-faire

   (C) Manifest Destiny

   (D) Gospel of wealth

3. Which of the following developments would be most consistent with the beliefs expressed in the excerpt?

   (A) Consolidation of wealth by an elite

   (B) Expansion of rights for women

   (C) Passage of anti-trust legislation

   (D) Spread of organized labor

Questions 4–5 refer to the cartoon below.

Source: *Literary Digest,* 1905. The Granger Collection, NYC

4. Which of the following groups would most likely support the sentiments behind this cartoon?

   (A) Proponents of Social Darwinism

   (B) Proponents of anti-monopoly legislation

   (C) Proponents of organizing unskilled workers

   (D) Proponents of the Interstate Commerce Commission

5. The kind of sentiments in the cartoon above contributed most directly to which of the following?

   (A) The sale of Standard Oil to J. P. Morgan for $900 million

   (B) The breakup of Standard Oil into competing oil companies

   (C) The replacement of kerosene lamps with the incandescent lights

   (D) The rise of the American Federation of Labor

Questions 6–8 refer to the excerpt below.

"You evidently have observed the growth of corporate wealth and influence. You recognize that wealth, in order to become more highly productive, is concentrated into fewer hands, and controlled by representatives and directors, and yet you sing the old siren song that the workingman should depend entirely upon his own 'individual effort.'

"The school of laissez-faire, of which you seem to be a pronounced advocate, has produced great men in advocating the theory of each for himself and his Satanic majesty taking the hindermost, but the most pronounced advocates of your school of thought in economics have, when practically put to the test, been compelled to admit that combination and organizations of the toiling masses are essential both to prevent the deterioration and to secure an improvement in the condition of the wage earners."

—Samuel Gompers, Letter to Judge Peter Grosscup,
"Labor in Industrial Society," 1894

6. This excerpt was written to most directly support which of the following?

   (A) Formation of trusts

   (B) Collective bargaining

   (C) The anti-trust movement

   (D) Employee ownership of business

7. According to the author, what has most contributed to the need for wage earners to organize?

   (A) The school of laissez-faire economics

   (B) The rise of the captains of industry

   (C) The concentration of corporate wealth and power

   (D) The belief in individualism and self-reliance

8. Which of the following was most closely allied to the sentiments in this excerpt?

   (A) The economic theory of wages by David Ricardo

   (B) The practice of horizontal integration

   (C) Pullman's company town for workers

   (D) American Federation of Labor

SHORT-ANSWER QUESTIONS

Use complete sentences; an outline or bulleted list alone is not acceptable.

Question 1. Answer (A), (B), and (C).

(A) Briefly explain ONE specific example of how government promoted the growth of railroads in the United States before 1900.

(B) Briefly explain ONE specific example of how the railroads promoted the development of the U.S. economy from 1865 to 1900.

(C) Briefly explain ONE significant effect of the overbuilding of the railroads on the U. S. economy from 1865 to 1900.

Question 2 is related to the excerpts below.

"We accept and welcome... the law of competition between these, as being not only beneficial, but essential for the progress of the race."

—Andrew Carnegie, Gospel of Wealth, 1889

"The struggle for the survival of the fittest . . . as well as the law of supply and demand, were observed in all ages past until Standard Oil company preached cooperation, and it did cooperate so successfully."

—John D. Rockefeller, Interview given around 1917

2. Using the excerpts, answer (A), (B), and (C).

(A) Briefly explain ONE significant difference between Carnegie's perspective and Rockefeller's perspective on the role of competition in industrial development.

(B) Briefly explain ONE historical event or development from Carnegie's career that supports his view on competition.

(C) Briefly explain ONE historical event or development from Rockefeller's career that supports his view on competition.

Question 3. Answer (A), (B), and (C).

(A) Briefly explain ONE business practice that caused or influenced the antitrust movement from 1865 to 1900.

(B) Briefly explain ONE example of an antitrust effort from 1865 to 1900.

(C) Briefly explain ONE reason why antitrust legislation was generally unsuccessful from 1865 to 1900.

Question 4 is related to the excerpt below.

"The continuing process of sorting out classes at the workplace and in metropolitan space made the denial of class more difficult in the post-Civil War America. . . . In nineteenth century America, 'middle class' represented a specific set of experiences, a specific style of living, and a specific social identity."

—Stuart M. Blumin, *The Emergence of the Middle Class*, 1989

4. Using the excerpt, answer (A), (B), and (C).
   (A) Briefly explain ONE specific cause of the "sorting out classes at the workplace" from 1865 to 1900.
   (B) Briefly explain ONE specific cause of the expansion of the middle class during the period from 1865 to 1900.
   (C) Briefly explain ONE specific example of the increased opportunities for working women during the period from 1865 to 1900.

THINK AS A HISTORIAN: STATEMENTS ABOUT CONTEXT

Which TWO of the following statements most clearly demonstrate the skill of placing an event in context?

1. Wages for American workers, though low, were higher than wages for similar workers in Europe.

2. The creation of time zones demonstrated the nationalization of events and behavior in the late 19th century.

3. Eugene Debs dedicated his adult life fighting for working people.

4. Thomas Edison deserves great credit for his contributions to modern life.

17

THE LAST WEST AND THE NEW SOUTH, 1865–1900

American social development has been continually beginning over again on the frontier. This perennial rebirth, this fluidity of American life, this expansion westward with its new opportunities, its continuous touch with the simplicity of primitive society, furnish the forces dominating American character. The true point of view in the history of this nation is not the Atlantic coast, it is the Great West.

Frederick Jackson Turner, 1893

During the post-Civil War era most of the large-scale industrial development took place in the Northeast and Midwest, while the South and West most often supplied raw materials and consumed northern manufactured goods. Some in the South and West resented this apparent colonial status, which helped to shape the politics in the final decades of the 19th century. However, the South and West were not defined by their economic roles alone. Their geography, people, and cultures shaped their regional characteristics well into the future.

The West: Settlement of the Last Frontier

After the Civil War, many Americans began settling in the vast arid territory in the West that included the Great Plains, the Rocky Mountains, and the Western Plateau. Before 1860, these lands between the Mississippi River and the Pacific Coast were known as "the Great American Desert" by pioneers passing through on the way to the green valleys of Oregon and the goldfields of California. The plains west of the 100th meridian had few trees and usually received less than 15 inches of rainfall a year, which was not considered enough moisture to support farming. While the winter blizzards and hot dry summers discouraged settlement, the open grasslands of the plains supported an estimated 15 million bison, or buffalo. The buffalo in turn provided food, clothing, shelter, and even tools for many of the 250,000 American Indians living in the West in 1865.

STATES ADMITTED TO THE UNION 1864–1896

In only 35 years, conditions on the Great Plains changed so dramatically that the frontier largely vanished. By 1900, the great buffalo herds had been wiped out. The open western lands were fenced in by homesteads and ranches, crisscrossed by steel rails, and modernized by new towns. Ten new western states had been carved out of the last frontier. Only Arizona, New Mexico, and Oklahoma remained as territories awaiting statehood. Progress came at a cost. The frenzied rush for the West's natural resources not only nearly exterminated the buffalo, but also seriously damaged the environment. Most significantly, the American Indians who lived in the region paid a high human and cultural price as land was settled by miners, ranchers, and farmers.

The Mining Frontier

The discovery of gold in California in 1848 caused the first flood of newcomers to the territory. The California Gold Rush was only the beginning of a feverish quest for gold and silver that would extend well into the 1890s and would help to settle much of the region. A series of gold strikes and silver strikes in what became the states of Colorado, Nevada, Idaho, Montana, Arizona, and South Dakota kept a steady flow of hopeful prospectors pushing into the western mountains. The discovery of gold near Pike's Peak, Colorado, in 1859 brought nearly 100,000 miners to the area. In the same year, the discovery of the fabulous Comstock Lode (which produced more than $340 million in gold and silver by 1890) was responsible for Nevada entering the Union in 1864. Idaho and Montana also received early statehood, largely because of mining booms.

California's great gold rush of 1849 set the pattern for other rushes. First, individual prospectors would look for traces of gold in the mountain streams by a method called placer mining, using simple tools such as shovels and washing pans. Such methods eventually gave way to deep-shaft mining that required expensive equipment and the resources of wealthy investors and corporations.

Rich strikes created boomtowns overnight—towns that became infamous for saloons, dance-hall girls, and vigilante justice. Many of these, however, became lonely ghost towns within a few years after the gold or silver ran out. Some towns, such as Nevada's Virginia City (created by the Comstock Lode), did grow, adding theaters, churches, newspapers, schools, libraries, railroads, and police. Mark Twain started his career as a writer working on a Virginia City newspaper in the early 1860s. A few towns that served the mines, such as San Francisco, Sacramento, and Denver, expanded into prosperous cities.

Chinese Exclusion Act Most of the mining towns that endured and grew were more like industrial cities than the frontier towns depicted in western films. As the mines developed, mining companies employed experienced miners from Europe, Latin America, and China. In many mining towns, half the population was foreign-born. About one-third of the western miners in the 1860s were Chinese immigrants. Native-born Americans resented the competition. In California, hostility to foreigners took the form of a Miner's Tax of $20 a month on all foreign-born miners. Political pressure from western states moved Congress to pass the Chinese Exclusion Act in 1882, which prohibited further immigration to the United States by Chinese laborers. Immigration from China was severely restricted until 1965. The 1882 law was the first major act of Congress to restrict immigration on the basis of race and nationality.

Mining not only stimulated the settlement of the West but also reshaped the economics and politics of the nation. The vast increase in the supply of silver created a crisis over the relative value of gold- and silver-backed currency, which became a bitter political issue in the 1880s and 1890s. The mining boom left environmental scars that remain visible today, and it had a disastrous effect on American Indians, who lost their lands to miners pursuing instant riches.

The Cattle Frontier

The economic potential of the vast open grasslands that reached from Texas to Canada was realized by ranchers in the decades after the Civil War. Earlier, cattle had been raised and rounded up in Texas on a small scale by Mexican cowboys, or *vaqueros*. The traditions of the cattle business in the late 1800s, like the hardy "Texas" longhorn cattle, were borrowed from the Mexicans. By the 1860s, wild herds of about 5 million head of cattle roamed freely over the Texas grasslands. The Texas cattle business was easy to get into because both the cattle and the grass were free.

The construction of railroads into Kansas after the war opened up eastern markets for the Texas cattle. Joseph G. McCoy built the first stockyards in the region, at Abilene, Kansas, to hold cattle destined for Chicago. There, they could be sold for the high price of $30 to $50 per head. Dodge City and other cow towns sprang up along the railroads to handle the millions of cattle driven up the Chisholm, Goodnight-Loving, and other trails out of Texas during the 1860s and 1870s. The cowboys, many of whom were African Americans or Mexicans, received about a dollar a day for their dangerous work.

The long cattle drives began to come to an end in the 1880s. Overgrazing destroyed the grass and a winter blizzard and drought of 1885–1886 killed off 90 percent of the cattle. Another factor that closed down the cattle frontier was the arrival of homesteaders, who used barbed wire fencing to cut off access to the formerly open range. Wealthy cattle owners turned to developing huge ranches and using scientific ranching techniques. They raised new breeds of cattle that produced more tender beef by feeding them hay and grains. The Wild West was largely tamed by the 1890s, but in these few decades, Americans' eating habits changed from pork to beef and people created the legend of the rugged, self-reliant American cowboy.

The Farming Frontier

The Homestead Act of 1862 encouraged farming on the Great Plains by offering 160 acres of public land free to any family that settled on it for a period of five years. The promise of free land combined with the promotions of railroads and land speculators induced hundreds of thousands of native-born and immigrant families to attempt to farm the Great Plains between 1870 and 1900. About 500,000 families took advantage of the Homestead Act. However, five times that number had to purchase their land, because the best public lands often ended up in the hands of railroad companies and speculators.

Problems and Solutions The first "sodbusters" on the dry and treeless plains often built their homes of sod bricks. Extremes of hot and cold weather, plagues of grasshoppers, and the lonesome life on the plains challenged even the most resourceful of the pioneer families. Water was scarce, and wood for fences was almost nonexistent. The invention of barbed wire by Joseph Glidden in 1874 helped farmers to fence in their lands on the lumber-scarce plains. Using mail-order windmills to drill deep wells provided some water. Even so, many homesteaders discovered too late that 160 acres was not adequate for farming the Great Plains. Long spells of severe weather, together with falling prices for their crops and the cost of new machinery, caused the failure of two-thirds of the homesteaders' farms on the Great Plains by 1900. Western Kansas alone lost half of its population between 1888 and 1892.

Those who managed to survive adopted "dry farming" and deep-plowing techniques to use the moisture available. They also learned to plant hardy strains of Russian wheat that withstood the extreme weather. Ultimately, dams and irrigation saved many western farmers, as humans reshaped the rivers and physical environment of the West to provide water for agriculture.

The Closing of the Frontier

The Oklahoma Territory, once set aside for the use of American Indians, was opened for settlement in 1889, and hundreds of homesteaders took part in the last great land rush in the West. The next year, the U.S. Census Bureau declared that the entire frontier—except for a few pockets—had been settled.

Turner's Frontier Thesis Reacting to the closing of the frontier, historian Frederick Jackson Turner wrote an influential essay, "The Significance of the Frontier in American History" (1893). Turner argued that 300 years of frontier experience had shaped American culture by promoting independence and individualism. The frontier was a powerful social leveler, breaking down class distinctions and thus fostering social and political democracy. Furthermore, the challenges of frontier life caused Americans to be inventive and practical-minded—but also wasteful in their attitude toward natural resources.

The closing of the frontier troubled Turner. He saw the availability of free land on the frontier as a safety valve for harmlessly releasing discontent in American society. The frontier had always held out the promise of a fresh start. Once the frontier was gone, would the United States be condemned to follow the patterns of class division and social conflict that troubled Europe?

While many debate the Turner thesis, historians acknowledge that by the 1890s the largest movement of Americans was to the cities and industrialized areas. Not only was the era of the western frontier coming to a close, but the dominance of rural America was also on a decline.

American Indians in the West

The American Indians who occupied the West in 1865 belonged to dozens of different cultural and tribal groups. In New Mexico and Arizona, Pueblo groups such as the Hopi and Zuni lived in permanent settlements as farmers raising corn and livestock. The Navajo and Apache peoples of the Southwest were nomadic hunter-gatherers who adapted a more settled way of life, not only raising crops and livestock but also producing arts and crafts. In the Pacific Northwest (Washington and Oregon), such tribes as the Chinook and Shasta developed complex communities based on abundant fish and game.

About two-thirds of the western tribal groups lived on the Great Plains. These nomadic tribes, such as the Sioux, Blackfoot, Cheyenne, Crow, and Comanche, had given up farming in colonial times after the introduction of the horse by the Spanish. By the 1700s, they had become skillful horse riders and developed a way of life centered on the hunting of buffalo. Although they belonged to tribes of several thousand, they lived in smaller bands of 300 to 500 members. In the late 19th century, their conflicts with the U.S. government were partly the result of white Americans having little understanding of the Plains people's loose tribal organization and nomadic lifestyle.

Reservation Policy In the 1830s, President Andrew Jackson's policy of removing eastern American Indians to the West was based on the belief that lands west of the Mississippi would permanently remain "Indian country."

This expectation soon proved false, as wagon trains rolled westward on the Oregon Trail, and plans were made for building a transcontenintal railroad. In 1851, in councils (negotiations) at Fort Laramie and Fort Atkinson, the federal government began to assign the Plains tribes large tracts of land—or reservations —with definite boundaries. Most Plains tribes, however, refused to restrict their movements to the reservations and continued to follow the migrating buffalo wherever they roamed.

Indian Wars In the late 19th century, the settlement of thousands of miners, ranchers, and homesteaders on American Indian lands led to violence. Fighting between U.S. troops and Plains Indians was often brutal, with the U.S. Army responsible for several massacres. In 1866, during the Sioux War, the tables were turned when an army column under Captain William Fetterman was wiped out by Sioux warriors. Following these wars, another round of treaties attempted to isolate the Plains Indians on smaller reservations with

AMERICAN INDIANS IN THE WEST

federal agents promising government support. However, gold miners refused to stay off American Indians' lands if gold was to be found on them, as indeed it was in the Dakotas' Black Hills. Soon, minor chiefs not involved in the treaty-making and younger warriors denounced the treaties and tried to return to ancestral lands.

A new round of conflicts in the West began in the 1870s. The Indian Appropriation Act of 1871 ended recognition of tribes as independent nations by the federal government and nullified previous treaties made with the tribes. Conflicts included the Red River War against the Comanche in the southern plains and a second Sioux War led by Sitting Bull and Crazy Horse in the northern plains. Before the Sioux went down to defeat, they ambushed and destroyed Colonel George Custer's command at Little Big Horn in 1876. Chief Joseph's courageous effort to lead a band of the Nez Percé into Canada ended in defeat and surrender in 1877. The constant pressure of the U.S. Army forced tribe after tribe to comply with Washington's terms. In addition, the slaughter of most of the buffalo by the early 1880s doomed the way of life of the Plains people.

The last effort of American Indians to resist U.S. government controls came through a religious movement known as the Ghost Dance. Leaders of the movements believed it could return prosperity to American Indians. In the government's campaign to suppress the movement, the famous Sioux medicine man Sitting Bull was killed during his arrest. Then in December 1890, the U.S. Army gunned down more than 200 American Indian men, women, and children in the "battle" (massacre) of Wounded Knee in the Dakotas. This final tragedy marked the end of the Indian Wars on the crimsoned prairie.

Assimilationists The injustices done to American Indians were chronicled in a best-selling book by Helen Hunt Jackson, *A Century of Dishonor* (1881). Although this book created sympathy for American Indians, especially in the eastern United States, it also generated support for ending Indian culture through assimilation. Reformers advocated formal education, job training, and conversion to Christianity. They set up boarding schools such as the Carlisle School in Pennsylvania to segregate American Indian children from their people and teach them white culture and farming and industrial skills.

Dawes Severalty Act (1887) A new phase in the relationship between the U.S. government and American Indians was incorporated in the Dawes Act of 1887. The act was designed to break up tribal organizations, which many felt kept American Indians from becoming "civilized" and law-abiding citizens. The Dawes Act divided the tribal lands into plots of up to 160 acres, depending on family size. U.S. citizenship was granted to those who stayed on the land for 25 years and "adopted the habits of civilized life."

Under the Dawes Act, as intended, the government distributed 47 million acres of land to American Indians. However, 90 million acres of former reservation land—often the best land—was sold over the years to white settlers by the government, speculators, or American Indians themselves. The new policy proved a failure. By the turn of the century, disease and poverty had reduced the American Indian population to just 200,000 persons, most of whom lived as wards of the federal government.

Changes in the 20th Century In 1924, in partial recognition that forced assimilation had failed, the federal government granted U.S. citizenship to all American Indians, whether or not they had complied with the Dawes Act. As part of President Franklin Roosevelt's New Deal in the 1930s, Congress adopted the Indian Reorganization Act (1934), which promoted the re-establishment of tribal organization and culture. Today, more than 3 million American Indians, belonging to 500 tribes, live within the United States.

The Latino Southwest

After the Mexican War ended in 1848, the Spanish-speaking landowners in California and the Southwest were guaranteed their property rights and granted citizenship. However, drawn-out legal proceedings often resulted in the sale or loss of lands to new Anglo arrivals. Hispanic culture was preserved in dominant Spanish-speaking areas, such as the New Mexico territories, the border towns, and the barrios of California.

Mexican Americans moved to find work, such as to the sugar beet fields and the mines of Colorado, and the building of western railroads. Before 1917, the border with Mexico was open and few records were kept for either seasonal workers or permanent settlers. Mexicans, like their European counterparts, were drawn by the explosive economic development of the region.

The Conservation Movement

The concerns over deforestation sparked the conservation movement, and the breathtaking paintings and photographs of western landscapes helped to push Congress to preserve such western icons as Yosemite Valley as a California state park in 1864 (a national park in 1890), and to dedicate the Yellowstone area as the first

Source: Logging in California, 1909. Library of Congress

National Park in 1872. Carl Schurz, as Secretary of the Interior in the 1880s, advocated creation of forest reserves and a federal forest service to protect federal lands from exploitation. Presidents Benjamin Harrison and Grover Cleveland reserved 33 million acres of national timber.

With the closing of the frontier era, Americans grew increasingly concerned about the loss of public lands and the natural treasures they contained. The Forest Reserve Act of 1891 and the Forest Management Act of 1897 withdrew federal timberlands from development and regulated their use. While most "conservationists" believed in scientific management and regulated use of natural resources, "preservationists," such as John Muir, a leading founder of the Sierra Club in 1892, went a step further, and aimed to preserve natural areas from human interference. The education efforts of the Arbor Day, Audubon Society, and the Sierra Club were another sign of a growing conservation movement by 1900.

The New South

While the West was being "won" by settlers and the U.S. Army, the South was recovering from the devastation of the Civil War. Some southerners promoted a new vision for a self-sufficient southern economy built on modern capitalist values, industrial growth, and improved transportation. Chief among them was Henry Grady, the editor of the *Atlanta Constitution*. Grady spread the gospel of the New South with editorials that argued for economic diversity and laissez-faire capitalism. To attract businesses, local governments offered tax exemptions to investors and the promise of low-wage labor.

Economic Progress

The growth of cities, the textual industry, and improved railroads symbolized efforts to create a "New South" in the late 19th century." Birmingham, Alabama, developed into one of the nation's leading steel producers. Memphis, Tennessee, prospered as a center for the South's growing lumber industry. Richmond, Virginia, the former capital of the Confederacy, became the capital of the nation's tobacco industry. Georgia, North Carolina, and South Carolina overtook the New England states as the chief producers of textiles. By 1900, the South had 400 cotton mills employing almost 100,000 white workers. Southern railroad companies rapidly converted to the standard-gauge rails used in the North and West, so the South was integrated into the national rail network. The South's rate of postwar growth from 1865 to 1900 equaled or surpassed that of the rest of the country in population, industry, and railroads.

Continued Poverty

Despite progress and growth, the South remained a largely agricultural section—and also the poorest region in the country. To a greater extent than before the war, northern financing dominated much of the southern economy. Northern investors controlled three-quarters of the southern railroads and by 1900 had control of the South's steel industry as well. A large share of the profits from the new industries went to northern banks and financiers. Industrial workers in the South (94 percent of whom were white) earned half of the national average and worked longer hours than elsewhere. Most southerners of both races remained in traditional roles and barely got by from year to year as sharecroppers and farmers.

The poverty of the majority of southerners was not caused by northern capitalists. Two other factors were chiefly responsible: (1) the South's late start at industrialization and (2) a poorly educated workforce. Only a small number of southerners had the technological skills needed for industrial development. The South failed to invest in technical and engineering schools as did the North. Furthermore, in the late 1800s, political leadership in the South provided little support for the education of either poor whites or poor African Americans. Without adequate education, the southern workforce faced limited economic opportunities in the fast-changing world of the late 19th century.

Agriculture

The South's postwar economy remained tied mainly to growing cotton. Between 1870 and 1900, the number of acres planted in cotton more than doubled. Increased productivity, however, only added to the cotton farmer's problems, as a glut of cotton on world markets caused cotton prices to decline by more than 50 percent by the 1890s. Per capita income in the South actually declined, and many farmers lost their farms. By 1900, more than half the region's white farmers and three-quarters of the black farmers were tenants (or sharecroppers), most of them straining to make a living from small plots of 15 to 20 acres. A shortage of credit forced farmers to borrow supplies from local merchants in the spring with a lien, or mortgage, on their crops to be paid at harvest. The combination of sharecropping and crop liens forced poor farmers to remain tenants, virtual serfs tied to the land by debt.

Some southern farmers sought to diversify their farming to escape the trap of depending entirely on cotton. George Washington Carver, an African-American scientist at Tuskegee Institute in Alabama, promoted the growing of such crops as peanuts, sweet potatoes, and soybeans. His work played an important role in shifting southern agriculture toward a more diversified base.

Even so, most small farmers in the South remained in the cycle of debt and poverty. As in the North and the West, hard times produced a harvest of discontent. By 1890, the Farmers' Southern Alliance claimed more than 1 million members. A separate organization for African Americans, the Colored Farmers' National Alliance, had about 250,000 members. Both organizations rallied behind political reforms to solve the farmers' economic problems. If poor black and poor white farmers in the South could have united, they would have been a potent political force, but the economic interests of the upper class and the powerful racial attitudes of whites stood in their way.

Segregation

With the end of Reconstruction in 1877, the North withdrew its protection of the freedmen and left southerners to work out solutions to their own social and economic problems. The Democratic politicians who came to power in the southern states after Reconstruction, known as redeemers, won support from two groups: the business community and the white supremacists. The latter group favored policies of separating, or segregating, public facilities for blacks and whites as a means of treating African Americans as social inferiors. The redeemers often used race as a rallying cry to deflect attention away from the real concerns of tenant farmers and the working poor. They discovered that they could exert political power by playing on the racial fears of whites.

Discrimination and the Supreme Court During Reconstruction, federal laws protected southern blacks from discriminatory acts by local and state governments. Starting in the late 1870s, however, the U.S. Supreme Court struck down one Reconstruction act after another applying to civil rights. In the *Civil Rights Cases* of 1883, the Court ruled that Congress could not legislate against the racial discrimination practiced by private citizens, which included railroads, hotels, and other businesses used by the public. Then, in 1896, in the landmark case of *Plessy v. Ferguson,* the Supreme Court upheld a Louisiana law requiring "separate but equal accommodations" for white and black passengers on railroads. The Court ruled that the Louisiana law did not violate the 14th Amendment's guarantee of "equal protection of the laws."

These federal court decisions supported a wave of segregation laws, commonly known as Jim Crow laws, that southern states adopted beginning in the 1870s. These laws required segregated washrooms, drinking fountains, park benches, and other facilities in virtually all public places. Only the use of streets and most stores was not restricted according to a person's race.

Loss of Civil Rights Other discriminatory laws resulted in the wholesale disfranchisement of black voters by 1900. In Louisiana, for example, 130,334 black voters were registered in 1896 but only 1,342 in 1904—a 99 percent decline. Various political and legal devices were invented to prevent southern blacks from voting. Among the most common obstacles were literacy tests, poll taxes, and political party primaries for whites only. Many southern states adopted so-called grandfather clauses, which allowed a man to vote only if his grandfather had cast ballots in elections before Reconstruction. The Supreme Court again gave its sanction to such laws in a case of 1898, in which it upheld a state's right to use literacy tests to determine citizens' qualifications for voting.

Discrimination took many forms. In southern courts, African Americans were barred from serving on juries. If convicted of crimes, they were often given stiffer penalties than whites. In some cases, African Americans accused of crimes were not even given the formality of a court-ordered sentence. Lynch mobs killed more than 1,400 men during the 1890s. Economic discrimination was also widespread, keeping most southern African Americans out of skilled trades and even factory jobs. Thus, while poor whites and immigrants learned the industrial skills that would help them rise into the middle class, African Americans remained engaged in farming and low-paying domestic work.

Responding to Segregation Segregation, disenfranchisement, and lynching left African Americans in the South oppressed but not powerless. Some responded with confrontation. Ida B. Wells, editor of the *Memphis Free Speech,* a black newspaper, campaigned against lynching and the Jim Crow laws. Death threats and the destruction of her printing press forced Wells to carry on her work from the North. Other black leaders advocated migration. Bishop Henry Turner formed the International Migration Society in 1894 to help blacks emigrate to Africa. Many African Americans moved to Kansas and Oklahoma.

A third response to oppression, advocated by Booker T. Washington, was to accommodate it. Washington, a former slave, had graduated from Hampton Institute in Virginia. In 1881, he established an industrial and agricultural school for African Americans in Tuskegee, Alabama. There, African Americans learned skilled trades while Washington preached the virtues of hard work, moderation, and economic self-help. Earning money, he said, was like having "a little green ballot" that would empower African Americans more effectively than a political ballot. Speaking at an exposition in Atlanta in 1895, Washington argued that "the agitation of the questions of social equality is the extremist folly." In 1900, he organized the National Negro Business League, which established 320 chapters across the country to support businesses owned and operated by African Americans. Washington's emphasis on racial harmony and economic cooperation won praise from many whites, including industrialist Andrew Carnegie and President Theodore Roosevelt.

Later civil rights leaders had mixed reactions to Washington's approach, especially his Atlanta speech. Some criticized him as too willing to accept discrimination. For example, after 1900, the younger African American leader W. E. B. Du Bois would demand an end to segregation and the granting of equal civil rights to all Americans. (See Chapter 21.) In contrast, other writers have praised Washington for paving the way for black self-reliance because of his emphasis on starting and supporting black-owned businesses.

Farm Problems: North, South, and West

By the end of the 1800s, farmers had become a minority within American society. While the number of U.S. farms more than doubled between 1865 and 1900, people working as farmers declined from 60 percent of the working population in 1860 to less than 37 percent in 1900. All farmers—white or black, westerner or southerner—faced similar problems.

Changes in Agriculture

With every passing decade in the late 1800s, farming became increasingly commercialized—and also more specialized. Northern and western farmers of the late 19th century concentrated on raising single cash crops, such as corn or wheat, for both national and international markets. As consumers, farmers began to procure their food from the stores in town and their manufactured goods from the mail-order catalogs sent to them by Montgomery Ward and Sears Roebuck. As producers, farmers became more dependent on large and expensive machines, such as steam engines, seeders, and reaper-thresher combines. Ever larger farms were run like factories. Unable to afford the new equipment, small, marginal farms could not compete and, in many cases, were driven out of business.

Falling Prices Increased American production as well as increased production in Argentina, Russia, and Canada drove prices down for wheat, cotton, and other crops. And since the money supply was not growing as fast as the economy, each dollar became worth more. This put more downward pressure on prices, or deflation. These figures tell the depressing story for farmers:

Wheat and Corn Prices per Bushel, 1867 and 1889		
Year	Wheat	Corn
1867	$2.01	$0.78
1889	$0.70	$0.28

Source: U.S. Bureau of the Census. *Historical Statistics of the United States, Colonial Times to 1970*

As prices fell, farmers with mortgages faced both high interest rates and the need to grow more and more to pay off old debts. Of course, increased production only lowered prices. The predictable results of this vicious circle were more debts, foreclosures by banks, and more independent farmers forced to become tenants and sharecroppers.

Rising Costs Farmers felt victimized by impersonal forces of the larger national economy. Industrial corporations were able to keep prices high on manufactured goods by forming monopolistic trusts. Wholesalers and retailers (known as "the middlemen") took their cut before selling to farmers. Railroads, warehouses, and elevators took what little profit remained by charging high or discriminatory rates for the shipment and storage of grain. Railroads would often charge more for short hauls on lines with no competition than for long hauls on lines with competition.

Taxes too seemed unfair to farmers. Local and state governments taxed property and land heavily but did not tax income from stocks and bonds. The tariffs protecting various American industries were viewed as just another unfair tax paid by farmers and consumers for the benefit of the industrialists.

Fighting Back

A long tradition of independence and individualism restrained farmers from taking collective action. Finally, however, they began to organize for their common interests and protection.

National Grange Movement The National Grange of Patrons of Husbandry was organized in 1868 by Oliver H. Kelley primarily as a social and educational organization for farmers and their families. Within five years, Granges existed in almost every state, with the most in the Midwest. As the Grange expanded, it became active in economics and politics to defend members against middlemen, trusts, and railroads. For example, Grangers established *cooperatives*—businesses owned and run by the farmers to save the costs charged by middlemen. In Illinois, Iowa, Minnesota, and Wisconsin, the Grangers, with help from local businesses, successfully lobbied their state legislatures to pass laws regulating the rates charged by railroads and elevators. Other Granger laws made it illegal for railroads to fix prices by means of pools and to give rebates to privileged customers. In the landmark case of *Munn v. Illinois* (1877), the Supreme Court upheld the right of a state to regulate businesses of a public nature, such as railroads.

Interstate Commerce Act (1886) The state laws regulating railroad rates ran into numerous legal problems, especially with railroads that crossed state lines. States could regulate only local or short-haul rates. Interstate commerce, on the other hand, was a federal matter, and railroad companies adapted to the Granger laws by simply raising their long-haul (interstate) rates. The Supreme Court ruled in the case of *Wabash v. Illinois* (1886) that individual states could not regulate interstate commerce. In effect, the Court's decision nullified many of the state regulations achieved by the Grangers.

Congress responded to the outcry of farmers and shippers by passing the first federal effort to regulate the railroads. The Interstate Commerce Act of 1886 required railroad rates to be "reasonable and just." It also set up the first federal regulatory agency, the Interstate Commerce Commission (ICC), which had the power to investigate and prosecute pools, rebates, and other discriminatory practices. Ironically, the first U.S. regulatory commission helped the railroads more than the farmers. The new commission lost most of its cases in the federal courts in the 1890s. On the other hand, the ICC helped railroads by stabilizing rates and curtailing destructive competition.

Farmers' Alliances Farmers also expressed their discontent by forming state and regional groups known as farmers' alliances. Like the Grange, the alliances taught about scientific farming methods. Unlike the Grange, alliances always had the goal of economic and political action. Hence, the alliance movement had serious potential for creating an independent national political party. By 1890, about 1 million farmers had joined farmers' alliances. In the South, both poor white and black farmers joined the movement.

Ocala Platform Potential nearly became reality in 1890 when a national organization of farmers—the National Alliance—met in Ocala, Florida, to address the problems of rural America. The alliance attacked both major parties as subservient to Wall Street bankers and big business. Ocala delegates created a platform that would significantly impact politics. They supported (1) direct election of U.S. senators (in the original U.S. Constitution, senators were selected by state legislatures), (2) lower tariff rates, (3) a graduated income tax (people with higher incomes would pay higher rates of tax), and (4) a new banking system regulated by the federal government.

In addition, the alliance platform demanded that Treasury notes and silver be used to increase the amount of money in circulation, which farmers hoped would create inflation and raise crop prices. The platform also proposed federal storage for farmers' crops and federal loans, which would free farmers from dependency on middlemen and creditors.

The alliances stopped short of forming a political party. Even so, their backing of local and state candidates who pledged support for alliance goals often proved decisive in the elections of 1890. Many of the reform ideas of the Grange and the farmers' alliances would become part of the Populist movement, which would shake the foundations of the two-party system in the elections of 1892 and 1896. (See Chapter 19.)

HISTORICAL PERSPECTIVES: HOW DID THE FRONTIER DEVELOP?

Frederick Jackson Turner set the agenda for generations of historians with his frontier thesis. He presented the settling of the frontier as an evolutionary process. The frontier, according to Turner, began as wilderness. The hunting frontier came first, which was followed by either the mining or the cattle frontier, and then the farming frontier. Finally, the founding of towns and cities completed the process.

Later historians challenged Turner's evolutionary view by arguing that frontier cities played an early and primary role in development. For example, Charles Glaab documented the role of town "boosters," who tried to create settlements on the frontier overnight in the middle of nowhere. After laying out town plots on paper, boosters of different western towns strove to establish their own town as a territory's central hub of development by competing to capture the county seat or state capital, a state asylum, a railroad depot, or a college. Many would-be towns, promoted as the next "Athens of the West," proved a booster's false prophecy and died as ghost towns.

Historian William Cronon argued that the frontier and cities grew up together, not sequentially. In his analysis of the growth of Chicago in the 19th century, (*Nature's Metropolis,* 1991) Cronon argued that the "frontier and the metropolis turn out to be two sides of the same coin. . . . The history of the Great West is a long dialogue between the place we call city and the place we call country." Urban markets made rural development possible. The cattle ranchers' frontier developed because it was linked by the railroads to Chicago and eastern markets. By "reading Turner backward," Cronon demonstrated how Chicago helped to create the mining, cattle, lumber, and farming frontiers as it developed into the great city of the West, or "nature's metropolis." By integrating the history of the city and the settlement of the frontier, Cronon challenged the perspective that urban areas and rural areas are necessarily in conflict. Not only the development of the American frontier, but the growth of cities and rural areas is clarified, when we begin to understand, as Cronon argued, "every city is nature's metropolis and every countryside its rural hinterland."

KEY TERMS BY THEME

Western Environment (GEO)
Great American Desert
100th meridian
buffalo herds
Great Plains
mineral resources

Western Development (WXT)
Chinese Exclusion Act of 1882
longhorns, vaqueros
cattle drives
barbed wire
Joseph Glidden
Homestead Act
dry farming

American Indians (MIG, POL)
federal treaty policies
causes of "Indian wars"
Little Big Horn
assimilationists
Helen Hunt Jackson
Dawes Act of 1887
Ghost Dance movement
Indian Reorganization Act of 1934

Mexican Americans (PEO)
Mexican War aftermath
Migration for jobs

Conservation Movement (GEO)
deforestation
Yellowstone, Yosemite
Department of Interior
conservationists and preservationists
Forest Reserve Act of 1891
Forest Management Act of 1897
John Muir, Sierra Club

Southern Development (WXT)
Birmingham (steel)
Memphis (lumber)
Richmond (tobacco)
integrated rail network
agriculture's dominance
George Washington Carver
Tuskegee Institute

Racial Discrimination (MIG, POL)
white supremacists
Civil Rights Cases of 1883
Plessy v. Ferguson
Jim Crow laws
literacy tests, poll taxes, grandfather clauses
white primaries, white juries
lynch mobs
economic discrimination

African American migration
Ida B. Wells
Booker T. Washington
economic cooperation

Farm Protests Movements (POL)
markets and farmers
crop price deflation
railroads and middlemen
National Grange Movement
cooperatives
Granger laws
Munn v. Illinois
Wabash v. Illinois
Interstate Commerce Commission
Ocala Platform of 1890

Frontier Closing (Soc)
census of 1890
Frederick Jackson Turner, "The Significance of the Frontier in American History"

Regions
mining frontier, boomtowns
commercial cities
Great Plains tribes
Southwest tribes
Spanish-speaking areas
"New South"
Henry Grady
sharecropping; tenant farmers
role of cities, "nature's metropolis"

MULTIPLE-CHOICE QUESTIONS

Questions 1–3 refer to the excerpt below.

"I attended a funeral once in Pickens County in my State. . . . They buried him in the heart of a pine forest, and yet the pine coffin was imported from Cincinnati. They buried him within touch of an iron mine, and yet the nails in his coffin and the iron in the shovel that dug his grave were imported from Pittsburgh . . . The South didn't furnish a thing on earth for that funeral but the corpse and the hole in the ground. There they put him away and the clods rattled down on his coffin, and they buried him in a New York coat and a Boston pair of shoes and a pair of breeches from Chicago and a shirt from Cincinnati, leaving him nothing to carry into the next world with him to remind him of the country in which he lived, and for which he fought for four years, but the chill of blood in his veins and the marrow in his bones."

—Henry Grady, Editor of the *Atlanta Constitution,* 1889

1. The key idea in the excerpt is that Grady believes
   (A) the Civil War damaged the southern economy
   (B) former Confederate soldiers deserved better treatment
   (C) the secession of the Confederacy was justified
   (D) the South needed to industrialize

2. Which of the following best demonstrates Henry Grady's vision for the South?
   (A) Birmingham, Alabama, became one of the nation's leading steel producers
   (B) Former slaves achieved semi-independence as tenant farmers
   (C) Northern investors controlled three-quarters of southern railroads
   (D) The southern economy remained mainly tied to agriculture

3. Henry Grady's comments best express the viewpoint of which group of people?
   (A) Advocates of a New South
   (B) Progressives
   (C) Redeemers
   (D) Supporters of Congressional Reconstruction

Questions 4–6 refer to the excerpt below from a statement by the National Alliance.

1. We demand the abolition of national banks.

2. We demand that the government shall establish sub-treasuries or depositories in the several states, which shall loan money direct to the people at a low rate of interest, not to exceed two per cent per annum, on non-perishable farm products, and also upon real estate . . . .

3. We demand that the amount of the circulating medium be speedily increased to not less than $50 per capita.

5. We condemn the silver bill recently passed by Congress, and demand in lieu there of the free and unlimited coinage of silver.

9. We further demand a removal of the existing heavy tariff tax from the necessities of life, that the poor of our land must have.

10. We further demand a just and equitable system of graduated tax on incomes.

13. We demand that the Congress of the United States submit an amendment to the Constitution providing for the election of United States Senators by direct vote of the people of each state.

—Ocala Platform, December 1890

4. The Ocala Platform resulted from a protest movement that primarily involved
   (A) labor unions
   (B) liberal reformers
   (C) northeastern conservatives
   (D) small farmers

5. The economic reasoning behind the Ocala Platform assumes that
   (A) federal income taxes fell mainly on average working Americans
   (B) large banks had formed a monopoly to lower interest rates
   (C) high tariffs had caused the rise in land prices
   (D) increasing the money supply would increase prices and incomes

6. The Ocala Platform proved an important link between which of the following groups?
   (A) Radical Republicans and Reconstruction
   (B) Farmer organizations and the Populist movement
   (C) Harrison Republicans and Cleveland Democrats
   (D) Rural and urban Progressive reformers

Questions 7–8 refer to the excerpt below.

"The white race deems itself to be the dominant race in this country. And so it is, in prestige, in achievements, in education, in wealth, and in power. . . . But in the view of the Constitution, in the eye of the law, there is in this country no superior, no dominant, ruling class of citizens. Our Constitution is color-blind and neither knows nor tolerates classes among citizens.

"In respect of civil rights, all citizens are equal before the law. The humblest is the peer of the most powerful. The laws regard man as man and take no account of his surroundings or his color when his civil rights as guaranteed by the supreme law of the land are involved. It is therefore to be regretted that this high tribunal, the final expositor of the fundamental law of the land, has reached the conclusion that it is competent for a state to regulate the enjoyment by citizens of their civil right solely upon the basis of race."

—Supreme Court Justice John Marshall Harlan, dissenting opinion in
Plessy v. Ferguson, 1896

7. Harlan's opinion goes against the majority opinion on the Supreme Court that

   (A) the 1st Amendment did not protect racist propaganda by the Ku Klux Klan and similar groups

   (B) African Americans were not citizens and could not vote or hold office

   (C) Jim Crow laws were a violation of the Constitution

   (D) facilities could be segregated by race if they were "separate but equal"

8. Harlan's opinion was consistent with the beliefs expressed by the

   (A) Supreme Court in the civil rights cases of 1883

   (B) writer W. E. B. Du Bois

   (C) supporters of Jim Crow laws

   (D) supporters of poll taxes

SHORT-ANSWER QUESTIONS

Use complete sentences; an outline or bulleted list alone is not acceptable.

Question 1 is based on the following excerpts.

"About the Indian wars that plagued the American West. . . . it is commonly believed that they might have been avoided but for the avarice [greed] and aggression of the white man. . . . The root of the trouble lay in the Plains Indian's rootlessness. It was freedom of movement, the privilege of ranging far and wide seasonally that gave his life meaning and dignity. . . . [T]hat given time and patience the Plains tribes could be persuaded to abandon their nomadic ways . . . was wishful thinking. . . . Civilization may have had a clear duty to save these people from themselves."

—S. L. A. Marshall, historian, *Crimsoned Prairie,* 1972

"The grand irony of the Great Plains is that none of the tribes with which the army would clash were native to the lands they claimed. All had been caught up in a vast migration, precipitated by the white settlements in the East. . . . As the dislocated Indians spilled onto the Plains, they jockeyed with native tribes for the choicest hunting grounds. In a real sense, then—and this cannot be over emphasized—the wars that were to come between the Indians and the government for the Great Plains . . . would represent a clash of emigrant peoples."

—Peter Cozzens, historian, *The Earth Is Weeping,* 2016

1. Using the excerpts above, answer (A), (B), and (C).
   - (A) Briefly describe ONE major difference between Marshall's and Cozzens's interpretation of the Indians Wars from 1865 to 1898.
   - (B) Briefly explain how ONE specific historical event or development that is not explicitly mentioned in the excerpts could be used to support Marshall's interpretation.
   - (C) Briefly explain how ONE specific historical event or development that is not explicitly mentioned in the excerpts could be used to support Cozzens's interpretation.

Question 2. Answer (A), (B), and (C).
   - (A) Briefly describe ONE specific effect on American culture or character that historian Frederick Jackson Turner attributed to the frontier experience.
   - (B) Briefly explain ONE specific effect of the closing of the frontier on American society that troubled Turner.
   - (C) Briefly explain ONE specific cause from 1865 to 1898 other than the frontier experience that shaped American culture or character.

Question 3. Answer (A), (B), and (C).

  (A) Briefly describe ONE specific change in the South that reflected the goals of the "New South" movement from 1865 to 1898.

  (B) Briefly explain ONE specific factor that limited the South from making more progress toward the goals of the "New South" movement from 1865 to 1898.

  (C) Briefly describe ONE specific way the Southern economy did not change during the period from 1865 to 1898.

Question 4 is based on the following excerpt.

"The wisest among my race understand that the agitation of questions of social equality is the extremist of folly, and that progress in the enjoyment of all privileges that will come to us must be the result of severe and constant struggle rather than of artificial forcing. No race that has anything to contribute to the markets of the world is long in any degree ostracized. It is important and right that all privileges of the law be ours, but it is vastly more important that we be prepared for the exercises of these privileges. The opportunity to earn a dollar in a factory just now is worth infinitely more than the opportunity to spend a dollar in an opera house."

—Booker T. Washington, Speech at Cotton States and International
Exposition, Atlanta, September 18, 1895

4. Using the excerpt, answer (A), (B), and (C).

  (A) Briefly describe ONE specific way that Booker T. Washington's policies were similar to the goals of the "New South" movement.

  (B) Briefly explain ONE specific accomplishment of Booker T. Washington that reflected policies described in the excerpt.

  (C) Briefly explain ONE specific form of discrimination against African Americans in the South that Booker T. Washington was trying to address in his policies or actions.

THINK AS A HISTORIAN: STATEMENTS ABOUT EVIDENCE

Which TWO of the following statements most clearly include evidence to support the claim it makes?

1. The Chinese Exclusion Act indicates the prejudice felt by many people in the United States in the late 19th century.

2. George Washington Carver and Ida B. Wells demonstrated different methods of combating racial prejudice.

3. Granges and cooperatives demonstrated the strong sense of community many Americans felt in the 19th century.

18

THE GROWTH OF CITIES AND AMERICAN CULTURE, 1865–1900

Give me your tired, your poor,
Your huddled masses yearning to breathe free,
The wretched refuse of your teeming shore,
Send these, the homeless, tempest-tossed, to me:
I lift my lamp beside the golden door.

Emma Lazarus, "The New Colossus," 1883
(Inscription on the base of the Statue of Liberty)

In 1893, Chicago hosted a world's fair known as the World's Columbian Exposition. More than 12 million people traveled to the White City, as Chicago's fairgrounds and gleaming white buildings were known. Visitors saw the progress of American civilization as represented by new industrial technologies and by the architects' grand visions of an ideal urban environment. In just six decades, Chicago's population had grown to more than one million. Its central business district was a marvel of modern urban structures: steel-framed skyscrapers, department stores, and theaters. Around this central hub lay a sprawling gridiron of workers' housing near the city's factories and warehouses, and a few miles beyond were tree-lined suburban retreats for the wealthy. The entire urban complex was connected by hundreds of miles of streetcars and railroads.

Visitors to Chicago also experienced a "gray city" of pollution, poverty, crime, and vice. Some complained of the confusion of tongues, "worse than the tower of Babel," for in 1893 Chicago was a city of immigrants. More than three-fourths of its population were either foreign-born or the children of the foreign-born. Both the real Chicago and the idealized "White City" represented the complex ways in which three great forces of change—industrialization, immigration, and urbanization—were transforming the nature of American society in the late 19th century. A previous chapter covered industrialization. This chapter focuses on immigration and urbanization.

A Nation of Immigrants

In the last half of the 19th century, the U.S. population more than tripled, from about 23.2 million in 1850 to 76.2 million in 1900. The arrival of 16.2 million immigrants fueled the growth. An additional 8.8 million more arrived during the peak years of immigration, 1901–1910.

Growth of Immigration

The growing connections between the United States and the world are evident during this period, especially in the area of immigration. A increased combination of "pushes" (negative factors from which people are fleeing) and "pulls" (positive attractions of the adopted country) increased migrations around the world. The negative forces driving Europeans to emigrate included (1) the poverty of displaced farmworkers driven from the land by political turmoil and the mechanization of farmwork, (2) overcrowding and joblessness in cities as a result of a population boom, and (3) religious persecution, particularly of Jews in eastern Europe. Positive reasons for moving to the United States included this country's reputation for political and religious freedom and the economic opportunities afforded by the settling of the West and the abundance of industrial jobs in U.S. cities. Furthermore, the introduction of large steamships and the relatively inexpensive one-way passage in the ships' "steerage" made it possible for millions of poor people to emigrate.

"Old" Immigrants and "New" Immigrants

Through the 1880s, the vast majority of immigrants came from northern and western Europe: the British Isles, Germany, and Scandinavia. Most of these "old" immigrants were Protestants, although many were Irish or German Catholics. Their language (mostly English-speaking) and high level of literacy and occupational skills made it relatively easy for these immigrants to blend into a mostly rural American society in the early decades of the 19th century.

New Immigrants Beginning in the 1890s and continuing to the outbreak of World War I in 1914, the national origins of most immigrants changed. The "new" immigrants came from southern and eastern Europe. They were Italians, Greeks, Croats, Slovaks, Poles, and Russians. Many were poor and illiterate peasants who had left autocratic countries and therefore were unaccustomed to democratic traditions. Unlike the earlier groups of Protestant immigrants, the newcomers were largely Roman Catholic, Greek Orthodox, Russian Orthodox, and Jewish. On arrival, most new immigrants crowded into poor ethnic neighborhoods in New York, Chicago, and other major U.S. cities.

An estimated 25 percent of them were "birds of passage," young men contracted for unskilled factory, mining, and construction jobs, who would return to their native lands once they had saved a fair sum of money to bring back to their families.

Restricting Immigration

In the 1870s, when the French sculptor Frédéric-Auguste Bartholdi began work on the Statue of Liberty, there were few legal restrictions on immigration to the United States. By 1886, however—the year that the great welcoming-statue was placed on its pedestal in New York Harbor—Congress had passed a number of new laws restricting immigration. First came the Chinese Exclusion Act of 1882, placing a ban on all new immigrants from China. As already noted in the last chapter, this hostility to the Chinese mainly came from the western states. Restrictions also came in 1882 on the immigration of "undesirable" persons, such as paupers, criminals, convicts, and those diagnosed as mentally incompetent. The Contract Labor Law of 1885 restricted temporary workers to protect American workers. A literacy test for immigrants was vetoed by President Cleveland, but passed in 1917. Soon after the opening of Ellis Island as an immigration center in 1892, new arrivals had to pass more rigorous medical examinations and pay a tax before entering the United States.

Efforts to restrict immigration were supported by diverse groups such as (1) labor unions, which feared that employers would use immigrants to depress wages and break strikes, (2) a nativist society, the American Protective Association, which was openly prejudiced against Roman Catholics, and (3) social Darwinists, who viewed the new immigrants as biologically inferior to English and Germanic stocks. During a severe depression in the 1890s, foreigners became a convenient scapegoat for jobless workers as well as for employers who blamed strikes and the labor movement on foreign agitators.

However, anti-immigrant feelings and early restrictions did not stop the flow of newcomers. At the turn of the century, almost 15 percent of the U.S. population were immigrants. The Statue of Liberty remained a beacon of hope for the poor and the oppressed of southern and eastern Europe until the 1920s, when the Quota Acts almost closed Liberty's golden door (see Chapter 23).

Urbanization

Urbanization and industrialization developed simultaneously. Cities provided both laborers for factories and a market for factory-made goods. The shift in population from rural to urban became more obvious with each passing decade. By 1900 almost 40 percent of Americans lived in towns or cities. By 1920, for the first time, more Americans lived in urban areas than in rural areas.

Those moving into the cities were both immigrants and internal migrants born in the rural United States. In the late 19th century, millions of young Americans from rural areas decided to seek new economic opportunities in the cities. They left the farms for industrial and commercial jobs, and few of them returned. Among those who joined the movement from farms to cities were African Americans from the South. Between 1897 and 1930, nearly 1 million southern blacks settled in northern and western cities.

Changes in the Nature of Cities

Cities of the late 19th century underwent significant changes not only in their size but also in their internal structure and design.

Streetcar Cities Improvements in urban transportation made the growth of cities possible. In the walking cities of the pre-Civil War era, people had little choice but to live within walking distance of their shops or jobs. Such cities gave way to streetcar cities, in which people lived in residences many miles from their jobs and commuted to work on horse-drawn streetcars. By the 1890s, both horse-drawn cars and cable cars were being replaced by electric trolleys, elevated railroads, and subways, which could transport people to urban residences even farther from the city's commercial center. The building of massive steel suspension bridges such as New York's Brooklyn Bridge (completed in 1883) also made possible longer commutes between residential areas and the center city.

Mass transportation had the effect of segregating urban workers by income. The upper and middle classes moved to streetcar suburbs to escape the pollution, poverty, and crime of the city. The exodus of higher-income residents left older sections of the city to the working poor, many of whom were immigrants. The residential areas of the cities and suburbs both reflected and contributed to the class, race, ethnic, and cultural divisions in American society.

Skyscrapers As cities expanded outward, they also soared upward, since increasing land values in the central business district dictated the construction of taller and taller buildings. In 1885, William Le Baron Jenny built the ten-story Home Insurance Company Building in Chicago—the first true skyscraper with a steel skeleton. Structures of this size were made possible by such innovations as the Otis elevator and the central steam-heating system with radiators in every room. By 1900 steel-framed skyscrapers for offices of industry had replaced church spires as the dominant feature of American urban skylines.

Ethnic Neighborhoods As affluent citizens moved out of residences near the business district, the poor moved into them. To increase their profits, landlords divided up inner-city housing into small, windowless rooms. The resulting slums and tenement apartments could cram more than 4,000 people into one city block. In an attempt to correct unlivable conditions, New York City passed a law in 1879 that required each bedroom to have a window. The cheapest way for landlords to respond to the law was to build the so-called dumbbell tenements, with ventilation shafts in the center of the building to provide windows for each room. However, overcrowding and filth in new tenements continued to promote the spread of deadly diseases, such as cholera, typhoid, and tuberculosis.

In their crowded tenement quarters, different immigrant groups created distinct ethnic neighborhoods where each group could maintain its own language, culture, church or temple, and social club. Many groups even supported their own newspapers and schools. While often crowded, unhealthy, and crime-ridden, these neighborhoods (sometimes called "ghettos") often served as springboards for ambitious and hardworking immigrants and their children to achieve their version of the American dream.

Residential Suburbs The residential pattern in the United States contrasted with that of Europe, where wealthy people remained near the business districts of modern cities and lower-income people live in the outlying areas. Five factors prompted Americans who could afford to move to the suburbs: (1) abundant land available at low cost, (2) inexpensive transportation by rail, (3) low-cost construction methods such as the wooden, balloon-frame house, (4) ethnic and racial prejudice, and (5) an American fondness for grass, privacy, and detached individual houses.

Landscape architect Frederick Law Olmsted, who designed New York's Central Park in the 1860s, went on to design suburban communities with graceful curved roads and open spaces—"a village in the park." By 1900, suburbs had grown up around every major U.S. city, and a single-family dwelling surrounded by an ornamental lawn soon became the American ideal of comfortable living. Thus began the world's first suburban nation.

Private City Versus Public City At first, city residents tried to carry on life in large cities much as they had in small villages. Private enterprise shaped the development of American cities, and provided services such as streetcars and utilities for a profit. In time, increasing disease, crime, waste, water pollution, and air pollution slowly convinced reform-minded citizens and city governments of the need for municipal water purification, sewerage systems, waste disposal, street lighting, police departments, and zoning laws to regulate urban development. In the 1890s, the "City Beautiful" movement advanced grand plans to remake American cities with tree-lined boulevards, public parks and public cultural attractions. The debate between the private good and the public good in urban growth and development has continued as an open issue.

Boss and Machine Politics

The consolidation of power in business had its parallel in urban politics. Political parties in major cities came under the control of tightly organized groups of politicians, known as political machines. Each machine had its boss, the top politician who gave orders to the rank and file and doled out government jobs to loyal supporters. Several political machines, such as Tammany Hall in New York City, started as social clubs and later developed into power centers to coordinate the needs of businesses, immigrants, and the underprivileged. In return, machines asked for people's votes on election day.

Successful party bosses knew how to manage the competing social, ethnic, and economic groups in the city. Political machines often brought modern services to the city, including a crude form of welfare for urban newcomers. The political organization would find jobs and apartments for recently arrived immigrants and show up at a poor family's door with baskets of food during hard times. But the political machine could be greedy as well as generous and often stole millions from the taxpayers in the form of graft and fraud. In New York City in the 1860s, for example, an estimated 65 percent of public building funds ended up in the pockets of Boss Tweed and his cronies.

Awakening of Reform

Urban problems, including the desperate poverty of working-class families, inspired a new social consciousness among the middle class. Reform movements begun in earlier decades increased strength in the 1880s and 1890s.

Books of Social Criticism A San Francisco journalist, Henry George, published a provocative book in 1879 that became an instant best-seller and jolted readers to look more critically at the effects of laissez-faire economics. George called attention to the alarming inequalities in wealth caused by industrialization. In his book *Progress and Poverty*, George proposed one innovative solution to poverty: replacing all taxes with a single tax on land. Another popular book of social criticism, *Looking Backward, 2000–1887*, was written by Edward Bellamy in 1888. It envisioned a future era in which a cooperative society had eliminated poverty, greed, and crime. So enthusiastic were many of the readers of George's and Bellamy's books that they joined various reform movements and organizations to try to implement the authors' ideas. Both books encouraged a shift in American public opinion away from pure laissez-faire and toward greater government regulation.

Settlement Houses Concerned about the lives of the poor, a number of young, well-educated women and men of the middle class settled into immigrant neighborhoods to learn about the problems of immigrant families first-hand. Living and working in places called settlement houses, the young reformers hoped to relieve the effects of poverty by providing social services for people in the neighborhood. The most famous such experiment was Hull House in Chicago, which was started by Jane Addams and a college classmate in 1889. Settlement houses taught English to immigrants, pioneered early-childhood education, taught industrial arts, and established neighborhood theaters and music schools. By 1910 there were more than 400 settlement houses in America's largest cities.

Settlement workers were civic-minded volunteers who created the foundation for the later job of social worker. They were also political activists who crusaded for child-labor laws, housing reform, and women's rights. Two settlement workers, Frances Perkins and Harry Hopkins, went on to leadership roles in President Franklin Roosevelt's reform program, the New Deal, in the 1930s.

Social Gospel In the 1880s and 1890s, a number of Protestant clergy espoused the cause of social justice for the poor—especially the urban poor. They preached what they called the Social Gospel, or the importance of applying Christian principles to social problems. Leading the Social Gospel movement in the late 19th and early 20th centuries was a Baptist minister from New York, Walter Rauschenbusch, who worked in the poverty-stricken neighborhood of New York City called Hell's Kitchen, wrote several books urging organized religions to take up the cause of social justice. His Social Gospel preaching linked Christianity with the Progressive reform movement (see Chapter 21) and encouraged many middle-class Protestants to attack urban problems.

Religion and Society All religions adapted to the stresses and challenges of modern urban living. Roman Catholicism grew rapidly from the influx of new immigrants. Catholic leaders such as Cardinal James Gibbons of Baltimore inspired the devoted support of old and new immigrants by defending the Knights of Labor and the cause of organized labor. Among Protestants, Dwight Moody, who founded the Moody Bible Institute in Chicago in 1889, would help generations of urban evangelists to adapt traditional Christianity to city life. The Salvation Army, imported from England in 1879, provided basic necessities to the homeless and the poor while preaching the Christian gospel.

Members of the urban middle class were attracted to the religious message of Mary Baker Eddy, who taught that good health was the result of correct thinking about "Father Mother God." By the time of her death in 1910, hundreds of thousands had joined the church she had founded, the Church of Christ, Scientist—popularly known as Christian Science.

Families in Urban Society Urban life placed severe strains on parents and their children by isolating them from the extended family (relatives beyond the family nucleus of parents and children) and village support. Divorce rates increased to one in 12 marriages by 1900, partly because a number of state legislatures had expanded the grounds for divorce to include cruelty and desertion. Another consequence of the shift from rural to urban living was a reduction in family size. Children were an economic asset on the farm, where their labor was needed at an early age. In the city, however, they were more of an economic liability. Therefore, in the last decades of the 19th century, the national average for birthrates and family size continued to drop.

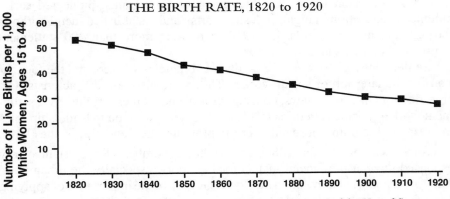

THE BIRTH RATE, 1820 to 1920

Source: U.S. Bureau of the Census. *Historical Statistics of the United States, Colonial Times to 1970*

Voting Rights for Women The cause of women's suffrage, launched at Seneca Falls in 1848, was vigorously carried forward by a number of middle-class women. In 1890, two of the pioneer feminists of the 1840s, Elizabeth Cady Stanton and Susan B. Anthony of New York, helped found the National American Woman Suffrage Association (NAWSA) to secure the vote for women.

A western state, Wyoming, was the first to grant full suffrage to women, in 1869. By 1900, some states allowed women to vote in local elections, and most allowed women to own and control property after marriage.

Temperance Movement Another cause that attracted the attention of urban reformers was temperance. Excessive drinking of alcohol by male factory workers was one cause of poverty for immigrant and working-class families. The Woman's Christian Temperance Union (WCTU) was formed in 1874. Advocating total abstinence from alcohol, the WCTU, under the leadership of Frances E. Willard of Evanston, Illinois, had 500,000 members by 1898. The Antisaloon League, founded in 1893, became a powerful political force and by 1916 had persuaded 21 states to close down all saloons and bars. Unwilling to wait for the laws to change, Carry A. Nation of Kansas created a sensation by raiding saloons and smashing barrels of beer with a hatchet.

Urban Reforms Across the country, grassroots efforts arose to combat corruption in city governments. In New York, a reformer named Theodore Roosevelt tried to clean up the New York City Police Department. As a result of his efforts, he became a vice-presidential nominee in 1896, and later the president. However, many of the reformers of the Gilded Age would not see their efforts reach fruition or have a national impact until the early 20th century.

Intellectual and Cultural Movements

The change from an agricultural to an industrial economy and from rural to urban living profoundly affected all areas of American life, including education, sciences, literature, arts, and popular entertainment.

Changes in Education

The growing complexity of life, along with reactions to Darwin's theory of evolution, raised challenging questions about what schools should teach.

Public Schools Elementary schools after 1865 continued to teach the 3 R's (reading, writing, arithmetic) and the traditional values promoted in the standard texts, McGuffey's readers. New compulsory education laws that required children to attend school, however, dramatically increased the number students enrolled. As a result, the literacy rate rose to 90 percent of the population by 1900. The practice of sending children to kindergarten (a concept borrowed from Germany) became popular and reflected the growing interest in early-childhood education in the United States.

Perhaps even more significant than lower-grade schools was the growing support for tax-supported public high schools. At first these schools followed the college preparatory curriculum of private academies, but soon the public high schools became more comprehensive. They began to provide vocational and citizenship education for a changing urban society.

Higher Education The number of U.S. colleges increased in the late 1800s largely as a result of: (1) land-grant colleges established under the federal Morrill acts of 1862 and 1890, (2) universities founded by wealthy philanthropists—the University of Chicago by John D. Rockefeller, for example, and (3) the founding of new colleges for women, such as Smith, Bryn Mawr, and Mount Holyoke. By 1900, 71 percent of the colleges admitted women, who represented more than one-third of the attending students.

The college curriculum also changed greatly in the late 19th century. Soon after becoming president of Harvard in 1869, Charles W. Eliot reduced the number of required courses and introduced electives (courses chosen by students) to accommodate the teaching of modern languages and the sciences: physics, chemistry, biology, and geology. Johns Hopkins University was founded in Baltimore in 1876 as the first American institution to specialize in advanced graduate studies. Following the model of German universities, Johns Hopkins emphasized research and free inquiry. As a result of such innovations in curriculum, the United States produced its first generation of scholars who could compete with the intellectual achievements of Europeans. As the curriculum was changing, colleges added social activities, fraternities, and intercollegiate sports, additions that soon dominated the college experience for many students.

Social Sciences The application of the scientific method and the theory of evolution to human affairs revolutionized the study of human society in the late 19th century. New fields, known as the social sciences, emerged, such as psychology, sociology, anthropology, and political science. Richard T. Ely of Johns Hopkins attacked laissez-faire economic thought as dogmatic and outdated and used economics to study labor unions, trusts, and other existing economic institutions not only to understand them but also to suggest remedies for economic problems of the day. Evolutionary theory influenced leading sociologists (Lester F. Ward), political scientists (Woodrow Wilson), and historians (Frederick Jackson Turner) to study the dynamic process of actual human behavior instead of logical abstractions.

One social scientist who used new statistical methods to study crime in urban neighborhoods was W. E. B. Du Bois. The first African American to receive a doctorate from Harvard, Du Bois was the leading black intellectual of the era. He advocated for equality for blacks, integrated schools, and equal access to higher education for the "talented tenth" of African Americans.

The Professions Scientific theory and methodology also influenced the work of doctors, educators, social workers, and lawyers. Oliver Wendell Holmes Jr. argued that the law should evolve with the times in response to changing needs and not remain restricted by legal precedents and judicial decisions of the past. Clarence Darrow, a famous lawyer, argued that criminal behavior could be caused by a person's environment of poverty, neglect, and abuse. These changes in the professions, along with changes in the universities, would provide a boost to progressive legislation and liberal reform in the 20th century.

Literature and the Arts

American writers and artists responded in diverse ways to industrialization and urban problems. In general, the work of the best-known innovators of the era reflected a new realism and an attempt to express an authentic American style.

Realism and Naturalism Many of the popular works of literature of the post-Civil War years were romantic novels that depicted ideal heroes and heroines. Breaking with this genteel literary tradition were regionalist writers such as Bret Harte, who depicted life in the rough mining camps of the West. Mark Twain (the pen name for Samuel L. Clemens) became the first great realist author. His classic work, *The Adventures of Huckleberry Finn* (1884), revealed the greed, violence, and racism in American society.

A younger generation of authors who emerged in the 1890s became known for their naturalism, which focused on how emotions and experience shaped human experience. In his naturalistic novel *Maggie: A Girl of the Streets* (1893), Stephen Crane told how a brutal urban environment could destroy the lives of young people. Crane also wrote the popular *Red Badge of Courage* about fear and human nature on the Civil War battlefield before dying himself of tuberculosis at only 29. Jack London, a young California writer and adventurer, portrayed the conflict between nature and civilization in novels such as *The Call of the Wild* (1903). A naturalistic book that caused a sensation and shocked the moral sensibilities of the time was Theodore Dreiser's novel about a poor working girl in Chicago, *Sister Carrie* (1900).

Painting Some American painters responded to the new emphasis on realism, while others continued to cater to the popular taste for romantic subjects. Winslow Homer, the foremost American painter of seascapes and watercolors, often rendered scenes of nature in a matter-of-fact way. Thomas Eakins's realism included paintings of surgical scenes and the everyday lives of working-class men and women. He also used the new technology of serial-action photographs to study human anatomy and paint it more realistically.

Source: George Bellows, *Cliff Dwellers,* 1913. Oil on Canvas.
Los Angeles County Museum of Art

James McNeill Whistler was born in Massachusetts but spent most of his life in Paris and London. His most famous painting, *Arrangement in Grey and Black* (popularly known as "Whistler's Mother"), hangs in the Louvre. This study of color, rather than subject matter, influenced the development of modern art. A distinguished portrait painter, Mary Cassatt, also spent much of her life in France where she learned the techniques of impressionism, especially in her use of pastel colors. As the 19th century ended, a group of social realists, such as George Bellows, of the "Ashcan School" painted scenes of everyday life in poor urban neighborhoods. Upsetting to realists and romanticists alike were the abstract, nonrepresentational paintings exhibited in the Armory Show in New York City in 1913. Art of this kind would be rejected by most Americans until the 1950s when it finally achieved respect among collectors of fine art.

Architecture In the 1870s, Henry Hobson Richardson changed the direction of American architecture. While earlier architects found inspiration in classical Greek and Roman styles, his designs were often based on the medieval Romanesque style of massive stone walls and rounded arches. Richardson gave a gravity and stateliness to functional commercial buildings. Louis Sullivan of Chicago went a step further by rejecting historical styles in his quest for a suitable style for the tall, steel-framed office buildings of the 1880s and 1890s. Sullivan's buildings achieved a much-admired aesthetic unity, in which the form of a building flowed from its function—a hallmark of the Chicago School of architecture. Frank Lloyd Wright, an employee of Sullivan's in the 1890s, developed an "organic" style of architecture that was in harmony with its natural surroundings. Wright's vision is exemplified in the long, horizontal lines of his prairie-style houses. Wright became the most famous American architect of the 20th century. Some architects, such as Daniel H. Burnham,

Frank Lloyd Wright, Robie House, Chicago, 1909. Library of Congress

who revived classical Greek and Roman architecture in his designs for the World's Columbian Exposition of 1893, continued to explore historical styles.

One of the most influential urbanists, Frederick Law Olmsted specialized in the planning of city parks and scenic boulevards, including Central Park in New York City and the grounds of the U.S. Capitol in Washington. As the originator of landscape architecture, Olmsted not only designed parks, parkways, campuses, and suburbs but also established the basis for later urban landscaping.

Music With the growth of cities came increasing demand for musical performances appealing to a variety of tastes. By 1900, most large cities had either an orchestra, an opera house, or both. In smaller towns, outdoor bandstands were the setting for the playing of popular marches by John Philip Sousa.

Among the greatest innovators of the era were African Americans in New Orleans. Jelly Roll Morton and Buddy Bolden expanded the audience for jazz, a musical form that combined African rhythms with European instruments, and mixed improvisation with a structured format. The remarkable black composer and performer Scott Joplin sold nearly a million copies of sheet music of his "Maple Leaf Rag" (1899). Also from the South came blues music that expressed the pain of the black experience. Jazz, ragtime, and blues music gained popularity during the early 20th century as New Orleans performers headed north into the urban centers of Memphis, St. Louis, Kansas City, and Chicago.

Popular Culture

Entertaining the urban masses became big business in the late 19th century. People wanted amusements as respites from their work.

Popular Press Mass-circulation newspapers had been around since the 1830s, but the first newspaper to exceed a million in circulation was Joseph Pulitzer's *New York World*. Pulitzer filled his daily paper with both sensational stories of crimes and disasters and crusading feature stories about political and economic corruption. Another New York publisher, William Randolph Hearst, pushed scandal and sensationalism to new heights (or lows).

Mass-circulation magazines also became numerous in the 1880s. Advertising revenues and new printing technologies made it possible for the *Ladies' Home Journal* and similar magazines to sell for as little as 10 cents a copy.

Amusements In addition to urbanization, other factors also promoted the growth of leisure-time activities: (1) a gradual reduction in the hours people worked, (2) improved transportation, (3) promotional billboards and advertising, and (4) the decline of restrictive Puritan and Victorian values that discouraged "wasting" time on play. Based on numbers alone, the most popular form of recreation in the late 19th century, despite the temperance movement, was drinking and talking at the corner saloon. Theaters that presented comedies and dramas flourished in most large cities, but vaudeville with its variety of acts drew the largest audiences. The national rail network encouraged traveling circuses such as Barnum and Bailey and the Ringling Brothers to create circus trains that moved a huge number of acts and animals from town to town, as the "Greatest Show on Earth." Also immensely popular was the Wild West show brought to urban audiences by William F. Cody ("Buffalo Bill") and headlining such personalities as Sitting Bull and the markswoman Annie Oakley.

Commuter streetcar and railroad companies also promoted weekend recreation in order to keep their cars running on Sundays and holidays. They created parks in the countryside near the end of the line so that urban families could enjoy picnics and outdoor recreation.

Spectator Sports Professional spectator sports originated in the late 19th century. Boxing attracted male spectators from all classes, and champions such as John L. Sullivan became national heroes. Baseball, while it recalled a rural past of green fields and fences, was very much an urban game that demanded the teamwork needed for an industrial age. Owners organized teams into leagues, much as trusts of the day were organized. In 1909, when President William Howard Taft started the tradition of the president throwing out the first ball of the season, baseball was the national pastime. However, Jim Crow laws and customs prevented blacks from playing on all-white big-league baseball teams between the 1890s and 1947.

Football developed primarily as a college activity, with the first game played by two New Jersey colleges, Rutgers and Princeton, in 1869. In the 1920s professional football teams and leagues were organized. Basketball was invented in 1891 at Springfield College, in Massachusetts. Within a few years, high schools and colleges across the nation had teams. The first professional basketball league was organized in 1898.

American spectator sports were played and attended by men. They were part of a "bachelor subculture" for single men in their twenties and thirties, whose lives centered around saloons, horse races, and pool halls. It took years for some spectator sports, such as boxing and football, to gain middle-class respectability.

Amateur Sports The value of sports as healthy exercise for the body gained acceptance by the middle and upper classes in the late 19th century. Women were considered unfit for most competitive sports, but they engaged in such recreational activities as croquet and bicycling. Sports such as golf and tennis grew, but mostly among the prosperous members of athletic clubs. The very rich pursued expensive sports of polo and yachting. Clubs generally discriminated against Jews, Catholics, and Africans Americans.

To what extent did immigrants give up their heritage to become American-ized, or fully assimilated into the existing culture? The prevailing view in the 19th and early 20th centuries was that the United States was a melting pot, in which immigrant groups quickly shed old-world characteristics in order to become successful citizens of their adopted country. This view was expressed as early as 1782 by a naturalized Frenchman, J. Hector St. John Crévecoeur. In his *Letters From an American Farmer*, Crévecoeur described how the American experience "melted" European immigrants "into a new race of men." The term "melting pot" became firmly associated with immigration in a popular play by that name: Israel Zangwill's *The Melting Pot* (1908). One line of this drama described "how the great Alchemist melts and fuses them [immigrants] with purging flames!"

In recent decades, the melting pot concept has come under intense scru-tiny and challenge by modern historians. Carl N. Degler, for example, has argued that a more accurate metaphor would be the salad bowl, in which each ingredient (ethnic culture) remains intact. To support this view, Degler points to the diversity of religions in the United States. Neither immigrants nor their descendants gave up their religions for the Protestantism of the American majority.

In his groundbreaking study of immigration, *The Uprooted* (1952), Oscar Handlin observed that newcomers to a strange land often became alienated from both their native culture and the culture of their new country. Accord-ing to Handlin, first-generation immigrants remained alienated and did not lose their cultural identity in the melting pot. Only the immigrants' children and children's children became fully assimilated into mainstream culture.

Many historians agree with Handlin that, after two or three generations, the melting pot, or assimilation, process reduced the cultural differences among most ethnic groups. However, certain groups have had a different experience. Historian Richard C. Wade has observed that African Americans who migrated to northern cities faced the special problem of racism, which has created seemingly permanent ghettos with "a growingly alienated and embittered group."

Historians remain divided in their analysis of the melting pot. Those who accept the concept see people of diverse ethnic backgrounds coming together to build a common culture. Others see American urban history characterized by intergroup hostility, alienation, crime, and corruption. The questions about past immigration shape current views of ethnic tensions in contemporary society. Is there a process, common to all groups, in which initial prejudice against the most recent immigrants fades after two or three generations? Is the cultural diversity in U.S. society today a permanent con-dition—or just unmelted bits of foreign ways that will someday fuse into a homogeneous culture?

KEY TERMS BY THEME

Immigration (MIG, POL)
causes of immigration
old immigrants
new Immigrants
Statue of Liberty
Chinese Exclusion Act
of 1882
Immigration Act of 1882
Contract Labor Act
of 1885
American Protective
Association
Ellis Island 1892
melting pot vs. cultural
diversity

City Growth (MIG, POL)
causes of migration
streetcar cities
steel-framed buildings
tenements, poverty
ethnic neighborhoods
residential suburbs
politic machines, "boss"
Tammany Hall
urban reformers
"City Beautiful"
movement

Reformers (SOC)
Henry George
Edward Bellamy
Jane Addams
settlement houses
Social Gospel
Walter Rauschenbusch
Cardinal Gibbons

Dwight Moody
Salvation Army
family size, divorce
Susan B. Anthony,
NAWSA
Francis Willard, WCTU
Antisaloon League
Carrie Nation

Education (SOC)
kindergarten
public high school
college elective system
Johns Hopkins
University

Professions (SOC)
new social sciences
Richard T. Ely
Oliver Wendell Holmes
Clarence Darrow
W.E.B. Du Bois

Arts and Writing (SOC)
realism, naturalism
Mark Twain
Stephen Crane
Jack London
Theodore Dreiser
Winslow Homer
Thomas Eakins
Impressionism
James Whistler
Mary Cassatt
Ashcan School
Armory Show
abstract art

Architecture (SOC)
Henry Hobson
Richardson
Romanesque style
Louis Sullivan
"form follows function"
Frank Lloyd Wright
organic architecture
Frederick Law Olmsted
landscape architecture

Popular Culture (SOC)
growth of leisure time
John Philip Sousa
jazz, blues, ragtime
Jelly Roll Morton
Scott Joplin
mass circulation
newspapers
Joseph Pulitzer
William Randolph
Hearst
Ladies' Home Journal
circus trains
Barnum & Bailey
"Greatest Show on
Earth"
"Buffalo Bill" Wild West
Show
spectator sports,
boxing, baseball
amateur sports,
bicycling, tennis
social class and
discrimination
country clubs, golf,
polo, yachts
corner saloon,
pool halls

Questions 1–2 refer to the graph below.

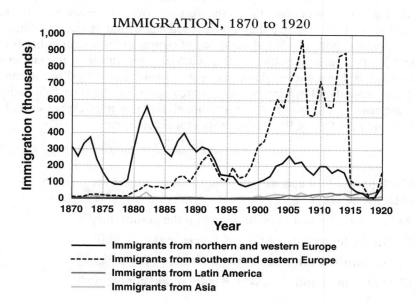

Source: U.S. Bureau of the Census. *Historical Statistics of the United States, Colonial Times to 1970*

1. In the chart above, the "new immigrants" include those who arrived in the United States from

   (A) northern and western Europe

   (B) southern and eastern Europe

   (C) Latin America

   (D) Asia

2. Which of the following most likely explains the significant reduction of immigration during the 1870s and 1890s to the United States?

   (A) Conflicts between the "old" and "new" immigrants.

   (B) Competition for jobs from Asian immigrations

   (C) Financial panics and depressions

   (D) Military conflicts in Europe

Questions 3–5 refer to the excerpt below.

"Today three-fourths of its [New York's] people live in tenements. . . .

"If it shall appear that the sufferings and the sins of the 'other half,' and the evil they breed, are but as a just punishment upon the community that gave it no other choice, it will be because that is the truth. . . . In the tenements all the influences make for evil; because they are the hotbeds of the epidemics that carry death to rich and poor alike; the nurseries of pauperism and crime that fill our jails and police courts; that throw off a scum of forty thousand human wrecks to the island asylums and workhouses year by year; that turned out in the last eight years around half million beggars to prey upon our charities; that maintain a standing army of ten thousand tramps with all that that implies; because above all, they touch the family life with deadly moral contagion. . . ."

—Jacob A. Riis, journalist, *How the Other Half Lives,* 1890

3. Which phrase best summarizes what Riis considers the cause of the problems he sees?
   (A) "are but as a just punishment upon the community"
   (B) "In the tenements all the influences make for evil"
   (C) "throw off a scum of forty thousand human wrecks"
   (D) "touch the family life with deadly moral contagion"

4. During the late 19th century, which of the following groups most benefited from the poverty described by Riis?
   (A) Salvation Army
   (B) Political machines
   (C) Social Darwinists
   (D) Social scientists

5. Which group would be most likely to oppose government intervention to improve the tenements?
   (A) Social scientists who used the scientific method to research poverty and urban problems
   (B) State governments in which representative districts were determined by area, not population
   (C) Protestant clergy who espoused the cause of social justice for the poor
   (D) Leaders and workers who provided services in the settlement house movement

Questions 6–8 refer to the excerpt below.

"I stand before you tonight under indictment for the alleged crime of having voted at the last presidential election, without having a lawful right to vote. It shall be my work this evening to prove to you that in thus voting, I not only committed no crime, but, instead, simply exercised my citizen's rights, guaranteed to me and all United States citizens by the National Constitution, beyond the power of any state to deny. . . . Are women persons? And I hardly believe any of our opponents will have the hardihood to say they are not. Being persons, then, women are citizens; and no state has a right to make any law, or to enforce any old law, that shall abridge their privileges or immunities. Hence, every discrimination against women in the constitutions and laws of the several states is today null and void, precisely as is every one against Negroes."

> —Susan B. Anthony, "Is It a Crime for a Citizen of the
> United States to Vote?" 1873

6. Susan B. Anthony was arrested and fined $100 for casting an illegal vote in the presidential election of 1872. She refused to pay the fine. Her protest was most similar to which of the following?

   (A) The dumping of chests of British tea into the Boston harbor by colonists disguised as American Indians

   (B) The jailing of Henry David Thoreau for not paying taxes for what he considered an immoral war

   (C) The federal suit to free the slave Dred Scott after he resided in a free state

   (D) The raid of abolitionists led by John Brown on the federal arsenal at Harpers Ferry

7. Susan B. Anthony's arguments for women's suffrage can best be understood in the context of

   (A) *Marbury v. Madison*

   (B) The Monroe Doctrine

   (C) The Reconstruction amendments

   (D) The American Protective Association

8. Anthony targeted the states as the parts of government discriminating against women primarily for which of the following reasons?

   (A) Except for the 14th and 15th amendments, the United States Constitution left the power to the states to determine who could vote

   (B) She believed that all states were in violation of federal voting laws

   (C) The states established marriage laws and at the time these laws kept women in an inferior legal position to men

   (D) The federal government already supported suffrage for women

SHORT-ANSWER QUESTIONS

Use complete sentences; an outline or bulleted list alone is not acceptable.

Question 1 is based on the following cartoon.

Source: *Frank Leslie's Illustrated Newspaper,* 1882. Library of Congress

1. Using the cartoon, answer (A), (B), and (C).

   (A) Briefly explain the cartoonist's point of view on immigration.

   (B) Briefly explain ONE specific cause of the anti-immigration sentiment in the period from 1865 to 1900.

   (C) Briefly explain ONE change in federal immigration policy from 1865 to 1900 that supported or opposed the cartoonist's viewpoint.

Question 2. Answer (A), (B), and (C).

   (A) Briefly explain ONE specific problem that was caused by the rapid growth of cities during the period from 1865 to 1900.

   (B) Briefly explain ONE reason that American cities were unprepared or slow to address problems such as the one identified above.

   (C) Briefly explain ONE specific reform movement that developed in the period from 1865 to 1900 to address one or more urban problems.

Question 3. Answer (A), (B), and (C). *(continued on the next page)*

   (A) Briefly explain ONE development in education that was influenced by the economic or cultural changes in the late 1800s.

   (B) Briefly explain ONE change in visual arts or architecture that was influenced by the economic and cultural changes in the late 1800s.

   (C) Briefly explain ONE change in literature or music that was influenced by the economic and cultural changes in the late 1800s.

Question 4 is based on the following excerpts.

"Between 1820 and 1930, over 62 million people uprooted themselves from their native countries to seek a better life in newer lands around the globe. Almost two-thirds of these enterprising souls came to the United States. . . . . Other new countries like Australia and Argentine, it is true, are as much the product of immigration as the United States, but all these such countries were peopled by a very narrow range of nationalities. . . . Only in America were many nationalities mixed together."

—Carl N. Degler, historian, *Out of Our Past,* 1970

"Relatively few outsiders entered the [Southern] region. The borders of the old Confederacy might as well have been a dam, so effectively did they turn aside immigrants and hold Southerners within the confines of Dixie. The percentage of foreign born in the South actually fell from 1860 to 1900. By 1910 only 2 percent of the Southern population had been born outside the United States, compared with 14.7 percent for the country as a whole. Immigrants avoided the South because of low wages, sharecropping."

—Richard White, historian, *The Republic for Which It Stands,* 2017

4. Using the excerpts, answer (A), (B), and (C).

   (A) Briefly describe ONE major difference between Degler's and White's historical interpretation of immigration to the United States.

   (B) Briefly explain how ONE specific historical event or development in the period 1865 to 1900 that is not explicitly mentioned in the excerpts could be used to support Degler's interpretation.

   (C) Briefly explain how ONE specific historical event or development in the period 1865 to 1900 that is not explicitly mentioned in the excerpts could be used to support White's interpretation.

THINK AS A HISTORIAN: STATEMENTS ABOUT INTERPRETATION

Which TWO statements most clearly express historical interpretations?

1. By giving people shared experiences as fans, spectator sports promoted the blending of diverse immigrants into Americans.

2. Globalization in recent years has caused historians to focus on European influences on American culture in the late 19th century.

3. People today still read the works of Jack London and Stephen Crane.

19

THE POLITICS OF
THE GILDED AGE,
1877–1900

*My country, 'is of thee, Once land of liberty, Of thee I sing.
Land of the Millionaire; Farmers with pockets bare;
Caused by the cursed snare—The Money Ring.*

Alliance Songster, 1890

Congress had enacted an ambitious reform program during the 1860s and 1870s—the era of Civil War and Reconstruction. After the election of President Rutherford B. Hayes and the Compromise of 1877, the national government settled into an era of stalemate and comparative inactivity. However, the causes of limited achievements and failure of politicians to address the growing problems related to industrialization and urbanization are often as instructive as periods of political achievements.

Politics in the Gilded Age

The expression "Gilded Age," first used by Mark Twain in 1873 as the title of a book, referred to the superficial glitter of the new wealth so prominently displayed in the late 19th century. Historians often criticize the politics of the era as more show than substance. It was the era of "forgettable" presidents, none of whom served two consecutive terms, and of politicians who largely ignored problems arising from the growth of industry and cities. The two major parties in these years often avoided taking stands on controversial issues.

Causes of Stalemate

Factors accounting for the complacency and conservatism of the era included (1) the prevailing political ideology of the time, (2) campaign tactics of the two parties, and (3) party patronage.

Belief in Limited Government The idea of "do-little" government was in tune with two other popular ideas of the time: laissez-faire economics and Social Darwinism. Furthermore, the federal courts narrowly interpreted the government's powers to regulate business, and this limited the impact of the few regulatory laws that Congress did pass.

Campaign Strategy The closeness of elections between 1876 and 1892 was one reason that Republicans and Democrats alike avoided taking strong positions on the issues. The Democrats won only two presidential contests in the electoral college (but four in the popular vote). They nevertheless controlled the House of Representatives after eight of the ten general elections. The result was divided government in Washington (except for two years of the Harrison administration, 1889–1891, when the Republicans were in control of both the presidency and the two houses of Congress). With elections so evenly matched, the objective was to get out the vote and not alienate voters on the issues.

Election campaigns of the time were characterized by brass bands, flags, campaign buttons, picnics, free beer, and crowd-pleasing oratory. Both parties had strong organizations, the Republicans usually on the state level and the Democrats in the cities. The irony is that the issue-free campaigns brought out nearly 80 percent of the eligible voters for presidential elections, much higher than elections in later periods. The high turnout was a function of strong party identification and loyalty, often connected with the regional, religious, and ethnic ties of voters.

Republicans In the North, Republican politicians kept memories of the Civil War alive during the Gilded Age by figuratively waving the "bloody shirt" in every campaign and reminding the millions of veterans of the Union army that their wounds had been caused by (southern) Democrats and that Abraham Lincoln had been murdered by a Democrat. The party of Lincoln, because of its antislavery past, kept the votes of reformers and African Americans. The core of Republican strength came from men in business and from middle-class, Anglo-Saxon Protestants, many of whom supported temperance or prohibition. Republicans followed the tradition of Hamilton and the Whigs, supporting a pro-business economic program of high protective tariffs.

Democrats After 1877, Democrats could count upon winning every election in the former states of the Confederacy. The solid South was indeed solidly Democratic until the mid-20th century. In the North, Democratic strength came from big-city political machines and the immigrant vote. Democrats were often Catholics, Lutherans, and Jews who objected to temperance and prohibition crusades conducted by Protestant (and largely Republican) groups. Democrats of the Gilded Age argued for states' rights and limiting powers for the federal government, following in the Jeffersonian tradition.

Party Patronage Since neither party had an active legislative agenda, politics in this era was chiefly a game of winning elections, holding office, and providing government jobs to the party faithful. In New York, for example, Republican Senator Roscoe Conkling became a powerful leader of his party by dictating who in the Republican ranks would be appointed to lucrative jobs in the New York Customs House. Conkling and his supporters were known as the Stalwarts, while their rivals for patronage were the Halfbreeds, led by James G. Blaine. Who got the patronage jobs within the party became a more important issue than any policy. Republicans who did not play the patronage game were ridiculed as the Mugwumps for sitting on the fence—their "mugs" on one side of the fence and "wumps" on the other. Historians generally consider this era a low point in American politics.

Political Party Affiliations in Congress, 1881–1901				
	House		Senate	
Year	Major Parties	Minor Parties	Major Parties	Minor Parties
1881–1883	R-147, D-135	11	R-37, D-37	1
1883–1885	D-197, R-118	10	R-38, D-36	2
1885–1887	D-183, R-140	2	R-43, D-34	0
1887–1889	D-169, R-152	4	R-39, D-37	0
1889–1891	R-166, D-159	0	R-39, D-37	0
1891–1893	D-235, R-88	9	R-47, D-39	2
1893–1895	D-218, R-127	11	D-44, R-38	3
1895–1897	R-244, D-105	7	R-43, D-39	6
1897–1899	R-204, D-113	40	R-47, D-34	7
1899–1901	R-185, D-163	9	R-53, D-26	8

R: Republican   D: Democrat

Source: U.S. Bureau of the Census. *Historical Statistics of the United States, Colonial Times to 1970*

Presidential Politics

The administrations of presidents Hayes, Garfield, and Arthur reflected the political stalemate and patronage problems of the Gilded Age.

Rutherford B. Hayes After being declared the winner of the disputed election of 1876, Rutherford B. Hayes's most significant act was to end Reconstruction by withdrawing the last federal troops from the South. President Hayes also attempted to re-establish honest government after the corrupt Grant administration. As temperance reformers, Hayes and his wife, "Lemonade Lucy," cut off the flow of liquor in the White House. Hayes vetoed efforts to restrict Chinese immigration.

James Garfield Republican politicians, more interested in spoils and patronage than reform, were happy to honor President Hayes's pledge in 1877 to serve only one term. In the election of 1880, the Republicans compromised on the nomination of "Halfbreed" James A. Garfield of Ohio (a key swing state of the times), and "Stalwart" Chester A. Arthur of New York as vice president. The Democrats nominated Winfield S. Hancock, a former Union general who had been wounded at Gettysburg. The Garfield-Arthur ticket defeated the Democratic war hero in a very close popular vote.

In his first weeks in office, Garfield was besieged in the White House by hordes of Republicans seeking some 100,000 federal jobs. Garfield's choice of Halfbreeds for most offices provoked a bitter contest with Senator Conkling and his Stalwarts. While the president was preparing to board a train for a summer vacation in 1881, a deranged office seeker who identified with the Stalwarts shot Garfield in the back. After an 11-week struggle, the gunshot wound proved fatal. Chester A. Arthur then became president.

Chester A. Arthur Arthur proved a much better president than people expected. He distanced himself from the Stalwarts, supported a bill reforming the civil service. This bill expanded the number of government employees hired based on their qualifications rather than their political connections. In addition, he approved the development of a modern American navy and began to question the high protective tariff. His reward was denial of renomination by the Republican party in 1884.

Congressional Leaders

Weak presidents do not necessarily mean strong Congresses. Lawmakers of the Gilded Age typically had long but undistinguished careers. John Sherman, brother of the famous Civil War general, was in Congress from 1855 to 1898 but did little other than allow his name to be attached to a number of bills, including the Sherman Antitrust Act of 1890. Thomas "Czar" Reed from Maine, a sharp-tongued bully, became Speaker of the House in 1890 and instituted an autocratic rule over the House that took years to break. Senator James G. Blaine, also from Maine, had the potential of being a great political leader and largely succeeded in reshaping the Republicans from an antislavery party into a well-organized, business-oriented party. However, Blaine's reputation was tarnished by links with railroad scandals and other corrupt dealings.

The Election of 1884

In 1884 the Republicans nominated Blaine for president, but suspicions about Blaine's honesty were enough for the reform-minded Mugwumps to switch allegiance and campaign for the Democratic nominee, Grover Cleveland. Unlike most Gilded Age politicians, Cleveland was honest, frugal, conscientious, and uncompromising. He had been an honest mayor of Buffalo and incorruptible governor of New York State. Republicans raised questions, however, about the New Yorker's private life, making much of the fact that Cleveland had fathered the child of a woman not his wife. In a notably dirty campaign, the Democrats were labeled the party of "Rum, Romanism, and Rebellion." Catholic voters were offended by the phrase, and their votes in key states such as New York may have been enough to ensure Cleveland's victory as the first Democrat to be elected president since Buchanan in 1856.

Cleveland's First Term

The Democratic president believed in frugal and limited government in the tradition of Jefferson. He implemented the new civil service system (see below) and vetoed hundreds of private pension bills for those falsely claiming to have served or been injured in the Civil War. He signed into law both (1) the Inter-state Commerce Act of 1887, the federal government's first effort to regulate business, and (2) the Dawes Act, which reformers hoped would benefit American Indians. Cleveland's administration also retrieved some 81 million acres of government land from cattle ranchers and the railroads.

Issues: Civil Service, Currency, and Tariffs

During the 1870s and 1880s, the Congresses in Washington were chiefly concerned with such issues as patronage, the money supply, and the tariff issue. They left the states and local governments to deal with the growing problems of the cities and industrialization.

Civil Service Reform Public outrage over the assassination of President Garfield in 1881 pushed Congress to remove certain government jobs from the control of party patronage. The Pendleton Act of 1881 set up the Civil Service Commission and created a system by which applicants for classified federal jobs would be selected on the basis of their scores on a competitive examination. The law also prohibited civil servants from making political contributions. At first, the law applied to only 10 percent of federal employees, but in later decades, the system was expanded until most federal jobs were classified (that is, taken out of the hands of politicians).

Politicians adapted to the reform by depending less on their armies of party workers and more on the rich to fund their campaigns. People still debate which approach is more harmful to democratic government.

Money Question The most hotly debated issues of the Gilded Age was how much to expand the money supply. For the economy to grow soundly, it needed more money in circulation. However, the money question reflected the growing tension in the era between the "haves" and the "have-nots."

Debtors, farmers, and start-up businesses wanted more "easy" or "soft" money in circulation, since this would enable them to (1) borrow money at lower interest rates and (2) pay off their loans more easily with inflated dollars. After the Panic of 1873, many Americans blamed the gold standard for restricting the money supply and causing the depression. To expand the supply of U.S. currency, easy-money advocates campaigned first for more paper money (greenbacks) and then for the unlimited minting of silver coins.

On the opposite side of the question, bankers, creditors, investors, and established businesses stood firm for "sound" or "hard" money—meaning currency backed by gold stored in government vaults. Supporters of hard money argued that dollars backed by gold would hold their value against inflation. Holders of money understood that as the U.S. economy and population grew faster than the number of gold-backed dollars, each dollar would gain in value. As predicted, the dollar did increase in value by as much as 300 percent between 1865 and 1895.

Greenback Party Paper money not backed by specie (gold or silver) had been issued by the federal government in the 1860s as an emergency measure for financing the Civil War. Northern farmers, who received high prices during the war, prospered from the use of "greenbacks." On the other hand, creditors and investors attacked the use of unbacked paper money as a violation of natural law. In 1875, Congress sided with the creditors, and passed the Specie Resumption Act, which withdrew all greenbacks from circulation.

Supporters of paper money formed a new political party, the Greenback party. In the congressional election of 1878, Greenback candidates received nearly 1 million votes, and 14 members were elected to Congress, including James B. Weaver of Iowa (a future leader of the Populist party). When the hard times of the 1870s ended, the Greenback party died out, but the goal of increasing the amount of money in circulation did not.

Demands for Silver Money In addition to removing greenbacks, Congress in the 1870s also stopped the coining of silver. Critics call this action "the Crime of 1873." Then silver discoveries in Nevada revived demands for the use of silver to expand the money supply. A compromise law, the Bland-Allison Act, was passed over Hayes's veto in 1878. It allowed only a limited coinage of between $2 million and $4 million in silver each month at the standard silver-to-gold ratio of 16 to 1. Not satisfied, farmers, debtors, and western miners continued to press for the unlimited coinage of silver.

Tariff Issue In the 1890s, tariffs provided more than half of federal revenue. Western farmers and eastern capitalists disagreed on the question of whether tariff rates on foreign imports should be high or low. During the Civil War, the Republican Congress had raised tariffs to protect U.S. industry and also fund the Union government. After the war, southern Democrats as well as some northern Democrats objected to high tariffs because these taxes raised the prices on consumer goods. Another result of the protective tariff was that other nations retaliated by placing taxes of their own on U.S. farm products. American farmers lost some overseas sales, contributing to surpluses of corn and wheat and resulting in lower farm prices and profits. From a farmer's point of view, industry seemed to be growing rich at the expense of rural America.

The Growth of Discontent, 1888–1896

The politics of stalemate and complacency would begin to lose their hold on the voters by the late 1880s. Discontent over government corruption, the money issue, tariffs, railroads, and trusts was growing. In response, politicians began to take small steps to respond to public concerns, but it would take a third party (the Populists) and a major depression in 1893 to shake the Democrats and the Republicans from their lethargy.

Harrison and the Billion-Dollar Congress

Toward the end of his first term, President Cleveland created a political storm by challenging the high protective tariff. He proposed that Congress set lower tariff rates, since there was a growing surplus in the federal treasury and the government did not need the added tax revenue.

The Election of 1888 With the tariff question, Cleveland introduced a real issue, the first in years that truly divided Democrats and Republicans. In the election of 1888, Democrats campaigned for Cleveland and a lower tariff; Republicans campaigned for Benjamin Harrison (grandson of the former president, William Henry Harrison) and a high tariff. The Republicans argued that a lower tariff would wreck business prosperity. They played upon this fear to raise campaign funds from big business and to rally workers in the North, whose jobs depended on the success of U.S. industry. The Republicans also attacked Cleveland's vetoes of pension bills to bring out the veteran vote. The election was extremely close. Cleveland received more popular votes than Harrison, but ended up losing the election because Harrison's sweep of the North gained the Republican ticket a majority of votes in the electoral college.

Billion-dollar Congress For the next two years, Republicans controlled the presidency and both houses of Congress—unusual for this era of close elections. The new Congress was the most active in years, passing the first billion-dollar budget in U.S. history. It enacted the following:

- The McKinley Tariff of 1890, which raised the tax on foreign products to a peacetime high of more than 48 percent
- Increases in the monthly pensions to Civil War veterans, widows, and children
- The Sherman Antitrust Act, outlawing "combinations in restraint of trade" (see Chapter 16)
- The Sherman Silver Purchase Act of 1890, which increased the coinage of silver, but too little to satisfy farmers and miners
- A bill to protect the voting rights of African Americans, passed by the House but defeated in the Senate

Return of the Democrats In the congressional elections of 1890, the voters, especially in the Midwest, replaced many Republicans with Democrats. They were reacting in part to unpopular measures passed by Republican state legislatures: prohibition of alcohol and laws requiring business to close on Sundays. Voters who were neither Anglo-Saxon nor Protestant rushed back to the Democrats, who had not tried to legislate public morality.

Rise of the Populists

Another factor in the Republican setbacks of 1890 was growing agrarian discontent in the South and West. Members of the Farmers' Alliances elected U.S. senators and representatives, the governors of several states, and majorities in four state legislatures in the West.

Omaha Platform The Alliance movement provided the foundation of a new political party—the People's, or Populist, party. Delegates from different states met in Omaha, Nebraska, in 1892 to draft a political platform and nominate candidates for president and vice president for the new party. Populists were determined to do something about the concentration of economic power in the hands of trusts and bankers. Their Omaha platform called for both political and economic reforms. Politically, it demanded an increase in the power of common voters through (1) direct popular election of U.S. senators (instead of indirect election by state legislatures) and (2) the use of initiatives and referendums, procedures that allowed citizens to vote directly on proposed laws. Economically, the Populist platform was even more ambitious. Populists advocated: (1) unlimited coinage of silver to increase the money supply, (2) a graduated income tax (the greater a person's income, the higher the percentage of the tax on his or her income), (3) public ownership of railroads by the U.S. government, (4) telegraph and telephone systems owned and operated by the government, (5) loans and federal warehouses for farmers to enable them to stabilize prices for their crops, and (6) an eight-hour day for industrial workers.

At the time, the Populist movement seemed revolutionary not only for its attack on laissez-faire capitalism but also for its attempt to form a political alliance between poor whites and poor blacks. In the South, Thomas Watson of Georgia appealed to poor farmers of both races to unite on their common economic grievances by joining the People's party.

The Election of 1892 In 1892, James Weaver of Iowa, the Populist candidate for president, won more than 1 million votes and 22 electoral votes, making him one of the few third-party candidates in U.S. history to win votes in the electoral college. Nevertheless, the Populist ticket lost badly in the South and failed to attract urban workers in the North. The fear of Populists uniting poor blacks and whites drove conservative southern Democrats to use every technique to disfranchise African Americans (see Chapter 17).

The two major parties provided a rematch between President Harrison and former president Cleveland. This time, Cleveland won a solid victory in both the popular and electoral vote. He won in part because of the unpopularity of the high-tax McKinley Tariff. Cleveland became the first and only former president thus far to return to the White House after having left it.

Depression Politics

No sooner did Cleveland take office than the country entered into one of its worst and longest depressions.

Panic of 1893 In the spring and summer of 1893, the stock market crashed as a result of overspeculation, and dozens of railroads went into bankruptcy as a result of overbuilding. The depression continued for almost four years. Farm foreclosures reached new highs, and the unemployed reached 20 percent of the workforce. Many people ended up relying on soup kitchens and riding the rails as hoboes. President Cleveland, more conservative than he had been in the 1880s, dealt with the crisis by championing the gold standard and otherwise adopting a hands-off policy toward the economy.

Gold Reserve and Tariff A decline in silver prices encouraged investors to trade their silver dollars for gold dollars. The gold reserve (bars of gold bullion stored by the U.S. Treasury) fell to a dangerously low level, and President Cleveland saw no alternative but to repeal the Sherman Silver Purchase Act of 1890.

This action, however, failed to stop the gold drain. The president then turned to the Wall Street banker J. P. Morgan to borrow $65 million in gold to support the dollar and the gold standard. This deal convinced many Americans that the government in Washington was only a tool of rich eastern bankers. Workers became further disenchanted with Cleveland when he used court injunctions and federal troops to crush the Pullman strike in 1894 (see Chapter 16).

The Democrats did enact one measure that was somewhat more popular. Congress passed the Wilson-Gorman Tariff in 1894, which (1) provided a moderate reduction in tariff rates and (2) included a 2 percent income tax on incomes of more than $2,000. Since the average American income at this time was less than $1,000, only those with higher incomes would be subject to the income tax. Within a year after the passage of the law, however, the conservative Supreme Court declared an income tax unconstitutional.

Jobless on the March As the depression worsened and the numbers of jobless people grew, conservatives feared class war between capital and labor. They were especially alarmed by a march to Washington in 1894 by thousands of the unemployed led by Populist Jacob A. Coxey of Ohio. "Coxey's Army" demanded that the federal government spend $500 million on public works programs to create jobs. Coxey and other protest leaders were arrested for trespassing, and the dejected marchers returned home.

Also in 1894, a little book by William H. Harvey presenting lessons in economics seemed to offer easy answers for ending the depression. Illustrated with cartoons, *Coin's Financial School* taught millions of discontented Americans that their troubles were caused by a conspiracy of rich bankers, and that prosperity would return if the government coined silver in unlimited quantities.

Turning Point in American Politics: 1896

National politics was in transition. The repeal of the Silver Purchase Act and Cleveland's handling of the depression thoroughly discredited the conservative leadership of the Democratic party. The Democrats were buried in the congressional elections of 1894 by the Republicans. At the same time, the Populists continued to gain both votes and legislative seats. The stage was set for a major reshaping of party politics in 1896.

The Election of 1896

The election of 1896 was one of the most emotional in U.S. history. It also would mark of the beginning of a new era in American politics.

Bryan, Democrats, and Populists Democrats were divided in 1896 between "gold" Democrats loyal to Cleveland and prosilver Democrats looking for a leader. Their national convention in Chicago in the summer of 1896 was dominated by the prosilver forces. Addressing the convention, William Jennings Bryan of Nebraska captured the hearts of the delegates with a speech that ended with these words: "We will answer their demands for a gold standard by saying to them: 'You shall not press down upon the brow of labor this crown of thorns, you shall not crucify mankind upon a cross of gold.'" So powerful was Bryan's "Cross of Gold" speech that it made him instantly the Democratic nominee for president. Bryan was only 36 years old.

The Democratic platform favored the unlimited coinage of silver at the traditional, but inflationary, ratio of 16 ounces of silver to one ounce of gold. (The market price then was about 32 to 1.) Thus, the Democrats had taken over the leading issue of the Populist platform. Given little choice, the Populist convention in 1896 also nominated Bryan and conducted a "fused" campaign for "free silver."

Unhappy with Bryan and free silver, the conservative faction of "Gold Bug" Democrats, including Cleveland, either formed the separate National Democratic party or voted Republican.

McKinley, Hanna, and Republicans For their presidential nominee, the Republicans nominated William McKinley of Ohio, best known for his support of a high protective tariff but also considered a friend of labor. Marcus (Mark) Hanna, who had made a fortune in business, was the financial power behind McKinley's nomination as well as the subsequent campaign for president. After blaming the Democrats for the Panic of 1893, the Republicans offered the American people the promise of a strong and prosperous industrial nation. The Republican platform proposed a high tariff to protect industry and upheld the gold standard against unlimited coinage of silver.

The Campaign The defection of "Gold Bug" Democrats over the silver issue gave the Republicans an early advantage. Bryan countered by turning the Democratic-Populist campaign into a nationwide crusade. Traveling by train from one end of the country to the other, the young candidate covered 18,000 miles and gave more than 600 speeches. His energy, positive attitude, and rousing oratory convinced millions of farmers and debtors that the unlimited coinage of silver was their salvation.

Mark Hanna meanwhile did most of the work of campaigning for McKinley. He raised millions of dollars for the Republican ticket from business leaders who feared that "silver lunacy" would lead to runaway inflation. Hanna used the money to sell McKinley through the mass media (newspapers, magazines), while the Republican candidate stayed home and conducted a safe, front-porch campaign, greeting delegations of supporters.

In the last weeks of the campaign, Bryan was hurt by (1) a rise in wheat prices, which made farmers less desperate, and (2) employers telling their workers that factories would shut down if Bryan was elected. On election day, McKinley carried all of the Northeast and the upper Midwest in a decisive victory over Bryan in both the popular vote (7.1 million to 6.5 million) and the electoral vote (271 to 176).

McKinley's Presidency

McKinley was lucky to take office just as the economy began to revive. Gold discoveries in Alaska in 1897 increased the money supply under the gold standard, which resulted in the inflation that the silverites had wanted. Farm prices rose, factory production increased, and the stock market climbed. The

Republicans honored their platform by enacting the Dingley Tariff of 1897 that increased the tariff to more than 46 percent, and, in 1900, making gold the official standard of the U.S. currency. McKinley was a well-liked, well-traveled president who tried to bring conflicting interests together. As leader during the war with Spain in 1898, he helped to make the United States a world power.

Significance of the Election of 1896

The election of 1896 had significant short-term and long-term consequences on American politics. It marked the end of the stalemate and stagnation that had characterized politics in the Gilded Age. In addition, the defeat of Bryan and the Populist free-silver movement initiated an era of Republican dominance of the presidency (seven of the next nine elections) and of both houses of Congress (17 of the next 20 sessions). Once the party of "free soil, free labor, and free men," the Republicans had become the party of business and industry, though it continued to advocate for a strong national government. The Democrats carried on in defeat as the sectional party of the South and host of whatever Populist sentiment remained.

Populist Demise The Populist party declined after 1896 and soon ceased to be a national party. In the South, Thomas Watson and other Populist leaders gave up trying to unite poor whites and blacks, having discovered the hard lesson that racism was stronger than common economic interests. Ironically, in defeat, much of the Populist reform agenda, such as the graduated income tax and popular election of senators, was adopted by both the Democrats and Republicans during the reform-minded Progressive era (1900–1917).

Urban Dominance The election of 1896 was a clear victory for big business, urban centers, conservative economics, and moderate, middle-class values. It proved to be the last hope of rural America to reclaim its former dominance in American politics. Some historians see the election marking the triumph of the values of modern industrial and urban America over the rural ideals of the America of Jefferson and Jackson.

Beginning of Modern Politics McKinley emerged as the first modern president, an active leader who took the United States from being relatively isolated to becoming a major player in international affairs. Mark Hanna, the master of high-finance politics, created a model for organizing and financing a successful campaign. McKinley's model focused on winning favorable publicity in the dominant mass media of his day: newspapers.

Historians debate whether the Populist crusade was realistic or romantic. Was it a practical, liberal response to problems or an idealistic, reactionary effort to bring back a farmer-dominated society?

Early histories of the Populists depicted them as farmers and small producers who challenged the abuses of industrial America and the corruption of the political system. As reformers, they were seeking only economic fairness and an honest democratic process. The reforms that they advocated in the Omaha platform of 1892 had long-term significance in preparing the way for similar reforms in the Progressive era (1900–1917) and the New Deal (1933–1939).

An alternative view of the Populists sees them largely as reactionaries who dreamed up conspiracies by eastern bankers instead of seriously trying to understand the complex causes of the decline of farm income. Critics argue that Populists—rather than dealing with the world as it was—isolated themselves from the new urban and industrial age and were often racists, nativists, anti-Semites, and anti-Catholics. Richard Hofstadter in *The Age of Reform* (1955) saw both positive and negative aspects in the Populist movement. He credited the Populists for insisting on the federal government's responsibility to promote the common good and deal with problems of industrialization. At the same time, Hofstadter criticized the Populists' backward-looking and nostalgic ideology and their hopeless quest to restore an agrarian golden age that existed only in myth.

Since Hofstadter, historians have returned to the view that the farmers' grievances were real and that American democracy was endangered by powerful economic groups. Members of the National Farmers' Alliance and the Populist movement were not ignorant of complex economic changes; instead, they worked to educate themselves about economics and politics. Nor were most of them bigoted. Walter Nugent in *The Tolerant Populists* (1963) depicts them as democratic humanists who welcomed into their ranks people of all races, creeds, and ethnic backgrounds.

As a style of politics, populism remains powerful. Michael Kazin in *The Populist Persuasion* (1995) analyzed populism as a political attitude and posture that combines anti-elitism with advocacy for the common people. According to Kazin, populism shifted to the right in the 1960s with the emergence of George Wallace and the presidency of Richard Nixon. The populist movements of the late 20th century were primarily conservative reactions against the increased role of government. Populist movements of the 2010s, such as the Tea Party, proved again the appeal of the outsiders and anti-establishment voices, and that the populist tradition remains a potent part of American politics.

KEY TERMS BY THEME

Political Stalemate (POL)
lassiez-faire economics and politics
divided electorate
identity politics
"Rum, Romanism, and Rebellion"
close elections
divided government
weak presidents
patronage politics
corrupt politicians

Republican Party (POL)
Union veterans, "bloody shirt"
Whig past, pro-business
Hamiltonian tradition
Social reformers, temperance
Anglo-Saxon heritage
Protestant religion
African Americans

Democratic Party (POL)
former Confederacy, "Solid South"
states' rights, limited government
Jeffersonian tradition
big-city political machines
immigrant vote
against prohibition
Catholics, Lutherans, Jews

Patronage Issue (POL)
federal government jobs
Stalwarts, Halfbreeds, and Mugwumps
Election of 1880

assassination of James Garfield
Chester Arthur
Pendleton Act of 1881
civil service reform
election of 1884
Grover Cleveland

Tariff Issue (POL, WXT)
high tariff
business vs. consumers
Cleveland threatens lower tariff
McKinley Tariff of 1890
Wilson-Gorman Tariff of 1894
Dingley Tariff of 1897–46.5 percent

Money Supply (WXT, POL)
"hard" money vs. "soft" money
banks, creditors vs. debtors
Panic of 1873, "Crime of 73"
Specie Resumption Act of 1875
Greenback party
James B. Weaver
Bland-Allison Act of 1878
Sherman Silver Purchase Act of 1890
run on gold reserves, J. P. Morgan bail out
repeal of Sherman Silver Purchase Act

Rise of Discontent (POL)
election of 1888, Harrison
"Billion Dollar Congress"
rise of the Populist Party
Farmers' Alliances in South and West
Alliance of whites and blacks in South
Thomas Watson
reformers vs. racism in South
Omaha Platform
government regulation and ownership
election of 1892, Cleveland returns
Panic of 1893
Coxey's Army, March on Washington
Coin's Financial School

Election of 1896 (POL)
William Jennings Bryan
"Cross of Gold" Speech
fusion of Democrats and Populists
unlimited coinage of silver at 16 to 1
"Gold Bug" Democrats
Mark Hanna, money and mass media
McKinley victory
gold standard and higher tariff
rise of modern urban-industrial society
decline of traditional rural-agricultural society
start of the modern presidency
era of Republican dominance

Questions 1–3 refer to the excerpt below.

"My Dear Nephew,

"Never allow yourself to lose sight of that fact that politics, and not poker, is our great American game. If this could be beaten into the heads of some presumably well-meaning but glaringly unpractical people, we should hear less idiotic talk about reform in connection with politics. Nobody ever dreams of organizing a reform movement in poker. . . .

"Mr. Lincoln, a very estimable and justly popular, but in some respects an impracticable man, formulated widely different error regard to politics. He held that ours is a government of the people, by the people, for the people. I maintain, on the contrary, that it is government of politicians, by politicians, for politicians. If your political career is to be a success, you must understand and respect this distinction with a difference."

> —William McElroy, journalist, "An Old War Horse to a Young Politician," published anonymously in the *Atlantic Monthly*, 1880

1. McElroy's letter uses humor to make a point. Which of the following statements reflects McElroy's true criticism?

   (A) Americans pay too much attention to politics

   (B) Elections were so close that for candidates it was similar to gambling

   (C) Lincoln was admired more than he deserved to be

   (D) Politics was primarily about holding office for personal gain

2. Voters demanded patronage reform in politics after

   (A) President James Garfield was assassinated

   (B) the Mugwumps sided with the opposing party

   (C) the Greenback Party won mid-year elections in 1878

   (D) Grover Cleveland threatened Republican dominance

3. Which of the following would the author, as a critic of the politics of the era, most likely oppose?

   (A) Laws limiting the number of terms one person could serve in an elective office

   (B) Rules reducing the number of patronage jobs controlled by politicians

   (C) Court decisions allowing unlimited campaign contributions by wealthy donors

   (D) Prosecutions of corruption in urban political parties and among political bosses

Questions 4–5 refer to the graph below.

U.S. TARIFFS, 1820 to 2000

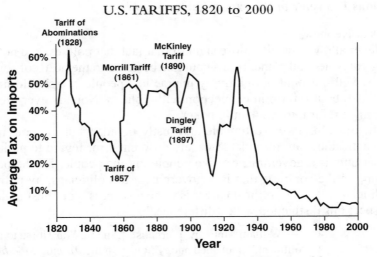

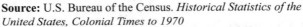

Source: U.S. Bureau of the Census. *Historical Statistics of the United States, Colonial Times to 1970*

4. Which of the following best explains the tariff rates during the period from 1865 to 1900?

(A) American farmers believed that high tariffs would result in high farm prices

(B) Republicans believed that high tariffs would protect American business from foreign competition

(C) Democrats believed that high tariffs would create jobs for American workers

(D) Consumers believed that high tariffs would result in high-quality manufactured goods made in the United States

5. Which statement best describes the level of tariffs in the United States in the 19th century?

(A) Tariffs were generally highest during Democratic administrations

(B) The election of Lincoln ushered in a period of high tariffs

(C) The election of McKinley resulted in a period of lower tariffs

(D) Tariffs were closely linked to the value of the U.S. dollar

Questions 6–8 refer to the table below.

Money in Circulation in the United States, 1865–1895		
Year	**Total Currency (in thousands of dollars)**	**Population (in thousands)**
1865	1,180,197	35,701
1870	899,876	39,905
1875	925,702	45,073
1880	1,185,550	50,262
1885	1,537,434	56,658
1890	1,685,123	63,056
1895	1,819,360	69,580

Source: U.S. Bureau of the Census. *Historical Statistics of the United States, Colonial Times to 1970*

6. Which of the following most likely explains the change in the amount of currency in circulation between 1865 and 1870?

(A) The decline of gold mining in the United States

(B) The withdrawal of "greenbacks" from circulation

(C) The refusal of Congress to purchase silver for coinage

(D) The increasing poverty of most Americans

7. Which of the following groups during the period from 1865 to 1895 most actively campaigned to increase the money supply?

(A) Farmers and debtors

(B) Bankers and lenders

(C) Merchants and consumers

(D) The federal and state governments

8. A decline in the amount of money in circulation in proportion to the population would most likely result in a(n)

(A) increase in prices and a decline in wages

(B) increase in the value of the dollar along with decrease in purchasing power

(C) increase in interest rates and a decline in prices

(D) decrease the value of the dollar and increase in prices

SHORT-ANSWER QUESTIONS

Use complete sentences; an outline or bulleted list alone is not acceptable.

Question 1. Answer (A), (B), and (C).

(A) Briefly explain ONE significant factor that influenced voting patterns during the period from 1865 to 1900.

(B) Briefly explain ONE cause of very high voter turnout during the period from 1865 to 1900.

(C) Briefly explain ONE cause of the often stalemated and ineffective government on a national level during the period from 1877 to 1900.

Question 2 is based on the following excerpts.

"The Populists looked backward with longing to the lost Eden, to the republican America of the early years of the nineteenth century in which there were few millionaires . . . when the laborer had excellent prospects and the farmers had abundance, when statesmen responded to the mood of the people and there was no such thing as the money power."

—Richard Hofstadter, *The Age of Reform*, 1955

"Populists sought to rethink the meaning of freedom to meet the exigencies of the 1890s. . . . Like the labor movement Populists rejected the era's laissez-faire orthodoxy. . . . a generation would pass before a major party offered so sweeping a plan for government action on the behalf of economic freedom as the Omaha platform."

—Eric Foner, *The Story of American Freedom*, 1998

2. Using the excerpts, answer (A), (B), and (C).

(A) Briefly explain ONE significant difference between Hofstadter's interpretation and Foner's interpretation of the Populists.

(B) Briefly explain ONE historical event or development from 1865 to 1900 that could support Hofstadter's interpretation of the Populists.

(C) Briefly explain ONE historical event or development from 1865 to 1900 that could support Foner's interpretation of the Populists.

Question 3. Answer (A), (B), and (C).

(A) Briefly explain ONE proposal of the Populist Party to reform politics or elections in the United States.

(B) Briefly explain ONE way the debate over the money supply affected the 1896 election.

(C) Briefly explain ONE specific result of the election of 1896 to support the interpretation that it was a turning point in American politics.

Question 4 is based on the following cartoon.

Source: 1896, The Granger Collection, NYC

4. Using the cartoon, answer (A), (B), and (C).

   (A) Briefly explain ONE historical perspective expressed by the artist about the changes in the economy from 1865 to 1900.

   (B) Briefly explain ONE development in the period from 1865 to 1900 that supported the perspective expressed by the artist.

   (C) Briefly explain ONE development in the period from 1865 to 1900 that challenged the perspective expressed by the artist.

THINK AS A HISTORIAN: STATING A THESIS ABOUT CAUSATION

The thesis statement is the organizing idea for an essay. It should express a clear idea that can be supported with evidence. Which THREE of the following statements would make the best thesis statements?

1. The Gilded Age shows that Hamilton, Clay, and Lincoln were right to advocate for a strong economic role for the federal government.

2. Racial conflict slowed the growth and development of the U.S. economy in the 19th century.

3. The energy and goals of the 19th-century populists make them my favorite movement in U.S. history.

4. James Garfield was the second president killed in less than 20 years.

5. The McKinley campaign of 1896 run by Mark Hanna set the pattern that most later candidates and presidents would follow.

Unit 6: Period 6 Review, 1865–1898

LONG ESSAY QUESTIONS

Directions: The suggested writing time for each question is 40 minutes. In your response you should do the following:

- **Thesis:** Make a defensible claim that establishes a line of reasoning and consists of one or more sentences found in one place.
- **Contextualization:** Relate the argument to a broader historical context.
- **Evidence:** Support an argument with specific and relevant historical evidence.
- **Reasoning:** Organize an argument using the skill in the question.
- **Analysis:** Demonstrate a complex understanding of the question using historical evidence to support, qualify, or modify an argument.

1. Compare the objectives and strategies of organized labor and the Populists for challenging the prevailing economic beliefs and practices of the Gilded Age.

2. Compare and contrast the roles of the federal government as both promoter and regulator of industrial development and market capitalism from 1865 to 1900.

3. Explain and analyze the impact of industrialization and expanding markets on the development of TWO of the following regions between 1865 and 1900.
   - Northeast/Midwest
   - South
   - West

4. Explain and analyze the impact of changes in transportation and marketing on both urban and rural consumers in the United States between 1865 and 1900.

5. Analyze the extent to which both external and internal migration changed over time from 1830 to 1900.

6. Analyze the extent to which TWO of the following groups changed their response over time to discrimination from 1830 to 1900.

- African Americans
- American Indians
- women

7. Analyze and evaluate ways in which TWO of the following areas reflected or challenged the dominate culture after the Civil War to 1900.

- architecture
- art and literature
- education
- religion

8. Analyze and evaluate the ways in which Social Darwinism and the Gospel of Wealth were used to defend the dominant economic and social order after the Civil War to 1900.

DOCUMENT-BASED QUESTION 1

Directions: Question 1 is based on the accompanying documents. The documents have been edited for the purpose of this exercise. You are advised to spend 15 minutes planning and 45 minutes writing your answer. In your response you should do the following:

- **Thesis:** Make a defensible claim that establishes a line of reasoning and consists of one or more sentences found in one place.
- **Contextualization:** Relate the argument to a broader historical context.
- **Document Evidence:** Use content from at least six documents.
- **Outside Evidence:** Use one piece of evidence not in the documents.
- **Document Sourcing:** Explain how or why the point of view, purpose, situation, or intended audience is relevant for at least three documents.
- **Analysis:** Show the relationships among pieces of historical evidence and use them to support, qualify, or modify an argument.

1. Some historians have characterized the industrial and business leaders of the 1865–1900 period as "robber barons," who used extreme methods to control and concentrate wealth and power. To what extent is that characterization justified based on the historical evidence?

Document 1

Source: Interview with William H. Vanderbilt, *Chicago Daily News,* 1882

Q: How is the freight and passenger pool working?

W.V.: Very satisfactorily. I don't like that expression "pool," however, that's a common construction applied by the people to a combination which the leading roads have entered into to keep rates at a point where they will pay dividends to the stockholders. The railroads are not run for the benefit of the "dear public"—that cry is all nonsense—they are built by men who invest their money and expect to get a fair percentage on the same.

Q: Does your limited express pay?

W.V.: No; not a bit of it. We only run it because we are forced to do so by the action of the Pennsylvania road. It doesn't pay expenses. We would abandon it if it was not for our competitor keeping its train on.

Q: But don't you run it for the public benefit?

W.V. The public be damned. What does the public care for the railroads except to get as much out of them for as small consideration as possible? I don't take any stock in this silly nonsense about working for anybody's good but our own.

Document 2

Source: Thomas Alva Edison, Letter written November 14, 1887

My laboratory will soon be completed. . . . I will have the best equipped and largest Laboratory extant, and the facilities incomparably superior to any other for rapid & cheap development of an invention, & working it up into Commercial shape with models, patterns & special machinery. In fact there is no similar institution in Existence. We do our own castings and forgings. Can build anything from a lady's watch to a Locomotive.

The Machine shop is sufficiently large to employ 50 men & 30 men can be worked in other parts of the works. Invention that formerly took months & cost a large sum can now be done in 2 or 3 days with very small expense, as I shall carry a stock of almost every conceivable material of every size, and with the latest machinery a man will produce 10 times as much as in a laboratory which has but little material, not of a size, delays of days waiting for castings and machinery not universal or modern. . . .

You are aware from your long acquaintance with me that I do not fly any financial Kites, or speculate, and that the works I control are well-managed. In the early days of the shops it was necessary that I should largely manage them [alone], first because the art had to be created, 2nd, because I could get no men who were competent in such a new business. But as soon as it was possible I put other persons in charge. I am perfectly well aware of the fact that my place is in the Laboratory; but I think you will admit that I know how a shop should be managed & also know how to select men to manage them

Document 3

Source: Andrew Carnegie, "Wealth," *North American Review,* 1889

The problem of our age is the proper administration of wealth so that the ties of brotherhood may still bind together the rich and poor in harmony. . . .

The price which society pays for the law of competition, like the price it pays for cheap comforts and luxuries, is also great; but the advantages of this law are also greater still. For it is to this law that we owe out wonderful material development which brings improved conditions. While the law may be sometimes hard for the individual, it is best for the race, because it insures the survival of the fittest in every department. We welcome, therefore, as conditions to which we must accommodate ourselves, great inequality of environment, the concentration of business, industrial and commercial, in the hands of a few; and the law of competition between these, as being not only beneficial, but essential for the future progress of the race.

Document 4

Source: James B. Weaver, "A Call to Action," 1892

It is clear that trusts are contrary to public policy and hence in conflict with the common law. They are monopolies organized to destroy competition and restrain trade. . . .

It is contended by those interested in trusts that they tend to cheapen production and diminish the price of the article to the consumer. . . . Trusts are speculative in their purpose and formed to make money. Once they secure control of a given line of business, they are masters of the situation and can dictate to the two great classes with which they deal—the producer of the raw material and the consumer of the finished product. They limit the price of the raw material so as to impoverish the producer, drive him to a single market, reduce the price of every class of labor connected with the trade, throw out of employment large numbers of persons who had before been engaged in a meritorious calling and finally . . . they increase the price to the consumer. . . . The main weapons of the trust are threats, intimidation, bribery, fraud, wreck, and pillage.

Document 5

Source: Standard Oil Company with tentacles, Library of Congress

Document 6

Source: Statement of Pullman Strikers, June 1894

Pullman, both the man and the town, is an ulcer on the body politic. He owns the houses, the schoolhouses, and the churches of God in the town he gave his once humble name. The revenue he derives from these wages he pays out with one hand—the Pullman Palace Car Company—he takes back with the other—the Pullman Land Association. He is able by this to bid under any contract car shop in this country. His competitors in business, to meet this, must reduce the wages of their men. This gives him the excuse to reduce ours to conform to the market. His business rivals must in turn scale down, so must he. And thus the merry war—the dance of skeletons bathed in human tears—goes on; and it will go on, brothers, forever unless you, the American Railway Union, stop it.

Document 7

Source: Major gifts by John D. Rockefeller before his death (1937)

American Baptist Foreign Mission Society New York City	$6,845,688.52
American Baptist Home Mission Society, New York City	6,994,831.62
American Baptist Missionary Society, Dayton, Ohio	1,902,132.58
General Education Board	129,209,167.10
Laura Spelman Rockefeller Memorial, New York	73,985,313.77
Minister and Missionaries Benefit Board of Northern Baptist Convention	7,090,579.06
Rockefeller Foundation, New York	182,851,480.90
Rockefeller Institute for Medical Research	59,931,891.60
University of Chicago, Chicago, Illinois	34,708,375.28
Yale University, New Haven	1,001,000.00
Y.M.C.A., International Committee	2,295,580.73
TOTAL	**$506,816,041.18**

DOCUMENT-BASED QUESTION 2

Directions: Question 2 is based on the accompanying documents. The documents have been edited for the purpose of this exercise. You are advised to spend 15 minutes planning and 45 minutes writing your answer.In your response you should do the following:

- **Thesis:** Make a defensible claim that establishes a line of reasoning and consists of one or more sentences found in one place.
- **Contextualization:** Relate the argument to a broader historical context.
- **Document Evidence:** Use content from at least six documents.
- **Outside Evidence:** Use one piece of evidence not in the documents.
- **Document Sourcing:** Explain how or why the point of view, purpose, situation, or intended audience is relevant for at least three documents.
- **Analysis:** Show the relationships among pieces of historical evidence and use them to support, qualify, or modify an argument.

1. "The politics of the Gilded Age failed to deal with the critical social and economic issues of the times." Assess the validity of this statement. Use both the documents and your knowledge of the United States from 1865 to 1900.

Document 1

Source: James Bryce, British commentator and later ambassador to the United States, *The American Commonwealth,* 1891

To explain the causes which keep much of the finest intellect of the country away from national business is one thing; to deny the unfortunate results would be quite another. Unfortunate they are. But the downward tendency observable since the end of the Civil War seems to have been arrested. When the war was over, the Union saved, the curse of slavery gone forever, there came a season of contentment and of lassitude. A nation which had surmounted such dangers seemed to have nothing more to fear. Those who had fought with tongue and pen and rifle might now rest on their laurels. After long continued strain and effort, the wearied nerve and muscle sought repose. It was repose from political warfare only. For the end of the war coincided with the opening of a time of swift material growth and abound ing material propensity in which industry and the development of the West absorbed more and more of the energy of the people. Hence a neglect of details of politics such as had never been seen before.

Document 2

Source: Henry Demarest Lloyd, financial writer and social reformer, "Lords of Industry," *North American Review,* June 1884

We have had an era of material inventions. We now need a renaissance of moral inventions. . . . Monopoly and anti-monopoly . . . represent the two great tendencies of our time: monopoly, the tendency to combination; anti-monopoly, the demand for social control of it. As the man is bent toward business or patriotism, he will negotiate combination or agitate for laws to regulate them. The first is capitalistic and the second is social. The first, industrial; the second, moral. The first promotes wealth; the second, citizenship. Our young men can no longer go west; they must go up or down. Not new land, but new virtue must be the outlet for the future.

Document 3

Source: J. Keppler, "The Bosses of the Senate," 1899. Library of Congress

Document 4

Source: The Interstate Commerce Act, 1887

Be it enacted by the Senate and House of Representatives of the United States of America in Congress assembled, that the provisions of this act shall apply to any common carriers engaged in the transportation of passengers or property wholly by railroad, . . . from one state or territory of the United States, or the District of Columbia, to any other state or territory of the United States, or the District of Columbia. . . .

Section 3. That it shall be unlawful for any common carrier subject to the provisions of this act to make or give any undue or unreasonable preference or advantage to any particular person, company, firm, corporation, or locality. . . .

Section 4. That it shall be unlawful for any common carrier subject to the provision of this act to charge or receive any greater compensation in the aggregate for the transportation of passengers or of like kind of property, under substantially similar circumstances and conditions, for a shorter than for a longer distance over the same line.

Document 5

Source: "Third Annual Report of the Factory Inspectors of the State of New York for the Year Ending December 1st, 1888," 1889

By the act of the legislature of 1888, the factory inspectors were required to enforce the law relating to the indenturing of apprentices. . . . The industrial conditions existing at, and previously to, the time of the passage of the Law of 1871 are so completely revolutionized that the old form of apprenticeship has become almost obsolete. Where, in former times, boys were expected to learn a trade in all its features, they are now simply put at a machine or at one branch of the craft, and no understanding exists that they shall be taught any other branch or the use of any other machine. Employers claim that these boys are not apprentices, and even if they so desired, could not teach . . . an apprentice all the intricacies of a trade, for the reason that where the skill and intelligence of a journeyman [trained] workman were once essential, a simple machine now unerringly performs the service, and consequently there is no occasion for an apprentice to learn to do the labor by hand. These were the principal reasons given by employers as to why the law had become inoperative.

Document 6

Source: Dr. Timothy D. Stow, Report of the Committee of the Senate Upon the Relations of Labor and Capital, 1890

The Chairman: We want to find out how the working people of Fall River [Massachusetts] are living and doing. . . . Just tell us the condition of the operatives there, in your own way.

The Witness: [Dr. Stow]: With regard to the effect of the present industrial system upon [the laboring classes'] physical and moral welfare, I should say it was of such a character as to need mending, to say the least. It needs some radical remedy. Our laboring population is made up very largely of foreigners, men, women, and children, who have either voluntarily come to Fall River or who have been induced to come there by the manufactures. As a class they are dwarfed physically. . . .

They are dwarfed, in my estimation, sir, as the majority of men and women who are brought up in factories must be dwarfed under the present industrial system; because by their long hours of indoor labor and their hard work they are cut off from the benefit of breathing fresh air and from the sights that surround a workman outside a mill. Being shut up all day long in the noise and in the high temperature of these mills they become physically weak.

Document 7

Source: Populist Party Platform, 1892

We have witnessed, for more than a quarter of a century the struggles of the two great political parties for power and plunder, while grievous wrongs have been inflicted upon the suffering people. We charge that the controlling influences dominating both these parties have permitted the existing dreadful conditions to develop without serious effort to prevent or restrain them.

Neither do they now promise us any substantial reform. They have agreed together to ignore, in the coming campaign, every issue but one. They propose to drown the outcries of a plundered people with the uproar of a sham battle over the tariff, so that capitalists, corporations, national banks, rings, trusts, watered stock, the demonetization of silver and the oppressions of the usurers may all be lost sight of. They propose to sacrifice our homes, lives, and children on the altar of mammon; to destroy the multitude in order to secure corruption funds from the millionaires.

UNIT 7: Period 7, 1890–1945

In less than one lifetime, Americans went from buggies to automobiles to airplanes. And in within three decades, they experienced two horrific wars and the worst depression in American history. Together, these events brought dramatic changes to how Americans lived and the role of their government.

Overview The era was shaped by continued industrialization, urbanization, and immigration. The role and size of government, especially on the federal level, expanded to meet the challenges of a boom-and-bust economy. However, this growth in government efforts to stabilize the economy and to assist the elderly and unemployed was controversial.

The federal government also grew in response to international affairs. When the United States went to war against Spain in 1898, the military was relatively small, and many people wanted to keep it that way. However, after fighting in two major world wars, the military had expanded, and it never returned to its pre-1898 size. The oceans that once kept the problems of Europe and Asia far from the United States no longer served that purpose. By 1945, the United States was the most powerful country in the world, both economically and politically.

Debates over the role of government, science and religion, culture and ethnic diversity created anxiety and conflicts. One extreme reaction to these changes was the rebirth of the Ku Klux Klan.

Alternate Views Historians who agree that this was a period of growth of government sometimes disagree on how to separate or combine events within it. For example, some see World War I and World II as distinct events, each with distinct causes. Other see them as two related events in a larger process of globalization. Similarly, some historians see the Progressive Era and the New Deal as separate events, with World War I and a conservative decade of the 1920s blocking any connection between them. Other historians view them as part of one larger reform movement.

20

BECOMING A WORLD POWER, 1865–1917

We are Anglo-Saxons, and must obey our blood and occupy new markets, and, if necessary, new lands.
Senator Albert Beveridge, April 27, 1898

Our form of government, our traditions, our present interests, and our future welfare, all forbid our entering upon a career of conquest.
William Jennings Bryan, December 13, 1898

Since the 1790s, U.S. foreign policy had centered on expanding westward, protecting U.S. interests abroad, and limiting foreign influences in the Americas. The period after the Civil War saw the development of a booming industrial economy, which created the basis for a major shift in U.S. relations with the rest of the world. Instead of a nation that—at least since the War of 1812— had been relatively isolated from European politics, the United States became a world power controlling territories in the Caribbean and extending across the Pacific to the Philippines. How and why did the United States acquire an overseas empire and intervene in the affairs of Cuba, Mexico, and other Latin American nations? The origins of these developments appear in the years just after the Civil War.

Seward, Alaska, and the French in Mexico

A leading Republican of the 1850s and 1860s, William H. Seward of New York served as secretary of state (1861–1869) under both Abraham Lincoln and Andrew Johnson. Seward was the most influential secretary of state since John Quincy Adams (who formulated the Monroe Doctrine in 1823). During the Civil War, Seward helped prevent Great Britain and France from entering the war on the side of the Confederacy. He led the drive to annex Midway Island in the Pacific, gained rights to build a canal in Nicaragua, and purchased the vast terriory of Alaska.

Though a powerful advocate for expansion, Seward did not get all he wanted. For example, he failed to convince Congress to annex Hawaii and to purchase the Danish West Indies.

The French in Mexico

Napoleon III (nephew of the famous emperor Napoleon Bonaparte) had taken advantage of U.S. involvement in the Civil War by sending French troops to occupy Mexico. As soon as the Civil War ended in 1865, Seward invoked the Monroe Doctrine and threatened U.S. military action unless the French withdrew. Napoleon III backed down, and the French troops left Mexico.

The Purchase of Alaska

For decades, Russia and Great Britain both claimed the vast territory of Alaska. Russia finally assumed control and established a small colony for seal hunting, but the territory soon became an economic burden because of the threat of a British takeover. Seeking buyers, Russia found Seward to be an enthusiastic champion of the idea of the United States purchasing Alaska. As result of Seward's lobbying, and also in appreciation of Russian support during the Civil War, Congress in 1867 agreed to buy Alaska for $7.2 million. However, for many years, Americans saw no value in Alaska and referred to it derisively as "Seward's Folly" or "Seward's Icebox."

The "New Imperialism"

As the United States industrialized in the late 19th century, it also intensified its foreign involvement, partly because it wanted both sources of raw materials for manufacturing and worldwide markets for its growing quantity of industrial and agricultural products. In addition, many conservatives hoped that overseas territories and adventures might offer a safety valve for unhappiness at home after the Panic of 1893. They were concerned about the growing violence of labor-management disputes and the unrest of farmers. For the most part, advocates of an expansionist policy hoped to achieve their ends by economic and diplomatic means, not by military action.

International Darwinism

Darwin's concept of the survival of the fittest was applied not only to competition in business but also to competition among nations and races for military advantage, colonies, and spheres of influence. Therefore, to demonstrate strength in the international arena, expansionists wanted to acquire territories overseas. They saw this expansion as an extension of the idea of manifest destiny into the Caribbean, Central America, and the Pacific Ocean.

Imperialism Americans were not alone in pursuing imperialism, which meant either acquiring territory or gaining control over the political or economic life of other countries. Britain, France, Germany, Russia, Japan, and other nations struggled to influence or possess weaker countries in Africa, Asia, and the Pacific Ocean. Some in the United States believed that the nation needed to compete with the imperialistic nations for new territory or it would be reduced to a second-class power. In the United States, advocates of American expansion included missionaries, politicians, naval strategists, and journalists.

Missionaries In his book *Our Country: Its Possible Future and Present Crisis* (1885), the Reverend Josiah Strong wrote that people of Anglo-Saxon stock were "the fittest to survive." He believed that Protestant Americans had a religious duty to colonize other lands in order to spread Christianity and the benefits of their "superior" civilization (medicine, science, and technology) to less fortunate peoples of the world. Many missionaries who traveled to Africa, Asia, and the Pacific islands believed in the racial superiority and natural supremacy of whites. Mission activities of their churches encouraged many Americans to support active U.S. government involvement in foreign affairs.

Politicians Many in the Republican party were closely allied with business leaders. Republican politicians therefore generally endorsed the use of foreign affairs to search for new markets. Congressional leaders such as Henry Cabot Lodge of Massachusetts and the Republican governor of New York, Theodore Roosevelt, were eager to build U.S. power through global expansion.

Naval Power U.S. Navy Captain Alfred Thayer Mahan wrote an important book, *The Influence of Sea Power Upon History* (1890), in which he argued that a strong navy was crucial to a country's ambitions of securing foreign markets and becoming a world power. Mahan's book was widely read by prominent American citizens—as well as by political leaders in Europe and Japan. Using arguments in Mahan's book, U.S. naval strategists persuaded Congress to finance the construction of modern steel ships and encouraged the acquisition of overseas islands, such as Samoa, that were desired as coaling and supply stations so that the new fleet could project its sea power around the world. By 1900, the United States had the third largest navy in the world.

Popular Press Newspaper and magazine editors found that they could increase circulation by printing adventure stories about distant and exotic places. Stories in the popular press increased public interest and stimulated demands for a larger U.S. role in world affairs.

Latin America

Beginning with the Monroe Doctrine in the 1820s, the United States had taken a special interest in problems of the Western Hemisphere and had assumed the role of protector of Latin America from European ambitions. Benjamin Harrison's Secretary of State James G. Blaine of Maine played a principal role in extending this tradition.

Blaine and the Pan-American Conference (1889) Blaine's repeated efforts to establish closer ties between the United States and its southern neighbors bore fruit in 1889 with the meeting of the first Pan-American Conference in Washington. Representatives from various nations of the Western Hemisphere decided to create a permanent organization for international cooperation on trade and other issues. Blaine had hoped to bring about reductions in tariff rates. Although this goal was not achieved, the foundation was established for the larger goal of hemispheric cooperation on both economic and political issues. The Pan-American Union continues today as part of the Organization of American States, which was established in 1948.

Cleveland, Olney, and the Monroe Doctrine One of the most important uses of the Monroe Doctrine in the 19th century concerned a boundary dispute between Venezuela and its neighbor—the British colony of Guiana. In 1895 and 1896, President Cleveland and Secretary of State Richard Olney insisted that Great Britain agree to arbitrate the dispute. The British initially said the matter was not the business of the United States. However, the United States argued that the Monroe Doctrine applied to the situation. If the British did not arbitrate, the United States would back up its argument with military force.

Deciding that U.S. friendship was more important to its long-term interests than a boundary dispute in South America, the British agreed to U.S. demands. As it turned out, the arbitrators ruled mainly in favor of Britain, not Venezuela. Even so, Latin American nations appreciated U.S. efforts to protect them from European domination. Most important, the Venezuela boundary dispute marked a turning point in U.S.–British relations. From 1895 on, the two countries cultivated a friendship rather than continuing their former rivalry. The friendship would prove vital for both nations in the 20th century.

The Spanish-American War

A principal target of American imperialism was the nearby Caribbean area. Expansionists from the South had coveted Cuba as early as the 1850s. Now, in the 1890s, large American investments in Cuban sugar, Spanish misrule of Cuba, and the Monroe Doctrine all provided justification for U.S. intervention in the Caribbean's largest island.

Causes of War

In the 1890s, American public opinion was being swept by a growing wave of *jingoism*—an intense form of nationalism calling for an aggressive foreign policy. Expansionists demanded that the United States take its place with the imperialist nations of Europe as a world power. Not everyone favored such a policy. Presidents Cleveland and McKinley were among many who thought military action abroad was both morally wrong and economically unsound. Nevertheless, specific events combined with background pressures led to overwhelming popular demand for war against Spain.

Cuban Revolt Cuban nationalists, after fighting but failing to overthrow Spanish colonial rule between 1868 and 1878, renewed the struggle in 1895. Through sabotage and laying waste to Cuban plantations, they hoped to either force Spain's withdrawal or pull in the United States as an ally. In response, Spain sent autocratic General Valeriano Weyler and over 100,000 troops to crush the revolt. Weyler forced civilians into armed camps, where tens of thousands died of starvation and disease, and gained him the title of "The Butcher" in the American press.

Yellow Press Actively promoting war fever in the United States was yellow journalism, sensationalistic reporting that featured bold and lurid headlines of crime, disaster, and scandal. Among the most sensationalistic were two New York newspapers, Joseph Pulitzer's World and William Randolph Hearst's *Journal,* which printed exaggerated and false accounts of Spanish atrocities in Cuba. Believing what they read daily in their newspapers, many Americans urged Congress and the president to intervene in Cuba for humanitarian reasons and put a stop to the atrocities and suffering.

De Lôme Letter (1898) One story that caused a storm of outrage was a Spanish diplomat's letter that was leaked to the press and printed on the front page of Hearst's *Journal.* Written by the Spanish minister to the United States, Dupuy de Lôme, the letter was highly critical of President McKinley. Many considered it an official Spanish insult against the U.S. national honor.

Sinking of the *Maine* Less than one week after the de Lôme letter made headlines, a far more shocking event occurred. On February 15, 1898, the U.S. battleship *Maine* was at anchor in the harbor of Havana, Cuba, when it suddenly exploded, killing 260 Americans on board. The yellow press accused Spain of deliberately blowing up the ship, even though experts later concluded that the explosion was probably an accident.

McKinley's War Message Following the sinking of the *Maine,* President McKinley issued an ultimatum to Spain demanding that it agree to a ceasefire in Cuba. Spain agreed to this demand, but U.S. newspapers and a majority in Congress kept clamoring for war. McKinley yielded to the public pressure in April by sending a war message to Congress. He offered four reasons for the United States to intervene in the Cuban revolution on behalf of the rebels:

1. "Put an end to the barbarities, bloodshed, starvation, and horrible miseries" in Cuba

2. Protect the lives and property of U.S. citizens living in Cuba

3. End "the very serious injury to the commerce, trade, and business of our people"

4. End "the constant menace to our peace" arising from disorder in Cuba

Teller Amendment Responding to the president's message, Congress passed a joint resolution on April 20 authorizing war. Part of the resolution, the Teller Amendment, declared that the United States had no intention of taking political control of Cuba and that, once peace was restored to the island, the Cuban people would control their own government.

Fighting the War

The first shots of the Spanish-American War were fired in Manila Bay in the Philippines, thousands of miles from Cuba. The last shots were fired only a few months later in August. So swift was the U.S. victory that Secretary of State John Hay called it "a splendid little war."

The Philippines Theodore Roosevelt, McKinley's assistant secretary of the navy, was an expansionist who was eager to show off the power of his country's new, all-steel navy. Anticipating war and recognizing the strategic value of Spain's territories in the Pacific, Roosevelt had ordered a fleet commanded by Commodore George Dewey to the Philippines. This large group of islands had been under Spanish control ever since the 1500s.

On May 1, shortly after war was declared, Commodore Dewey's fleet fired on Spanish ships in Manila Bay. The Spanish fleet was soon pounded into submission by U.S. naval guns. The fight on land took longer. Allied with Filipino rebels, U.S. troops captured the city of Manila on August 13.

Invasion of Cuba More troublesome than the Philippines was the U.S. effort in Cuba. An ill-prepared, largely volunteer force landed in Cuba by the end of June. Here the most lethal enemy proved to be not Spanish bullets but tropical diseases. More than 5,000 American soldiers died of malaria, typhoid, and dysentery, while fewer than 500 died in battle.

Attacks by both American and Cuban forces succeeded in defeating the much larger but poorly led Spanish army. Next to Dewey's victory in Manila Bay, the most celebrated event of the war was a cavalry charge up San Juan Hill in Cuba by the Rough Riders, a regiment of volunteers led by Theodore Roosevelt, who had resigned his navy post to take part in the war. Roosevelt's volunteers were aided in victory by veteran regiments of African Americans. Less heroic but more important than the taking of San Juan Hill was the success of the U.S. Navy in destroying the Spanish fleet at Santiago Bay on July 3. Without a navy, Spain realized that it could not continue fighting, and in early August 1898 asked for U.S. terms of peace.

Annexation of Hawaii

Since the mid-1800s, American missionaries and entrepreneurs had settled in the Pacific islands of Hawaii. Expansionists coveted the islands and, in 1893, American settlers aided in the overthrow of the Hawaiian monarch, Queen Liliuokalani. However, President Cleveland opposed imperialism and blocked Republican efforts to annex Hawaii. Then the outbreak of war in the Philippines gave Congress and President McKinley the pretext to complete annexation in July 1898. The Hawaiian islands became a territory of the United States in 1900 and the fiftieth state in the Union in August 1959.

Controversy Over the Treaty of Peace

Far more controversial than the war itself were the terms of the treaty of peace signed in Paris on December 10, 1898. It provided for (1) recognition of Cuban independence, (2) U.S. acquisition of two Spanish islands—Puerto Rico in the Caribbean and Guam in the Pacific, and (3) U.S. acquisition of the Philippines in return for payment to Spain of $20 million. Since the avowed purpose of the U.S. war effort was to liberate Cuba, Americans accepted this provision of the treaty. However, many were not prepared for taking over a large Pacific island nation, the Philippines, as a colony.

The Philippine Question Controversy over the Philippine question took many months longer to resolve than the brief war with Spain. Opinion both in Congress and the public at large became sharply divided between imperialists who favored annexing the Philippines and anti-imperialists who opposed it. In the Senate, where a two-thirds vote was required to ratify the Treaty of Paris, anti-imperialists were determined to defeat the treaty because of its provision for acquiring the Philippines. Anti-imperialists argued that, for the first time, the United States would be taking possession of a heavily populated area whose people were of a different race and culture. Such action, they thought, violated the principles of the Declaration of Independence by depriving Filipinos of the right to "life, liberty, and the pursuit of happiness," and also would entangle the United States in the political conflicts of Asia.

On February 6, 1899, the the Treaty of Paris (including Philippine annexation) came to a vote in Congress. The treaty was approved 57 to 27, just one vote more than the two-thirds majority required by the Constitution for ratification. The anti-imperialists fell just two votes short of defeating the treaty.

The people of the Philippines were outraged that their hopes for national independence from Spain were now being denied by the United States. Filipino nationalist leader Emilio Aguinaldo had fought alongside U.S. troops during the Spanish-American War. Now he led bands of guerrilla fighters in a war against U.S. control. It took U.S. troops three years and cost thousands of lives on both sides before the insurrection finally ended in 1902.

Other Results of the War

Imperialism remained a major issue in the United States even after ratification of the Treaty of Paris. An Anti-Imperialist League, led by William Jennings Bryan, rallied opposition to further acts of expansion in the Pacific.

Insular Cases. One question concerned the constitutional rights of the Philippine people: Did the Constitution follow the flag? In other words, did the provisions of the U.S. Constitution apply to whatever territories fell under

U.S. control, including the Philippines and Puerto Rico? Bryan and other anti-imperialists argued in the affirmative, while leading imperialists argued in the negative. The issue was resolved in favor of the imperialists in a series of Supreme Court cases (1901–1903) known as the insular (island) cases. The Court ruled that constitutional rights were not automatically extended to territorial possessions and that the power to decide whether or not to grant such rights belonged to Congress.

Cuba and the Platt Amendment (1901) Previously, the Teller Amendment to the war resolution of 1898 had guaranteed U.S. respect for Cuba's sovereignty as an independent nation. Nevertheless, U.S. troops remained in Cuba from 1898 until 1901. In the latter year, Congress made withdrawal of troops conditional upon Cuba's acceptance of terms included in an amendment to an army appropriations bill—the Platt Amendment of 1901. Bitterly resented by Cuban nationalists, the Platt Amendment required Cuba to agree (1) to never sign a treaty with a foreign power that impaired its independence, (2) to permit the United States to intervene in Cuba's affairs to preserve its independence and maintain law and order, and (3) to allow the U.S. to maintain naval bases in Cuba, including one permanent base at Guantanamo Bay.

A Cuban convention reluctantly accepted these terms, adding them to its country's new constitution. In effect, the Platt Amendment made Cuba a U.S. protectorate. As a result, Cuba's foreign policy would, for many years, be subject to U.S. oversight and control.

Election of 1900 The Republicans renominated President McKinley, along with war hero and New York Governor Theodore Roosevelt for vice president. The Democrats, as they had in 1896, nominated William Jennings Bryan. He again argued for free silver and vigorously attacked the growth of American imperialism. However, most Americans accepted the recently enacted gold standard and saw the new territory, including the Philippines, acquired during the war as an accomplished fact. With growing national economic prosperity, the electorate gave McKinley a larger margin of victory than in 1896.

Recognition of U.S. Power One consequence of the Spanish-American War was its effect on the way both Americans and Europeans thought about U.S. power. The decisive U.S. victory in the war filled Americans with national pride. Southerners shared in this pride and became more attached to the Union after their bitter experience in the 1860s. At the same time, France, Great Britain, and other European nations recognized that the United States was a first-class power with a strong navy and a new willingness to take an active role in international affairs.

Open Door Policy in China

Europeans were further impressed by U.S. involvement in global politics as a result of John Hay's policies toward China. As McKinley's secretary of state, Hay was alarmed that the Chinese empire, weakened by political corruption and failure to modernize, was falling under the control of various outside powers. In the 1890s, Russia, Japan, Great Britain, France, and Germany had all established *spheres of influence* in China, meaning that they could dominate trade and investment within their sphere (a particular port or region of China) and shut out competitors. To prevent the United States from losing access to the lucrative China trade, Hay dispatched a diplomatic note in 1899 to nations controlling spheres of influence. He asked them to accept the concept of an Open Door, by which all nations would have equal trading privileges in China. The replies to Hay's note were evasive. However, because no nation rejected the concept, Hay declared that all had accepted the Open Door policy. The press hailed Hay's initiative as a diplomatic triumph.

Boxer Rebellion (1900) As the 19th century ended, nationalism and *xenophobia* (hatred and fear of foreigners) were on the rise in China. In 1900, a secret society of Chinese nationalists—the Society of Harmonious Fists, or Boxers—attacked foreign settlements and murdered dozens of Christian missionaries. To protect American lives and property, U.S. troops participated in an international force that marched into Peking (Beijing) and quickly crushed the rebellion of the Boxers. The countries forced China to pay a huge sum in indemnities, which further weakened the imperial regime.

Hay's Second Round of Notes Hay feared that the expeditionary force in China might attempt to occupy the country and destroy its independence. In 1900, therefore, he wrote a second note to the imperialistic powers stating U.S. commitment to (1) preserve China's territorial integrity as well as (2) safeguard "equal and impartial trade with all parts of the Chinese empire." Hay's first and second notes set U.S. policy on China not only for the administrations of McKinley and Theodore Roosevelt but also for future presidents. In the 1930s, this Open Door policy for China would strongly influence U.S. relations with Japan.

Hay's notes in themselves did not deter other nations from exploiting the situation in China. For the moment, European powers were kept from grabbing larger pieces of China by the political rivalries among themselves.

Theodore Roosevelt's Big-Stick Policy

In 1901, only a few months after being inaugurated president for a second time, McKinley was fatally shot by an anarchist (person who opposed all government). Succeeding him in office was the Republican vice president—the young expansionist and hero of the Spanish-American War, Theodore Roosevelt. Describing his foreign policy, the new president had once said that it was his motto to "speak softly and carry a big stick." The press therefore applied the label "big stick" to Roosevelt's aggressive foreign policy. By acting boldly and decisively in a number of situations, Roosevelt attempted to build the reputation of the U.S. as a world power. Imperialists applauded his every move, but critics disliked breaking the tradition of noninvolvement in global politics.

The Panama Canal

As a result of the Spanish-American War, the new American empire stretched from Puerto Rico in the Caribbean to the Philippines in the Pacific. As a strategic necessity for holding on to these far-flung islands, the United States desired a canal through Central America to connect the Atlantic and Pacific oceans. However, building a canal would be difficult. The French had already failed to complete a canal through the tropic jungles. And before the United States could even try, it needed to negotiate an agreement with the British to abrogate (cancel) an earlier treaty of 1850 in which any canal in Central America was to be under joint British-U.S. control. This agreement, called the Hay-Pauncefote Treaty, was signed in 1901. With the British agreement to let United States build a canal alone, the young and activist President Roosevelt took charge.

Revolution in Panama Roosevelt was eager to begin the construction of a canal through the narrow but rugged terrain of the isthmus of Panama. He was frustrated, however, by Colombia's control of this isthmus and its refusal to agree to U.S. terms for digging the canal through its territory. Losing patience with Colombia's demands of more money and sovereignty over the canal, Roosevelt orchestrated a revolt for Panama's independence in 1903. With the support of the U.S. Navy, the rebellion succeeded immediately and almost without bloodshed. However, the new government of an independent Panama had to sign the Hay-Bunau-Varilla Treaty of 1903 granting the United States all rights over the 51-mile-long and 10-mile-wide Canal Zone as "if it were sovereign . . . in perpetuity" to keep U.S. protection. Years later, Roosevelt boasted, "I took Canal Zone and let Congress debate."

Building the Canal Started in 1904, the Panama Canal was completed in 1914. Hundreds of laborers lost their lives in the effort. The work was completed thanks in great measure to the skills of two Army colonels—George Goethals, the chief engineer of the canal, and Dr. William Gorgas, whose efforts eliminated the mosquitoes that spread deadly yellow fever.

Most Americans approved of Roosevelt's determination to build the canal, but many were unhappy with his high-handed tactics to secure the Canal Zone. Latin Americans were especially resentful. To compensate, Congress finally voted in 1921 to pay Colombia an indemnity of $25 million for its loss of Panama. In 1999, United States returned the Canal Zone to the Republic of Panama to end the growing bitterness over the original treaty (See Chapter 29).

The Roosevelt Corollary to the Monroe Doctrine

Another application of Roosevelt's big-stick diplomacy involved Latin American nations that were in deep financial trouble and could not pay their debts to European creditors. For example, in 1902, the British dispatched warships to Venezuela to force that country to pay its debts. In 1904, it appeared that European powers stood ready to intervene in Santo Domingo (the Dominican

Republic) for the same reason. Rather than let Europeans intervene in Latin America—a blatant violation of the Monroe Doctrine—Roosevelt declared in December 1904 that the United States would intervene instead, whenever necessary. This policy became known as the Roosevelt Corollary to the Monroe Doctrine. It meant that the United States would send gunboats to a Latin American country that was delinquent in paying its debts. U.S. sailors and marines would then occupy the country's major ports to manage the collection of customs taxes until European debts were satisfied.

Over the next 20 years, U.S. presidents used the Roosevelt Corollary to justify sending U.S. forces into Haiti, Honduras, the Dominican Republic, and Nicaragua. One long-term result of such interventions was poor U.S. relations with the entire region of Latin America.

East Asia

As the 20th century began, Japan and the United States were both relatively new imperialist powers in East Asia. Their relationship during Theodore Roosevelt's presidency, though at first friendly, grew increasingly competitive.

Russo-Japanese War Imperialist rivalry between Russia and Japan led to war in 1904, a war Japan was winning. To end the conflict, Roosevelt arranged a diplomatic conference between the two foes at Portsmouth, New Hampshire, in 1905. Although both Japan and Russia agreed to the Treaty of Portsmouth, Japanese nationalists blamed the United States for not giving their country all that they believed they deserved from Russia.

"Gentlemen's Agreement" A major cause of friction between Japan and the United States concerned the laws of California, which discriminated against Japanese Americans. San Francisco's practice of requiring Japanese American children to attend segregated schools was considered a national insult in Japan. In 1908, President Roosevelt arranged a compromise by means of an informal understanding, or "gentlemen's agreement." The Japanese government secretly agreed to restrict the emigration of Japanese workers to the United States in return for Roosevelt persuading California to repeal its discriminatory laws.

Great White Fleet To demonstrate U.S. naval power to Japan and other nations, Roosevelt sent a fleet of battleships on an around-the-world cruise (1907–1909). The great white ships made an impressive sight, and the Japanese government warmly welcomed their arrival in Tokyo Bay.

Root-Takahira Agreement (1908) An important executive agreement was concluded between the United States and Japan in 1908. Secretary of State Elihu Root and Japanese Ambassador Takahira exchanged notes pledging mutual respect for each nation's Pacific possessions and support for the Open Door policy in China.

Peace Efforts

Roosevelt saw his big-stick policies as a way to promote peaceful solutions to international disputes. For his work in settling the Russo-Japanese War, Roosevelt was awarded the Nobel Peace Prize in 1906. In the same year, he helped arrange and direct the Algeciras Conference in Spain, which succeeded in settling a conflict between France and Germany over claims to Morocco. The president also directed U.S. participation at the Second International Peace Conference at the Hague in 1907, which discussed rules for limiting warfare. As an expansionist, interventionist, and finally as an internationalist, Theodore Roosevelt embodied the vigor of a youthful nation arriving on world stage.

William Howard Taft and Dollar Diplomacy

Roosevelt's successor, William Howard Taft (1909–1913), did not carry a big stick. He adopted a foreign policy that was mildly expansionist but depended more on investors' dollars than on the navy's battleships. His policy of promoting U.S. trade by supporting American enterprises abroad was known as *dollar diplomacy*.

Dollar Diplomacy in East Asia and Latin America

Taft believed that private American financial investment in China and Central America would lead to greater stability there, while at the same time promoting U.S. business interests. His policy, however, was thwarted by one major obstacle: growing anti-imperialism both in the United States and overseas.

Railroads in China Taft first tested his policy in China. Wanting U.S. bankers to be included in a British, French, and German plan to invest in railroads in China, Taft succeeded in securing American participation in an agreement signed in 1911. In the northern province of Manchuria, however, the United States was excluded from an agreement between Russia and Japan to build railroads there. In direct defiance of the U.S. Open Door policy, Russia and Japan agreed to treat Manchuria as a jointly held sphere of influence.

Intervention in Nicaragua To protect American investments, the United States intervened in Nicaragua's financial affairs in 1911, and sent in marines when a civil war broke out in 1912. The marines remained, except for a short period, until 1933.

The Lodge Corollary

Henry Cabot Lodge, a Republican senator from Massachusetts, was responsible for another action that alienated both Latin America and Japan. A group of Japanese investors wanted to buy a large part of Mexico's Baja Peninsula, extending south of California. Fearing that Japan's government might be secretly scheming to acquire the land, Lodge introduced and the Senate in 1912 passed a resolution known as the Lodge Corollary to the Monroe Doctrine. The resolution stated that non-European powers (such as Japan) would be excluded from owning territory in the Western Hemisphere. President Taft opposed the corollary, which also offended Japan and angered Latin American countries.

Woodrow Wilson and Foreign Affairs

In his campaign for president in 1912, the Democratic candidate Woodrow Wilson called for a *New Freedom* in government and promised a moral approach to foreign affairs. Wilson said he opposed imperialism and the big-stick and dollar-diplomacy policies of his Republican predecessors.

Wilson's Moral Diplomacy

In his first term as president (1913–1917), Wilson had limited success applying a high moral standard to foreign relations. He and Secretary of State William Jennings Bryan hoped to demonstrate that the United States respected other nations' rights and would support the spread of democracy. Hoping to demonstrate that his presidency was opposed to self-interested imperialism, Wilson took steps to correct what he viewed as wrongful policies of the past.

U.S. TERRITORIES AND PROTECTORATES, 1917

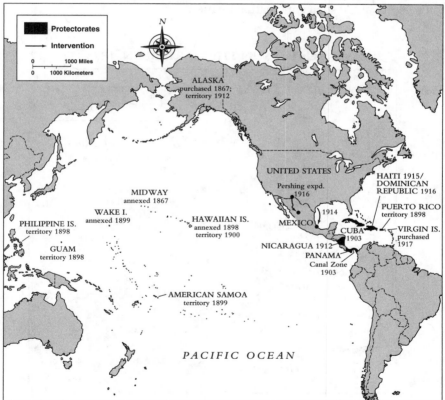

The Philippines Wilson won passage of the Jones Act of 1916, which (1) granted full territorial status to that country, (2) guaranteed a bill of rights and universal male suffrage to Filipino citizens, and (3) promised independence for the Philippines as soon as a stable government was established.

Puerto Rico An act of Congress in 1917 granted U.S. citizenship to all the inhabitants and also provided for limited self-government.

The Panama Canal Wilson persuaded Congress in 1914 to repeal an act that had granted U.S. ships an exemption from paying the standard canal tolls charged other nations. Wilson's policy on Panama Canal tolls angered American nationalists such as Roosevelt and Lodge but pleased the British, who had strongly objected to the U.S. exemption.

Conciliation Treaties Wilson's commitment to the ideals of democracy and peace was fully shared by his famous secretary of state, William Jennings Bryan. Bryan's pet project was to negotiate treaties in which nations pledged to (1) submit disputes to international commissions and (2) observe a one-year cooling-off period before taking military action. Bryan arranged, with Wilson's approval, 30 such conciliation treaties.

U.S. INTERVENTION IN THE CARIBBEAN, 1898 TO 1917

Military Intervention Under Wilson

Wilson's commitement to democracy and anticolonialm had a blind spot with respect to the Mexico and countries of Central America and the Caribbean. He went far beyond both Roosevelt and Taft in his use of U.S. marines to straighten out financial and political troubles in the region. He kept marines in Nicaragua and ordered U.S. troops into Haiti in 1915 and the Dominican Republic in 1916. He argued that such intervention was necessary to maintain stability in the region and protect the Panama Canal.

Wilson's moral approach to foreign affairs was severely tested by a revolution and civil war in Mexico. As a supporter of democracy, Wilson refused to recognize the military dictatorship of General Victoriano Huerta, who had seized power in 1913 by having the democratically elected president killed.

Tampico Incident To aid revolutionaries fighting Huerta, Wilson called for an arms embargo against the Mexican government and sent a fleet to blockade the port of Vera Cruz. In 1914, several U.S. sailors went ashore at Tampico where they were arrested by Mexican authorities. They were soon released. However, Huerta refused to apologize, as demanded by a U.S. naval officer. Wilson retaliated by ordering the U.S. Navy to occupy Veracruz. War seemed imminent. It was averted, however, when South America's ABC powers—Argentina, Brazil, and Chile—offered to mediate the dispute. This was the first dispute in the Americas to be settled through joint mediation.

Pancho Villa and the U.S. Expeditionary Force Huerta fell from power in late 1914. Replacing him was a more democratic regime led by Venustiano Carranza. Almost immediately, the new government was challenged by a band of rebels loyal to Pancho Villa. Hoping to destabilize his opponent's government, Villa led raids across the U.S.–Mexican border and murdered several people in Texas and New Mexico. In March 1916, President Wilson ordered General John J. Pershing and an "expeditionary force" to pursue Villa into northern Mexico. They failed to capture Villa. President Carranza protested the American presence in Mexico. In January 1917, the growing possibility of U.S. entry into World War I caused Wilson to withdraw Pershing's troops.

For most of the 20th century, historians writing on U.S. emergence as a world power stressed economic motives as the principal reason for the imperialism. Whether explaining the Spanish-American War or later actions, historians such as William Appelman Williams and Walter La Feber focused on U.S. desires for overseas markets, raw materials, and investments.

Some historians have challenged this economic explanation of U.S. imperialism. In the Spanish-American War, historians note that business interests initially opposed U.S. intervention in Cuba because they feared that it would disrupt commerce. Only later did bankers and manufactures support the war as a stabilizing influence. The change in view may have occurred only after war had started.

Other critics of the economic interpretation of imperialism stress the importance of noneconomic motives. Influenced by shocking stories in the yellow press, Americans public opinion seemed to express genuine humanitarian impulses—and also nationalistic outrage over the sinking of the *Maine*. Other historians, studying the motives of nationalist leaders like Theodore Roosevelt and Henry Cabot Lodge, have concluded that their chief interest was in establishing U.S. power on the world stage. In securing U.S. control of the Philippines, Roosevelt's role was crucial, and he was motivated by strategic considerations (establishing a naval base in the Pacific), not by economics. In response, those stressing economic motives argue that, even if Roosevelt had not ordered Dewey to Manila Bay, the Philippines would soon have become a target of U.S. ambitions.

Other historians believe that a new generation of foreign-policy makers had come to power around 1900. These talented leaders— chiefly Theodore Roosevelt and Woodrow Wilson—were critical of the mediocre leadership in Washington in the post-Civil War years and were eager to take bold new directions. Historians taking this view portray Theodore Roosevelt as a realist who saw diplomacy as a question of balance-of-power politics, as opposed to the idealist, Woodrow Wilson, who approached foreign policy as a matter of morals and legality.

Historian Richard Hofstadter interpreted the Spanish-American War from the perspective of social psychology. He argued that the popular support for war resulted from a psychic crisis in the nation. In Hofstadter's view, the American people were expressing aggression built up by economic depressions, the closing of the frontier, the rise of big business, and fears of labor radicalism.

KEY TERMS BY THEME

Overseas Involvement (WOR)
William Seward
Monroe Doctrine
French in Mexico
Alaska purchase (1867)
Pan-American Conference (1889)
James Blaine
Venezuela boundary dispute
Cleveland and Olney
Hawaii
Pearl Harbor
Queen Liliuokalani
Cleveland blocks annexation

Causes of U.S. Imperialism (WOR, NAT)
international Darwinism
business and imperialist competitors
spreading religion and science
Josiah Strong
expansionist politicians
steel and steam navy
Alfred Thayer Mahan
nationalist media

Spanish-American War, (WOR, POL)
Cuban revolt
Valeriano Weyler
"jingoism"
"yellow journalism"
De Lôme Letter
sinking of the *Maine*
Teller Amendment
"a splendid little war"
invade the Philippines

George Dewey
Rough Riders
Theodore Roosevelt
Treaty of Paris: Puerto Rico
Guam and Philippines annexation dispute
Emilio Aguinaldo
Anti-Imperialist League
Insular cases
Platt Amendment (1901)

China Policy (WOR)
spheres of influence
John Hay
Open Door policy
Boxer Rebellion
U.S. joined international force
Second Hay Note

TR Policies (WOR)
"big-stick policy"
TR supports Panama revolt
Hay-Bunau-Varilla Treaty (1903)
building the Panama Canal
George Goethals
William Gorgas
Roosevelt Corollary
Santo Domingo
Russo-Japanese War
Treaty of Portsmouth (1905)

Noble Peace Prize (1906)
segregation in San Francisco schools
gentlemen's agreement
Great White Fleet
Algeciras Conference (1906)
Hague Conference 1907)
Root-Takahira Agreement (1908)

Dollar Diplomacy (WOR, WXT)
William Howard Taft
role of American money
railroads in China
Manchurian problem
intervention in Nicaragua
Henry Cabot Lodge
Lodge Corollary

Moral Diplomacy (WOR)
Woodrow Wilson
anti-imperialism
William Jennings Bryan
Jones Act (1916)
Puerto Rico citizenship
Conciliation treaties
military intervention
Mexican civil war
General Huerta
Tampico incident
ABC powers
Pancho Villa
expeditionary force
John J. Pershing

Questions 1–3 refer to the newspaper below.

Source: *New York Journal,* February 17, 1898. The Granger Collection, NYC

1. Newspaper headlines such as those above most directly contributed to which of the following?
   (A) The capture of the terrorists by American authorities
   (B) The selection of Theodore Roosevelt as a vice-presidential candidate
   (C) The declaration of war against Spain by the U.S. Congress
   (D) The attack by the U.S. Navy on Manila Bay

2. Who of the following would most strongly support the sentiments in these headlines?
   (A) Members of Protestant missionary societies
   (B) Midwestern and western Democrats
   (C) President William McKinley
   (D) Expansionists such as Henry Cabot Lodge

3. The point of view of this newspaper most clearly reflects
   (A) the theory of the safety-valve
   (B) the concept of jingoism
   (C) the idea of isolationism
   (D) the views of the pro-business lobby

Questions 4–6 refer to the excerpt below.

"We hold that the policy known as imperialism is hostile to liberty and tends toward militarism, an evil from which it has been our glory to be free. We regret that it has become necessary in the land of Washington and Lincoln to reaffirm that all men, of whatever race or color, are entitled to life, liberty, and the pursuit of happiness. . . .

"We earnestly condemn the policy of the present national administration in the Philippines. It seeks to extinguish the spirit of 1776 in those islands. . . . We denounce the slaughter of the Filipinos as a needless horror. We protest against the extension of American sovereignty by Spanish methods. We demand the immediate cessation of the war against liberty, begun by Spain and continued by us. We urge that Congress be promptly convened to announce to the Filipinos our purpose to concede to them the independence for which they have so long fought and which of right is theirs."

—Platform of the American Anti-Imperialist League, October 17, 1899

4. With which of the following would supporters of this excerpt most likely agree?
   (A) The peoples of Asia had a right to govern themselves without outside interference.
   (B) The United States had a duty to bring a new civilization and religion to the former Spanish colonies.
   (C) The people of the Philippines were unprepared and unfit to govern themselves.
   (D) The United States should control weak countries that might fall to other great powers.

5. Which of the following most directly contributed to the anti-imperialist sentiments expressed in the excerpt?
   (A) The sensationalism of the popular press of the time
   (B) The provisions of the peace treaty ending the Spanish-American War
   (C) The expansionist politics of Theodore Roosevelt and Henry Cabot Lodge
   (D) The debate over the Platt Amendment and its consequences

6. Which of the following represents a policy that the authors of the excerpt would most likely support?
   (A) Secretary John Hay's Open Door Policy
   (B) President Roosevelt's "gentlemen's agreement"
   (C) President Taft's "dollar diplomacy"
   (D) President Wilson's signing of the Jones Act in 1916

Questions 7–8 refer to the excerpt below.

"Chronic wrongdoing, or an impotence which results in a general loosening of the ties of civilized society, may in America, as elsewhere, ultimately require intervention by some civilized nation, and in the Western Hemisphere the adherence of the United States to the Monroe Doctrine may force the United States, however reluctantly, in flagrant cases of such wrongdoing or impotence, to the exercise of international police power . . .

"We would interfere with them only in the last resort, and then only if it became evident that their inability or unwillingness to do justice at home and abroad had violated the rights of the United States or has invited foreign aggression to the detriment of the entire body of American nations."

—Theodore Roosevelt, Speech to Congress, Dec. 6, 1904

7. This excerpt most directly reflects the continuation of the policy that
   (A) the United States should remain neutral and impartial in European conflicts
   (B) the United States should exercise international police power
   (C) the independent nations of the Americas should remain free from European intervention
   (D) the United States should civilize and educate other nations in the Americas

8. Which of the following was the most direct result of the policy stated in this excerpt?
   (A) The United States aided the Cuban rebels against their Spanish rulers
   (B) The United States intervened in many American countries in the early 20th century
   (C) U.S. troops helped American settlers overthrow the monarchy in Hawaii
   (D) President Roosevelt was awarded the Nobel Peace Prize in 1906

SHORT-ANSWER QUESTIONS

Use complete sentences; an outline or bulleted list alone is not acceptable.

Question 1. Answer (A), (B), and (C).

(A) Briefly explain ONE historical event or development that supports the view that humanitarian concerns caused the Spanish-American War.

(B) Briefly explain ONE historical event or development that supports the view that imperialist motives caused the Spanish-American War.

(C) Briefly explain ONE historical event or development that supports the view that the Spanish-American War caused changes in American foreign policy.

Question 2 is based on the excerpts below.

"Theodore Roosevelt, who was widely traveled, easily ranks as the most internationally minded President of his generation. He understood the role of the United States in the world of power politics more clearly than any of his predecessors and most of his successors. . . . He is far better known for his efforts at peacemaking than at warmaking. And, what is more, he deserved this acclaim."

—Thomas B. Bailey, *A Diplomatic History of the American People,* 1974

"[Theodore Roosevelt was] a person of his times. . . . He hailed the advance of Western and especially Anglo-Saxon civilization as world movement, the key to peace and progress. . . . He viewed "barbaric" people as the major threat to civilization and had no difficulty rationalizing the use of force to keep them in line. . . . He was less clear how to keep peace among the so-called civilized nations."

—George C. Herring, historian, *From Colony to Superpower,* 2008

2. Using the excerpts above, answer (A), (B), and (C).

(A) Briefly describe ONE major difference between Bailey's and Herring's historical interpretation of Theodore Roosevelt's foreign policy.

(B) Briefly explain ONE specific historical event or development that is not explicitly mentioned in the excerpts that could be used to support Bailey's interpretation of Theodore Roosevelt's foreign policy.

(C) Briefly explain ONE specific historical event or development that is not explicitly mentioned in the excerpts that could be used to support Herring's interpretation of Theodore Roosevelt's foreign policy.

Question 3. Answer (A), (B), and (C). *continued on the next page*

(A) Briefly explain ONE specific historical event or development that improved American-British relations from 1865 to 1917.

(B) Briefly explain ONE specific historical event or development that worsened American-Japanese relations from 1865 to 1917.

(C) Briefly explain ONE specific historical event or development that shaped American-Mexican relations from 1865 to 1917.

Question 4 is based on the cartoon below.

Source: 1914,
The Granger
Collection, NYC

4. Using the cartoon, answer (A), (B), and (C). The teacher represents Woodrow Wilson. The board says, "We can have no sympathy with those who seek to seize the power of government to advance their own personal interests or ambition." The hats say Venezuela, Nicaragua, and Mexico.

   (A) Briefly explain ONE perspective expressed by the artist about Woodrow Wilson's foreign policy.

   (B) Briefly explain ONE specific event or development that contributed to this perspective during the Woodrow Wilson administration.

   (C) Briefly explain ONE difference or similarity between the policies of Wilson and either Theodore Roosevelt or William Howard Taft.

THINK AS A HISTORIAN: CHOOSING A POSITION ABOUT CONTINUITY

Which events listed below indicate that American foreign policy after 1896 was a continuation of earlier policies and which that it was a change from them?

1. Washington's Farewell Address

2. Monroe Doctrine

3. Treaty of Guadalupe Hidalgo

4. Kanagawa Treaty

5. Purchase of Alaska

21

THE PROGRESSIVE ERA, 1901–1917

I am, therefore, a Progressive because we have not kept up with our own changes of conditions, either in the economic field or in the political field. We have not kept up as well as other nations have. We have not adjusted our practices to the facts of the case. . . .

Woodrow Wilson, campaign speech, 1912

Large-scale industrialization, immigration, and urban expansion changed the United States dramatically during the last quarter of the 19th century. (See Chapters 16, 18, and 19.) By the turn of the century, a reform movement had developed that included a wide range of groups and individuals with a common desire to improve life in the industrial age. Their ideas and work became known as *progressivism,* because they wanted to build on the existing society, making moderate political changes and social improvements through government action. Most Progressives were not revolutionaries but shared the goals of limiting the power of big business, improving democracy for the people, and strengthening social justice. Achieving these goals often included a more active role for the federal government. This chapter will examine the origins, efforts, and accomplishments of the Progressive era. While Progressives did not cure all of America's problems, they improved the quality of life, provided a larger role for the people in their democracy, and established a precedent for a more active role for the federal government.

Origins of Progressivism

Although the Progressive movement had its origins in the state reforms of the early 1890s, it acquired national momentum only with the dawn of a new century and the unexpected swearing into office of a young president, Theodore Roosevelt, in 1901. The Progressive era lasted through the Republican presidencies of Roosevelt (1901–1909) and William Howard Taft (1909–1913), and the first term of the Democrat Woodrow Wilson (1913–1917). U.S. entry into World War I in 1917 diverted public attention away from domestic issues and brought the era to an end—but not before major regulatory laws had been enacted by Congress and various state legislatures.

Attitudes and Motives

As they entered a new century, most Americans were well aware of rapid changes in their country. The relatively homogeneous, rural society of independent farmers of the past was transforming into an industrialized nation of mixed ethnicity centered in the growing cities. For decades, middle-class Americans had been alarmed by the rising power of big business, the uncertainties of business cycles, the increasing gap between rich and poor, the violent conflict between labor and capital, and the dominance of corrupt political machines in the cities. Most disturbing to minorities were the racist Jim Crow laws in the South that relegated African Americans to the status of second-class citizens. Crusaders for women's suffrage added their voices to the call for greater democracy.

Who Were the Progressives? The groups participating in the Progressive movement were extremely diverse. Protestant church leaders championed one set of reforms, African Americans proposed other reforms, union leaders sought public support for their goals, and feminists lobbied their state legislatures for votes for women. Loosely linking these reform efforts under a single label, Progressive, was a belief that society badly needed changes and that government was the proper agency for correcting social and economic ills.

Urban Middle Class Unlike the Populists of the 1890s, whose strength came from rural America, most Progressives were middle-class men and women who lived in cities. The urban middle class had steadily grown in the final decades of the 19th century. In addition to doctors, lawyers, ministers, and storekeepers (the heart of the middle class in an earlier era), thousands of white-collar office workers and middle managers employed in banks, manufacturing firms, and other businesses formed a key segment of the economy.

Professional Class Members of this business and professional middle class took their civic responsibilities seriously. Some were versed in scientific and statistical methods and the findings of the new social sciences. They belonged to the hundreds of national business and professional associations that provided platforms to address corrupt business and government practices and urban social and economic problems.

Religion A missionary spirit inspired some middle-class reformers. Protestant churches preached against vice and taught a code of social responsibility, which included caring for the less fortunate and insisting on honesty in public life. The Social Gospel popularized by Walter Rauschenbusch (see Chapter 18) was an important element in Protestant Christians' response to the problem of urban poverty. Most of these Protestants were native-born and older stock Americans, often from families of older elites who felt that their central role in society had been replaced by wealthy industrialists and urban political machines.

Leadership Without strong leadership, the diverse forces of reform could not have overcome conservatives' resistance to change. Fortunately for the Progressives, a number of dedicated and able leaders entered politics at the turn of the century to challenge the status quo. Theodore Roosevelt and Robert La Follette in the Republican party and William Jennings Bryan and Woodrow Wilson in the Democratic party demonstrated a vigorous style of political leadership that had been lacking from national politics during the Gilded Age.

The Progressives' Philosophy The reform impulse was hardly new. In fact, many historians see progressivism as just one more phase in a reform tradition going back to the Jeffersonians in the early 1800s, the Jacksonians in the 1830s, and the Populists in the 1890s. Without doubt, the Progressives—like American reformers before them—were committed to democratic values and shared in the belief that honest government and just laws could improve the human condition.

Pragmatism A revolution in thinking occurred at the same time as the Industrial Revolution. Charles Darwin, in his *Origin of Species,* presented the concept of evolution, which had an impact well beyond simply justifying the accumulation of wealth (see Chapter 16). The way people thought and reasoned was challenged, and the prevailing philosophy of romantic transcendentalism in America gave way to a balanced *pragmatism.* In the early 20th century, William James and John Dewey were two leading American advocates of this new philosophy. They defined "truth" in a way that many Progressives found appealing. James and Dewey argued that the "good" and the "true" could not be known in the abstract as fixed and changeless ideals. Rather, they said, people should take a pragmatic, or practical, approach to morals, ideals, and knowledge. They should experiment with ideas and laws and test them in action until they found something that would produce a well-functioning democratic society.

Progressive thinkers adopted the new philosophy of pragmatism because it enabled them to challenge fixed notions that stood in the way of reform. For example, they rejected laissez-faire theory as impractical. The old standard of rugged individualism no longer seemed viable in a modern society dominated by impersonal corporations.

Scientific Management Another idea that gained widespread acceptance among Progressives came from the practical studies of Frederick W. Taylor. By using a stopwatch to time the output of factory workers, Taylor discovered ways of organizing people in the most efficient manner—the scientific management system. Many Progressives believed that government too could be made more efficient if placed in the hands of experts and scientific managers. They objected to the corruption of political bosses partly because it was anti-democratic and partly because it was an inefficient way to run things.

The Muckrakers

Before the public could be roused to action, it first had to be well-informed about the scandalous realities of politics, factories, and slums. Newspaper and magazine publishers found that their middle-class readers loved to read about underhanded schemes in politics. Therefore, many publications featured in-depth, investigative stories. Writers specializing in such stories were referred to as "muckrakers" by President Theodore Roosevelt.

Origins One of the earliest muckrakers was Chicago reporter Henry Demarest Lloyd, who in 1881 wrote a series of articles for the *Atlantic Monthly* attacking the practices of the Standard Oil Company and the railroads. Published in book form in 1894, Lloyd's *Wealth Against Commonwealth* fully exposed the corruption and greed of the oil monopoly but failed to suggest how to control it.

Magazines An Irish immigrant, Samuel Sidney McClure, founded *McClure's Magazine* in 1893, which became a major success by running a series of muckraking articles by Lincoln Steffens (*Tweed Days in St. Louis,* 1902) and another series by Ida Tarbell (*The History of the Standard Oil Company,* also in 1902). Combining careful research with sensationalism, these articles set a standard for the deluge of muckraking that followed. Popular 10- and 15-cent magazines such as *McClure's, Collier's,* and *Cosmopolitan* competed fiercely to outdo their rivals with shocking exposés of political and economic corruption.

Books The most popular series of muckraking articles were usually collected and published as best-selling books. Articles on tenement life by Jacob Riis, one of the first photojournalists, were published as *How the Other Half Lives* (1890). Lincoln Steffens' *The Shame of the Cities* (1904) also caused a sensation by describing in detail the corrupt deals that characterized big-city politics from Philadelphia to Minneapolis.

Many of the muckraking books were novels. Two of Theodore Dreiser's novels, *The Financier* and *The Titan,* portrayed the avarice and ruthlessness of an industrialist. Fictional accounts such as Frank Norris' *The Octopus* (on the tyrannical power of railroad companies) and *The Pit* (grain speculation) were more effective than many journalistic accounts in stirring up public demands for government regulations.

Decline of Muckraking The popularity of muckraking books and magazine articles began to decline after 1910 for several reasons. First, writers found it more and more difficult to top the sensationalism of the last story. Second, publishers were expanding and faced economic pressures from banks and advertisers to tone down their treatment of business. Third, by 1910 corporations were becoming more aware of their public image and developing a new specialty: the field of public relations. Nevertheless, muckraking had a lasting effect on the Progressive era. It exposed inequities, educated the public about corruption in high places, and prepared the way for corrective action.

Political Reforms in Cities and States

The cornerstone of Progressive ideology was faith in democracy. Progressives believed that, given a chance, the majority of voters would elect honest officials instead of the corrupt ones backed by boss-dominated political machines.

Voter Participation

Progressives advocated a number of reforms for increasing the participation of the average citizen in political decision-making.

Australian, or Secret, Ballot Political parties could manipulate and intimidate voters by printing lists (or "tickets") of party candidates and watching voters drop them into the ballot box on election day. In 1888, Massachusetts was the first state to adopt a system successfully tried in Australia of issuing ballots printed by the state and requiring voters to mark their choices secretly within a private booth. By 1910, all states had adopted the secret ballot.

Direct Primaries In the late 19th century, Republicans and Democrats commonly nominated candidates for state and federal offices in state conventions dominated by party bosses. In 1903, the Progressive governor of Wisconsin, Robert La Follette, introduced a new system for bypassing politicians and placing the nominating process directly in the hands of the voters—the direct primary. By 1915, some form of the direct primary was used in every state. The system's effectiveness in overthrowing boss rule was limited, as politicians devised ways of confusing the voters and splitting the antimachine vote. Some southern states even used white-only primaries to exclude African Americans from voting.

Direct Election of U.S. Senators Traditionally, U.S. senators had been chosen by the state legislatures rather than by direct vote of the people. Progressives believed this was a principal reason that the Senate had become a millionaires' club dominated by big business. Nevada in 1899 was the first state to give the voters the opportunity to elect U.S. senators directly. By 1912, a total of 30 states had adopted this reform, and in 1913, adoption of the 17th Amendment required that all U.S. senators be elected by popular vote.

Initiative, Referendum, and Recall If politicians in the state legislatures balked at obeying the "will of the people," then Progressives proposed two methods for forcing them to act. Amendments to state constitutions offered voters (1) the *initiative*—a method by which voters could compel the legislature to consider a bill and (2) the *referendum*—a method that allowed citizens to vote on proposed laws printed on their ballots. A third Progressive measure, the *recall,* enabled voters to remove a corrupt or unsatisfactory politician from office by majority vote before that official's term had expired.

Between 1898, when South Dakota adopted the initiative and referendum, and 1918 (the end of World War I), a total of 20 states—most of them west of the Mississippi—offered voters the initiative and the referendum, while 11 states offered the recall.

Municipal Reform

City bosses and their corrupt alliance with local businesses (trolley lines and utility companies, for example) were the first target of Progressive leaders. In Toledo, Ohio, in 1897, a self-made millionaire with strong memories of his origins as a workingman became the Republican mayor. Adopting "golden rule" as both his policy and his middle name, Mayor Samuel M. "Golden Rule" Jones delighted Toledo's citizens by introducing a comprehensive program of municipal reform, including free kindergartens, night schools, and public playgrounds. Another Ohioan, Tom L. Johnson, devoted himself to tax reform and three-cent trolley fares for the people of Cleveland. As Cleveland's mayor from 1901–1909, Johnson fought hard—but without success—for public ownership and operation of the city's public utilities and services (water, electricity, and trolleys).

Controlling Public Utilities Reform leaders arose in other cities throughout the nation seeking to break the power of the city bosses and take utilities out of the hands of private companies. By 1915 fully two-thirds of the nation's cities owned their own water systems. As a result of the Progressives' efforts, many cities also came to own and operate gas lines, electric power plants, and urban transportation systems.

Commissions and City Managers New types of municipal government were another Progressive innovation. In 1900, Galveston, Texas, was the first city to adopt a commission plan of government, in which voters elected the heads of city departments (fire, police, and sanitation), not just the mayor. Ultimately proving itself more effective than the commission plan was a system first tried in Dayton, Ohio, in 1913, in which an expert manager was hired by an elected city council to direct the work of the various departments of city government. By 1923, more than 300 cities had adopted the manager-council plan of municipal government.

State Reform

At the state level, reform governors battled corporate interests and championed such measures as the initiative, the referendum, and the direct primary to give common people control of their own government. In New York, Charles Evans Hughes battled fraudulent insurance companies. In California, Hiram Johnson successfully fought against the economic and political power of the Southern Pacific Railroad. In Wisconsin, Robert La Follette established a strong personal following as the governor (1900–1904) who won passage of the "Wisconsin Idea"—a series of Progressive measures that included a direct primary law, tax reform, and state regulatory commissions to monitor railroads, utilities, and business such as insurance.

Temperance and Prohibition Whether or not to shut down saloons and prohibit the drinking of alcohol was one issue over which the champions of reform were sharply divided. While urban Progressives recognized that saloons were often the neighborhood headquarters of political machines, they generally had little sympathy for the temperance movement. Rural reformers, on the other hand, thought they could clean up morals and politics in one stroke by abolishing liquor. The drys (prohibitionists) were determined and well organized. By 1915, they had persuaded the legislatures of two-thirds of the states to prohibit the sale of alcoholic beverages.

Social Welfare Urban life in the Progressive era was improved not only by political reformers but also by the efforts of settlement house workers (see Chapter 18) and other civic-minded volunteers. Jane Addams, Florence Kelley, and other leaders of the social justice movement found that they needed political support in the state legislatures for meeting the needs of immigrants and the working class. They lobbied vigorously and with considerable success for better schools, juvenile courts, liberalized divorce laws, and safety regulations for tenements and factories. Believing that criminals could learn to become effective citizens, reformers fought for such measures as a system of parole, separate reformatories for juveniles, and limits on the death penalty.

Child and Women Labor Progressives were most outraged by the treatment of children by industry. The National Child Labor Committee proposed model state child labor laws that were passed by two-thirds of the states by 1907. Ultimately state compulsory school attendance laws proved most effective in keeping children out of the mines and factories.

Florence Kelley and the National Consumers' League promoted the passage of state laws to protect women from long working hours. While in *Lochner v. New York* (1905) the Supreme Court ruled against a state law limiting workers to a ten-hour workday, later in *Muller v. Oregon* (1908) the high court ruled that health of women needed special protection from long hours. The Triangle Shirtwaist fire (1911) in a New York City high-rise garment factory took 146 lives, mostly women. The tragedy sparked greater women's activism and motivated states to pass laws to improve safety and working conditions in factories. One unforeseen consequence of efforts to protect women in the workplace was that the legislation kept women out of physically demanding but higher paying jobs in industry and mining. Later, many in the women's movement wanted these restrictions lifted so that women could compete as equals with men.

Political Reform in the Nation

While Progressive governors and mayors were battling conservative forces in the state houses and city halls, three presidents—Roosevelt, Taft, and Wilson—sought broad reforms and regulations at the national level.

Theodore Roosevelt's Square Deal

Following President McKinley's assassination in September 1901, Theodore Roosevelt became, at the age of 42, the youngest president in U.S. history. He was also one of the most athletic. He was unusual not simply because of his age and vigor but also because he believed that the president should do much more than lead the executive departments. He thought it was the president's job to set the legislative agenda for Congress as well. Thus, by the accident of McKinley's death, the Progressive movement suddenly shot into high gear under the dynamic leadership of an activist, reform-minded president.

"Square Deal" for Labor Presidents in the 19th century had consistently taken the side of owners in conflicts with labor (most notably Hayes in the railroad strike of 1877 and Cleveland in the Pullman strike of 1894). However, in the first economic crisis in his presidency, Roosevelt quickly demonstrated that he favored neither business nor labor but insisted on a *Square Deal* for both. The crisis involved a strike of anthracite coal miners through much of 1902. If the strike continued, many Americans feared that—without coal—they would freeze to death when winter came. Roosevelt took the unusual step of trying to mediate the labor dispute by calling a union leader and coal mine owners to the White House. The mine owners' stubborn refusal to compromise angered the president. To ensure the delivery of coal to consumers, he threatened to take over the mines with federal troops. The owners finally agreed to accept the findings of a special commission, which granted a 10 percent wage increase and a nine-hour workday to the miners. However, the owners did not have to recognize the union.

Voters seemed to approve of Roosevelt and his Square Deal. They elected him by a landslide in 1904.

Trust-Busting Roosevelt further increased his popularity by being the first president since the passage of the Sherman Antitrust Act in 1890 to enforce that poorly written law. The trust that he most wanted to bust was a combination of railroads known as the Northern Securities Company. Reversing its position in earlier cases, the Supreme Court in 1904 upheld Roosevelt's action in breaking up the railroad monopoly. Roosevelt later directed his attorney general to take antitrust action against Standard Oil and more than 40 other large corporations. Roosevelt did make a distinction between breaking up "bad trusts," which harmed the public and stifled competition, and regulating "good trusts," which through efficiency and low prices dominated a market.

Railroad Regulation President Roosevelt also took the initiative in persuading a Republican majority in Congress to pass two laws that significantly strengthened the regulatory powers of the Interstate Commerce Commission (ICC). Under the Elkins Act (1903), the ICC had greater authority to stop railroads from granting rebates to favored customers. Under the Hepburn Act (1906), the commission could fix "just and reasonable" rates for railroads.

Consumer Protection *The Jungle,* a muckraking book by Upton Sinclair, described in horrifying detail the conditions in the Chicago stockyards and meatpacking industry. The public outcry following the publication of Sinclair's novel caused Congress to enact two regulatory laws in 1906:

1. The *Pure Food and Drug Act* forbade the manufacture, sale, and transportation of adulterated or mislabeled foods and drugs.

2. The *Meat Inspection Act* provided that federal inspectors visit meatpacking plants to ensure that they met minimum standards of sanitation.

Conservation As a lover of the wilderness and the outdoor life, Roosevelt enthusiastically championed the cause of conservation. In fact, Roosevelt's most original and lasting contribution in domestic policy may have been his efforts to protect the nation's natural resources. Three actions were particularly important.

1. Roosevelt made repeated use of the Forest Reserve Act of 1891 to set aside 150 million acres of federal land as a national reserve that could not be sold to private interests.

2. In 1902, Roosevelt won passage of the Newlands Reclamation Act, a law providing money from the sale of public land for irrigation projects in western states.

3. In 1908, the president publicized the need for conservation by hosting a White House Conference of Governors to promoted coordinated conservation planning by federal and state governments. Following this conference, a National Conservation Commission was established under Gifford Pinchot of Pennsylvania, whom Roosevelt had earlier appointed to be the first director of the U.S. Forest Service.

Taft's Presidency

The good-natured William Howard Taft had served in Roosevelt's cabinet as secretary of war. Honoring the two-term tradition, Roosevelt refused to seek reelection and picked Taft to be his successor. The Republican party readily endorsed Taft as its nominee for president in 1908 and, as expected, defeated for a third time the Democrats' campaigner, William Jennings Bryan.

More Trust-Busting and Conservation Taft continued Roosevelt's Progressive policies. As a trustbuster, Taft ordered the prosecution of almost twice the number of antitrust cases as his predecessor. Among these cases was one against U.S. Steel, which included a merger approved by then President Theodore Roosevelt. An angry Roosevelt viewed Taft's action as a personal attack on his integrity. As a conservationist, Taft established the Bureau of Mines, added large tracts in the Appalachians to the national forest reserves, and set aside federal oil lands (the first president to do so).

Two other Progressive measures were at least equal in importance to legislation enacted under Roosevelt. The Mann-Elkins Act of 1910 gave the Interstate Commerce Commission the power to suspend new railroad rates and oversee telephone, telegraph, and cable companies. The Sixteenth Amendment, ratified by the states in 1913, authorized the U.S government to collect an income tax. (This reform was originally proposed by the Populists in their 1892 platform.) Progressives heartily approved the new tax because, at first, it applied only to the very wealthy.

Split in the Republican Party Progressives in the Republican party were unimpressed with Taft's achievements. In fact, they became so disenchanted with his leadership that they accused him of betraying their cause and joining the conservative wing of the party. These were their reasons:

1. Payne-Aldrich Tariff During his 1908 campaign, Taft had promised to lower the tariff. Instead, conservative Republicans in *Congress* passed the Payne-Aldrich Tariff in 1909, which raised the tariff on most imports. Taft angered Progressives in his party not only by signing the tariff bill but by making a public statement in its defense.

2. Pinchot-Ballinger Controversy The Progressives respected the chief of the Forest Service, Gifford Pinchot, as a dedicated conservationist. On the other hand, they distrusted Taft's secretary of the interior, Richard Ballinger, especially after he opened public lands in Alaska for private development. In 1910, when Pinchot criticized Ballinger, Taft stood by his cabinet member and fired Pinchot for insubordination. Conservatives applauded; Progressives protested.

3. House Speaker Joe Cannon Taft angered Progressive Republicans when he failed to support their effort to reduce the dictatorial powers of Congress' leading conservative, Speaker of the House Joseph Cannon.

4. Midterm Elections Fighting back against his Progressive critics, Taft openly supported conservative candidates for Congress in the midterm elections of 1910. It was a serious political mistake. Progressive Republicans from the Midwest easily defeated the candidates endorsed by Taft. After this election, the Republican party was split wide open between two opposing groups: a conservative faction loyal to Taft and a Progressive faction. The latter group of Republicans fervently hoped that their ex-president and hero, Theodore Roosevelt, would agree to become their candidate again in 1912.

Rise of the Socialist Party

A third party developed in the first decade of the 1900s that was dedicated to the welfare of the working class. Originally called the Socialist Labor party in 1897, it changed its name in 1901 to the Socialist Party of America. The Socialist platform called for more radical reforms than the Progressives favored: public ownership of the railroads, utilities, and even of major industries such as oil and steel.

Eugene V. Debs One of the Socialist party's founders, Eugene Debs, was the party's candidate for president in five elections from 1900 to 1920. A former railway union leader, Debs adopted socialism while jailed for the Pullman strike. He was an outspoken critic of business and a champion of labor.

Influence On such issues as workers' compensation and minimum wage laws, Progressives and some Socialists joined forces. For the most part, however, Progressives wanted to distance themselves from the ideas of Socialists, since the majority of voters favored only mild reforms, not radical causes. Eventually, however, some Socialist ideas were accepted: public ownership of utilities, the eight-hour workday, and pensions for employees.

The Election of 1912

Reform efforts dominated a campaign that involved four notable presidential candidates.

Candidates President Taft was renominated by the Republicans after his supporters excluded Theodore Roosevelt's delegates from the party's convention. Progressive Republicans then formed a new party and nominated Theodore Roosevelt. (Roosevelt's claim that he was as strong as a bull moose gave the new Progressive party its nickname: the Bull Moose party.) After lengthy balloting, Democrats united behind Woodrow Wilson, a newcomer who had first been elected to office in 1910 as governor of New Jersey. The Socialist party, at the peak of its strength, again nominated Eugene V. Debs.

Campaign With Taft enjoying little popularity and Debs considered too radical, the election came down to a battle between Theodore Roosevelt and Woodrow Wilson. Roosevelt called for a New Nationalism, with more government regulation of business and unions, women's suffrage, and more social welfare programs. Wilson pledged a New Freedom, which would limit both big business and big government, bring about reform by ending corruption, and revive competition by supporting small business.

Results Wilson won less than a majority of the popular vote, but with the Republicans split, he won a landslide in the electoral college and the Democrats gained control of Congress. The overwhelming support for the Progressive presidential candidates ensured that reform efforts would continue under Wilson, while the failure of the Progressive party to elect local candidates suggested that the new party would not last. But the idea contained in Roosevelt's New Nationalism—of strong federal government regulations helping the people—did have a lasting influence for much of the century (see, in Chapter 24, the New Deal, and, in Chapter 28, the Great Society).

PRESIDENTIAL ELECTION, 1912

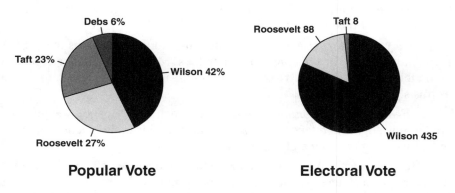

Debs 6%
Taft 23%
Wilson 42%
Roosevelt 27%

Popular Vote

Roosevelt 88
Taft 8
Wilson 435

Electoral Vote

Source: U.S. Bureau of the Census. *Historical Statistics of the United States, Colonial Times to 1970*

Woodrow Wilson's Progressive Program

Wilson, who grew up in Virginia during the Civil War, was only the second Democrat elected president since the war (Cleveland was the other), and the first southerner to occupy the White House since Zachary Taylor (1849–1850). Wilson was idealistic, intellectual, righteous, and inflexible. Like Roosevelt, he believed that a president should actively lead Congress and, as necessary, appeal directly to the people to rally support for his legislative program.

In his inaugural address in 1913, the Democratic president pledged again his commitment to a New Freedom. To bring back conditions of free and fair competition in the economy, Wilson attacked "the triple wall of privilege": tariffs, banking, and trusts.

Tariff Reduction Wasting no time to fulfill a campaign pledge, Wilson on the first day of his presidency called a special session of Congress to lower the tariff. Past presidents had always sent written messages to Congress, but Wilson broke this longstanding tradition by addressing Congress in person about the need for lower tariff rates to bring consumer prices down. Passage of the Underwood Tariff in 1913 substantially lowered tariffs for the first time in over 50 years. To compensate for the reduced tariff revenues, the Underwood bill included a graduated income tax with rates from 1 to 6 percent.

Banking Reform Wilson's next major initiative concerned the banking system and the money supply. He was persuaded that the gold standard was inflexible and that banks, rather than serving the public interest, were too much influenced by stock speculators on Wall Street. The president again went directly to Congress in 1913 to propose a plan for building both stability and flexibility into the U.S. financial system. Rejecting the Republican proposal for a private national bank, he proposed a national banking system with 12 district banks supervised by a Federal Reserve Board. After months of debate, Congress finally passed the Federal Reserve Act in 1914. Ever since, Americans have purchased goods and services using the Federal Reserve Notes (dollar bills) issued by the federally regulated banking system.

Business Regulation Two major pieces of legislation in 1914 completed Wilson's New Freedom program:

1. Clayton Antitrust Act This act strengthened the provisions in the Sherman Antitrust Act for breaking up monopolies. Most important for organized labor, the new law contained a clause exempting unions from being prosecuted as trusts.

2. Federal Trade Commission The new regulatory agency was empowered to investigate and take action against any "unfair trade practice" in every industry except banking and transportation.

Other Reforms Wilson was at first opposed to any legislation that seemed to favor special interests, such as farmers' groups and labor unions. He was finally persuaded, however, to extend his reform program to include the following Progressive measures:

1. Federal Farm Loan Act In 1916, 12 regional federal farm loan banks were established to provide farm loans at low interest rates.

2. Child Labor Act This measure, long favored by settlement house workers and labor unions alike, was enacted in 1916. It prohibited the shipment in interstate commerce of products manufactured by children under 14 years old. However, the Supreme Court found this act to be unconstitutional in the 1918 case of *Hammer v. Dagenhart*.

African Americans in the Progressive Era

In championing greater democracy for the American people, most leaders of the Progressive movement thought only in terms of the white race. African Americans were, for the most part, ignored by Progressive presidents and governors. President Wilson, with a strong southern heritage and many of the racist attitudes of the times, acquiesced to the demands of southern Democrats and permitted the segregation of federal workers and buildings.

The status of African Americans had declined steadily since Reconstruction. With the Supreme Court's "separate but equal" decision in *Plessy v. Ferguson* (1896), racial segregation had been the rule in the South and, unofficially, in much of the North. Ironically and tragically, the Progressive era coincided with years when thousands of blacks were lynched by racist mobs. Few Progressives did anything about segregation and lynching. Most shared in the general prejudice of their times. In addition, many considered other reforms (such as lower tariffs) to be more important than antilynching laws because such reforms benefited everyone, not just one group.

Two Approaches: Washington and Du Bois

Though lacking widespread white support, African-Americans took action to alleviate poverty and discrimination. Economic deprivation and exploitation was one problem; denial of civil rights was another. Which problem was primary was a difficult question that became the focus of a debate between two African American leaders: Booker T. Washington and W. E. B. Du Bois.

Washington's Stress on Economics The most influential African American at the turn of the century was the head of the Tuskegee Institute in Alabama, Booker T. Washington. In his Atlanta Exposition speech in 1895, Washington argued that blacks' needs for education and economic progress were of foremost importance, and that they should concentrate on learning industrial skills for better wages. Only after establishing a secure economic base, said Washington, could African Americans hope to realize their other goal of political and social equality. (See Chapter 17.)

Du Bois' Stress on Civil Rights Unlike Washington, who had been born into slavery on a southern plantation, W. E. B. Du Bois was a northerner with a college education, who became a distinguished scholar and writer. In his book

The Souls of Black Folk (1903), Du Bois criticized Booker T. Washington's approach and demanded equal rights for African Americans. He argued that political and social rights were a prerequisite for economic independence.

Washington's pragmatic approach to economic advancement and Du Bois' militant demands for equal rights framed a debate in the African American community that continued throughout much of the 20th century.

The Great "Migration"

At the close of the 19th century, about nine out of ten African Americans lived in the South. In the next century, this ratio steadily shifted toward the North. This internal migration began in earnest between 1910 and 1930 when about a million people traveled north to seek jobs in the cities. Motivating their decision to leave the South were: (1) deteriorating race relations, (2) destruction of their cotton crops by the boll weevil, and (3) job opportunities in northern factories that opened up when white workers were drafted in World War I. The Great Depression in the 1930s slowed migration, but World War II renewed it. Between 1940 and 1970, over 4 million African Americans moved north. Although many succeeded in improving their economic conditions, the newcomers to northern cities also faced racial tension and discrimination.

Civil Rights Organizations

Racial discrimination during the Progressive era prompted black leaders to found three powerful civil rights organizations in a span of just six years.

1. In 1905, W. E. B. Du Bois met with a group of black intellectuals in Niagara Falls, Canada, to discuss a program of protest and action aimed at securing equal rights for blacks. They and others who later joined the group became known as the *Niagara Movement*.

2. On Lincoln's birthday in 1908, Du Bois, other members of the Niagara Movement, and a group of white Progressives founded the National Association for the Advancement of Colored People (NAACP). Their mission was no less than to abolish all forms of segregation and to increase educational opportunities for African American children. By 1920, the NAACP was the nation's largest civil rights organization, with over 100,000 members.

3. Another organization, the National Urban League, was formed in 1911 to help people migrating from the South to northern cities. The league's motto, "Not Alms But Opportunity," reflected its emphasis on self-reliance and economic advancement.

Women, Suffrage, and the Progressive Movement

The Progressive era was a time of increased activism and optimism for a new generation of feminists. By 1900, the older generation of suffrage crusaders led by Susan B. Anthony and Elizabeth Cady Stanton had passed the torch to younger women. They sought allies among male Progressives, but not always with success. For example, President Wilson refused to support the suffragists' call for a national amendment until late in his presidency.

The Campaign for Women's Suffrage

Carrie Chapman Catt, an energetic reformer from Iowa, became the new president of the National American Woman Suffrage Association (NAWSA) in 1900. Catt argued for the vote as a broadening of democracy which would empower women, thus enabling them to more actively care for their families in an industrial society. At first, Catt continued NAWSA's drive to win votes for women at the state level before changing strategies and seeking a suffrage amendment to the U.S. Constitution.

Militant Suffragists A more militant approach to gaining the vote was adopted by some women, who took to the streets with mass pickets, parades, and hunger strikes. Their leader, Alice Paul of New Jersey, broke from NAWSA in 1916 to form the National Woman's party. From the beginning, Paul focused on winning the support of Congress and the president for an amendment to the Constitution.

Nineteenth Amendment (1920) The dedicated efforts of women on the home front in World War I finally persuaded a two-thirds majority in Congress to support a women's suffrage amendment. Its ratification as the Nineteenth Amendment in 1920 guaranteed women's right to vote in all elections at the local, state, and national levels. Following the victory of her cause, Carrie Chapman Catt organized the League of Women Voters, a civic organization dedicated to keeping voters informed about candidates and issues.

Other Issues

In addition to winning the right to vote, Progressive women worked on other issues as well. Margaret Sanger advocated birth-control education, especially among the poor. Over time, the movement developed into the Planned Parenthood organization. Women made progress in securing educational equality, liberalizing marriage and divorce laws, reducing discrimination in business and the professions, and recognizing women's rights to own property.

CAUSES

Growth of
Industries

Growth of
Cities

THE PROGRESSIVE MOVEMENT

EFFECTS

Political	Social	Economic
• Party primaries • Split in Republican party, 1912 • Decline of machine politics • Votes for women	• Laws protecting workers • Settlement houses and social work • Birth control for women • Beginning of civil rights movement for African Americans	• Conservation of land and water • Regulation of business • Lower tariffs • Reformed banking system • Federal income tax

HISTORICAL PERSPECTIVES: REFORM OR REACTION?

Historians have generally agreed that the Progressive movement was a response to industrialization and urbanization. They do not agree, however, on whether the Progressives were truly seeking to move society in new directions or whether they were reacting *against* new trends and attempting to maintain society as it once was.

Progressives saw themselves as genuine reformers, and for many years, historians accepted this view. Historians said that Progressives were simply acting in the tradition of earlier reformers: the Jeffersonians, Jacksonians, and Populists. William Allen White argued that the Progressives adopted the complete Populist package of reforms except for free silver. Historian Arthur M. Schlesinger, Jr., thought that U.S.

history moved in a liberal-conservative cycle and that progressivism was a predictable phase in that cycle following the conservatism of late-19th century politics.

Another, complementary view of the Progressives, depicts them not as democratic champions of "the people" but as modernizers who wanted to apply rational, scientific methods to the operations of social and political institutions. Samuel P. Hay's study of municipal reform, for example, shows that Progressive leaders were an educated, upper-class elite working to make government more efficient under the direction of skilled experts. Some historians fault the Progressive movement's emphasis on scientific expertise, boards, and commissions for creating institutions that seem to take away power from the voters and elected officials. For example, the chair of the Federal Reserve Board is often considered the second most powerful person in government after the president, but once appointed, this individual is largely independent of the president and Congress.

Those historians who view Progressives as conservatives in disguise—or even as reactionaries—stress how disturbed these citizens were by labor strife, by the agrarian discontent of the Populists, and by signs of revolutionary ferment among the urban masses. Gabriel Kolko argues that the business elite, far from being opposed to government regulation, in fact wanted regulation as a means of stabilizing industry. Kolko points out that the regulation of the meatpacking industry, although inspired by muckraking literature, benefitted the large meatpackers, who lobbied behind the scenes for government controls.

Historians have debated the relationship between Progressives and the working class. Did the middle-class Progressives act out of sympathy for the workers or out of fear of a socialist revolution? George Mowry in the early 1950s characterized the Progressive movement as a reaction of middle-class professionals and small-business owners to pressures both from above (large corporations) and from below (labor unions). In this view, the middle class was attempting to maintain its traditional leadership of society by directing reform. The neglect of unions and African Americans by Progressives provides further evidence that the reformers were conservative at heart.

On the other hand, some historians argue that middle-class motives for reform might have been an expression of that group's strong sense of social conscience. The Protestant churches had cultivated a sense of responsibility and justice. The muckrakers' articles stirred their readers' conscience and aroused genuine feelings of guilt with respect to the poor and outrage with respect to dishonest politics.

KEY TERMS BY THEME

Progressive Movement (SOC, ARC)
urban middle class
male and female
white, old stock
Protestants
professional associations
Pragmatism
William James
John Dewey
Frederick W. Taylor
scientific management

Muckrakers (SOC)
Henry Demarest Lloyd
Standard Oil Company
Lincoln Steffans
Ida Tarbell
Jacob Riis
Theodore Dreiser

Voting Rights (POL)
Australian ballot
direct primary
Robert La Follett
Seventeenth
Amendment
direct election of
senators
initiative, referendum,
and recall

City and State Government (POL)
municipal reform
Samuel M. Jones
Tom L. Johnson
commission plan
city manager plan
Charles Evans
Hughes Hiram Johnson
"Wisconsin Idea"
regulatory commissions

Social and Labor Reform (POL)
state Prohibition laws
state regulation of education and safety
National Child Labor
Committee
compulsory school
attendance
Florence Kelley
National Consumers'
League
Lochner v. New York
Muller v. Oregon
Triangle Shirtwaist fire

Theodore Roosevelt Presidency (POL, GEO)
Square Deal
anthracite coal miners'
strike (1902)
trust-busting
bad vs. good trusts
Elkins Act (1903)
Hepburn Act (1906)
Upton Sinclair
The Jungle; Pure Food
and Drug Act (1906)
Meat Inspection Act
(1906)
conservation of public
lands
Newlands Reclamation
Act (1902)
White House Conference
Gifford Pinchot

Election of 1912 (POL)
Socialist Party of
America
Eugene V. Debs
Bull Moose party
New Nationalism New
Freedom

William Howard Taft Presidency (POL)
Mann-Elkins Act (1910)
Sixteenth Amendment,
federal income tax
Payne-Aldrich Tariff
(1909)
firing of Pinchot

Woodrow Wilson Presidency (POL)
Underwood Tariff (1913)
Federal Reserve Act
(1914)
Federal Reserve Board
Clayton Antitrust Act
(1914)
Federal Trade Commission
Federal Farm Loan Act
(1916)

African Americans (NAT)
racial segregation laws
increased lynching
Booker T. Washington
W. E. B. Du Bois
National Association for
the Advancement of
Colored People
National Urban League

Women's Movement (NAT, POL)
Carrie Chapman Catt
National American
Woman Suffrage
Association
Alice Paul
National Woman's party
Nineteenth Amendment
League of Women Voters
Margaret Sanger

MULTIPLE-CHOICE QUESTIONS

Question 1–3 refer to the excerpt below.

"To be sure, much of progressivism was exclusionary. Yet we can now recognize not a singular political persuasion, but rather a truly plural set of progressivisms, with workers, African Americans, women, and even Native Americans—along with a diverse and contentious set of middling folk—taking up the language and ideas of what was once conceived of as an almost entirely white, male, middle-class movement. As for the dreams of democracy from the period: despite the frequent blindness of those who embodied them, they remain bold, diverse, and daring. It is for this reason that democratic political theorists . . . have looked so longingly at the active citizenship of the Progressive Era, seeking ways to rekindle the democratic impulses of a century ago."

—Robert D. Johnston, historian, "The Possibilities of Politics," 2011

1. Which of the following interpretations of progressivism would most likely support this excerpt?
   (A) Progressives were mostly conservatives in disguise
   (B) Progressives were almost entirely white, middle class, and urban
   (C) Progressives were educated modernizers interested in efficiency
   (D) Progressives were a diverse group who supported various reforms

2. Which of the following would most directly support the argument that Progressives were "exclusionary"?
   (A) Rural agrarian reformers played little role in the movement
   (B) Women's movements were sidelined by male-dominated governments
   (C) Progressives did little to end the segregation of African Americans
   (D) Most Progressive wanted to keep immigrants and laborers from voting

3. Which of the following Progressive reforms most directly promoted "active citizenship"?
   (A) City manager laws
   (B) Breaking up trusts
   (C) The direct election of senators
   (D) Regulatory commissions

Questions 4–6 refer to the excerpt below.

"Worst of any, however, were the fertilizer men, and those who served in the cooking rooms. These people could not be shown to the visitor— for the odor of a fertilizer man would scare any ordinary visitor at a hundred yards, and as for other men, who worked in tank rooms full of steam, their peculiar trouble was that they fell into the vats; and when they were fished out, there was never enough of them left to be worth exhibiting — sometimes they would be overlooked for days, till all but the bones of them has gone out to the world as Durham's Pure Leaf Lard!"

—Upton Sinclair, *The Jungle,* 1906

4. The above excerpt is most closely associated with which sector of the Progressive movement?
   (A) Politicians who supported state regulatory commissions to curtail abuses in business
   (B) Reformers who fought to break up monopolies and trusts
   (C) Investigative journalists and authors known as "muckrakers"
   (D) The union movement associated with the American Federation of Labor

5. *The Jungle* most directly contributed to which of the following?
   (A) Federal regulations to promote safety and health protection for industrial workers
   (B) A federal inspection system to ensure minimum standards for processed meats and food
   (C) The shutdown of Chicago meatpacking factories by the state of Illinois
   (D) Pressure on publishers to reduce sensational articles and books attacking businesses

6. Which of the following most effectively addressed the concerns that Upton Sinclair and others had for industrial workers?
   (A) State legislation that limited the hours and working conditions for women and children
   (B) President Theodore Roosevelt's promise for an impartial set of rules, or "Square Deal," for labor
   (C) Legislation passed during the Wilson presidency to legalize the organization of labor unions
   (D) The formation of the Socialist Party under the leadership of Eugene Debs

Questions 7–8 refer to the excerpt below.

"We believe that God created both man and woman in His own image, and, therefore, we believe in one standard of purity for both men and women, and in equal rights of all to hold opinions and to express the same with equal freedom.

"We believe in a living wage; in an eight-hour day; in courts of conciliation and arbitration; in justice as opposed to greed of gain; in 'peace on earth and goodwill to men.'

"We therefore formulate and, for ourselves, adopt the following pledge, asking our sisters and brothers of a common danger and a common hope to make common cause with us in working its reason able and helpful precepts into the practice of everyday life:

"I hereby solemnly promise, God helping me, to abstain from all distilled, fermented, and malt liquors, including wine, beer, and cider, and to employ all proper means to discourage the use of and traffic in the same."

—National Woman's Christian Temperance Union, Annual Leaflet, 1902

7. The above excerpt most directly reflects that the temperance movement
   (A) started out as an unpopular women's fringe group
   (B) appealed to a varied constituency of reformers
   (C) drew strong support from immigrant groups
   (D) gained support by opposing the "liquor trust"

8. The Prohibition movement was similar to other Progressive reforms because it
   (A) began on the local and state levels before becoming national
   (B) started out under the leadership of the Christian clergy
   (C) primarily was concerned about poor immigrant workers
   (D) aimed to reduce immorality destroying family life

Use complete sentences; an outline or bulleted list alone is not acceptable.

Question 1 is based on the cartoon below.

Source: Clifford Berryman, *Washington Evening Star,* 1907. Library of Congress

1. Using the cartoon, answer (A), (B), and (C).

    (A) Briefly explain the point of view of the cartoon on Theodore Roosevelt's approach to trusts.

    (B) Briefly explain the point of view of the cartoon on Theodore Roosevelt's distinction between "good" and "bad" trusts.

    (C) Briefly explain ONE way that the antitrust policies of Woodrow Wilson differed from those of Theodore Roosevelt.

Question 2. Answer (A), (B), and (C).

    (A) Briefly explain ONE significant contribution of the philosophy of pragmatism to the Progressive movement.

    (B) Briefly explain ONE significant contribution of either scientific management or regulatory commissions to the Progressive movement.

    (C) Briefly explain ONE reason why the Progressives thought government needed to play a more active role in solving America's problems.

Question 3 is based on the excerpts below.

"According to the liberal view of the Progressive Era, the major political innovations of reform involved the equalization of political power through the primary, the direct election of public officials, and the initiative, referendum, and recall. . . . But they provided at best only an occasional and often incidental process of decision-making. Far more important in continuous, sustained, day-to-day processes of government were those innovations which centralized decision-making in the hands of fewer and fewer people."

—Samuel L. Hays, *The Politics of Reform in Municipal Government in the Progressive Era,* 1964.

"Progressivism owed much to it success to a distinctive method of reform. . . . They typically began by organizing voluntary associations, investigating a problem, gathering relevant facts, and analyzing them. From such analysis a proposed solution would emerge, be popularized through campaigns of education and moral suasion, and . . . to be taken over by some level of government as a public function. . . . These tactics were pioneered in many cases by women. . . . It fell to women to invent their own means to improve the world."

—Richard L. McCormick, *Public Life in Industrial America, 1877–1917,* 1997

3. Using the excerpts, answer (A), (B), and (C).

   (A) Briefly describe ONE major difference between Hays's and McCormick's historical interpretation of the Progressive Era.

   (B) Briefly explain how ONE specific historical event or development that is not explicitly mentioned in the excerpts could be used to support Hays's interpretation of the Progressive Era.

   (C) Briefly explain how ONE specific historical event or development that is not explicitly mentioned in the excerpts could be used to support McCormick's interpretation of the Progressive Era.

Question 4. Answer (A), (B), and (C).

   (A) Briefly explain ONE specific way the Wilson administration fulfilled the goals of reforming the United States banking system.

   (B) Briefly explain ONE specific way the Wilson administration fulfilled the goals of reforming federal tariffs and taxation.

   (C) Briefly explain how ONE reform identified above either reflected or violated Wilson's New Freedom policies.

THINK AS A HISTORIAN: MAKING A CHOICE ABOUT CONTINUITY

If you were writing a history of women in the United States, what years would you include in a chapter title "Women in the Progressive Era"? Explain your choices.

22

WORLD WAR I AND ITS AFTERMATH, 1914–1920

It breaks his heart that kings must murder still,
That all his hours of travail here for men
Seem in vain. And who will bring white peace
That he may sleep upon his hill again?

Vachel Lindsay, "Abraham Lincoln Walks at Midnight," 1914

The sequence of events in 1914 leading from peace in Europe to the outbreak of a general war occurred with stunning rapidity:

- SARAJEVO, JUNE 28: A Serbian nationalist assassinates Austrian Archduke Francis Ferdinand—the heir apparent to the throne of the Austro-Hungarian empire—and his wife.

- VIENNA, JULY 23: The Austrian government issues an ultimatum threatening war against Serbia and invades that country four days later.

- ST. PETERSBURG, JULY 31: Russia, as an ally of Serbia, orders its army to mobilize against Austria.

- BERLIN, AUGUST 1: Germany, as Austria's ally, declares war against Russia.

- BERLIN, AUGUST 3: Germany declares war against France, an ally of Russia, and immediately begins an invasion of neutral Belgium because it offers the fastest route to Paris.

- LONDON, AUGUST 4: Great Britain, as an ally of France, declares war against Germany.

The assassination of the archduke sparked the war, but the underlying causes were (1) nationalism, (2) imperialism, (3) militarism, and (4) a combination of public and secret alliances, as explained above, which pulled all the major European powers into war before calm minds could prevent it. It was a tragedy that haunted generations of future leaders and that motivated President Woodrow Wilson to search for a lasting peace.

President Wilson's first response to the outbreak of the European war was a declaration of U.S. neutrality, in the tradition of Washington and Jefferson, and he called upon the American people to support his policy by not taking sides. However, in trying to steer a neutral course, Wilson soon found that it was difficult—if not impossible—to protect U.S. trading rights and maintain a policy that favored neither the Allied Powers (Great Britain, France, and Russia) nor the Central Powers (Germany, Austria-Hungary, and the Ottoman Empires of Turkey). During a relatively short period (1914–1919), the United States and its people rapidly moved through a wide range of roles: first as a contented neutral country, next as a country waging a war for peace, then as a victorious world power, and finally, as an alienated and isolationist nation.

Neutrality

In World War I (as in the War of 1812), the trouble for the United States arose as the belligerent powers tried to stop supplies from reaching the enemy. Having the stronger navy, Great Britain was the first to declare a naval blockade against Germany by mining the North Sea and seizing ships—including U.S. ships—attempting to run the blockade. President Wilson protested British seizure of American ships as a violation of a neutral nation's right to freedom of the seas.

Submarine Warfare

Germany's one hope for challenging British power at sea lay with a new naval weapon, the submarine. In February 1915, Germany answered the British blockade by announcing a blockade of its own and warned that ships attempting to enter the "war zone" (waters near the British Isles) risked being sunk on sight by German submarines.

Lusitania **Crisis** The first major crisis challenging U.S. neutrality occurred on May 7, 1915, when German torpedoes hit and sank a British passenger liner, the *Lusitania*. Most of the passengers drowned, including 128 Americans. In response, Wilson sent Germany a strongly worded diplomatic message warning that Germany would be held to "strict accountability" if it continued its policy of sinking unarmed ships. Secretary of State William Jennings Bryan objected to this message as too warlike and resigned from the president's cabinet.

Other Sinkings In August 1915, two more Americans lost their lives at sea as the result of a German submarine attack on another passenger ship, the *Arabic*. This time, Wilson's note of protest prevailed upon the German government to pledge that no unarmed passenger ships would be sunk without warning, which would allow time for passengers to get into lifeboats.

Germany kept its word until March 1916 when a German torpedo struck an unarmed merchant ship, the *Sussex*, injuring several American passengers. Wilson threatened to cut off U.S. diplomatic relations with Germany—a step preparatory to war. Once again, rather than risk U.S. entry into the war on the British side, Germany backed down. Its reply to the president, known as the Sussex pledge, promised not to sink merchant or passenger ships without giving due warning. For the remainder of 1916, Germany was true to its word.

Economic Links with Britain and France

Even though the United States was officially a neutral nation, its economy became closely tied to that of the Allied powers, Great Britain and France. In early 1914, before the war began, the United States had been in a business recession. Soon after the outbreak of war, the economy rebounded in part because of orders for war supplies from the British and the French. By 1915, U.S. businesses had never been so prosperous.

In theory, U.S. manufacturers could have shipped supplies to Germany as well, but the British blockade effectively prevented such trade. Wilson's policy did not deliberately favor the Allied powers. Nevertheless, because the president more or less tolerated the British blockade while restricting Germany's submarine blockade, U.S. economic support was going to one side (Britain and France) and not the other. Between 1914 and 1917, U.S. trade with the Allies quadrupled while its trade with Germany dwindled to the vanishing point.

Loans In addition, when the Allies could not finance the purchase of everything they needed, the U.S. government permitted J. P. Morgan and other bankers to extend as much as $3 billion in secured credit to Britain and France. These loans promoted U.S. prosperity as they sustained the Allies' war effort.

Public Opinion

If Wilson's policies favored Britain, so did the attitudes of most Americans. In August 1914, as Americans read in their newspapers about German armies marching ruthlessly through Belgium, they perceived Germany as a cruel bully whose armies were commanded by a mean-spirited autocrat, Kaiser Wilhelm. The sinking of the *Lusitania* reinforced this negative view of Germany.

Ethnic Influences In 1914, first- and second-generation immigrants made up over 30 percent of the U.S. population. They were glad to be out of the fighting and strongly supported neutrality. Even so, their sympathies reflected their ancestries. For example, German Americans strongly identified with the struggles of their "homeland." And many Irish Americans, who hated Britain because of its oppressive rule of Ireland, openly backed the Central Powers. On the other hand, when Italy joined the Allies in 1915, Italian Americans began cheering on the Allies in their desperate struggle to fend off German assaults on the Western Front (entrenched positions in France).

Overall, though, the majority of native-born Americans wanted the Allies to win. Positive U.S. relations with France since the Revolutionary War bolstered public support for the French. Americans also tended to sympathize with

Britain and France because of their democratic governments. President Wilson himself, as a person of Scotch-English descent, had long admired the British political system.

British War Propaganda Not only did Britain command the seas but it also commanded the war news that was cabled daily to U.S. newspapers and magazines. Fully recognizing the importance of influencing U.S. public opinion, the British government made sure the American press was well supplied with stories of German soldiers committing atrocities in Belgium and the German-occupied part of eastern France.

The War Debate

After the *Lusitania* crisis, a small but vocal minority of influential Republicans from the East—including Theodore Roosevelt—argued for U.S. entry into the war against Germany. Foreign policy realists believed that a German victory would change the balance of power and United States needed a strong British navy to protect the status-quo. However, the majority of Americans remained thankful for a booming economy and peace.

Preparedness

Eastern Republicans such as Roosevelt were the first to recognize that the U.S. military was hopelessly unprepared for a major war. They clamored for "preparedness" (greater defense expenditures) soon after the European war broke out.

At first, President Wilson opposed the call for preparedness, but in late 1915, he changed his policy. Wilson urged Congress to approve an ambitious expansion of the armed forces. The president's proposal provoked a storm of controversy, especially among Democrats, who until then were largely opposed to military increases. After a nationwide speaking tour on behalf of preparedness, Wilson finally convinced Congress to pass the National Defense Act in June 1916, which increased the regular army to a force of nearly 175,000. A month later, Congress approved the construction of more than 50 warships (battleships, cruisers, destroyers, and submarines) in just one year.

Opposition to War

Many Americans, especially in the Midwest and West, were adamantly opposed to preparedness, fearing that it would soon lead to U.S. involvement in the war. The antiwar activists included Populists, Progressives, and Socialists. Leaders among the peace-minded Progressives were William Jennings Bryan, Jane Addams, and Jeannette Rankin—the latter the first woman to be elected to Congress. Woman suffragists actively campaigned against any military buildup (although after the U.S. declaration of war in 1917, they supported the war effort).

The Election of 1916

President Wilson was well aware that, as a Democrat, he had won election to the presidency in 1912 only because of the split in Republican ranks between Taft conservatives and Roosevelt Progressives. Despite his own Progressive record, Wilson's chances for reelection did not seem strong after Theodore Roosevelt declined the Progressive party's nomination for president in 1916 and rejoined the Republicans. (Roosevelt's decision virtually destroyed any chance of the Progressive party surviving.) Charles Evans Hughes, a Supreme Court justice and former governor of New York, became the presidential candidate of a reunited Republican party.

"He Kept Us Out of War" The Democrats adopted as their campaign slogan: "He kept us out of war." The peace sentiment in the country, Wilson's record of Progressive leadership, and Hughes' weakness as a candidate combined to give the president the victory in an extremely close election. Democratic strength in the South and West overcame Republican power in the East.

Peace Efforts

Wilson made repeated efforts to fulfill his party's campaign promise to keep out of the war. Before the election, in 1915, he had sent his chief foreign policy adviser, Colonel Edward House of Texas, to London, Paris, and Berlin to negotiate a peace settlement. This mission, however, had been unsuccessful. Other efforts at mediation also were turned aside by both the Allies and the Central Powers. Finally, in January 1917, Wilson made a speech to the Senate declaring U.S. commitment to his idealistic hope for "peace without victory."

Decision for War

In April 1917, only one month after being sworn into office a second time, President Wilson went before Congress to ask for a declaration of war against Germany. What had happened to change his policy from neutrality to war?

Unrestricted Submarine Warfare

Most important in the U.S. decision for war was a sudden change in German military strategy. The German high command had decided in early January 1917 to resume unrestricted submarine warfare. Germany recognized the risk of the United States entering the war but believed that, by cutting off supplies to the Allies, they could win the war before Americans could react. Germany communicated its decision to the U.S. government on January 31. A few days later, Wilson broke off U.S. diplomatic relations with Germany.

Immediate Causes

Wilson still hesitated, but a series of events in March 1917 as well as the president's hopes for arranging a permanent peace in Europe convinced him that U.S. participation in the war was now unavoidable.

Zimmermann Telegram On March 1, U.S. newspapers carried the shocking news of a secret offer made by Germany to Mexico. Intercepted by British intelligence, a telegram to Mexico from the German foreign minister, Arthur Zimmermann, proposed that Mexico ally itself with Germany in return for Germany's pledge to help Mexico recover lost territories: Texas, New Mexico, and Arizona. The Zimmermann Telegram aroused the nationalist anger of the American people and convinced Wilson that Germany fully expected a war with the United States.

Russian Revolution Applying the principle of moral diplomacy, Wilson wanted the war to be fought for a worthy purpose: the triumph of democracy. It bothered him that one of the Allies was Russia, a nation governed by an autocratic czar. This barrier to U.S. participation was suddenly removed on March 15, when Russian revolutionaries overthrew the czar's government and proclaimed a republic. (Only later in November would the revolutionary government be taken over by Communists.)

Renewed Submarine Attacks In the first weeks of March, German submarines sank five unarmed U.S. merchant ships. Wilson was ready for war.

Declaration of War

On April 2, 1917, President Wilson stood before a special session of senators and representatives and solemnly asked Congress to recognize that a state of war existed between Germany and the United States. His speech condemned Germany's submarine policy as "warfare against mankind" and declared: "The world must be made safe for democracy." On April 6, an overwhelming majority in Congress voted for a declaration of war, although a few pacifists, including Robert La Follette and Jeanette Rankin, defiantly voted no.

Mobilization

U.S. mobilization for war in 1917 was a race against time. Germany was preparing to deliver a knockout blow to end the war on German terms. Could the United States mobilize its vast economic resources fast enough to make a difference? That was the question Wilson and his advisers confronted in the critical early months of U.S. involvement in war.

Industry and Labor

The Wilson administration, with Progressive efficiency, created hundreds of temporary wartime agencies and commissions staffed by experts from business and government. The legacy of this mobilization of the domestic economy under governmental leadership proved significant in the Great Depression New Deal programs. For example:

- Bernard Baruch, a Wall Street broker, volunteered to use his extensive contacts in industry to help win the war. Under his direction, the War Industries Board set production priorities and established centralized control over raw materials and prices.

- Herbert Hoover, a distinguished engineer, took charge of the Food Administration, which encouraged American households to eat less meat and bread so that more food could be shipped abroad for the French and British troops. The conservation drive paid off; in two years, U.S. overseas shipment of food tripled.

- Harry Garfield volunteered to head the Fuel Administration, which directed efforts to save coal. Nonessential factories were closed, and daylight saving time went into effect for the first time.

- Treasury Secretary William McAdoo, headed the Railroad Administration which took public control of the railroads to coordinate traffic and promoted standardized railroad equipment.

- Former president William Howard Taft helped arbitrate disputes between workers and employers as head of the National War Labor Board. Labor won concessions during the war that had earlier been denied. Wages rose, the eight-hour day became more common, and union membership increased

Finance

Paying for the costly war presented a huge challenge. Wilson's war government managed to raise $33 billion in two years by a combination of loans and taxes. It conducted four massive drives to convince Americans to put their savings into federal government Liberty Bonds. Congress also increased both personal income and corporate taxes and placed an excise tax on luxury goods.

Public Opinion and Civil Liberties

The U.S. government used techniques of both patriotic persuasion and legal intimidation to ensure public support for the war effort. Journalist George Creel took charge of a propaganda agency called the Committee on Public Information, which enlisted the voluntary services of artists, writers, vaudeville performers, and movie stars to depict the heroism of the "boys" (U.S. soldiers) and the villainy of the kaiser. They created films, posters, pamphlets, and volunteer speakers—all urging Americans to watch out for German spies and to "do your bit" for the war.

War hysteria and patriotic enthusiasm provided an excuse for nativist groups to take out their prejudices by charging minorities with disloyalty. One such group, the American Protective League, mounted "Hate the Hun" campaigns and used vigilante actions to attack all things German—from the performing of Beethoven's music to the cooking of sauerkraut. Under the order of the U.S. Secretary of Labor, manufacturers of war materials could refuse to hire and could fire American citizens of German extraction.

Espionage and Sedition Acts A number of socialists and pacifists bravely risked criticizing the government's war policy. The Espionage Act (1917) provided for imprisonment of up to 20 years for persons who either tried to incite rebellion in the armed forces or obstruct the operation of the draft. The Sedition Act (1918) went much further by prohibiting anyone from making "disloyal" or "abusive" remarks about the U.S. government. About 2,000 people were prosecuted under these laws, half of whom were convicted and jailed. Among them was the Socialist leader Eugene Debs, who was sentenced to ten years in federal prison for speaking against the war.

Case of *Schenck v. United States* The Supreme Court upheld the constitutionality of the Espionage Act in a case involving a man who had been imprisoned for distributing pamphlets against the draft. In 1919, Justice Oliver Wendell Holmes concluded that the right to free speech could be limited when it represented a "clear and present danger" to the public safety.

Armed Forces

As soon as war was declared, thousands of young men voluntarily enlisted for military service. Still, the military felt it needed more soldiers and sailors.

Selective Service Act (1917) To meet this need, Secretary of War Newton D. Baker devised a "selective service" system to conscript (draft) men into the military. He wanted a democratic method run by local boards for ensuring that all groups in the population would be called into service. The government required all men between 21 and 30 (and later between 18 and 45) to register for possible induction into the military. Under the Selective Service Act, about 2.8 million men were eventually called by lottery, in addition to the almost 2 million who volunteered to serve. About half of all those in uniform made it to the Western Front.

African Americans Racial segregation applied to the army as it did to civilian life. Almost 400,000 African Americans served in World War I in segregated units. Only a few were permitted to be officers, and all were barred from the Marine Corps. Nevertheless, W. E. B. Du Bois believed that the record of service by African Americans, fighting to "make the world safe for democracy," would earn them equal rights at home when the war ended. However, he would be bitterly disappointed.

Effects on American Society

All groups in American society—business and labor, women and men, immigrants and native-born—had to adjust to the realities of a wartime economy.

More Jobs for Women As men were drafted into the military, the jobs they vacated were often taken by women, thousands of whom entered the workforce for the first time. Women's contributions to the war effort, both as volunteers and wage earners, finally convinced Wilson and Congress to support the 19th Amendment.

Migration of Mexicans and African Americans Job opportunities in wartime America, together with the upheavals of the revolution in Mexico, caused thousands of Mexicans to cross the border to work in agriculture and mining. Most were employed in the Southwest, but a significant number also traveled to the Midwest for factory jobs. African Americans also took advantage of job opportunities opened up by the war and migrated north.

African American Population, 1900 to 1960			
Region	1900	1930	1960
Northeast	385,000	1,147,000	3,028,000
Midwest	496,000	1,262,000	3,446,000
South	7,923,000	9,362,000	11,312,000
West	30,000	120,000	1,086,000

Source: U.S. Bureau of the Census. *Historical Statistics of the United States, Colonial Times to 1970.* All numbers in the above table are rounded.

Fighting the War

By the time the first U.S. troops were shipped overseas in late 1917, millions of European soldiers on both sides had already died in trench warfare made more murderous in the industrial age by heavy artillery, machine guns, poison gas, tanks, and airplanes. A second revolution in Russia by Bolsheviks (or Communists) took that nation out of the war. With no Eastern Front to divide its forces, Germany concentrated on one all-out push to break through Allied lines in France.

Naval Operations

Germany's policy of unrestricted submarine warfare was having its intended effect. Merchant ships bound for Britain were being sunk at a staggering rate: 900,000 tons of shipping was lost in just one month (April 1917). U.S. response to this Allied emergency was to undertake a record-setting program of ship construction. The U.S. Navy also implemented a convoy system of armed escorts for groups of merchant ships. By the end of 1917, the system was working well enough to ensure that Britain and France would not be starved into submission.

American Expeditionary Force

Unable to imagine the grim realities of trench warfare, U.S. troops were eager for action. The idealism of both the troops and the public is reflected in the popular song of George M. Cohan that many were singing:

> Over there, over there,
> Send the word, send the word over there
> That the Yanks are coming,
> The Yanks are coming,
> The drums rum-tumming ev'ry where—

The American Expeditionary Force (AEF) was commanded by General John J. Pershing. The first U.S. troops to see action were used to plug weaknesses in the French and British lines, but by the summer of 1918, as American forces arrived by the hundreds of thousands, the AEF assumed independent responsibility for one segment of the Western Front.

Last German Offensive Enough U.S. troops were in place in spring 1918 to hold the line against the last ferocious assault by German forces. At Château-Thierry on the Marne River, Americans stopped the German advance (June 1918) and struck back with a successful counterattack at Belleau Wood.

Drive to Victory In August, September, and October, an Allied offensive along the Meuse River and through the Argonne Forest (the Meuse–Argonne offensive) succeeded in driving an exhausted German army backward toward the German border. U.S. troops participated in this drive at St. Mihiel—the southern sector of the Allied line. On November 11, 1918, the Germans signed an armistice in which they agreed to surrender their arms, give up much of their navy, and evacuate occupied territory.

U.S. Casualties After only a few months of fighting, U.S. combat deaths totaled nearly 49,000. Many more thousands died of disease, including a flu epidemic in the training camps, bringing total U.S. fatalities in World War I to 112,432.

Making the Peace

During the war, Woodrow Wilson never lost sight of his ambition to shape the peace settlement when the war ended. In January 1917 he had said that the United States would insist on "peace without victory." A year later he presented to Congress a detailed list of war aims, known as the Fourteen Points, designed to address the causes of World War I and prevent another world war.

The Fourteen Points

Several of the president's Fourteen Points related to specific territorial questions: for example, Germany had to return the regions of Alsace and Lorraine to France, and to evacuate Belgium in the west and Romania and Serbia in the east. Of greater significance were the following broad principles for securing the peace:

- Recognition of freedom of the seas

- An end to the practice of making secret treaties

- Reduction of national armaments

- An "impartial adjustment of all colonial claims"

- Self-determination for the various nationalities

- Removal of trade barriers

- "A general association of nations . . . for the purpose of affording mutual guarantees of political independence and territorial integrity to great and small states alike"

The last point was the one that Wilson valued the most. The international peace association that he envisioned would soon be named the League of Nations.

The Treaty of Versailles

The peace conference following the armistice took place in the Palace of Versailles outside Paris, beginning in January 1919. Every nation that had fought on the Allied side in the war was represented. No U.S. president had ever traveled abroad to attend a diplomatic conference, but President Wilson decided that his personal participation at Versailles was vital to defending his Fourteen Points. Republicans criticized him for being accompanied to Paris by several Democrats, but only one Republican, whose advice was never sought.

EUROPE AFTER WORLD WAR I (1919)

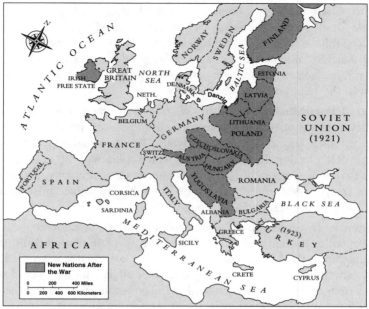

The Big Four Other heads of state at Versailles made it clear that their nations wanted both revenge against Germany and compensation in the form of indemnities and territory. They did not share Wilson's idealism, which called for a peace without victory. David Lloyd George of Great Britain, Georges Clemenceau of France, and Vittorio Orlando of Italy met with Wilson almost daily as the Big Four. After months of argument, the president reluctantly agreed to compromise on most of his Fourteen Points. He insisted, however, that the other delegations accept his plan for a League of Nations.

Peace Terms When the peace conference adjourned in June 1919, the Treaty of Versailles included the following terms:

1. Germany was disarmed and stripped of its colonies in Asia and Africa. It was also forced to admit guilt for the war, accept French occupation of the Rhineland for 15 years, and pay a huge sum of money in reparations to Great Britain and France.

2. Applying the principle of self-determination, territories once controlled by Germany, Austria-Hungary, and Russia were taken by the Allies; independence was granted to Estonia, Latvia, Lithuania, Finland, and Poland; and the new nations of Czechoslovakia and Yugoslavia were established.

3. Signers of the treaty would join an international peacekeeping organization, the League of Nations. Article X of the covenant (charter) of the League called on each member nation to stand ready to protect the independence and territorial integrity of other nations.

The Battle for Ratification

Returning to the United States, President Wilson had to win approval of two-thirds of the Senate for all parts of the Treaty of Versailles, including the League of Nations covenant. Republican senators raised objections to the League, especially to Article X, arguing that U.S. membership in such a body might interfere with U.S. sovereignty and might also cause European nations to interfere in the Western Hemisphere (a violation of the Monroe Doctrine).

Increased Partisanship After the War Wilson made winning Senate ratification difficult. In October 1918 he had asked voters to support Democrats in the midterm elections as an act of patriotic loyalty. This political appeal had backfired badly. In the 1918 election, Republicans had won a solid majority in the House and a majority of two in the Senate. In 1919 Wilson needed Republican votes in the Senate to ratify the Treaty of Versailles. Instead, he faced the determined hostility of a leading Senate Republican, Henry Cabot Lodge.

Opponents: Irreconcilables and Reservationists Senators opposed to the Treaty of Versailles formed two groups. The irreconcilable faction could not accept U.S. membership in the League, no matter how the covenant was worded. The reservationist faction, a larger group led by Senator Lodge, said they could accept the League if certain reservations were added to the covenant. Wilson had the option of either accepting Lodge's reservations or fighting for the treaty as it stood. He chose to fight.

Wilson's Western Tour and Breakdown Believing that his policy could prevail if he could personally rally public support, Wilson boarded a train and went on an arduous speaking tour to the West to make speeches for the League of Nations. On September 25, 1919, he collapsed after delivering a speech in Colorado. He returned to Washington and a few days later suffered a massive stroke from which he never fully recovered.

Rejection of the Treaty The Senate defeated the treaty without reservations. When it came up with reservations, the ailing Wilson directed his Senate allies to reject the compromise, and they joined with the irreconcilables in defeating the treaty a second time.

After Wilson left office in 1921, the United States officially made peace with Germany. It never ratified the Versailles Treaty nor joined the League of Nations.

Postwar Problems

Americans had trouble adjusting from the patriotic fervor of wartime to the economic and social stresses of postwar uncertainties.

Demobilization

During the war, 4 million American men had been taken from civilian life and the domestic economy. Not all the returning soldiers could find jobs right away, but many who did took employment from the women and African Americans who, for a short time, had thrived on war work. The business boom of wartime also went flat, as factory orders for war production fell off. With European farm products back on the market, farm prices fell, which hurt U.S. farmers. In the cities, consumers went on a buying spree, leading to inflation and a short boom in 1920. The spree did not last. In 1921, business plunged into a recession, and 10 percent of the American workforce was unemployed.

The Red Scare

In 1919, the country suffered from a volatile combination of unhappiness with the peace process, fears of communism fueled by the Communist takeover in Russia, and worries about labor unrest at home. The anti-German hysteria of the war years turned quickly into anti-Communist hysteria known as the Red Scare. These anti-radical fears also fueled xenophobia that resulted in restrictions on immigration in the 1920s.

Palmer Raids A series of unexplained bombings caused Attorney General A. Mitchell Palmer to establish a special office under J. Edgar Hoover to gather information on radicals. Palmer also ordered mass arrests of anarchists, socialists, and labor agitators. From November 1919 through January 1920, over 6,000 people were arrested, based on limited criminal evidence. Most of the suspects were foreign born, and 500 of them, including the outspoken radical Emma Goldman, were deported.

The scare faded almost as quickly as it arose. Palmer warned of huge riots on May Day, 1920, but they never took place. His loss of credibility, coupled with rising concerns about civil liberties, caused the hysteria to recede.

Labor Conflict

In a nation that valued free enterprise and rugged individualism, a large part of the American public regarded unions with distrust. Their antiunion attitude softened during the Progressive era. Factory workers and their unions were offered a "square deal" under Theodore Roosevelt and protection from lawsuits under the Clayton Antitrust Act of 1914. During the war, unions made important gains. In the postwar period, however, a series of strikes in 1919 as well as fear of revolution turned public opinion against unions.

Strikes of 1919 The first major strike of 1919 was in Seattle in February. Some 60,000 unionists joined shipyard workers in a peaceful strike for higher pay. Troops were called out, but there was no violence. In Boston, in September, police went on strike to protest the firing of a few police officers who tried to unionize. Massachusetts Governor Calvin Coolidge sent in the National Guard to break the strike. Also in September, workers for the U.S. Steel Corporation struck. State and federal troops were called out and, after considerable violence, the strike was broken in January 1920.

Race Riots

The migration of African Americans to northern cities during the war increased racial tensions. Whites resented the increased competition for jobs and housing. During the war, race riots had erupted, the largest in East St. Louis, Illinois, in 1917. In 1919, racial tensions led to violence in many cities. The worst riot was in Chicago, where 40 people were killed and 500 were injured. Conditions were no better in the South, as racial prejudice and fears of returning African American soldiers led to an increase in racial violence and lynchings by whites.

HISTORICAL PERSPECTIVES: WAS WILSON A GOOD PRESIDENT?

Analysis of U.S. involvement in World War I focuses on two questions: (1) Why did the United States go to war, and (2) how did the peace treaty fail? Central to answering both questions is an understanding of the leadership and personality of Woodrow Wilson. Historical interpretations of Wilson from the 1920s to our own times are widely divergent.

Within ten years of the end of World War I, historians such as Harry Elmer Barnes offered highly critical studies of Wilson's policies and motives. They argued that Wilson had strong pro-British sympathies, that his policies favored Britain throughout the period of neutrality, and that the interests of U.S. bankers and arms manufacturers in making war profits influenced Wilson's decision for war. Historians, like most Americans, looked back upon World War I as a tragic mistake. This view remained common through the 1930s.

In the 1940s, after U.S. entry into World War II, historians adopted a "realist" perspective on Wilson. They saw the decision for war as a necessary and unavoidable response to German submarine attacks. They also looked positively on Wilson's commitment to the League of Nations as a pioneering step toward the formation of the United Nations in 1945. The diplomat and historian George F. Kennan argued that Wilson was a pragmatist in foreign policy who recognized the dire consequences to U.S. security if Germany were permitted to overthrow the balance of power in Europe.

More recent historians have looked on Wilson favorably. Arthur S. Link portrayed him as a gifted leader who responded appropriately to both British and German violations of U.S. neutral rights and who was forced by events outside his control into a war he did not want. Link also believes that the primary motivation for Wilson's war message of 1917 was his desire for the United States to play a leading role in the peacemaking process. Arno J. Mayer and Gordon Levin believed that Wilson skillfully combined his democratic ideals with consideration for U.S. economic and strategic interests. They pointed out how the president's efforts to ensure free trade and self-determination and to end colonialism and militarism served the purpose of advancing liberal capitalism. According to Levin, Wilson's motivations went beyond economics. His championing of the League of Nations transcended narrow U.S. self-interest and reflected a vision of a new world order based on collective security.

KEY TERMS BY THEME

Causes of WWI (WOR)
Allied power
Central Powers
neutrality
submarine warfare
Lusitania
Sussex pledge
propaganda
ethnic support

Debate over War (WOR)
preparedness
election of 1916
Robert LaFollette
Jeannette Rankin
Edward House
Zimmermann telegram
Russian Revolution
declaration of war

Mobilization (POL)
war industry boards
Food Administration
Railroad Administration
National War Labor Board
taxes and bonds
Selective Service Act
service of African Americans

Civil Liberties (POL)
Committee on Public Information
George Creel
anti-German hysteria
Espionage Act (1917)
Sedition Act (1918)
Eugene Debs
Schenck v. United States

Social Impact of the War (MIG, WXT)
wartime jobs for women
attitudes toward suffrage
migration of blacks and Hispanics

Fighting in Europe, (WOR)
Bolsheviks withdraw
American Expeditionary Force
John J. Pershing
Western front
November 11, 1918

Peace Treaty (WOR)
"peace without victory"
Fourteen Points
Wilson in Paris
Big Four
Treaty of Versailles
self-determination
League of Nations
Article X

Debate over Treaty (POL)
election of 1918
Henry Cabot Lodge
Irreconcilables
Reservationists
Wilson's stroke
rejection of treaty

Aftermath of War (WXT, POL, MIG)
recession, loss of jobs
falling farm prices
Red Scare
anti-radical hysteria
Palmer raids
xenophobia
strikes of 1919
Boston police strike
race riots

Questions 1–3 refer to the excerpt below.

"On the first of February, we intend to begin submarine warfare unrestricted. In spite of this it is our intention to keep neutral the United States of America.

"If this attempt is not successful we propose an alliance on the following basis with Mexico: that we shall make war together and together make peace. We shall give financial support, and it is understood that Mexico is to reconquer the lost territory in New Mexico, Texas and Arizona. The details are left for your settlement."

—Arthur Zimmermann, German Foreign Minister, January 19, 1917

1. Which of the following does this excerpt support as the primary cause of the U.S. declaration of war in April 1917?
   (A) Mexico's plan to invade the United States
   (B) Germany's violations of U.S. neutral rights
   (C) Pro-British intelligence and propaganda
   (D) Germany's violation of the Monroe Doctrine

2. When the Zimmermann message was made public, most people in the United States
   (A) viewed it as a threat by Germany against Mexico
   (B) feared that a German victory would split the United States
   (C) expressed nationalist anger against Germany
   (D) assumed it was the result of Allied propaganda

3. The issue of freedom of the seas in World War I most closely resembles the cause of which of the following conflicts?
   (A) War of 1812
   (B) Mexican War of 1846
   (C) The American Civil War
   (D) Spanish-American War of 1898

Questions 4–6 refer to the excerpt below.

"I think all men recognize that in time of war the citizen must surrender some rights for the common good which he is entitled to enjoy in time of peace. But sir, the right to control their own government, according to constitutional forms, is not one of the rights that the citizens of this country are called upon to surrender in time of war. . . .

"Mr. President, our Government, above all others, is founded on the right of the people freely to discuss all matters pertaining to their Government, in war not less than in peace. . . . How can the popular will express itself between elections except by meetings, by speeches, by publications, by petitions, and by addresses to the representatives of the people?

"Any man who seeks to set a limit upon these rights, whether in war or peace, aims a blow at the most vital part of our Government."

—Robert M. Lafollette, *Congressional Record,* October 6, 1917

4. What does the author imply by the phrase, "not one of the rights that the citizens of this country are called upon to surrender in time of war"?

   (A) Citizens do not lose their freedom of speech during war

   (B) Citizens should not have to pay taxes during war

   (C) The Constitution protects the rights of people to disrupt the draft

   (D) The Constitution allows people to fight for the opponent in a war

5. Which of the following during World War I proved the most direct threat to the perspective on civil rights in this excerpt?

   (A) Spread of the Bolshevik Revolution

   (B) The Espionage and Sedition Acts

   (C) The Committee for Public Information

   (D) *Schenck v. United States*

6. Which of the following conflicts raised the most similar concerns about the violation of civil rights as did World War I?

   (A) War of 1812

   (B) Mexican War of 1846

   (C) The American Civil War

   (D) Spanish-American War of 1898

Source: Frederick Strothmann, 1918. Poster from the Third Liberty Loan Drive. Library of Congress

7. During World War I, the government propaganda, such as poster shown above, most likely contributed to which of the following?

   (A) The decline of votes for the Socialist Party

   (B) Increased fear of foreigners and immigrants

   (C) Increased popularity of the Democratic Party

   (D) Decline in trade with Germany

8. During the war, a government agency named the Committee of Public Information, headed by George Creel, was

   (A) unsuccessful in enlisting movie stars as volunteers

   (B) infiltrated by German spies and saboteurs

   (C) the source of the most accurate information about the war

   (D) the producer of a vast number of posters, pamphlets, and films

SHORT-ANSWER QUESTIONS

Use complete sentences; an outline or bulleted list alone is not acceptable.

Question 1. Answer (A), (B), and (C).

(A) Briefly explain ONE specific example of how the government mobilized industry or labor during World War I.

(B) Briefly explain ONE specific example of how the federal government restricted freedom of speech during World War I.

(C) Briefly explain ONE specific example of how World War I affected either women or African Americans during this period.

Question 2 is based on the photo below.

2. Using the photo, answer (A), (B), and (C).

(A) Briefly explain ONE perspective expressed in this photo about United States foreign policy during World War I.

(B) Briefly explain ONE specific action taken by the Wilson administration in response to the issues raised by this document.

(C) Briefly explain the similarity or difference between a World War I event and ONE other specific historical event or development that involved rights of United States during wartime.

Question 3 is based on the excerpts below.

"The League of Nations failed to take hold in America because the country was not yet ready for so global a role. Nevertheless, Wilson's intellectual victory proved more seminal than any political victory could have been. For, whenever America has faced the task of constructing a new world order, it has returned in one way or another to Woodrow Wilson's precepts."

—Henry Kissinger, former secretatary of state, *Diplomacy,* 1994

"The United States would never ratify the treaty and would never join the League of Nations. Many newspapers and commentators expressed regret at the outcome, and most laid the blame on Wilson — properly so. Brandegee's cruel remark about Wilson's strangling his own child was not far off the mark. Wilson had blocked every effort at compromise."

—John Milton Cooper Jr., historian, *Woodrow Wilson,* 2009

3. Using the excerpts, answer (A), (B), and (C).

   (A) Briefly describe ONE major difference between the two interpretation about the Versailles Treaty and the League of Nations.

   (B) Briefly explain how ONE specific historical event that is not noted in the excerpts could be used to support Kissinger's interpretation.

   (C) Briefly explain how ONE specific historical event that is not noted in the excerpts could be used to support Cooper's interpretation.

Question 4. Answer (A), (B), and (C).

   (A) Briefly explain ONE specific example of how the Red Scare was related to World War I.

   (B) Briefly explain ONE specific example of how the post-war labor problems were related to World War I.

   (C) Briefly explain ONE specific example of how the racial conflicts of 1917 to 1919 were related to World War I.

THINK AS A HISTORIAN: ORGANIZING EVIDENCE FOR COMPARISONS

In a comparison essay, a writer might describe one topic and then the other, and end by making comparisons in the final paragraph. Or writers might describe one trait at a time, comparing topics as they go. Is each example below organized by topic or by trait?

1. In government, both the United States and Great Britain were democracies with free elections and basic civil liberties.

2. Great Britain was a democracy, a long-standing world power, and ethnically homogenous. The United States was a democracy, new on the world stage, and ethnically diverse.

23

THE MODERN ERA OF THE 1920S

My candle burns at both ends;
It will not last the night;
But ah, my foes, and oh, my friends—
It gives a lovely light!

Edna St. Vincent Millay, "First Fig," 1920

The armistice ending World War I was two years in the past in November 1920 when the American people—women as well as men—went to the polls to cast their votes for president. Their choice was between two men from Ohio: Governor James Cox, a Democrat who urged the adoption of the League of Nations, and Senator Warren G. Harding, a Republican who was unclear about where he stood on every issue. The only memorable phrase in Harding's campaign was his assertion that the American people wanted a "return to normalcy." Harding apparently was right, because he was elected by a landslide. It was a sign that the idealism and activism that had characterized the prewar years of the Progressive era were over.

Republican Control

Through the 1920s, three Republican presidents would control the executive branch. Congress too was solidly Republican through a decade in which U.S. business boomed, while farmers and unions struggled.

Business Doctrine

The great leader of the progressive wing of the Republican party, Theodore Roosevelt, died in 1919. This loss, combined with public disillusionment over the war, allowed the return of the old-guard (conservative) Republicans. Unlike the Republicans of the Gilded Age, however, Republican leadership in the 1920s did not preach laissez-faire economics but rather accepted the idea of limited government regulation as an aid to stabilizing business. The regulatory commissions established in the Progressive era were now administered by appointees who were more sympathetic to business than to the general public. The prevailing idea of the Republican party was that the nation would benefit if business and the pursuit of profits took the lead in developing the economy.

The Presidency of Warren Harding

Harding had been a newspaper publisher in Ohio before entering politics. He was handsome and well-liked among the Republican political cronies with whom he regularly played poker. His abilities as a leader, however, were less than presidential. When the Republican national convention of 1920 deadlocked, the party bosses decided "in a smoke-filled room" to deliver the nomination to Harding as a compromise choice.

A Few Good Choices Harding recognized his limitations and hoped to make up for them by appointing able men to his cabinet. He appointed the former presidential candidate and Supreme Court justice Charles Evans Hughes to be secretary of state; the greatly admired former mining engineer and Food Administration leader Herbert Hoover to be secretary of commerce; and the Pittsburgh industrialist and millionaire Andrew Mellon to be secretary of the treasury. When the Chief Justice's seat on the Supreme Court became vacant, Harding filled it by appointing former President William Howard Taft.

Domestic Policy Harding did little more than sign into law the measures adopted by the Republican Congress. He approved (1) a reduction in the income tax, (2) an increase in tariff rates under the Fordney-McCumber Tariff Act of 1922, and (3) establishment of the Bureau of the Budget, with procedures for all government expenditures to be placed in a single budget for Congress to review and vote on.

Harding did surprise many people, particularly his conservative allies, by pardoning and releasing from federal prison Socialist leader Eugene Debs. Debs had been convicted of violating the Espionage Act during World War I. Though in prison, Debs received 920,000 votes in the 1920 presidential election. Harding's decision to pardon Deb's was prompted by the president's generous spirit.

Scandals and Death Curiously, Harding's postwar presidency was marked by scandals and corruption similar to those that had occurred under an earlier postwar president, Ulysses S. Grant. Having appointed some excellent officials, Harding also selected a number of incompetent and dishonest men to fill important positions, including Secretary of the Interior Albert B. Fall and Attorney General Harry M. Daugherty. In 1924, Congress discovered that Fall had accepted bribes for granting oil leases near Teapot Dome, Wyoming. Daugherty also took bribes for agreeing not to prosecute certain criminal suspects.

However, in August 1923, shortly before these scandals were uncovered publicly, Harding died suddenly while traveling in the West. He was never implicated in any of the scandals.

The Presidency of Calvin Coolidge

Harding's vice president and successor, Calvin Coolidge, had won popularity in 1919 as the Massachusetts governor who broke the Boston police strike. He was a man of few words who richly deserved the nickname "Silent Cal." Coolidge once explained why silence was good politics. "If you don't say anything," he said, "you won't be called on to repeat it." Also unanswerable was the president's sage comment: "When more and more people are thrown out of work, unemployment results." Coolidge summarized both his presidency and his era in the phrase: "The business of America is business."

The Election of 1924 After less than a year in office, Coolidge was the overwhelming choice of the Republican party as their presidential nominee in 1924. The Democrats nominated a conservative lawyer from West Virginia, John W. Davis, and tried to make an issue of the Teapot Dome scandal. Unhappy with conservative dominance of both parties, liberals formed a new Progressive party led by its presidential candidate, Robert La Follette of Wisconsin. Coolidge won the election easily, but the Progressive ticket did extremely well for a third party in a conservative era. La Follette received nearly 5 million votes, chiefly from discontented farmers and laborers.

Vetoes and Inaction Coolidge believed in limited government that stood aside while business conducted its own affairs. Little was accomplished in the White House except keeping a close watch on the budget. Cutting spending to the bone, Coolidge vetoed even the acts of the Republican majority in Congress. He would not allow bonuses for World War I veterans and vetoed a bill (the McNary-Haugen Bill of 1928) to help farmers as crop prices fell.

Hoover, Smith, and the Election of 1928

Coolidge declined to run for the presidency a second time. The Republicans therefore turned to an able leader with a spotless reputation, self-made millionaire and Secretary of Commerce Herbert Hoover. Hoover had served three presidents (Wilson, Harding, and Coolidge) in administrative roles but had never before campaigned for elective office. Nevertheless, in 1928, he was made the Republican nominee for president.

Hoover's Democratic opponent was the governor of New York, Alfred E. Smith. As a Roman Catholic and an opponent of Prohibition, Smith appealed to many immigrant voters in the cities. Many Protestants, however, were openly prejudiced against Smith.

Republicans boasted of "Coolidge Prosperity," which Hoover promised to extend. He even suggested (ironically, as it proved) that poverty would soon be ended altogether. Hoover won in a landslide and even took a large number of the electoral votes in the South. In several southern states—including Texas, Florida, and Virginia—the taste of prosperity and general dislike for Smith's religion outweighed the voters' usual allegiance to the Democratic party.

Mixed Economic Development

Politics took a backseat in the 1920s, as Americans adapted to economic growth and social change. The decade began with a brief postwar recession (1921), included a lengthy period of business prosperity (1922–1928), and ended in economic disaster (October 1929) with the nation's worst stock market crash. During the boom years, unemployment was usually below 4 percent. The standard of living for most Americans improved significantly. Indoor plumbing and central heating became commonplace. By 1930, two-thirds of all homes had electricity. Real income for both the middle class and the working class increased substantially.

The prosperity, however, was far from universal. In fact, during the 1920s as many as 40 percent of U.S. families in both rural and urban areas had incomes in the poverty range—they struggled to live on less than $1,500 a year. Farmers in particular did not share in the booming economy.

Causes of Business Prosperity

The business boom—led by a spectacular rise of 64 percent in manufacturing output between 1919 and 1929—resulted from several factors.

Increased Productivity Companies made greater use of research, expanding their use of Frederick W. Taylor's time-and-motion studies and principles of scientific management. The manufacturing process was made more efficient by the adoption of improved methods of mass production. In 1914, Henry Ford had perfected a system for manufacturing automobiles by means of an assembly line. Instead of losing time moving around a factory as in the past, Ford's workers remained at one place all day and performed the same simple operation over and over again at rapid speed. In the 1920s, most major industries adopted the assembly line and realized major gains in worker productivity.

Energy Technologies Another cause of economic growth was the increased use of oil and electricity, although coal was still used for the railroads and to heat most homes. Increasingly, oil was used to power factories and to provide gasoline for the rapidly increasing numbers of automobiles. By 1930, oil would account for 23 percent of U.S. energy (up from a mere 3 percent in 1900). Electric motors in factories and new appliances at home increased electrical generation over 300 percent during the decade.

Government Policy Government at all levels in the 1920s favored the growth of big business by offering corporate tax cuts and doing almost nothing to enforce the antitrust laws of the Progressive era. Large tax cuts for higher-income Americans also contributed to the imbalance in incomes and increased speculation in markets. The Federal Reserve contributed to the overheated economic boom first through low interest rates and relaxed regulation of banks and then by tightening the money supply at the wrong time.

Consumer Economy

Electricity in their homes enabled millions of Americans to purchase the new consumer appliances of the decade—refrigerators, vacuum cleaners, and washing machines. Automobiles became more affordable and sold by the millions, making the horse-and-buggy era a thing of the past. Advertising expanded as businesses found that consumers' demand for new products could be manipulated by appealing to their desires for status and popularity. Stores increased sales of the new appliances and automobiles by allowing customers to buy on credit. Later, as consumers faced more "easy monthly payments" than they could afford, they curtailed buying, contributing to the collapse of the economic boom. Chain stores, such as Woolworth's and the A & P, proliferated. Their greater variety of products were attractively displayed and often priced lower than the neighborhood stores, which they threatened to displace.

Impact of the Automobile More than anything else, the automobile changed society. By 1929, a total of 26.5 million automobiles were registered, compared to 1.2 million in 1913. The enormous increase in automobile sales meant that, by the end of the decade, there was an average of nearly one car per American family. In economic terms, the production of automobiles replaced the railroad industry as the key promoter of economic growth. Other industries—steel, glass, rubber, gasoline, and highway construction—now depended on automobile sales. In social terms, the automobile affected all that Americans did: shopping, traveling for pleasure, commuting to work, even dating. Of course, there were new problems as well: traffic jams in the cities, injuries and deaths on roads and highways.

Farm Problems

Farmers did not share in the Coolidge prosperity. Their best years had been 1916–1918, when crop prices had been kept artificially high by (1) wartime demand in Europe and (2) the U.S. government's wartime policy of guaranteeing a minimum price for wheat and corn. When the war ended, so did farm prosperity. Farmers who had borrowed heavily to expand during the war were now left with a heavy burden of debt. New technologies (chemical fertilizers, gasoline tractors) helped farmers increase their production in the 1920s, but did not solve their problems. In fact, productivity only served to increase their debts, as growing surpluses produced falling prices.

Labor Problems

Wages rose during the 1920s, but the union movement went backward. Membership in unions declined 20 percent, partly because most companies insisted on an *open shop* (keeping jobs open to nonunion workers). Some companies also began to practice welfare capitalism—voluntarily offering their employees improved benefits and higher wages in order to reduce their interest in organizing unions. In the South, companies used police, state militia, and local mobs to violently resist efforts to unionize the textile industry.

In an era that so strongly favored business, union efforts at strikes usually failed. The United Mine Workers, led by John L. Lewis, suffered setbacks in a series of violent and ultimately unsuccessful strikes in Pennsylvania, West Virginia, and Kentucky. Conservative courts routinely issued injunctions against strikes and nullified labor laws aimed at protecting workers' welfare.

A New Culture

The Census of 1920 reported that, for the first time, more than half of the American population lived in urban areas. The culture of the cities was based on popular tastes, morals, and habits of mass consumption that were increasingly at odds with the strict religious and moral codes of rural America. Moralists of the 1920s blamed the automobile, "a bordello on wheels," for the breakdown of morals, especially among the young, but soon the music, dances, movies and fashions were added to the list.

The Jazz Age

High school and college youth expressed their rebellion against their elders' culture by dancing to jazz music. Brought north by African American musicians, jazz became a symbol of the "new" and "modern" culture of the cities. The proliferation of phonographs and radios made this new style of music available to a huge (and chiefly youthful) public.

Entertainment Newspapers had once been the only medium of mass communication and entertainment. In the 1920s, a new medium—the radio—suddenly appeared. The first commercial radio station went on the air in 1920 and broadcast music to just a few thousand listeners. By 1930 there were over 800 stations broadcasting to 10 million radios—about a third of all U.S. homes. The organization of the National Broadcasting Company (NBC) in 1924 and the Columbia Broadcasting System (CBS) in 1927 provided networks of radio stations that enabled people from coast to coast to listen to the same programs: news broadcasts, sporting events, soap operas, quiz shows, and comedies.

The movie industry centered in Hollywood, California, became big business in the 1920s. Going to the movies became a national habit in cities, suburbs, and small towns. Sexy and glamorous movie stars such as Greta Garbo and Rudolf Valentino were idolized by millions. Elaborate movie theater "palaces" were built for the general public. With the introduction of talking (sound) pictures in 1927, the movie industry reached new heights. By 1929, over 80 million tickets to the latest Hollywood movies were sold each week.

Popular Heroes In an earlier era, politicians such as William Jennings Bryan, Theodore Roosevelt, and Woodrow Wilson had been popularly viewed as heroic figures. In the new age of radio and movies, Americans radically shifted their viewpoint and adopted as role models the larger-than-life personalities celebrated on the sports page and the movie screen. Every sport had its superstars who were nationally known. In the 1920s, people followed the knockouts of heavyweight boxer Jack Dempsey, the swimming records of Gertrude Ederle, the touchdowns scored by Jim Thorpe, the home runs hit by Babe Ruth, and the golf tournaments won by Bobby Jones.

Of all the popular heroes of the decade, the most celebrated was a young aviator who, in 1927, thrilled the nation and the entire world by flying nonstop across the Atlantic from Long Island to Paris. Americans listened to the radio for news of Charles Lindbergh's flight and welcomed his return to the United States with ticker tape parades larger than the welcome given to the returning soldiers of World War I.

Gender Roles, Family, and Education

The passage of the Nineteenth Amendment did not change either women's lives or U.S. politics as much as had been anticipated. Voting patterns in the election of 1920 showed that women did not vote as a bloc, but adopted the party preferences of their husbands or fathers.

Women at Home The traditional separation of labor between men and women continued into the 1920s. Most middle-class women expected to spend their lives as homemakers and mothers. The introduction into the home of such laborsaving devices as the washing machine and vacuum cleaner eased but did not substantially change the daily routines of the homemaker.

Women in the Labor Force Participation of women in the workforce remained about the same as before the war. Employed women usually lived in the cities, were limited to certain categories of jobs as clerks, nurses, teachers, and domestics, and received lower wages than men.

Revolution in Morals Probably the most significant change in the lives of young men and women of the 1920s was their revolt against sexual taboos. Some were influenced by the writings of the Austrian psychiatrist Sigmund Freud, who stressed the role of sexual repression in mental illness. Others, who perhaps had never heard of Freud, took to premarital sex as if it were—like radio and jazz music—one of the inventions of the modern age. Movies, novels, automobiles, and new dance steps (the fox-trot and the Charleston) also encouraged greater promiscuity. The use of contraceptives for birth control was still against the law in almost every state. Even so, the work of Margaret Sanger and other advocates of birth control achieved growing acceptance in the twenties.

A special fashion that set young people apart from older generations was the flapper look. Influenced by movie actresses as well as their own desires for independence, young women shocked their elders by wearing dresses hemmed at the knee (instead of the ankle), "bobbing" (cutting short) their hair, smoking cigarettes, and driving cars. High school and college graduates also took office jobs until they married. Then, as married women, they were expected to abandon the flapper look, quit their jobs, and settle down as wives and mothers.

Divorce As a result of women's suffrage, state lawmakers were now forced to listen to feminists, who demanded changes in the divorce laws to permit women to escape abusive and incompatible husbands. Liberalized divorce laws were one reason that one in six marriages ended in divorce by 1930—a dramatic increase over the one-in-eight ratio of 1920.

Education Widespread belief in the value of education, together with economic prosperity, stimulated more state governments to enact compulsory school laws. Universal high school education became the new American goal. By the end of the 1920s, the number of high school graduates had doubled to over 25 percent of the school-age young adults.

The Literature of Alienation

Scorning religion as hypocritical and bitterly condemning the sacrifices of wartime as a fraud perpetrated by money interests were two dominant themes of the leading writers of the postwar decade. This disillusionment caused the writer Gertrude Stein to call these writers a "lost generation." The novels of F. Scott Fitzgerald, Ernest Hemingway, and Sinclair Lewis, the poems of Ezra Pound and T. S. Eliot, and the plays of Eugene O'Neill expressed disillusionment with the ideals of an earlier time and with the materialism of a business-oriented culture. Fitzgerald and O'Neill took to a life of drinking, while Eliot and Hemingway expressed their unhappiness by moving into exile in Europe.

Art and Architecture

The fusion of art and technology during the 1920s and 1930s created a new profession of industrial designers. Influenced by Art Deco and streamlining styles, they created functional products from toasters to locomotives that had aesthetic appeal. Many skyscrapers, such as the Chrysler and Empire State buildings in New York, were also built in the Art Deco style that captured modernist simplification of forms, while using the machine age materials.

Painters, such as Edward Hopper, were inspired by the architecture of American cities to explore loneliness and isolation of urban life. Regional artists, such as Grant Wood and Thomas Hart Benton, celebrated the rural people and scenes of the heartland of America.

On the stage, Jewish immigrants played a major role in the development of the American musical theatre during this era. For example, composer George Gershwin, the son of Russian-Jewish immigrants, blended jazz and classical music in his symphonic *Rhapsody in Blue* and the folk opera *Porgy and Bess*.

The Chrysler Building, New York City
Source: Carol M. Highsmith / Library of Congress

Harlem Renaissance

By 1930, almost 20 percent of African Americans lived in the North, as migration from the South continued. In the North, African Americans still faced discrimination in housing and jobs, but they found at least some improvement in their earnings and material standard of living. The largest African American community developed in the Harlem section of New York City. With a population of almost 200,000 by 1930, Harlem became famous in the 1920s for its concentration of talented actors, artists, musicians, and writers. Because of their artistic achievements this period is known as the Harlem Renaissance.

Poets and Musicians The leading Harlem poets included Countee Cullen, Langston Hughes, James Weldon Johnson, and Claude McKay. Commenting on the African American heritage, their poems expressed a range of emotions, from bitterness and resentment to joy and hope.

African American jazz musicians such as Duke Ellington and Louis Armstrong were so popular among people of all races that the 1920s is often called the Jazz Age. Other great performers included blues singer Bessie Smith and the multitalented singer and actor Paul Robeson. While these artists sometimes performed before integrated audiences in Harlem, they often found themselves and their audiences segregated in much of the rest of the nation.

Marcus Garvey In 1916, the United Negro Improvement Association (UNIA) was brought to Harlem from Jamaica by a charismatic immigrant, Marcus Garvey. Garvey advocated individual and racial pride for African Americans and developed political ideas of black nationalism. Going beyond the efforts of W. E. B. Du Bois, Garvey established an organization for black separatism, economic self-sufficiency, and a back-to-Africa movement. Garvey's sale of stock in the Black Star Steamship line led to federal charges of fraud. In 1925, he was tried, convicted, and jailed. Later, he was deported to Jamaica and his movement collapsed.

W. E. B. Du Bois and other African American leaders disagreed with Garvey's back-to-Africa idea but endorsed his emphasis on racial pride and self-respect. In the 1960s, Garvey's thinking helped to inspire a later generation to embrace the cause of black pride and nationalism.

Values in Conflict

The dominant social and political issues of the 1920s expressed sharp divisions in U.S. society between the young and the old, between urban modernists and rural fundamentalists, between prohibitionists and antiprohibitionists, and between nativists and the foreign-born.

Religion

Divisions among Protestants reflected the tensions in society between the traditional values of rural areas and the modernizing forces of the cities.

Modernism A range of influences, including the changing role of women, the Social Gospel movement, and scientific knowledge, caused large numbers of Protestants to define their faith in new ways. Modernists took a historical and critical view of certain passages in the Bible and believed they could accept Darwin's theory of evolution without abandoning their religious faith.

Fundamentalism Protestant preachers in rural areas condemned the modernists and taught that every word in the Bible must be accepted as literally true. A key point in fundamentalist doctrine was that creationism (the idea that God had created the universe in seven days, as stated in the Book of Genesis) explained the origin of all life. Fundamentalists blamed the liberal views of modernists for causing a decline in morals.

Revivalists on the Radio Ever since the Great Awakening of the early 1700s, religious revivals swept through America periodically. Revivalists of the 1920s preached a fundamentalist message but did so for the first time making full use of the new tool of mass communication, the radio. The leading radio evangelists were Billy Sunday, who drew large crowds as he attacked drinking, gambling, and dancing; and Aimee Semple McPherson, who condemned the twin evils of communism and jazz music from her pulpit in Los Angeles.

Fundamentalism and the Scopes Trial

More than any other single event, a much-publicized trial in Tennessee focused the debate between religious fundamentalists in the rural South and modernists of the northern cities. Tennessee, like several other southern states, outlawed the teaching of Darwin's theory of evolution in public schools. To challenge the constitutionality of these laws, the American Civil Liberties Union persuaded a Tennessee biology teacher, John Scopes, to teach the theory of evolution to his high school class. For doing so, Scopes was arrested and tried in 1925.

The Trial The entire nation followed the Scopes trial both in newspapers and by radio. Defending Scopes was the famous lawyer Clarence Darrow. Representing the fundamentalists was three-time Democratic candidate for president William Jennings Bryan, who testified as an expert on the Bible.

Aftermath As expected, Scopes was convicted, but the conviction was later overturned on a technicality. Laws banning the teaching of evolution remained on the books for years, although they were rarely enforced. The northern press asserted that Darrow and the modernists had thoroughly discredited fundamentalism. However, to this day, questions about the relationship between religion and the public schools remain controversial and unresolved.

Prohibition

Another controversy that helped define the 1920s concerned people's conflicting attitudes toward the 18th Amendment. Wartime concerns to conserve grain and maintain a sober workforce moved Congress to pass this amendment, which strictly prohibited the manufacture and sale of alcoholic beverages, including liquors, wines, and beers. It was ratified in 1919. The adoption of the Prohibition amendment and a federal law enforcing it (the Volstead Act, 1919) were the culmination of many decades of crusading by temperance forces.

Defying the Law Prohibition did not stop people from drinking alcohol either in public places or at home. Especially in the cities, it became fashionable to defy the law by going to clubs or bars known as speakeasies, where bootleg (smuggled) liquor was sold. City police and judges were paid to look the other way. Even elected officials such as President Harding served alcoholic drinks to guests. Liquors, beers, and wines were readily available from bootleggers who smuggled them from Canada or made them in their garages or basements.

Rival groups of gangsters, including a Chicago gang headed by Al Capone, fought for control of the lucrative bootlegging trade. Organized crime became big business. The millions made from the sale of illegal booze allowed the gangs to expand other illegal activities: prostitution, gambling, and narcotics.

Political Discord and Repeal Most Republicans publicly supported the "noble experiment" of Prohibition (although in private, many politicians drank). Democrats were divided on the issue, with southerners supporting it and northern city politicians calling for repeal. Supporters of the 18th Amendment pointed to declines in alcoholism and alcohol-related deaths, but as the years passed, they gradually weakened in the face of growing public resentment and clear evidence of increased criminal activity. With the coming of the Great Depression, economic arguments for repeal were added to the others. In 1933, the 21st Amendment repealing the Eighteenth was ratified, and millions celebrated the new year by toasting the end of Prohibition.

Nativism

The world war had interrupted the flow of immigrants to the United States, but as soon as the war ended, immigration shot upward. Over a million foreigners entered the country between 1919 and 1921. Like the immigrants of the prewar period, the new arrivals were mainly Catholics and Jews from eastern and southern Europe. Once again, nativist prejudices of native-born Protestants were aroused. Workers feared competition for jobs. Isolationists wanted minimal contact with Europe and feared that immigrants might foment revolution. In response to public demands for restrictive legislation, Congress acted quickly.

Quota Laws Congress passed two laws that severely limited immigration by setting quotas based on nationality. The first quota act of 1921 limited immigration to 3 percent of the number of foreign-born persons from a given nation counted in the 1910 Census (a maximum of 357,000). To reduce the number of immigrants from southern and eastern Europe, Congress passed a second quota act in 1924 that set quotas of 2 percent based on the Census of 1890 (before the arrival of most of the "new" immigrants). Although there were quotas for all European and Asian nationalities, the law chiefly restricted those groups considered "undesirable" by the nativists. By 1927, the quota for all Asians and eastern and southern Europeans had been limited to 150,000, with all Japanese immigrants barred. With these acts, the traditional United States policy of unlimited immigration ended.

Canadians and Latin Americans were exempt from restrictions. Almost 500,000 Mexicans migrated legally to the Southwest during the 1920s.

Case of Sacco and Vanzetti Although liberal American artists and intellectuals were few in number, they loudly protested against racist and nativist prejudices. They rallied to the support of two Italian immigrants, Nicola Sacco and Bartolomeo Vanzetti, who in 1921 had been convicted in a Massachusetts court of committing robbery and murder. Liberals protested that the two men were innocent, and that they had been accused, convicted, and sentenced to die simply because they were poor Italians and anarchists (who were against all government). After six years of appeals and national and international debates over the fairness of their trial, Sacco and Vanzetti were executed in 1927.

Ku Klux Klan

The most extreme expression of nativism in the 1920s was the resurgence of the Ku Klux Klan. Unlike the original Klan of the 1860s and 1870s, the new Klan founded in 1915 was as strong in the Midwest as in the South. The Klan attracted new members because of the popular silent film, *Birth of a Nation,* which portrayed the KKK during Reconstruction as the heroes, and from the white backlash to the race riots of 1919. The new Klan used modern advertising techniques to grow to 5 million members by 1925. It drew most of its support from lower-middle-class white Protestants in small cities and towns. Northern branches of the KKK directed their hostility not only against blacks but also against Catholics, Jews, foreigners, and suspected Communists.

Tactics The Klan employed various methods for terrorizing and intimidating anyone targeted as "un-American." Dressed in white hoods to disguise their identity, Klan members would burn crosses and apply vigilante justice, punishing their victims with whips, tar and feathers, and even the hangman's noose. In its heyday in the early 1920s, the Klan developed strong political influence. In Indiana and Texas, its support became crucial for candidates hoping to win election to state and local offices.

Decline At first, the majority of native-born white Americans appeared to tolerate the Klan because it vowed to uphold high standards of Christian morality and drive out bootleggers, gamblers, and adulterers. Beginning in 1923, however, investigative reports in the northern press revealed that fraud and corruption in the KKK were rife. In 1925, the leader of Indiana's Klan, Grand Dragon David Stephenson, was convicted of murder. After that, the Klan's influence and membership declined rapidly. Nevertheless, it continued to exist and advocate for white supremacy into the 1960s.

Foreign Policy: The Fiction of Isolation

During the 1920s, widespread disillusionment with World War I, Europe's postwar problems, and communism in the Soviet Union (as Russia was renamed) made Americans fearful of being pulled into another foreign war. But despite the U.S. refusal to join the League of Nations, the makers of U.S. foreign policy did not retreat to the isolationism of the Gilded Age. Instead, they actively pursued arrangements in foreign affairs that would advance American interests while also maintaining world peace.

Disarmament and Peace

The Republican presidents of the 1920s tried to promote peace and also scale back expenditures on defense by arranging treaties of disarmament. The most successful disarmament conference—and the greatest achievement of Harding's presidency—was held in Washington, D.C., in 1921.

Washington Conference (1921) Secretary of State Charles Evans Hughes initiated talks on naval disarmament, hoping to stabilize the size of the U.S. Navy relative to that of other powers and to resolve conflicts in the Pacific.

Representatives to the Washington Conference came from Belgium, China, France, Great Britain, Italy, Japan, the Netherlands, and Portugal. Three agreements to relieve tensions resulted from the discussions:

1. Five-Power Treaty Nations with the five largest navies agreed to maintain the following ratio with respect to their largest warships, or battleships: the United States, 5; Great Britain, 5; Japan, 3; France, 1.67; Italy, 1.67. Britain and the United States also agreed not to fortify their possessions in the Pacific, while no limit was placed on the Japanese.

2. Four-Power Treaty The United States, France, Great Britain, and Japan agreed to respect one another's territory in the Pacific.

3. Nine-Power Treaty All nine nations represented at the conference agreed to respect the Open Door policy by guaranteeing the territorial integrity of China.

Kellogg-Briand Pact American women took the lead in a peace movement committed to outlawing future wars. (For her efforts on behalf of peace, Jane Addams won the Nobel Peace Prize in 1931.) The movement achieved its greatest success in 1928 with the signing of a treaty arranged by U.S. Secretary of State Frank Kellogg and the French foreign minister Aristide Briand. Almost all the nations of the world signed the Kellogg-Briand Pact, which renounced the aggressive use of force to achieve national ends. This international agreement would prove ineffective, however, since it (1) permitted defensive wars and (2) failed to provide for taking action against violators of the agreement.

Business and Diplomacy

Republican presidents believed that probusiness policies brought prosperity at home and at the same time strengthened U.S. dealings with other nations. Thus, they found it natural to use diplomacy to advance American business interests in Latin America and other regions.

Latin America Mexico's constitution of 1917 mandated government ownership of all that nation's mineral and oil resources. U.S. investors in Mexico feared that the government might confiscate their properties. A peaceful resolution protecting their interests was negotiated by Coolidge's ambassador to Mexico, Dwight Morrow, in 1927.

Elsewhere in Latin America, Coolidge kept U.S. troops in Nicaragua and Haiti but withdrew them from the Dominican Republic in 1924. While American military influence declined, American economic impact increased. U.S. investments in Latin America doubled between 1919 and 1929.

Middle East The oil reserves in the Middle East were becoming recognized as a major source of potential wealth. British oil companies had a large head start in the region, but Secretary of State Hughes succeeded in winning oil-drilling rights for U.S. companies.

Tariffs Passed by Congress in 1922, the Fordney-McCumber Tariff increased the duties on foreign manufactured goods by 25 percent. It was protective of U.S. business interests in the short run but destructive in the long run. Because of it, European nations were slow to recover from the war and had difficulty repaying their war debts to the United States. They responded to the high U.S. tariffs by imposing tariffs of their own on American imports. Ultimately, these obstacles to international trade weakened the world economy and were one reason for the Great Depression of the 1930s.

War Debts and Reparations

Before World War I, the United States had been a debtor nation, importing more than it exported. It emerged from the war as a creditor nation, having lent more than $10 billion to the Allies. Harding and Coolidge insisted that Britain and France pay back every penny of their war debts. The British and French objected. They pointed out that they suffered much worse losses than the Americans during the war, that the borrowed money had been spent in the United States, and that high U.S. tariffs made it more difficult to pay the debts. To be sure, the Treaty of Versailles required Germany to pay $30 billion in reparations to the Allies. But how were Britain and France to collect this money? Germany was bankrupt, had soaring inflation, and was near anarchy.

Dawes Plan Charles Dawes, an American banker who would become Coolidge's vice president, negotiated a compromise that was accepted by all sides in 1924. The Dawes Plan established a cycle of payments flowing from the United States to Germany and from Germany to the Allies. U.S. banks would lend Germany huge sums to rebuild its economy and pay reparations to Britain and France. In turn, Britain and France would use the reparations money to pay their war debts to the United States. This cycle helped to ease financial problems on both sides of the Atlantic. After the stock market crash of 1929, however, U.S. bank loans stopped and the prosperity propped up by the Dawes Plan collapsed.

Legacy Ultimately, Finland was the only nation to repay its war debts in full. The unpaid debts of the other nations left bad feelings on all sides. Many Europeans resented what they saw as American greed, while Americans saw new reasons to follow an isolationist path in the 1930s.

HISTORICAL PERSPECTIVES: HOW CONSERVATIVE WERE THE 1920S?

By the 1930s, the 1920s seemed to be a unique decade—a period of social fun and business boom wedged between two calamities, World War I and the Great Depression. In his popular history *Only Yesterday* (1931), Frederick Lewis Allen gave support to the ideas of the leading social critics of the 1920s, H. L. Mencken and Sinclair Lewis. He portrayed the period as one of narrow-minded materialism in which the middle class abandoned Progressive reforms, embraced conservative Republican policies, and either supported or condoned nativism, racism, and fundamentalism. Historian Arthur Schlesinger Jr. generally accepted this view of the twenties, seeing it within the framework of his cyclical view of history. He argued that the politics of the decade represented a conservative reaction to the liberal reforms of the Progressive era.

Revisionist historians of the 1950s questioned whether the 1920s truly broke with the Progressive past. They argued that the period continued earlier protest movements such as Populism. Richard Hofstadter and other "consensus" writers distinguished between two middle classes: a new urban group with modern values and an older middle class with traditional values. William Leuchtenburg in *The Perils of Prosperity* (1958) portrayed the traditionalists as threatened by cultural pluralism and modern ideas.

A third assessment took a more positive view of the traditionalists. Some historians, including Alan Brinkley in the 1980s, argued that people in the "old" middle class, including fundamentalists and nativists, were understandably trying to protect their own economic and social self-interests. At the same time, they were seeking to preserve individual and community freedom in face of the modernist movement toward centralized bureaucratic and national control. This effort to maintain local control and independence from big government is seen as continuing from the 1920s to the present.

Given the extreme and deeply felt differences between the modernists and the traditionalists, some historians have wondered why there was not more conflict in the twenties. One explanation, which has grown from the 1960s to the present, is the importance of the consumer culture. Historians, including Stuart Ewen and Roland Marchand, have in diverse ways shown how the influence of growing materialism and prosperity caused people to accept increased bureaucratic control of their lives. They place varying emphasis on the ways in which material affluence, consumer goods, advertising, and a homogeneous mass culture redefined U.S. social and political values. Though these historians agree on consumer culture's importance, they differ greatly on its positive and negative impact. By focusing on materialism and consumption, historians have returned to the views of Mencken, Lewis, and Allen.

KEY TERMS BY THEME

1920s Politics (POL)
Warren Harding
Charles Evans Hughes
Andrew Mellon
Harry Daugherty
Albert Fall
Teapot Dome
Fordney-McCumber
  Tariff Act
Bureau of the Budget
Calvin Coolidge
Herbert Hoover
Alfred E. Smith

1920s Economy (WXT)
business prosperity
standard of living
scientific management
Henry Ford
assembly line
open shop
welfare capitalism
consumerism
electric appliances
impact of the
  automobile

A Modern Culture (SOC, ARC)
jazz age
radio, phonographs
national networks
Hollywood
movie stars
movie palaces
popular heroes
role of women
Sigmund Freud
morals and fashions
Margaret Sanger
high school education
consumer culture
Frederick Lewis Allen
Only Yesterday

Literature and the Arts (SOC)
Gertrude Stein
Lost Generation
F. Scott Fitzgerald
Ernest Hemingway
Sinclair Lewis
Ezra Pound
T. S. Eliot
Eugene O'Neill
industrial design
Art Deco
Edward Hopper
regional artists
Grant Wood
George Gershwin

African American Identity (SOC, ID)
northern migration
Harlem Renaissance
Countee Cullen
Langston Hughes
James Weldon Johnson
Claude McKay
Duke Ellington
Louis Armstrong
Bessie Smith
Paul Robeson
Back to Africa
  movement
Marcus Garvey
black pride

Conflict over Religion (SOC)
modernism
fundamentalism
revivalists: Billy
  Sunday, Aimee
  Semple McPherson
Scopes trial
Clarence Darrow

Conflict over Prohibition (SOC, POL)
Volstead Act (1919)
rural vs. urban
organized crime
Al Capone
21st Amendment

Conflict over Immigration (SOC, POL, NAT)
quota laws of 1921
  and 1924
Sacco and Vanzetti
  Case
Ku Klux Klan
Birth of a Nation
blacks, Catholics and
  Jews
foreigners and
  Communists

Foreign Policy (WOR)
disarmament
Washington Conference (1921)
Five-Power Naval
  treaty
Nine-Power China
  Treaty
Kellogg-Briand Pact
  (1928)
Latin America policy
war debts
reparations
Dawes Plan (1924)

MULTIPLE-CHOICE QUESTIONS

Questions 1–3 refer to the excerpt below.

"A widely held view of the Republican administrations of the 1920s is that they represented a return to an older order that had existed before Theodore Roosevelt and Woodrow Wilson became the nation's chief executives. Harding and Coolidge especially are seen as latter-day McKinleys, political mediocrities who peopled their cabinets with routine, conservative party hacks of the kind almost universal in Washington from the end of the Civil War until the early 20th century. In this view, the 1920s politically were an effort to set back the clock."

—David A. Shannon, historian, *Between the Wars: America, 1919–1941*, 1965

1. Which of the following groups from the 1920s most likely would have supported the perspective of this excerpt?
   (A) Business and financial leaders
   (B) Democrats and Republicans who supported Progressive reforms
   (C) Supporters of reduced government spending and tax cuts
   (D) Native-born and older Americans with traditional values

2. Which of the following from the 1920s mostly clearly challenges the interpretation expressed in the excerpt?
   (A) The disarmament agreement among the great powers to limit warships and aggression
   (B) The passage of legislation to increase tariff rates and cut income taxes
   (C) The leasing of public lands to private oil companies
   (D) The reduction of federal regulations for businesses and the banking system

3. Which of the following groups of politicians from between 1865 and 1900 most closely resemble the corrupt politicians during the Harding administration?
   (A) Politicians who failed to protect the freedmen in the South
   (B) Politicians who took shares of railroad stock in return for government subsidies
   (C) Politicians who gave government jobs to their political supporters as rewards
   (D) Politicians who violated the temperance laws and their professed moral beliefs

Questions 4–6 refer to the advertisement below.

Source: General Motors, 1925. The Granger Collection, NYC

4. Which of the following trends of the 1920s is most clearly portrayed in this advertisement?

   (A) The expansion of auto dealers throughout the country

   (B) The use of extended payment plans to purchase consumer goods

   (C) The emergence of General Motors as the largest company

   (D) The growth of middle-class incomes

5. Many historians criticize the economy that developed during the 1920s. Which of the following statements best supports that point of view?

   (A) Consumerism weakened the moral character of the nation

   (B) The growth of the auto industry badly hurt the railroads

   (C) Advertising was based on gaining status and popularity

   (D) The boom was based on speculation and borrowed money

6. Which of the following groups faced the most difficult economic conditions during the 1920s?

   (A) Non-unionized workers in older industries

   (B) Assembly line workers in factories

   (C) Farmers and many rural areas

   (D) Businesses that did not accept credit cards

Questions 7–8 refer to the excerpt below.

The problem of birth control has arisen directly from the efforts of the feminine spirit to free itself from bondage. . . .

The basic freedom of the world is woman's freedom. A free race cannot be born of slave mothers. A woman enchained cannot choose but give a measure of that bondage to her sons and daughters. No woman can call herself free who does not own and control her body. No woman can call herself free until she can choose consciously whether she will or will not be a mother.

—Margaret Sanger, *Woman and the New Race,* 1920

7. Which of the following developments in the 1920s would most directly support the author's sentiments in the excerpt?
   (A) Liberalized divorce laws
   (B) Labor-saving household appliances
   (C) Employment as secretaries, nurses, and teachers
   (D) New fashions and hair styles

8. Which of the following most influenced thinking about sexual behavior during the 1920s?
   (A) Research of Frederick Taylor
   (B) Writing of the Lost Generation
   (C) Advertising of consumer products
   (D) Popularization of Sigmund Freud

SHORT-ANSWER QUESTIONS

Use complete sentences; an outline or bulleted list alone is not acceptable.

Question 1 is based on the excerpt below.

"Through his artistic efforts the Negro is smashing this immemorial stereotype faster than he has ever done through any other method he has been able to use. . . . He is impressing upon the national mind the conviction that he is an active and important force in American life; that he is a creator as well as a creature; that he has given as well as received; that he is the potential giver of larger and richer contributions. . . .

"I do not think it too much to say that through artistic achievement the Negro has found a means of getting at the very core of the prejudice against him by challenging the Nordic superiority complex. A great deal has been accomplished in this decade of 'renaissance.'"

—James Weldon Johnson, poet and NAACP, *Harper's,* 1928

1. Using the excerpt, answer (A), (B), and (C).
   (A) Briefly explain ONE specific example of an African American artist's achievement from the era that would support Johnson's perspective.
   (B) Briefly explain ONE specific factor that helped African American artists reach a wider audience in the 1920s.
   (C) Briefly explain ONE specific example of what Johnson most likely meant by "the very core of prejudice" faced by African Americans in the 1920s.

Question 2. Answer (A), (B), and (C).

   (A) Briefly explain ONE specific example of how religion and science were a source of conflict in American society during the 1920s.
   (B) Briefly explain ONE specific development during the 1920s that changed public attitudes toward Prohibition.
   (C) Briefly explain ONE specific difference in the immigrant legislation of the 1920s in comparison to the period from 1865 to 1914.

Question 3. Answer (A), (B), and (C).

   (A) Briefly explain ONE specific example of how the media of the 1920s contributed to development of a shared national culture.
   (B) Briefly explain ONE specific development that caused the disillusionment among writers of the 1920s.
   (C) Briefly explain ONE specific artistic response during the 1920s and 1930s to industrial development or the urban experience.

Question 4 is based on the excerpts below.

"Nor was this new material advance essentially gross and philistine [unsophisticted], as the popular historiography of the 1920s has it, 'a drunken fiesta' ... Intellectuals are a little too inclined to resent poorer people acquiring for the first time material possessions, and especially luxuries. ... During the 1920s, in fact, America began suddenly to acquire a cultural density ... which it had never before possessed."

—Paul Johnson, historian, *A History of the American People,* 1997

"Never was a decade snuffed out so quickly as the 1920s. The stock market crash was taken as a judgment pronounced on the whole era, and, in the grim days of the depression, the 1920s were condemned as a time of irresponsibility and immaturity."

—William E. Leuchtenburg, historian, *The Perils of Prosperity,* 1959

4. Using the excerpts, answer (A), (B), and (C).
   (A) Briefly describe ONE major difference between Leuchtenburg's and Johnson's historical interpretation of the 1920s in the United States.
   (B) Briefly explain how ONE specific historical event or development that is not explicitly mentioned in the excerpts could be used to support Leuchtenburg's interpretation.
   (C) Briefly explain how ONE specific historical event or development that is not explicitly mentioned in the excerpts could be used to support Johnson's interpretation.

THINK AS A HISTORIAN: ADDING DETAILS FOR CONTEXTUALIZATION

Adding information about the historical context of an event helps the reader understand its significance. Which THREE of the sentences below best demonstrates the use of contextualization?

1. The corruption in the Harding administration involving Albert Fall and Harry Daugherty was serious.

2. The Kellogg-Briand Pact expressed a reaction against war that could be seen throughout Europe and eastern Asia.

3. In his novels, F. Scott Fitzgerald reflected the consumer culture, materialism, and fascination with wealth that dominated the 1920s.

4. The Harlem Renaissance was even more impressive because it occurred during a period when the KKK and anti-immigrant feelings were on the increase.

5. Grant Wood appreciated the subtle beauty of Iowa and other rural parts of the United States.

24

THE GREAT DEPRESSION AND THE NEW DEAL, 1929–1939

Once I built a tower, to the sun.
Brick and rivet and lime,
Once I built a tower,
Now it's done,
Brother, can you spare a dime?

E. Y. Harburg and Jay Gorney,
"Brother, Can You Spare a Dime?," 1932

When the new Democratic president, Franklin D. Roosevelt, said in his 1933 inaugural address, "the only thing we have to fear is fear itself," he struck a note that the millions who listened to him on the radio could well understand. In 1933, after having experienced nearly four years of the worst economic depression in U.S. history, Americans were gripped by fear for their survival.

In the past, overproduction and business failures had periodically caused economic downturns measured in months that would be followed by recovery and eventual prosperity. These depressions and recessions were thought to be nothing more than part of the natural rhythm of the business cycle in a free market economy. However, depressions that included widespread bank failures and the collapse of investment and credit systems often resulted in long-term and deeper depressions extending several years, such as the depressions of 1837, 1873, and 1893.

This depression of the 1930s felt different. It lasted far longer, caused more business failures and unemployment, and affected more people—both middle class and working class—than any preceding period of hard times. This was in fact not just an ordinary depression, but the *Great Depression*. Before it was over, two presidents—Herbert Hoover and Franklin Roosevelt—would devote 12 years to seeking the elusive path toward recovery.

Causes and Effects of the Depression, 1929–1933

What caused the spectacular business boom of the 1920s to collapse dramatically in October 1929?

Wall Street Crash

The ever-rising stock prices had become both a symbol and a source of wealth during the prosperous 1920s. A "boom" was in full force both in the United States and in the world economy in the late 1920s. On the stock exchange on Wall Street in New York City, stock prices had kept going up and up for 18 months from March 1928 to September 1929. On September 3, the Dow Jones Industrial Average of major stocks had reached an all-time high of 381. An average investor who bought $1,000 worth of such stocks at the time of Hoover's election (November 1928) would have doubled his or her money in less than a year. Millions of people did invest in the boom market of 1928— and millions lost their money in October 1929, when it collapsed.

Black Thursday and Black Tuesday Although stock prices had fluctuated greatly for several weeks preceding the crash, the true panic did not begin until a Thursday in late October. On this Black Thursday—October 24, 1929—there was an unprecedented volume of selling on Wall Street, and stock prices plunged. The next day, hoping to stave off disaster by stabilizing prices, a group of bankers bought millions of dollars of stocks. The strategy worked for only one business day, Friday. The selling frenzy resumed on Monday. On Black Tuesday, October 29, the bottom fell out, as millions of panicky investors ordered their brokers to sell —but almost no buyers could be found.

From that day on, prices on Wall Street kept going down and down. By late November, the Dow Jones index had fallen from its September high of 381 to 198. Three years later, stock prices would finally hit bottom at 41, less then one-ninth of their peak value.

Causes of the Crash

While the collapse of the stock market in 1929 may have triggered economic turmoil, it alone was not responsible for the Great Depression. The depression throughout the nation and the world was the result of a combination of factors, and economists continue to debate their relative importance.

Uneven Distribution of Income Wages had risen relatively little compared to the large increases in productivity and corporate profits. Economic success was not shared by all, as the top 5 percent of the richest Americans received over 33 percent of all income. Once demand for their products declined, businesses laid off workers contributing to a downward spiral in demand, and more layoffs.

Stock Market Speculation Many people in all economic classes believed that they could get rich by "playing the market." People were no longer investing their money in order to share in the profits of a company—they were speculating that the price of a stock would go up and that they could sell it for a quick profit. *Buying on margin* allowed people to borrow most of the cost of the stock, making down payments as low as 10 percent. Investors depended on the price of the stock increasing so that they could repay the loan. When stock prices dropped, the market collapsed, and many lost everything they had borrowed and invested.

Excessive Use of Credit Low interest rates and a belief of both consumers and business that the economic boom was permanent led to increased borrowing and installment buying. This over-indebtedness would result in defaults on loans and bank failures.

Overproduction of Consumer Goods Business growth, aided by increased productivity and use of credit, had produced a volume of goods that workers with stagnant wages could not continue to purchase.

Weak Farm Economy The prosperity of the 1920s never reached farmers, who had suffered from overproduction, high debt, and low prices since the end of World War I. As the depression continued through the 1930s, severe weather and a long drought added to farmers' difficulties.

Government Policies During the 1920s, the government had complete faith in business and did little to control or regulate it. Congress enacted high tariffs which protected U.S. industries but hurt farmers and international trade.

Some economists have concentrated blame on the Federal Reserve for its tight money policies, as hundreds of banks failed. Instead on trying to stabilize banks, the money supply, and prices, The Federal Reserve tried to preserve the gold standard. Without depositors' insurance, people panicked to get their money out of the banks, which caused more bank failures.

Global Economic Problems Nations had become more interdependent because of international banking, manufacturing, and trade. Europe had never recovered from World War I, but the United States failed to recognize Europe's postwar problems (The United States reacted differently after World War II. See Chapter 26). Instead, U.S. insistence on loan repayment in full and high tariffs policies weakened Europe and contributed to the worldwide depression.

Effects

It is difficult to imagine the pervasive impact of the Great Depression. While in retrospect it can be seen that the economic decline reached bottom in 1932, complete recovery came only with the beginning of another world war, in 1939. The Great Depression's influence on American thinking and policies has even extended beyond the lifetimes of those who experienced it.

Various economic statistics serve as indicators that track the health of a nation's economy. The U.S. Gross National Product—the value of all the goods and services produced by the nation in one year—dropped from $104 billion to $56 billion in four years (1929 to 1932), while the nation's income declined by over 50 percent. Some 20 percent of all banks closed, wiping out 10 million savings accounts. As banks failed, the money supply contracted by 30 percent. By 1933, the number of unemployed had reached 13 million people, or 25 percent of the workforce, not including farmers.

The crash ended Republican domination of government. People accepted dramatic changes in policies and the expansion of the federal government.

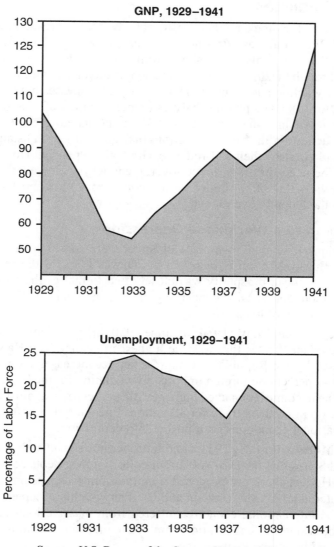

GNP, 1929–1941

Unemployment, 1929–1941

Percentage of Labor Force

Source: U.S. Bureau of the Census. *Historical Statistics of the United States, Colonial Times to 1970*

The social effects of the depression were felt by all classes. Those who had never fully shared in the prosperity of the 1920s, such as farmers and African Americans, had increased difficulties. Poverty and homelessness increased, as did the stress on families, as people searched for work. Mortgage foreclosures and evictions became commonplace. The homeless traveled in box cars and lived in shantytowns, named "Hoovervilles," in mock honor of their president.

Hoover's Policies

At the time of the stock market crash, nobody could foresee how long the downward slide would last. President Hoover was wrong—but hardly alone—in thinking that prosperity would soon return. The president believed the nation could get through the difficult times if the people took his advice about exercising voluntary action and restraint. Hoover urged businesses not to cut wages, unions not to strike, and private charities to increase their efforts for the needy and the jobless. Until the summer of 1930, he hesitated to ask Congress for legislative action on the economy, afraid that government assistance to individuals would destroy their self-reliance. Gradually, President Hoover came to recognize the need for more direct government action. However, he took the traditional view that public relief should come from state and local governments, not the federal government.

Responding to a Worldwide Depression

Repercussions from the crash on Wall Street were soon felt in the financial centers of Europe. Through trade and the Dawes Plan for the repayment of war debts, European prosperity was closely tied to that of the United States. Hoover's first major decision concerning the international situation was one of the worst mistakes of his presidency.

Hawley-Smoot Tariff (1930) In June 1930, the president signed into law a schedule of tariff rates that was the highest in history. The Hawley-Smoot Tariff passed by the Republican Congress set tax increases ranging from 31 percent to 49 percent on foreign imports. In retaliation for the U.S. tariff, however, European countries enacted higher tariffs of their own against U.S. goods. The effect was to reduce trade for all nations, meaning that both the national and international economies sank further into depression.

Debt Moratorium By 1931, conditions became so bad both in Europe and the United States that the Dawes Plan for collecting war debts could no longer continue. Hoover therefore proposed a moratorium (suspension) on the payment of international debts. Britain and Germany readily accepted, but France balked. The international economy suffered from massive loan defaults, and banks on both sides of the Atlantic scrambled to meet the demands of the many depositors withdrawing their money.

Domestic Programs: Too Little, Too Late

By 1931, Hoover was convinced that some federal action was needed to pull the U.S. economy out of its doldrums. He therefore supported and signed into law programs that offered assistance to indebted farmers and struggling businesses.

Federal Farm Board The Farm Board was actually created in 1929, before the stock market crash, but its powers were later enlarged to meet the economic crisis. The board was authorized to help farmers stabilize prices by temporarily holding surplus grain and cotton in storage. The program, however, was far too modest to handle the continued overproduction of farm goods.

Reconstruction Finance Corporation (RFC) This federally funded, government-owned corporation was created by Congress early in 1932 as a measure for propping up faltering railroads, banks, life insurance companies, and other financial institutions. The president reasoned that emergency loans from the RFC would help to stabilize these key businesses. The benefits would then "trickle down" to smaller businesses and ultimately bring recovery. Democrats scoffed at this measure, saying it would only help the rich.

Despair and Protest

By 1932, millions of unemployed workers and impoverished farmers were in a state bordering on desperation. Some decided to take direct action to battle the forces that seemed to be crushing them.

Unrest on the Farms In many communities, farmers banded together to stop banks from foreclosing on farms and evicting people from their homes. Farmers in the Midwest formed the Farm Holiday Association, which attempted to reverse the drop in prices by stopping the entire crop of grain harvested in 1932 from reaching the market. The effort collapsed after some violence.

Bonus March Also in the desperate summer of 1932, a thousand unemployed World War I veterans marched to Washington, D.C., to demand immediate payment of the bonuses promised them at a later date (1945). They were eventually joined by thousands of other veterans who brought their wives and children and camped in improvised shacks near the Capitol. Congress failed to pass the bonus bill they sought. When two veterans were killed in a clash with police, Hoover ordered the army to break up the encampment. General Douglas MacArthur, the army's chief of staff, used tanks and tear gas to destroy the shantytown and drive the veterans from Washington. The incident caused many Americans to regard Hoover as heartless and uncaring.

The Election of 1932

The depression's worst year, 1932, happened to be a presidential election year. The disheartened Republicans renominated Hoover, who warned that a Democratic victory would only result in worse economic problems.

Democrats At their convention, the Democrats nominated New York Governor Franklin D. Roosevelt for president and Speaker of the House John Nance Garner of Texas for vice president. As a candidate, Roosevelt pledged a "new deal" for the American people, the repeal of Prohibition, aid for the unemployed, and cuts in government spending.

Results In voters' minds, the only real issue was the depression, and which candidate—Hoover or Roosevelt—could do a better job of ending the hard times. Almost 60 percent of them concluded that it was time for a change. The Roosevelt-Garner ticket carried all but six states, Republican strongholds in the Northeast. Desperate for change, many Socialists deserted their candidate,

Norman Thomas, to support Roosevelt. Not only was the new president a Democrat but both houses of Congress had large Democratic majorities.

Hoover as "Lame-Duck" President For the four months between Roosevelt's election and his inauguration in March 1933, Hoover was still president. However, as a "lame duck," Hoover was powerless to cope with the depression, which continued to get worse. He offered to work with the president-elect through the long period, but Roosevelt declined, not wanting to be tied to any of the Republican president's ideas. The Twentieth Amendment (known as the *lame-duck amendment*), passed in February 1933 and ratified by October 1933, shortened the period between presidential election and inauguration. The amendment set the start of each president's term for January 20.

Franklin D. Roosevelt's New Deal

The new president was a distant cousin of President Theodore Roosevelt and was married to Theodore's niece, Eleanor. More than any other president, Franklin Delano Roosevelt—popularly known by his initials, FDR—expanded the size of the federal government, altered its scope of operations, and greatly enlarged presidential powers. He would dominate the nation and the government for an unprecedented stretch of time, 12 years and two months. FDR became one of the most influential world leaders of the 20th century.

FDR: The Man

Franklin Roosevelt was the only child of a wealthy New York family. He personally admired cousin Theodore and followed in his footsteps as a New York state legislator and then as U.S. assistant secretary of the navy. Unlike Republican Theodore, however, Franklin was a Democrat. In 1920 he was the Democratic nominee for vice president. He and James Cox, the presidential candidate, lost badly in Warren G. Harding's landslide victory.

Disability In the midst of a promising career, Roosevelt was paralyzed by polio in 1921. Although he was wealthy enough to retire, he labored instead to resume his career in politics and eventually regained the full power of his upper body, even though he could never again walk unaided and required the assistance of crutches, braces, and a wheelchair. Roosevelt's greatest strengths were his warm personality, his gifts as a speaker, and his ability to work with and inspire people. In 1928, campaigning from a car and in a wheelchair, FDR was elected governor of New York. In this office, he instituted a number of welfare and relief programs to help the jobless.

Eleanor Roosevelt Roosevelt's wife, Eleanor, emerged as a leader in her own right. She became the most active first lady in history, writing a newspaper column, giving speeches, and traveling the country. Though their personal relationship was strained, Eleanor and Franklin Roosevelt had a strong mutual respect. She served as the president's social conscience and influenced him to support minorities and the less fortunate.

New Deal Philosophy

In his campaign for president in 1932, Roosevelt offered vague promises but no concrete programs. He did not have a detailed plan for ending the depression, but he was committed to action and willing to experiment with political solutions to economic problems.

The Three R's In his acceptance speech at the Democratic convention in 1932, Roosevelt had said: "I pledge you, I pledge myself, to a new deal for the American people." He had further promised in his campaign to help the "forgotten man at the bottom of the economic pyramid." During the early years of his presidency, it became clear that his New Deal programs were to serve three R's: *relief* for people out of work, *recovery* for business and the economy as a whole, and *reform* of American economic institutions.

Brain Trust and Other Advisers In giving shape to his New Deal, President Roosevelt relied on a group of advisers who had assisted him while he was governor of New York. Louis Howe was to be his chief political adviser. For advice on economic matters, Roosevelt turned to a group of university professors, known as the Brain Trust.

The people that Roosevelt appointed to high administrative positions were the most diverse in U.S. history, with a record number of African Americans, Catholics, Jews, and women. For example, his secretary of labor was Frances Perkins, the first woman ever to serve in a president's cabinet.

The First Hundred Days

With the nation desperate and close to the brink of panic, the Democratic Congress looked to the new president for leadership, which Roosevelt was eager to provide. Immediately after being sworn into office on March 4, 1933, Roosevelt called Congress into a hundred-day-long special session. During this brief period, Congress passed into law every request of President Roosevelt, enacting more major legislation than any single Congress in history. Most of the new laws and agencies were commonly referred to by their initials: WPA, AAA, CCC, NRA.

Bank Holiday In early 1933, banks were failing at a frightening rate, as depositors flocked to withdraw funds. As many banks failed in 1933 (over 5,000) as had failed in all the previous years of the depression. To restore confidence in those banks that were still solvent, the president ordered the banks closed for a bank holiday on March 6, 1933. He went on the radio to explain that the banks would be reopened after allowing enough time for the government to reorganize them on a sound basis.

Repeal of Prohibition The new president kept a campaign promise to enact repeal of Prohibition and also raised needed tax money by having Congress pass the Beer-Wine Revenue Act, which legalized the sale of beer and wine. Later in 1933, the ratification of the Twenty-First Amendment repealed the Eighteenth Amendment, bringing Prohibition to an end.

Fireside Chats Roosevelt went on the radio on March 12, 1933, to present the first of many fireside chats to the American people. The president assured his listeners that the banks which reopened after the bank holiday were safe. The public responded as hoped, with the money deposited in the reopened banks exceeding the money withdrawn.

Financial Recovery and Reform Programs As the financial part of his New Deal, FDR persuaded Congress to enact the following measures:

- The Emergency Banking Relief Act authorized the government to examine the finances of banks closed during the bank holiday and reopen those judged to be sound.

- The Glass-Steagall Act increased regulation of the banks and limited how banks could invest customers' money. The Federal Deposit Insurance Corporation (FDIC) guaranteed individual bank deposits. The gold standard was restricted to international transactions, and the Americans could no longer exchange their dollars for gold.

- The Home Owners Loan Corporation (HOLC) provided refinancing of small homes to prevent foreclosures.

- The Farm Credit Administration provided low-interest farm loans and mortgages to prevent foreclosures on the property of indebted farmers.

Relief for the Unemployed A number of programs created during the Hundred Days addressed the needs of the millions of unemployed workers. These plans created jobs with government stimulus dollars to provide both relief and to create more demand for goods and services, which it hoped would create more jobs in the private sector.

- The Federal Emergency Relief Administration (FERA) offered outright grants of federal money to states and local governments that were operating soup kitchens and other forms of relief for the jobless and homeless. The director of FERA was Harry Hopkins, one of the president's closest friends and advisers.

- The Public Works Administration (PWA), directed by Secretary of the Interior Harold Ickes, allotted money to state and local governments for building roads, bridges, dams, and other public works. Such construction projects were a source of thousands of jobs.

- The Civilian Conservation Corps (CCC) employed young men on projects on federal lands and paid their families small monthly sums.

- The Tennessee Valley Authority (TVA) was a huge experiment in regional development and public planning. As a government corporation, it hired thousands of people in one of the nation's poorest regions, the Tennessee Valley, to build dams, operate electric power plants, control flooding and erosion, and manufacture fertilizer. The TVA sold electricity to residents of the region at rates that were well below those previously charged by a private power company.

Industrial Recovery Program The key measure in 1933 to combine immediate relief and long-term reform was the National Recovery Administration (NRA). Directed by Hugh Johnson, the NRA was an attempt to guarantee reasonable profits for business and fair wages and hours for labor. With the antitrust laws temporarily suspended, the NRA could help each industry (such as steel, oil, and paper) set codes for wages, hours of work, levels of production, and prices of finished goods. The law creating the NRA also gave workers the right to organize and bargain collectively. The complex program operated with limited success for two years before the Supreme Court declared the NRA unconstitutional (*Schechter v. U.S.*) in 1935.

Farm Production Control Program Farmers were offered a program similar in concept to what the NRA did for industry. The Agricultural Adjustment Administration (AAA) encouraged farmers to reduce production (and thereby boost prices) by offering to pay government subsidies for every acre they plowed under. The AAA met the same fate as the NRA. It was declared unconstitutional in a 1935 Supreme Court decision.

Other Programs of the First New Deal

Congress adjourned briefly after its extraordinary legislative record in the first Hundred Days of the New Deal. Roosevelt, however, was not finished devising new remedies for the nation's ills. In late 1933 and through much of 1934, the Democratic Congress was easily persuaded to enact the following:

- The Civil Works Administration (CWA) was added to the PWA and other programs for creating jobs. This agency hired laborers for temporary construction projects sponsored by the federal government.

- The Securities and Exchange Commission (SEC) was created to regulate the stock market and to place strict limits on the kind of speculative practices that had led to the Wall Street crash in 1929. The SEC also required full audits of and financial disclosure by corporations to protect investors from fraud and insider trading.

- The Federal Housing Administration (FHA) gave both the construction industry and homeowners a boost by insuring bank loans for building new houses and repairing old ones.

- A new law took the United States off the gold standard in an effort to halt deflation (falling prices). The value of the dollar was set at $35 per ounce of gold, but paper dollars were no longer redeemable in gold.

The Second New Deal

Roosevelt's first two years in office were largely focused on achieving one of the three R's: recovery. Democratic victories in the congressional elections of 1934 gave the president the popular mandate he needed to seek another round of laws and programs. In the summer of 1935, he launched the second New Deal, which concentrated on the other two R's: relief and reform.

Relief Programs

Harry Hopkins became even more prominent in Roosevelt's administration with the creation in 1935 of a new and larger relief agency.

Works Progress Administration (WPA) Much bigger than the relief agencies of the first New Deal, the WPA spent billions of dollars between 1935 and 1940 to provide people with jobs. After its first year of operation under Hopkins, it employed 3.4 million men and women who had formerly been on the relief rolls of state and local governments. It paid them double the relief rate but less than the going wage for regular workers. Most WPA workers were put to work constructing new bridges, roads, airports, and public buildings. Unemployed artists, writers, actors, and photographers were paid by the WPA to paint murals, write histories, and perform in plays.

One part of the WPA, the National Youth Administration (NYA), provided part-time jobs to help young people stay in high school and college or until they could get a job with a private employer.

Resettlement Administration (RA) Placed under the direction of one of the Brain Trust, Rexford Tugwell, the Resettlement Administration provided loans to sharecroppers, tenants, and small farmers. It also established federal camps where migrant workers could find decent housing.

Source: Carl Morris, Eugene, Oregon, Post Office, c. 1939, WPA Federal Arts Project. Oregon Scenic County Images

Reforms

The reform legislation of the second New Deal reflected Roosevelt's belief that industrial workers and farmers needed to receive more government help than members of the business and privileged classes.

National Labor Relations (Wagner) Act (1935) This major labor law of 1935 replaced the labor provisions of the National Industrial Recovery Act, after that law was declared unconstitutional. The Wagner Act guaranteed a worker's right to join a union and a union's right to bargain collectively. It also outlawed business practices that were unfair to labor. A new agency, the National Labor Relations Board (NLRB), was empowered to enforce the law and make sure that workers' rights were protected.

Rural Electrification Administration (REA) This new agency provided loans for electrical cooperatives to supply power in rural areas.

Federal Taxes A revenue act of 1935 significantly increased the tax on incomes of the wealthy few. It also increased the tax on large gifts from parent to child and on capital gains (profits from the sale of stocks or other properties).

The Social Security Act

The reform that, for generations afterward, would affect the lives of nearly all Americans was the passage in 1935 of the Social Security Act. It created a federal insurance program based upon the automatic collection of payments from employees and employers throughout people's working careers. The Social Security trust fund would then be used to make monthly payments to retired persons over the age of 65. Also receiving benefits under this new law were workers who lost their jobs (unemployment compensation), persons who were blind or otherwise disabled, and dependent children and their mothers.

The Election of 1936

The economy was improving but still weak and unstable in 1936 when the Democrats nominated Roosevelt for a second term. Because of his New Deal programs and active style of personal leadership, the president was now enormously popular among workers and small farmers. Business, however, generally disliked and even hated him because of his regulatory programs and prounion measures such as the Wagner Act.

Alf Landon Challenging Roosevelt was the Republican nominee for president, Alfred (Alf) Landon, the progressive-minded governor of Kansas. Landon criticized the Democrats for spending too much money but in general accepted most of the New Deal legislation.

Results Roosevelt swamped Landon, winning every state except Maine and Vermont and more than 60 percent of the popular vote. Behind their president's New Deal, the Democratic party could now count on the votes of a new coalition of popular support. Through the 1930s and into the 1960s, the Democratic or New Deal coalition would consist of the Solid South, white ethnic groups in the cities, midwestern farmers, and labor unions and liberals. In addition, new support for the Democrats came from African Americans, mainly in northern cities, who left the Republican party of Lincoln because of Roosevelt's New Deal.

Opponents of the New Deal

Opinion polls and election results showed that a large majority of Americans supported Roosevelt. Nevertheless, his New Deal programs were extremely controversial and became the target of vitriolic attacks by liberals, conservatives, and demagogues.

Liberal Critics

Socialists and extreme liberals in the Democratic party criticized the New Deal (especially the first New Deal of 1933–1934) for doing too much for business and too little for the unemployed and the working poor. They charged that the president failed to address the problems of ethnic minorities, women, and the elderly.

Conservative Critics

More numerous were those on the right who attacked the New Deal for giving the federal government too much power. These critics charged that relief programs such as the WPA and labor laws such as the Wagner Act bordered on socialism or even communism. Business leaders were alarmed by (1) increased regulations, (2) the second New Deal's prounion stance, and (3) the financing of government programs by means of borrowed money—a practice known as *deficit financing*. Conservative Democrats, including former presidential candidates Alfred E. (Al) Smith and John W. Davis, joined with leading Republicans in 1934 to form an anti-New Deal organization called the American Liberty League. Its avowed purpose was to stop the New Deal from "subverting" the U.S. economic and political system.

Demagogues

Several critics played upon the American people's desperate need for immediate solutions to their problems. Using the radio to reach a mass audience, they proposed simplistic schemes for ending "evil conspiracies" (Father Coughlin), guaranteeing economic security for the elderly (Dr. Townsend), and redistributing wealth (Huey Long).

Father Charles E. Coughlin This Catholic priest attracted a huge popular following in the early 1930s through his weekly radio broadcasts. Father Coughlin founded the National Union for Social Justice, which called for issuing an inflated currency and nationalizing all banks. His attacks on the New Deal became increasingly anti-Semitic and Fascist until his superiors in the Catholic Church ordered him to stop his broadcasts.

Dr. Francis E. Townsend Before the passage of the Social Security Act, a retired physician from Long Beach, California, became an instant hero to millions of senior citizens by proposing a simple plan for guaranteeing a secure income. Dr. Francis E. Townsend proposed that a 2 percent federal sales tax be used to create a special fund, from which every retired person over 60 years old would receive $200 a month. By spending their money promptly, Townsend argued, recipients would stimulate the economy and soon bring the depression to an end. The popularity of the Townsend Plan persuaded Roosevelt to substitute a more moderate plan of his own, which became the Social Security system.

Huey Long From Roosevelt's point of view, the most dangerous of the depression demagogues was the "Kingfish" from Louisiana, Senator Huey Long. Immensely popular in his own state, Long became a prominent national figure by proposing a "Share Our Wealth" program that promised a minimum annual income of $5,000 for every American family, to be paid for by taxing the wealthy. In 1935, Huey Long challenged Roosevelt's leadership of the Democratic party by announcing his candidacy for president. Both his candidacy and his populist appeal were abruptly ended when he was killed by an assassin.

The Supreme Court

Of all the challenges to Roosevelt's leadership in his first term in office, the conservative decisions of the U.S. Supreme Court proved the most frustrating. In two cases in 1935, the Supreme Court effectively killed both the NRA for business recovery and the AAA for agricultural recovery by deciding that the laws creating them were unconstitutional. Roosevelt interpreted his landslide reelection in 1936 as a mandate to end the obstacles posed by the Court.

Court Reorganization Plan President Roosevelt did not have an opportunity to appoint any Justices to the Supreme Court during his first term. He hoped to remove the Court as an obstacle to the New Deal by proposing a judicial-reorganization bill in 1937. It proposed that the president be authorized to appoint to the Supreme Court an additional justice for each current justice who was older than a certain age (70 ½ years). In effect, the bill would have allowed Roosevelt to add up to six more justices to the Court—all of them presumably of liberal persuasion. Critics called it a "Court-packing" bill.

Reaction Republicans and many Democrats were outraged by what they saw as an attempt to tamper with the system of checks and balances. They accused the president of wanting to give himself the powers of a dictator. Roosevelt did not back down—and neither did the congressional opposition. For the first time in Roosevelt's presidency, a major bill that he proposed went down to decisive defeat by a defiant Congress. Even a majority of Democratic senators refused to support him on this controversial measure.

Aftermath Ironically, while Roosevelt was fighting to "pack" the Court, the justices were already backing off their former resistance to his program. In 1937, the Supreme Court upheld the constitutionality of several major New Deal laws, including the Wagner (Labor) Act and the Social Security Act. Also, as it happened, several justices retired during Roosevelt's second term, enabling him to appoint new justices who were more sympathetic to his reforms.

Rise of Unions

Two New Deal measures—the National Industrial Recovery Act of 1933 and the Wagner Act of 1935—caused a lasting change in labor-management relations by legalizing labor unions. Union membership, which had slumped badly under the hostile policies of the 1920s, shot upward. It went from less than 3 million in the early 1930s to over 10 million (more than one out of four non-farm workers) by 1941.

Formation of the C.I.O.

As unions grew in size, tensions and conflicts between rival unions grew in intensity. The many different unions that made up the American Federation of Labor (A.F. of L.) were dominated by skilled white male workers and were organized according to crafts. A group of unions within the A.F. of L. wanted union membership to be extended to all workers in an industry regardless of their race and sex, including those who were unskilled. In 1935, the industrial unions, as they were called, joined together as the Committee of Industrial Organizations (C.I.O.). Their leader was John L. Lewis, president of the United Mine Workers union. In 1936, the A.F. of L. suspended the C.I.O. unions. Renamed the *Congress* of Industrial Organizations, the C.I.O. broke away from the A.F. of L. and became its chief rival. It concentrated on organizing unskilled workers in the automobile, steel, and southern textile industries.

Strikes

Even though collective bargaining was now protected by federal law, many companies still resisted union demands. Strikes were therefore a frequent occurrence in the depression decade.

Automobiles At the huge General Motors plant in Flint, Michigan, in 1937, the workers insisted on their right to join a union by participating in a sit-down strike (literally sitting down at the assembly line and refusing to work). Neither the president nor Michigan's governor agreed to the company's request to intervene with troops. Finally, the company yielded to striker demands by recognizing the United Auto Workers union (U.A.W.). Union organizers at the Ford plant in Michigan, however, were beaten and driven away.

Steel In the steel industry, the giant U.S. Steel Corporation voluntarily recognized one of the C.I.O. unions, but smaller companies resisted. On Memorial Day, 1937, a demonstration by union picketers at Republic Steel in Chicago ended in four deaths, as the police fired into the crowd. However, eventually almost all the smaller steel companies agreed to deal with the C.I.O. by 1941.

Fair Labor Standards Act

A final political victory for organized labor in the 1930s also represented the last major reform of the New Deal. In 1938, Congress enacted the Fair Labor Standards Act, which established several regulations on businesses in interstate commerce:

- a minimum wage, initially fixed at 40 cents an hour

- a maximum standard workweek of 40 hours, with extra pay ("time-and-a-half") for overtime

- child-labor restrictions on hiring people under 16 years old

Previously, the Supreme Court had declared unconstitutional a 1916 law prohibiting child labor. However, in 1941, in the case of *U.S. v. Darby Lumber Co.*, the Supreme Court reversed its earlier ruling by upholding the child-labor provisions of the Fair Labor Standards Act.

Last Phase of the New Deal

Passage of the Fair Labor Standards Act was not only the last but also the only major reform of Roosevelt's second term. The New Deal lost momentum in the late 1930s for both economic and political reasons.

Recession, 1937–1938

From 1933 to 1937 (Roosevelt's first term), the economy showed signs of gradually pulling out of its nosedive. Banks were stablizing, business earnings were increasing, and unemployment, though still high at 15 percent, had declined from the 25 percent figure in 1933. In the winter of 1937, however, the economy once again had a backward slide and entered into a recessionary period.

Causes Government policy was at least partly to blame. The new Social Security tax reduced consumer spending at the same time that Roosevelt was curtailing expenditures for relief and public works. In reducing spending for relief, the president hoped to balance the budget and reduce the national debt.

Keynesian Economics The writings of the British economist John Maynard Keynes taught Roosevelt that he had made a mistake in attempting to balance the budget. According to Keynesian theory, deficit spending was helpful in difficult times because the government needed to spend well above its tax revenues in order to initiate economic growth. Deficit spending "prime the pump" to increase investment and create jobs. Roosevelt's economic advisers adopted this theory in 1938 with positive results. As federal spending on public works and relief went up, so too did employment and industrial production.

Weakened New Deal

Although the economy improved, there was no boom and problems remained. After the Court-packing fight of 1937, the people and Congress no longer automatically followed FDR, and the 1938 elections brought a reduced Democratic majority in Congress. A coalition of Republicans and conservative Democrats blocked further New Deal reform legislation. Also, beginning in 1938, fears about the aggressive acts of Nazi Germany diverted attention from domestic concerns toward foreign affairs.

Life During the Depression

Millions of people who lived through the Great Depression and hard times of the 1930s never got over it. They developed a "depression mentality"—an attitude of insecurity and economic concern that would always remain, even in times of prosperity.

Women

During the depression, added pressures were placed on the family as unemployed fathers searched for work, and declining incomes presented severe challenges for mothers in the feeding and clothing of their children. To supplement the family income, more women sought work, and their percentage of the total labor force increased. Women were accused of taking jobs from men, even though they did not get the heavy factory jobs that were lost to all, and most men did not seek the types of jobs available to women. Even with Eleanor Roosevelt championing women's equality, many New Deal programs allowed women to receive lower pay than men.

Dust Bowl Farmers

As if farmers did not already have enough problems, a severe drought in the early 1930s ruined crops in the Great Plains. This region became a *dust bowl,* as poor farming practices coupled with high winds blew away millions of tons of dried topsoil. With their farms turned to dust, and their health often compromised, thousands of "Okies" from Oklahoma and surrounding states migrated westward to California in search of farm or factory work that often could not be found. The novelist John Steinbeck wrote about their hardships in his classic study of economic heartbreak, *The Grapes of Wrath* (1939).

In response to one of the worst ecological disasters in American history, the federal government created the Soil Conservation Service in 1935 to teach and subsidize the plains farmers to rotate crops, terrace fields, use contour plowing, and plant trees to stop soil erosion and conserve water. For those who could stay behind, the region recovered, but environmental issues remained.

African Americans

Racial discrimination continued in the 1930s with devastating effects on African Americans, who were the last hired, first fired. Their unemployment rate was higher than the national average. Black sharecroppers were forced off the land in the South because of cutbacks in farm production. Often, despite their extreme poverty, jobless African Americans were excluded from state and local relief programs. Hard times increased racial tensions, particularly in the South where lynchings continued. Civil rights leaders could get little support from President Roosevelt, who feared the loss of white southern Democratic votes.

Improvements Some New Deal programs, such as the WPA and the CCC did provide low-paying jobs for African Americans, though these jobs were often segregated. Blacks also received moral support from Eleanor Roosevelt and Secretary of the Interior Harold Ickes in a famous incident in 1939. The distinguished African American singer Marian Anderson had been refused the use of Constitution Hall in Washington, D.C., by the all-white Daughters of the American Revolution. Eleanor Roosevelt and Ickes promptly arranged for Anderson to give a special concert at the Lincoln Memorial.

Over one hundred African Americans were appointed to middle-level positions in federal departments by President Roosevelt. One of them, Mary McLeod Bethune, had been a longtime leader of efforts for improving education and economic opportunities for women. Invited to Washington to direct a division of the National Youth Administration, she established the Federal Council on Negro Affairs for the purpose of increasing African American involvement in the New Deal.

Fair Employment Practices Committee An executive order in 1941 set up a committee to assist minorities in gaining jobs in defense industries. President Roosevelt took this action only after A. Philip Randolph, head of the Railroad Porters Union, threatened a march on Washington to demand equal job opportunities for African Americans.

American Indians

John Collier, a long-time advocate of American Indian rights, was appointed commissioner of the Bureau of Indian Affairs in 1933. He established conservation and CCC projects on reservations and gained American Indian involvement in the WPA and other New Deal programs.

Indian Reorganization (Wheeler-Howard) Act (1934) Collier won Roosevelt's support for a major change in policy. In 1934, Congress repealed the Dawes Act of 1887, which had encouraged American Indians to be independent farmers, and replaced it with the Indian Reorganization Act. The new measure returned lands to the control of tribes and supported preservation of Indian cultures. Despite this major reform, critics later accused the New Deal of being paternalistic and withholding control from American Indians.

Mexican Americans

Mexican Americans also suffered from discrimination in the 1930s. In California and the Southwest, they had been a principal source of agricultural labor in the 1920s. However, during the depression, high unemployment and drought in the Plains and the Midwest caused a dramatic growth in white migrant workers who pushed west in search of work. Discrimination in New Deal programs and competition for jobs forced many thousands of Mexican Americans to return to Mexico.

Roosevelt's New Deal was unique. In later decades, there would be nothing quite like it in terms of either the challenges faced or the legislative record achieved. Recognizing its scope, historians have debated whether the New Deal represented a revolutionary break with the past or an evolutionary outgrowth of earlier movements.

The first historical interpretations tended to praise the New Deal as a continuation or revival of the Progressive reform movement. In the late 1950s, Arthur M. Schlesinger Jr. saw the New Deal in terms of his theory of a recurring political cycle from a period of liberal reforms to a period of conservative reaction and back again to reform.

Some liberal historians such as Carl Degler went further and characterized the New Deal as a third American Revolution that went far beyond earlier reforms. They argued that such measures as the NRA, the WPA, and the Social Security Act redefined the role of government in American society. In his *Age of Reform* (1955), Richard Hofstadter agreed that the New Deal had ventured beyond traditional reform movements. It was unique, he said, because it concentrated not on regulating corporate abuses as in the past but on providing social-democratic guarantees for different groups in such forms as Social Security, housing credits, and minimum wage laws.

Revisionists of the 1960s and 1970s viewed the New Deal differently. William E. Leuchtenburg in *Franklin D. Roosevelt and the New Deal* (1963) depicted a "halfway revolution" that helped some (farmers and labor unions), ignored others (African Americans), and implemented changes without being either completely radical or conservative. Leuchtenburg believed Roosevelt did the best he could given both his own personal ideas and the political realities of the time. A highly critical interpretation came from New Left scholars (radical thinkers of the 1970s), who argued that the New Deal was a missed opportunity that did not do enough to meet society's needs. They saw New Deal measures as conservative in purpose, aimed at preserving capitalism from a worker revolution. New Left historians have been criticized for judging the New Deal in terms of the 1970s rather than the 1930s.

In recent years, some historians have questioned whether it is useful to characterize the New Deal as either conservative on the one hand or revolutionary on the other. They see the New Deal as nothing more or less than a pragmatic political response to various groups. In their view, Roosevelt and his political advisers had no central plan but simply responded to the different needs of special interests (farmers, business, labor, and elderly). In defense of Roosevelt, they ask: If the nation in general and the South in particular was essentially conservative, then how far could the New Deal go in improving race relations? If the government bureaucracy was relatively small in the 1930s, how could it be expected to implement massive new programs?

KEY TERMS BY THEME

Causes of the Depression (WXT)
stock market crash
Black Tuesday
Dow Jones index
buying on margin
uneven income
  distribution
excessive debt
overproduction
Federal Reserve
postwar Europe
debts and high tariffs

Effect of the Depression (WXT)
Gross National Product
unemployment
bank failures
poverty and homeless

Hoover Administration (POL)
Herbert Hoover
self-reliance
Hawley-Smoot Tariff
  (1930)
debt moratorium
Farm Board
Reconstruction Finance
  Corporation
bonus march (1932)
Twentieth Amendment
  ("lame-duck")

Roosevelt Administration (POL)
Franklin D. Roosevelt
Eleanor Roosevelt
New Deal
relief, recovery, reform
Brain Trust
Frances Perkins
Hundred Days
bank holiday
repeal of Prohibition
fireside chats
Federal Deposit
  Insurance
  Corporation
Public Works
  Administration
Harold Ickes
Civilian Conservation
  Corps
Tennessee Valley
  Authority
National Recovery
  Administration
Schechter v. U.S.
Securities and Exchange
  Commission
Federal Housing
  Administration

Second New Deal (POL)
Works Progress
  Administration
Harry Hopkins
National Labor Rela-
  tions (Wagner) Act
  (1935)
Social Security Act
  (1935)

election of 1936
New Deal coalition
John Maynard Keynes
recession of 1937

New Deal Opponents (POL)
Father Charles Coughlin
Francis Townsend
Huey Long
Supreme Court
  reorganization plan
conservative coalition

Rise of Unions (WXT)
Congress of Industrial
  Organizations
John L. Lewis
sit-down strike
Fair Labor Standards Act
minimum wage

Impact on Americans (MIG)
depression mentality
drought; dust bowl;
  Okies
John Steinbeck, The
  Grapes of Wrath
Marian Anderson
Mary McLeod Bethune
Fair Employment
  Practices Committee
A. Philip Randolph
Indian Reorganization
  (Wheeler-Howard) Act
  (1934)
Mexican deportation

MULTIPLE-CHOICE QUESTIONS

Questions 1–3 refer to the excerpt below.

"The farmers are being pauperized by the poverty of industrial populations and the industrial populations are being pauperized by the poverty of the farmers. Neither has the money to buy the product of the other, hence we have over-production and under consumption at the same time and in the same country.

"I have not come here to stir you in a recital of the necessity for relief for our suffering fellow citizens. However, unless something is done for them and done soon, you will have a revolution on hand. . . .

"There is a feeling among the masses that something is radically wrong . . . . they say that this government is a conspiracy against the common people to enrich the already rich."

> —Oscar Ameringer, editor of the *Oklahoma Daily Leader,* testimony to
> the House Committee on Labor, February, 1932

1. Which of the following most directly supports the author's analysis?
   (A) Gross national product fell from $104 billion in 1929 to $56 billion in 1932
   (B) Bank assets fell from $72 billion in 1929 to $51 billion in 1932
   (C) Farm income fell from $11.4 billion in 1929 to $6.3 billion in 1932
   (D) Government spending rose from $3.2 billion in 1929 to $4.6 billion in 1932

2. Which of the following was most directly related to the phrase in the testimony "the necessity for relief for our suffering fellow citizens"?
   (A) Twenty percent of the banks were closed
   (B) The Dawes Plan was suspended
   (C) The Federal Farm Board was created
   (D) Twenty-five percent of the workforce was unemployed

3. Which of the following would most likely support a belief that the government was "against the common people"?
   (A) Creation of the Reconstruction Finance Corporation
   (B) Treatment of the Bonus Marchers
   (C) Efforts to stabilize farm prices
   (D) Passage of the Hawley-Smoot Tariff

Questions 4–6 refer to the excerpt below.

"Illumined by the stern-lantern of history, the New Deal can be seen to have left in place a set of institutional arrangement that constituted a more coherent pattern than is dreamt of in many philosophies. That pattern can be summarized in a single word: security—security for vulnerable individuals, to be sure, as Roosevelt famously urged in his campaign for the Social Security Act of 1935, but security for capitalists and consumers, for workers and builders as well. Job-security, life-cycle security, financial security, market security—however it might be defined, achieving security was the leitmotif of virtually everything the New Deal attempted."

—David M. Kennedy, historian, *Freedom From Fear,* 1999

4. Which of the following groups would most likely oppose the philosophy of the New Deal as explained in this excerpt?
   (A) Advocates of unregulated markets and balanced budgets
   (B) Many academics, especially in the fields of economics and social sciences
   (C) Critics who thought that the New Deal did not go far enough to address poverty and inequality
   (D) Consumers who depended on the banking system and the stock markets

5. Which of the following New Deal policies most directly addressed "security for capitalists"?
   (A) Roosevelt's "bank holiday" and examination of banks' records
   (B) Federal funding of construction projects that pumped money into the economy
   (C) The creation of the FDIC to insure individual bank deposits up to $5,000
   (D) Regulations to curtail fraud in investment banking and the stock markets

6. Which of the following New Deal policies most clearly addressed "job security" for workers?
   (A) Programs to construct roads, bridges, airports, and public buildings
   (B) Laws to guarantee worker rights to collective bargaining, minimum wage, and fair treatment
   (C) Federal programs to collect funds for retirement, unemployment, and injuries on the job
   (D) Government program to employ young men in conservation projects on federal lands

Questions 7–8 refer to the excerpt below.

"Though Franklin himself never tried to discourage me and was undisturbed by anything I wanted to say or do, other people were frequently less happy about my actions. I knew, for instance, that many of my racial beliefs and activities in the field of social work caused . . . grave concern. They were afraid that I would hurt my husband politically and socially, and I imagine they thought I was doing many things without Franklin's knowledge and agreement. On occasion they blew up to him and to other people. I knew it at the time, but there was no use in my trying to explain, because our basic values were very different."

—Eleanor Roosevelt, *This I Remember,* 1949

7. Eleanor Roosevelt expressed the most independence from President Franklin Roosevelt and his advisers in her
   (A) support for socialism
   (B) support for American Indians
   (C) opposition to racial discrimination
   (D) opposition to social work

8. The excerpt suggests that Eleanor Roosevelt knew that her positions could most harm her husband's standing with which of the following groups?
   (A) The Catholic Church
   (B) White ethnic groups
   (C) Wall Street capitalists
   (D) Southern Democrats

SHORT-ANSWER QUESTIONS

Use complete sentences; an outline or bulleted list alone is not acceptable.

Question 1. Answer (A), (B), and (C).

(A) Briefly explain the composition of the New Deal political coalition.

(B) Briefly explain ONE specific way the New Deal caused a long-term realignment in U.S. politics.

(C) Briefly explain ONE specific political challenge to Franklin Roosevelt and his policies.

Queston 2. Answer (A), (B), and (C).

(A) Briefly explain ONE specific historical event or development that contributed to the kind of internal migration depicted in the photo.

(B) Briefly explain ONE specific historical event or development that contributed to the migration of either African Americans or Mexican Americans during the 1930s.

(C) Briefly explain ONE specific way that New Deal policies specifically impacted Native Americans.

Question 3. Answer (A), (B), and (C).

(A) Briefly explain ONE specific similarity or difference between the Great Depression of 1929 and depressions from 1865 to 1900.

(B) Briefly explain ONE specific similarity between policies of the Progressive era and New Deal era.

(C) Briefly explain ONE specific New Deal reform that went beyond the reforms of the Progressive era.

Question 4 is based on the excerpts below.

"When the New Deal was over, capitalism remained intact. The rich still controlled the nation's wealth, as well as its laws, courts, police, newspaper, churches, colleges. Enough help had been given to enough people to make Roosevelt a hero to millions, but the same system that had brought depression and crisis—the system of waste, of inequality, of concern for profit over human need—remained."

—Howard Zinn, *A People's History of the United States,* 1999

"Most of Roosevelt's solutions did little. The public hoopla of 'job programs' barely dented unemployment numbers, which still stood at 12.5 percent in 1939, or ten times what they had been under Coolidge. . . . Did FDR do anything right? Yes. By taking the United States off the gold standard, he saved what was left of the banking system. But as they say, even a blind squirrel finds a nut once in a while."

—Larry Schweikart, *48 Liberal Lies about American History,* 2008

4. Using the excerpts, answer (A), (B), and (C).

   (A) Briefly describe ONE major difference between Zinn's and Schweikart's historical interpretation about the effectiveness of Franklin Roosevelt and the New Deal.

   (B) Briefly explain how ONE specific historical event or development that is not explicitly mentioned in the excerpts could be used to support Zinn's interpretation.

   (C) Briefly explain how ONE specific historical event or development that is not explicitly mentioned in the excerpts could be used to support Schweikart's interpretation.

THINK AS A HISTORIAN: USING DOCUMENTS IN ARGUMENTS

When using information from sources in an essay or document-based question (DBQ), identify the source by the author's name rather than its document or page number and quote only the key words. Add clarifying information as needed. Which of the following uses information from a source more effectively?

1. Eleanor Roosevelt was aware that her advocacy for civil rights caused "grave concern" among her husband's political advisers.

2. In the quotation from Eleanor Roosevelt on page 518, she says that "I knew, for instance, that many of my racial beliefs and activities in the field of social work caused . . . grave concern."

25

DIPLOMACY AND WORLD WAR II, 1929–1945

*We seek peace—enduring peace. More than an end to war,
we want an end to the beginnings of all wars.*

Franklin D. Roosevelt, April 13, 1945

President Roosevelt's fervent desire for peace was hardly new. World War I, after all, was meant to be a "war to end all wars" and, as Woodrow Wilson had said, a war "to make the world safe for democracy." In 1933, however, few people believed that the fragile peace established by the Treaty of Versailles would hold up for much longer. In Asia, Japan was threatening China. In Europe, the Nazi party under Adolf Hitler had come to power in Germany with promises of reasserting German nationalism and militarism. In the United States, worries about the depression overshadowed concerns about a second world war. Even if war did break out, most Americans were determined not to send troops abroad again.

However, a second world war did occur, and the United States played a major role in fighting it. How and why U.S. foreign policy changed from disengagement to neutrality and from neutrality to total involvement is the subject of this chapter. Moreover, the war transformed American economy and society in many ways more dramatically than the New Deal.

Herbert Hoover's Foreign Policy

Hoover concurred with the prevailing opinion of the American people that the United States should not enter into firm commitments to preserve the security of other nations. Such an opinion, in the 1930s, would be labeled "isolationism."

Japanese Aggression in Manchuria

In the early 1930s, Japan posed the greatest threat to world peace. Defying both the Open Door policy and the covenant of the League of Nations, Japanese troops marched into Manchuria in September 1931, renamed the territory Manchukuo, and established a puppet government.

JAPANESE AGGRESSION IN ASIA IN THE 1930s

Despite its commitment to taking action against blatant aggression, the League of Nations did nothing except to pass a resolution condemning Japan for its actions in Manchuria. The Japanese delegation then walked out of the League, never to return. In the Manchuria crisis, the League, through its failure to take action, showed its inability to maintain peace. Its warnings would never be taken seriously by potential aggressors.

Stimson Doctrine U.S. response to Japan's violation of the Open Door policy was somewhat stronger than the League's response—but no more effective in deterring further aggression. Secretary of State Henry Stimson declared in 1932 that the United States would honor its treaty obligations under the Nine-Power Treaty (1922) by refusing to recognize the legitimacy of any regime like "Manchukuo" that had been established by force. The League of Nations readily endorsed the Stimson Doctrine and issued a similar declaration.

Latin America

Hoover actively pursued friendly relations with the countries of Latin America. In 1929, even before being inaugurated, the president-elect went on a goodwill tour of the region. As president, he ended the interventionist policies of Taft and Wilson by (1) arranging for U.S. troops to leave Nicaragua by 1933 and (2) negotiating a treaty with Haiti to remove all U.S. troops by 1934.

Franklin Roosevelt's Policies, 1933–1938

In his first term, Roosevelt's concentration on dealing with the economic crisis at home kept him from giving much thought to shaping foreign policy. He did, however, extend Hoover's efforts at improving U.S. relations with Latin America by initiating a good-neighbor policy.

Good-Neighbor Policy

In his first inaugural address in 1933, Roosevelt promised a "policy of the good neighbor" toward other nations of the Western Hemisphere. First, interventionism in support of dollar diplomacy no longer made economic sense, because U.S. businesses during the depression lacked the resources to invest in foreign operations. Second, the rise of militarist regimes in Germany and Italy prompted Roosevelt to seek Latin American's cooperation in defending the region from potential danger. FDR implemented his good-neighbor policy through several actions.

Pan-American Conferences At Roosevelt's direction, the U.S. delegation at the Seventh Pan-American Conference in Montevideo, Uruguay, in 1933, pledged never again to intervene in the internal affairs of a Latin American country. In effect, Franklin Roosevelt repudiated the policy of his older cousin, Theodore, who had justified intervention as a corollary to the Monroe Doctrine. Another Pan-American conference was held in Buenos Aires, Argentina, in 1936. Roosevelt himself attended the conference. He personally pledged to submit future disputes to arbitration and also warned that if a European power such as Germany attempted "to commit acts of aggression against us," it would find "a hemisphere wholly prepared to consult together for our mutual safety and our mutual good."

Cuba Cubans had long resented the Platt Amendment, which had made their country's foreign policy subject to U.S. approval. In 1934, President Roosevelt persuaded Congress to nullify the Platt Amendment, retaining only the U.S. right to keep its naval base at Guantanamo Bay.

Mexico Mexico tested U.S. patience and commitment to the good-neighbor policy in 1938 when its president, Lázaro Cárdenas, seized oil properties owned by U.S. corporations. Roosevelt rejected corporate demands to intervene and encouraged American companies to negotiate a settlement.

Economic Diplomacy

Helping the U.S. economy was the chief motivation for Roosevelt's policies toward other foreign policy issues in his first term.

Recognition of the Soviet Union The Republican presidents of the 1920s had refused to grant diplomatic recognition to the Communist regime that ruled the Soviet Union. Roosevelt promptly changed this policy by granting recognition in 1933. His reason for doing so, he said, was to increase U.S. trade and thereby boost the economy.

Philippines Governing the Philippines cost money. As an economy measure, Roosevelt persuaded Congress to pass the Tydings-McDuffie Act in 1934, which provided for the independence of the Philippines by 1946 and the gradual removal of U.S. military presence from the islands.

Reciprocal Trade Agreements Acting in the tradition of Progressive Democrats such as William Jennings Bryan and Woodrow Wilson, President Roosevelt favored lower tariffs as a means of increasing international trade. In 1934, Congress enacted a plan suggested by Secretary of State Cordell Hull, which gave the president power to reduce U.S. tariffs up to 50 percent for nations that reciprocated with comparable reductions for U.S. imports.

Events Abroad: Fascism and Aggressive Militarism

The worldwide depression soon proved to have alarming repercussions for world politics. Combined with nationalist resentments after World War I, economic hardships gave rise to military dictatorships in Italy in the 1920s and Japan and Germany in the 1930s. Eventually, in 1940, Japan, Italy, and Germany signed a treaty of alliance which formed the Axis Powers.

Italy A new regime seized power in Italy in 1922. Benito Mussolini led Italy's Fascist party, which attracted dissatisfied war veterans, nationalists, and those afraid of rising communism. Dressed in black shirts, the Fascists marched on Rome and installed Mussolini in power as "Il Duce" (the Leader). Fascism—the idea that people should glorify their nation and their race through an aggressive show of force—became the dominant ideology in European dictatorships in the 1930s.

Germany The Nazi party was the German equivalent of Italy's Fascist party. It arose in the 1920s in reaction to deplorable economic conditions after the war and national resentments over the Treaty of Versailles. The Nazi leader, Adolf Hitler, used bullying tactics against Jews as well as Fascist ideology to increase his popularity with disgruntled, unemployed German workers. Hitler seized the opportunity presented by the depression to play upon anti-Semitic hatreds. With his personal army of "brown shirts," Hitler gained control of the German legislature in early 1933.

Japan Nationalists and militarists in Japan increased their power in the 1920s and 1930s. As economic conditions worsened, they persuaded Japan's nominal ruler, the emperor, that the best way to ensure access to basic raw materials (oil, tin, and iron) was to invade China and Southeast Asia and thereby give Japan control over what their leaders proclaimed to be the Greater East Asia Co-Prosperity Sphere.

American Isolationists

Public opinion in the United States was also nationalistic but expressed itself in an opposite way from fascism and militarism. Disillusioned with the results of World War I, American isolationists wanted to make sure that the United States would never again be drawn into a foreign war. Japanese aggression in Manchuria and the rise of fascism in Italy and Germany only increased the determination of isolationists to avoid war at all costs. Isolationist sentiment was strongest in the Midwest and among Republicans.

The Lesson of World War I In the early 1930s, Americans commonly felt that U.S. entry into World War I had been a terrible mistake. An investigating committee led by Senator Gerald Nye of North Dakota bolstered this view when it concluded in 1934 that the main reason for U.S. participation in the world war was to serve the greed of bankers and arms manufacturers. This committee's work influenced isolationist legislation in the following years.

Neutrality Acts Isolationist senators and representatives in both parties held a majority in Congress through 1938. To ensure that U.S. policy would be strictly neutral if war broke out in Europe, Congress adopted a series of neutrality acts, which Roosevelt signed with some reluctance. Each law applied to nations that the president proclaimed to be at war.

- The *Neutrality Act of 1935* authorized the president to prohibit all arms shipments and to forbid U.S. citizens to travel on the ships of belligerent nations.

- The *Neutrality Act of 1936* forbade the extension of loans and credits to belligerents.

- The *Neutrality Act of 1937* forbade the shipment of arms to the opposing sides in the civil war in Spain.

Spanish Civil War The outbreak of civil war in Spain in 1936 was viewed in Europe and the United States as an ideological struggle between the forces of fascism, led by General Francisco Franco, and the forces of republicanism, called Loyalists. Roosevelt and most Americans sympathized with the Loyalists but, because of the Neutrality Acts, could not aid them. Ultimately, in 1939, Franco's Fascists prevailed and established a military dictatorship.

America First Committee In 1940, after World War II had begun in Asia and Europe, isolationists became alarmed by Roosevelt's pro-British policies. To mobilize American public opinion against war, they formed the America First Committee and engaged speakers such as Charles Lindbergh to travel the country warning against reengaging in Europe's troubles.

Prelude to War

In the years 1935 to 1938, a series of aggressive actions by the Fascist dictatorships made democratic governments in Britain and France extremely nervous. It was known that Hitler was creating an air force more powerful than anything they could match. Hoping to avoid open conflict with Germany, the democracies adopted a policy of appeasement—allowing Hitler to get away with relatively small acts of aggression and expansion. The United States went along with the British and French policy.

Appeasement The following events showed how unprepared the democracies were to challenge Fascist aggression.

1. Ethiopia, 1935 In a bid to prove fascism's military might, Mussolini ordered Italian troops to invade Ethiopia. The League of Nations and the United States objected but did nothing to stop the Italian aggressor, which succeeded in conquering the African country after a year of bitter fighting.

2. Rhineland, 1936 This region in western Germany was supposed to be permanently demilitarized, according to the Versailles Treaty. Hitler openly defied the treaty by ordering German troops to march into the Rhineland.

3. China, 1937 Full-scale war between Japan and China erupted in 1937 as Japan's troops invaded its weaker neighbor. A U.S. gunboat in China, the *Panay,* was bombed and sunk by Japanese planes. Japan's apology for the sinking was quickly accepted by the U.S. government.

4. Sudetenland, 1938 In Europe, Hitler insisted that Germany had a right to take over a strip of land in Czechoslovakia, the Sudetenland, where most people were German-speaking. To maintain peace, the British prime minister, Neville Chamberlain, and the French president, Édouard Daladier, with Roosevelt's support, met with Hitler and Mussolini in Munich. At this conference in September 1938, the British and French leaders agreed to allow Hitler to take the Sudetenland unopposed. The word "Munich" has since become synonymous with appeasement.

Quarantine Speech Roosevelt recognized the dangers of Fascist aggression but was limited by the isolationist feelings of the majority of Americans. When Japan invaded China in 1937, he tested public opinion by making a speech proposing that the democracies act together to "quarantine" the aggressor. Public reaction to the speech was overwhelmingly negative, and Roosevelt dropped the quarantine idea as politically unwise.

Preparedness Like Wilson in 1916, Roosevelt argued for neutrality and an arms buildup at the same time. Congress went along with his request in late 1938 by increasing the military and naval budgets by nearly two-thirds. Some isolationists accepted the increased defense spending, thinking it would be used only to protect against possible invasion of the Western Hemisphere.

AXIS AGGRESSION IN THE 1930s

Germany and Italy (Axis Powers)

(1935) Date of Annexation, Occupation, or Invasion

0   100   200 Miles
0   100   200 Kilometers

From Neutrality to War, 1939–1941

In March 1939, Hitler broke the Munich agreement by sending troops to occupy all of Czechoslovakia. After this, it became clear that Hitler's ambitions had no limit and that war was probably unavoidable.

Outbreak of War in Europe

Recognizing the failure of appeasement, Britain and France pledged to fight if Poland was attacked. They had always assumed that they could count on the Soviet leader, Joseph Stalin, to oppose Hitler, since communism and fascism were ideological enemies. The democracies were therefore shocked in August 1939 when Stalin and Hitler signed a nonaggression pact. Secretly, the Soviet and German dictators agreed to divide Poland between them.

Invasion of Poland On September 1, 1939, German tanks and planes began a full-scale invasion of Poland. Keeping their pledge, Britain and France declared war against Germany—and soon afterward, they were also at war with its Axis allies, Italy and Japan. World War II in Europe had begun.

Blitzkrieg Poland was the first to fall to Germany's overwhelming use of air power and fast-moving tanks—a type of warfare called *blitzkrieg* (lightning war). After a relatively inactive winter, the war was resumed in the spring of 1940 with Germany attacking its Scandinavian neighbors to the north and its chief enemy, France, to the west. Denmark and Norway surrendered in a few days, France in only a week. By June 1940, the only ally that remained free of German troops was Great Britain.

Changing U.S. Policy

President Roosevelt countered isolationism in the United States by gradually giving aid to the Allies, especially Great Britain. Now that war had actually begun, most Americans were alarmed by news of Nazi tanks, planes, and troops conquering one country after another. They were strongly opposed to Hitler but still hoped to keep their country out of the war. President Roosevelt believed that British survival was crucial to U.S. security. The relationship that was built over the coming years between British Prime Minister Winston Churchill and FDR proved one of keys to Allied success in the war. The president chipped away at the restrictive neutrality laws until practically nothing remained to prevent him from giving massive aid to Britain. After the surrender of France to the Germans in 1940, most Americans accepted the need to strengthen U.S. defenses, but giving direct aid to Britain was controversial.

"Cash and Carry" The British navy still controlled the seas. Therefore, if the United States ended its arms embargo, it would help only Britain, not Germany. Roosevelt persuaded Congress in 1939 to adopt a less restrictive Neutrality Act, which provided that a belligerent could buy U.S. arms if it used its own ships and paid cash. Technically, "cash and carry" was neutral, but in practice, it strongly favored Britain.

Selective Service Act (1940) Without actually naming Germany as the potential enemy, Roosevelt pushed neutrality back one more step by persuading Congress to enact a law for compulsory military service. The Selective Training and Service Act of September 1940 provided for the registration of all American men between the ages of 21 and 35 and for the training of 1.2 million troops in just one year. There had been a military draft in the Civil War and World War I but only when the United States was officially at war. Isolationists strenuously opposed the peacetime draft, but they were now outnumbered as public opinion shifted away from strict neutrality.

Destroyers-for-Bases Deal In September 1940, Britain was under constant assault by German bombing raids. German submarine attacks threatened British control of the Atlantic. Roosevelt knew that selling U.S. destroyers to the British outright would outrage the isolationists. He therefore cleverly arranged a trade. Britain received 50 older but still serviceable U.S. destroyers and gave the United States the right to build military bases on British islands in the Caribbean.

The Election of 1940

Adding to suspense over the war was uncertainty over a presidential election. Might Franklin Roosevelt be the first president to break the two-term tradition and seek election to a third term? For months, the president gave an ambiguous reply, causing frenzied speculation in the press. At last, he announced that, in those critical times, he would not turn down the Democratic nomination if it were offered. Most Democrats were delighted to renominate their most effective campaigner. During the campaign, Roosevelt made the rash pronouncement: "Your boys are not going to be sent into any foreign wars."

Wendell Willkie The Republicans had a number of veteran politicians who were eager to challenge the president. Instead, they chose a newcomer to public office: Wendell Willkie, a lawyer and utility executive with a magnetic personality. Although he criticized the New Deal, Willkie largely agreed with Roosevelt on preparedness and giving aid to Britain short of actually entering the war. His strongest criticism of Roosevelt was the president's decision to break the two-term tradition established by George Washington.

Results Roosevelt won with 54 percent of the popular vote—a smaller margin than in 1932 and 1936. Important factors in the president's reelection were (1) a strong economic recovery enhanced by defense purchases and (2) fear of war, which caused voters to stay with the more experienced leader.

Arsenal of Democracy

Roosevelt viewed Germany's conquest of most of Europe as a direct threat both to U.S. security and to the future of democratic governments everywhere. After his reelection, he believed that he was in a stronger position to end the appearance of U.S. neutrality and give material aid to Britain. In a December 1940 fireside chat to the American people, he explained his thinking and concluded: "We must be the great arsenal of democracy."

Four Freedoms Addressing Congress on January 6, 1941, the president delivered a speech that proposed lending money to Britain for the purchase of U.S. war materials. He justified such a policy by arguing that the United States must help others nations defend "four freedoms:" freedom of speech, freedom of religion, freedom from want, and freedom from fear.

Lend-Lease Act Roosevelt proposed ending the cash-and-carry requirement of the Neutrality Act and permitting Britain to obtain all the U.S. arms it needed on credit. The president said it would be like lending a neighbor a garden hose to put out a fire. Isolationists in the America First Committee campaigned vigorously against the lend-lease bill. By now, however, majority opinion had shifted toward aiding Britain, and the Lend-Lease Act was signed into law in March 1941.

Atlantic Charter With the United States actively aiding Britain, Roosevelt knew that the United States might soon enter the war. He arranged for a secret meeting in August with British Prime Minister Winston Churchill aboard a ship off the coast of Newfoundland. The two leaders drew up a document known as the Atlantic Charter that affirmed that the general principles for a sound peace after the war would include self-determination for all people, no territorial expansion, and free trade.

Shoot-on-Sight In July 1941, the president extended U.S. support for Britain even further by protecting its ships from submarine attack. He ordered the U.S. Navy to escort British ships carrying lend-lease materials from U.S. shores as far as Iceland. On September 4, the American destroyer *Greer* was attacked by a German submarine it had been hunting. In response, Roosevelt ordered the navy to attack all German ships on sight. In effect, this meant that the United States was now fighting an undeclared naval war against Germany.

Disputes with Japan

Meanwhile, through 1940 and 1941, U.S. relations with Japan were becoming increasingly strained as a result of Japan's invasion of China and ambitions to extend its conquests to Southeast Asia. Beginning in 1940, Japan was allied with Germany and Italy as one of the Axis powers. Hitler's success in Europe enabled Japanese expansion into the Dutch East Indies, British Burma, and French Indochina—territories still held as European colonies.

U.S. Economic Action When Japan joined the Axis in September 1940, Roosevelt responded by prohibiting the export of steel and scrap iron to all countries except Britain and the nations of the Western Hemisphere. His action was aimed at Japan, which protested that it was an "unfriendly act." In July 1941, Japanese troops occupied French Indochina. Roosevelt then froze all Japanese credits in the United States and also cut off Japanese access to vital materials, including U.S. oil.

Negotiations Both sides realized that Japan needed oil to fuel its navy and air force. If the U.S. embargo on oil did not end, Japan would likely seize the oil resources in the Dutch East Indies. At the same time, Japan's invasion of China was a blatant violation of the Open Door policy, to which the United States was still committed. Roosevelt and Secretary of State Cordell Hull insisted that Japan pull its troops out of China, which Japan refused to do. The Japanese ambassador to the United States tried to negotiate a change in U.S. policy regarding oil. Agreement, however, seemed most unlikely. In October, a new Japanese government headed by General Hideki Tojo made a final attempt at negotiating an agreement. Neither side, however, changed its position.

U.S. military leaders hoped to delay armed confrontation with Japan until U.S. armed forces in the Pacific were strengthened. Japan, on the other hand, believed that quick action was necessary because of its limited oil supplies.

Pearl Harbor

The U.S. fleet in the Pacific was anchored at Pearl Harbor, Hawaii. On Sunday morning, December 7, 1941, while most American sailors were still asleep in their bunks, Japanese planes from aircraft carriers flew over Pearl Harbor bombing every ship in sight. The surprise attack lasted less than two hours. In that time, 2,400 Americans were killed (including over 1,100 when the battleship *Arizona* sank), almost 1,200 were wounded, 20 warships were sunk or severely damaged, and approximately 150 airplanes were destroyed.

Partial Surprise The American people were stunned by the attack on Pearl Harbor. High government officials, however, knew that an attack somewhere in the Pacific was imminent because they had broken the Japanese codes. They did not know the exact target and date for the attack, which many felt would be in the Philippines, the Dutch East Indies, or Malaya.

Declaration of War Addressing Congress on the day after Pearl Harbor, Roosevelt described December 7th as "a date which will live in infamy." He asked Congress to declare "that since the unprovoked and dastardly attack by Japan on December 7, 1941, a state of war has existed between the United States and the Japanese Empire." On December 8, Congress acted immediately by declaring war, with only one dissenting vote. Three days later, Germany and Italy honored their treaty with Japan by declaring war on the United States.

Soviet Union Invaded By December 1941, the battlefront in Europe had shifted from the west to the east. Breaking his nonaggression pact with Stalin, Hitler had ordered an invasion of the Soviet Union. Thus, the principal Allies fighting Nazi Germany from 1942 to 1945 were Britain, the United States, and the Soviet Union. The three Allied leaders—Churchill, Roosevelt, and Stalin—agreed to concentrate on the war in Europe before shifting their resources to counter Japanese advances in the Pacific.

World War II: The Home Front

FDR compared the transition after Pearl Harbor to a patient with new problems. It was time for Dr. Win-the-War to take over from Dr. New Deal.

Mobilization

The success of U.S. and Allied armed forces depended on mobilizing America's people, industries, and creative and scientific communities. The role of federal government expanded well beyond the anything in World War I or the New Deal.

Federal Government As in World War I, the U.S. government organized a number of special agencies to mobilize U.S. economic and military resources for the wartime crisis. Early in 1942, the War Production Board (WPB) was established to manage war industries. Later the Office of War Mobilization (OWM) set production priorities and controlled raw materials. The government used a cost-plus system, in which it paid war contractors the costs of production plus a certain percentage for profit. One federal agency, the Office of Price Administration (OPA), regulated almost every aspect of civilians' lives by freezing prices, wages, and rents and rationing such commodities as meat, sugar, gasoline, and auto tires, primarily to fight wartime inflation.

Deficit spending during the depression was dwarfed by the deficits incurred during the war. Federal spending increased 1,000 percent between 1939 and 1945. As a result the gross national product grew by 15 percent or more a year. World War II proved what the New Deal did not, that the government could spend its way of a depression. By war's end, the national debt had reached the then staggering figure of $250 billion, five times what it had been in 1941.

Business and Industry Stimulated by wartime demand and government contracts, U.S. industries did a booming business, far exceeding their production and profits of the 1920s. The depression was over, vanquished at last by the coming of war. By 1944, unemployment had practically disappeared.

War-related industrial output in the United States was astonishing. By 1944, it was twice that of all the Axis powers combined. Instead of automobiles, tanks and fighter planes rolled off the assembly lines. American factories produced over 300,000 planes, 100,000 tanks, and ships with a total capacity of 53 million tons. So efficient were production methods that Henry Kaiser's giant shipyard in California could turn out a new ship in just 14 days. The war concentrated production in the largest corporations, as smaller business lost out on government contracts to larger businesses with more capacity. The 100 largest corporations accounted for up to 70 percent of wartime manufacturing.

Research and Development Government worked closely not only with industries, but also universities and research labs to create and improve technologies that could be used to defeat the enemy. The Office of Research and Development was established to contract scientists and universities to help in the development of electronics, such as radar and sonar, medicines such as penicillin, jet engines, rockets, and in the top secret Manhattan Project, the atomic bomb. Ironically, many of the European scientists that had to flee Fascist persecution would contribute to its defeat working in United States.

Workers and Unions Labor unions and large corporations agreed that while the war lasted, there would be no strikes. Workers became disgruntled, however, as their wages were frozen while corporations made large profits. John L. Lewis therefore called a few strikes of coal unions. The Smith-Connally Anti-Strike Act of 1943, passed over Roosevelt's veto, empowered the government to take over war-related businesses whose operations were threatened by a strike. In 1944, Roosevelt had occasion to use this law when he ordered the army to operate the nation's railroads for a brief period.

Financing the War The government paid for its huge increase in spending ($100 billion spent on the war in 1945 alone) by (1) increasing the income tax and (2) selling war bonds. For the first time, most Americans were required to pay an income tax, and in 1944, the practice was begun of automatically deducting a withholding tax from paychecks. Borrowing money by selling $135 billion in war bonds supplemented the tax increase. In addition, the shortage of consumer goods made it easier for Americans to save.

Wartime Propaganda Few people opposed the war, so the government's propaganda campaign of posters, songs, and news bulletins was primarily to maintain public morale, to encourage people to conserve resources, and to increase war production. The Office of War Information controlled news about troop movements and battles. Movies, radio, and popular music all supported and reflected a cheerful, patriotic view of the war. For example, Norman Rockwell's popular illustrations of the "Four Freedoms" captured the liberties and values at stake in the war. The unity of Americans behind the war's democratic ideals helped that generation remember it as "the Good War."

The War's Impact on Society

Every group in the U.S. population adjusted to the unique circumstances of wartime. The increase in factory jobs caused millions to leave rural areas for industrial jobs in the Midwest and on the Pacific Coast, especially California. Entirely new communities arose around the construction of new factories and military bases. Many of the new defense installations were located in the South because of that region's warm climate and low labor costs. The wartime expansion set the stage for a post-war migration to the Sunbelt.

African Americans Attracted by jobs in the North and West, over 1.5 million African Americans left the South. In addition, a million young men left home to serve in the armed forces. Whether as soldiers or civilians, all faced continued discrimination and segregation. White resentment in urban areas led to dozens dying in race riots in New York and Detroit during the summer of 1943. Civil rights leaders encouraged African Americans to adopt the "Double V" slogan—one for victory over fascism abroad and one for equality at home.

Membership in the NAACP increased during the war. Another civil rights organization, the Congress of Racial Equality (CORE), was formed in 1942 to work more militantly for African American interests. After black leaders threatened a protest march on Washington, the Roosevelt administration issued an executive order to prohibit discrimination in government and in businesses that received federal contracts. One judicial victory was achieved in the Supreme Court case of *Smith v. Allwright* (1944), which ruled that it was unconstitutional to deny membership in political parties to African Americans as a way of excluding them from voting in primaries.

Mexican Americans Many Mexican Americans worked in defense industries, and over 300,000 served in the military. A 1942 agreement with Mexico allowed Mexican farmworkers, known as *braceros*, to enter the United States in the harvest season without going through formal immigration procedures.

The sudden influx of Mexican immigrants into Los Angeles stirred white resentment and led to the so-called zoot suit riots in the summer of 1943, in which whites and Mexican Americans battled on the streets.

American Indians American Indians also contributed to the war effort. Approximately 25,000 served in the military, and thousands more worked in defense industries. Having discovered the opportunities off their reservations, more than half never returned.

Japanese Americans More than any other ethnic group, Japanese Americans suffered from their association with a wartime enemy. Almost 20,000 native-born Japanese Americans served loyally in the military. Nevertheless, following the attack on Pearl Harbor, Japanese Americans were suspected of being potential spies and saboteurs, and a Japanese invasion of the West Coast was considered imminent by many. In 1942, these irrational fears as well as racism prompted the U.S. government to order over 100,000 Japanese Americans on the West Coast to leave their homes and reside in the barracks of internment camps. Japanese Americans living in other parts of the U.S., including Hawaii, did not come under this order. In the case of *Korematsu v. U.S.* (1944), the Supreme Court upheld the U.S. government's internment policy as justified in wartime. Years later, in 1988, the federal government agreed the ruling was unjust and awarded financial compensation to those still alive who had been interned.

Women The war also changed the lives of women. Over 200,000 women served in uniform in the army, navy and marines, but in noncombat roles. As in World War I, an acute labor shortage caused women to take jobs vacated by men in uniform. Almost 5 million women entered the workforce, many of them working in industrial jobs in the shipyards and defense plants. The number of married women in the workforce increased to 24 percent. A song about "Rosie the Riveter" was used to encourage women to take defense jobs. However, they received pay well below that of male factory workers.

Wartime Solidarity The New Deal helped immigrant groups feel more included, and serving together as "bands of brothers" in combat or working together for a common cause in defense plants helped to reduce prejudices based on nationality, ethnicity and religion. The wartime migrations also helped to soften regional differences, and open the eyes of many Americans to the injustice of racial discrimination.

The Election of 1944

With the war consuming most of people's attention, the presidential election of 1944 had less interest than usual.

Again, FDR Many felt that, in the war emergency, there should be no change in leadership. The president therefore sought and received the Democratic nomination for the fourth time. There was a change, however, in the Democrats' choice of a vice presidential running mate. Party leaders felt that Roosevelt's third-term vice president, Henry Wallace, was too radical and unmanageable. With Roosevelt's agreement, they replaced Wallace with Harry

S. Truman, a Missouri senator with a national reputation for having conducted a much-publicized investigation of war spending. Although Roosevelt publicly denied medical problems, those near him recognized his uncertain health.

Thomas Dewey The Republicans nominated the 42-year-old governor of New York, Thomas Dewey, who had a strong record of prosecuting corruption and racketeering. The Republican candidate was unable to offer any real alternative to Roosevelt's leadership or generate enthusiasm for change.

Results Winning 53 percent of the popular vote and an overwhelming 432–99 victory in the electoral college, the president was elected to an unprecedented fourth term. As it proved, however, FDR would live for less than three months after his inauguration. Most of his term would be served by Truman.

World War II: The Battlefronts

The fighting of World War II was waged on two fronts, or "theaters of operation." In the Pacific, Japanese forces reached the height of their power in 1942, occupying islands throughout the western Pacific Ocean. In Europe, much of the fighting in the first year of war was between the Germans and the Soviets, as the latter fought desperately to prevent the conquest of Russia.

Fighting Germany

The high tide of the German advance ended in 1942, partly as a result of U.S. entry into the war but mainly because of a Soviet victory at Stalingrad in the winter of that year.

Defense at Sea, Attacks by Air Coordinating their military strategy, the British and Americans concentrated on two objectives in 1942: (1) overcoming the menace of German submarines in the Atlantic and (2) beginning bombing raids on German cities. The protracted naval war to control the shipping lanes was known as the Battle of the Atlantic. German submarines sank over 500 Allied ships in 1942. Gradually, however, the Allies developed ways of containing the submarine menace through the use of radar, sonar, and the bombing of German naval bases. The U.S bombers carried out daylight "strategic bombing" raids on military targets in Europe, but the lines between military and civilian targets became blurred as the war carried on, especially in Japan,

From North Africa to Italy The Allies had the daunting task of driving German occupying forces out of their advance positions in North Africa and the Mediterranean. They began their North Africa campaign, Operation Torch, in November 1942. Led by U.S. General Dwight Eisenhower and British General Bernard Montgomery, Allied forces succeeded in taking North Africa from the Germans by May 1943.

The next U.S.–British target was the Mediterranean island of Sicily, which they occupied in the summer of 1943, preparatory to an invasion of Italy. Mussolini fell from power during the summer, but Hitler's forces rescued him and gave him nominal control of northern Italy. In fact, German troops controlled much of Italy at the time that the Allies invaded the peninsula in September 1943. The Germans put up a determined resistance to the Allied offensive, holding much of northern Italy until their final surrender in May 1945.

From D-Day to Victory in Europe The Allied drive to liberate France began on June 6, 1944, with the largest invasion by sea in history. On D-Day, as the invasion date was called, British, Canadian, and U.S. forces under the command of General Eisenhower secured several beachheads on the Normandy coast. After this bloody but successful attack, the Allied offensive moved rapidly to roll back German occupying forces. By the end of August, Paris was liberated. By September, Allied troops had crossed the German border for a final push toward Berlin. The Germans launched a desperate counterattack in Belgium in December 1944 in the Battle of the Bulge. After this setback, however, Americans reorganized and resumed their advance.

German Surrender and Discovery of the Holocaust Since 1942, Allied bombing raids over Germany had reduced that nation's industrial capacity and ability to continue fighting. Recognizing that the end was near, as the Russian army closed in on Berlin, Hitler committed suicide on April 30, 1945. The unconditional surrender of the Nazi armies took place a week later, on May 7.

As U.S. troops advanced through Germany, they came upon German concentration camps and witnessed the horrifying extent of the Nazis' program of genocide against the Jews and others. Americans and the world were shocked to learn that 6 million Jewish civilians and several million non-Jews had been systematically murdered by Nazi Germany.

Fighting Japan

In Europe, British, Soviet, and U.S. forces were jointly responsible for defeating Germany, but in the Pacific, it was largely the U.S. armed forces that challenged the Japanese. After the Pearl Harbor attack, Japan seized control of much of East Asia and Southeast Asia. By early 1942, Japanese troops occupied Korea, eastern China, the Philippines, British Burma and Malaya, French Indochina (Vietnam, Cambodia, and Laos), the Dutch East Indies (Indonesia), and most of the Pacific islands west of Midway Island.

Turning Point, 1942 The war in the Pacific was dominated by naval forces battling over a vast area. Intercepting and decoding Japanese messages enabled U.S. forces to destroy four Japanese carriers and 300 planes in the decisive Battle of Midway on June 4–7. This battle ended Japanese expansion.

Island-Hopping After the victory at Midway, the United States began a long campaign to get within striking distance of Japan's home islands by seizing strategic locations in the Pacific. Using a strategy called "island-hopping," commanders bypassed strongly held Japanese posts and isolated them with naval and air power. Allied forces moved steadily toward Japan.

Major Battles Early in 1942, the Japanese had conquered the Philippines. When General Douglas MacArthur, the commander of army units in the Southern Pacific, was driven from the islands, he famously vowed, "I shall return." The conflict that prepared the way for U.S. reoccupation of the Philippines was the largest naval battle in history. At the Battle of Leyte Gulf in October 1944, the Japanese navy was virtually destroyed. For the first time in the war, the Japanese used *kamikaze* pilots to make suicide attacks on U.S. ships. Kamikazes also inflicted major damage in the colossal Battle of Okinawa (April to June 1945). Before finally succeeding in taking this island near Japan, U.S. forces suffered 50,000 casualties and killed 100,000 Japanese.

Atomic Bombs After Okinawa, a huge invasion force stood ready to attack Japan. Extremely heavy casualties were feared. By this time, however, the United States had developed a frightfully destructive new weapon. The top-secret Manhattan Project had begun in 1942. Directed by the physicist J. Robert Oppenheimer, the project employed over 100,000 people and spent $2 billion to develop a weapon whose power came from the splitting of the atom. The atomic bomb, or A-bomb, was successfully tested on July 16, 1945, at Alamogordo, New Mexico. The new president, Harry Truman, and his wartime allies called on Japan to surrender unconditionally or face "utter destruction." When Japan gave an unsatisfactory reply, Truman consulted with his advisers and decided to use the new weapon on two Japanese cities. On August 6, an A-bomb was dropped on Hiroshima, and on August 9, a second bomb was dropped on Nagasaki. About 250,000 Japanese died, either immediately or after a prolonged period of suffering, as a result of the two bombs.

Japan Surrenders Within a week after the second bomb fell, Japan agreed to surrender if the Allies would allow the emperor to remain as a titular (powerless) head of state. General MacArthur received Japan's formal surrender on September 2, 1945, in Tokyo harbor aboard the battleship *Missouri*.

Wartime Conferences

During the war, the Big Three (leaders of the United States, the Soviet Union, and Great Britain) arranged to confer secretly to coordinate their military strategies and to lay the foundation for peace terms and postwar involvement.

Casablanca The first conference involved only two of the Big Three. In January 1943, Roosevelt and Churchill agreed on the grand strategy to win the war, including to invade Sicily and Italy and to demand "unconditional surrender" from the Axis powers.

Teheran The Big Three—Roosevelt, Churchill, and Stalin—met for the first time in the Iranian city of Teheran in November 1943. They agreed that the British and Americans would begin their drive to liberate France in the spring of 1944 and that the Soviets would invade Germany and eventually join the war against Japan.

Yalta In February 1945, the Big Three conferred again at Yalta, a resort town on the Black Sea coast of the Soviet Union. Their agreement at Yalta would prove the most historic of the three meetings. After victory in Europe was achieved, Roosevelt, Churchill, and Stalin agreed that

- Germany would be divided into occupation zones

- there would be free elections in the liberated countries of Eastern Europe (even though Soviet troops controlled this territory)

- the Soviets would enter the war against Japan, which they did on August 8, 1945—just as Japan was about to surrender

- the Soviets would control the southern half of Sakhalin Island and the Kurile Islands in the Pacific and would have special concessions in Manchuria

- a new world peace organization (the future United Nations) would be formed at a conference in San Francisco

Death of President Roosevelt When the president returned from Yalta and informed Congress of his agreement with Churchill and Stalin, it was apparent that his health had deteriorated. On April 12, 1945, while resting in a vacation home in Georgia, an exhausted Franklin Roosevelt died suddenly. News of his death shocked the nation almost as much as Pearl Harbor. Harry S. Truman entered the presidency unexpectedly to assume enormous responsibilities as commander in chief of a war effort that had not yet been won.

Potsdam In late July, after Germany's surrender, only Stalin remained as one of the Big Three. Truman was the U.S. president, and Clement Attlee had just been elected the new British prime minister. The three leaders met in Postsdam, Germany (July 17–August 2, 1945) and agreed (1) to demand that Japan surrender unconditionally, and (2) to hold war-crime trials of Nazi leaders.

The War's Legacy

The most destructive war in the history of the world had profound effects on all nations, including the United States.

Costs

The deadliest war in human history resulted in the deaths of some 50 million military personnel and civilians worldwide. Fifteen million Americans served in uniform and approximately 300,000 Americans lost their lives either in Europe or the Pacific, and 800,000 were wounded. Excluding the Civil War, more Americans died in World War II than in all other U.S. wars combined. The war left the country with a huge national debt, but domestically the United States had suffered little compared to others.

The United Nations

Unlike the rejection of the League of Nations following World War I, Congress readily accepted the peacekeeping organization that was conceived during World War II and put in place immediately after the war. Meeting in 1944 at Dumbarton Oaks near Washington, D.C., Allied representatives from the United States, the Soviet Union, Great Britain, and China proposed an international organization to be called the United Nations. Then in April 1945, delegates from 50 nations assembled in San Francisco, where they took only eight weeks to draft a charter for the United Nations. The Senate quickly voted to accept U.S. involvement in the U.N. On October 24, 1945, the U.N. came into existence when the majority of member-nations ratified its charter.

Expectations

In a final speech, which he never delivered, Franklin Roosevelt wrote: "The only limit to our realization of tomorrow will be the doubts of today." There were doubts, to be sure, about the new world order to emerge from World War II. Initially at least, there were also widely shared hopes that life would be better and more prosperous after the war than before. While other combatants, such as China, France, Germany, Great Britain, Italy, Japan, and the Soviet Union, had suffered extensive damage from the war, the cities of the United States had remained unscarred. Without a doubt, the United States in 1945 was at once the most prosperous and the most powerful nation in the world. It had played a major role in defeating the Fascist dictators. Now people looked forward with some optimism to both a more peaceful and more democratic world. Unfortunately, the specters of the Soviet Union and the A-bomb would soon dim these expectations of a brighter tomorrow.

HISTORICAL PERSPECTIVES: WAS PEARL HARBOR AVOIDABLE?

At first it seemed that U.S. entry into World War II was simply a reaction to Japan's attack on Pearl Harbor. Probing more deeply, some historians placed part of the blame for the outbreak of World War II on U.S. policies in the late 1930s. They argued that U.S. isolationism emboldened the Fascist dictators and also left U.S. territories vulnerable to attack through military unpreparedness.

In the late 1940s, revisionists wrote that the Pearl Harbor attack could have been avoided if the diplomacy of Roosevelt and Secretary of State Hull had been more flexible. Charles A. Beard took the extreme view that Roosevelt intended the embargo on raw materials to force Japan into war. Many of the revisionists believed that Roosevelt wanted the United States in the war because of his anti-Fascist beliefs and pro-British sympathies.

Later revisionist criticisms of the 1950s and 1960s asked why naval authorities at Pearl Harbor were unprepared for an attack since the United States had broken the Japanese code. Presumably, officials knew that a Japanese attack was coming but could not determine precisely when and where it would be.

For many, the definitive study of Pearl Harbor is Gordon W. Prange's *At Dawn We Slept* (1981). While Prange believes the government could have done better predicting and preparing for an attack, he finds no evidence of a secret plot to allow Pearl Harbor to happen. His key point is that the Japanese had brilliantly planned and executed an attack that was inconceivable to most Americans at that time.

Taking the opposite position is John Toland's *Infamy: Pearl Harbor and Its Aftermath* (1982). Toland argues that Roosevelt had advance knowledge of the attack but withheld any warning so that a surprise attack would bring the United States into the war. A major problem with this argument is that the author presents no direct evidence for his conclusion.

The divergent views on the Pearl Harbor attack show the difference between historical *analysis* of how and why events occurred and historical *judgment* of a leader's underlying motives. In judging motives, historians often show their own values.

KEY TERMS BY THEME

Hoover-FDR Policies (WOR)
Good Neighbor policy
Pan-American conferences
Soviet Union recognized
Independence for Philippines
reciprocal trade agreements

Militarist/Fascist Aggression (WOR)
Japan takes Manchuria
Stimson Doctrine
fascism
Italian Fascist party
Benito Mussolini
Ethiopia
German Nazi party
Adolf Hitler
Axis Powers
Spanish Civil War
Francisco Franco
Rhineland
Sudetenland
Munich
appeasement
Poland; blitzkrieg

Isolationist Response (WOR)
isolationism
Nye Committee
Neutrality Acts
America First Committee
Charles Lindbergh

FDR's Response (WOR)
Quarantine speech
cash and carry
Selective Training and-Service Act (1940)
destroyers-for-bases deal
FDR, third term
Wendell Willkie
Four Freedoms speech
Lend-Lease Act (1941)
Atlantic Charter
escort convoys
oil and steel embargo
Pearl Harbor

Mobilization (WXT, POL)
War Production Board
Office of Price Administration
government spending, debt
role of large corporations
research and development
Manhattan Project
Office of War Information
"the Good War"

Home Front (MIG, POL)
wartime migration
civil rights, "Double V"
executive order on jobs
Smith v. Allwright
Braceros program
Japanese internment
Korematsu v. U.S.
"Rosie the Riveter"
wartime solidarity
election of 1944
Harry S. Truman

Wartime Strategies (WOR)
Battle of the Atlantic
strategic bombing
Dwight Eisenhower
D-Day
Holocaust
island-hopping
Battle of Midway
Douglas MacArthur
kamikaze attacks
J. Robert Oppenheimer
atomic bomb
Hiroshima; Nagasaki

Wartime Diplomacy (WOR)
Big Three
Casablanca Conference
unconditional surrender
Tehran, Yalta, Potsdam
United Nations

Questions 1–3 refer to the cartoon below.

The Only Way We Can Save Her

Source: Carey Orr, 1939. Granger Collection, NYC

1. Which of the following attitudes most directly contributed to the perspective of this cartoon?

   (A) The priority of President Roosevelt to protect Latin American nations

   (B) The strong opposition to helping the Soviet Union under Joseph Stalin

   (C) The isolationist sentiment that developed after World War I

   (D) The antiwar policies of the Franklin Roosevelt administration

2. Which of the following events most directly conflicted with the perspective of this cartoon?

   (A) Congressional hearings into the causes of U.S. entry into World War I

   (B) The Spanish Civil War between the fascist and the republican forces

   (C) Passage of laws prohibiting arms sales, bank loans, and travel to nations at war

   (D) Roosevelt's call for democracies to "quarantine" aggressive nations

3. Which of the following individuals and groups most directly supported the perspective of this cartoon?

   (A) Herbert Hoover and East Coast leaders of the Republican Party

   (B) Charles Lindbergh and Midwest and rural newspapers and voters

   (C) American men who were eligible for the military draft

   (D) Wendell Willkie and the progressive wing of the Republican Party

Questions 4–6 refer to the excerpt below.

"It has been said, times without number, that if Hitler cannot cross the English Channel he cannot cross three thousand miles of sea. But there is only one reason why he has not crossed the English Channel. That is because forty-five million determined Britons, in a heroic resistance, have converted their island into a armed base, from which proceeds a steady stream of sea and air power. As Secretary Hull has said: "It is not the water that bars the way. It is the resolute determination of British arms. Were the control of the seas by Britain lost, the Atlantic would no longer be an obstacle—rather, it would become a broad highway for a conqueror moving westward."

—*The New York Times,* April 30, 1941

4. Which of the following would the author(s) of this excerpt most likely support?
   (A) Aiding the Soviet Union in case the British surrendered
   (B) Extending the Good Neighbor Policy to Great Britain
   (C) Prohibiting travel on ships of belligerent nations
   (D) Passing the Lend Lease Act to provide arms on credit to Great Britain

5. Which of the following statements best characterizes American opinion about involvement in World War II at the time this excerpt was published?
   (A) The United States should increase defense spending, but providing direct aid to Britain is controversial.
   (B) Britain faces certain defeat by Germany and the United States should stay out of the war.
   (C) The Atlantic Ocean is an effective barrier to a military invasion by Germany.
   (D) The United States should immediately come to the aid of Britain against Germany.

6. Which of the following caused the greatest shift in American opinion about World War II?
   (A) The re-election of President Franklin Roosevelt for a third term in 1940
   (B) The invasion of the Soviet Union by Hitler's Germany
   (C) The Japanese attack on Pearl Harbor and the Philippines
   (D) The British victory over the German and Italian armies in North Africa

Questions 7–8 refer to the excerpt below.

"Rationing is a vital part of your country's war effort. Any attempt to violate the rules is an effort to deny someone his share and will create hardship and help the enemy. This book is our Government's assurance of your right to buy your fair share of certain goods made scare by war. Price ceilings have also been established for your protection. Dealers must post these prices conspicuously. Don't pay more. Give your whole support to rationing and thereby conserve our vital goods. Be guided by the rule: "If you don't need it, DON'T BUY IT."

"IMPORTANT: When you used your ration, salvage the TIN CANS and WASTE FATS. They are needed to make munitions for our fighting men. Cooperate with your local Salvage Committee."

—War Ration Books 3 and 4, Office of Price Administration, 1943

7. Which of the following was the primary economic purpose for the rationing program found in the above document?

   (A) Control inflation caused by shortages of consumer goods

   (B) Discourage the development of black markets

   (C) Encourage industries to stop making consumer products

   (D) Encourage workers and unions not to demand higher wages

8. Which of the following best explains the campaign behind the above government documents?

   (A) Governments needed to control civilian behavior during wartime to reassure people that they were still in control

   (B) Industrial production was essential to successful modern warfare and it required an effort by the entire nation

   (C) Salvaging waste materials promoted patriotism by giving everyone a way to support the war effort

   (D) Governments had to stop civilian hoarding during wartime so that people would not focus their anger on each other

SHORT-ANSWER QUESTIONS

Use complete sentences; an outline or bulleted list alone is not acceptable.

Question 1 is based on the excerpt below.

"Whereas the successful prosecution of the war requires every possible protection against espionage and against sabotage to national-defense. . . . I hereby authorize and direct the Secretary of War . . . to prescribe military areas . . . from which any and all persons may be excluded, and with respect to which, the right of any person to enter, remain in, or leave shall be subject to whatever restrictions the Secretary of War or the appropriate Military Commander may impose in his discretion."

—Executive Order 9066, February 19, 1942

1. Using the excerpt, answer (A), (B), and (C).
   (A) Briefly explain ONE specific effect that this order had on Japanese Americans.
   (B) Briefly explain ONE specific Constitutional issue that was raised by this order.
   (C) Briefly explain ONE additional effect that the wartime experience had on the civil rights movement in the United States.

Question 2. Answer (A), (B), and (C).

   (A) Briefly explain ONE historical event or development that caused Americans to view the war as a struggle for the survival of democracy against fascism and militarism.
   (B) Briefly explain ONE specific military strategy or tactic that contributed to the U. S. victory in World War II.
   (C) Briefly explain ONE important factor or development that contributed to the emergence of the United States as the most powerful and leading nation after World War II.

Question 3. Answer (A), (B), and (C).

   (A) Briefly explain ONE specific effect that federal mobilization policies had on the American economy and businesses during World War II.
   (B) Briefly explain ONE specific effect that World War II had on opportunities for women.
   (C) Briefly explain ONE specific example of how technological and scientific advances contributed to U.S. military victories.

Question 4 is based on the excerpts below.

"Each of the tiny steps [Roosevelt] took was designed to keep the US out of the war... The only conclusion to be reached is Britain in 1940 and 1941 survived with no significant outside help except that freely given by the Dominions, especially Canada. . . . The defender of liberal democracy in 1940–41 was not Britain along with the United States. . . . They fought freedom's battle while the largest democracy on earth occasionally threw them some crumbs."

—Robin Prior, historian, *When Britain Saved The West,* 2015

"Roosevelt took the lead in educating Americans to this new perspective on world affairs. He has been criticized for his timidity. . . . But he had vivid memories of Wilson's defeat and feared getting too far out in front of public opinion. . . . Step by step between 1939 and 1941, he abandoned neutrality and, through aid to Britain and other nations fighting Hitler, took the United States to the brink of war. . . . He set forth the intellectual underpinnings for an American globalism that would take form in World War II and flourish in the postwar years."

—George C. Herring, historian, *From Colony to Superpower,* 2008

4. Using the excerpts, answer (A), (B), and (C).

   (A) Briefly describe ONE major difference between Prior's and Herring's historical interpretation about Roosevelt's role in World War II.

   (B) Briefly explain how ONE specific historical event or development that is not explicitly mentioned in the excerpts could be used to support Prior's interpretation.

   (C) Briefly explain how ONE specific historical event or development that is not explicitly mentioned in the excerpts could be used to support Herring's interpretation.

THINK AS A HISTORIAN: SELECTING RELEVANT EVIDENCE

Which THREE of the following would be most relevant for an essay about whether wars increase or decrease acts of prejudice?

1. *Korematsu v. United States*

2. *Smith v. Allwright*

3. Four Freedoms speech

4. zoot suit riots

UNIT 7: Period 7 Review, 1890–1945

LONG ESSAY QUESTIONS

Directions: The suggested writing time for each question is 40 minutes. In your response you should do the following:

- **Thesis:** Make a defensible claim that establishes a line of reasoning and consists of one or more sentences found in one place.
- **Contextualization:** Relate the argument to a broader historical context.
- **Evidence:** Support an argument with specific and relevant historical evidence.
- **Reasoning:** Organize an argument using the skill in the question.
- **Analysis:** Demonstrate a complex understanding of the question using historical evidence to support, qualify, or modify an argument.

1. Analyze how TWO of the following helped to shape the national identity in the 20th century.
   - Spanish American War
   - World War I
   - Great Depression/New Deal
   - World War II

2. Analyze how women's identity was influenced by both peacetime and wartime experiences in the period from 1900 to 1945.

3. Compare and contrast the beliefs and strategies of TWO of the following to address the needs of the U.S. economic system.
   - Progressives
   - Economic conservatives of the 1920s and 1930s
   - New Deal

4. Compare and contrast the effects of TWO of the following on business and labor.
   - World War I
   - Great Depression
   - New Deal
   - World War II

5. Analyze the causes and effects of changes in immigration patterns and polices from 1900 to 1945.

6. Analyze the causes and effects of changes in internal migration patterns from 1900 to 1945.

7. Analyze to what extent the increased role of the federal government in the U.S. economy was an important political development between 1900 and 1945.

8. Analyze to what extent federal wartime policies threatened or changed civil liberties for Americans during the period from 1898 to 1945.

9. Compare and contrast the goals of U.S. policy makers in the Spanish American War, World War I and World War II.

10. Compare and contrast the influence of TWO of the following wars on postwar foreign policy.

   • Spanish-American War

   • World War I

   • World War II

11. Analyze to what extent the arts and popular culture, including immigrant and African-American artists, contributed to changes in American values and attitudes between 1900 and 1945.

12. Analyze to what extent science and technological innovations contribute to American values and attitudes between 1900 and 1945.

Directions: Question 1 is based on the accompanying documents. The documents have been edited for the purpose of this exercise. You are advised to spend 15 minutes planning and 45 minutes writing your answer. In your response you should do the following:

- **Thesis:** Make a defensible claim that establishes a line of reasoning and consists of one or more sentences found in one place.
- **Contextualization:** Relate the argument to a broader historical context.
- **Document Evidence:** Use content from at least six documents.
- **Outside Evidence:** Use one piece of evidence not in the documents.
- **Document Sourcing:** Explain how or why the point of view, purpose, situation, or intended audience is relevant for at least three documents.
- **Analysis:** Show the relationships among pieces of historical evidence and use them to support, qualify, or modify an argument.

1. "The ideals used to justify U.S. involvement in World War I disguised the real reasons for Wilson's change in policy from neutrality to war and, in fact, violated the traditional values of the American nation." Assess this statement and the reasons for the change in U.S. policy in 1917 AND whether these reasons were consistent with traditional American values.

Document 1

Source: Oswald Garrison Villard, writer and journalist, *Annals of the American Academy of Political and Social Science,* July 1916

Now, the real significance of this [campaign for preparedness] is that we have all at once, in the midst of a terrifying cataclysm, abjured our faith in many things American. We no longer believe, as for 140 years, in the moral power of an America unarmed and unafraid; we believe suddenly that the influence of the United States is to be measured only by the numbers of our soldiery and our dreadnoughts—our whole history to the contrary notwithstanding.

Next, the preparedness policy signifies an entire change in our attitude toward the military as to whom we inherited from our forefathers suspicions and distrust. A cardinal principle of our polity has always been the subordination of the military to the civil authority as a necessary safeguard for the republic."

Document 2

Source: U.S. Bureau of the Census. *Historical Statistics of the United States,*

VALUE OF UNITED STATES IMPORTS AND EXPORTS, 1914 to 1919

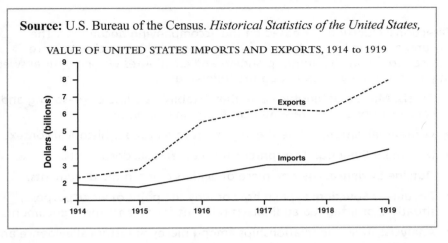

Document 3

Source: President Woodrow Wilson, War Message to Congress, April 2, 1917

We are glad, now that we see the facts with no veil of false pretense about them, to fight thus for the ultimate peace of the world and for the liberation of its peoples, the German peoples included: for the rights of nations great and small and the privilege of men everywhere to choose their way of life and of obedience. The world must be made safe for democracy. Its peace must be planted upon the tested foundations of political liberty. We have no selfish ends to serve. We desire no conquest, no dominion. We seek no indemnities for ourselves, no material compensation for the sacrifices we shall freely make. We are but one of the champions of the rights of mankind. We shall be satisfied when those rights have been made as secure as the faith and the freedom of nations can make them.

Document 4

Source: Senator George W. Norris, Speech in the U.S. Senate, April 4, 1917

We are taking a step today that is fraught with untold danger. We are going into war upon the command of gold. We are going to run the risk of sacrificing millions of our countrymen's lives in order that other countrymen may coin their lifeblood into money. . . . We are about to do the bidding of wealth's terrible mandate. By our act we will make millions of our countrymen suffer, and the consequences of it may well be that millions of our brethren must shed their lifeblood, millions of broken-hearted women must weep, millions of children must suffer with cold, and millions of babes must die from hunger, and all because we want to preserve the commercial right of American citizens to deliver munitions of war to belligerent nations.

Document 5

Source: Library of Congress

I WANT YOU
FOR U.S. ARMY
NEAREST RECRUITING STATION

Document 6

Source: Norman Thomas, socialist and pacifist, *The New Republic,* May 26, 1917

Tolerance arises from the existence of varying types of doers, all willing to respect one another's special competence. It is not too extreme to assert that in wartime (as in peacetime) some of the most heroic deeds are performed by those who do not (and, if called upon, would not) take up arms in defense of the cause. There are other forms of bravery than the purely military one. Let us be reasonable.

In bringing the gift of freedom to the distant unemancipated, shall we betray so precious a cause by brute denial of freedom to those of our own blood and tradition, to our own freedom lovers within the gate? What a sorry, tragical miscarriage of wisdom!

Document 7

Source: Theodore Roosevelt, Pledge of Loyalty, September 11, 1917

We ask that good Americans . . . uphold the hands of the government at every point efficiently and resolutely against our foreign and domestic foes, and that they constantly spur the government to speedier and more effective action. Furthermore, we ask that, where government action cannot be taken, they arouse an effective and indignant public opinion against the enemies of our country, whether these enemies masquerade as pacifists, or proclaim themselves the enemies of our allies, or act through organizations such as the I.W.W. and the Socialist Party machine, or appear nakedly as the champions of Germany. Above all, we ask that they teach our people to spurn any peace save the peace of overwhelming victory in the war to which we have set our hands.

DOCUMENT-BASED QUESTION 2

Directions: Question 1 is based on the accompanying documents. The documents have been edited for the purpose of this exercise. You are advised to spend 15 minutes planning and 45 minutes writing your answer. In your response you should do the following:

- **Thesis:** Make a defensible claim that establishes a line of reasoning and consists of one or more sentences found in one place.
- **Contextualization:** Relate the argument to a broader historical context.
- **Document Evidence:** Use content from at least six documents.
- **Outside Evidence:** Use one piece of evidence not in the documents.
- **Document Sourcing:** Explain how or why the point of view, purpose, situation, or intended audience is relevant for at least three documents.
- **Analysis:** Show the relationships among pieces of historical evidence and use them to support, qualify, or modify an argument.

2. "To a greater or lesser extent, three factors were involved in explaining U.S. response to Japanese and German aggression: (a) economics, (b) national security, and (c) democratic values." Drawing upon the documents that follow as well as your knowledge of history, write an essay analyzing to what extent these factors influenced foreign policy from 1937 through 1941.

Document 1

Source: Council on Foreign Relations, *The United States in World Affairs, 1937*, 1938

The Commandant of the Third Naval District expressed "hearty accord" with President Roosevelt's proposal to increase the nation's naval strength by a huge and extraordinary appropriation of public funds. "A navy second to none," said he, was needed as a "contribution to world peace," and he denounced "all foolish nations which through mistaken ideas of altruism were unprepared to defend themselves when attacked."

In the stock markets [according to the *New York Herald Tribune*, December 30], "intermittent buying in aircrafts, steels, and a selected assortment of heavy industrials pushed prices substantially higher, demand apparently being based on expectations of large rearmament expenditures by the national government.

Document 2

Source: Advertisement, *New York Times,* June 10, 1940

If Hitler wins in Europe—if the strength of the British and French armies and navies is forever broken—the United States will find itself alone in a barbaric world—a world ruled by Nazis, with "spheres of influence" assigned to their totalitarian allies. However different the dictatorships may be, racially, they all agree on one primary objective: "Democracy must be wiped from the face of the earth."

The world will be placed on a permanent war footing. Our country will have to pile armaments upon armaments to maintain even the illusion of security. We shall have no other business, no other aim in life, but primitive self-defense. We shall exist only under martial law—or the law of the jungle."

Document 3

Source: Wendell Willkie, Acceptance Speech at the Republican National Convention, August 17, 1940

I cannot ask the American people to put their faith in me without recording my conviction that some form of selective service is the only democratic way in which to secure the trained and competent manpower we need for national defense.

Also, in the light of my principle, we must honestly face our relationship with Great Britain. We must admit that the loss of the British Fleet would greatly weaken our defense. This is because the British Fleet has for years controlled the Atlantic, leaving us free to concentrate in the Pacific. If the British Fleet were lost or captured, the Atlantic might be dominated by Germany, a power hostile to our way of life, controlling in that event most of the ships and shipbuilding facilities of Europe.

This would be calamity for us. We might be exposed to attack on the Atlantic. Our defense would be weakened until we could build a navy and air force strong enough to defend both coasts. Also, our foreign trade would be profoundly affected. That trade is vital to our prosperity. But if we had to trade with a Europe dominated by the present German trade policies, we might have to change our methods to some totalitarian form. This is a prospect that any lover of democracy must view with consternation.

Document 4

Source: Brown Brothers

Document 5

Source: Franklin Roosevelt, Speech to Congress, "Four Freedoms," January 6, 1941

Our national policy is this:

First, by an impressive expression of the public will and without regard to partisanship, we are committed to all-inclusive national defense.

Second, by an impressive expression of the public will and without regard to partisanship, we are committed to full support of all those resolute people everywhere who are resisting aggression and are thereby keeping war away from our hemisphere. By this support we express our determination that the democratic cause shall prevail, and we strengthen the defense and the security of our own nation. . . .

Let us say to the democracies: "We Americans are vitally concerned in your defense of freedom. We are putting forth our energies, our resources and our organizing powers to give you the strength to regain and maintain a free world. We shall send you in ever-increasing numbers, ships, planes, tanks, guns. That is our purpose and our pledge.

Document 6

Source: Adapted from Gilbert C. Fite, Jim E. Reese, *An Economic History of the United States,* 1959

The Effect of World War II on Industry			
Category	1939	1940	1941
Index of manufacturing output (1939 = 100)	100	116	154
Corporate profits before taxes (billions of dollars)	6.4	9.3	17.0
Corporate profits before taxes (billions of dollars)	5.0	6.5	9.4
Business failures	14,768	13,619	11,848

Document 7

Source: Charles A. Lindbergh, Speech in New York City, April 23, 1941

The United States is better situated from a military standpoint than any other nation in the world. Even in our present condition of unpreparedness no foreign power is in a position to invade us today. If we concentrate on our own defenses and build the strength that this nation should maintain, no foreign army will ever attempt to land on American shores.

War is not inevitable for this country. Such a claim is defeatism in the true sense. No one can make us fight abroad unless we ourselves are willing to do so. No one will attempt to fight us here if we arm ourselves as a great nation should be armed. Over 100 million people in this nation are opposed to entering the war. If the principles of democracy mean anything at all, that is reason enough for us to stay out.

UNIT 8: Period 8, 1945–1980

In 1945, the United States emerged from World War II with the world's largest and strongest economy. Americans were happy to get back to civilian life. However, people feared that without the stimulus of war-time spending, the country might return to the economic depression of the 1930s. What no one could predict with any confidence was how the fall of colonial empires, the spread of Communism, and changes in the global economy would impact American lives in the future.

Overview Despite the worries about an economic slow-down, Americans enjoyed mostly robust economic growth through the 1950s and 1960s. In part, this success was because the country faced little competition, as the rest of world's economies recovered from the destruction of factories, roads, railways, and harbors during World War II. Democrats, expanding on the New Deal, enacted major domestic programs. Among these were Medicare to provide health care for the elderly, aid to education, and civil rights for African Americans and women.

In foreign affairs, the Cold War against Communist governments in the Soviet Union, China, and other countries dominated U.S. policy. The threat of the use of nuclear weapons kept the great powers from attacking each other. However, limited "hot" wars in Korea and Vietnam resulted in the deaths of more than 100,000 Americans and millions of Koreans and Vietnamese.

By the late 1960s, frustration over the Vietnam War, opposition to civil rights reforms and other liberal domestic programs, and increased civil unrest weakened the Democratic majority. Liberal views slowly gave way during the 1970s to a conservative resurgence in 1980.

Alternate Views Historians debate when postwar optimism and prosperity gave way to pessimism and a declining standard of living for many Americans. Historians who focus on cultural attitudes identify 1968, a year of assassinations, riots, and intense conflict over the Vietnam War, as a turning point. People were losing confidence in government's ability to solve problems and in the effectiveness of universities, the media, and other institutions. Other historians, who focus on economic changes, point to the mid-1970s, when wage growth stagnated for average Americans.

26

TRUMAN AND THE COLD WAR, 1945–1952

Communism holds that the world is so deeply divided into opposing classes that war is inevitable. Democracy holds that free nations can settle differences justly and maintain lasting peace.

President Harry S. Truman,
Inaugural Address, January 20, 1949

World War II dramatically changed the United States from an isolationist country into a military superpower and a leader in world affairs. After the war, most of the Americans at home and the millions coming back from military service wished to return to normal domestic life and enjoy the revitalized national economy. However, during the Truman presidency, the growing conflict between the Communist Soviet Union and the United States—a conflict that came to be known as the Cold War—dampened the nation's enjoyment of the postwar boom.

Postwar America

The 15 million American soldiers, sailors, and marines returning to civilian life in 1945 and 1946 faced the problem of finding jobs and housing. Many feared that the end of the war might mean the return of economic hard times. Happily, the fears were not realized because the war years had increased the per-capita income of Americans. Much of that income was tucked away in savings accounts, since wartime shortages meant there had been few consumer goods to buy. Pent-up consumer demand for autos and housing combined with government road-building projects quickly overcame the economic uncertainty after the war and introduced an era of unprecedented prosperity and economic growth. By the 1950s, Americans enjoyed the highest standard of living achieved by any society in history.

GI Bill—Help for Veterans

The Servicemen's Readjustment Act of 1944, popularly known as the GI Bill of Rights, proved a powerful support during the transition of 15 million veterans to a peacetime economy. More than half the returning GIs (as the men and women in uniform were called) seized the opportunity afforded by the GI Bill to continue their education at government expense. Over 2 million GIs attended college, which started a postwar boom in higher education. The veterans also received over $16 billion in low-interest, government-backed loans to buy homes and farms and to start businesses. By focusing on a better educated workforce and also promoting new construction, the federal government stimulated the postwar economic expansion.

Baby Boom

One sign of the basic confidence of the postwar era was an explosion in marriages and births. Younger marriages and larger families resulted in 50 million babies entering the U.S. population between 1945 and 1960. As the *baby boom* generation gradually passed from childhood to adolescence to adulthood, it profoundly affected the nation's social institutions and economic life in the last half of the 20th century. Initially, the baby boom tended to focus women's attention on raising children and homemaking. Nevertheless, the trend of more women in the workplace continued. By 1960, one-third of all married women worked outside the home.

Suburban Growth

The high demand for housing after the war resulted in a construction boom. William J. Levitt led in the development of postwar suburbia with his building and promotion of Levittown, a project of 17,000 mass-produced, low-priced family homes on Long Island, New York. Low interest rates on mortgages that were both government-insured and tax deductible made the move from city to suburb affordable for even families of modest means. In a single generation, the majority of middle-class Americans became suburbanites. For many older inner cities, the effect of the mass movement to suburbia was disastrous. By the 1960s, cities from Boston to Los Angeles became increasingly poor and racially divided.

Rise of the Sunbelt

Uprooted by the war, millions of Americans made moving a habit in the postwar era. A warmer climate, lower taxes, and economic opportunities in defense-related industries attracted many GIs and their families to the Sunbelt states from Florida to California. By transferring tax dollars from the Northeast and Midwest to the South and West, military spending during the Cold War helped finance the shift of industry, people, and ultimately political power from one region to the other.

Postwar Politics

Harry S. Truman, a moderate Democratic senator from Missouri, replaced the more liberal Henry Wallace as FDR's vice president in the 1944 election. Thrust into the presidency after Roosevelt's death in April 1945, Truman matured into a decisive leader whose basic honesty and unpretentious style appealed to average citizens. Truman attempted to continue in the New Deal tradition of his predecessor.

Economic Program and Civil Rights

Truman's proposals for full employment and for civil rights for African Americans ran into opposition from conservatives in Congress.

Employment Act of 1946 In September 1945, during the same week that Japan formally surrendered, Truman urged Congress to enact a series of progressive measures, including national health insurance, an increase in the minimum wage, and a bill to commit the U.S. government to maintaining full employment. After much debate, the watered-down version of the full-employment bill was enacted as the Employment Act of 1946. It created the Council of Economic Advisers to counsel both the president and Congress on means of promoting national economic welfare. Over the next seven years, a coalition between Republicans and conservative Southern Democrats, combined with the beginning of the Cold War, hindered passage of most of Truman's domestic program.

Inflation and Strikes Truman urged Congress to continue the price controls of wartime in order to hold inflation in check. Instead, southern Democrats joined with Republicans to relax the controls of the Office of Price Administration. The result was an inflation rate of almost 25 percent during the first year and a half of peace.

Workers and unions wanted wages to catch up after years of wage controls. Over 4.5 million workers went on strike in 1946. Strikes by railroad and mine workers threatened the national safety. Truman took a tough approach to this challenge, seizing the mines and using soldiers to keep them operating until the United Mine Workers finally called off its strike.

Civil Rights Truman was the first modern president to use the powers of his office to challenge racial discrimination. Bypassing southern Democrats who controlled key committees in Congress, the president used his executive powers to establish the Committee on Civil Rights in 1946. He also strengthened the civil rights division of the Justice Department, which aided the efforts of black leaders to end segregation in schools. Most importantly, in 1948 he ordered the end of racial discrimination throughout the federal government, including the armed forces. The end of segregation changed life on military bases, many of which were in the South.

Recognizing the odds against passage of civil rights legislation, Truman nevertheless urged Congress to create a Fair Employment Practices Commission that would prevent employers from discriminating against the hiring of African Americans. Southern Democrats blocked the legislation.

Republican Control of the Eightieth Congress

Unhappy with inflation and strikes, voters were in a conservative mood in the fall of 1946 when they elected Republican majorities in both houses of Congress. Under Republican control, the Eightieth Congress attempted to pass two tax cuts for upper-income Americans, but Truman vetoed both measures. More successful were Republican efforts to amend the Constitution and roll back some of the New Deal gains for labor.

Twenty-second Amendment (1951) Reacting against the election of Roosevelt as president four times, the Republican-dominated Congress proposed a constitutional amendment to limit a president to a maximum of two full terms in office. The 22nd Amendment was ratified by the states in 1951.

Taft-Hartley Act (1947) In 1947, Congress passed the probusiness Taft-Hartley Act. Truman vetoed the measure as a "slave-labor" bill, but Congress overrode his veto. The one purpose of the Republican-sponsored law was to check the growing power of unions. Its provisions included

- outlawing the closed shop (contract requiring workers to join a union *before* being hired)

- permitting states to pass "right to work" laws outlawing the union shop (contract requiring workers to join a union *after* being hired)

- outlawing secondary boycotts (the practice of several unions supporting a striking union by joining a boycott of a company's products)

- giving the president the power to invoke an 80-day cooling-off period before a strike endangering the national safety could be called

For years afterward, unions sought unsuccessfully to repeal the Taft-Hartley Act. The act became a major issue dividing Republicans and Democrats in the 1950s.

The Election of 1948

As measured by opinion polls, Truman's popularity was at a low point as the 1948 campaign for the presidency began. Republicans were confident of victory, especially after both a liberal faction and a conservative faction in the Democratic party abandoned Truman to organize their own third parties. Liberal Democrats, who thought Truman's aggressive foreign policy threatened world peace, formed a new Progressive party that nominated former vice president Henry Wallace. Southern Democrats also bolted the party in reaction to Truman's support for civil rights. Their States' Rights party, better known as the Dixiecrats, chose Governor J. Strom Thurmond of South Carolina as its presidential candidate.

The Republicans once again nominated New York Governor Thomas E. Dewey, who looked so much like a winner from the outset that he conducted an overly cautious and unexciting campaign. Meanwhile, the man without a chance toured the nation by rail, attacking the "do-nothing" Republican Eightieth Congress with "give-'em-hell" speeches. The feisty Truman confounded the polling experts with a decisive victory over Dewey, winning the popular vote by 2 million votes and winning the electoral vote 303 to 189. The president had succeeded in reuniting Roosevelt's New Deal coalition, except for four southern states that went to Thurmond and the Dixiecrats.

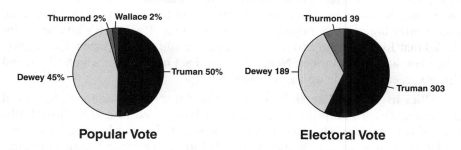

PRESIDENTIAL ELECTION, 1948

Thurmond 2% Wallace 2%

Dewey 45% Truman 50%

Popular Vote

Thurmond 39

Dewey 189 Truman 303

Electoral Vote

Source: U.S. Bureau of the Census. *Historical Statistics of the United States, Colonial Times to 1970*

The Fair Deal

Fresh from victory, Truman launched an ambitious reform program, which he called the *Fair Deal*. In 1949, he urged Congress to enact national health care insurance, federal aid to education, civil rights legislation, funds for public housing, and a new farm program. Conservatives in Congress blocked most of the proposed reforms, except for an increase in the minimum wage (from 40 to 75 cents an hour) and the inclusion of more workers under Social Security.

Most of the Fair Deal bills were defeated for two reasons: (1) Truman's political conflicts with Congress, and (2) the pressing foreign policy concerns of the Cold War. Nevertheless, liberal defenders of Truman praised him for at least maintaining the New Deal reforms of his predecessor and making civil rights part of the liberal agenda.

Origins of the Cold War

The Cold War dominated international relations from the late 1940s to the collapse of the Soviet Union in 1991. The conflict centered around the intense rivalry between two superpowers: the Communist empire of the Soviet Union and the leading Western democracy, the United States. Superpower competition usually was through diplomacy rather than armed conflict, but, in several instances, the Cold War took the world dangerously close to a nuclear war.

Among historians there is intense debate over how and why the Cold War began. Many analysts see Truman's policies as a reasonable response to Soviet efforts to increase their influence in the world. However, some critics argue that Truman misunderstood and overreacted to Russia's historic need to secure its borders. Other critics have attacked his administration as being weak or "soft" on communism.

U.S.-Soviet Relations to 1945

The wartime alliance between the United States and the Soviet Union against the Axis powers was actually a temporary halt in their generally poor relations of the past. Since the Bolshevik Revolution that established a Communist government in Russia in 1917, Americans had viewed the Soviets as a threat to all capitalistic countries. In the United States, it led to the Red Scare of 1919. The United States refused to recognize the Soviet Union until 1933. Even then, after a brief honeymoon period of less than a year, Roosevelt's advisers concluded that Joseph Stalin and the Communists could not be trusted. Confirming their view was the notorious Nonaggression Pact of 1939, in which Stalin and Hitler agreed to divide up Eastern Europe.

Allies in World War II In 1941, Hitler's surprise invasion of the Soviet Union and Japan's surprise attack on Pearl Harbor led to a U.S.–Soviet alliance of convenience—but not of mutual trust. Stalin bitterly complained that the British and Americans waited until 1944 to open a second front in France. Because of this wait, the Soviets bore the brunt of fighting the Nazis. By some estimates, half of all deaths in World War II were Soviets. The postwar conflicts over Central and Eastern Europe were already evident in the negotiations between Britain, the Soviet Union, and the U.S. at Yalta and Potsdam in 1945. Roosevelt hoped that personal diplomacy might keep Stalin in check, but when Truman came to power, he quickly became suspicious of the Soviets.

Postwar Cooperation and the U.N. The founding of the United Nations in the fall of 1945 provided one hopeful sign for the future. The General Assembly of the United Nations was created to provide representation to all member nations, while the 15-member Security Council was given the primary responsibility within the U.N. for maintaining international security and authorizing peacekeeping missions. The five major allies of wartime—the United States, Great Britain, France, China, and the Soviet Union—were granted permanent seats and veto power in the U.N. Security Council. Optimists hoped that these nations would be able to reach agreement on international issues. In addition, the Soviets went along with a U.S. proposal to establish an Atomic Energy Commission in the United Nations. They rejected, however, a plan proposed by Bernard Baruch for regulating nuclear energy and eliminating atomic weapons. Rejection of the Baruch Plan was interpreted by some American leaders as proof that Moscow did not have peaceful intentions.

The United States also offered the Soviets participation in the new International Bank for Reconstruction and Development (World Bank) created at the Bretton Woods Conference in 1944. The bank's initial purpose was to fund rebuilding of a war-torn world. The Soviets, however, declined to participate because they viewed the bank as an instrument of capitalism. The Soviets did join the other Allies in the 1945–1946 Nuremberg trials of 22 top Nazi leaders for war crimes and violations of human rights.

Satellite States in Eastern Europe Distrust turned into hostility beginning in 1946, as Soviet forces remained in occupation of the countries of Central and Eastern Europe. Elections were held by the Soviets—as promised by Stalin at Yalta—but the results were manipulated in favor of Communist candidates. One by one, from 1946 to 1948, Communist dictators, most of them loyal to Moscow, came to power in Poland, Romania, Bulgaria, Albania, Hungary, and Czechoslovakia. Apologists for the Soviets argued that Russia needed buffer states or satellites (nations under the control of a great power), as a protection against another Hitler-like invasion from the West.

The U.S. and British governments were alarmed by the Soviet takeover of Eastern Europe. They regarded Soviet actions in this region as a flagrant violation of self-determination, genuine democracy, and open markets. The British especially wanted free elections in Poland, whose independence had been the issue that started World War II.

Occupation Zones in Germany At the end of the war, the division of Germany and Austria into Soviet, French, British, and U.S. zones of occupation was meant to be only temporary. In Germany, however, the eastern zone under Soviet occupation gradually evolved into a new Communist state, the German Democratic Republic. The conflict over Germany was at least in part a conflict over differing views of national security and economic needs. The Soviets wanted a weak Germany for security reasons and large war reparations for economic reasons. The United States and Great Britain refused to allow reparations from their western zones because both viewed the economic recovery of Germany as important to the stability of Central Europe. The Soviets, fearing a restored Germany, tightened their control over East Germany. Also, since Berlin lay within their zone, they attempted to force the Americans, British, and French to give up their assigned sectors of the city.

Iron Curtain "I'm tired of babying the Soviets," Truman told Secretary of State James Byrnes in January 1946. News of a Canadian spy ring stealing atomic secrets for the Soviets and continued Soviet occupation of northern Iran further encouraged a get-tough policy in Washington.

In March 1946, in Fulton, Missouri, Truman was present on the speaker's platform as former British Prime Minister Winston Churchill declared: "An iron curtain has descended across the continent" of Europe. The iron curtain metaphor was later used throughout the Cold War to refer to the Soviet satellite states of Eastern Europe. Churchill's "iron curtain" speech called for a partnership between Western democracies to halt the expansion of communism. Did the speech anticipate the Cold War—or help to cause it? Historians still debate this question.

Containment in Europe

Early in 1947, Truman adopted the advice of three top advisers in deciding to "contain" Soviet aggression. His containment policy, which was to govern U.S. foreign policy for decades, was formulated by the secretary of state, General George Marshall; the undersecretary of state, Dean Acheson; and an expert on Soviet affairs, George F. Kennan. In an influential article, Kennan had written that only "a long-term, patient but firm and vigilant containment of Russian expansive tendencies" would eventually cause the Soviets to back off their Communist ideology of world domination and live in peace with other nations.

Did the containment policy attempt to do too much? Among the critics who argued that it did was journalist Walter Lippmann, who had coined the term "Cold War." Lippmann argued that some areas were vital to U.S. security, while others were merely peripheral; some governments deserved U.S. support, but others did not. American leaders, however, had learned the lesson of Munich (when leaders had given into demands by Hitler for land in 1938) and appeasement well and felt that Communist aggression, wherever it occurred, must be challenged.

The Truman Doctrine

Truman first implemented the containment policy in response to two threats: (1) a Communist-led uprising against the government in Greece, and (2) Soviet demands for some control of a water route in Turkey, the Dardanelles. In what became known as the Truman Doctrine, the president asked Congress in March 1947 for $400 million in economic and military aid to assist the "free people" of Greece and Turkey against "totalitarian" regimes. While Truman's alarmist speech may have oversimplified the situation in Greece and Turkey, it gained bipartisan support from Republicans and Democrats in Congress.

The Marshall Plan

After the war, Europe lay in ruins, short of food and deep in debt. The harsh winter of 1946–1947 further demoralized Europeans, who had already suffered through years of depression and war. Discontent encouraged the growth of the Communist party, especially in France and Italy. The Truman administration feared that the western democracies might vote the Communists into power.

In June 1947, George Marshall outlined an extensive program of U.S. economic aid to help European nations revive their economies and strengthen democratic governments. In December, Truman submitted to Congress a $17 billion European Recovery Program, better known as the Marshall Plan. In 1948, $12 billion in aid was approved for distribution to the countries of Western Europe over a four-year period. The United States offered Marshall Plan aid to the Soviet Union and its Eastern European satellites, but the Soviets refused it, fearing that it would lead to dependence on the United States.

Effects The Marshall Plan worked exactly as Marshall and Truman had hoped. The massive infusion of U.S. dollars helped Western Europe achieve self-sustaining growth by the 1950s and ended any real threat of Communist political successes in that region. It also bolstered U.S. prosperity by greatly increasing U.S. exports to Europe. At the same time, however, it deepened the rift between the non-Communist West and the Communist East.

The Berlin Airlift

A major crisis of the Cold War focused on Berlin. In June 1948, the Soviets cut off all access by land to the German city. Truman dismissed any plans to withdraw from Berlin, but he also rejected using force to open up the roads through the Soviet-controlled eastern zone. Instead, he ordered U.S. planes to fly in supplies to the people of West Berlin. Day after day, week after week, the massive airlift continued. At the same time, Truman sent 60 bombers capable of carrying atomic bombs to bases in England. The world waited nervously for the outbreak of war, but Stalin decided not to challenge the airlift. (Truman's stand on Berlin was partly responsible for his victory in the 1948 election.)

By May 1949, the Soviets finally opened up the highways to Berlin, thus bringing their 11-month blockade to an end. A major long-term consequence of the Berlin crisis was the creation of two Germanies: the Federal Republic of Germany (West Germany, a U.S. ally) and the German Democratic Republic (East Germany, a Soviet satellite).

NATO and National Security

Ever since Washington's farewell address of 1796, the United States had avoided permanent alliances with European nations. Truman broke with this tradition in 1949 by recommending that the United States join a military defense pact to protect Western Europe. The Senate readily gave its consent. Ten European nations joined the United States and Canada in creating the North Atlantic Treaty Organization (NATO), a military alliance for defending all members from outside attack. Truman selected General Eisenhower as NATO's first Supreme Commander and stationed U.S. troops in Western Europe as a deterrent against a Soviet invasion. Thus, the containment policy led to a military buildup and major commitments abroad. The Soviet Union countered in 1955 by forming the Warsaw Pact, a military alliance for the defense of the Communist states of Eastern Europe.

EUROPE AFTER WORLD WAR II: THE COLD WAR

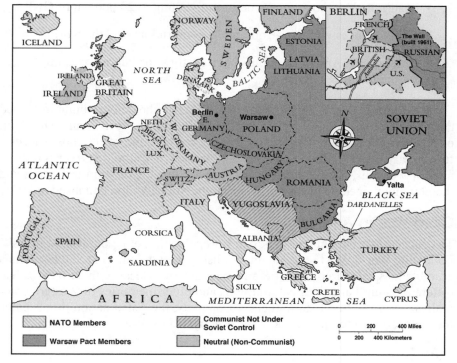

National Security Act (1947) The United States had begun to modernize its military capability in 1947 by passing the National Security Act. It provided for (1) a centralized Department of Defense (replacing the War Department) to coordinate the operations of the army, navy, and air force; (2) the creation of the National Security Council (NSC) to coordinate the making of foreign policy in the Cold War; and (3) the creation of the Central Intelligence Agency (CIA) to employ spies to gather information on foreign governments. In 1948, the Selective Service System and a peacetime draft were instituted.

Atomic Weapons After the Berlin crisis, teams of scientists in both the Soviet Union and the United States were engaged in an intense competition— or *arms race*—to develop superior weapons systems. For a period of just four years (1945–1949), the United States was the only nation to have the atomic bomb. It also developed in this period a new generation of long-range bombers for delivering nuclear weapons.

The Soviets tested their first atomic bomb in the fall of 1949. Truman then approved the development of a bomb a thousand times more powerful than the A-bomb that had destroyed Hiroshima. In 1952, this hydrogen bomb (or H-bomb) was added to the U.S. arsenal. Earlier, in 1950, the National Security Council had recommended, in a secret report known as NSC-68, that the following measures were necessary for fighting the Cold War:

- quadruple U.S. government defense spending to 20 percent of GNP

- form alliances with non-Communist countries around the world

- convince the American public that a costly arms buildup was imperative for the nation's defense

Evaluating U.S. Policy Critics of NATO and the defense buildup argued that the Truman administration intensified Russian fears and started an unnecessary arms race. Regardless, NATO became one of the most successful military alliances in history. In combination with the deterrent power of nuclear weapons, NATO effectively checked Soviet expansion in Europe and thereby maintained an uneasy peace until the Soviet Union collapsed in 1991.

Cold War in Asia

The successful containment policy in Europe could not be duplicated in Asia. Following World War II, the old imperialist system in India and Southeast Asia crumbled, as former colonies became new nations. Because these nations had different cultural and political traditions and bitter memories of Western colonialism, they resisted U.S. influence. Ironically, the Asian nation that became most closely tied to the U.S. defense system was its former enemy, Japan.

Japan

Unlike Germany, Japan was solely under the control of the United States. General Douglas MacArthur took firm charge of the reconstruction of Japan. Seven

Japanese generals, including Premier Hideki Tojo, were tried for war crimes and executed. Under MacArthur's guidance, the new constitution adopted in May 1947 set up a parliamentary democracy. It retained Emperor Hirohito as the ceremonial head of state, but the emperor gave up his claims to divinity. The new constitution also renounced war as an instrument of national policy and provided for only limited military capability. As a result, Japan depended on the military protection of the United States.

U.S.-Japanese Security Treaties With the signing of two treaties in 1951, Japan surrendered its claims to Korea and islands in the Pacific, and the United States ended formal occupation of Japan. One of the treaties also provided for U.S. troops to remain in military bases in Japan for that country's protection against external enemies, particularly Communists. Japan became a strong ally and prospered under the American shield.

The Philippines and the Pacific

On July 4, 1946, in accordance with the act passed by Congress in 1934, the Philippines became an independent republic, but the United States retained important naval and air bases there throughout the Cold War. This, together with U.S. control of the United Nations trustee islands taken from Japan at the end of the war, began to make the Pacific Ocean look like an American lake.

China

Since coming to power in the late 1920s, Chiang Kai-shek (Jiang Jie-shi) had used his command of the Nationalist, or Kuomintang, party to control China's central government. During World War II, the United States had given massive military aid to Chiang to prevent all of China from being conquered by Japan. As soon as the war ended, a civil war dating back to the 1930s was renewed between Chiang's Nationalists and the Chinese Communists led by Mao Zedong. The Nationalists were losing the loyalty of millions of Chinese because of runaway inflation and widespread corruption, while the well-organized Communists successfully appealed to the poor landless peasants.

U.S. Policy The Truman administration sent George Marshall in 1946 to China to negotiate an end to the civil war, but his compromise fell apart in a few months. By 1947, Chiang's armies were in retreat. Truman seemed unsure of what to do, after ruling out a large-scale American invasion to rescue Chiang. In 1948, Congress voted to give the Nationalist government $400 million in aid, but 80 percent of the U.S. military supplies ended up in Communist hands because of corruption and the collapse of the Nationalist armies.

Two Chinas By the end of 1949, all of mainland China was controlled by the Communists. Chiang and the Nationalists had retreated to an island once under Japanese rule, Formosa (Taiwan). From there, Chiang still claimed to be the legitimate government for all of China. The United States continued to support Chiang and refused to recognize Mao Zedong's regime in Beijing (the People's Republic of China) until 30 years later, in 1979.

In the United States, Republicans blamed the Democrats for the "loss of China" to the Communists. In 1950, the two Communist dictators, Stalin and Mao, signed a Sino-Soviet pact, which seemed to provide further proof of a worldwide Communist conspiracy.

The Korean War

After the defeat of Japan, its former colony Korea was divided along the 38th parallel by the victors. Soviet armies occupied Korean territory north of the line, while U.S. forces occupied territory to the south. By 1949 both armies were withdrawn, leaving the North in the hands of the Communist leader Kim Il Sung and the South under the conservative nationalist Syngman Rhee.

Invasion On June 25, 1950, the North Korean army surprised the world, possibly even Moscow, by invading South Korea. Truman took immediate action, applying his containment policy to this latest crisis in Asia. He called for a special session of the U.N. Security Council. Taking advantage of a temporary boycott by the Soviet delegation, the Security Council under U.S. leadership authorized a U.N. force to defend South Korea against the invaders. Although other nations participated in this force, U.S. troops made up most of the U.N. forces sent to help the South Korean army. Commanding the expedition was General Douglas MacArthur. Congress supported the use of U.S. troops in the Korean crisis but failed to declare war, accepting Truman's characterization of U.S. intervention as merely a "police action."

Counterattack At first the war in Korea went badly, as the North Koreans pushed the combined South Korean and American forces to the tip of the peninsula. However, General MacArthur reversed the war with a brilliant amphibious assault at Inchon behind the North Korean lines. U.N. forces then proceeded to destroy much of the North Korean army, advancing northward almost as far as the Chinese border. MacArthur failed to heed China's warnings that it would resist threats to its security. In November 1950, masses of Chinese troops crossed the border into Korea, overwhelmed U.N. forces in one of the worst defeats in U.S. military history, and drove them out of North Korea.

Truman Versus MacArthur MacArthur stabilized the fighting near the 38th parallel. At the same time, he called for expanding the war, including bombing and invading mainland China. As commander in chief, Truman cautioned MacArthur about making public statements that suggested criticism of official U.S. policy. The general spoke out anyway. In April 1951, Truman, with the support of the Joint Chiefs of Staff, recalled MacArthur for insubordination.

MacArthur returned home as a hero. Most Americans understood his statement, "There is no substitute for victory," better than the president's containment policy and concept of "limited war." Critics attacked Truman and the Democrats as appeasers for not trying to destroy communism in Asia.

Armistice In Korea, the war was stalemated along a front just north of the 38th parallel. At Panmunjom, peace talks began in July 1951. The police action dragged on for another two years, however, until an armistice was finally

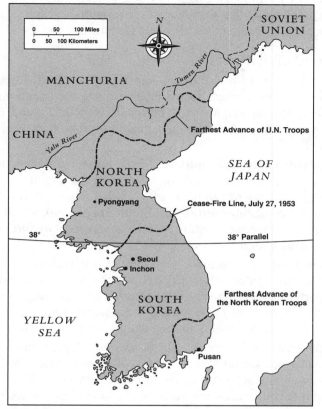

THE KOREAN WAR

signed in 1953 during the first year of Eisenhower's presidency. More than 2.5 million people died in the Korean conflict, including 54,000 Americans.

Political Consequences From the perspective of the grand strategy of the Cold War, Truman's containment policy in Korea worked. It stopped Communist aggression without allowing the conflict to develop into a world war. The Truman administration used the Korean War as justification for dramatically expanding the military, funding a new jet bomber (the B-52), and stationing more U.S. troops in overseas bases.

However, Republicans were far from satisfied. The stalemate in Korea and the loss of China led Republicans to characterize Truman and the Democrats as "soft on communism." They attacked leading Democrats as members of "Dean Acheson's Cowardly College of Communist Containment." (In 1949, Acheson had replaced George Marshall as secretary of state.)

The Second Red Scare

Just as a Red Scare had followed U.S. victory in World War I, a second Red Scare followed U.S. victory in World War II. The Truman administration's tendency to see a Communist conspiracy behind civil wars in Europe and Asia contributed to the belief that Communist conspirators and spies had infiltrated American society, including the U.S. State Department and the U.S. military.

Security and Civil Rights

In 1947, the Truman administration—under pressure from Republican critics—set up a Loyalty Review Board to investigate the background of more than 3 million federal employees. Thousands of officials and civil service employees either resigned or lost their jobs in a probe that went on for four years (1947–1951).

Prosecutions Under the Smith Act In addition, the leaders of the American Communist party were jailed for advocating the overthrow of the U.S. government. In the case of *Dennis et al. v. United States* (1951), the Supreme Court upheld the constitutionality of the Smith Act of 1940, which made it illegal to advocate or teach the overthrow of the government by force or to belong to an organization with this objective.

McCarran Internal Security Act (1950) Over Truman's veto, Congress passed the McCarran Internal Security Act, which (1) made it unlawful to advocate or support the establishment of a totalitarian government, (2) restricted the employment and travel of those joining Communist-front organizations, and (3) authorized the creation of detention camps for subversives.

Un-American Activities In the House of Representatives, the Un-American Activities Committee (HUAC), originally established in 1939 to seek out Nazis, was reactivated in the postwar years to find Communists. The committee not only investigated government officials but also looked for Communist influence in such organizations as the Boy Scouts and in the Hollywood film industry. Actors, directors, and writers were called before the committee to testify. Those who refused to testify were tried for contempt of Congress. Others were blacklisted from the industry.

Cultural Impact The Second Red Scare had a chilling effect on freedom of expression. Creators of the gritty crime dramas in the film noir style, and playwrights, such as Arthur Miller (*Death of a Salesman,* 1949) came under attacks as anti-American. Rodgers and Hammerstein's musical, *South Pacific* (1949), was criticized, especially by southern politicians, as a communistic assault on racial segregation. Loyalty oaths were commonly required of writers and teachers as a condition of employment. The American Civil Liberties Union and other opponents of these security measures argued that the 1st Amendment protected the free expression of unpopular political views and membership in political groups, including the Communist party.

Espionage Cases

The fear of a Communist conspiracy bent on world conquest was supported by a series of actual cases of Communist espionage in Great Britain, Canada, and the United States. The methods used to identify Communist spies, however, raised serious questions about whether the government was going too far and violating civil liberties in the process.

Hiss Case Whittaker Chambers, a confessed Communist, became a star witness for the House Un-American Activities Committee in 1948. His testimony, along with the investigative work of a young member of Congress from California named Richard Nixon, led to the trial of Alger Hiss, a prominent official in the State Department who had assisted Roosevelt at the Yalta Conference. Hiss denied the accusations that he was a Communist and had given secret documents to Chambers. In 1950, however, he was convicted of perjury and sent to prison. Many Americans could not help wondering whether the highest levels of government were infiltrated by Communist spies.

Rosenberg Case When the Soviets tested their first atomic bomb in 1949, many Americans were convinced that spies had helped them to steal the technology from the United States. Klaus Fuchs, a British scientist who had worked on the Manhattan Project, admitted giving A-bomb secrets to the Russians. An FBI investigation traced another spy ring to Julius and Ethel Rosenberg in New York. After a controversial trial in 1951, the Rosenbergs were found guilty of treason and executed in 1953. Civil rights groups charged that anticommunist hysteria was responsible for the conviction and punishment of the Rosenbergs.

The Rise of Joseph McCarthy

Joseph McCarthy, a Republican senator from Wisconsin, used the growing concern over communism in his reelection campaign. In a speech in 1950, he charged that 205 Communists were still working for the State Department. This sensational accusation was widely publicized in the American press. McCarthy then rode the wave of anticommunist feelings to make himself one of the most powerful men in America. His power was based entirely on people's fear of the damage McCarthy could do if his accusing finger pointed their way.

McCarthy's Tactics Senator McCarthy used a steady stream of unsupported accusations about Communists in government to keep the media focus on himself and to discredit the Truman administration. Working-class Americans at first loved his "take the gloves off" hard-hitting remarks, which were often aimed at the wealthy and privileged in society. While many Republicans disliked McCarthy's ruthless tactics, he was primarily hurting the Democrats before the election of Eisenhower in 1952. He became so popular, however, that even President Eisenhower would not dare to defend his old friend, George Marshall, against McCarthy's untruths.

Army-McCarthy Hearings Finally, in 1954, McCarthy's "reckless cruelty" was exposed on television. A Senate committee held televised hearings on Communist infiltration in the army, and McCarthy was seen as a bully by millions of viewers. In December, Republicans joined Democrats in a Senate censure of McCarthy. The "witch hunt" for Communists (McCarthyism) had played itself out. Three years later, McCarthy died a broken man.

Truman in Retirement

The second Red Scare, the stalemate in Korea, the loss of China, and scandals surrounding several of Truman's advisers made his prospects of reelection unlikely. Truman decided to return to private life in Missouri—a move that he jokingly called his "promotion." In the election of 1952, Republicans blamed Truman for "the mess in Washington." In time, however, even Truman's critics came to respect his many tough decisions and admire his direct, frank character.

HISTORICAL PERSPECTIVES: WHO STARTED THE COLD WAR?

Among U.S. historians, the traditional, or orthodox, view of the origins of the Cold War is that the Soviet government under Stalin started the conflict by subjugating the countries of Eastern Europe in the late 1940s. Historians who share this view criticize FDR for failing to understand the Soviets' aggressive intentions and for the agreement at Yalta. The traditional view holds that the Truman Doctrine, Marshall Plan, and NATO finally checked Soviet expansion in Europe. The United States in the Cold War (as in both world wars) was viewed as the defender of the "free world."

In the 1960s, during the time of public unhappiness over the Vietnam War, revisionist historians began to argue that the United States contributed to starting the Cold War. These historians praised Roosevelt for understanding Russia's historical needs for security on its eastern borders. On the other hand, they blamed Truman for antagonizing the Soviets with his blunt challenge of their actions in Poland and the Balkans. Gar Alperovitz (*The Decision to Use the Atomic Bomb*, 1995) concluded that Truman had dropped atomic bombs on Japan primarily to warn Stalin to remove his troops from Eastern Europe. Other revisionists have also argued that U.S. capitalism's need for open markets in Europe and Asia was the main reason for the U.S. government's anti-communist policies.

In the 21st century, John L. Gaddis (*The Cold War: A New History,* 2005), recognized by some as "the dean of Cold War historians," argued that the causes of the Cold War were rooted in the Big Three's failure "to reconcile divergent political objectives even as they pursued a common military task" during World War II. Gaddis suggested that objective observers would not have expected a different outcome given that great power rivalries are the normal pattern in history. However, he credits both Truman and Stalin for recognizing how atomic weapons changed the context of war and making decisions that avoided a nuclear war. Gaddis concluded that the most important aspect of the Cold War is what did not happen—a nuclear holocaust.

KEY TERMS BY THEME

Postwar Society (WXT, SOC)
Servicemen's Readjustment Act (GI Bill) (1944)
early marriages
baby boom
suburban growth
Levittown
Sunbelt
Harry Truman
Employment Act of 1946
Council of Economic Advisers
inflation and labor unions
Committee on Civil Rights
racial integration of military
22nd Amendment
Taft-Hartley Act (1947)

Election of 1948 (POL)
Progressive party
Henry Wallace
States-Rights party (Dixiecrats)
J. Strom Thurmond
Thomas Dewey
Fair Deal

Origins of the Cold War (WOR)
Cold War
Soviet Union
Joseph Stalin
United Nations
Security Council
World Bank
Communist satellites
Occupation zones
Iron Curtain
Winston Churchill
historians: traditionalists vs. revisionists

Containment in Europe (WOR)
George Kennan
Dean Acheson
containment policy
Truman Doctrine
Marshall Plan
Berlin airlift
East Germany
West Germany
North Atlantic Treaty Organization
National Security Act (1947)
Nuclear arms race
NSC-68

Cold War in Asia (WOR)
U.S.-Japanese Security Treaty
Douglas MacArthur
Chinese civil war
Chiang Kai-shek
Taiwan
Mao Zedong
People's Republic of China
Korean War
Kim Il Sung
Syngman Rhee
U.N. police action
38th parallel
"soft on communism"

Second Red Scare (POL, SOC)
Loyalty Review Board
Smith Act (1940)
Dennis et al. v. United States
McCarran Internal Security Act (1950)
House Un-American Activities Committee
Hollywood blacklists
freedom of expression in arts
Alger Hiss
Whittaker Chambers
Rosenberg case
Joseph McCarthy
McCarthyism

Questions 1–3 refer to the excerpt below.

"It is clear that the main element of any United States policy towards the Soviet Union must be that of a long-term, patient but firm and vigilant containment of Russian expansive tendencies. . . . It is clear that the United States cannot expect in the foreseeable future to enjoy political intimacy with the Soviet regime. It must continue to regard the Soviet Union as a rival, not a partner, in the political arena. It must continue to expect that Soviet policies will reflect no abstract love of peace and stability, no real faith in the possibility of a permanent happy coexistence of the Socialist and capitalist worlds, but rather a cautious, persistent pressure towards the disruption and weakening of all rival influence and rival power."

—Mr. X (George F. Kennan), State Department professional, "The Sources of Soviet Conduct," *Foreign Affairs,* July 1947

1. Which one of the following best reflected the policies advocated in the above excerpt?

(A) The proposal to miltarily roll back Communism in Eastern Europe

(B) General MacArthur's criticism of the concept of limited wars

(C) The Truman Doctrine of aid to Greece and Turkey

(D) George Marshall's negotiations to end the Chinese civil war

2. Which of the following actions would best implement the goals and strategy of George Kennan?

(A) Offering economic aid to Eastern Europe and the Soviet Union

(B) Using the U.S. Army to invade East Germany and liberate West Berlin

(C) Reorganizing all military services under the Department of Defense

(D) Using economic aid to block the appeal of Communism in Western Europe

3. To implement the policies based on this excerpt, the United States for the first time had to

(A) create permanent peacetime alliances with other nations

(B) turn over the command of U.S. troops to foreign nations

(C) employ spies to gather information on foreign governments

(D) get involved in civil wars and nation building

Questions 4–5 refer to the photo below.

Levittown, Long Island, New York, c. 1948. photos.com

4. Levittown is most closely associated with which of the following?
   (A) The baby boom that occurred after World War II
   (B) The mass production of affordable suburban housing
   (C) The impact of the G.I. Bill of Rights on economic development
   (D) The focus of women after World War II on full time homemaking

5. Which of the following best explains the dramatic increase in personal ownership of homes after World War II?
   (A) Americans were marrying younger and having larger families
   (B) Second incomes of married women helped to finance home purchases
   (C) Mortgages were at low rates, government-insured, and tax deductible
   (D) Population was shifting to the Southern and Western states

Questions 6–8 refer to the excerpt below.

"Truman found saving the free world easier than governing America. . . .

"By the time war broke out in Korea, the Fair Deal was over, Truman had tried to accomplish too much with too little, ending up with practically nothing. Without a liberal majority in Congress there could not be much in the way of liberal legislation.

"Through the Truman years domestic politics was a thing of rags and patches, a time when problems were ignored, programs shelved, and partisanship allowed to run rampant. Yet a recent history of the period 1945–1950 is called The Best Years because that is how they were remembered."

—William L. O'Neill, historian, *American High*, 1986

6. Which of the following actions is an example of a Fair Deal reform that would best support the passage that "problems were ignored, programs shelved"?

   (A) Establishing a committee on civil rights

   (B) Passing national health care insurance

   (C) Outlawing the practice of closed shop

   (D) Limiting individuals to two terms as president

7. Which of the following coalitions provided the strongest opposition to Truman's domestic programs?

   (A) Republicans and Roosevelt Democrats

   (B) Antiwar Progressives and Republicans

   (C) Dixiecrats and the members of the Progressive party

   (D) Republicans and southern Democrats

8. Which of the following most advanced liberal domestic policies during the Truman administration?

   (A) The ratification of the 22nd Amendment

   (B) The executive order ending racial discrimination in the military

   (C) The passage of the Taft-Hartley Act to outlaw closed shops

   (D) The successful implementation of wage and price controls

SHORT-ANSWER QUESTIONS

Use complete sentences; an outline or bulleted list alone is not acceptable.

Question 1 is based on the excerpt below.

"The reason why we find ourselves in a position of impotency is . . . because of the traitorous actions of those who have been treated so well by this Nation. It has not been the less fortunate or members of minority groups who have been selling this Nation out, but rather those who have had all the benefits that the wealthiest nation on earth has to offer—the finest homes, the finest college education, and the finest jobs in Government.

"This is glaringly true in the State Department. There the bright young men who are born with silver spoons in their mouths are the ones who have been the worst. . . . In my opinion, the State Department . . . is thoroughly infested with Communists. I have in my hand 57 cases of individuals who would appear to be either card-carrying members or certainly loyal to the Communist Party, but who nevertheless are still helping to shape our foreign policy."

—Joseph R. McCarthy, Speech,Wheeling, West Virginia, February 1950

1. Using the excerpt, answer (A), (B), and (C).
   (A) Briefly explain ONE specific postwar event that would support the rhetoric of this excerpt.
   (B) Briefly explain ONE specific tactic used by Joseph McCarthy that was condemned as a "witch hunt" or "McCarthyism."
   (C) Briefly explain ONE specific cause of McCarthy's appeal to blue-collar Americans.

Question 2.   Answer (A), (B), and (C).

   (A) Briefly explain ONE specific historical event or development during the Truman administration that provided economic aid to bolster non-Communist governments in Europe or Asia.
   (B) Briefly explain ONE specific historical event or development during the Truman administration that promoted collective security.
   (C) Briefly explain ONE specific difference between U.S. foreign policy after World War II and U.S. foreign policy after World War I.

Question 3.   Answer (A), (B), and (C).

   (A) Briefly explain ONE reason higher education expanded after 1945.
   (B) Briefly explain ONE specific change in the American family from the period 1929 to 1945 to the period 1945 to 1960.
   (C) Briefly explain ONE cause of Sun Belt growth after World War II.

Question 4 is based on the following excerpts.

"I find it increasingly difficult, given what we know now, to imagine the Soviet Union or the Cold War without Stalin. . . . If one could have eliminated Stalin, alternative paths become quite conceivable. . . . And given his propensity for cold wars, a tendency firmly rooted long before he had even heard of Harry Truman. . . . it is equally clear that there was going to be a Cold War whatever the West did. Who then was responsible? The answer, I think, is authoritarianism in general, and Stalin in particular."

—John Lewis Gaddis, *We Know Now: Rethinking the Cold War,* 1997

"No one leader or nation caused the Cold War. . . . Nevertheless, from the Potsdam Conference through the Korean War, [President Truman] contributed significantly to the growing Cold War and the militarism of American foreign policy. . . . Throughout his presidency, Truman remained a parochial [narrow-minded] nationalist who lacked the leadership to move America away from conflict toward detente. Instead, he promoted an ideology and politics of Cold War confrontation that became the modus operandi [common method] of successor administrations and the United States for the next two generations."

—Arnold A. Offner, *Diplomatic History,* Spring 1999

4. Using the excerpts above, answer (A), (B), and (C).
   (A) Briefly describe ONE specific difference between Gaddis's and Offner's historical interpretation of the origins of the Cold War.
   (B) Briefly explain ONE specific historical event or development that is not explicitly mentioned in the excerpts that could be used to support Gaddis's interpretation of the origins of the Cold War.
   (C) Briefly explain ONE specific historical event or development that is not explicitly mentioned in the excerpts that could be used to support Offner's interpretation of the origins of the Cold War.

THINK AS A HISTORIAN: INTRODUCING AN INTERPRETATION

The first sentence of an essay should catch the reader's attention with a surprising fact, personal connection, or dramatic comment. The first sentence should make the reader want to read more. Which TWO of the following would be the best first sentences in essays about the impact of the Cold War on the culture of the United States?

1. Fighting the Cold War threatened to destroy the values it was being fought to defend.

2. The Cold War was not the deadliest war, but it was among the costliest.

3. The Cold War was between the United States and the Soviet Union.

27

THE EISENHOWER YEARS, 1952–1960

*We conclude that in the field of public education
the doctrine of "separate but equal" has no place.
Separate educational facilities are inherently unequal.*

Earl Warren, *Brown v. Board of Education of Topeka*, May 17, 1954

The 1950s have the popular image of the "happy days," when the nation prospered and teens enjoyed the new beat of rock-and-roll music. This nostalgic view of the fifties is correct—but limited. The decade started with a war in Korea and the incriminations of McCarthyism. From the point of view of African Americans, what mattered most about the 1950s was not so much the music of Elvis Presley but the resistance of Rosa Parks and Martin Luther King Jr. to segregation in the South. While middle-class suburbanites enjoyed their chrome-trimmed cars and tuned in to *I Love Lucy* on their new television sets, the Cold War and threat of nuclear destruction loomed in the background.

Eisenhower Takes Command

Much as Franklin Roosevelt dominated the 1930s, President Dwight ("Ike") Eisenhower personified the 1950s. The Republican campaign slogan, "I Like Ike," expressed the genuine feelings of millions of middle-class Americans. They liked his winning smile and trusted and admired the former general who had successfully commanded Allied forces in Europe in World War II.

The Election of 1952

In 1952, the last year of Truman's presidency, Americans were looking for relief from the Korean War and an end to political scandals commonly referred to as "the mess in Washington." Republicans looked forward with relish to their first presidential victory in 20 years. In the Republican primaries, voters had a choice between the Old Guard's favorite, Senator Robert Taft of Ohio, and the war hero, Eisenhower. Most of them liked "Ike," who went on to win the Republican nomination. Conservative supporters of Taft balanced the ticket by persuading Eisenhower to choose Richard Nixon for his running mate. This young California senator had made a name for himself attacking Communists in the Alger Hiss case.

The Democrats selected popular Illinois Governor Adlai Stevenson, whose wit, eloquence, and courage in confronting McCarthyism appealed to liberals.

Campaign Highlights A nonpolitician, Eisenhower had a spotless reputation for integrity that was almost spoiled by reports that his running mate, Richard Nixon, had used campaign funds for his own personal use. Nixon was almost dropped from the ticket. However, he saved his political future by effectively defending himself using the new medium of television. In his so-called Checkers speech, Nixon won the support of millions of viewers by tugging at their heartstrings. With his wife and daughters around him, he emotionally vowed never to return the gift of their beloved dog, Checkers.

What really put distance between the Republicans and the Democrats was Eisenhower's pledge during the last days of the campaign to go to Korea and end the war. The Eisenhower-Nixon ticket went on to win over 55 percent of the popular vote and an electoral college landslide of 442 to Stevenson's 89.

Domestic Policies

As president, Eisenhower adopted a style of leadership that emphasized the delegation of authority. He filled his cabinet with successful corporate executives who gave his administration a businesslike tone. His secretary of defense, for example, was Charles Wilson, the former head of General Motors. Eisenhower was often criticized by the press for spending too much time golfing and fishing and perhaps entrusting important decisions to others. However, later research showed that behind the scenes Eisenhower was in charge.

Modern Republicanism Eisenhower was a fiscal conservative whose first priority was balancing the budget after years of deficit spending. Although his annual budgets were not always balanced, he came closer to curbing federal spending than any of his successors. As a moderate on domestic issues, he accepted most of the New Deal programs as a reality of modern life and even extended some of them. During Eisenhower's two terms in office, Social Security was extended to 10 million more citizens, the minimum wage was raised, and additional public housing was built. In 1953, Eisenhower consolidated welfare programs by creating the Department of Health, Education, and Welfare (HEW) under Oveta Culp Hobby, the first woman in a Republican cabinet. For farmers, a soil-bank program was initiated as means of reducing farm production and thereby increasing farm income. On the other hand, Eisenhower opposed the ideas of federal health care insurance and federal aid to education.

As the first Republican president since Hoover, Eisenhower called his balanced and moderate approach "modern Republicanism." His critics called it "the bland leading the bland."

Interstate Highway System The most permanent legacy of the Eisenhower years was the passage in 1956 of the Highway Act, which authorized the construction of 42,000 miles of interstate highways linking all the nation's major cities. When completed, the U.S. highway system became a model for the rest of the world. The justification for new taxes on fuel, tires, and vehicles was to improve national defense. At the same time, this immense public works project created jobs, promoted the trucking industry, accelerated the growth of the suburbs, and contributed to a more homogeneous national culture. The emphasis on cars, trucks, and highways, however, hurt the railroads and ultimately the environment. Little attention was paid to public transportation, on which the old and the poor depended.

Prosperity Eisenhower's domestic legislation was modest. During his years in office, however, the country enjoyed a steady growth rate, with an inflation rate averaging a negligible 1.5 percent. Although the federal budget had a small surplus only three times in eight years, the deficits fell in relation to the national wealth. For these reasons, some historians rate Eisenhower's economic policies the most successful of any modern president's. Between 1945 and 1960, the per-capita disposable income of Americans more than tripled. By the mid-1950s, the average American family had twice the real income of a comparable family during the boom years of the 1920s. The postwar economy gave Americans the highest standard of living in the world.

The Election of 1956

Toward the end of his first term, in 1955, Eisenhower suffered a heart attack and had major surgery in 1956. Democrats questioned whether his health was strong enough for election to a second term. Four years of peace and prosperity, however, made Ike more popular than ever, and the Eisenhower-Nixon ticket was enthusiastically renominated by the Republicans. The Democrats again nominated Adlai Stevenson. In this political rematch, Eisenhower won by an even greater margin than in 1952. It was a personal victory only, however, as the Democrats retained control of both houses of Congress.

Eisenhower and the Cold War

Most of Eisenhower's attention in both his first and second terms focused on foreign policy and various international crises arising from the Cold War. The experienced diplomat who helped to shape U.S. foreign policy throughout Eisenhower's presidency was Secretary of State John Foster Dulles.

Dulles' Diplomacy

Dulles had been critical of Truman's containment policy as too passive. He advocated a "new look" to U.S. foreign policy that took the initiative in challenging the Soviet Union and the People's Republic of China. He talked of "liberating captive nations" of Eastern Europe and encouraging the Nationalist government of Taiwan to assert itself against "Red" (Communist) China. Dulles pleased conservatives—and alarmed many others—by declaring that, if the United States pushed Communist powers to the brink of war, they would back down because of American nuclear superiority. His hard line became known as "brinkmanship." In the end, however, Eisenhower prevented Dulles from carrying his ideas to an extreme.

Massive Retaliation Dulles advocated placing greater reliance on nuclear weapons and air power and spending less on conventional forces of the army and navy. In theory, this would save money ("more bang for the buck"), help balance the federal budget, and increase pressure on potential enemies. In 1953, the United States developed the hydrogen bomb, which could destroy the largest cities. Within a year, however, the Soviets caught up with a hydrogen bomb of their own. To some, the policy of massive retaliation looked more like a policy for mutual extinction. Nuclear weapons indeed proved a powerful deterrent against the superpowers fighting an all-out war between themselves, but such weapons could not prevent small "brushfire" wars from breaking out in the developing nations of Southeast Asia, Africa, and the Middle East. However, Eisenhower refused to use even small nuclear weapons in these conflicts.

Unrest in the Third World

Decolonization, or the collapse of colonial empires, after World War II may have been the single most important development of the postwar era. Between 1947 and 1962, dozens of colonies in Asia and Africa gained their independence from former colonial powers such as Britain, France, and the Netherlands. In Asia, India and Pakistan became new nations in 1947, and the Dutch East Indies became the independent country of Indonesia in 1949. In Africa, Ghana threw off British colonial rule in 1957, and a host of other nations followed. These new Third World countries (in contrast to the industrialized nations of the Western bloc and the Communist bloc) often lacked stable political and economic institutions. Their need for foreign aid from either the United States or the Soviet Union often made them into pawns of the Cold War.

Covert Action Part of the new look in Eisenhower's conduct of U.S. foreign policy was the growing use of covert action. Undercover intervention in the internal politics of other nations seemed less objectionable than employing U.S. troops and also proved less expensive. In 1953, the CIA helped overthrow a government in Iran that had tried to nationalize the holding of foreign oil companies. The overthrow of the elected government allowed for the return of Reza Pahlavi as shah (monarch) of Iran. The shah in return provided the West with favorable oil prices and made enormous purchases of American arms.

In Guatemala, in 1954, the CIA overthrew a leftist government that threatened American business interests. U.S. opposition to communism seemed to drive Washington to support corrupt and often ruthless dictators, especially in Latin America. In addition, the CIA, acting in secret and under lax control by civilian officials, planned assassinations of national leaders, such as Fidel Castro of Cuba. CIA operations fueled anti-American feelings, especially in Latin America, but the long-term damage was to U.S. relations with Iran.

Asia

During Eisenhower's first year in office, some of the most serious Cold War challenges concerned events in East Asia and Southeast Asia.

Korean Armistice Soon after his inauguration in 1953, Eisenhower kept his election promise by going to Korea to visit U.N. forces and see what could be done to stop the war. He understood that no quick fix was possible. Even so, diplomacy, the threat of nuclear war, and the sudden death of Joseph Stalin in March 1953 finally moved China and North Korea to agree to an armistice and an exchange of prisoners in July 1953. The fighting stopped and most (but not all) U.S. troops were withdrawn. Korea would remain divided near the 38th parallel, and despite years of futile negotiations, no peace treaty was ever concluded between North Korea and South Korea.

Fall of Indochina After losing their Southeast Asian colony of Indochina to Japanese invaders in World War II, the French made the mistake of trying to retake it. Wanting independence, native Vietnamese and Cambodians resisted. French imperialism had the effect of increasing support for nationalist and Communist leader Ho Chi Minh. By 1950, the anticolonial war in Indochina became part of the Cold War rivalry between Communist and anticommunist powers. Truman's government started to give U.S. military aid to the French, while China and the Soviet Union aided the Viet Minh guerrillas led by Ho Chi Minh. In 1954, a large French army at Dien Bien Phu was trapped and forced to surrender. After this disastrous defeat, the French tried to convince Eisenhower to send in U.S. troops, but he refused. At the Geneva Conference of 1954, France agreed to give up Indochina, which was divided into the independent nations of Cambodia, Laos, and Vietnam.

Division of Vietnam By the terms of the Geneva Conference, Vietnam was to be temporarily divided at the 17th parallel until a general election could be held. The new nation remained divided, however, as two hostile governments took power on either side of the line. In North Vietnam, Ho Chi Minh established a Communist dictatorship. In South Vietnam, a government emerged under Ngo Dinh Diem, whose support came largely from anticommunist, Catholic, and urban Vietnamese, many of whom had fled from Communist rule in the North. The general election to unite Vietnam was never held, largely because South Vietnam's government feared that the Communists would win.

From 1955 to 1961, the United States gave over $1 billion in economic and military aid to South Vietnam in an effort to build a stable, anticommunist state. In justifying this aid, President Eisenhower made an analogy to a row of dominoes. According to this *domino theory* (later to become famous), if South Vietnam fell under Communist control, one nation after another in Southeast Asia would also fall, until Australia and New Zealand were in dire danger.

SEATO To prevent South Vietnam, Laos, and Cambodia from "falling" to communism, Dulles put together a regional defense pact called the Southeast Asia Treaty Organization (SEATO). Agreeing to defend one another in case of an attack within the region, eight nations signed the pact in 1954: the United States, Great Britain, France, Australia, New Zealand, the Philippines, Thailand, and Pakistan.

The Middle East

In the Middle East, the United States tried to balance maintaining friendly ties with the oil-rich Arab states while at the same time supporting the new state of Israel. The latter nation was created in 1948 under U.N. auspices, after a civil war in the British mandate territory of Palestine left the land divided between the Israelis and the Palestinians. Israel's neighbors, including Egypt, had fought unsuccessfully to prevent the Jewish state from being formed.

Suez Crisis Led by the Arab nationalist General Gamal Nasser, Egypt asked the United States for funds to build the ambitious Aswan Dam project on the Nile River. The United States refused, in part because Egypt threatened Israel's security. Nasser turned to the Soviet Union to help build the dam. The Soviets agreed to provide limited financing for the project. Seeking another source of funds, Nasser precipitated an international crisis in July 1956 by seizing and nationalizing the British- and French-owned Suez Canal that passed through Egyptian territory. Loss of the canal threatened Western Europe's supply line to Middle Eastern oil. In response to this threat, Britain, France, and Israel carried out a surprise attack against Egypt and retook the canal.

Eisenhower, furious that he had been kept in the dark about the attack by his old allies the British and French, sponsored a U.N. resolution condemning the invasion of Egypt. Under pressure from the United States and world public opinion, the invading forces withdrew.

Eisenhower Doctrine The United States quickly replaced Britain and France as the leading Western influence in the Middle East, but it faced a growing Soviet influence in Egypt and Syria. In a policy pronouncement later known as the *Eisenhower Doctrine,* the United States in 1957 pledged economic and military aid to any Middle Eastern country threatened by communism. Eisenhower first applied his doctrine in 1958 by sending 14,000 marines to Lebanon to prevent a civil war between Christians and Muslims.

OPEC and Oil In Eisenhower's last year in office, 1960, the Arab nations of Saudi Arabia, Kuwait, Iraq, and Iran joined Venezuela to form the Organization of Petroleum Exporting Countries (OPEC). Oil was shaping up to be a critical foreign policy issue. The combination of Western dependence on Middle East oil, Arab nationalism, and a conflict between Israelis and Palestinian refugees would trouble American presidents in the coming decades.

U.S.-Soviet Relations

For U.S. security, nothing was more crucial than U.S. diplomatic relations with its chief political and military rival, the Soviet Union. Throughout Eisenhower's presidency, the relations between the two superpowers fluctuated between periods of relative calm and extreme tension.

Spirit of Geneva After Stalin's death in 1953, Eisenhower called for a slowdown in the arms race and presented to the United Nations an *atoms for peace* plan. The Soviets also showed signs of wanting to reduce Cold War tensions. They withdrew their troops from Austria (once that country had agreed to be neutral in the Cold War) and established peaceful relations with Greece and Turkey. By 1955, a desire for improved relations on both sides resulted in a summit meeting in Geneva, Switzerland, between Eisenhower and the new Soviet premier, Nikolai Bulganin. At this conference, the U.S. president proposed an "open skies" policy over each other's territory—open to aerial photography by the opposing nation—in order to eliminate the chance of a surprise nuclear attack. The Soviets rejected the proposal. Nevertheless, the "spirit of Geneva," as the press called it, produced the first thaw in the Cold War. Even more encouraging, from the U.S. point of view, was a speech by the new Soviet leader Nikita Khrushchev in early 1956 in which he denounced the crimes of Joseph Stalin and supported "peaceful coexistence" with the West.

MIDDLE EAST AREAS OF CONFLICT, 1948–1990

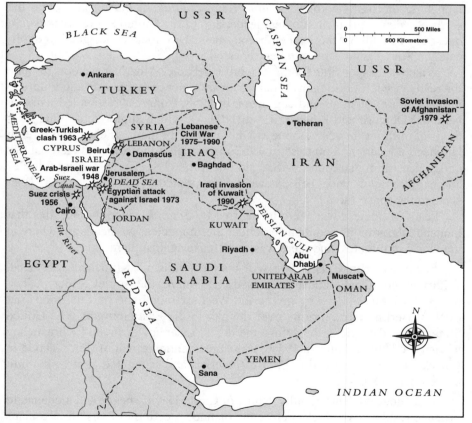

Hungarian Revolt The relaxation in the Cold War encouraged workers in East Germany and Poland to demand reforms from their Communist governments. In October 1956, a popular uprising in Hungary actually succeeded in overthrowing a government backed by Moscow. The new, more liberal leaders wanted to pull Hungary out of the Warsaw Pact, the Communist security organization. This was too much for the Kremlin, and Khrushchev sent in Soviet tanks to crush the freedom fighters and restore control over Hungary. The United States took no action in the crisis. Eisenhower feared that sending troops to aid the Hungarians would touch off a major war in Europe. In effect, by allowing Soviet tanks to roll into Hungary, the United States gave de facto recognition to the Soviet sphere of influence in Eastern Europe and ended Dulles' talk of "liberating" this region. Soviet suppression of the Hungarian revolt also ended the first thaw in the Cold War.

***Sputnik* Shock** In 1957, the Soviet Union shocked the United States by launching the first satellites, *Sputnik I* and *Sputnik II*, into orbit around the earth. Suddenly, the technological leadership of the United States was open to question. To add to American embarrassment, U.S. rockets designed to duplicate the Soviet achievement failed repeatedly.

What was responsible for this scientific debacle? American schools became the ready target for criticism of their math and science instruction and failure to produce more scientists and engineers. In 1958, Congress responded with the National Defense and Education Act (NDEA), which authorized giving hundreds of millions in federal money to the schools for math, science, and foreign language education. Congress in 1958 also created the National Aeronautics and Space Administration (NASA), to direct the U.S. efforts to build missiles and explore outer space. Billions were appropriated to compete with the Russians in the space race.

Fears of nuclear war were intensified by *Sputnik*, since the missiles that launched the satellites could also deliver thermonuclear warheads anywhere in the world in minutes, and there was no defense against them.

Second Berlin Crisis "We will bury capitalism," Khrushchev boasted. With new confidence and pride based on *Sputnik*, the Soviet leader pushed the Berlin issue in 1958 by giving the West six months to pull its troops out of West Berlin before turning over the city to the East Germans. The United States refused to yield. To defuse the crisis, Eisenhower invited Khrushchev to visit the United States in 1959. At the presidential retreat of Camp David in Maryland, the two agreed to put off the crisis and scheduled another summit conference in Paris for 1960.

U-2 Incident The friendly "spirit of Camp David" never had a chance to produce results. Two weeks before the planned meeting in Paris, the Russians shot down a high-altitude U.S. spy plane—the U-2—over the Soviet Union. The incident exposed a secret U.S. tactic for gaining information. After its open-skies proposals had been rejected by the Soviets in 1955, the United

States had decided to conduct regular spy flights over Soviet territory to find out about its enemy's missile program. Eisenhower took full responsibility for the flights—*after* they were exposed by the U-2 incident—but his honesty proved to be a diplomatic mistake. Khrushchev denounced the United States and walked out of the Paris summit to temporarily end the thaw in the Cold War.

Communism in Cuba

Perhaps more alarming than any other Cold War development during the Eisenhower years was the loss of Cuba to communism. A bearded revolutionary, Fidel Castro, overthrew the Cuban dictator Fulgencio Batista in 1959. At first, no one knew whether Castro's politics would be better or worse than those of his ruthless predecessor. Once in power, however, Castro nationalized American-owned businesses and properties in Cuba. Eisenhower retaliated by cutting off U.S. trade with Cuba. Castro then turned to the Soviets for support. He also revealed that he was a Marxist and soon proved it by setting up a Communist totalitarian state. With communism only 90 miles off the shores of Florida, Eisenhower authorized the CIA to train anticommunist Cuban exiles to retake their island, but the decision to go ahead with the scheme was left up to the next president, Kennedy.

Eisenhower's Legacy

After leaving the White House, Eisenhower claimed credit for checking Communist aggression and keeping the peace without the loss of American lives in combat. He also started the long process of relaxing tensions with the Soviet Union. In 1958, he initiated the first arms limitations by voluntarily suspending above-ground testing of nuclear weapons.

"Military-Industrial Complex" In his farewell address as president, Eisenhower spoke out against the negative impact of the Cold War on U.S. society. He warned the nation to "guard against the acquisition of unwarranted influence . . . by the military-industrial complex." If the outgoing president was right, the arms race was taking on a momentum and logic all its own. It seemed to some Americans in the 1960s that the United States was in danger of going down the path of ancient Rome by turning into a military, or imperial, state.

The Civil Rights Movement

While Eisenhower was concentrating on Cold War issues, events with revolutionary significance to race relations were developing within the United States.

Origins of the Movement

The baseball player Jackie Robinson had broken the color line in 1947 by being hired by the Brooklyn Dodgers as the first African American to play on a major league team since the 1880s. President Truman integrated the armed forces in 1948 and introduced civil rights legislation in Congress. These were the first well-publicized indications that race relations after World War II were changing. As the 1950s began, however, African Americans in the South were still by law segregated from whites in schools and in most public facilities. They were also kept from voting by poll taxes, literacy tests, grandfather clauses, and intimidation. Social segregation left most of them poorly educated, while economic discrimination kept them in a state of poverty.

Changing Demographics The origins of the modern civil rights movement can be traced back to the movement of millions of African Americans from the rural South to the urban centers of the South and the North. In the North, African Americans, who joined the Democrats during the New Deal, had a growing influence in party politics in the 1950s.

Changing Attitudes in the Cold War The Cold War also played an indirect role in changing both government policies and social attitudes. The U.S. reputation for freedom and democracy was competing against Communist ideology for the hearts and minds of the peoples of Africa and Asia. Against this global background, racial segregation and discrimination stood out as glaring wrongs that needed to be corrected. President Truman took one step in this direction by desegregation the military in 1948.

Desegregating the Schools

The NAACP had been working through the courts for decades trying to overturn the Supreme Court's 1896 decision, *Plessy v. Ferguson*, which allowed segregation in "separate but equal" facilities. In the late 1940s, the NAACP won a series of cases involving higher education.

Brown Decision One of the great landmark cases in Supreme Court history was argued in the early 1950s by a team of NAACP lawyers led by Thurgood Marshall. In *Brown v. Board of Education of Topeka,* they argued that segregation of black children in the public schools was unconstitutional because it violated the 14th Amendment's guarantee of "equal protection of the laws." In May 1954, the Supreme Court agreed with Marshall and overturned the Plessy case. Writing for a unanimous Court, Chief Justice Earl Warren ruled that (1) "separate facilities are inherently unequal" and unconstitutional, and (2) school segregation should end with "all deliberate speed."

Resistance in the South Opposition to the Brown decision erupted throughout the South. To start with, 101 members of Congress signed the "Southern Manifesto" condemning the Supreme Court for a "clear abuse of judicial power." States fought the decision several ways, including the temporary closing of the public schools and setting up private schools. The Ku Klux Klan made a comeback, and violence against blacks increased. In Arkansas in

1956, Governor Orval Faubus used the state's National Guard to prevent nine African American students from entering Little Rock Central High School, as ordered by a federal court. President Eisenhower then intervened. While the president did not actively support desegregation or the Brown decision, he understood his constitutional duty to uphold federal authority. Eisenhower ordered federal troops to stand guard in Little Rock and protect black students. Resistance remained stubborn. In 1964, ten years after the Supreme Court decision, less than 2 percent of blacks in the South attended integrated schools.

Source: Marion Post Wolcott, Memphis, 1939. Library of Congress

Montgomery Bus Boycott

In 1955, as a Montgomery, Alabama, bus took on more white passengers, the driver ordered a middle-aged black woman to give up her seat to one of them. Rosa Parks refused and her arrest for violating the segregation law sparked a massive African American protest in the form of a boycott of the city buses. The Reverend Martin Luther King Jr., minister of the Baptist church where the boycott started, soon emerged as the inspirational leader of a nonviolent movement to end segregation. The protest touched off by Rosa Parks and the Montgomery boycott resulted in the Supreme Court ruling that segregation laws were unconstitutional. The boycott also sparked other civil rights protests that reshaped America over the coming decades.

Federal Laws

Signed into law by President Eisenhower, two civil rights laws of 1957 and 1960 were the first such laws to be enacted by the U.S. Congress since Reconstruction. They were modest in scope, providing for a permanent Civil Rights Commission and giving the Justice Department new powers to protect the voting rights of blacks. Despite this legislation, southern officials still used an arsenal of obstructive tactics to discourage African Americans from voting.

Nonviolent Protests

What the government would not do, the African American community did for itself. In 1957, Martin Luther King Jr. formed the Southern Christian Leadership Conference (SCLC), which organized ministers and churches in the South to get behind the civil rights struggle. In February 1960, college students in Greensboro, North Carolina, started the sit-in movement after being refused service at a segregated Woolworth's lunch counter. To call attention to the injustice of segregated facilities, students would deliberately invite arrest by sitting in restricted areas. The Student Nonviolent Coordinating Committee (SNCC) was formed a few months later to keep the movement organized. In the 1960s, African Americans used the sit-in tactic to integrate restaurants, hotels, buildings, libraries, pools, and transportation throughout the South.

The results of the boycotts, sit-ins, court rulings, and government responses to pressure marked a turning point in the civil rights movement. Progress was slow, however. In the 1960s, a growing impatience among many African Americans would be manifested in violent confrontations in the streets.

Immigration Issues in the Postwar Years

Congress dropped the bans on Chinese and other Asian immigrants and eliminated "race" as a barrier to naturalization, but the quota system remained in place until 1965. Puerto Ricans, as American citizens, could enter the United States without restrictions. However, Mexicans faced a choice of working under contract in the *braceros* program, entering as a regulated legal immigrant, or crossing the border as "illegals." In the early 1950s, U.S. officials, responding to complaints from native-born workers and from Mexico, launched Operation Wetback, which forced an estimate 3.8 million people to return to Mexico. Mexicans migrants remaining in the United States often faced discrimination and exploitation by commercial farmers.

Popular Culture in the Fifties

Among white suburbanites, the 1950s were marked by similarities in social norms. Consensus about political issues and conformity in social behavior were safe harbors for Americans troubled by the foreign ideology of communism. At the same time, consensus and conformity were the hallmarks of a consumer-driven mass economy.

Consumer Culture and Conformity

Television, advertising, and the middle-class movement to the suburbs contributed mightily to the growing homogeneity of American culture.

Television Little more than a curiosity in the late 1940s, television suddenly became a center of family life in millions of American homes. By 1961, there were 55 million TV sets, about one for every 3.3 Americans. Television programming in the fifties was dominated by three national networks, which presented viewers with a bland menu of situation comedies, westerns, quiz shows, and professional sports. FCC chairman Newton Minnow criticized television as a "vast wasteland" and worried about the impact on children of a steady dose of five or more hours of daily viewing. Yet the culture portrayed on television—especially for third and fourth generations of white ethnic Americans—provided a common content for their common language.

Advertising In all the media (television, radio, newspapers, and magazines), aggressive advertising by name brands promoted common material wants, and the introduction of suburban shopping centers and the plastic credit card in the 1950s provided a quick means of satisfying them. The phenomenal proliferation of chains of fast food restaurants on the roadside was one measure of success for the new marketing techniques and standardized products as the nation turned from "mom and pop" stores to franchise operations.

Paperbacks and Records Despite television, Americans read more than ever. Paperback books, an innovation in the 1950s, were selling almost a million copies a day by 1960. Popular music was revolutionized by the mass marketing of inexpensive, long-playing (LP) record albums and stacks of 45 rpm records. Teenagers fell in love with rock-and-roll music, a blend of African American rhythm and blues with white country music, popularized by the gyrating Elvis Presley.

Corporate America In the business world, conglomerates with diversified holdings began to dominate such industries as food processing, hotels, transportation, insurance, and banking. For the first time in history, more American workers held white-collar jobs than blue-collar jobs. To work for one of *Fortune* magazine's top 500 companies seemed to be the road to success. Large corporations of this era promoted teamwork and conformity, including a dress code for male workers of a dark business suit, white shirt, and a conservative tie. The social scientist William Whyte documented this loss of individuality in his book *The Organization Man* (1956).

Big unions became more powerful after the merger of the AF of L and the CIO in 1955. They also became more conservative, as blue-collar workers began to enjoy middle-class incomes.

For most Americans, conformity was a small price to pay for the new affluence of a home in the suburbs, a new automobile every two or three years, good schools for the children, and maybe a vacation at the recently opened Disneyland (1955) in California.

Religion Organized religions expanded dramatically after World War II with the building of thousands of new churches and synagogues. Will Herberg's book *Protestant, Catholic, Jew* (1955) commented on the new religious tolerance of the times and the lack of interest in doctrine, as religious membership became a source of both individual identity and socialization.

Women's Roles

The baby boom and running a home in the suburbs made homemaking a full-time job for millions of women. The traditional view of a woman's role as caring for home and children was reaffirmed in the mass media and in the best-selling self-help book, *Baby and Child Care* (1946) by Dr. Benjamin Spock.

At the same time, evidence of dissatisfaction was growing, especially among well-educated women of the middle class. More married women, especially as they reached middle age, entered the workforce. Yet male employers in the 1950s saw female workers primarily as wives and mothers, and women's lower wages reflected this attitude.

Social Critics

Not everybody approved of the social trends of the 1950s. In *The Lonely Crowd* (1958), Harvard sociologist David Riesman criticized the replacement of "inner-directed" individuals in society with "other-directed" conformists. In *The Affluent Society* (1958), economist John Kenneth Galbraith wrote about the failure of wealthy Americans to address the need for increased social spending for the common good. (Galbraith's ideas were to influence the Kennedy and Johnson administrations in the next decade.) Sociologist C. Wright Mills portrayed dehumanizing corporate worlds in *White Collar* (1951) and threats to freedom in *The Power Elite* (1956).

Novels Some of the most popular novelists of the 1950s wrote about the individual's struggle against conformity. J. D. Salinger provided a classic commentary on "phoniness" as viewed by a troubled teenager in *The Catcher in the Rye* (1951). Joseph Heller satirized the stupidity of the military and war in *Catch-22* (1961).

"Beatniks" A group of rebellious writers and intellectuals made up the Beat Generation of the 1950s. Led by Jack Kerouac (*On the Road,* 1957) and poet Allen Ginsberg ("Howl," 1956), they advocated spontaneity, use of drugs, and rebellion against societal standards. The beatniks would become models for the youth rebellion of the 1960s.

HISTORICAL PERSPECTIVES: A SILENT GENERATION?

Among intellectuals, a commonly held view of the 1950s was that Americans had become complacent in their political outlook— a "silent generation" presided over by a grandfatherly and passive President Eisenhower. Liberal academics believed that McCarthyism had stopped any serious or critical discussion of the problems in American society. Eisenhower's policies and their general acceptance by most voters seemed a bland consensus of ideas that would bother no one. Critics contrasted the seeming calm of the 1950s with the more "interesting" social and cultural revolution of the next decade.

Over time, historians have treated the 1950s with more respect. Research into the Eisenhower papers has revealed a president who used a hidden-hand approach to leadership. Behind the scenes, he was an active and decisive administrator who was in full command of his presidency. His domestic policies achieved sustained economic growth, and his foreign policy relaxed international tensions. Such accomplishments no longer looked boring to historians writing after decades of economic dislocations and stagnant or declining incomes.

Reflecting this more generous view of Eisenhower is William O'Neill's *American High: The Years of Confidence, 1945–1960* (1987). O'Neill argues that Eisenhower led a needed and largely successful economic and social postwar "reconstruction." He and other historians emphasize that the 1950s prepared the way for both the liberal reforms of the 1960s and the conservative politics of the 1980s. Achievements of women, African Americans, and other minorities in a later era were made possible by changes in the fifties. Furthermore, the integration of Catholics, Jews, and other white ethnics into American society during the postwar years made it possible for Kennedy to be elected the first Irish Catholic president in 1960.

KEY TERMS BY THEME

Domestic Politics (POL)
elections of 1952, 1956
Dwight Eisenhower
Adlai Stevenson
Richard Nixon
modern Republicanism
Dept. of Health, Education and Welfare (HEW)
soil-bank program
Highway Act (1956); interstate highway system

"New Look" Foreign Policy (WOR)
John Foster Dulles
"brinksmanship"
massive retaliation
decolonization
India, Pakistan, Indonesia
Third World
CIA, covert action
Iranian overthrow

US Policy in Asia (WOR)
Korean armistice
Indochina
Ho Chi Minh
Geneva Conference (1954)
division of Vietnam
domino theory
Southeast Asia Treaty Organization (1954)

US Policy in Middle East (WOR)
State of Israel (1948)
Arab nationalism
Suez Canal crisis (1956)
Eisenhower Doctrine
Organization of Petroleum Exporting Countries (OPEC)

US-Soviet Relations (WOR)
atoms for peace
"spirit of Geneva"
open-skies
Nikita Khrushchev
peaceful coexistence
Hungarian revolt
Warsaw Pact
Sputnik (1957)
NDEA, NASA
U-2 incident
Cuba, Fidel Castro
military-industrial complex

Civil Rights in 1950s (POL, NAT)
Jackie Robinson
causes of movement
NAACP
desegregation
Thurgood Marshall
Brown v. Board of Education of Topeka (1954)

Earl Warren
Southern Manifesto
Little Rock crisis
Rosa Parks
Montgomery bus boycott
Martin Luther King Jr.
Civil Rights acts of 1957, 1960
Civil Rights Commission
Southern Christian Leadership Conference
nonviolent protest
sit-in movement
Student Nonviolent Coordinating Committee
immigration issues
Operation Wetback

1950s Culture (SOC)
homogeneity
popular culture
paperbacks
television
rock and roll
consumer culture
fast food
credit cards
conglomerates
social critics
The Lonely Crowd
The Affluent Society
The Catcher in the Rye
Catch-22
beatniks

MULTIPLE-CHOICE QUESTIONS

Questions 1–2 refer to the excerpt below.

"Does segregation of children in public schools solely on the basis of race even though the physical facilities and other 'tangible' factors may be equal, deprive the children of the minority group of equal education opportunities? We believe that it does.

"[I]n finding that a segregated law school for Negroes could not provide them equal educational opportunities, this court relied in large part on 'those qualities which are incapable of objective measurement but which make for greatness in a law school.'

"Such considerations apply with added force to children in grade and high schools. To separate them from others of similar age and qualifications solely because of their race generates a feeling of inferiority as to their status in the community that may affect their hearts and minds in a way unlikely ever to be undone. . . .

"We conclude that in the field of public education the doctrine of 'separate but equal' has no place. Separate educational facilities are inherently unequal. Therefore, we hold that the plaintiffs . . . [are] deprived of the equal protection of the laws guaranteed by the 14th Amendment."

—Supreme Court, *Brown v. Board of Education of Topeka,*
May 17, 1954

1. The *Brown* decision was controversial for a variety of reasons, but which of the following is most evident in this selection?

   (A) Most of the all-black schools were not physically equal

   (B) The decision was based on tangible, or physical, factors

   (C) The Court condemned segregated schools only in the South

   (D) The Court used psychological evidence to support their case

2. Which of the following best describes the initial reaction to the *Brown* decision?

   (A) Southern leaders supported the decision, but the voters did not

   (B) President Eisenhower provided active support for the decision

   (C) Resistance was widespread and initially few schools were integrated

   (D) It was implemented with little opposition in larger cities

Questions 3–5 refer to the excerpt below.

"Why is it that in the twelve years that have passed since the end of World War II, the United States which was so far in the lead has been losing its lead to the Russians. . . .

"Our people have been led to believe in the enormous fallacy that the highest purpose of the American social order is to multiply the enjoyment of consumer goods. As a result, our public institutions, particularly those having to do with education and research, have been . . . scandalously starved.

"With prosperity acting as a narcotic . . . our public life has been increasingly doped and without purpose. With the President in a kind of partial retirement . . . we drift, with no one to state our purposes and to make policy."

—Walter Lippmann, journalist, essay written six days
after *Sputnik,* October 1957

3. Which of the following would most likely support the recommendations of this excerpt?
   (A) Building more suburban shopping centers
   (B) Increasing the sales of televisions
   (C) Creating the National Aeronautic and Space Administration
   (D) Expanding tax breaks for American corporations

4. Which of the following took the most criticism after the shocking success of Russia's *Sputnik*?
   (A) American educational system
   (B) United States Air Force
   (C) Television programming
   (D) United States Congress

5. Recent historians would argue that Lippmann was
   (A) not concerned enough about the strength of the Soviet Union
   (B) unaware of how engaged Eisenhower actually was
   (C) right to be critical of American culture in the 1950s
   (D) expressing a view commonly held by Republicans

Questions 6–8 refer to the excerpt below.

"Eisenhower was the first American president to have atomic weapons and not use them. . . . He refused when his advisers begged him to use those weapons and when they urged him to develop plans for fighting smaller nuclear wars in remote areas of the world. We can only wonder how humanity's course might have been different if Eisenhower acceded to those who believed America would have been best served by use of the weapons under his control.

"But, he was not always right. He was enamored of covert action, and he did not fully apprehend the moral imperatives of civil rights. . . . If Earl Warren and the Supreme Court sometimes baffled or annoyed him . . . when the South threatened to defy the court, Ike restored order and supremacy by force, as only he could."

—Jim Newton, historian, *Eisenhower: The White House Years,* 2011

6. Which of the following would best support the sentiments found in this excerpt?

   (A) Poor advisers in the White House resulted in poor policies

   (B) Small tactical nuclear weapons could be used as battlefield weapons

   (C) Eisenhower was baffled by many of the problems that faced him

   (D) Eisenhower was a decisive president who avoided nuclear war

7. Which of the following would most likely support the author's perspective that Eisenhower "was not always right"?

   (A) Eisenhower's leadership style emphasized the delegation of authority

   (B) Eisenhower supported the overthrow of the elected government of Iran

   (C) Eisenhower failed to balance five out of the eight federal budgets

   (D) Eisenhower ignored the environmental impact of the Interstate Highway Act

8. Which of the following best supports the observation that "Ike restored order and supremacy by force"?

   (A) Using "modern Republicanism" to defeat the Democrats

   (B) Sending U.S. troops into Indochina

   (C) Ordering federal troops to Little Rock Central High School

   (D) Supporting the "brinkmanship" policies of John Foster Dulles

SHORT-ANSWER QUESTIONS

Use complete sentences; an outline or bulleted list alone is not acceptable.

Question 1. Answer (A), (B), and (C).

(A) Briefly explain ONE specific historical example of how the foreign policy of President Eisenhower's was similar to that of President Truman's.

(B) Briefly explain ONE specific historical example of how the foreign policy of President Eisenhower's was different from that of President Truman's.

(C) Briefly explain ONE specific historical example of how the Cold War fluctuated between periods of confrontation and peaceful coexistence during the 1950s.

Question 2 is based on the following photo.

Source:
©ClassicStock/
Alamy

2. Using the photo, answer (A), (B), and (C).

(A) Briefly analyze ONE effect of television on society during the 1950s.

(B) Briefly explain ONE criticism of television during the 1950s.

(C) Briefly explain the primary role of women during the 1950s.

Question 3. Answer (A), (B), and (C).

(A) Briefly explain ONE impact of "modern Republicanism" on the Republican Party.

(B) Briefly explain ONE effect of the Highway Act of 1956.

(C) Briefly explain ONE of Eisenhower's concerns about the "military-industrial complex."

Question 4 is based on the excerpts below.

"In the 1950s critics launched a devastating attack on the consumer culture for fostering a docile, standardized nation. Wherever they looked—toward a woman's place in the home or antiseptic one-class suburb or the comatose campus—America seemed . . . routinized. One writer described the United States as 'The Packaged Society, for we are all items in a national supermarket—categorized, processed, labeled, priced, and readied for merchandising.'"

—William E. Leuchtenburg, historian, *A Troubled Feast: American Society Since 1945,* 1973

"The Truman-Eisenhower period is regarded as conservative and backward looking. . . . But what this view obscures is the extent to which, without anyone realizing it, the preconditions for social change and reform were being established. . . . Before Selma there was Montgomery. . . . before the hippies were the Beats. . . . Withal, it had been a time of hope, a time of growth, and, in its best moments, even a time of glory."

—William L. O'Neill, historian, *American High: The Years of Confidence, 1945–1960,* 1986

4. Using the excerpts, answer (A), (B), and (C).

   (A) Briefly describe ONE major difference between Leuchtenburg's and O'Neill's historical interpretation of the 1950s.

   (B) Briefly explain ONE specific historical event or development that is not explicitly mentioned in the excerpts that could be used to support Leuchtenburg's interpretation of the 1950s.

   (C) Briefly explain ONE specific historical event or development that is not explicitly mentioned in the excerpts that could be used to support O'Neill's interpretation of the 1950s.

THINK AS A HISTORIAN: STATING A CONCLUSION

Often, an essay's conclusion includes a statement summarizing the points of the essay by combining them. Which ONE of the following statements most clearly expresses a combining of information?

1. The success of Jackie Robinson in integrating major league baseball demonstrates how race relations were changing.

2. *The Catcher in the Rye* is an example of the conflict between individualism and conformity.

3. In the 1950s, U.S.–Soviet tensions, division in Germany, and the Suez Crisis showed how quickly relations among countries change.

4. Later events in Southeast Asia provided evidence that the domino theory about the spread of communism was not correct.

28

PROMISE AND TURMOIL, THE 1960S

Let the word go forth from this time and place, to friend and foe alike, that the torch has been passed to a new generation of Americans—born in this century, tempered by war, disciplined by a hard and bitter peace, proud of our ancient heritage. . . . Let every nation know, whether it wishes us well or ill, that we shall pay any price, bear any burden, meet any hardship, support any friend, oppose any foe to assure the survival and success of liberty.

John F. Kennedy, Inaugural Address, January 20, 1961

The 1960s were in many ways both the best and the worst of times. On the one hand, the postwar economic prosperity peaked in the 1960s. At the same time, racial strife, a controversial war in Vietnam, and student radicalism started to tear the country apart. The proud superpower began to learn its limits both in the jungles of Vietnam and on the streets at home.

John F. Kennedy's New Frontier

The decade began with an election that proved symbolic of the changes that were to come.

The Election of 1960

President Eisenhower had not been able to transfer his popularity to other Republicans, and the Democrats retained control of Congress through Eisenhower's last two years in office.

Nixon At their 1960 convention, the Republicans unanimously nominated Richard Nixon for president. During his eight years as Eisenhower's vice president, Nixon had gained a reputation as a statesman in his diplomatic travels to Europe and South America. In a visit to Moscow, he stood up to Nikita Khrushchev in the so-called kitchen debate (which took place in a model of an American kitchen) over the relative merits of capitalism and communism. Still young at 47, Nixon was known to be a tough and seasoned campaigner.

Kennedy Early in 1960, several Democrats believed they had a chance at the nomination. Liberal Democrats Hubert Humphrey of Minnesota and Adlai Stevenson of Illinois were in the contest, and southern Democrats supported the Senate majority leader, Lyndon B. Johnson of Texas. In the primaries, however, a charismatic, wealthy, and youthful 43-year-old senator from Massachusetts, John F. Kennedy, defeated his rivals. Going into the convention, he had just enough delegates behind him to win the nomination. To balance the ticket, the New Englander chose a Texan, Lyndon B. Johnson, to be his vice presidential running mate—a choice that proved critical in carrying southern states in the November election.

Campaign The new medium of television was perhaps the most decisive factor in the close race between the two youthful campaigners, Nixon and Kennedy. In the first of four televised debates—the first such debates in campaign history—Kennedy appeared on-screen as more vigorous and comfortable than the pale and tense Nixon. On the issues, Kennedy attacked the Eisenhower administration for the recent recession and for permitting the Soviets to take the lead in the arms race. In reality, what Kennedy called a "missile gap" was actually in the U.S. favor, but his charges seemed plausible after *Sputnik*. As the first Catholic presidential candidate since Al Smith (1928), Kennedy's religion became an issue in the minds of some voters. Religious loyalties helped Nixon in rural Protestant areas but helped Kennedy in the large cities.

Results In one of the closest elections in U.S. history, Kennedy defeated Nixon by a little more than 100,000 popular votes, and by a slightly wider margin of 303 to 219 in the electoral college. Many Republicans, including Nixon, felt the election had been stolen by Democratic political machines in states like Illinois and Texas by stuffing ballot boxes with "votes" of the deceased.

Domestic Policy

At 43, Kennedy was the youngest candidate ever to be elected president. His energy and sharp wit gave a new, personal style to the presidency. In his inaugural address, Kennedy spoke of "the torch being passed to a new generation" and promised to lead the nation into a New Frontier. The Democratic president surrounded himself with both business executives such as Secretary of Defense Robert McNamara and academics such as economist John Kenneth Galbraith. For the sensitive position of attorney general, the president chose his younger brother, Robert. John Kennedy and his wife, Jacqueline ("Jackie"), brought style, glamour, and an appreciation of the arts to the White House. The press loved Kennedy's news conferences, and some later likened his administration to the mythical kingdom of Camelot and the court of King Arthur, the subject of a then-popular Broadway musical.

New Frontier Programs The promises of the New Frontier proved difficult to keep. Kennedy called for aid to education, federal support of health care, urban renewal, and civil rights, but his domestic programs languished in Congress. While few of Kennedy's proposals became law during his thousand-day administration, most were passed later under President Johnson.

On economic issues, Kennedy had some success. He faced down big steel executives over a price increase he charged was inflationary and achieved a price rollback. In addition, the economy was stimulated by increased spending for defense and space exploration, as the president committed the nation to land on the moon by the end of the decade.

Foreign Affairs

With his domestic programs often blocked, Kennedy increasingly turned his attention to foreign policy issues. In 1961, he set up the Peace Corps, an organization that recruited young American volunteers to give technical aid to developing countries. Also in 1961, he organized the Alliance for Progress, which promoted land reform and economic development in Latin America. Kennedy did persuade Congress to pass the Trade Expansion Act of 1962, which authorized tariff reductions with the recently formed European Economic Community (Common Market) of Western European nations.

Bay of Pigs Invasion (1961) Kennedy made a major blunder shortly after entering office. He approved a Central Intelligence Agency scheme planned under the Eisenhower administration to use Cuban exiles to overthrow Fidel Castro's regime in Cuba. In April 1961, the CIA-trained force of Cubans landed at the Bay of Pigs in Cuba but failed to set off a general uprising as planned. Trapped on the beach, the anti-Castro Cubans had little choice but to surrender after Kennedy rejected the idea of using U.S. forces to save them. Castro used the failed invasion to get even more aid from the Soviet Union and to strengthen his grip on power.

Berlin Wall Trying to shake off the embarrassment of the Bay of Pigs defeat, Kennedy agreed to meet Soviet premier Khrushchev in Vienna in the summer of 1961. Khrushchev seized the opportunity in Vienna to threaten the president by renewing Soviet demands that the United States pull its troops out of Berlin. Kennedy refused. In August, the East Germans, with Soviet backing, built a wall around West Berlin. Its purpose was to stop East Germans from fleeing to West Germany. As the wall was being built, Soviet and U.S. tanks faced off in Berlin. Kennedy called up the reserves, but he made no move to stop the completion of the wall. In 1963, the president traveled to West Berlin to assure its residents of continuing U.S. support. To cheering crowds, he proclaimed: "Freedom has many difficulties and democracy is not perfect, but we have never had to put up a wall to keep our people in. . . . As a free man, I take pride in the words, *'Ich bin ein Berliner'* [I am a Berliner]."

The Berlin Wall stood as a gloomy symbol of the Cold War until it was torn down by rebellious East Germans in 1989.

Cuban Missile Crisis (1962) The most dangerous challenge from the Soviets came in October 1962. U.S. reconnaissance planes discovered that the Russians were building underground sites in Cuba for the launching of offensive missiles that could reach the United States in minutes. Kennedy responded by announcing to the world that he was setting up a naval blockade of Cuba until the weapons were removed. A full-scale nuclear war between the superpowers seemed likely if Soviet ships challenged the U.S. naval blockade. After days of tension, Khrushchev finally agreed to remove the missiles from Cuba in exchange for Kennedy's pledge not to invade the island nation and to later remove some U.S. missiles from Turkey.

The Cuban missile crisis had a sobering effect on both sides. Soon afterward, a telecommunications hotline was established between Washington and Moscow to make it possible for the leaders of the two countries to talk directly during a crisis. In 1963, the Soviet Union and the United States—along with nearly 100 other nations—signed the Nuclear Test Ban Treaty to end the testing of nuclear weapons in the atmosphere. This first step in controlling the testing of nuclear arms was offset by a new round in the arms race for developing missile and warhead superiority.

THE CARIBBEAN AND CENTRAL AMERICA

Flexible Response A different Cold War challenge were the many "brush-fire wars" in Africa and Southeast Asia, in which insurgent forces were often aided by Soviet arms and training. Such conflicts in the Congo (later renamed Zaire) in Africa and in Laos and Vietnam in Southeast Asia convinced the Kennedy administration to adopt a policy of flexible response. Moving away from Dulles' idea of massive retaliation and reliance on nuclear weapons, Kennedy and McNamara increased spending on conventional (nonnuclear) arms and mobile military forces. While the flexible-response policy reduced the risk of using nuclear weapons, it also increased the temptation to send elite special forces, such as the Green Berets, into combat all over the globe.

Assassination in Dallas

After just two and a half years in office, President Kennedy's "one brief, shining moment" was cut short on November 22, 1963, in Dallas, Texas, as two bullets from an assassin's rifle found their mark. After the shocking news of Kennedy's murder, millions of stunned Americans were fixed to their televisions for days and even witnessed the killing of the alleged assassin, Lee Harvey Oswald, just two days after the president's death. The Warren Commission, headed by Chief Justice Earl Warren, concluded that Oswald was the lone assassin. For years afterward, however, unanswered questions about the events in Dallas produced dozens of conspiracy theories pointing to possible involvement by organized crime, Castro, the CIA, and the FBI. For many Americans, the tragedy in Dallas and doubts about the Warren Commission marked the beginning of a loss of credibility in government.

In Retrospect At the time, John Kennedy's presidency inspired many idealistic young Americans to take seriously his inaugural message and to "ask not what your country can do for you—ask what you can do for your country." However, more recently, his belligerent Cold War rhetoric has drawn criticism from some historians. Nevertheless, the Kennedy legend has endured.

Lyndon Johnson's Great Society

Two hours after the Kennedy assassination, Lyndon Johnson took the presidential oath of office aboard a plane at the Dallas airport. On the one hand, as a native of rural west Texas and a graduate of a little-known teacher's college, he seemed very unsophisticated compared to the wealthy, Harvard-educated Kennedy. On the other hand, Johnson was a skilled politician who had started his career as a devoted Roosevelt Democrat during the Great Depression.

As the new president, Johnson was determined to expand the social reforms of the New Deal. During his almost 30 years in Congress, he had learned how to get things done. Shortly after taking office, Johnson persuaded Congress to pass (1) an expanded version of Kennedy's civil rights bill, and (2) Kennedy's proposal for an income tax cut. The latter measure sparked an increase in jobs, consumer spending, and a long period of economic expansion in the sixties.

The War on Poverty

Michael Harrington's best-selling book on poverty, *The Other America* (1962), helped to focus national attention on the 40 million Americans still living in poverty. Johnson responded by declaring in 1964 an "unconditional war on poverty." The Democratic Congress gave the president almost everything that he asked for by creating the Office of Economic Opportunity (OEO) and providing this antipoverty agency with a billion-dollar budget. The OEO sponsored a wide variety of self-help programs for the poor, such as Head Start for preschoolers, the Job Corps for vocational education, literacy programs, and legal services. The controversial Community Action Program allowed the poor to run antipoverty programs in their own neighborhoods.

Like the New Deal, some of Johnson's programs produced results, while others did not. Nevertheless, before being cut back to pay for the far more costly Vietnam War, the War on Poverty did significantly reduce the number of American families living in poverty.

The Election of 1964

Johnson and his running mate, Senator Hubert Humphrey, went into the 1964 election with a clearly liberal agenda. In contrast, the Republicans nominated a staunch conservative, Senator Barry Goldwater of Arizona, who advocated ending the welfare state, including TVA and Social Security. A TV ad by the Democrats pictured Goldwater as a dangerous extremist, who would be quick to involve the United States in nuclear war. However, the doomed Goldwater campaign did energize young conservatives and introduced new conservative voices, such as former film actor and TV host, Ronald Reagan of California.

Johnson won the election by a landslide, taking 61 percent of the popular vote—a higher figure than FDR's landslide of 1936. In addition, Democrats now controlled both houses of Congress by better than a two-thirds margin. A Democratic president and Congress were in a position to pass the economic and social reforms originally proposed by President Truman in the 1940s.

Great Society Reforms

Johnson's list of legislative achievements from 1963 to 1966 is long and includes new programs that would have lasting effects on U.S. society. Several of the most significant ones are listed in the table below.

Great Society Programs		
Title	Year Passed	Program
Food Stamp Act	1964	Expanded the federal program to help poor people buy food
National Foundation on the Arts and Humanities	1965	Provided federal funding for the arts and for creative and scholarly projects
Medicare	1965	Provided health insurance for all people 65 and older
Medicaid	1965	Provided funds to states to pay for medical care for the poor and disabled
Elementary and Secondary Education Act	1965	Provided federal funds to poor school districts; funds for special education programs; and funds to expand Head Start, an early childhood education program
Higher Education Act	1965	Provided federal scholarships for post-secondary education
Immigration Act	1965	Abolished discriminatory quotas based on national origins
Child Nutrition Act	1966	Added breakfasts to the school lunch program

In addition to the programs listed in the table, Congress increased funding for mass transit, public housing, rent subsidies for low-income people, and crime prevention, Johnson also established two new cabinet departments: the Department of Transportation (DOT), and the Department of Housing and Urban Development (HUD). Congress, in response to Ralph Nader's book *Unsafe at Any Speed* (1965), also passed regulations of the automobile industry that would save hundreds of thousands of lives in the following years. Clean air and water laws were enacted in part as a response to Rachel Carson's exposé of pesticides, *Silent Spring* (1962). Federal parks and wilderness areas were expanded. LBJs wife, Lady Bird Johnson, contributed to improving the environment with her Beautify America campaign, which resulted in the Highway Beautification Act that removed billboards from federal roads.

Evaluating the Great Society Critics have attacked Johnson's Great Society for making unrealistic promises to eliminate poverty, for creating a centralized welfare state, and for being inefficient and very costly. On the other hand, defenders point out that these programs gave vitally needed assistance to millions of Americans who had previously been forgotten or ignored—the poor, the disabled, and the elderly. Johnson himself would jeopardize the Democrat's vast domestic achievements by escalating the war in Vietnam—a war that resulted in higher taxes and inflation.

Civil Rights Acts of 1964 and 1965

Ironically, a southern president succeeded in persuading Congress to enact the most important civil rights laws since Reconstruction. Even before the 1964 election, Johnson managed to persuade both a majority of Democrats and some Republicans in Congress to pass the 1964 Civil Rights Act, which made segregation illegal in all public facilities, including hotels and restaurants, and gave the federal government additional powers to enforce school desegregation. This act also set up the Equal Employment Opportunity Commission to end discrimination in employment on the basis of race, religion, sex, or national origin. Also in 1964, the 24th Amendment was ratified. It abolished the practice of collecting a poll tax, one of the measures that, for decades, had discouraged poor people from voting.

The following year, after the killings and brutality in Selma, Alabama, against the voting rights marches led by Martin Luther King Jr., President Johnson persuaded Congress to pass the Voting Rights Act of 1965. This act ended literacy tests and provided federal registrars in areas where blacks were kept from voting. The impact was most dramatic in the Deep South, where African Americans could vote for the first time since the Reconstruction era.

Civil Rights and Conflict

The civil rights movement gained momentum during the Kennedy and Johnson presidencies. A very close election in 1960 influenced President Kennedy not to press the issue of civil rights, lest he alienate white voters. But the defiance of the governors of Alabama and Mississippi to federal court rulings on integration forced a showdown. In 1962, James Meredith, a young African American air force veteran, attempted to enroll in the University of Mississippi. A federal court guaranteed his right to attend. Supporting Meredith and the court order, Kennedy sent in 400 federal marshals and 3,000 troops to control mob violence and protect Meredith's right to attend class.

A similar incident occurred in Alabama in 1963. Governor George Wallace tried to stop an African American student from entering the University of Alabama. Once again, President Kennedy sent troops to the scene, and the student was admitted.

The Leadership of Dr. Martin Luther King Jr.

Civil rights activists and freedom riders who traveled through the South registering African Americans to vote and integrating public places were met with beatings, bombings, and murder by white extremists. Recognized nationally as the leader of the civil rights movement, Dr. Martin Luther King Jr. remained committed to nonviolent protests against segregation. In 1963, he and some followers were jailed in Birmingham, Alabama, for what local authorities judged to be an illegal march. The jailing of King, however, proved to be a milestone in the civil rights movement because most Americans believed King to have been jailed unjustly. From his jail cell, King wrote an essay, "Letter from Birmingham Jail," in which he argued:

> [W]e need emulate neither the "do-nothingism" of the complacent nor the hatred and despair of the black nationalist. For there is the more excellent way of love and nonviolent protest. I am grateful to God that, through the influence of the Negro church, the way of nonviolence became an integral part of our struggle. . . .
>
> One day the South will know that when these disinherited children of God sat down at lunch counters, they were in reality standing up for what is best in the American dream and for the most sacred values in our Judeo-Christian heritage, thereby bringing our nation back to those great wells of democracy which were dug deep by the founding fathers in their formulation of the Constitution and the Declaration of Independence. . . .

King's letter moved President Kennedy to support a tougher civil rights bill.

March on Washington (1963) In August 1963, King led one of the largest and most successful demonstrations in U.S. history. About 200,000 blacks and whites took part in the peaceful March on Washington in support of the civil rights bill. The highlight of the demonstration was King's impassioned "I Have a Dream" speech, which appealed for the end of racial prejudice and ended with everyone in the crowd singing "We Shall Overcome."

March to Montgomery (1965) A voting rights march from Selma, Alabama, to the state capitol of Montgomery was met with beatings and tear gas in what became known as "Bloody Sunday." Televised pictures of the violence proved a turning point in the civil rights movement. The national outrage moved President Johnson to send federal troops to protect King and other marchers in another attempt to petition the state government. As a result, Congress passed the powerful Voting Rights Act of 1965. Nevertheless, young African Americans were losing patience with the slow progress toward equality and the continued violence against their people by white extremists.

Black Muslims and Malcolm X

Seeking a new cultural identity based on Africa and Islam, the Black Muslim leader Elijah Muhammad preached black nationalism, separatism, and self-improvement. The movement had already attracted thousands of followers by the time a young man became a convert while serving in prison. He adopted the name Malcolm X. Leaving prison in 1952, Malcolm X acquired a reputation as the movement's most controversial voice. He criticized King as "an Uncle Tom" (subservient to whites) and advocated self-defense—using black violence to counter white violence. He eventually left the Black Muslims and moved away from defending violence, but he was assassinated by black opponents in 1965. *The Autobiography of Malcolm X* remains an engaging testimony to one man's development from a petty criminal into a major leader.

Race Riots and Black Power

The radicalism of Malcolm X influenced the thinking of young blacks in civil rights organizations such as the Student Nonviolent Coordinating Committee (SNCC) and the Congress of Racial Equality (CORE). Stokely Carmichael, the chairman of SNCC, repudiated nonviolence and advocated "black power" (especially economic power) and racial separatism. In 1966, the Black Panthers were organized by Huey Newton, Bobby Seale, and other militants as a revolutionary socialist movement advocating self-rule for American blacks.

Riots Shortly after the passage of the Voting Rights Act of 1965, the arrest of a young black motorist by white police in the black neighborhood of Watts in Los Angeles sparked a six-day race riot that killed 34 people and destroyed over 700 buildings. Race riots continued to erupt each summer in black neighborhoods of major cities through 1968 with increasing casualties and destruction of property. Rioters shouting slogans—"Burn baby, burn" and "Get whitey"—made whites suspect that black extremists and revolutionaries were behind the violence. There was little evidence, however, that the small Black Power movement was responsible for the violence. A federal investigation of the many riots, the Kerner Commission, concluded in late 1968 that racism and segregation were chiefly responsible and that the United States was becoming "two societies, one black, one white—separate and unequal." By the mid-1960s, the issue of civil rights had spread far beyond *de jure* segregation practiced under the law in the South and now included the de facto segregation and discrimination caused by racist attitudes in the North and West.

Murder in Memphis Martin Luther King, Jr., received the Nobel Peace Prize in 1964, but his nonviolent approach was under increasing pressure from all sides. His effort to use peaceful marches in urban centers of the North, such as Chicago, met with little success. King also broke with President Johnson over the Vietnam War because that war was beginning to drain money from social programs. In April 1968, the nation went into shock over the news that King, while standing on a motel balcony in Memphis, Tennessee, had been shot and killed by a white man. Massive riots erupted in 168 cities across the country, leaving at least 46 people dead. The violence did not reflect the ideals of the murdered leader, but it did reveal the anger and frustrations among African Americans in both the North and the South. The violence also fed a growing "white backlash," especially among white blue-collar voters, to the civil rights movement, which was soon reflected in election results.

The Warren Court and Individual Rights

As chief justice of the Supreme Court from 1953 to 1969, Earl Warren had an impact on the nation comparable to that of John Marshall in the early 1800s. Warren's decision in the desegregation case of *Brown v. Board of Education of Topeka* (1954) was by far the most important case of the 20th century involving race relations. Then in the 1960s the Warren Court made a series of decisions that profoundly affected the criminal justice system, state political systems, and the definition of individual rights. Before Warren's tenure as chief justice, the Supreme Court had concentrated on protecting property rights. During and after his tenure, the Court focused more on protecting individual rights.

Criminal Justice

Several decisions of the Warren Court concerned a defendant's rights. Four of the most important were the following:

- *Mapp v. Ohio* (1961) ruled that illegally seized evidence cannot be used in court against the accused.

- *Gideon v. Wainwright* (1963) required that state courts provide counsel (services of an attorney) for indigent (poor) defendants.

- *Escobedo v. Illinois* (1964) required the police to inform an arrested person of his or her right to remain silent.

- *Miranda v. Arizona* (1966) extended the ruling in *Escobedo* to include the right to a lawyer being present during questioning by the police.

Reapportionment

Before 1962, many states included at least one house of its legislature (usually the senate) that had districts that strongly favored rural areas to the disadvantage of cities. In the landmark case of *Baker v. Carr* (1962), the Warren Court declared this practice unconstitutional. In *Baker* and later cases, the Court established the principle of "one man, one vote," meaning that election districts would have to be redrawn to provide equal representation for all citizens.

Freedom of Expression and Privacy

Other rulings by the Warren Court extended the rights mentioned in the 1st Amendment to protect the actions of protesters, to permit greater latitude under freedom of the press, to ban religious activities sponsored by public schools, and to guarantee adults' rights to use contraceptives.

- *Yates v. United States* (1957) said that the 1st Amendment protected radical and revolutionary speech, even by Communists, unless it was a "clear and present danger" to the safety of the country.

- *Engel v. Vitale* (1962) ruled that state laws requiring prayers and Bible readings in the public schools violated the 1st Amendment's provision for separation of church and state.

- *Griswold v. Connecticut* (1965) ruled that, in recognition of a citizen's right to privacy, a state could not prohibit the use of contraceptives by adults. (This privacy case provided the foundation for later cases establishing a woman's right to an abortion.)

The Warren Court's defense of the rights of unpopular individuals, including people accused of crimes, provoked a storm of controversy. Critics called for Warren's impeachment. Both supporters and critics agreed that the Warren Court profoundly changed the interpretation of constitutional rights.

Social Revolutions and Cultural Movements

In the early and mid-1960s, various liberal groups began to identify with blacks' struggle against oppressive controls and laws. The first such group to rebel against established authority were college and university students.

Student Movement and the New Left

In 1962, a newly formed radical student organization called Students for a Democratic Society (SDS) held a meeting in Port Huron, Michigan. Following the leadership of Tom Hayden, the group issued a declaration of purposes known as the Port Huron Statement. It called for university decisions to be made through participatory democracy, so that students would have a voice in decisions affecting their lives. Activists and intellectuals who supported Hayden's ideas became known as the New Left.

The first major student protest took place in 1964 on the Berkeley campus of the University of California. Calling their cause the Free Speech Movement, Berkeley students demanded an end to university restrictions on student political activities. By the mid-1960s, students across the country were protesting a variety of university rules, including those against drinking and dorm visits by members of the opposite sex. They also demanded a greater voice in the government of the university. Student demonstrations grew with the escalation of U.S. involvement in the Vietnam War. Hundreds of campuses were disrupted or closed down by antiwar protests.

The most radical fringe of the SDS, known as the Weathermen, embraced violence and vandalism in their attacks on American institutions. In the eyes of most Americans, the Weathermen's extremist acts and language discredited the early idealism of the New Left.

Counterculture

The political protests of the New Left went hand in hand with a new counterculture that was expressed by young people in rebellious styles of dress, music, drug use, and, for some, communal living. The apparent dress code of the "hippies" and "flower children" of the 1960s included long hair, beards, beads, and jeans. The folk music of Joan Baez and Bob Dylan gave voice to the younger generation's protests, while the rock music of the Beatles, the Rolling Stones, Jim Morrison, and Janis Joplin provided the beat and lyrics for the counterculture. In 1969, a gathering of thousands of young people at the Woodstock Music Festival in upper New York State reflected the zenith of the counterculture. However, as a result of experimenting with hallucinogenic drugs such as LSD or becoming addicted to various other drugs, some young people destroyed their lives. The counterculture's excesses and the economic uncertainties of the times led to its demise in the 1970s.

In Retrospect The generation of baby boomers that came of age in the 1960s believed fervently in the ideals of a democratic society. They hoped to slay the dragons of unresponsive authority, poverty, racism, and war. However, the impatience of some activists with change, the use of violence, and the spread of self-destructive behavior discredited their cause in the eyes of others, particularly older Americans.

Sexual Revolution

One aspect of the counterculture that continued beyond the 1960s was a change in many Americans' attitudes toward sexual expression. Traditional beliefs about sexual conduct had originally been challenged in the late 1940s and 1950s by the pioneering surveys of sexual practice conducted by Alfred Kinsey. His research indicated that premarital sex, marital infidelity, and homosexuality were more common than anyone had suspected. Medicine (antibiotics for venereal disease) and science (the introduction of the birth control pill in 1960) also contributed to changing attitudes about engaging in casual sex with a number of partners. Moreover, overtly sexual themes in advertisements, magazines, and movies made sex appear to be just one more consumer product.

How deeply the so-called sexual revolution changed the behavior of the majority of Americans is open to question. There is little doubt, however, that premarital sex, contraception, abortion, and homosexuality became practiced more openly. Later, in the 1980s, there was a general reaction against the loosened moral codes as many blamed it for an increase in illegitimate births, especially among teenagers, an increase in rape and sexual abuse, and the spread of a deadly new disease, AIDS (acquired immune deficiency syndrome).

The Women's Movement

The increased education and employment of women in the 1950s, the civil rights movement, and the sexual revolution all contributed to a renewal of the women's movement in the 1960s. Betty Friedan's book *The Feminine Mystique* (1963) gave the movement a new direction by encouraging middle-class women to seek fulfillment in professional careers in addition to filling the roles of wife, mother, and homemaker. In 1966, Friedan helped found the National Organization for Women (NOW), which adopted the activist tactics of other civil rights movements to secure equal treatment of women, especially for job opportunities. By this time, Congress had already enacted two antidiscriminatory laws: the Equal Pay Act of 1963 and the Civil Rights Act of 1964. These measures prohibited discrimination in employment and compensation on the basis of gender, but had been poorly enforced.

Campaign for the ERA Feminists achieved a major legislative victory in 1972 when Congress passed the Equal Rights Amendment (ERA). This proposed constitutional amendment stated: "Equality of rights under the law shall not be denied or abridged by the United States or by any state on account of sex." Although NOW and other groups campaigned hard for the ratification of the ERA, it just missed acceptance by the required 38 states. It was defeated in part because of a growing reaction against feminism by conservatives who feared the movement threatened the traditional roles of women.

Achievements Even without the ERA, the women's movement accomplished fundamental changes in attitudes and hiring practices. In increasing numbers, women moved into professions previously dominated by men: business, law, medicine, and politics. Although women still experienced the "glass ceiling" in the corporate world, American society at the beginning of the 21st century was less and less a man's world.

The Vietnam War to 1969

None of the divisive issues in the 1960s was as tragic as the war in Vietnam. Some 2.7 million Americans served in the conflict and 58,000 died in a failed effort to prevent the takeover of South Vietnam by communist North Vietnam.

Early Stages

Vietnam was hardly mentioned in the election debates of 1960 between Nixon and Kennedy. U.S. involvement was minimal at that time, but every year thereafter, it loomed larger and eventually dominated the presidency of Lyndon Johnson and the thoughts of the nation.

Buildup Under Kennedy President Kennedy adopted Eisenhower's domino theory that, if Communist forces overthrew South Vietnam's government, they would quickly overrun other countries of Southeast Asia—Laos, Cambodia, Thailand, Malaysia, and Indonesia. Kennedy therefore continued U.S. military aid to South Vietnam's regime and significantly increased the number of military "advisers," who trained the South Vietnamese army and guarded weapons and facilities. By 1963, there were more than 16,000 U.S. troops in South Vietnam in support, not combat, roles. They provided training and supplies for South Vietnam's armed forces and helped create "strategic hamlets" (fortified villages).

However, the U.S. ally in South Vietnam, Ngo Dinh Diem, was not popular. He and his government steadily lost the support of peasants in the countryside, while in the capital city of Saigon, Buddhist monks set themselves on fire in the streets to protest Diem's policies. Kennedy began to question whether the South Vietnamese could win "their war" against Communist insurgents. Just two weeks before Kennedy himself was assassinated in Dallas, Diem was overthrown and killed by South Vietnamese generals. Historians later learned that the generals acted with the knowledge of the Kennedy administration.

Tonkin Gulf Resolution Lyndon Johnson became president just as things began to fall apart in South Vietnam. The country had seven different governments in 1964. During the U.S. presidential campaign, Republican candidate Barry Goldwater attacked the Johnson administration for giving only weak support to South Vietnam's fight against the Vietcong (Communist guerrillas). In August 1964, President Johnson and Congress took a fateful turn in policy. Johnson made use of a naval incident in the Gulf of Tonkin off Vietnam's coast to secure congressional authorization for U.S. forces going into combat. Allegedly, North Vietnamese gunboats had fired on U.S. warships in the Gulf of Tonkin. The president persuaded Congress that this aggressive act was sufficient reason for a military response by the United States. Congress voted its approval of the Tonkin Gulf Resolution, which basically gave the president, as commander in chief, a blank check to take "all necessary measures" to protect U.S. interests in Vietnam.

Critics later called the full-scale use of U.S. forces in Vietnam an illegal war, because the war was not declared by Congress, as the Constitution requires. Congress, however, did not have this concern and did not withdraw its resolution. Until 1968, most Americans supported the effort to contain communism in Southeast Asia. Johnson was caught in a political dilemma to which there was no good solution. How could he stop the defeat of a weak and unpopular government in South Vietnam without making it into an American war—a war whose cost would doom his Great Society programs? If he pulled out, he would be seen as weak and lose public support.

Escalating the War

In 1965, the U.S. military and most of the president's foreign policy advisers recommended expanding operations in Vietnam to save the Saigon government. After a Vietcong attack on the U.S. base at Pleiku in 1965, Johnson authorized Operation Rolling Thunder, a prolonged air attack using B-52 bombers against targets in North Vietnam. In April, the president decided to use U.S. combat troops for the first time to fight the Vietcong. By the end of 1965, over 184,000 U.S. troops were in Vietnam, and most were engaged in a combat role. Johnson continued a step-by-step escalation of U.S. involvement in the war. Hoping to win a war of attrition, American generals used search-and-destroy tactics, which only further alienated the peasants. By the end of 1967, the United States had over 485,000 troops in Vietnam (the peak was 540,000 in March 1969), and 16,000 Americans had already died in the conflict. Nevertheless, General William Westmoreland, commander of the U.S. forces in Vietnam, assured the American public that he could see "light at the end of the tunnel."

Controversy

Misinformation from military and civilian leaders combined with Johnson's reluctance to speak frankly with the American people about the scope and the costs of the war created what the media called a *credibility gap*. Johnson always hoped that a little more military pressure would bring the North Vietnamese to the peace table. The most damaging knowledge gap, however, may have been within the inner circles of government. Years later, Robert McNamara in his memoirs concluded that the leaders in Washington had failed to understand both the enemy and the nature of the war.

THE VIETNAM WAR

Hawks versus Doves The supporters of the war, the "hawks," believed that the war was an act of Soviet-backed Communist aggression against South Vietnam and that it was part of a master plan to conquer all of Southeast Asia. The opponents of the war, the "doves," viewed the conflict as a civil war fought by Vietnamese nationalists and some Communists who wanted to unite their country by overthrowing a corrupt Saigon government.

Some Americans opposed the war because of its costs in lives and money. They believed the billions spent in Vietnam could be better spent on the problems of the cities and the poor in the United States. By far the greatest opposition came from students on college campuses who, after graduation, would become eligible to be drafted into the military and shipped off to Vietnam. In November 1967, the antiwar movement was given a political leader when scholarly Senator Eugene F. McCarthy of Minnesota became the first antiwar advocate to challenge Johnson for the 1968 Democratic presidential nomination.

Tet Offensive On the occasion of their Lunar New Year (Tet) in January 1968, the Vietcong launched an all-out surprise attack on almost every provincial capital and American base in South Vietnam. Although the attack took a fearful toll in the cities, the U.S. military counterattacked, inflicted much heavier losses on the Vietcong, and recovered the lost territory. Even so, in political terms, the American military victory proved irrelevant to the way the Tet Offensive was interpreted at home. The destruction viewed by millions on the TV news appeared as a colossal setback for Johnson's Vietnam policy. Thus, for the Vietcong and North Vietnamese, Tet was a tremendous political victory in demoralizing the American public. In the New Hampshire primary in February, the antiwar McCarthy took 42 percent of the vote against Johnson.

LBJ Ends Escalation The Joint Chiefs of Staff responded to Tet by requesting 200,000 more troops to win the war. By this time, however, the group of experienced Cold War diplomats who advised Johnson had turned against further escalation of the war. On March 31, 1968, President Johnson went on television and told the American people that he would limit the bombing of North Vietnam and negotiate peace. He then surprised everyone by announcing that he would not run again for president.

In May 1968, peace talks between North Vietnam, South Vietnam, and the United States started in Paris, but they were quickly deadlocked over minor issues. The war continued, and tens of thousands more died. But the escalation of the number of U.S. troops in Vietnam had stopped, and under the next administration it would be reversed.

Coming Apart at Home, 1968

Few years in U.S. history were as troubled or violent as 1968. The Tet offensive and the withdrawal of Johnson from the presidential race were followed by the senseless murder of Martin Luther King Jr. and destructive riots in cities across the country. As the year unfolded, Americans wondered if their nation was coming apart from internal conflicts over the war issue, the race issue, and the generation gap between the baby boomers and their parents.

Second Kennedy Assassination

In 1964, Kennedy's younger brother, Robert Kennedy, had become a senator from New York. Four years later, he decided to enter the presidential race after McCarthy's strong showing in New Hampshire. Bobby Kennedy was more effective than McCarthy in mobilizing the traditional Democratic blue-collar and minority vote. On June 5, 1968, he won a major victory in California's primary, but immediately after his victory speech, he was shot and killed by a young Arab nationalist who opposed Kennedy's support for Israel.

The Election of 1968

After Robert Kennedy's death, the election of 1968 turned into a three-way race between two conservatives—George Wallace and Richard Nixon— and one liberal, Vice President Hubert Humphrey.

Democratic Convention at Chicago When the Democrats met in Chicago for their party convention, it was clear that Hubert Humphrey had enough delegates to win the nomination. As vice president, he had loyally supported Johnson's domestic and foreign policies. He controlled the convention, but the antiwar demonstrators were determined to control the streets. Chicago's mayor Richard Daley had the police out in mass, and the resulting violence went out on television across the country as a "police riot." Humphrey left the convention as the nominee of a badly divided Democratic party, and early polls showed he was a clear underdog in a nation sick of disorder and protest.

White Backlash and George Wallace The growing hostility of many whites to federal desegregation, antiwar protests, and race riots was tapped by Governor George Wallace of Alabama. Wallace was the first politician of late-20th-century America to marshal the general resentment against the Washington establishment ("pointy-head liberals," as he called them) and the two-party system. He ran for president as the self-nominated candidate of the American Independent party, hoping to win enough electoral votes to throw the election into the House of Representatives.

Return of Richard Nixon Many observers thought Richard Nixon's political career had ended in 1962 after his unsuccessful run for governor of California. In 1968, however, a new, more confident and less negative Nixon announced his candidacy and soon became the front-runner in the Republican primaries. The favorite of the party regulars, he had little trouble securing his nomination at the Republican convention. For his running mate, he selected Governor Spiro Agnew of Maryland, whose rhetoric was similar to that of George Wallace. Nixon was a "hawk" on the Vietnam War and ran on the slogans of "peace with honor" and "law and order."

Results Wallace and Nixon started strong, but the Democrats began to catch up, especially in northern urban centers, as Humphrey preached to the faithful of the old New Deal coalition. On election night, Nixon defeated Humphrey by a very close popular vote but took a substantial majority of the electoral vote (301 to 191), ending any threat that the three-candidate election would end up in the House of Representatives.

The significance of the 1968 election is clear in the combined total of Nixon's and Wallace's popular vote of almost 57 percent. Apparently, most Americans wanted a time out to heal the wounds inflicted on the national psyche by the upheavals of the 1960s. Supporters of Nixon and Wallace had had enough of protest, violence, permissiveness, the counterculture, drugs, and federal intervention in social institutions. Elections in the 1970s and 1980s would confirm that the tide was turning against New Deal liberalism in favor of the conservatives.

HISTORICAL PERSPECTIVES: WHAT ARE THE LESSONS OF VIETNAM?

The U.S. war in Vietnam had been long and deadly. Marked by failures in both political and military leadership, the war initiated a period of widespread distrust of the government. What went wrong? Critics of the war argued that the United States failed in Vietnam because neither the government nor the military understood the nature of the war. Eisenhower, Kennedy, Johnson, and Nixon viewed the conflict strictly in Cold War terms as an act of aggression by the Communist "monolith" to take over another part of the world, instead of a civil war in which a former colony was trying to gain its independence from Western colonialism. Former Secretary of Defense Robert McNamara, in his book *In Retrospect: The Tragedy and Lessons of Vietnam* (1995), laments that members of the Johnson administration lacked Asian experts to advise them on the formulation of Vietnam policy.

In contrast, General William Westmoreland and other military leaders of the era blamed the civilian government for placing restrictions on the conduct of the war that prevented the military from winning it. In their view, the war could have been won if only the U.S. military had been permitted to take the offensive and bring the war to a swift conclusion. The generals blamed the media for turning the American people against the war. Westmoreland and others argued that the telecasts of the Tet Offensive forced a change in the conduct of the war, just at the point that the U.S. military was beginning to win it.

Many observers have attempted to extract lessons from Vietnam, hoping that the mistakes of the past can be avoided in the future. To many critics of the war, it appeared that the most important mistake was attempting to impose an unsatisfactory regime on a country and that the United States should not go into a war if no vital national interests are at stake. Many critics concluded that a president and Congress should not lead the nation into future war unless they are confident that they can rally and sustain the support of the American people behind the effort over time.

KEY TERMS BY THEME

Kennedy: Domestic Issues (POL)
Election of 1960
John F. Kennedy
New Frontier
Robert Kennedy
Jacqueline Kennedy
race to the moon
assassination in Dallas
Warren Commission

Kennedy: Foreign Policy (WOR)
Peace Corps
Alliance for Progress
Trade Expansion Act (1962)
Bay of Pigs
Berlin Wall
Cuban missile crisis (1962)
flexible response
Nuclear Test Ban Treaty

Johnson: Domestic Programs (POL, WXT)
Lyndon Johnson
Great Society
War on Poverty
Michael Harrington, *The Other America*
Election of 1964
Barry Goldwater
Medicare; Medicaid
Elementary and Secondary Education Act (1965)
Immigrant Act (1965)
National Foundation on the Arts and Humanities
DOT and HUD
Ralph Nader, *Unsafe at Any Speed*
Rachel Carson, *Silent Spring*

Lady Bird Johnson
Civil Rights Act of 1964
Equal Employment Opportunity Commission
24th Amendment
Voting Rights Act of 1965

Civil Rights and Black Power (NAT, POL)
James Meredith
George Wallace
Martin Luther King Jr.
March on Washington (1963)
"I Have a Dream" speech
March to Montgomery
Black Muslims
Malcolm X
Student Nonviolent Coordinating Committee
Congress of Racial Equality
Stokely Carmichael
Black Panthers
Watts riots, race riots
de facto segregation
Kerner Commission
King assassination (1968)

Rights of Americans (POL)
Warren Court
Mapp v. Ohio
Gideon v. Wainwright
Escobedo v. Illinois
Miranda v. Arizona
reapportionment
Baker v. Carr
"one man, one vote"
Yates v. United States
separation of church and state

Engel v. Vitale
Griswold v. Connecticut
privacy and contraceptives

Social Conflict (NAT, SOC)
Students for a Democratic Society
New Left
Weathermen
counterculture
Woodstock
Alfred Kinsey
sexual revolution
women's movement
Betty Friedan, *The Feminine Mystique*
National Organization for Women
Equal Pay Act (1963)
Equal Rights Amendment (ERA)

Vietnam War to 1969 (WOR)
military "advisers"
fall of Diem
Tonkin Gulf Resolution
escalation of troops
General Westmoreland
credibility gap
Tet Offensive
hawks and doves

1968 Election (POL)
LBJ withdraws
Eugene McCarthy
Robert Kennedy
RFK assassination
Hubert Humphrey
Chicago convention
white backlash
George Wallace
Richard Nixon

MULTIPLE-CHOICE QUESTIONS

Questions 1–3 refer to the excerpt below.

"We will stay (in Vietnam) because a just nation cannot leave to the cruelties of its enemies a people who have staked their lives and independence on America's solemn pledge—a pledge which had grown through the commitment of three American Presidents.

"We will stay because in Asia—and around the world—are countries whose independence rests, in large measure, on confidence in America's word and in American protection. To yield to force in Vietnam would weaken that confidence, would undermine the independence of many lands, and would whet the appetite of aggression. We would have to fight in one land, and then we would have to fight in another—or abandon much of Asia to the domination of Communists."

—Lyndon B. Johnson, State of the Union Message, January 12, 1966

1. The foreign policy position for Vietnam explained in the excerpt is most directly based on
   (A) the practice of brinkmanship
   (B) the process of decolonization
   (C) the belief in the domino theory
   (D) the principle of mutually assured destruction

2. In which way did Johnson most significantly depart from the policies of prior presidents?
   (A) He used U.S. troops in a combat role in Vietnam
   (B) He attempted to negotiate with North Vietnam
   (C) He limited the number of troops sent to Vietnam
   (D) He turned over all decision making to the generals

3. Which of the following best characterizes the position of the president's antiwar critics?
   (A) The war primarily enriched the military-industrial complex
   (B) The conflict was primarily a civil war between factions in Vietnam
   (C) The containment policy would not work in Asia
   (D) Johnson did not want to look soft on Communism

Source: Selma to Montgomery march, 1965, Bruce Davidson/Magnum Photo/Library of Congress

4. Which of the following best explains the result of the 1965 march from Selma to Montgomery?

   (A) The marchers, along with Dr. King, were jailed for civil disobedience

   (B) Under pressure, Congress passed the most effective voting rights legislation since Reconstruction

   (C) There was white backlash against blacks for demanding too much

   (D) Race riots were sparked in cities across the nation

5. Which of the following best reflects the loss of faith by younger African Americans in the non-violent civil rights movement after the March to Montgomery?

   (A) The events that started the Watts Riot in Los Angles

   (B) The conversion of Malcolm X to the Black Muslims

   (C) The shift in tactics of SNCC under Stokely Carmichael

   (D) The reaction to the Kerner Commission's findings on racism

Questions 6–8 refer to the excerpt below.

"We, men and women who hereby constitute ourselves as the National Organization for Women, believe that the time has come for a new movement toward equality for all women in America, and towards a full equal partnership of the sexes. . . .

NOW Bill of Rights:

Equal Rights Constitutional Amendment

Enforce Law Banning Sex Discrimination in Employment

Maternity Leave Rights in Employment and in Social Security Benefits

Tax Deduction for Home and Child Care Expenses for Working Parents

Child Care Centers

Equal and Unsegregated Education

Equal Job training Opportunities and Allowances for Women in Poverty

Rights of Women to Control Their Reproductive Lives"

—National Organization for Women, June 1966

6. The 1966 NOW statement, although broadened during the conference, most emphasized which of the following?
   (A) Child care
   (B) Empowerment of wives
   (C) Job opportunities
   (D) Reproduction rights

7. Which of the following goals from the NOW Bill of Rights did the feminist movement most clearly fail to achieve?
   (A) Greater assistance with child care
   (B) New employment opportunities
   (C) Passage of the Equal Rights Amendment
   (D) Increased reproductive rights

8. Which of the following most clearly reflects the main argument in Betty Friedan's *The Feminine Mystique?*
   (A) Women should earn college degrees and avoid early marriages.
   (B) Women should avoid the male-dominated business world by cooperating with other businesswomen.
   (C) Women should have separate finances to protect themselves from the rising divorce rate.
   (D) Women should seek fulfillment in professional careers in addition to their roles as wives and mothers.

SHORT-ANSWER QUESTIONS

Use complete sentences; an outline or bulleted list alone is not acceptable.

Question 1. Answer (A), (B), and (C).

(A) Briefly explain ONE specific historical event or development that supports the argument that the Kennedy administration placed less reliance on massive retaliation and nuclear weapons than did other administrations.

(B) Briefly explain ONE specific historical event or development that supports the argument that Cold War tensions increased during the 1960s.

(C) Briefly explain ONE specific historical event or development that supports the Vietnam War perspectives of either the pro-war "hawks" or the anti-war "doves" during the 1960s.

Question 2 is based on the excerpt below.

"In your time we have the opportunity to move not only toward the rich society and the powerful society, but upward to the Great Society. The Great Society rests on abundance and liberty for all. It demands an end to poverty and racial injustice, to which we are totally committed in our time. . . .

The Great Society is a place where every child can find knowledge to enrich his mind and to enlarge his talents."

—Lyndon B. Johnson, Commencement Address at the
University of Michigan, May 1964

2. Using the excerpt, answer (A), (B), and (C).

(A) Briefly explain ONE way the Great Society attacked poverty.

(B) Briefly explain ONE way the Great Society tried to improve education.

(C) Briefly explain ONE of Johnson's health care programs that had a lasting impact on American society.

Question 3. Answer (A), (B), and (C).

(A) Briefly explain ONE specific ruling of the Warren Court that expanded the rights of defendants in the criminal justice system.

(B) Briefly explain ONE specific ruling of the Warren Court that expanded the 1st Amendment.

(C) Briefly analyze ONE specific impact of the court's "one man, one vote" ruling on American politics.

Question 4 is based on the excerpts below.

"So it proved for the 1960's policymakers, whose ignorance and misconceptions of Southeast Asian history, culture and politics pulled America progressively deeper into the war. LBJ, Rusk, McNamara. . . . mistakenly viewed Vietnam through the simplistic prism of the Cold War. They perceived a deeply complex and ambiguous regional struggle, as a grave challenge to world order and stability. . . . Vietnam exposed the limitations and contradictions of this static doctrine in a world of flux. . . . Vietnam represented a failure not just of American foreign policy, but also of American statesmanship."

—Brian VanDemark, *Into the Quagmire: Lyndon Johnson and the Evolution of the Vietnam War,* 1991

"America's military bureaucracy depends on weapons, increasingly complex, difficult to maintain and expensive. . . . Our marvelously clever technology did not help us to understand the [Vietnam] war and, in fact, confused us even more because it created our unquestioning faith in our own power. . . . If we exploded enough bombs and fired enough rounds, we assumed the enemy would quit. . . . The utter failure of military tactics to utilize technology was not the fault of civilians. . . . By the sheer force of firepower the military won battles, but it could never have made these victories add up to victory."

—Leon Baritz, historian, *A History of How American Culture Led Us into Vietnam and Made Us Fight the Way We Did,* 1985

4. Using the excerpts, answer (A), (B), and (C).

(A) Briefly describe ONE specific difference between VanDemark's and Baritz's historical interpretation of the U. S. policies in Vietnam.

(B) Briefly explain ONE specific historical event or development that is not explicitly mentioned in the excerpts that could be used to support VanDemark's interpretation of U.S. policies in Vietnam during the 1960s.

(C) Briefly explain ONE specific historical event or development that is not explicitly mentioned in the excerpts that could be used to support Baritz's interpretation of U.S. policies in Vietnam during the 1960s.

THINK AS A HISTORIAN: WRITING WITH PRECISE WORDS

Strong essays use words that express the writer's ideas clearly with carefully chosen words rather than bland, general words. In each pair of sentences below, choose the sentence that uses the most precise words.

1. John Kennedy

   A. The death of Kennedy was a sad day for many people.

   B. The assassination of Kennedy shocked Americans.

2. Lyndon Johnson

   A. Johnson had spent many years in Congress trying to pass laws.

   B. Johnson was a veteran legislator, skilled at getting laws passed.

3. George Wallace

   A. Lots of people liked Wallace because they opposed things that were happening.

   B. Wallace expressed the conservative anger at integration.

29

LIMITS OF A SUPERPOWER, 1969–1980

If, when the chips are down, the world's most powerful nation, the United States, acts like a pitiful, helpless giant, the forces of totalitarianism and anarchy will threaten free nations and free institutions throughout the world.
Richard Nixon, Address to the Nation, April 30, 1970

In 1969, television viewers around the world witnessed the astonishing sight of two American astronauts walking on the moon's surface. This event, followed by a series of other successes for the U.S. space program, represented some of the high points of the 1970s. Offsetting these technological triumphs, however, were shocking revelations about White House participation in the Watergate crime, a stagnant economy, and the fall of South Vietnam to communism. Increased foreign economic competition, oil shortages, rising unemployment, and high inflation made Americans aware that even the world's leading superpower would have to adjust to a fast-changing, less manageable world.

Richard Nixon's Foreign Policy

In his January 1969 inaugural address, President Nixon promised to bring Americans together after the turmoil of the 1960s. However, suspicious and secretive by nature, Nixon soon began to isolate himself in the White House and create what Arthur Schlesinger Jr. called an "imperial presidency." Nixon's first interest was international relations, not domestic policy. Together with his national security adviser, Henry Kissinger (who became secretary of state during Nixon's second term), Nixon fashioned a pragmatic foreign policy that reduced the tensions of the Cold War.

Vietnam

When Nixon took office, more than half a million U.S. troops were in Vietnam. His principal objective was to find a way to reduce U.S. involvement in the war while at the same time avoiding the appearance of conceding defeat. In a word, Nixon said the United States was seeking nothing less than "peace with honor."

"Vietnamization." Almost immediately, the new president began the process called "Vietnamization." He announced that he would gradually withdraw U.S. troops from Vietnam and give the South Vietnamese the money, the weapons, and the training that they needed to take over the full conduct of the war. Under this policy, U.S. troops in South Vietnam went from over 540,000 in 1969 to under 30,000 in 1972. Extending the idea of disengagement to other parts of Asia, the president proclaimed the *Nixon Doctrine,* declaring that in the future Asian allies would receive U.S. support but without the extensive use of U.S. ground forces.

Opposition to Nixon's War Policies Nixon's gradual withdrawal of forces from Vietnam reduced the number of antiwar protests. However, in April 1970, the president expanded the war by using U.S. forces to invade Cambodia in an effort to destroy Vietnamese Communist bases in that country. A nationwide protest on college campuses against this action resulted in the killing of four youths by National Guard troops at Kent State in Ohio and two students at Jackson State in Mississippi. In reaction to the escalation of the war, the U.S. Senate (but not the House) voted to repeal the Gulf of Tonkin Resolution.

Also in 1970, the American public was shocked to learn about a 1968 massacre of women and children by U.S. troops in the Vietnamese village of My Lai. Further fueling the antiwar sentiment was the publication by the *New York Times* of the Pentagon Papers, a secret government history documenting the mistakes and deceptions of government policy-makers in dealing with Vietnam. The papers had been turned over, or "leaked," to the press by Daniel Ellsberg, a former Defense Department analyst.

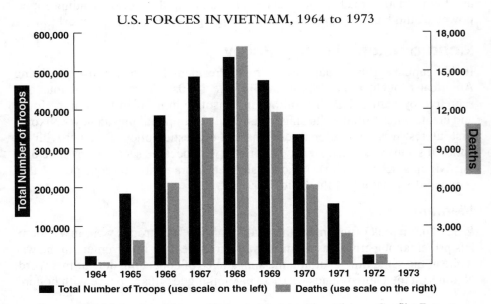

Source: U.S. National Archives and Records Administration. Vietnam Conflict Extract Data File and other sources.

Peace Talks, Bombing Attacks, and Armistice On the diplomatic front, Nixon had Kissinger conduct secret meetings with North Vietnam's foreign minister, Le Duc Tho. Kissinger announced in the fall of 1972 that "peace is at hand," but this announcement proved premature. When the two sides could not reach a deal, Nixon ordered a massive bombing of North Vietnam (the heaviest air attacks of the long war) to force a settlement. After several weeks of B-52 bomber attacks, the North Vietnamese agreed to an armistice, in which the United States would withdraw the last of its troops and get back over 500 prisoners of war (POWs). The Paris Accords of January 1973 also promised a cease-fire and free elections. In practice, however, the armistice did not end the war between the North and the South and left tens of thousands of enemy troops in South Vietnam. Before the war ended, the death toll probably numbered more than a million.

The armistice finally allowed the United States to extricate itself from a war that had claimed over 58,000 American lives. The $118 billion spent on the war began an inflationary cycle that racked the U.S. economy for years afterward.

Détente with China and the Soviet Union

Nixon and Kissinger strengthened the U.S. position in the world by taking advantage of the rivalry between the two Communist giants, China and the Soviet Union. Their diplomacy was praised for bringing about *détente*—a deliberate reduction of Cold War tensions. Even after Watergate ended his presidency in disgrace, Nixon's critics would admit that his conduct of foreign affairs had enhanced world peace.

Visit to China Nixon knew that only an outspoken critic of communism like himself could take the bold step of improving relations with "Red" China (Mao Zedong's Communist regime) without being condemned as "soft" on communism. After a series of secret negotiations with Chinese leaders, Nixon astonished the world in February 1972 by traveling to Beijing to meet with Mao. His visit initiated diplomatic exchanges that ultimately led to U.S. recognition of the Communist government in 1979.

Arms Control with the U.S.S.R. Nixon used his new relationship with China to put pressure on the Soviets to agree to a treaty limiting antiballistic missiles (ABMs), a new technology that would have expanded the arms race. After the first round of Strategic Arms Limitations Talks (SALT I), U.S. diplomats secured Soviet consent to a freeze on the number of ballistic missiles carrying nuclear warheads. While this agreement did not end the arms race, it was a significant step toward reducing Cold War tensions and bringing about détente.

Nixon's Domestic Policy

Throughout the 1970s, the Democrats continued to hold majorities in both houses of Congress. The Republican president had to live with this reality and obtain some concessions from Congress through moderation and compromise. At the same time, Nixon laid the foundation for a shift in public opinion toward conservatism and for Republican gains that would challenge and overthrow the Democratic control of Congress in the 1980s and 1990s.

The New Federalism

Nixon tried to slow down the growth of Johnson's Great Society programs by proposing the Family Assistance Plan, which would have replaced welfare by providing a guaranteed annual income for working Americans. The Democratic majority in Congress easily defeated this initiative. The Republican president did succeed, however, in shifting some of the responsibility for social programs from the federal to the state and local levels. In a program known as revenue sharing, or the New Federalism, Congress approved giving local governments $30 billion in block grants over five years to address local needs as they saw fit (instead of specific uses of federal money being controlled by Washington). Republicans hoped revenue sharing would check the growth of the federal government and return responsibility to the states, where it had rested before the New Deal.

Nixon attempted to bypass Congress by impounding (not spending) funds appropriated for social programs. Democrats protested that such action was an abuse of executive powers. The courts agreed with the president's critics, arguing that it was a president's duty to carry out the laws of Congress, whether or not the president agreed with them.

Nixon's Economic Policies

Starting with a recession in 1970, the U.S. economy throughout the 1970s faced the unusual combination of economic slowdown and high inflation—a condition referred to as *stagflation* (*stag*nation plus in*flation*). To slow inflation, Nixon at first tried to cut federal spending. However, when this policy contributed to a recession and unemployment, he adopted Keynesian economics and deficit spending so as not to alienate middle-class and blue-collar Americans. In August 1971, he surprised the nation by imposing a 90-day wage and price freeze. Next, he took the dollar off the gold standard, which helped to devalue it relative to foreign currencies. This action, combined with a 10 percent surtax on all imports, improved the U.S. balance of trade with foreign competitors.

By the election year of 1972, the recession was over. Also in that year, Congress approved automatic increases for Social Security benefits based on the annual rise in the cost of living. This measure protected seniors, the poor, and the disabled from the worst effects of inflation but also contributed to budget problems in the future. In 1972, Congress also passed Title IX, a statue to end sex discrimination in schools that receive federal funding. Though far-reaching, the law is best known for its requirement that schools provide girls with equal athletic opportunities. Many believe that these new opportunities in athletics proved to be a key step in promoting women's equality.

Southern Strategy

Having received just 43 percent of the popular vote in 1968, Nixon was well aware of being a minority president. He devised a political strategy to form a Republican majority by appealing to the millions of voters who had become disaffected by antiwar protests, black militants, school busing to achieve racial balance, and the excesses of the youth counterculture. Nixon referred to these conservative Americans as the "silent majority." Many of them were Democrats, including southern whites, northern Catholic blue-collar workers, and recent suburbanites who disagreed with the liberal drift of their party.

To win over the South, the president asked the federal courts in that region to delay integration plans and busing orders. He also nominated two southern conservatives (Clement Haynsworth and G. Harold Carswell) to the Supreme Court. Though the courts rejected his requests and the Senate refused to confirm the two nominees, his strategy played well with southern white voters. At the same time, Nixon authorized Vice President Spiro Agnew to make verbal assaults on war protesters and to attack the press as liberal.

The Burger Court

As liberal justices of the Supreme Court retired, Nixon replaced them with more conservative members. However, like other presidents, Nixon found that his appointees did not always rule as he had hoped. In 1969, after Chief Justice Earl Warren resigned, Nixon appointed Warren E. Burger of Minnesota to replace him. The Burger Court was more conservative than the Warren Court, but several of its major decisions angered conservatives. For example, in 1971 the court ordered busing to achieve racial balance in the schools, and in 1972 it issued strict guidelines that made carrying out the death penalty more difficult. The court's most controversial ruling was *Roe v. Wade* (1973). In this 7–2 decision, the high court struck down many state laws prohibiting abortions as a violation of a women's right to privacy. Finally, in the last days of Nixon's Watergate agony (described later in this chapter), the court that he tried to shape denied his claims to executive privilege and ordered him to turn over the Watergate tapes (*United States v. Nixon,* 1974).

The Election of 1972

The success of Nixon's southern strategy became evident in the presidential election of 1972 when the Republican ticket won majorities in every southern state. Nixon's reelection was practically assured by (1) his foreign policy successes in China and the Soviet Union, (2) the removal of George Wallace from the race by an assassin's bullet that paralyzed the Alabama populist, and (3) the nomination by the Democrats of a very liberal, antiwar, antiestablishment candidate, Senator George McGovern of South Dakota.

McGovern's campaign quickly went off track. After some indecision, he dropped his vice presidential candidate, Senator Thomas Eagleton of Missouri, when it was discovered that he had undergone electroschock treatment for depression. On election day, Nixon overwhelmed McGovern in a landslide victory that carried every state but Massachusetts and won 61 percent of the popular vote. The Democrats still managed to keep control of both houses of Congress. Nevertheless, the voting patterns for Nixon indicated the start of a major political realignment of the Sunbelt and suburban voters, who were forming a new Republican majority. Nixon's electoral triumph in 1972 made the Watergate revelations and scandals of 1973 all the more surprising.

Watergate

The tragedy of Watergate went well beyond the public humiliation of Richard Nixon and the conviction and jailing of 26 White House officials and aides. Watergate had a paralyzing effect on the political system in the mid-1970s, a critical time both at home and overseas, when the country needed respected, strong, and confident leadership.

White House Abuses

In June 1972, a group of men hired by Nixon's reelection committee were caught breaking into the offices of the Democratic national headquarters in the Watergate complex in Washington, D.C. This break-in and attempted bugging were only part of a series of illegal activities and "dirty tricks" conducted by the Nixon administration and the Committee to Re-Elect the President (CREEP).

Earlier, Nixon had ordered wiretaps on government employees and reporters to stop news leaks such as one that had exposed the secret bombing of Cambodia. The president's aides created a group, called the "plumbers," to stop leaks as well as to discredit opponents. Before Watergate, the "plumbers" had burglarized the office of psychiatrist of Daniel Ellsberg, the person behind the leaking of the Pentagon Papers, in order to obtain information to discredit Ellsberg. The White House had also created an "enemies list" of prominent Americans who opposed Nixon, the Vietnam War, or both. People on this list were investigated by government agencies, such as the IRS. The illegal break-in at Watergate reflected the attitude in the Nixon administration that any means could be used to promote the national security—an objective that was often confused with protecting the Nixon administration from its critics.

Watergate Investigation

No solid proof demonstrated that President Nixon ordered any of these illegal activities. However, after months of investigation, it became clear that Nixon did engage in an illegal cover-up to avoid scandal. Tough sentencing of the Watergate burglars by federal judge John Sirica led to information about the use of money and a promise of pardons by the White House staff to keep the burglars quiet. A Senate investigating committee headed by Democrat Sam Ervin of North Carolina brought the abuses to the attention of Americans through televised hearings. A highlight of these hearings was the testimony of a White House lawyer, John Dean, who linked the president to the cover-up. Nixon's top aides, H. R. Haldeman and John Ehrlichman, resigned to protect him and were later indicted, as were many others, for obstructing justice.

The discovery of a taping system in the Oval Office led to a year-long struggle between Nixon, who claimed executive privilege for the tapes, and investigators, who wanted the tapes to prove the cover-up charges.

The Nixon administration received another blow in the fall of 1973, when Vice President Agnew had to resign because he had taken bribes when governor of Maryland. Replacing him was Michigan Representative Gerald Ford.

Other Developments in 1973

Although the Watergate affair absorbed most of Nixon's attention during his shortened second term, important developments occurred at home and abroad.

War Powers Act Further discrediting Nixon was the news that he had authorized 3,500 secret bombing raids in Cambodia, a neutral country. Congress used the public uproar over this information to attempt to limit the president's powers over the military. In November 1973, after a long struggle, Congress finally passed the War Powers Act over Nixon's veto. This law required Nixon and any future president to report to Congress within 48 hours after taking military action. It further provided that Congress would have to approve any military action that lasted more than 60 days.

October War and Oil Embargo In world politics, the most important event of 1973 was the outbreak of another Middle Eastern war. On October 6, on the Jewish holy day of Yom Kippur, the Syrians and Egyptians launched a surprise attack on Israel in an attempt to recover the lands lost in the Six-Day War of 1967. President Nixon ordered the U.S. nuclear forces on alert and airlifted almost $2 billion in arms to Israel to stem their retreat. The tide of battle quickly shifted in favor of the Israelis, and the war was soon over.

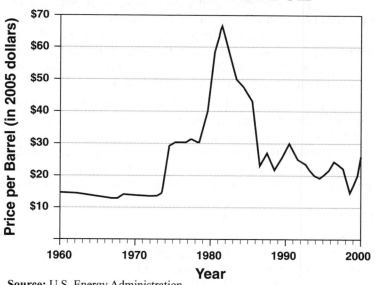

WORLD PRICE OF CRUDE OIL

Source: U.S. Energy Administration

The United States was made to pay a huge price for supporting Israel. The Arab members of the Organization of Petroleum Exporting Countries (OPEC) placed an embargo on oil sold to Israel's supporters. The embargo caused a worldwide oil shortage and long lines at gas stations in the United States. Even worse was the impact on the U.S. economy, which now suffered from runaway inflation, the loss of manufacturing jobs, and a lower standard of living for blue-collar workers. Consumers switched from big American-made cars to smaller, more fuel-efficient Japanese cars, which cost U.S. automobile workers over 225,000 jobs. Congress responded by enacting a 55-miles-per-hour speed limit to save gasoline and approving construction of a controversial oil pipeline to tap American oil reserves in Alaska. No government program, however, seemed to bolster the sluggish economy or stem high inflation rates, which continued to the end of the decade.

Resignation of a President

In 1974, Nixon made triumphal visits to Moscow and Cairo, but at home his reputation continued to slide. In October 1973, the president appeared to be interfering with the Watergate investigation when he fired Archibald Cox, the special prosecutor assigned to the case. In protest, the U.S. attorney general resigned. The House of Representatives began impeachment hearings, which caused Nixon to reveal transcripts of some of the Watergate tapes in April 1974. Still, it took a Supreme Court decision in July to force him to turn over the tapes to the courts and Congress. Included on one tape made just days after the Watergate burglary was an 18 ½-minute gap that had been erased. Meanwhile, the House Judiciary Committee voted three articles of impeachment: (1) obstruction of justice, (2) abuse of power, and (3) contempt of Congress.

The conversations recorded on the tapes shocked friends and foes alike. The transcript of one such White House conversation clearly implicated Nixon in the cover-up only days after the Watergate break-in. Faced with certain impeachment in the House and a trial in the Senate, Richard Nixon chose to resign on August 9, 1974. Vice President Gerald Ford then took the oath of office as the first unelected president in U.S. history.

Significance To some, the final outcome of the Watergate scandal (Nixon leaving office under pressure) proved that the U.S. constitutional system of checks and balances worked as it was intended. For others, the scandal underlined the dangerous shift of power to the presidency that began with Franklin Roosevelt and had been expanded during the Cold War. Without a doubt, Watergate contributed to a growing loss of faith in the federal government.

Gerald Ford in the White House

Before Nixon chose him to replace Vice President Agnew in 1973, Gerald Ford had served in Congress for years as a representative from Michigan and as the Republican minority leader of the House. Ford was a likeable and unpretentious man, but many questioned his ability to be president.

Pardoning of Nixon

In his first month in office, President Ford lost the goodwill of many by granting Nixon a full and unconditional pardon for any crime that he might have committed. The pardon was extended even before any formal charges or indictment had been made by a court of law. Ford was accused of making a "corrupt bargain" with Nixon, but he explained that the purpose of the pardon was to end the "national nightmare," instead of prolonging it for months, if not years. Critics were angered that the full truth of Nixon's deeds never came out.

Investigating the CIA

During Ford's presidency (1974–1977), the Democratic Congress continued to search for abuses in the executive branch, especially in the CIA. This intelligence agency was accused of engineering the assassination of foreign leaders, among them the Marxist president of Chile, Salvador Allende. Ford appointed former Texas Congressman George H. W. Bush to reform the agency.

Failure of U.S. Policy in Southeast Asia

President Ford was unable to get additional funds from Congress for the South Vietnamese, who in 1974 were facing strong attack from Communist forces.

Fall of Saigon In April 1975, the U.S.-supported government in Saigon fell to the enemy, and Vietnam became one country under the rule of the Communist government in Hanoi (North Vietnam's capital). Just before the final collapse, the United States was able to evacuate about 150,000 Vietnamese who had supported the United States and now faced certain persecution. The fall of South Vietnam marked a low point of American prestige overseas and confidence at home.

Genocide in Cambodia Also in 1975, the U.S.-supported government in Vietnam's neighbor, Cambodia, fell to the Khmer Rouge, a radical Communist faction that killed over a million of its own people in a brutal relocation program to rid the country of western influence. Together the wars in Southeast Asia created 10 million refugees, many of whom fled to the United States.

Future of Southeast Asia The fall of Cambodia seemed to fulfill Eisenhower's domino theory, but in fact the rest of Southeast Asia did not fall to communism. Instead, nations such as Singapore, Thailand, and Malaysia emerged as the "little tigers" of the vigorously growing Asian (Pacific Rim) economy. Some argued that U.S. support of South Vietnam was not a waste, because it bought time for other nations of East Asia and Southeast Asia to develop and better resist communism.

The Economy and Domestic Policy

On domestic matters, Ford proved less accommodating and more conservative than Nixon. His chief concern was bringing inflation under control. He urged voluntary measures on the part of businesses and consumers, including the wearing of WIN buttons (Whip Inflation Now). Not only did inflation continue, but the economy also sank deeper into recession, with the unemployment rate reaching more than 9 percent. Ford finally agreed to a Democratic package to stimulate the economy, but he vetoed 39 other Democratic bills.

Bicentennial Celebration In 1976, the United States celebrated its 200th birthday. Americans' pride in their history helped to put Watergate and Vietnam behind them. Even the lackluster presidency of Gerald Ford served the purpose of restoring candor and humility to the White House.

The Election of 1976

Watergate still cast its gloom over the Republican party in the 1976 elections. President Ford was challenged for the party's nomination by Ronald Reagan, a former actor and ex-governor of California, who enjoyed the support of the more conservative Republicans. Ford won the nomination in a close battle, but the conflict with Reagan hurt him in the polls.

Emergence of Jimmy Carter A number of Democrats competed for their party's nomination, including a little-known former governor of Georgia, James Earl (Jimmy) Carter. With Watergate still on voters' minds, Carter had success running as an outsider against the corruption in Washington. His victories in open primaries reduced the influence of more experienced Democratic politicians. After watching his huge lead in the polls evaporate in the closing days of the campaign, Carter managed to win a close election (287 electoral votes to 241 for Ford) by carrying most of the South and getting an estimated 97 percent of the African American vote. In the aftermath of Watergate, the Democrats also won strong majorities in both houses of Congress.

Jimmy Carter's Presidency

The informal style of Jimmy Carter signaled an effort to end the imperial presidency. On his inaugural day, he walked down Pennsylvania Avenue to the White House instead of riding in the presidential limousine. Public images of the president carrying his own luggage may have impressed average Americans. However, veteran members of Congress always viewed Carter as an outsider who depended too much on his politically inexperienced advisers from Georgia. Even Carter's keen intelligence and dedication to duty may have been partly a liability in causing him to pay close attention to all the details of government operations. Critics observed that, when it came to distinguishing between the forest and the trees, Carter was a "leaf man."

Foreign Policy

The hallmark of Carter's foreign policy was human rights, which he preached with Wilsonian fervor to the world's dictators.

Human Rights Diplomacy Carter appointed Andrew Young, an African American, to serve as U.S. ambassador to the United Nations. Carter and Young championed the cause of human rights around the world, especially by opposing the oppression of the black majority in South Africa and Rhodesia (Zimbabwe) by all-white governments. In Latin America, human rights violations by the military governments of Argentina and Chile caused Carter to cut off U.S. aid to those countries.

Panama Canal The Carter administration attempted to correct inequities in the original Panama Canal Treaty of 1903 by negotiating a new treaty. In 1978, after long debate, the Senate ratified a treaty that would gradually transfer operation and control of the Panama Canal from the United States to the Panamanians, a process to be completed by the year 2000. Opponents would remember Carter's "giveaway" of the canal in the 1980 election.

Camp David Accords (1978) Perhaps Carter's single greatest achievement as president was arranging a peace settlement between Egypt and Israel. In 1977, Egyptian President Anwar Sadat took the first courageous step toward Middle East peace by visiting Israeli Prime Minister Menachem Begin in Jerusalem. President Carter followed this bold initiative by inviting Sadat and Begin to meet again at the presidential retreat in Camp David, Maryland. With Carter acting as an intermediary, the two leaders negotiated the Camp David Accords (September 1978), which provided a framework for a peace settlement between their countries.

Later, as a result of a peace treaty concluded in 1979, Egypt became the first Arab nation to recognize the nation of Israel. In return, Israel withdrew its troops from the Sinai territory taken from Egypt in the Six-Day War of 1967. The treaty was opposed by the Palestine Liberation Organization (PLO) and most of the Arab world, but it proved the first step in the long road to a negotiated peace in the Middle East.

Iran and the Hostage Crisis The Middle East provided Carter's greatest frustration. In Iran, anti-American sentiment had been strong since the United States had helped overthrow the country's democratically elected leader in 1953 and install a dictatorial government. In 1979, Islamic fundamentalists in Iran, led by the Ayatollah Khomeini, overthrew the shah who was then leading the Iranian government. The shah had kept the oil flowing for the West during the 1970s, but his autocratic rule and policy of westernization had alienated a large part of the Iranian population.

With the ayatollah and fundamentalists in power, Iranian oil production ground to a halt, causing the second worldwide oil shortage of the decade and another round of price increases. U.S. impotence in dealing with the crisis became more evident in November 1979 when Iranian militants seized the U.S. embassy in Teheran and held more than 50 members of the American staff as prisoners and hostages. The hostage crisis dragged out through the remainder of Carter's presidency. In April 1980, Carter approved a rescue mission, but the breakdown of the helicopters over the Iranian desert forced the United States to abort the mission. For many Americans, Carter's unsuccessful attempts to free the hostages became a symbol of a failed presidency.

Cold War President Carter attempted to continue the Nixon-Ford policy of détente with China and the Soviet Union. In 1979, the United States ended its official recognition of the Nationalist Chinese government of Taiwan and completed the first exchange of ambassadors with the People's Republic of China. At first, détente also moved ahead with the Soviet Union with the signing in 1979 of a SALT II treaty, which provided for limiting the size of each superpower's nuclear delivery system. The Senate never ratified the treaty, however, as a result of a renewal of Cold War tensions over Afghanistan.

In December 1979, Soviet troops invaded Afghanistan—an aggressive action that ended a decade of improving U.S.-Soviet relations. The United States feared that the invasion might lead to a Soviet move to control the oil-rich Persian Gulf. Carter reacted by (1) placing an embargo on grain exports and the sale of high technology to the Soviet Union, and (2) boycotting the 1980 Olympics in Moscow. After having campaigned for arms reduction, Carter now had to switch to an arms buildup.

Domestic Policy: Dealing with Inflation

At home, the biggest issue was the growing inflation rate. At first Carter tried to check inflation with measures aimed at conserving oil energy and reviving the U.S. coal industry. However, the compromises that came out of Congress failed either to reduce the consumption of oil or to check inflation. In 1979–1980, inflation seemed completely out of control and reached the unheard of rate of 13 percent.

Troubled Economy Inflation slowed economic growth as consumers and businesses could no longer afford the high interest rates that came with high prices. The chairman of the Federal Reserve Board, Paul Volcker, hoped to break the back of inflation by pushing interest rates even higher, to 20 percent in 1980. These rates especially hurt the automobile and building industries, which laid off tens of thousands of workers. Inflation also pushed middle-class taxpayers into higher tax brackets, which led to a "taxpayers' revolt." Government social programs that were indexed to the inflation rate helped to push the federal deficit to nearly $60 billion in 1980. Many Americans had to adjust to the harsh truth that, for the first time since World War II, their standard of living was on the decline.

Loss of Popularity

The Iranian hostage crisis and worsening economic crisis hurt Carter in the opinion polls. In 1979, in what the press called Carter's "national malaise" speech, he blamed the problems of the United States on a "moral and spiritual crisis" of the American people. By that time, however, many Americans blamed the president for weak and indecisive leadership. By the election year 1980 his approval rating had fallen to only 23 percent. In seeking a second term, the unpopular president was clearly vulnerable to political challenges from both Democrats and Republicans.

American Society in Transition

Social changes in the 1970s were of potentially even greater significance than politics. By the end of the decade, for the first time, half of all Americans lived in the fastest-growing sections of the country—the South and the West. Unlike the previous decade, which was dominated by the youth revolt, Americans were conscious in the seventies that the population was aging. The fastest growing age group consisted of senior citizens over 65.

The country's racial and ethnic composition was also changing noticeably in the late 20th century. By 1990, minority groups made up 25 percent of the population. The Census Bureau predicted that, by 2050, as much as half the population would be Hispanic American, African American, or Asian

American. Cultural pluralism was replacing the melting pot as the model for U.S. society, as diverse ethnic and cultural groups strove not only to end discrimination and improve their lives, but also to celebrate their unique traditions.

Growth of Immigration

Before the 1960s, most immigrants to the United States had come from Europe and Canada. By the 1980s, 47 percent of immigrants came from Latin America, 37 percent from Asia, and less than 13 percent from Europe and Canada. In part, this dramatic shift was caused by the arrival of refugees leaving Cuba and Vietnam after the Communist takeovers of these countries. Of far greater importance was the impact of the Immigration Act of 1965, which ended the ethnic quota acts of the 1920s favoring Europeans and thereby opened the United States to immigrants from all parts of the world.

Undocumented Immigrants How many immigrants entered the United States illegally every year could only be estimated, but by the mid-1970s, as many as 12 million foreigners were in the U.S. illegally. The rise in immigrants from countries of Latin America and Asia led to the Immigration Reform and Control Act of 1986, which penalized employers for hiring immigrants who had entered the country illegally or had overstayed their visas, while also granting amnesty to undocumented immigrants arriving by 1982. Even so, many Americans concluded that the nation had lost control of its own borders, as both legal and undocumented immigrants continued to flock to the United States at an estimated million persons a year.

Demands for Minority Rights

One aspect of the protest movements of the 1960s that continued into later decades was the movement by a variety of minorities to gain both relief from discrimination and recognition for their contributions to U.S. society.

Hispanic Americans Most Hispanic Americans before World War II lived in the southwestern states, but in the postwar years new arrivals from Puerto Rico, Cuba, and South and Central America increasingly settled in the East and Midwest. Mexican workers, after suffering deportation during the Great Depression, returned to the United States in the 1950s and 1960s to take low-paying agricultural jobs. They were widely exploited before a long series of boycotts led by Cesar Chavez and the United Farm Workers Organization finally gained collective bargaining rights for farm workers in 1975. Mexican American activists also won a federal mandate for bilingual education requiring schools to teach Hispanic children in both English and Spanish. In the 1980s, a growing number of Hispanic Americans were elected to public office, including as mayors of Miami, San Antonio, and other large cities. The Census Bureau reported that, in 2000, Hispanics, including Cubans, Puerto Ricans, and other Latin Americans, had become the country's largest minority group.

American Indian Movement In the 1950s, the Eisenhower administration had made an unsuccessful attempt to encourage American Indians to leave reservations and assimilate into urban America. American Indian leaders resisted the loss of cultural identity that would have resulted from such a policy. To achieve self-determination and revival of tribal traditions, the American Indian Movement (AIM) was founded in 1968. Militant actions soon followed, including AIM's takeover of the abandoned prison on Alcatraz Island in San Francisco Bay in 1969. AIM members also occupied Wounded Knee, South Dakota, in 1973, site of the infamous massacre of American Indians by the U.S. cavalry in 1890.

American Indians had a number of successes in both Congress and the courts. Congress' passage of the Indian Self-Determination Act of 1975 gave reservations and tribal lands greater control over internal programs, education, and law enforcement. American Indians also used the federal courts successfully to regain property or compensation for treaty violations. They attacked widespread unemployment and poverty on reservations by improving education, through the Tribally Controlled Community College Assistance Act of 1978, and by building industries and gambling casinos on reservations, under the self-determination legislation. Interest in the cultural heritage of American Indians was also overcoming old prejudices. By the 2010 census, nearly three million people identified themselves as American Indian or Alaska Native, and and over two million more identified themselves as a combination of American Indian or Alaska Native and some other ethnic group.

American Indian Population of the United States, 1950 to 2010		
Year	Total	Percentage
1950	343,410	0.2
1960	508,675	0.3
1970	827,255	0.4
1980	1,420,400	0.6
1990	1,959,234	0.8
2000	2,475,956	0.9
2010	2,932,248	0.9

Figures include Alaska Natives
Source: U.S. Census Bureau

Asian Americans Americans of Asian descent had become the fastest growing ethnic minority by the 1980s. The largest group of Asian Americans were of Chinese ancestry, followed by Filipinos, Japanese, Indians, Koreans, and Vietnamese. A strong dedication to education resulted in Asian Americans being well represented in the best colleges and universities. However, at times, Asian Americans suffered from discrimination, envy, and Japan-bashing, while the less educated immigrants earned well below the national average.

Gay Liberation Movement In 1969, a police raid on the Stonewall Inn, a gay bar in New York City, sparked both a riot and the gay rights movement. Gay activists urged homosexuals to be open about their identity and to work to end discrimination and violent abuse. By the mid-1970s, homosexuality was no longer classified as a mental illness and the federal Civil Service dropped its ban on employment of homosexuals. In 1993, President Clinton attempted to end discrimination against gays and lesbians in the military, but settled for the compromise "don't ask, don't tell" policy. People would not be asked or expected to describe their sexual identity, but the military could still expel people for being gay or lesbian.

The Environmental Movement

While the Progressive era conservation movement was fairly small and led by politicians such as Theodore Roosevelt, the modern environmental movement had wide spread popular support. The participation of 20 million citizens in the first Earth Day in 1970 reflected the nation's growing concerns over air and water pollution and the destruction of the natural environment, including wildlife. Media coverage of industrial disasters increased public questioning of the benefits of industry and new technologies, in what some called a "post-modern" culture. Massive oil spills around the world, from off the coast of Santa Barbara California in 1969 to the *Exxon Valdez* oil tanker accident in Alaska in 1989, reinforced fears about the deadly combination of human error and modern technology. Public opinion also turned against building additional nuclear power plants after an accident at the Three Mile Island power plant in Pennsylvania (1979) and the deadly explosion of the Chernobyl nuclear reactor in the Soviet Union (1986).

Protective Legislation The environmental movement borrowed tactics from other protest movements to secure legislation to stop pollution and destruction of nature. In 1970, Congress passed the Clean Air Act and created the Environmental Protection Agency (EPA) and followed this legislation in 1972 with the Clean Water Act, and the Endangered Species Act of 1973. In 1980, the Superfund was created to clean up toxic dumps, such as Love Canal in Niagara Falls, New York. These laws regulated toxic substances, public drinking water systems, dumping of waste, and protected natural environments and wildlife, such as the American bald eagle. In the 1980s, the backlash from business and industry would try to reverse the impact of this legislation.

Conservative Shift

The protest movements by diverse groups in American society seemed to produce more social stress and fragmentation. Combined with a slowing economy and a declining standard of living, these forces left many Americans feeling angry and bitter. A conservative reaction to the liberal policies of the New Deal and the Great Society was gaining strength in the late 1970s and would prove a powerful force in the politics of the next decade.

HISTORICAL PERSPECTIVES: END OF THE IMPERIAL PRESIDENCY?

The Cold War, and the Vietnam War in particular, caused critics in the 1970s to fear the expansion and abuse of power by presidents. They saw parallels between the decline of the Roman Republic and the rise of the powerful emperor system of the Roman Empire during Rome's expansion, and the developments in the political system of the United States during its emergence as a superpower after World War II. The actions of Richard Nixon and the Watergate scandals confirmed many Americans' fears.

Arthur Schlesinger Jr. argued in his book *The Imperial Presidency* (1973) that the United States' exercise of world leadership had gradually undermined the original intent of the Constitution and the war powers of Congress. Cold War presidents had used national security, the need for secrecy, executive privilege, and the mystique of the high office to concentrate power into the White House. The end of the Vietnam War, the resignation of Richard Nixon, and the War Powers Act of 1973 seemed to end the dangers of the imperial presidency. Presidents Ford and Carter proved comparatively weak presidents, and power had seemed to shift back to the Congress, as the Founders had intended.

Schlesinger concluded that the U.S. would continue to need a strong president, but one working within the limits of the Constitution. The issue of the proper constitutional limits on presidential powers reemerged after the terrorist attacks of September 11, 2001. What are the constitutional limits on presidential powers to fight terrorists given invasive reach of the newest electronic and military technologies?

KEY TERMS BY THEME

Nixon Foreign Policy (WOR)
Henry Kissinger
Vietnamization
Nixon Doctrine
Kent State
My Lai
Pentagon Papers
Paris Accords of 1973
détente
China visit
antiballistic missiles
Strategic Arms Limitation Talks (SALT)
Middle East War (1973)
OPEC; oil embargo

Nixon Domestic Policy (POL)
New Federalism
stagflation
southern strategy
wage and price controls
off the gold standard
cost of living indexed
Title IX
Burger Court
Roe v. Wade (1973)
election of 1972
George McGovern
Watergate cover-up
"plumbers"
"enemies list"
United States v. Nixon
War Powers Act (1973)
impeachment and resignation
"imperial presidency"

Ford Presidency (POL, WOR)
Gerald Ford
pardon of Nixon
reform of CIA
fall of Saigon
Cambodia genocide
battle over inflation
Bicentennial
election of 1976

Carter Presidency (WOR, POL)
James Earl (Jimmy) Carter
human rights
Panama Canal Treaty (1978)
Camp David Accords (1978)
Iranian hostage crisis
recognition of China
Soviet Afghanistan invasion
Paul Volcker, high interest rates
"malaise" speech

American Identities (NAT, PEO)
cultural pluralism
impact of 1965 immigration law
Immigration Reform and Control Act (1986)
Hispanic Americans
Cesar Chavez
American Indian Movement
Indian Self-Determination Act (1975)
gaming casinos
Asian Americans
gay liberation movement

Environmental Movement (GEO)
Earth Day (1970)
Exxon Valdez accident
Three Mile Island
Chernobyl meltdown
Clean Air Act (1970)
Environmental Protection Agency (EPA)
Clean Water Act (1972)
Environmental Superfund (1980)
Endangered Species Act (1973)

Questions 1–3 refer to the excerpt below.

"Unlike some anticommunists . . . I have always believed that we can and must communicate and, when possible, negotiate with Communist nations. . . .

"There were, however, a few things in our favor. The most important and interesting was the Soviet split with China. . . .

"It was often said that the key to a Vietnam settlement lay in Moscow and Peking rather than in Hanoi. . . . Aside from wanting to keep Hanoi from going over to Peking, Moscow had little stake in the outcome of the North Vietnamese cause, especially as it increasingly worked against Moscow's own major interests vis-à-vis the United States. While I understood that the Soviets were not entirely free agents where their support for North Vietnam was concerned, I nonetheless planned to bring maximum pressure to bear on them in this area."

—Richard Nixon, *RN: Memoirs of Richard Nixon,* 1978

1. Which of the following best explains why Nixon's foreign policy was a departure from the previous administrations'?
   (A) He was the first president willing to negotiate with Communist leaders
   (B) He was willing to use massive bombing to force an issue
   (C) He turned over his foreign policy to his national security advisor
   (D) He exploited that Communism was not a unified world movement

2. Nixon's bold move to open up relations with Communist China was helped most by
   (A) the support of the Communist leaders in the Soviet Union
   (B) his long history of being a hard-line opponent of communism
   (C) Mao Zedong's belief that the Cultural Revolution had failed
   (D) his belief that Americans trusted China more than the Soviet Union

3. Which of the following was Nixon able to negotiate as a result of his new relationship with China?
   (A) Withdrawal of Chinese troops from Vietnam
   (B) Autonomy for Poland in Eastern Europe
   (C) Freeze on the number of US and USSR ballistic missiles
   (D) A peace treaty between South and North Korea

Questions 4–5 refer to the following cartoon.

Source: A 1974 Herblock Cartoon, © The Herb
Block Foundation

4. Richard Nixon claimed that "I am not a crook," but which of the
   following best explains his crime?
   (A) Destroying evidence that was on the tapes
   (B) Covering up illegal activities of his reelection campaign
   (C) Firing the special prosecutors and his attorney general
   (D) Lying to the grand jury during the investigation

5. Which best explains the role of the tapes in Nixon's fall?
   (A) Transcripts of the tapes were published in the newspapers
   (B) The tapes used in *United States v. Nixon* proved that he was lying
   (C) The tapes provided evidence that he was involved in the cover-up
   (D) The tapes turned his closest advisers against him

"Our people are losing faith, not only in government itself but in their ability as citizens to serve as the ultimate rulers and shapers of our democracy.

"We were sure that ours was a nation of the ballot, not the bullet, until the murders of John Kennedy and Robert Kennedy and Martin Luther King Jr. We were taught that our armies were always invincible and our causes were always just, only to suffer the agony of Vietnam. We respected the Presidency as a place of honor until the shock of Watergate.

"We remember when the phrase 'sound as a dollar' was an expression of absolute dependability, until ten years of inflation began to shrink our dollar and our savings. We believed that our Nation's resources were limitless until 1973, when we had to face a growing dependence on foreign oil."

—Jimmy Carter, *Public Papers of the Presidents of the United States,* 1979

6. Which of the following would most strongly support Carter's contention in his phrase "we were taught that our armies were always invincible"?

   (A) The secret expansion of the Vietnam War into Cambodia by Nixon

   (B) The killing of protesters at Kent State and Jackson State Universities

   (C) The decision by newspapers to publish the Pentagon Papers

   (D) The defeat of South Vietnam by North Vietnam in 1975

7. Why might Carter and historians consider 1973 a turning point in Americans' confidence in the economy?

   (A) Nixon devaluated the dollar by taking it off of the gold standard

   (B) Nixon imposed a wage and price freeze to fight inflation

   (C) The OPEC oil embargo caused runaway inflation and loss of jobs

   (D) President Ford would not take strong measures to fight inflation

8. Which of the following best identifies the effect of the speech from which the above excerpt is taken?

   (A) Consumers increased their efforts to conserve energy

   (B) Americans blamed Carter for weak and ineffective leadership

   (C) Carter increased his approval ratings with his honesty

   (D) The Federal Reserve raised interest rates to support the President

Use complete sentences; an outline or bulleted list alone is not acceptable.

Question 1. Answer (A), (B), and (C).

(A) Briefly explain ONE specific historical event or development during the 1970s that caused a decline in public confidence and trust in the federal government to solve America's problems.

(B) Briefly explain ONE specific historical event or development during the 1970s that promoted the growing clash between liberals and conservatives over social and cultural issues.

(C) Briefly explain ONE specific strategy that President Nixon developed to help make the Republicans the majority political party in the United States.

Question 2. Answer (A), (B), and (C).

(A) Briefly explain ONE specific historical event or development that helped to mobilize either the American Indian movement or the Latino movement to address social and economic inequality or past injustices during the period from 1960 to 1980.

(B) Briefly explain ONE specific historical event or development that helped to mobilize either feminist rights or gay rights during the period from 1960 to 1980.

(C) Briefly explain ONE specific historical event or development that contributed to a growing environmental movement to combat pollution and protect natural resources during the period from 1960 to 1980.

Question 3 is based on the excerpts below.

"Nixon defied simple political characterizations. . . . On most domestic issues he adopted centrist positions, bobbing and weaving in an effort to maintain support from both the liberal and conservative wings of the Republican Party. . . . Nixon hoped to win over some traditionally Democratic constituencies to ensure his reelection and to rebuild the Republican Party as a national party. To woo them, he supported the core of New Deal economic and social programs from which they benefited, even as he took conservative positions on other issues. Sometimes taken with thinking of himself as a Tory [a type of conservative] reformer, Nixon proved willing to take innovative steps most conservatives would blanch at."

—Joshua B. Freeman, historian, *American Empire,* 2012

"At [Nixon's] funeral, Senator Bob Dole prophesied the 'the second half of the twentieth century will be known as the age of Nixon.' What Richard Nixon left behind was the very terms of our national self-image: a notion that there are two kinds of Americans. On the one side, that 'Silent Majority.' The "nonshouters'. . . . [the] coalition who call themselves, now 'Value voters,' "people of faith,' 'patriots,'. . . . who feel themselves condescended to by snobby opinion-making elites. . . . On the other side are 'liberals,' the 'cosmopolitans,' the 'intellectuals,' the 'professionals,' . . . . who say shouting in opposition to injustice is a higher form of patriotism. . . . And both have learned to consider the other not quite Americans at all. The argument over Richard Nixon, pro and con, gave us the language for this war."

—Rick Perlstein, historian and journalist, *Nixonland,* 2008

3. Using the excerpts, answer (A), (B), and (C).

   (A) Briefly describe ONE major difference between Freeman's and Perlstein's historical interpretation of the Nixon presidency.

   (B) Briefly explain ONE specific historical event or development that is not explicitly mentioned in the excerpts that could be used to support Freeman's interpretation of the Nixon presidency.

   (C) Briefly explain ONE specific historical event or development that is not explicitly mentioned in the excerpts that could be used to support Perlstein's interpretation of the Nixon presidency.

Question 4 is based on the following graphs.

IMMIGRATION TO THE UNITED STATES

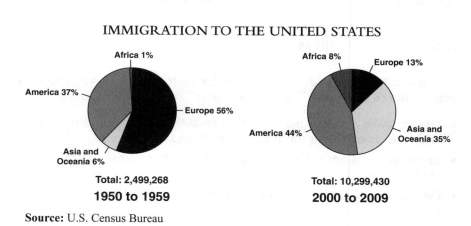

Total: 2,499,268
1950 to 1959

Total: 10,299,430
2000 to 2009

Source: U.S. Census Bureau

4. Using the graphs, answer (A), (B), and (C).

(A) Briefly explain ONE specific change in immigration patterns from the 1950s to the first decade of the 2000s.

(B) Briefly analyze ONE specific way the Immigration Act of 1965 contributed to the changes in immigration patterns.

(C) Briefly explain ONE additional cause of the changes in immigration patterns from the 1950s to the first decade of the 2000s.

THINK AS A HISTORIAN: WRITING CLEAR SENTENCES

In effective writing, each sentence is clear and understandable. Which ONE of the following sentences is most clearly written?

1. U.S. foreign policy, under Nixon, who was complex, was changed in direction.

2. A complex Nixon in foreign policy changed U.S. direction.

3. A complex man, Nixon changed the direction of U.S foreign policy.

UNIT 8: Period 8, 1945–1980

LONG ESSAY QUESTIONS

Directions: The suggested writing time for each question is 40 minutes. In your response you should do the following:

- **Thesis:** Make a defensible claim that establishes a line of reasoning and consists of one or more sentences found in one place.
- **Contextualization:** Relate the argument to a broader historical context.
- **Evidence:** Support an argument with specific and relevant historical evidence.
- **Reasoning:** Organize an argument using the skill in the question.
- **Analysis:** Demonstrate a complex understanding of the question using historical evidence to support, qualify, or modify an argument.

1. Analyze how the Cold War altered the role of the United States in the world from 1945 to 1980.

2. Analyze the impact of the Cold War on domestic politics from 1945 to 1980.

3. Compare and contrast the policies of the New Deal with the Great Society.

4. Compare and contrast the policies and effects of the Quota Acts of 1921 and 1924 with the Immigration Act of 1965.

5. Analyze the changes and continuity in U.S. environmental policies of the Progressive era with the period from 1945 to 1980.

6. Analyze the changes and continuity in the identity and roles of American women from 1945 to 1980.

7. Analyze THREE developments in popular culture that had an impact on American society from 1945 to 1980.

8. Analyze THREE events or developments that had a significant impact on race relations in the United States in the period from 1945 to 1980.

9. Analyze the changing impact on American workers of U.S. interconnection with other world economies during the period from 1945 to 1980.

10. Analyze how the role of the federal government in the American economy changed during the period from 1945 to 1980.

DOCUMENT-BASED QUESTION

Directions: Question 1 is based on the accompanying documents. The documents have been edited for the purpose of this exercise. You are advised to spend 15 minutes planning and 45 minutes writing your answer. In your response you should do the following:

- **Thesis:** Make a defensible claim that establishes a line of reasoning and consists of one or more sentences found in one place.
- **Contextualization:** Relate the argument to a broader historical context.
- **Document Evidence:** Use content from at least six documents.
- **Outside Evidence:** Use one piece of evidence not in the documents.
- **Document Sourcing:** Explain how or why the point of view, purpose, situation, or intended audience is relevant for at least three documents.
- **Analysis:** Show the relationships among pieces of historical evidence and use them to support, qualify, or modify an argument.

1. Compare and contrast the roles of the federal government and the civil rights activists in achieving the goals of the civil rights movement from 1945 through 1968.

Document 1

> **Source:** Harry S. Truman, *Establishing the President's Committee on Equality of Treatment and Opportunity in the Armed Services,* July 1948
>
> "Whereas it is essential that there be maintained in the armed services of the United States the highest standards of democracy, with equality of treatment and opportunity for all those who serve in our country's defense:
>
> "1. It is hereby declared to be the policy of the President that there shall be equality of treatment and opportunity for all persons in the armed forces without regard to race, color, religion, or national origin. This policy shall be put into effect as rapidly as possible, having regard to the time required to effectuate any necessary changes without impairing efficiency or morale."

Document 2

Source: Jo Ann Gibson Robinson, civil rights organizer, *The Montgomery Bus Boycott and the Women Who Started It,* 1987

"The news [of Mrs. Parks' arrest] traveled like wildfire into every black home. Telephones jangled; people congregated on street corners and in homes and talked. But nothing was done. A numbing helplessness seemed to paralyze everyone. . . .

"Lost in thought, I was startled by the telephone's ring. Black attorney Fred Gray. . . . had just gotten back and was returning the phone message I had left him about Mrs. Parks' arrest.

"Fred was shocked by the news of Mrs. Parks' arrest. I informed him that I already was thinking that the WPC [Women's Political Council] should distribute thousands of notices calling for all bus riders to stay off the buses. . . . 'Are you ready?' he asked. Without hesitation, I assured him that we were. With that he hung up, and I went to work.

"I made some notes on the back of an envelope: 'The Women's Political Council will not wait for Mrs. Parks' consent to call for a boycott of city buses. On Friday, December 1, 1955, the women of Montgomery will call for a boycott to take place on Monday, December 5.'"

Document 3

Source: Governor George C. Wallace, Proclamation at the University of Alabama, June 11, 1963

"I stand here today, as Governor of this sovereign State, and refuse to willingly submit to illegal usurpation of power by the Central Government. I claim today for all the people of the State of Alabama those rights reserved to them under the Constitution of the United States. Among those powers so reserved and claimed is the right of state authority in the operation of the public schools, colleges, and universities.

My action does not constitute disobedience to legislative and constitutional provisions. It is not defiance for defiance sake, but for the purpose of raising basic and fundamental constitutional questions. My action is raising a call for strict adherence to the Constitution of the United States as it was written—for a cessation of usurpation and abuses. My action seeks to avoid having state sovereignty sacrificed on the altar of political expediency."

Document 4

Source: March on Washington for Jobs and Freedom, August 28, 1963. Library of Congress

Document 5

Source: Malcolm X's Speech in Cleveland, Ohio, April 3, 1964

"The question tonight, as I understand it, is 'The Negro Revolt, and Where Do We Go From Here?', or 'What Next?'" In my little humble way of understanding it, it points toward either the ballot or the bullet. . . .

"The black nationalists aren't going to wait. Lyndon B. Johnson is the head of the Democratic Party. If he's for civil rights, let him go into the Senate next week and declare himself. Let him go in there right now and declare himself. Let him go in there and denounce the Southern branch of his party. Let him go in there right now and take a moral stand—right now, not later. Tell him, don't wait until election time. If he waits too long, brothers and sisters, he will be responsible for letting a condition develop in this country which will create a climate that will bring seeds up out of the ground with vegetation on the end of them looking like something these people never dreamed of. In 1964, it's the ballot or the bullet."

Document 6

Source: Martin Luther King Jr. Acceptance speech for the Nobel Peace Prize, December 10, 1964

"I accept the Nobel Prize for Peace at a moment when 22 million Negroes of the United States of America are engaged in a creative battle to end the long night of racial injustice. I accept this award on behalf of a civil rights movement which is moving with determination and a majestic scorn for risk and danger to establish a reign of freedom and a rule of justice. I am mindful that only yesterday in Birmingham, Alabama, our children, crying out for brotherhood, were answered with fire hoses, snarling dogs and even death. I am mindful that only yesterday in Philadelphia, Mississippi, young people seeking to secure the right to vote were brutalized and murdered. And only yesterday more than 40 houses of worship in the State of Mississippi alone were bombed or burned because they offered a sanctuary to those who would not accept segregation. I am mindful that debilitating and grinding poverty afflicts my people and chains them to the lowest rung of the economic ladder.

"The tortuous road which has led from Montgomery, Alabama, to Oslo bears witness to this truth [nonviolence]. This is a road over which millions of Negroes are travelling to find a new sense of dignity. This same road has opened for all Americans a new era of progress and hope. It has led to a new Civil Rights Bill, and it will, I am convinced, be widened and lengthened into a super highway of justice as Negro and white men in increasing numbers create alliances to overcome their common problems."

Document 7

Source: President Lyndon B. Johnson, Speech to Congress and the Nation, March 15, 1965

"At times, history and fate meet at a single time in a single place to shape a turning point in man's unending search for freedom. So it was at Lexington and Concord. So it was a century ago at Appomattox. So it was last week in Selma, Alabama. There, long suffering men and women peacefully protested the denial of their rights as Americans. Many of them were brutally assaulted. One good man—a man of God—was killed. . . .

"But I want to really discuss with you now briefly the main proposals of this legislation. This bill will strike down restrictions to voting in all elections—federal, state, and local—which have been used to deny Negroes the right to vote.
. . .

"But even if we pass this bill, the battle will not be over. What happened in Selma is part of a far larger movement, which reaches into every section and State of America. It is the effort of American Negroes to secure for themselves the full blessings of American life. Their cause must be our cause too. Because it is not just Negroes, but really it is all of us, who must overcome the crippling legacy of bigotry and injustice. And we shall overcome."

UNIT 9: Unit 9, 1980–Present

Chapter 30 *Conservative Resurgence, 1980–2000*

Chapter 31 *Challenges of the 21st Century, 2000–Present*

The election of Ronald Reagan in 1980 signaled the closing of the chapter on the post-war era. The United States entered a more conservative political era in which Republicans would hold the White House for most of the following four decades.

Overview The decline of faith in the federal government's ability to solve social and economic problems, the championing of unregulated markets by American corporations, and the growth of religious fundamentalism combined to give conservatism new life. The demographic growth of the Sunbelt and the shift of Southern white conservative voters to the Republican party also helped create an electoral majority. Conservatives achieved some of their goals, but the enduring popularity of government programs such as Social Security and Medicare limited the amount of actual change.

The Reagan administration pursued an aggressive anti-communist foreign policy, but the end of the Cold War took away the 45-year focus of U.S. foreign policy. After the terrorists' attacks of September 11, 2001, the United States quickly became involved in wars in Afghanistan and Iraq and adopted a new focus on homeland security.

The Great Recession of 2008 and demographic and cultural changes deepened the political divide in the nation between an older white population who dominated the Tea Party movement and a younger multicultural society who represented the new emerging majority. This divide showed clearly in the bitterly fought presidential election between Hillary Clinton and Donald Trump in 2016. Trump won, but narrowly. With the changing of a very small percentage of the votes in a few states, Clinton would have won.

Alternate View Some analysts of American politics doubted whether the country was becoming more conservative or more divided. While politicians who identified as conservative did well in elections, polls suggested that the American population was becoming more liberal. Majorities supported traditionally liberal positions such as shifting the tax burden toward the wealthy, passing laws to protect the environment, and ending discrimination against people who were gay or lesbian.

Further, some argued that the division in the country reflected realignments of the parties more than any consistent change in the overall political attitudes. That is, while elected Democrats were more consistently liberal and elected Republicans were more consistently conservative than ever, the American people as a whole were not shifting significantly in any direction.

30

CONSERVATIVE RESURGENCE, 1980-2000

In this present crisis, government is not the solution to our problem;
government is the problem.

President Ronald Reagan, Inaugural Address, January 20, 1981

The most important changes during the 1980s and 1990s included the collapse of communism in Eastern Europe, the breakup of the Soviet Union, and the end of the Cold War. In the post-Cold War world, older ethnic and religious conflicts reemerged to threaten the peace with civil wars and terrorism. On the domestic scene, the conservative agenda of the Reagan administration (1981–1989)—for a stronger military, lower taxes, fewer social programs, and traditional cultural values—helped the Republicans to dominate much of national politics in the 1980s and 1990s.

The Rise of Conservatism

Even though Barry Goldwater was defeated in a landslide in the election of 1964, his campaign for the presidency marked the beginning of the resurgence of conservatism. The policies of presidents Nixon and Ford and the writings of the conservative political commentator William F. Buckley Jr. and the free-market economist Milton Friedman gave evidence in the 1970s of a steady shift to the right, away from the liberalism of the 1960s. By 1980, a loose coalition of economic and political conservatives, religious fundamentalists, and political action committees (PACs) had become a potent force for change. These groups opposed big government, New Deal liberalism, gun control, feminism, gay rights, welfare, affirmative action, sexual permissiveness, abortion, and drug use. They believed that these issues were undermining family and religious values, the work ethic, and national security.

Leading Issues

By 1980, various activists had taken the lead in establishing a conservative agenda for the nation, which included such diverse causes as lower taxes, changed morals, and reduced emphasis on affirmative action.

Taxpayers' Revolt In 1978, California voters led the revolt against increasing taxes by passing Proposition 13, a measure that sharply cut property taxes. Nationally, conservatives promoted economist Arthur Laffer's belief that tax cuts would increase government revenues. Two Republican members of Congress, Jack Kemp and William Roth, proposed legislation to reduce federal taxes by 30 percent, which became the basis for the Reagan tax cuts.

Conservative Religious Revival Moral decay was a weekly theme of religious leaders on television such as Pat Robertson, Oral Roberts, and Jim Baker. By 1980, televangelists had a combined weekly audience of between 60 and 100 million viewers. Religion became an instrument of electoral politics when an evangelist from Virginia, Jerry Falwell, founded the Moral Majority, which financed campaigns to unseat liberal members of Congress. Religious fundamentalists attacked "secular humanism" as a godless creed taking over public education and also campaigned for the return of prayers and the teaching of the Biblical account of creation in public schools. The legalization of abortion in the *Roe* v. *Wade* (1973) decision sparked the right-to-life movement. This movement united Catholics and fundamentalist Protestants, who believed that human life begins at the moment of conception.

Elimination of Racial Preferences In 1965, President Johnson had committed the U.S. government to a policy of affirmative action to ensure that underprivileged minorities and women would have equal access to education, jobs, and promotions. Suffering through years of recession and stagflation in the 1970s, many whites blamed their troubles on affirmative action, calling it "reverse discrimination." In a landmark court case challenging the admissions policies of one medical school, *Regents of the University of California* v. *Bakke* (1978), the Supreme Court ruled that while race could be considered, the school had created racial quotas, which were unconstitutional. Using this decision, conservatives intensified their campaign to end all preferences based on race and ethnicity.

De-Regulation of Business Starting in the 1970s, business interests launched a very successful campaign to mobilize and influence federal and state governments to curtail regulations, lower taxes, and weaken labor unions. Business donors created "think tanks," such as the American Enterprise Institute, the Heritage Foundation, and the Cato Institute, to promote free-market ideas, while the U.S. Chamber of Commerce lobbied for pro-business legislation.

Ronald Reagan and the Election of 1980

Ronald Reagan, a well-known movie and television actor, gained fame among Republicans as an effective political speaker in the 1964 Goldwater campaign. He was soon elected the governor of California, the nation's most populous state. By 1976, Reagan was the party's leading spokesperson for conservative positions, and he almost defeated President Ford for the nomination. Handsome and vigorous in his late sixties, he proved a master of the media and was seen by millions as a likable and sensible champion of average Americans. In 1980, Reagan won the Republican nomination.

Campaign for President, 1980 Senator Edward Kennedy's challenge to President Carter for the Democratic nomination left Carter battered in the polls.

As the Republican nominee, Reagan attacked the Democrats for expanding government and for undermining U.S. prestige abroad. (Throughout the campaign, American hostages remained in the hands of Iranian radicals.) Reagan also pointed to a "misery index" of 28 (rate of inflation added to the rate of unemployment) and concluded his campaign by asking a huge television audience, "Are you better off now than you were four years ago?" The voters' rejection of Carter's presidency and the growing conservative mood gave Reagan 51 percent of the popular vote and almost 91 percent of the electoral vote. Carter received 41 percent of the popular vote. A third candidate, John Anderson, a moderate Republican running as an independent, received 8 percent.

Significance Reagan's election broke up a key element of the New Deal coalition by taking more than 50 percent of the blue-collar vote. The defeat of 11 liberal Democratic senators targeted by the Moral Majority gave the Republicans control of the Senate for the first time since 1954. The Republicans also gained 33 seats in the House, which when combined with the votes of conservative southern Democrats, would give them a working majority on many key issues. The 1980 election ended a half-century of Democratic dominance of Congress.

The Reagan Revolution

On the very day that Reagan was inaugurated, the Iranians released the 52 American hostages, giving his administration a positive start. Two months later, the president survived a serious gunshot wound from an assassination attempt. Reagan handled the crisis with such humor and charm that he emerged from the ordeal as an even more popular leader. He pledged that his administra- tion would lower taxes, reduce government spending on welfare, build up the U.S. armed forces, and create a more conservative federal court. He delivered on all four promises—but there were costs.

Supply-Side Economics ("Reaganomics")

The Reagan administration advocated supply-side economics, arguing that tax cuts and reduced government spending would increase investment by the private sector, which would lead to increased production, jobs, and prosperity. This approach contrasted with the Keynesian economics long favored by the Democrats, which relied on government spending during economic downturns to boost consumer income and demand. Critics of the supply-side theory compared it to the "trickle-down" economics of the 1920s, in which wealthy Americans prospered, and some of their increased spending benefited the middle class and the poor.

Federal Tax Reduction The legislative activity early in Reagan's presidency reminded some in the media of FDR's Hundred Days. Congress passed the Economic Recovery Act of 1981, which included a 25 percent decrease in personal income taxes over three years. Cuts in the corporate income tax, capital gains tax, and gift and inheritance taxes guaranteed that a large share of the tax relief went to upper-income taxpayers. Under Reagan, the top income

Source: Len Boro/Rothco

tax rate was reduced to 28 percent. At the same time, small investors were also helped by a provision that allowed them to invest up to $2,000 a year in Individual Retirement Accounts (IRAs) without paying taxes on this money.

Spending Cuts With the help of conservative southern Democrats ("boll weevils"), the Republicans cut more than $40 billion from domestic programs, such as food stamps, student loans, and mass transportation. However, these savings were offset by a dramatic increase in military spending. Reagan pushed through no cuts in Medicare or Social Security, but he did support and sign into law a bipartisan bill to strengthen Social Security. The law increased what individuals paid into the system, raised the age at which they could get full benefits to 67, and taxed some benefits paid to upper-income recipients.

Deregulation

Following up on the promise of "getting government off the backs of the people," the Reagan administration reduced federal regulations on business and industry—a policy of deregulation begun under Carter. Restrictions were eased on savings and loan institutions, mergers and takeovers by large corporations, and environmental protection. To help the struggling American auto industry, regulations on emissions and auto safety were also reduced. Secretary of the Interior James Watt opened federal lands for increased coal and timber produc- tion and offshore waters for oil drilling.

Labor Unions

Despite having once been the president of the Screen Actors Guild, Reagan took a tough stand against unions. He fired thousands of striking federal air traffic controllers for violating their contract and decertified their union (PATCO). Many businesses followed this action by hiring striker replacements in labor conflicts. These anti-union policies along with the loss of manufacturing jobs hastened the decline of union membership among nonfarm workers from more than 30 percent in 1962 to only 12 percent in the late 1990s. In addition, the recession of 1982 and foreign competition had a dampening effect on workers' wages.

Recession and Recovery

In 1982, the nation suffered the worst recession since the 1930s. Banks failed and unemployment reached 11 percent. However, the recession, along with a fall in oil prices, reduced the double-digit inflation rate of the late 1970s to less than 4 percent. As the policies of Reaganomics took hold, the economy rebounded and beginning in 1983 entered a long period of recovery. However, the recovery only widened the income gap between rich and poor. While upper-income groups, including well-educated workers and "yuppies" (young urban professionals) enjoyed higher incomes from a deregulated marketplace, the standard of living of the middle class remained stagnant or declined. Not until the late 1990s did the middle class gain back some of its losses.

Social Issues

President Reagan followed through on his pledge to appoint conservative judges to the Supreme Court by nominating Sandra Day O'Connor, the first woman on the Court, as well as Antonin Scalia and Anthony Kennedy. Led by a new chief justice, William Rehnquist, the Supreme Court scaled back affirmative action in hiring and promotions, and limited *Roe* v. *Wade* by allowing states to impose certain restrictions on abortion, such as requiring minors to notify their parents before having an abortion.

The Election of 1984

The return of prosperity, even if not fully shared by all Americans, restored public confidence in the Reagan administration. At their convention in 1984, Republicans nominated their popular president by acclamation. Among Democrats, Jesse Jackson became the first African American politician to make a strong run for the presidency by seeking the support of all minority groups under the banner of the National Rainbow Coalition. However, Democrats nominated Walter Mondale, Carter's vice president, to be their presidential candidate. For vice president, they chose Representative Geraldine Ferraro of New York, the first woman to run for vice president on a major party ticket.

President Reagan campaigned on an optimistic "It's Morning Again in America" theme. Reagan took every state except Mondale's home state of Minnesota. Two-thirds of white males voted for Reagan. Analysis of voting returns indicated that only two groups still favored the Democrats: African Americans and those earning less than $12,500 a year.

Budget and Trade Deficits

By the mid-1980s, Reagan's tax cuts combined with large increases in military spending were creating federal deficits of more than $200 billion a year. Over the course of Reagan's two terms as president, the national debt tripled from about $900 billion to almost $2.7 trillion. The tax cuts, designed to stimulate investments, seemed only to increase consumption, especially of foreign-made luxury and consumer items. As a result, the U.S. trade deficit reached a then-staggering $150 billion a year. The cumulative trade imbalance of $1 trillion during the 1980s contributed to a dramatic increase in the foreign ownership of U.S. real estate and industry. In 1985, for the first time since the World War I era, the United States became a debtor nation.

In an effort to reduce the federal deficit, Congress in 1985 passed the Gramm-Rudman-Hollings Balanced Budget Act, which provided for across-the-board spending cuts. Court rulings and later congressional changes kept this legislation from achieving its full purpose, but Congress was still able to reduce the deficit by $66 billion from 1986 to 1988.

Impact of Reaganomics

President Reagan's two terms reduced restrictions on a free-market economy and put more money in the hands of investors and higher income Americans. Reagan's policies also succeeded in containing the growth of the New Deal-Great Society welfare state. Another legacy of the Reagan years were the huge federal deficits of $200 to 300 billion a year, which changed the context of future political debates. With yearly deficits running between $200 and $300 billion, it no longer seemed reasonable for either Democrats or Republicans to propose new social programs, such as universal health coverage. Instead of asking what new government programs might be needed, Reaganomics changed the debate to issues of which government programs to cut and by how much.

Foreign Policy During the Reagan Years

Reagan started his presidency determined to restore the military might and superpower prestige of the United States and to intensify the Cold War competition with the Soviet Union. He called the Soviet Communists "the evil empire" and "focus of evil in the modern world." Reagan was prepared to use military force to back up his rhetoric. During his second term, however, he proved flexible enough in his foreign policy to respond to significant changes in the Soviet Union and its satellites in Eastern Europe.

Renewing the Cold War

Increased spending for defense and aid to anti-communist forces in Latin America were the hallmarks of Reagan's approach to the Cold War during his first term.

Military Buildup The Reagan administration spent billions to build new weapons systems, such as the B-1 bomber and the MX missile, and to expand the U.S. Navy from 450 to 600 ships. The administration also increased spending on the Strategic Defense Initiative (SDI), an ambitious plan for building a high-tech system of lasers and particle beams to destroy enemy missiles before they could reach U.S. territory. Critics called the SDI "Star Wars" and argued that the costly program would only escalate the arms race and could be overwhelmed by the Soviets building more missiles. Although Congress made some cuts in the Reagan proposals, the defense budget grew from $171 billion in 1981 to more than $300 billion in 1985.

Central America In the Americas, Reagan supported "friendly" right-wing dictators to keep out communism. In Nicaragua in 1979, a Marxist movement known as the Sandinistas had overthrown the country's dictator. In response, the United States provided significant military aid to the "contras" in their effort to dislodge the Sandinistas. In 1985, Democrats opposed to the administration's policies in Nicaragua passed the Boland Amendment, which prohibited further aid to the contras.

In El Salvador, meanwhile, the Reagan administration spent nearly $5 billion to support the Salvadoran government against a coalition of leftist guerrillas. Many Americans protested the killing of more than 40,000 civilians, including American missionaries, by right-wing "death squads" with connections to the El Salvador army.

Grenada On the small Caribbean island of Grenada, a coup led to the establishment of a pro-Cuban regime. In October 1983, President Reagan ordered a small force of marines to invade the island in order to prevent the establishment of a strategic Communist military base in the Americas. The invasion quickly succeeded in re-establishing a pro-U.S. government in Grenada.

Iran-Contra Affair If Grenada was the notable military triumph of Reagan's presidency, his efforts to aid the Nicaraguan contras involved him in a serious blunder and scandal. The so-called Iran-contra affair had its origins in U.S. troubles with Iran. Since 1980, Iran and Iraq had been engaged in a bloody war. Reagan aides came up with the plan—kept secret from the American public—of selling U.S. antitank and anti-aircraft missiles to Iran's government for its help in freeing the Americans held hostage by a radical Arab group. In 1986, another Reagan staff member had the "great idea" to use the profits of the arms deal with Iran to fund the contras in Nicaragua.

President Reagan denied that he had knowledge of the illegal diversion of funds—illegal in that it violated both the Boland Amendment and congressional budget authority. The picture that emerged from a televised congressional investigation was of an uninformed, hands-off president who was easily manipulated by his advisers. Reagan suffered a sharp, but temporary, drop in the popularity polls.

Lebanon, Israel, and the PLO

Reagan suffered a series of setbacks in the Middle East. In 1982, Israel (with U.S. approval) invaded southern Lebanon to stop Palestinian Liberation Organization (PLO) terrorists from raiding Israel. Soon the United States sent peacekeeping forces into Lebanon in an effort to contain that country's bitter civil war. In April 1983, an Arab suicide squad bombed the U.S. embassy in Beirut, killing 63 people. A few months later, another Arab terrorist drove a bomb-filled truck into the U.S. Marines barracks, killing 241 servicemen. In 1984, Reagan pulled U.S. forces out of Lebanon, with little to show for the effort and loss of lives.

Secretary of State George Schultz pushed for a peaceful settlement of the Palestinian-Israeli conflict by setting up a homeland for the PLO in the West

Bank territories occupied by Israel since the 1967 war. Under U.S. pressure, PLO leader Yasser Arafat agreed in 1988 to recognize Israel's right to exist.

Improved U.S.-Soviet Relations

The Cold War intensified in the early 1980s as a result of both Reagan's arms buildup and the Soviet deployment of a larger number of missiles against NATO countries. In 1985, however, a dynamic reformer, Mikhail Gorbachev, became the new Soviet leader. Gorbachev attempted to change Soviet domestic politics by introducing two major reforms: (1) *glasnost,* or openness, to end political repression and move toward greater political freedom for Soviet citizens, and (2) *perestroika,* or restructuring of the Soviet economy by introducing some free-market practices. To achieve his reforms, Gorbachev wanted to end the costly arms race and deal with a deteriorating Soviet economy. In 1987, President Reagan challenged the Soviet leader to follow through with his reforms. In front of Brandenburg Gate and the Berlin Wall, a divisive symbol of the Cold War, Reagan ended his speech with the line, "Mr. Gorbachev, tear down this wall."

Gorbachev and Reagan did agree to remove and destroy all intermediate-range missiles (the INF agreement). In 1988, Gorbachev further reduced Cold War tensions by starting the pullout of Soviet troops from Afghanistan. He also cooperated with the United States in putting diplomatic pressure on Iran and Iraq to end their war. By the end of Reagan's second term, superpower relations had so improved that the end of the Cold War seemed at hand.

Assessing Reagan's Policy The Reagan administration argued that its military buildup forced the Soviet Union to concede defeat and abandon the

'I CAN'T BELIEVE MY EYES!'

Cold War. Some have concluded that Gorbachev ended the Cold War in order to reform the troubled Communist economic and political system. And yet others have given credit to George Kennan's containment policies. Whatever caused the Soviets to change their policy, Reagan responded by seizing the opportunity to end the Cold War.

Source: Edmund S. Valtman / Library of Congress. 1991

By the end of Reagan's second term in 1988, "the Great Communicator's" combination of style, humor, and expressions of patriotism had won over the electorate. He would leave office as one of the most popular presidents of the 20th century. In addition, he changed the politics of the nation for at least a generation by bringing many former Democrats into the Republican party.

George H. W. Bush and the End of the Cold War

The Cold War had threatened the very existence of humankind. At the same time, ever since 1945, the conflict had given clear purpose and structure to U.S. foreign policy. What would be the role of the United States in the world *after* the Cold War? George H. W. Bush, a former ambassador to the United Nations and director of the CIA (and the father of President George W. Bush), became the first president to define the country's role in the new era.

The Election of 1988

The Democrats regained control of the Senate in 1986 and expected that the Iran-contra scandal and the huge deficits under Reagan would hurt the Republicans in the presidential race of 1988. Michael Dukakis, governor of Massachusetts, won the Democratic nomination and balanced the ticket by selecting Senator Lloyd Bentsen of Texas as his running mate. The Republican candidates were Reagan's vice president, George H. W. Bush, and a young Indiana senator, Dan Quayle. Bush did not have Reagan's ease in front of the camera, but he quickly overtook an expressionless Dukakis by charging that the Democrat was soft on crime (for furloughing criminals) and weak on national defense. Bush also appealed to voters by promising not to raise taxes: "Read my lips—no new taxes."

The Republicans won a decisive victory in November by a margin of 7 million votes. Once again, the Democrats failed to win the confidence of most white middle-class voters. Nevertheless, the voters sent mixed signals by returning larger Democratic majorities to both the House and the Senate. Americans evidently believed in the system of checks and balances, but it often produced legislative gridlock in Washington.

The Collapse of Soviet Communism and the Soviet Union

The first years of the Bush administration were dominated by dramatic changes in the Communist world.

Tiananmen Square In China during the spring of 1989, prodemocracy students demonstrated for freedom in Beijing's Tiananmen Square. Television cameras from the West broadcast the democracy movement around the world. Under the cover of night, the Chinese Communist government crushed the protest with tanks, killing hundreds and ending the brief flowering of an open political environment in China.

Eastern Europe Challenges to communism in Eastern Europe produced more positive results. Gorbachev declared that he would no longer support the various Communist governments of Eastern Europe with Soviet armed forces.

Starting in Poland in 1989 with the election of Lech Walesa, the leader of the once-outlawed Solidarity movement, the Communist party fell from power in one country after another—Hungary, Czechoslovakia, Bulgaria, and Romania. The Communists in East Germany were forced out of power after protesters tore down the Berlin Wall, the hated symbol of the Cold War. In October 1990, the two Germanys, divided since 1945, were finally reunited with the blessing of both NATO and the Soviet Union.

Breakup of the Soviet Union The swift march of events and the nationalist desire for self-determination soon overwhelmed Gorbachev and the Soviet Union. In 1990 the Soviet Baltic republics of Estonia, Latvia, and Lithuania declared their independence. After a failed coup against Gorbachev by Communist hard-liners, the remaining republics dissolved the Soviet Union in December 1991, leaving Gorbachev a leader with no country. Boris Yeltsin, president of the Russian Republic, joined with nine former Soviet republics to form a loose confederation, the Commonwealth of Independent States (CIS). Yeltsin disbanded the Communist party in Russia and attempted to establish a democracy and a free-market economy.

End of the Cold War Sweeping agreements to dismantle their nuclear weapons were one piece of tangible proof that the Cold War had ended. Bush and Gorbachev signed the START I agreement in 1991, reducing the number of nuclear warheads to under 10,000 for each side. In late 1992, Bush and Yeltsin agreed to a START II treaty, which reduced the number of nuclear weapons to just over 3,000 each. The treaty also offered U.S. economic assistance to the troubled Russian economy.

EASTERN EUROPE AFTER THE FALL OF COMMUNISM

Even as Soviet Communism collapsed, President Bush, a seasoned diplomat, remained cautious. Instead of celebrating final victory in the Cold War, Americans grew concerned about the outbreak of civil wars and violence in the former Soviet Union. In Eastern Europe, Yugoslavia started to disintegrate in 1991, and a civil war broke out in the province of Bosnia and Herzegovina in 1992. At home, the end of the Cold War raised questions about whether the United States still needed such heavy defense spending and as many U.S. military bases around the world.

Invasion of Panama

Since the outbreak of the Cold War in the 1940s, U.S. intervention in foreign conflicts had been consistently tied to the containment of communism. In December 1989, U.S. troops were used for a different purpose, as Bush ordered the invasion of Panama to remove the autocratic General Manuel Noriega. The alleged purpose of the invasion was to stop Noriega from using his country as a drug pipeline to the United States. U.S. troops remained until elections established a more credible government.

Persian Gulf War

President Bush's hopes for a "new world order" of peace and democracy were challenged in August 1990 when Iraq's dictator, Saddam Hussein, invaded oil-rich but weak Kuwait. This move threatened Western oil sources in Saudi Arabia and the Persian Gulf. President Bush successfully built a coalition of United Nations members to pressure Hussein to withdraw from Kuwait. However, a U.N. embargo against Iraq had little effect. Bush won congressional approval for a military campaign to roll back Iraq's aggression. In January 1991, in a massive operation called Desert Storm, more than 500,00 Americans were joined by military units from 28 other nations. Five weeks of relentless air strikes were followed by a brilliant invasion led by U.S. General Norman Schwarzkopf. After only 100 hours of fighting on the ground, Iraq conceded defeat.

Some Americans were disappointed that the United States stopped short of driving Saddam Hussein from power in Iraq. Nevertheless, after the victory, Bush enjoyed a boost in his approval rating to nearly 90 percent.

Domestic Problems

President Bush's political future seemed secure based on his foreign policy successes, but a host of domestic problems dogged his administration.

Nomination of Clarence Thomas The president's nomination of Clarence Thomas to the Supreme Court to replace the retiring Thurgood Marshall proved extremely controversial. Thomas's conservative views on judicial issues and charges of sexual harassment against him particularly angered African Americans and women. Nevertheless, the Senate confirmed him.

Taxes and the Economy Americans were shocked to learn that the government's intervention to save weak savings and loan institutions (S&Ls) and to pay insured depositors for funds lost in failed S&Ls would cost the taxpayers more than $250 billion. Also disturbing were the federal budget deficits of more than $250 billion a year. Many Republicans felt betrayed when, in 1990, Bush violated his campaign pledge of "no new taxes" by agreeing to accept the Democratic Congress' proposed $133 billion in new taxes. The unpopular tax law increased the top income tax rate to 31 percent and raised federal excise taxes on beer, wine, cigarettes, gasoline, luxury cars, and yachts. Most damaging of all for Bush's re-election prospects was a recession starting in 1990 that ended the Reagan era of prosperity, increased unemployment, and decreased average family income.

Political Inertia President Bush began his administration calling for "a kinder, gentler America" and declaring himself the "education president." He did sign into law the Americans With Disabilities Act (1990), which prohibited discrimination against citizens with physical and mental disabilities in hiring, transportation, and public accommodation. Outside of this accomplishment, the president offered little in the way of domestic policy. In the midst of recession, he emphasized cuts in federal programs. This seemed to offer little hope to growing numbers of Americans left behind by the "Reagan revolution."

The Clinton Years: Prosperity and Partisanship

During the last years of the 20th century, the United States enjoyed a period of unrivaled economic growth and technological innovation. The end of the Cold War allowed Americans to focus more on economic and domestic issues. But, during this period, American politics became more divided and bitter.

Anti-Incumbent Mood

A stagnant economy, huge budget deficits, and political deadlock fueled a growing disillusionment with government, especially as practiced in the nation's capital. The movement to impose term limits on elected officials gained popularity on the state level, but the Supreme Court ruled in *U.S. Term Limits Inc. v. Thorton* (1995) that the states could not limit the tenure of federal lawmakers without a constitutional amendment.

Another reflection of Americans' disillusionment with Washington politics was the ratification in 1992 of the 27th Amendment. First proposed by James Madison in 1789, this amendment prohibited members of Congress from raising their own salaries. Future raises could not go into effect until the next session of Congress.

The Election of 1992

As expected, George H. Bush was nominated by the Republicans for a second term. After a long career in public service, the president seemed tired and out of touch with average Americans, who were more concerned about their paychecks than with Bush's foreign policy successes.

William Jefferson Clinton Among Democrats, Bill Clinton, the youthful governor of Arkansas, emerged from the primaries as his party's choice for president. The first member of the baby-boom generation to be nominated for president, Clinton proved an articulate and energetic campaigner. He presented himself as a moderate "New Democrat," who focused on economic issues such as jobs, education, and health care, which were important to the "vital center" of the electorate. The strategy was known among his political advisers as: "It's the economy, stupid!"

H. Ross Perot Ross Perot, a Texas billionaire, entered the 1992 race for president as an independent. Able to use his own resources to finance a series of TV commercials, Perot appealed to millions with his anti-Washington, anti-deficit views. On election day, Perot captured nearly 20 percent of the popular vote for the best third-party showing since Theodore Roosevelt and the Bull Moose campaign of 1912.

Results Despite the serious challenge from Perot, the front-runners still divided up all the electoral votes: 370 for Clinton (and 43 percent of the popular vote), 168 for Bush (37 percent of the popular vote). Clinton and his running mate, Senator Albert Gore of Tennessee, did well in the South and recaptured the majority of the elderly and blue-collar workers from the Republicans. In addition, the Democrats again won control of both houses of Congress. The new Congress better reflected the diversity of the U.S. population. Among its 66 minority members and 48 women was Carol Moseley-Braun of Illinois, the first African American woman to be elected to the Senate.

Clinton's First Term (1993–1997)

During the first two years of the Clinton administration, Senate Republicans used filibusters to kill the president's economic stimulus package, campaign-finance reform, environmental bills, and health care reform. The president assigned his wife, Hillary Rodham Clinton, to head a task force to propose a plan for universal health coverage, which had been a goal of the Democrats since the Truman presidency. The complicated health care proposal ran into determined opposition from the insurance industry, small business organizations, and the Republicans, and it failed to pass again. Clinton also failed to end discrimination against gays in the military and settled for the rule, "Don't ask, don't tell." Under this policy, members of the military could still be expelled for being gay or lesbian, but they would not routinely be asked or expected to volunteer information about their sexual orientation.

Early Accomplishments The Democratic Congress was able to pass the Family and Medical Leave Act and the "motor-voter" law that enabled citizens to register to vote as they received their driver's licenses. The Brady Handgun bill, which mandated a five-day waiting period for the purchase of handguns, was enacted. In 1994, Congress enacted Clinton's Anti-Crime Bill, which provided $30 billion in funding for more police protection and crime-prevention programs. The legislation also banned the sale of most assault rifles, which angered the gun lobby led by the National Rifle Association (NRA). After protracted negotiation and compromise, Congress passed a deficit-reduction budget that included $255 billion in spending cuts and $241 billion in tax increases. Incorporated in this budget were the president's requests for increased appropriations for education and job training. Clinton also won a notable victory by signing the North American Free Trade Agreement (NAFTA), which created a free-trade zone with Canada and Mexico. Despite these accomplishments, Clinton's apparent waffling on policies and his eagerness to compromise confirmed his image among his critics, who nicknamed him "Slick Willie."

Republicans Take Over Congress

In the midterm elections of November 1994, the Republicans gained control of both houses of Congress for the first time since 1954. They benefited from a well-organized effort to promote a short list of policy priorities they called the "Contract with America." In addition, the Democratic Congress was unpopular because it had raised taxes and limited gun ownership. President Clinton adjusted to his party's defeat by declaring in his 1995 State of the Union address, "The era of big government is over."

Zealous Reformers Newt Gingrich, the newly elected Speaker of the House, led the Republicans in an attack on federal programs and spending outlined in their campaign manifesto, "Contract with America." While the president and moderates agreed with the goal of a balanced budget, Clinton proposed a "leaner, not meaner" budget. This confrontation resulted in two shutdowns of the federal government in late 1995, which many Americans blamed on overzealous Republicans in Congress. Antigovernment reformers were not helped by the mood after the bombing in 1995 of a federal building in Oklahoma City by militia-movement extremists. The bombing took 169 lives, the worst act of domestic terrorism in the nation's history until the attacks on September 11, 2001.

Balanced Budget Finally, in the 1996 election year, Congress and the president compromised on a budget that left Medicare and Social Security benefits intact, limited welfare benefits to five years under the Personal Responsibility and Work Opportunity Act, set some curbs on immigrants, increased the minimum wage, and balanced the budget. The spending cuts and tax increases made during Clinton's first term, along with record growth in the economy, helped to eliminate the deficit in federal spending in 1998 and produced the first federal surplus since 1969. In his battle with the Republican Congress, President Clinton captured the middle ground by successfully characterizing the Republicans as extremists, and by taking over their more popular positions, such as balancing the budget and reforming welfare. He was also aided in the 1996 election by a fast-growing economy that had produced more than 10 million new jobs.

The Election of 1996

Senator Bob Dole of Kansas, the majority leader of the Senate, became Clinton's Republican opponent. His campaign, which proposed a 15 percent tax cut, never captured voters' imagination. Character attacks and massive campaign spending by both sides did little to bring more people to the polls, and the turn-out dropped below 50 percent of eligible voters.

The Clinton-Gore ticket won with 379 electoral votes (49.2 percent of the popular vote), while Dole and his running mate, Jack Kemp, captured 159 electoral votes (40.8 percent of the popular vote). Ross Perot ran again, but had little impact on the election. Clinton became the first Democrat since Franklin Roosevelt to be re-elected president. The Republicans could celebrate retaining control of both houses of Congress, which they had not done since the 1920s.

The Technology Boom

During President Clinton's two terms the United States enjoyed the longest peacetime economic expansion in its history, with annual growth rates of more than 4 percent. Technological innovations in personal computers, software, the Internet, cable, and wireless communications fueled increased national productivity (a gain of more than 5 percent in 1999) and made "e- (or electronic) commerce" part of American life. High-tech companies, such as Apple, Intel, and Microsoft, were joined during the "dot-com" boom by the likes of Amazon, AOL, Yahoo, and Google.

After years of heavy competition with Europe and Asia, American businesses had become proficient in cutting costs, which both increased their profitability and held down the U.S. inflation rate to below 3 percent a year. Investors were rewarded with record gains of more than 22 percent in the stock market. The number of households worth $1 million or more quadrupled in the 1990s, to more than 8 million, or one in 14 households. The unemployment rate fell from 7.5 percent in 1992 to a 30-year low of 3.9 percent in 2000. The unemployment of African Americans and Hispanics was the lowest on record. During the peak of prosperity from 1997 to 1999, average and lower-income Americans experienced the first gains in real income since 1973. However, the economic boom was over by 2001, and both investors and wage earners faced another recession.

Clinton's Second Term: Politics of Impeachment

The prosperity of the late 1990s shifted the debate in Washington to what to do with the federal government's surplus revenues, projected to be $4.6 trillion over the first ten years of the 21st century. In 1997, Congress and the president did compromise on legislation that cut taxes on estates and capital gains, and gave tax credits for families with children and for higher education expenses. As Clinton's second term progressed, the struggle between the Democratic president and the Republican Congress intensified. The Republicans pressed for more tax revenue cuts, such as the elimination of the estate tax (the "death tax") and taxes on two-income families (the "marriage penalty"), while the president held out for using the projected surplus to support Social Security, expand Medicare, and reduce the national debt.

Investigations and Impeachment From the early days of the Clinton presidency, President Clinton, his wife, Hillary, cabinet members, and other associates had been under investigation by Congress and by congressionally appointed independent prosecutors (a legacy of the independent prosecutor law of the Watergate era). Some Democrats viewed these investigations as a "right-wing conspiracy" to overturn the elections of 1992 and 1996. After long and expensive investigations, the Clintons were not charged with any illegalities in the Whitewater real estate deal, the firings of White House staff ("Travelgate"), or the political use of FBI files ("Filegate"). However, independent prosecutor Kenneth Starr charged that President Clinton, during his deposition in a civil suit about alleged sexual harassment while governor of Arkansas, had lied about his relations with a young woman who was a White House intern.

Impeachment In December 1998, the House voted to impeach the president on two counts, perjury and obstruction of justice. Members of both parties and the public condemned Clinton's reckless personal behavior, but popular opinion did not support the Republican impeachment of Clinton for lying about his personal life. In the fall elections, Democrats gained House seats and Newt Gingrich resigned as speaker. In February 1999, after a formal trial in the Senate, neither impeachment charge was upheld even by a Senate majority, much less the two-thirds vote needed to remove a president from office. However, the Republicans damaged Clinton's reputation by making him the first president to be impeached since 1868. A weary Congress in 2000 allowed the controversial law establishing the independent prosecutor's office to lapse.

Foreign Policy in the Clinton Administration

The end of the Cold War, while taking away the Soviet threat, exposed dozens of long-standing ethnic, religious, and cultural conflicts around the world. During Clinton's first term, Secretary of State Warren Christopher conducted a low-key foreign policy, which critics thought lacked coherent purpose. In 1997 Madeleine K. Albright became the first woman to serve as secretary of state. She proved more assertive in the use of American power, but questions still remained about the role of the United States, especially the use of its armed forces for peacekeeping in foreign nations' internal conflicts.

Peacekeeping The first deaths of U.S. soldiers in humanitarian missions during the Clinton administration came in the civil war in Somalia in 1993. In 1994, after some reluctance, the president sent 20,000 troops into Haiti to restore its elected president, Jean-Bertrand Aristide, after a military coup and deteriorating economic conditions had caused an exodus of Haitians to Florida. The United States also played a key diplomatic role in negotiating an end to British rule and the armed conflict in Northern Ireland in 1998.

Europe The European Union (EU) became a unified market of 15 nations, 12 of which adopted a single currency, the euro, in 2002. The EU grew to include 27 European nations by 2007, including ten former satellites of the USSR, such as Poland, Bulgaria, and Romania.

Under President Boris Yeltsin, Russia struggled to reform its economy and to fight rampant corruption. In 2000 Yeltsin's elected successor, Vladimir Putin, took office. Relations with the United States were strained by Russia's brutal repression of the civil war in Chechnya, by NATO's admittance in 1999 of the Czech Republic, Hungary, and Poland, and by Russia's support of Serbia in the Balkan wars of the 1990s.

The Serbian dictator, Slobodan Milosevic, carried out a series of armed conflicts to suppress independence movements in the former Yugoslav provinces of Slovenia, Croatia, Bosnia-Herzegovina, and Kosovo. Hundreds of thousands of members of ethnic and religious minorities, including many Muslims, were killed in the brutal "ethnic cleansing." A combination of diplomacy, bombing, and troops from NATO countries, including the United States, stopped the bloodshed first in Bosnia in 1995 and again in Kosovo in 1999. These Balkan wars proved to be the worst conflict Europe had seen since World War II, and were a troubling reminder of how World War I had started.

Asia Nuclear proliferation became a growing concern in the 1990s, when North Korea stepped up its nuclear reactor and missile programs, and India and Pakistan tested nuclear weapons for the first time in 1998. North Korea agreed to halt the development of nuclear weapons after direct negotiations with the Clinton administration, but later secretly restarted the program. In 1995, 20 years after the fall of Saigon to the Communists, the United States established diplomatic relations with Vietnam. The Clinton administration continued to sign trade agreements with China through his second term, hoping to improve diplomatic relations and encourage reform within China, despite protests from human rights activists and labor unions at home, and Chinese threats to the still-independent island nation of Taiwan.

Middle East Iraqi leader Saddam Hussein's continued defiance of U.N. weapons inspectors led to the suspension of all inspections in 1998. President Clinton responded with a series of air strikes against Iraq, but Hussein remained in power, as support for U.S. economic sanctions declined in Europe and the Middle East. The United States had some success in the Israeli-Palestinian peace process. Israel granted home rule to the Palestinians in the Gaza Strip and parts of the West Bank territories, and signed a peace treaty with Jordan in 1994. The peace process slowed after the assassination of Israeli Prime Minister Yitzak Rabin in 1995, and it broke down late in 2000 over issues of Israeli security and control of Jerusalem. Renewed violence in Israel also provoked a new round of anti-American sentiment in the Islamic world.

Globalization The surging increases in trade, communications, and the movement of capital around the world during this era were key parts of the process of globalization. Globalization promoted the development of global and regional economic organizations. The World Trade Organization (WTO) was established in 1994 to oversee trade agreements, enforce trade rules, and settle disputes. The powerful International Monetary Fund (IMF) and the World Bank made loans to and supervised the economic policies of poorer nations with debt troubles.

The Group of Eight (G-8), the world's largest industrial powers (Canada, France, Germany, Italy, Japan, Russia, the United Kingdom, and the United

States), which controlled two-thirds of the world's wealth, remained the leading economic powers. However, China, India, and Brazil would soon surpass many of the older industrial powers in the 21st century. The growing gap between the rich and poor nations of the world caused tensions, especially over the debts the poor nations owed to powerful banks and the richest nations. Workers and unions in the richest nations often resented globalization, because they lost their jobs to cheaper labor markets in the developing world.

American Society in 2000

According to the 2000 census, the resident population of the United States was 281.4 million, making it the third most populous nation in the world. The fastest growing regions of the United States in the 1990s continued to be in the West and in the South. With the growth in population came greater political power as a result of the shift of congressional representatives and electoral votes to these regions. The 2000 census reported that 50 percent of U.S. residents lived in suburbs, 30 percent in central cities, and only 20 percent in rural regions.

Immigration The Immigration Reform and Control Act of 1986 attempted to create a fair entry process for immigrants, but failed to stop the problem of illegal entry into the United States from Mexico. The law was also criticized for granting amnesty to some undocumented immigrants from Mexico and the Americas. In 2000, the Hispanic population was the fastest growing segment of the population and emerged as the largest minority group in the nation. Asian Americans also represented another fast-growing part of society, with a population of more than 10 million.

By 2000, 10.4 percent of the population was foreign-born, a high percentage but well below the levels of the 1870s through the 1920s. Immigration accounted for 27.8 percent of the population increase in the 1990s, and was a key stimulus to the economic growth during the decade. Without immigration, the United States was on a path to experience a negative population growth by 2030.

Aging and the Family As the United States became more ethnically diverse, the population was also "graying," with a steady increase in life expectancy. By 2000, 35 million people were over 65, but the fastest growing segment of the population was those 85 and over. As the baby-boom generation aged, concern about health care, prescription drugs, senior housing, and Social Security increased. It is estimated that in 2030 that there will be only about two workers for every person receiving Social Security.

The decline of the traditional family and the growing number of single-parent families was another national concern. The number of families headed by a female with no husband soared from 5.5 million in 1970 to 12.8 million in 2000. Single women headed 47.2 percent of black families in 2000, but the same trend was also evident in white and Hispanic households with children under 18. Children in these families often grew up in poverty and without adequate support.

Income and Wealth In many ways, Americans were achieving the American dream. Homeownership continued to climb during the prosperity of the 1990s to 67.4 percent of all households. The economy was continuing to generate more and more wealth. Per-capita money income in constant (inflation-adjusted) dollars rose dramatically, from $12,275 in 1970 to $22,199 in 2000. However, in 1999 the top fifth of American households received more than half of all income. The average after-tax income for the lowest three-fifths of households actually declined between 1977 and 1997. In addition, the distribution of income varied widely by race, gender, and education. For example, the median income in 2000 was $53,256 for white families, $35,054 for Hispanic families, and $34,192 for black families. High school graduates earned only half the income of college graduates. The United States was the richest country in the world, but among industrialized nations, it had the largest gap between lowest and highest paid workers and the greatest concentration of wealth among the top-earning households. This concentration reminded some of the Gilded Age.

HISTORICAL PERSPECTIVES: WHAT DOES FREEDOM MEAN?

Freedom is a main theme of American history, but people disagree on what "freedom" means. Eric Foner in *The Story of American Freedom* (1999) traced America's thoughts about freedom from the struggle for independence through the Reagan era. In the Civil War, both sides fought in the name of freedom, but for Confederates the right to enslave others was a "freedom." The Reconstruction, Progressive, New Deal, and Civil Rights eras enlarged the meaning of freedom to include equal rights for all and increased political and economic protections, largely guaranteed by the federal government. During the Reagan Revolution, freedom was frequently defined as the liberation from "big government" and federal regulations. Foner attributed this change to reactions to forced desegregation in the 1950s and 1960s and federal court rulings promoting equality, privacy, abortion rights, and other issues. The Cold War also encouraged some to equate American freedom with unregulated capitalism.

While Foner saw freedom "as an essentially contested concept," David Hackett Fischer in *Liberty and Freedom* (2005) pursued its meaning through American visual expressions, customs, and what Tocqueville called "habits of the heart." Fischer's analysis of the images and symbols from the Liberty Trees of the American Revolution through the protest posters of the late 20th century revealed the rich diversity of traditions about freedom that eluded abstract definitions. Hackett concluded that the United States remains free because of its diversity of traditions about freedom. He believes that the gravest threat to freedom comes from those incapable of imagining any vision of freedom except their own.

KEY NAMES, EVENTS, AND TERMS

Conservative Movement, (POL, SOC)
Milton Freidman
political action committees (PACs)
Proposition 13
Arthur Laffer
religious fundamentalism
televangelists
Moral Majority
abortion rights; *Roe v. Wade*
reverse discrimination
Regents of University of California v. Bakke

Reagan Revolution (POL, WXT)
election of 1980
Ronald Reagan
supply-side economics (Reaganomics)
"trickle down" economics
Economic Recovery Tax Act (1981)
business deregulation
PACTO strike
Sandra Day O'Connor
William Rehnquist
growth of upper incomes
budget and trade deficits
election of 1984

Reagan Foreign Policy (WOR)
Expand military
Strategic Defense Initiative (Star Wars)
Nicaragua; Sandinistas
Boland Amendment
Iran-contra affair
Beirut bombings

Palestine Liberation Organization (PLO)
Yasser Arafat
"evil empire"
Mikhail Gorbachev; *glasnost, perestroika*
"tear down this wall"
INF agreement

End of Cold War (WOR)
Tiananmen Square (1989)
Soviet satellites
Poland, Lech Walesa
Berlin Wall falls (1989)
Soviet Union breakup
Russia Republic, CIS
Boris Yeltsin
START I and II
Yugoslavia civil war

George H. W. Bush Policies (POL, WOR)
election of 1988
George H. W. Bush
Panama invasion (1989)
Saddam Hussein
Persian Gulf War (1991)
Operation Desert Storm
Clarence Thomas
"no new taxes"
Americans With Disabilities Act (1990)

Clinton Era Politics (POL, WXT)
election of 1992
William (Bill) Clinton
H. Ross Perot
failure of health reform
"don't ask, don't tell"
NAFTA
Brady Bill
National Rifle Association (NRA)
deficit reduction budget

Anti-Crime Bill
Election of 1994
Newt Gingrich
Contract with America
government shutdowns
Oklahoma City bombing
welfare reform
balanced budgets
election of 1996
Clinton impeachment

Post-Cold War Policies, (WOR)
Madeleine K. Albright
humanitarian missions
Northern Ireland accords
Yugoslavia breakup
Balkan Wars: Bosnia, Kosovo
"ethnic cleansing"
nuclear proliferation
West Bank, Gaza Strip

Globalization (WOR)
European Union (EU); euro
World Trade Organization
World Bank, G-8
China, India, Brazil
effects on jobs

2000 American Society (WXT, NAT)
prosperity of 1990s
technology boom
Internet, e-commerce
rise of South and West
Immigration Act of 1986
growth of Hispanics
"graying" America
single-parent families
distribution of income
concentration of wealth
debate over freedom

Questions 1–3 refer to the excerpt below.

"In this present crisis, government is not the solution to our problem; government is the problem. From time to time we've been tempted to believe that society has become too complex to be managed by self-rule, that government by an elite group is superior to government for, by, and of the people. . . .

"It is my intention to curb the size and influence of the federal establishment and to demand recognition of the distinction between the powers granted to the Federal government and those reserved to the States or to the people. . . .

"In the days ahead I will propose removing the roadblocks that have slowed our economy and reduced productivity. . . . It is time to reawaken this industrial giant, to get government back within its means, and to lighten our punitive tax burden. And these will be our first priorities, and on these principles there will be no compromise."

—President Ronald Reagan, Inaugural Address, January 20, 1981

1. Which of the following was an accomplishment by Reagan that fulfilled the pledges made in this excerpt?
   (A) Balancing the federal budget
   (B) Cutting military spending through greater efficiency
   (C) Strengthening environmental protections of federal lands
   (D) Reducing taxes for businesses and upper-income individuals

2. Which of the following points of view most closely resembles the one expressed in this excerpt?
   (A) Government spending is a useful tool to boost the economy and consumer demand.
   (B) The federal government is in a better position to manage the economy than the states.
   (C) Federal taxes should be used to reduce the income inequality among Americans.
   (D) Privately owned businesses are the key to economic growth

3. Which of the following would best support President Reagan's views on "removing roadblocks that have slowed our economy?"
   (A) Cutting restrictions on financial institutions
   (B) Improving mass transportation for workers
   (C) Promoting college education with student loans
   (D) Requiring older Americans to work longer

Questions 4–6 refer to the excerpt below.

"While the world waited, Saddam Hussein met every overture of peace with open contempt. While the world prayed for peace, Saddam prepared for war. . . . Tonight, 28 nations—countries from five continents, Europe and Asia, Africa and the Arab League—have forces in the Gulf area standing shoulder to shoulder against Saddam Hussein. . . .

"This is an historic moment. We have in this past year made great progress in ending the long era of conflict and cold war. We have before us the opportunity to forge for ourselves and for future generations a new world order—a world where the rule of law, not the law of the jungle, governs the conduct of nations. . . . [W]e have a real chance at this new world order, an order in which a credible United Nations can use its peacekeeping role to fulfill the promise and vision of the U.N.'s founders."

—President George H. W. Bush, Address to the Nation,
January 16, 1991

4. Which of the following best explains the purpose of this speech?
   (A) Aid Iran and Saudi Arabia in their conflict with Iraq
   (B) Force the Iraqi military forces out of Kuwait
   (C) Promote democracy in the Middle East
   (D) Remove weapons of mass destruction from Hussein's Iraq

5. In this speech, Bush is most clearly expressing the concept in foreign policy called
   (A) collective security
   (B) containment
   (C) isolationism
   (D) mutual assured destruction

6. Which of the following best explains the result of the foreign policy effort described in this excerpt?
   (A) Saddam Hussein, the dictator of Iraq, was removed from power
   (B) The Soviet Union joined in support of the operation
   (C) United States and its allies became bogged down in a lengthy war
   (D) President Bush's approval rating increased to 90 percent

Questions 7–8 refer to the excerpt below.

"Clinton was widely hailed, even by some of his detractors, as the most gifted politician of his generation—but the political task presented to him required continual bobbing and weaving, compromising and negotiation, retreating so as to advance. . . . Clinton was forced to establish a position independent of both the hostile Republican majority and the impotent Democratic minority. The ensuing confrontations that led to a federal government shutdown, Clinton's recovery in the election of 1996, and the impeachment proceeding two years later all stemmed from the political realities surrounding the Clinton White House. . . .

Clinton and his advisors figured out a great deal on the run. . . . Clinton was also hunted and accused of wrongdoing as few previous presidents had been. . . . Under siege, though, Clinton survived to become, by the end of his second term, a singularly admired if controversial leader."

—Sean Wilentz, historian, *The Age of Reagan: A History 1974–2008,* 2008

7. Passage of which of the following is an example of Clinton's success in "compromising and negotiation, retreating so as to advance?"

   (A) Bill ending discrimination against gays in the military

   (B) Brady Bill and ban on assault rifles

   (C) Health Care Reform Act

   (D) Welfare and budget reform

8. Which of the following best explains the general popularity of the Clinton presidency?

   (A) Clinton survived an unpopular impeachment effort led by his political opponents

   (B) Clinton presided over eight years of prosperity and improved middle-class incomes

   (C) Clinton organized successful peace-keeping efforts in the former Yugoslavia

   (D) Clinton negotiated a plan to stabilize Social Security and Medicare for seniors

SHORT-ANSWER QUESTIONS

Use complete sentences; an outline or bulleted list alone is not acceptable.

Question 1. Answer (A), (B), and (C).

(A) Briefly explain ONE specific historical development that made a significant contribution to conservative resurgence in the 1980s.

(B) Briefly explain ONE specific economic legislative or policy achievement of the Reagan administration and its impact.

(C) Briefly explain ONE specific technological innovation of the 1980s and 1990s and its impact.

Question 2 is based on the following graphs.

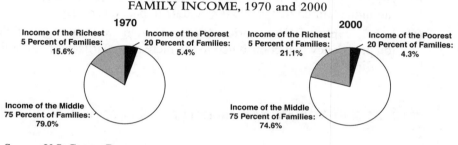

FAMILY INCOME, 1970 and 2000

Source: U.S. Census Bureau

2. Using the graphs, answer (A), (B), and (C).

(A) Briefly explain ONE specific historical event or development that contributed to the increase in family income of the richest Americans during the period from 1970 to 2000.

(B) Briefly explain ONE specific historical event or development that contributed to the decrease in family income of the middle and poorest groups of Americans during the period from 1970 to 2000.

(C) Briefly explain ONE specific historical effect that resulted from the change depicted in the chart.

Question 3. Answer (A), (B), and (C).

(A) Briefly explain how ONE specific historical event or development contributed to support the position that the Reagan administration helped to end the Cold War.

(B) Briefly explain ONE specific historical event or development to support the position that political changes in USSR and Eastern Europe helped to end the Cold War.

(C) Briefly explain ONE specific historical foreign policy challenge for the United States that resulted from the aftermath of the Cold War.

Question 4. Answer (A), (B), and (C).

(A) Briefly explain ONE specific change in immigration patterns in the United States from 1970 to 2000 and its impact on diversity.

(B) Briefly explain ONE specific way that family structures were changing in the United States by 2000 and its impact on society.

(C) Briefly explain ONE historical event or development during the Clinton presidency that contributed to the increasing partisan or cultural conflicts.

THINK AS A HISTORIAN: WRITING EFFECTIVE PARAGRAPHS

Effective paragraphs include a topic sentence that states a main idea, which other sentences support with facts, examples, or reasons. Which TWO of the following statements best support this topic sentence? "Popular presidents often mix liberal and conservative policies."

1. Ronald Reagan negotiated an arms control deal with the Soviets.

2. George H. W. Bush tried to cut social programs during a recession.

3. Bill Clinton reduced government spending on welfare.

31

CHALLENGES OF THE 21ST CENTURY, 2000–PRESENT

*There is not a Black America and a White America and Latino America
and Asian America—there's the United States of America.*
Barack Obama, Democratic Convention Keynote Address, 2004

The United States entered the 21st century with unrivaled economic and military dominance in the world. However, international terrorism, economic problems, and partisan politics exposed the nation's vulnerability.

Political Polarization

The elections of the early 21st century revealed a nation closely divided between the conservative South, Great Plains, and Mountain States, and the more moderate-to-liberal Northeast, Midwest, and West Coast. As a result of this division, a few swing states, such as Ohio and Florida, determined federal elections. The more traditional, religious, and limited- or anti-government rural areas and many suburban areas went Republican, while the more diverse large urban centers and internationally minded coasts voted Democrat.

The shift of southern white conservatives after the 1960s from the Democratic to the Republican party transformed American politics. In the 1990s, southern conservatives took over the leadership of the Republican party, making it more conservative and partisan. As the party of Lincoln became the party of Ronald Reagan, moderate Republicans lost influence and primary contests to conservatives. In the state legislatures, both parties gerrymandered congressional districts to create "safe seats," which rewarded partisanship and discouraged compromise in Congress.

Disputed Election of 2000

The presidential election of 2000 was the closest since 1876 and the first ever to be settled by the Supreme Court. President Clinton's vice president, Al Gore, easily gained the nomination of the Democratic party, selecting Senator Joseph Lieberman of Connecticut as his running mate. Governor George W. Bush of Texas, eldest son of former President George H. W. Bush, won the nomination of the

Republican party, and selected Dick Cheney, a veteran of the Reagan and elder Bush administrations, as his running mate. Both candidates fought over the moderate and independent vote, Gore as a champion of "working families" and Bush running as "a compassionate conservative." Ralph Nader, the candidate for the Green party, ran a distant third, but he probably took enough votes from Gore to make a difference in Florida and other states.

Gore received more than 500,000 more popular votes nationwide than Bush, but victory hinged on who won Florida's 25 electoral votes. Bush led by only 537 popular votes in Florida after a partial recount. Then the Democrats asked for manual recounts of the error-prone punch cards. The Supreme Court of Florida ordered recounts of all the votes, but the U.S. Supreme Court overruled them in a split 5-4 decision that matched the party loyalty of the justices. In *Bush v. Gore*, the majority ruled that the varying standards used in Florida's recount violated the Equal-Protection Clause of the 14th Amendment. Al Gore ended the election crisis by accepting the ruling. Governor Bush won with 271 electoral votes against Gore's 266. (One elector abstained.)

PRESIDENTIAL ELECTION 2000, ELECTORAL VOTES BY STATE

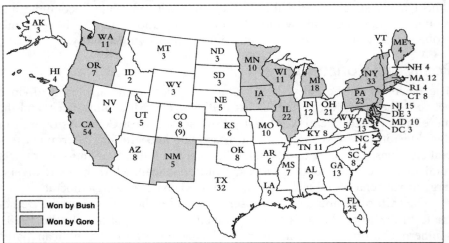

Domestic Policies of the George W. Bush Administration

President George W. Bush aggressively pushed his conservative agenda: tax cuts, deregulation, federal aid to faith-based organizations, pro-life legislation, school choice, privatization of Social Security and Medicare, drilling for oil and gas in the Alaska wildlife refuge, and voluntary environmental standards for industry.

Republican Tax Cuts In 2001, Congress, enjoying rare budget surpluses, passed a $1.35 trillion dollar tax cut spread over ten years. The bill lowered the top tax bracket, gradually eliminated estate taxes, increased the child tax credit and limits for IRA and 401(k) contributions, and gave all taxpayers an immediate tax rebate. In 2003, President Bush pushed through another round of tax cuts for stock dividends, capital gains, and married couples. Democrats criticized the tax cuts for giving most of the benefits to the richest 5 percent of the population and for contributing to the doubling of the national debt during the Bush presidency from about $5 trillion to $10 trillion.

Education and Health Reform President Bush championed the bipartisan No Child Left Behind Act. It aimed to improve student performance and close the gap between well-to-do and poor students in the public schools through testing of all students nationwide, granting students the right to transfer to better schools, funding stronger reading programs, and training high-quality teachers. Republicans also passed laws to give seniors in Medicare the option to enroll in private insurance companies. Congress also fulfilled a campaign promise by President Bush to provide prescription drug coverage for seniors. Democrats criticized the legislation as primarily designed to profit insurance and drug companies.

Economic Bubbles and Corruption The technology boom of the 1990s peaked in 2000 and was over by 2002. The stock market crashed; the Dow Jones Industrial Average fell by 38 percent. The unemployment rate climbed to 6 percent, and the number of people living in poverty increased for the first time in eight years. Fraud and dishonesty committed by business leaders also hurt the stock market and consumer confidence in the economy. For example, the large corporations Enron and WorldCom had "cooked their books" (falsified stated earnings and profits) with the help of accounting companies. The Federal Reserve fought the recession by cutting interest rates to 1.25 percent, the lowest in fifty years. The end of the technology boom-bust cycle (1995–2002) encouraged many investors to move their money into real estate, which created another speculative "bubble" (2002–2007) that would burst with even more tragic consequences in Bush's second term.

The War on Terrorism

Terrorism dominated U.S. foreign policy after September 11, 2001. George W. Bush entered the White House with no foreign policy experience but surrounded himself with veterans of prior Republican administrations, such as his vice president, Dick Cheney, who served as secretary of defense under his father. General Colin Powell became his secretary of state, the first African American to hold the job. President Bush's confident and aggressive approach against terrorism won over many Americans, but his administration often alienated other nations.

Roots of Terrorism The United States was faulted by many in the Arab world for siding with Israel in the deadly cycle of Palestinian terror-bombing and Israeli reprisals. However, the causes of anti-Americanism often went deeper. After World War I, the Ottoman Empire, the last of the Islamic empires, was replaced in the Middle East by Western-style, secular nation-states. Religious fundamentalists decried modernization and the corruption of the "House of Islam," an ancient Islamic ideal of a realm governed by the precepts of the Koran and Sharia law. The stationing of U.S. troops in the Middle East after the Gulf War was seen as another violation of their lands. Islamic extremists, such as

Osama bin Laden and the supporters of Al-Qaeda ("The Base"), preached jihad, which they defined as a holy war against the "Jews and Crusaders" to restore an Islamic caliphate, or realm, from Africa and the Middle East through East Asia. The restrictive economic and political conditions in the Middle East also provided a fertile breeding ground for recruiting extremists.

Early Terrorist Attacks A truck bombing of the World Trade Center in New York City in 1993 that killed six people brought home for the first time the threat posed by Islamic extremists. In 1998, the United States responded to the terrorist bombing of two U.S. embassies in Kenya and Tanzania by bombing Al-Qaeda camps in Afghanistan and the Sudan. The leader of Al-Qaeda, Osama bin Laden, had fled to Afghanistan and allied himself with the Taliban, the Islamic fundamentalists who had taken over Afghanistan. In 2000, U.S. armed forces learned the nature of "asymmetric" warfare conducted by terrorists when two suicide bombers in a small rubber boat nearly sank a billion-dollar warship, the USS *Cole*, docked in Yemen.

Source: World Trade Center, September 11, 2001. Wikimedia Commons/Michael Foran

September 11, 2001 The coordinated attacks by Al-Qaeda terrorists in commercial airliners on the twin towers of the World Trade Center in New York City and the Pentagon near Washington, D.C., and involving a fourth plane that crashed in Pennsylvania claimed nearly 3,000 lives. The attacks galvanized public opinion as nothing had since the Japanese attack on Pearl Harbor in 1941, and they empowered the Bush administration to take action.

War in Afghanistan President Bush declared that he wanted Osama bin Laden and other Al-Qaeda leaders "dead or alive." After the Taliban refused to turn over bin Laden and his associates, their government was quickly overthrown in the fall of 2001 by a combination of U.S. bombings, U.S. special forces, and Afghan troops in the anti-Taliban Northern Alliance. American and Afghan forces continued to pursue the remnants of Al-Qaeda in the mountains bordering Pakistan, but they failed to capture bin Laden. Hamid Karzai, with U.S. support, became head of the government in Kabul, but Afghanistan remained unstable and divided by the Taliban insurgency and tribal conflicts.

Homeland Security After the 9/11 attacks, most Americans were willing to accept background checks and airport searches. The Patriot Acts of 2001 and 2003 gave unparalleled powers to the U.S. government to obtain information and expand surveillance and arrest powers. However, many Americans were troubled by unlimited wiretaps, the collection of records about cell phone calls and emails, the use of military tribunals to try suspects accused of terrorism, and the imprisonment of suspects indefinitely at a U.S. prison in Guantánamo, Cuba.

To enhance security, the Bush administration created a new Department of Homeland Security by combining more than 20 federal agencies with 170,000 employees, including the Secret Service, the Coast Guard, and ones dealing with customs and immigration. This was the largest reorganization of government since the creation of the Department of Defense after World War II. Many in Congress questioned why the FBI and CIA were left out of the new department. In 2004, a bipartisan commission on terrorism criticized the FBI and the CIA, as well as the Defense Department, for failing to work together to "connect the dots" that may have uncovered the 9/11 plot. Congress followed up on their recommendations, creating a director of national intelligence with the difficult job of coordinating the intelligence activities of all agencies.

George W. Bush Foreign Policy President Bush worked with European nations to expand the European Union and NATO, supported admission of China to the World Trade Organization, and brokered conflicts between India and Pakistan. However, the Bush administration refused to join the Kyoto Accord to prevent global warming, walked out of a U.N. conference on racism, abandoned the 1972 Anti-Ballistic Missile Treaty with Russia, and for years would not negotiate with North Korea or Iran. Critics questioned whether the administration valued cooperation with the nations of the world or instead followed a unilateralist approach. The president argued, in what became known as the "Bush Doctrine," that the old policies of containment and deterrence were no longer effective in a world of stateless terrorism. To protect America, the president claimed that the United States would be justified in using preemptive attacks to stop the acquisition and use of weapons of mass destruction (WMDs) by terrorists and by nations that support terrorism.

Iraq War President Bush, in his 2002 State of the Union address, singled out Iraq, North Korea, and Iran as the "axis of evil." While U.S. intelligence agencies were finding no link between Iraq's Saddam Hussein and the September 11, 2001, attacks, the Bush administration pursued a preemptive attack on Iraq before Saddam Hussein could build and distribute WMDs (nuclear and biological) to terrorists. Late in 2002, Secretary of State Powell negotiated an inspection plan with the U.N. Security Council, which Iraq accepted. In the following months, the U.N. inspectors failed to find WMDs in Iraq. Nevertheless, the Bush administration continued to present claims of their existence based on intelligence information that proved false.

Operation Iraqi Freedom In early 2003, President Bush declared that Iraq had not complied with numerous U.N. resolutions and that "the game was over." Without support of the U.N. Security Council, the United States launched air attacks on Iraq on March 19. In less than four weeks, U.S. armed forces, with the support of the British and other allies, overran Iraqi forces, captured the capital city, Baghdad, and ended Hussein's dictatorship. When U.S. forces could not find WMDs in Iraq, criticism of the "war of choice" and the "regime change" mounted both at home and overseas.

The defeat of the Iraqi army and the capture of Saddam Hussein in late 2003 did not end the violence in Iraq. Diverse groups of insurgents (Sunni followers of the former dictator, Shiite militias, and foreign fighters, including Al-Qaeda) continued to attacked U.S. and allied troops and one another. Millions of Iraqis fled the country or were displaced by the sectarian attacks. The Bush administration was widely criticized for going into Iraq without sufficient troops to control the country and for disbanding the Iraqi army. Pictures of the barbaric treatment of prisoners by U.S. troops at Abu Ghraib further diminished America's reputation in Iraq and around the world.

Elections of 2004 and a Bush Second Term

The Democrats approached the elections of 2004 optimistic that they could unseat the incumbent president burdened by an increasingly unpopular war and limited economic recovery. Democratic voters selected Senator John Kerry of Massachusetts as their presidential candidate. The Republicans successfully energized their conservative base on issues such as the war against terrorism, more tax cuts, and opposition to gay marriage and abortion.

President Bush received 51 percent of the popular vote and captured 286 electoral votes to Kerry's 252. The Republicans also expanded their majorities in the Senate and House and continued to gain on the state level, especially in the South. This left the party in its strongest position since the 1920s.

Four More Years at War The reconstruction of Iraq had made some headway by 2005, when the Iraqis held their first election, created a national assembly, and selected a prime minister and cabinet ministries, but the violence continued. On average, 100 Americans and 3,000 Iraqis were killed each month. In an attempt to reduce the violence, President Bush sent a "surge" of an additional 30,000 U.S. troops in early 2007. By late 2008, militia violence and American deaths were down in Iraq, and the United States had started to turn over control of the provinces to the Iraqi government.

In Afghanistan, the Taliban stepped up their attacks. For the first time, the number of Americans killed there outnumbered those killed in Iraq. President Bush turned over to the next president two unresolved wars and incomplete efforts to deal with nuclear threats from Iran and North Korea. The Bush administration, though, did have the satisfaction of knowing that there had not been another major terrorist attack in the United States since September 11, 2001.

Washington Politics After his reelection victory in 2004, President Bush pushed Congress without success to privatize Social Security by encouraging Americans to invest part of their Social Security payroll deductions in various market investments. His administration also argued for immigration reform, which was blocked by conservatives who criticized it as "amnesty" for undocumented immigrants. President Bush, however, did leave a lasting impact on the federal courts by appointing two conservatives to the Supreme Court—John Roberts (as Chief Justice) and Samuel Alito—and increasing conservative majorities in the federal appellate courts.

When Hurricane Katrina hit the Gulf Coast hard and flooded New Orleans in August 2005, the Federal Emergency Management Agency (FEMA) failed both to anticipate and respond to the crisis. More than 1,000 people died, and tens of thousands of others (mostly poor people) were left in desperate conditions. Public dissatisfaction with the Katrina response, the Iraq War, and a variety of Republican congressional scandals involving bribery, perjury, and obstruction of justice helped the Democrats win control of both houses of Congress in 2006.

The Great Recession The housing boom of 2002–2007 was fueled by subprime and fraudulent mortgage lending and runaway real estate speculation. Wall Street firms packaged these high-risk loans into a variety of complex investments (securitization) and sold them to unsuspecting investors around the world. However, as soon as housing prices started to dip, the bubble burst. Prices collapsed, foreclosures climbed, and investments worth trillions of dollars lost value. Investors panicked, which caused many banks and financial institutions at home and overseas to face failure. This resulted in a credit, or liquidity, crisis because banks either lacked funds or were afraid to make the loans to businesses and consumers necessary for the day-to-day functioning of the economy.

As the crisis deepened within credit markets, Americans were also hit with soaring gas prices (well over $4 a gallon), stock market declines of more than 40 percent, and rising unemployment. In early 2008, the federal government tried a $170 billion stimulus package and took over a few critical financial institutions, such as quasi-governmental mortgage institutions Fannie Mae and Freddie Mac.

However, the crisis was not over. In September, the bankruptcy of the large Wall Street investment bank Lehman Brothers led to panic in the financial industry. This forced the Bush administration to ask Congress for additional funds to help U.S. banks and restore the credit markets. The controversial Economic Stabilization Act of 2008 was passed, creating a $700 billion Troubled Assets Relief Program (TARP) to purchase failing assets that included mortgages and mortgage-related securities from financial institutions. Conservatives attacked TARP as "socialism" while liberals attacked it as a bailout of the Wall Street executives who had caused the problems.

As with the Great Depression of 1929, the causes of this crash will be debated for years. Some blamed the Federal Reserve for keeping interest rates too low. Others criticized excessive deregulation of the financial industry. And others saw the cause in government efforts to promote home ownership. Moreover, real estate bank fraud and Ponzi schemes that cost investors tens of billions of dollars in losses also helped to destroy investor confidence. Whatever its causes, the crisis significantly affected the 2008 election.

Election of 2008

After a long primary battle with former first lady and U.S. Senator Hillary Clinton, the forty-seven-year-old, charismatic, African American junior senator from Illinois, Barack Obama, captured the Democratic nomination for president. Obama chose as his running mate Joseph Biden of Delaware, an experienced member of the Senate. In the shadow of the unpopular Bush administration, the Republicans nominated Senator John McCain of Arizona, a Vietnam War hero and a political "maverick" who hoped to appeal to undecided voters.

Senator McCain briefly led in the polls, but the economic crisis, Obama's message for change, and a well-funded grassroots campaign helped the Democrats win in November. Obama won with a decisive 364 electoral votes to McCain's 174 by taking eight states (including Florida, Ohio, Virginia, and North Carolina) that had been won by Bush in 2004. The Democrats also increased their majorities in the House and Senate well beyond their victories in 2006.

The election of the first African American president of the United States was historic. However, Barack Obama and the Democrats faced the country's worst economic crisis since the Great Depression, two unfinished U.S. wars, and a world increasingly skeptical of U.S. power and leadership.

Domestic Policy During the Obama Presidency

President Obama appointed his Democratic primary foe, Hillary Clinton, as secretary of state and Eric Holder as the first African American attorney general. Obama reappointed a Republican, Robert Gates, as secretary of defense to provide operational continuity in the Iraq and Afghanistan wars.

The Transition The rapidly growing economic crisis dominated the transition between President Bush and President Obama. Congress approved the use of the second half of the controversial TARP funding—$350 billion. At Obama's request, Bush used more than $10 billion of TARP funds to support the failing automakers General Motors (GM) and the Chrysler Corporation.

Presidential Initiatives President Obama signed a number of executive orders to overturn actions of the Bush administration. He placed a formal ban on torture by requiring that army field manuals be used as the guide for interrogating terrorist suspects. The new president expanded stem cell research and ended restrictions on federal funding of overseas health organizations. One of the first bills passed by Congress that Obama signed was the Lilly Ledbetter Fair Pay Act that strengthened protection of equal pay for female employees. He had promised to close the U.S. prison at Guantánamo Bay, Cuba, but failed to win needed congressional support.

Republicans largely rejected the president's efforts at bipartisanship legislation. However, during his first term, Democrats controlled the House and briefly had enough Senate votes to stop filibusters and so could pass legislation with little Republican support. Several Republicans did vote to confirm Sonia Sotomayor and Elena Kagan to the Supreme Court. Since the new justices replaced other liberals, Justice Anthony Kennedy remained the swing vote in many 5-4 decisions.

Economic Stimulus The "Great" (or "Long") Recession started in late 2007 in the United States. During the downturn, the stock market lost half of its value and unemployment peaked at more than 10 percent. Based on Keynesian economic ideas to avoid a greater depression, Obama and the Democrats enacted a number of programs to promote recovery and financial reform.

The American Recovery and Reinvestment Act of 2009 provided a $787 billion economic stimulus package designed to create or save 3.5 million jobs. Included was $288 billion for tax cuts to stimulate spending and $144 billion to help state and local governments maintain jobs and services. The balance of the package was for construction projects, health care, education, and renewable energy. The Federal Reserve, under the leadership of economist and scholar of the Great Depression Ben Bernanke, also promoted recovery. It lowered interest rates and injected $600 billion dollars into the banking system.

With the domestic auto industry near collapse, the federal government became deeply involved in its recovery. The government temporarily took over General Motors ("Government Motors") while it went through bankruptcy and guided the sale of Chrysler to Fiat, an Italian automaker. The popular "Cash for Clunkers" program provided $3 billion in incentives to U.S. residents to scrap old cars in order to promote sales and to purchase new, more fuel-efficient vehicles.

The Great Recession revealed serious flaws in the federal oversight of financial institutions. The comprehensive Dodd-Frank Wall Street Reform and Consumer Protection Act (2010) was designed to improve regulations of banking and investment firms and to protect taxpayers from future bailouts of "too big to fail" businesses. The act also set up a new Consumer Financial Protection Bureau (CFPB) to regulate consumer products, such as mortgages and credit cards. Some criticized the act for not breaking up the big banks that contributed to the meltdown of the economy and needed the bailouts.

By late 2016, the economy looked far stronger than in 2010. It had added 15 million jobs, the unemployment rate had fallen to 4.6 percent, and the Dow Jones Industrial Average was up 210 percent. The new CFPB had already investigated nearly one million consumer banking and credit card complaints and provided $11.7 billion in relief for more than 27 million consumers. However, the Obama administration was still criticized for a slow recovery, and a lower percentage of Americans were working than before the recession.

Health Care The U.S. "fee for service" medical system was the most expensive in the world but produced mixed results. It promoted innovation but left more than 45 million people outside the system to seek medical care in emergency rooms. The Patient Protection and Affordable Care Act of 2010 ("Obamacare") aimed to extend affordable health care insurance to an additional 25 million Americans through combinations of subsidies, mandates, insurance exchanges, and expansion of Medicaid while introducing medical and insurance reforms to control health care costs. The act required insurance companies to accept patients regardless of preexisting conditions, allowed children to remain on their parents' insurance until age twenty-six, and funded wellness exams and women's medical needs. Republicans opposed the law for its regulations and costs, but after a slow roll out, nearly 20 million Americans gained coverage through private health insurance or Medicaid.

Environment and Climate Change The Obama administration used the stimulus bill to promote reduced reliance on oil and increased development of alternative energy sources, such as solar and wind. Auto manufacturers were encouraged to produce more hybrid and electric cars. In 2015, the United States joined 195 other nations in the Paris Agreement to reduce global carbon emissions. However, many in Congress disagreed with the science behind global warming and opposed tighter controls of greenhouse gases.

Education In the stimulus package, Obama promoted reforms in early childhood and K-12 education (Race to the Top), including more private-public partnerships and more use of charter schools. Democrats attacked the growing college loan debt crisis by cutting out private banks in the federal college loan program. The bipartisan Every Student Succeeds Act was signed into law in 2015 to replace No Child Left Behind, which had been attacked for excessive testing and for supporting efforts to develop common curriculum standards across the country. The new law placed more emphasis on local and state flexibility.

Budget Deficits The recession both decreased federal tax income receipts and increased federal spending to avoid a depression. The total national debt under Obama ballooned from $10.6 to $19.9 trillion dollars, an 88 percent increase. Congressional efforts to reduce deficit spending were stymied by Democrats who opposed cuts to social services and by Republicans who fought tax increases: *compromise* had become a dirty word in Washington. Despite the stalemate in Congress, renewed economic growth reduced the annual deficit from over 9 percent of GDP at the depth of the recession to about 3 percent in 2016.

The Tea Party The opposition to the growing national debt and to "Obamacare" coalesced in a loosely united conservative and libertarian movement known as the Tea Party. While many in the movement focused on debt and health care, others emphasized expanding gun rights, outlawing abortions, and preventing undocumented immigration. Fueled by Tea Party energy, the Republicans in 2010 took control of the House with a 242 to 193 majority and reduced the Democrats' majority in the Senate to 53 votes, which included two independents.

Elections and Money In 2010, the Supreme Court ruled in *Citizens United v. Federal Election Commission* that corporations were "legal persons" and had the same rights as individuals to buy ads to influence political elections. This ruling opened a flood of new money into politics from wealthy donors. As individual donors replaced traditional party fund-raising, parties became weaker.

Election of 2012 The presidential election of 2012 was dominated by issues related to the Great Recession, the Affordable Care Act, illegal immigration, and the long-term fiscal health of the United States. Republicans conducted a long, hard-fought battle for their party's nomination before selecting Mitt Romney, former governor of Massachusetts. President Obama defeated Romney 332 to 206 in the Electoral College and by five million popular votes. The president ran strongly among Hispanics, winning 71 percent of their votes.

In Congress, Republicans could celebrate after the election of 2012 by keeping their strong majority in the House of Representatives, while the Democrats retained control of the Senate. However, the election of 2014 again proved the strength of the Republican turnout in nonpresidential elections as the Republicans took control of both House and Senate.

Government in Deadlock During Obama's first term, the divisions between the Democratic president and the Republican-controlled Congress were so serious that Standard & Poor's downgraded the government's credit rating. These divisions continued through the last four years of Obama's presidency. Compromise was difficult and rare, and as a result, little significant legislation was signed into law. Divided government produced budget stalemates and even a Republican threat to default on the national debt.

One high-profile point conflict was the Affordable Care Act. After Republicans regained control of the House, they tried more than 50 times to overturn or defund the ACA without success.

The two parties did pass one major tax compromise in January 2013. It preserved the Bush tax cuts for incomes of $400,000 and less and allowed the top tax rate to rise to 39.6 percent for higher incomes. However, Congress was unable to compromise on the annual budget, so sequestrations (automatic cuts) across both domestic and defense spending, went into effect. Neither party liked the impact on the military and domestic programs, but the deep divisions prevented compromise. In October 2013, Republicans carried out their threat to shut down the federal government, which remained closed for sixteen days.

The unexpected death of Justice Antonin Scalia in February 2016 led to a new arena for conflict. Senate Republicans refused to hold hearings for Obama's Supreme Court nominee, Merrick Garland. As a result, the Supreme Court went thirteen months with only eight members. When the Court deadlocked 4–4, it could not rule on decisions made in the lower federal courts.

LGBT Rights The gay rights movement achieved significant gains during the Obama presidency. In 2009, Congress made it a federal crime to assault someone because of sexual orientation or gender identity. The next year, Congress repealed "Don't Ask, Don't Tell" to end discrimination against gays and lesbians in the military. In 2012, President Obama came out in support of equal marriage rights. In 2013, the Supreme Court, in a 5–4 ruling, declared the 1996 Defense of Marriage Act unconstitutional and let stand a California court's overturning of a state law banning same-sex marriage. Within a few years, over 30 states allowed same-sex marriage by legislation or by court order. Finally, in a 5–4 decision, the Supreme Court ruled in *Obergefell v. Hodges* (2015) that the 14th Amendment protects the right of same-sex couples to marry.

Gun Rights and Gun Violence The Supreme Court in 2008 had ruled in *District of Columbia v. Heller* that the 2nd Amendment protects an individual's right to possess a firearm unconnected with service in a militia. However, the mass shooting of 26 children and teachers in Connecticut and the murder of 9 African Americans in a South Carolina church sparked another debate over gun rights. President Obama's proposals to tighten gun laws and background checks to keep guns out of the hands of people with mental health problems went nowhere in Congress because of opposition from the gun advocates, such as the National Rifle Association (NRA). The killing of unarmed black teenagers and men by police during arrests sparked a "Black Lives Matter" movement to demand reforms in police training and arrest procedures.

Immigration The Obama administration had no more success than the Bush administration in getting immigration reform through Congress. In 2012, Obama took executive action to protect undocumented young people brought to the United States as children (known as "Dreamers") from deportation and allow them to continue their education and apply for work permits. The program was controversial. Further action to expand it in 2014 was challenged by lawsuits from 26 states and blocked by a federal judge. Anger at Obama's immigration policies increased even though the number of border guards was increased, deportations for undocumented immigrants increased, and the total undocumented immigrant population decreased during his presidency.

Terrorism at Home The fear of homegrown terrorists, self-radicalized by extremist Islamic propaganda, was fueled by the Fort Hood, Texas, shooting (2009); the Boston Marathon bombings (2013); the San Bernadino, California, shooting (2015); and the killing of 49 persons at an Orlando, Florida, nightclub (2016). The Bush and Obama administrations spent billions on intelligence, airport security, federal agents, and support for local and state governments to stop terrorist attacks, but the acts of isolated individuals proved difficult to stop.

Foreign Policy During the Obama Presidency

Barack Obama was elected in part because of his opposition to the Iraq War and his promise to end the unilateral approach overseas that had damaged the reputation of the United States during the Bush presidency. In general, the Obama administration was reluctant to use large-scale military actions that would put many U.S. troops on the ground. Instead, they opted for negotiations, targeted operations by special forces, and drone attacks. Critics attacked Obama for "leading from behind," but the issue remained unresolved whether more troops would solve or worsen conflicts in the Middle East and elsewhere.

Iraq In early 2009, the United States continued to wind down ground combat operations in Iraq. U.S. military support and air power helped the Iraqi forces battle insurgents through 2011, when the last of U.S. forces were withdrawn. However, sectarian violence between Sunni and Shiite Muslims erupted again.

Afghanistan The Obama campaign charged that the Bush administration had ignored Afghanistan in order to invade Iraq. As president, Obama made fighting Al-Qaeda and the Taliban in Afghanistan a priority. He approved adding 17,000 troops to the U.S. forces in Afghanistan in 2009 and then 30,000 more in 2010. The counterterrorism surge proved effective in Afghanistan, but the increased use of pilotless drone attacks on terrorists in Pakistan intensified anger against the United States. In 2012, President Obama and President Karzai of Afghanistan signed a long-term partnership agreement. After 2014, the new focus for U.S. forces was to train and support the Afghan military.

Death of Osama bin Laden In May 2011, Osama bin Laden, the leader of Al-Qaeda, was killed in Pakistan in a clandestine operation of the CIA and Navy SEALs. The death of bin Laden and other top leaders of Al-Qaeda raised the question of whether the U.S. role in the area was completed.

Arab Spring In June of 2009, President Obama traveled to Egypt and gave a speech at the University of Cairo calling for a "new beginning" in relations between the Islamic world and the United States. In 2010, President Obama was soon tested by a wave of protests across the Middle East and North Africa, known as the "Arab Spring." Civil unrest and armed rebellion toppled governments in Tunisia, Libya (the leader, Muammar Gaddafi, was killed), Egypt (the leader, Hosni Mubarak, was imprisoned), and Yemen. However, the civil war in Syria created a greater humanitarian crisis as 12.5 million Syrian refugees tried to escape to safety, often to neighboring countries in the Middle East and Europe. President Obama was widely criticized for not intervening more effectively.

Rise of ISIS In Syria and Iraq, another terrorist movement, ISIS (Islamic State of Iraq and Syria, also known as ISIL) vowed to create a worldwide caliphate under strict Islamic law. This well-financed movement used social media to recruit fighters from around the world. Former members of the Iraqi military, driven from power in the U.S. invasion of Iraq in 2003, also joined ISIS. President Obama, while reluctant to return American soldiers to fight in Iraq and Syria, did commit American air power and trainers to help Iraq regain lost territories. By 2016, the United States had around 5,000 military personnel in Iraq.

Iran The Obama Administration joined other world powers in a 2015 agreement that would prevent Iran from developing and producing nuclear bombs for at least fifteen years. Republicans opposed the agreement because it released the frozen assets of Iran, which it could use for conventional weapons and terrorism.

Asia Events in the Middle East limited President Obama's planned "pivot" to Asia. The administration understood that America's economic and strategic future was closely tied to the Pacific Rim. The United States and 11 other Pacific countries (excluding China) negotiated the Trans-Pacific Partnership (TPP) trade agreement in 2016. However, American public opinion turned against globalization, and the U.S. Senate did not ratify the TPP. China's move to create new territories on islands in the South China Sea threatened Southeast Asian nations and free passage through international waters guarded by the U.S. Navy. The most immediate threat to U.S. interests in Asia came from North Korea, which was developing nuclear weapons and long-range missiles.

Europe After the Great Recession, the European Union struggled with a debt crisis, especially in countries with weaker economies, such as Greece. It took German leadership to save the euro as a common currency. However, the resulting fiscal austerity programs and the EU open borders policies alienated many working-class people. This promoted a resurgence of nationalism among people who worried that they were losing their jobs and national identities.

Russia In 2014, Ukraine's pro-Russian government was overthrown by a popular pro-Western movement. Russia, under Vladimir Putin, responded by orchestrating a revolt of pro-Russian partisans in eastern Ukraine and annexing the militarily strategic Crimea region. The United States and European nations retaliated by placing economic sanctions on Russia and its leaders. A resurgent Russia also intervened in Syria's civil war, making it a player in Middle Eastern politics once again. By the end of the Obama administration, U.S.-Russia relations were at the lowest point since the end of the Cold War.

Cuba President Obama started a slow normalization of relations with Cuba. In 2015, the two countries agreed to open embassies in Havana and Washington and to resume direct flights for the first time since the Eisenhower administration. Against some Republican opposition, American travelers and businesses took advantage of the thaw in relations with the former Cold War enemy.

Cyber Attacks The greatest new threats to the nation's security in the 21st century included cybercrime, such as stealing digital data, and cyber warfare, such as incapacitating the computerized networks that operate another country's electric power grid. Russians, Chinese, Iranians, and others used cyber attacks to steal U.S. private and governmental digital data, including credit card and personnel records. In 2016, Russian agents hacked into emails of the Hillary Clinton campaign and distributed the information through the antisecrecy group WikiLeaks in an effort to disrupt the U.S. election.

The Trump Presidency

The flood of more than one million refugees and immigrants into Europe from the Middle East and Africa in 2015 fueled a backlash against worldwide globalization trends. Many struggling middle-class families felt that their jobs, safety, and cultural identities were under attack, which sparked the rise of more nationalistic politics. Anti-immigration sentiment was a major factor in the 2016 "Brexit" vote by Great Britain to leave the 28-nation European Union. In the United States, the unsolved issues of 11 million undocumented immigrants and the loss of manufacturing jobs to lower-wage countries in Asia and Latin America set the stage for another political upset.

2016 Election In the United States, the most vocal leader against globalization was Donald J. Trump, a well-known real estate developer and reality TV show personality. He attacked Washington politicians ("drain the swamp"), unwanted immigration ("build a wall"), and international trade deals, such as NAFTA, while promoting a nationalist movement to "Make America Great Again." Trump's effective use of slogans, social media (Twitter), and large rallies helped him to defeat 13 other candidates and capture the Republican party presidential nomination. In the Democratic party, Hillary Clinton, former secretary of state, U.S. senator, and first lady, became the first woman from a major party to run for the presidency of the United States.

The polls favored Clinton to win. However, a controversy over her "extremely careless" use of a personal computer server fed the perception that she was untrustworthy. Meanwhile, Trump's bold attacks energized non-college educated and working-class voters, adding them to the traditional Republican base. On election night, Trump surprised media predictions by winning

Source: Getty Images

Pennsylvania, Michigan, and Wisconsin along with traditional swing states, and captured 306 electoral votes against Clinton's 232 votes. Clinton did win the popular vote by almost 3 million. The Republican party also held firm control of both the House and Senate, giving them the best opportunity to enact their agenda since 2006.

Trump Administration While President Trump had no prior experience in political office or the military, he had selected an experienced politician, Governor Michael Pence of Indiana, as his vice president. Trump's "Make America Great Again" policies emphasized tax cuts, deregulation, trade protection, and controlling immigration. In 2017, the president signed the Tax Cuts and Jobs Act, which cut corporate tax rate from 35 to 21 percent and lowered personal tax brackets and the threshold for estate taxes. The Republicans, with a control of both houses of Congress, dismantled parts of the Dodd-Frank Act that regulates banks and consumer borrowing. The president also weakened the Democrat's Affordable Health Care Act by eliminating the mandate to buy health insurance and overturned DACA, an Obama program that protected from deportation children who had come into the country with their families. President Trump also fulfilled another campaign promise by filling vacancies in the federal courts with conservative judges, such as Supreme Court judges Neil Gorsuch and Brett Kavanaugh. The first two years of Trump's presidency enjoyed low unemployment, strong job growth, and a positive business climate, which Republicans credited to tax cuts and deregulation.

President Trump implemented his "America First" campaign in foreign affairs by negotiating a new trade agreement with Canada and Mexico to replace NAFTA. Trump unilaterally canceled U.S. participation in the Trans-Pacific Partnership, the Paris Climate, and the Iran Nuclear agreements. He ordered tariffs to protect American steel and aluminum industries against foreign competition, and initiated additional tariffs against Chinese imports, which threatened trade wars. The administration increased its support among conservatives by recognizing Jerusalem as the capital of Israel, to which it moved the U.S. embassy. President Trump also started personal negotiations with North Korean dictator Kim Jong-un to end their nuclear weapons and missiles threat. The administration proposed the withdrawal of U.S. troops from Syria, Iraq, and Afghanistan, but supported a successful war to destroy the ISIS caliphate. The president disrupted U.S. long-standing allies by criticizing the European Union, NATO, and other nations for taking advantage of the United States. Critics of Trump thought he was friendlier to Russian and North Korean dictators than long-standing democratic allies, such as Canada, France, and Germany.

Turmoil in Washington Intelligence agencies uncovered Russian interference in the 2016 election, such as hacking into the Democratic National Committee computers and the creation of hundreds of fake social media accounts to spread divisions and false stories among the electorate. Former FBI director Robert Mueller was appointed special counsel to investigate the Russian interference and possible coordination with members of the Trump campaign. Dozens of Russians and six Americans associated with the Trump campaign were indicted as part of grand jury investigations. The firing of FBI director James Comey by President Trump and other political pressures on the Department of Justice also raised questions of obstruction of justice. President Trump dismissed the investigation as a "witch hunt." In March 2019, Mueller released his report to the attorney general, who announced that it cleared President Trump of charges of coordination with Russia, but did not take a clear stand on possible obstruction charges.

In the 2018 midterm elections, concerns about health insurance, gun violence, trade wars, and President Trump's provocative style helped the Democrats capture control of the House by a 35-seat majority. However, Republicans gained Senate seats in states where President Trump was popular, expanding their majority to 6. In early 2019, a partial shutdown of the federal government resulted, when the President and Congress disagreed over funding to build a wall along the Mexican border. The longest shutdown in history lasted 35 days, before Congressional Republicans persuaded President Trump to accept a compromise. Unhappy over the compromise, the president sought to build a border wall with his presidential emergency powers. Conflicts over the wall, the Mueller Report, and other investigations of President Trump, along with long-standing deep partisan divisions, left Washington observers skeptical about the ability of Congress and the president to reach additional compromises.

Developing Domestic Issues Americans continued to debate immigration policies, income inequality, health care, racial prejudice, and gun violence, especially on school campuses, but the late 2010s revealed others areas of growing national concern.

Opioid Epidemic Drugs heralded in the 1990s as breakthroughs in pain treatment became a major health crisis in the 21st century, as opioid overdoses took an estimated 400,000 lives between 1999 and 2017. For example in 2017, there were more than 72,000 drug overdose deaths in the United States, including 49,068 that involved an opioid. During the same time, an estimated 11.4 million Americans misused prescription pain medicine. Drug makers, such as Purdue Pharma, were found guilty of misleadingly physicians that opioids, such as OxyContin, were safe. Drug distributors who dispensed large amounts of opioids were also prosecuted. In 2018, federal funds were provided for treatment of opioid addiction, which often developed after people took medicine for dental pain, back surgery, or sports injuries.

#MeToo In October 2017, a movement against sexual assault and harassment went viral on social media sites, such as Twitter and Facebook. The hashtag MeToo was used in 12 million posts during the first 24 hours. At first sexual-abuse allegations were against well-known Hollywood, media, and political personalities, but the movement opened up discussion of sexual harassment and abuse in business, education, health care, churches, and society at large. In response, many businesses examined improving sexual harassment policies and gender-based pay differences. A priority for #MeToo was to change the laws surrounding sexual harassment and assault, and giving sufferers the ability to file complaints without retaliation. These widespread allegations raised issues about due process for the accused, yet the movement continued to expand in the United States and around the world.

Source: Shutterstock

Digital Security and Privacy Investigations into foreign hacking and use of social media to disrupt elections exposed abuses by large Internet companies such as Facebook and Google. These companies became wealthy and powerful through the extraction and analysis of personal data of hundreds of millions of their users for focused advertisements and resale of data to third parties. Fearful of discouraging innovation, government exercised little regulation of the industry. Congressional hearings exposed the failure of the Internet companies to monitor how the data was used or to protect it from cyber attacks. Some saw the rise of "surveillance capitalism" as a growing threat to Americans' privacy, security, and tradition of self-government.

HISTORICAL PERSPECTIVES: WHAT CAUSES BOOMS AND BUSTS?

The Great Recession renewed the debate over the causes of depressions and the government's role in the economy. Economic collapses caused by financial crises, such as the Panic of 1837, have been far more severe and long lasting than those caused by industrial overproduction. Kevin Phillips in *Bad Money* (2008) argued that the danger to the U.S. economy increased after the 1970s because financial services became more profitable than manufacturing. He viewed this "financialization" of the economy as dangerous because it will lead to national decline as it did for the Spanish, the Dutch, and the British in the past.

At the heart of many debates among economists is their confidence in markets. Has history shown that markets are free and rational or that they are often inefficient and easily manipulated? The conservative view, expressed by Friedrich Hayek and Milton Friedman, is that markets have worked so well that government should stay out of them. In contrast, liberal Joseph Stiglitz pointed out that markets can fail because of imperfect or false information, such as the fraudulent sale of repackaged subprime mortgage debt. Stiglitz argued that markets need government supervision to avoid economic calamities that harm ordinary working people.

The Great Recession caused former Federal Reserve Chair Alan Greenspan to modify his views. Though a free-market conservative, he admitted that he had been wrong and that "curative" regulation of banks was needed to counter the "animal spirits" of euphoria, greed, and fear in the financial markets.

KEY TERMS BY THEME

Politics in the 2000s (POL, ARC)
political polarization
southern white
  conservatives
gerrymandered "safe
  seats"
election of 2000
George W. Bush
Al Gore
Bush v. Gore
Bush tax cuts
No Child Left Behind Act
Enron, corporate
  corruption
campaign finance
  reform
housing bubble
election of 2004
John Kerry
privatization of Social
  Security
Hurricane Katrina
John Roberts
Samuel Alito
border security

War on Terrorism (WOR)
Colin Powell
Islamic roots of
  anti-Americanism
Al-Qaeda
Osama bin Laden
asymmetric warfare
bombing of U.S.
  embassies
USS Cole
World Trade Center
September 11, 2001
Afghanistan, Taliban
Hamid Karzai
Homeland Security
  Department
"connect the dots"

Director of National
  Intelligence
Kyoto Accord
Bush Doctrine
unilateralist approach
"axis of evil"
WMDs
Saddam Hussein
UN inspections
Operation Iraq Freedom
"regime change"
"war of choice"
Sunni vs. Shiite
Abu Ghraib prison
2007 troop surge

Great Recession (WXT)
securitization
liquidity crisis
Fannie Mae, Freddie
  Mac
Lehman Brothers
Troubled Assets Relief
  Program (TARP)
poor regulation of
  financial institutions

Obama Presidency (POL)
election of 2008
Hillary Clinton
Barack Obama
John McCain
Sonia Sotomayor
Elena Kagan
2009 stimulus bill
Federal Reserve
Dodd-Frank Act
Consumer Financial Pro-
  tection Bureau
aid to auto industry
Affordable Care Act
Paris Agreement (2015)
budget deficits
Tea Party

election of 2012
Mitt Romney
Latino voters
sequester cuts
2013 shutdown of
  government
LGBT rights
repeal of "Don't Ask,
  Don't Tell"
gun violence
Black Lives Matter
Boston Marathon
  bombing
Dreamers

Obama Foreign Policy (WOR)
ban on torture
withdrawal from Iraq
Afghanistan surge
death of bin Laden
drawdown in
  Afghanistan
Arab Spring
fall of dictatorships
civil war in Syria
ISIS
"pivot" to Asia
euro crisis
Vladimir Putin
Conflict in Ukraine
Cyber attacks
WikiLeaks
Cuban relations
Brexit
antiglobalization
Election of 2016
Donald J. Trump

Roberts Court (POL, SOC)
D.C. v. Heller (2008)
Citizens United (2010)
Obergefell v. Hodges
  (2015)

Questions 1–2 refer to the excerpt below.

"These militants are not just the enemies of America or the enemies of Iraq. They are the enemies of Islam, and they're the enemies of humanity.

[I]t is cowardice that seeks to kill children and the elderly with car bombs, and cuts the throat of a bound captive, and targets worshipers leaving a mosque. It is courage that liberated more than 50 million people from tyranny. And it is courage in the cause of freedom that will once again destroy the enemies of freedom!

Islamic radicalism, like the ideology of communism, contains inherent contradictions that doom it to failure. By fearing freedom, by distrusting human creativity, and punishing change, and limiting the contributions of half a population, this ideology undermines the very qualities that make human progress possible and human societies successful. The only thing modern about the militants' vision is the weapons they want to use against us. The rest of their grim vision is defined by a warped image of the past, a declaration of war on the idea of progress itself."

—George W. Bush, Veterans Day speech, November 11, 2005

1. Which of the following best explains the context for this speech by President Bush?

   (A) The attack on the Twin Towers in New York

   (B) The resurgence of the Taliban in Afghanistan

   (C) The challenge to control the violence in Iraq

   (D) The breakdown of relations with Iran

2. Which of the following best supports President Bush's comparison of Islamic radicalism to communism?

   (A) Neither saw universal education as a path to progress

   (B) Neither valued freedom of the individual

   (C) Both opposed cultural change

   (D) Both opposed advances in personal communications

Questions 3–5 refer to the excerpt below.

"The fact is our economy did not fall into decline overnight. Nor did all of our problems begin when the housing market collapsed or the stock market sank. We have known for decades that our survival depends on finding new sources of energy. . . . The cost of health care eats up more and more of our savings each year, yet we keep delaying reform. Our children will compete for jobs in a global economy that too many of our schools do not prepare them for. . . .

A surplus became an excuse to transfer wealth to the wealthy instead of an opportunity to invest in our future. Regulations were gutted for the sake of a quick profit at the expense of a healthy market. People bought homes they knew they couldn't afford from banks and lenders who pushed those bad loans anyway. . . .

Well that day of reckoning has arrived, and the time to take charge of our future is here."

—Barack Obama, Speech to Congress, February 24, 2009

3. Which of the following would best support the text, "A surplus became an excuse to transfer wealth to the wealthy?"

   (A) The tax cuts in 2001 and 2003 under George W. Bush

   (B) The 1996 budget compromise under Clinton

   (C) The bailout of the savings and loans under George H. W. Bush

   (D) The 25 percent tax cuts passed under Ronald Reagan

4. Among the issues identified in the speech, which of the following became the signature accomplishment of the Obama administration in the first term?

   (A) Legislation providing for energy independence in ten years

   (B) Breakup of the banks that contributed to the recession

   (C) Takeover of home mortgages to keep people in their homes

   (D) Health insurance reform and expansion of the Americans insured

5. Which of the following became law to achieve the "healthy market" goal in the excerpt?

   (A) The federal stimulus package to create 3.5 million jobs and tax cuts to stimulate spending

   (B) The reform of banking and financial institutions and the creation of the Bureau of Consumer Protection

   (C) Federal rebates for consumers to promote sales of new and more energy efficient automobiles

   (D) A bipartisan budget that increased taxes, cut federal spending, and secured the future of Social Security and Medicare

Questions 6–8 refer to the excerpt below.

"Obama's foreign policy has, above all, been characterized by strategic restraint. . . . He has been wary of grand declaration and military interventions.

"Obama came to office believing that the U.S. had overextended itself militarily. He believed that the cost of extravagant involvement in Iraq and Afghanistan had been the erosion of ties with allies and the worsening of relations with adversaries. . . .

"Such restraint is much harder to execute than it may appear. In a world without a serious military rival, the U.S. becomes the world's emergency call center. . . .

"The president whom Obama resembles most in this respect is an unlikely one: Dwight Eisenhower. . . . Eisenhower refused to support America's closest allies, the British and French, when they—with Israel—invaded Egypt. . . . He declined to send forces to help the French in Vietnam. . . . Eisenhower—the greatest military hero of World War II—could stay sane and resist calls for action."

—Fareed Zakaria, commentator and journalist,"Why Barack Is
Like Ike," *Time*, December 31, 2012

6. Which of the following best explains the context for "Obama came to office believing that the U.S. had overextended itself militarily"?

   (A) President Reagan's expansion of the U.S. military spending

   (B) The failures of presidents Clinton and Bush to capture Osama bin Laden

   (C) President Bush's decision to go to war in Iraq

   (D) The application of the containment policy in the war on terrorism

7. The restraint shown by President Obama in foreign affairs was most evident in his policies regarding

   (A) the imprisonment of Hosni Mubarak in Egypt

   (B) the death of Muammar Gaddafi in Libya

   (C) the crackdown on protesters in Saudi Arabia

   (D) the civil war in Syria

8. President Obama best resembled President Eisenhower in his preference for

   (A) using nuclear brinkmanship to force opponents to yield

   (B) relying on relatively small secret operations to carry out policies

   (C) challenging the military-industrial complex over spending

   (D) giving the impression that he was not in charge by playing golf

SHORT-ANSWER QUESTIONS

Use complete sentences; an outline or bulleted list alone is not acceptable.

Question 1 is based on the following cartoon.

Source: Otherwords.org

1. Using the cartoon, answer (A), (B), and (C).
   (A) Briefly explain ONE specific historical event or development from the period 2000 to 2017 that caused the United States to increase its involvement in the Middle East.
   (B) Briefly explain ONE specific historical impact of increased U.S. involvement in the Middle East on that region.
   (C) Briefly explain ONE specific historical impact of increased U.S. involvement in the Middle East on U.S. domestic policies or politics.

Question 2. Answer (A), (B), and (C).

   (A) Briefly explain ONE specific way that the South and West influenced American politics after 1980.
   (B) Briefly explain ONE specific way that increased immigration from Latin America influenced American politics after 1980.
   (C) Briefly explain ONE specific way that issues related to guns influenced American politics after 1980.

Question 3. Answer (A), (B), and (C).

(A) Briefly explain ONE specific historical event or development that contributed to the economic bubbles of the 1990s or 2000s.

(B) Briefly explain ONE specific historical impact of the Great Recession of 2008 in addition to rising unemployment and job loss.

(C) Briefly explain ONE specific program created by the George W. Bush or Barack Obama administrations to deal with the Great Recession or to reform the economy.

Question 4. Answer (A), (B), and (C).

(A) Briefly explain ONE specific way the environment contributed to increased political and cultural conflicts after 2000.

(B) Briefly explain ONE specific way gender-related issues contributed to increased political and cultural conflicts after 2000.

(C) Briefly explain ONE specific way a ruling of the Supreme Court contributed to increased political and cultural conflicts after 2000.

THINK AS A HISTORIAN: WRITING A COHERENT ESSAY

Connecting words such as "in addition" and "however" help readers follow a train of thought. Which THREE of the following sentences best starts a paragraph that would support the argument emphasizing differences between presidents George W. Bush and Barack Obama?

1. In contrast, Obama emphasized international action in foreign policy.

2. Similarly, Obama attended Harvard after graduating from a prestigious undergraduate school.

3. Unlike Bush, the new president entered office while the nation was in the midst of an economic crisis.

4. Many of Obama's supporters were disappointed that he continued or extended several of Bush's policies on national security.

5. Reporters who covered both men's presidential campaigns noted the contrasts in how each one treated the press.

UNIT 9: Period 9 Review, 1980–Present

LONG ESSAY QUESTIONS

Directions: The suggested writing time for each question is 40 minutes. In your response you should do the following:

- **Thesis:** Make a defensible claim that establishes a line of reasoning and consists of one or more sentences found in one place.
- **Contextualization:** Relate the argument to a broader historical context.
- **Evidence:** Support an argument with specific and relevant historical evidence.
- **Reasoning:** Organize an argument using the skill in the question.
- **Analysis:** Demonstrate a complex understanding of the question

1. Analyze to what extent the conservative resurgence changed the economic and social policies of the United States government from 1980 to 2008.
2. Analyze to what extent the end of the Cold War changed United States foreign policies from 1991 to 2012.
3. Compare and contrast the leadership and economic policies of presidents Ronald Reagan and Franklin Roosevelt.
4. Compare and contrast the chief successes and failures of TWO of the following presidential administrations.
   - George H. W. Bush
   - Bill Clinton
   - George W. Bush
   - Barack Obama

U.S. History
Practice Examination

Section 1

Part A: Multiple Choice—55 minutes, 55 questions

Directions: *Two to four questions are in sets that focus on a primary source, secondary source, or other historical issue. Each question has four answers or completions. Select the best one for each question or statement.*

Questions 1–4 on this page and the next refer to the excerpt below.

"Part of the myth about the first Americans is that all of them . . . had one culture . . . the white man turned everything upside down. Three elements were important in the early influence: the dislodgement of eastern tribes, the introduction of the horse, and metal tools and firearms.

"The British invaders of the New World, and to lesser degree the French, came to colonize. They came in thousands to occupy the land. They were, therefore, in direct competition with the Indians and acted accordingly, despite their verbal adherence to fine principles of justice and fair dealing. The Spanish came quite frankly to conquer, to Christianize. . . . They came in small numbers. . . . and the Indian labor force was essential to their aims. Therefore they did not dislodge or exterminate the Indians. . . .

"The Spanish, then did not set populations in motion. That was done chiefly from the east. The great Spanish contribution was the horse."

—Oliver LaFarge, anthropologist, "Myths That Hide the American Indian," *The American Indian: Past and Present*, 1971

1. During the early years of colonization, the French policy in North America was based primarily on
   (A) settling on lands controlled by American Indians
   (B) controlling the fur trade
   (C) farming in the Mississippi River Valley
   (D) establishing a series of Catholic missions

2. United States policy toward the American Indians in the 19th century was most similar to the colonial Indian policy of the

(A) British

(B) Dutch

(C) French

(D) Spanish

3. Which of the following best describes something Europeans introduced in the Americas that helped American Indians survive colonization?

(A) European introduced new farming methods, which enabled American Indians to maintain their agricultural heritage

(B) Europeans introduced metal tools, which led to increased trade and better relationships with Europeans

(C) Europeans introduced horses, which transformed the cultures of American Indians on the Great Plains

(D) Europeans introduced Christianity, which brought unity among American Indians

4. Which of the following generalizations best describes a similarity among Europeans who colonized North America?

(A) All wanted to convert American Indians to Catholicism

(B) All emphasized developing extensive trade with American Indians

(C) All attempted to dominate American Indians in some way

(D) All intended to exterminate or remove American Indians

Questions 5–7 refer to the excerpt below.

"We want peace and good order at the South; but it can only come by the fullest recognition of the rights of all classes. . . .

"We simply demand the practical recognition of the rights given us in the Constitution and laws. . . .

"The vicious and exceptional political action had by the White League in Mississippi has been repeated in other contests and in other states of the South, and the colored voters have been subjected therein to outrages upon their rights similar to those perpetrated in my own state at the recent election . . . and we ask such action as will not only protect us in the enjoyment of our constitutional rights but will preserve the integrity of our republican institutions."

—Senator Blanche K. Bruce, African American U.S. Senator from Mississippi, speech to the Senate, 1876

5. Examples of actions that responded to Senator Bruce's plea in the excerpt included the

   (A) formation of the NAACP in 1909

   (B) civil rights legislation of 1964 and 1965

   (C) *Brown v. Board of Education* decision in 1954

   (D) March on Washington in 1963

6. An accepted response to Bruce's call for action in the excerpt was Booker T. Washington's program based on which of the following?

   (A) Active participation in the Republican Party

   (B) Migration back to Africa

   (C) Economic self-help

   (D) An agricultural based society

7. The end of Senator Bruce's senate career and African American political power in the South was ensured by which of the following?

   (A) Removal of federal troops from the South

   (B) A divided Republican party

   (C) Election of a Democrat as president

   (D) Rebirth of the Ku Klux Klan

Questions 8–10 refer to the excerpt below.

"Instructions to you, Vicente de Zaldivar. . . . of the expedition to New Mexico. . . . for the punishment of the pueblo of Acoma for having killed . . . soldiers. . . .

"Since the good success of the undertaking depends on the pleasure of God our Lord in directing you to appropriate and effective methods, it is right that you should seek to prevent public or private offenses to Him in the expedition. . . . You will proceed over the shortest route. . . . At the places and pueblos that you pass through on the way you will treat the natives well and not allow harm to be done them. . . .

"If God shall be so merciful as to grant us victory, you will arrest all of the people, young and old, without sparing anyone. Inasmuch as we have declared war on them without quarter, you will punish all those of fighting age as you deem best, as a warning to everyone in this kingdom."

—Don Juan de Oñate, Colonizer of New Mexico, 1599

8. The first Spanish explorers in the Americas provided a strong motivation for colonization by other Europeans, who saw that the Spanish
   (A) found abundant fertile land
   (B) established political freedom
   (C) won many religious conversions
   (D) found large amounts of gold and silver

9. Which of the following best explains why the natives of America became so important to the Spanish empire?
   (A) Natives could be enslaved by the Spanish settlers
   (B) Natives provided most of the labor on Spanish land
   (C) Natives often joined the Spanish military
   (D) Natives were primarily trading partners of the Spanish

10. The authority of the leaders in the Spanish colonies to order the actions described in this excerpt came from which of the following?
    (A) Elected governors
    (B) Pope
    (C) King
    (D) Church

Questions 11–13 refer to the excerpt below.

"Now we all found the loss of Captain Smith; yea, his greatest maligners could now curse his loss. As for corn provision and contribution from the savages, we had nothing but mortal wounds, with clubs and arrows. . . .

"Nay, so great was our famine that a savage we slew and buried, the poorer sort took him up again and ate him; and so did diverse one another boiled and stewed with roots and herbs. . . .

"This was that time, which still to this day, we called the starving time. It were too vile to say, and scarce to be believed, what we endured; but the occasion was our own for want of providence, industry, and government, and not the barrenness and defect of the country. . . . For till then in three years, for the numbers were landed us, we have never from England provision sufficient for six months."

—John Smith, description of "starving time" in Virginia, 1607–1614

11. When the Virginia colony was first formed, control over it rested with
    (A) an elected assembly
    (B) the king
    (C) Captain John Smith
    (D) shareholders of the joint-stock company

12. During the "starving time," the Jamestown colony depended on which of the following form of charter for its support?
    (A) Joint-stock company
    (B) Proprietary colony
    (C) Royal colony
    (D) Church-based company

13. Both the Virginia and Plymouth colonists shared a commitment to
    (A) equal rights for all
    (B) religious freedom
    (C) good relations with the American Indians
    (D) representative government

Questions 14–16 refer to the photograph below.

Source: Madison, Wisconsin, 1967. AP Photo/Neal Ulevich

14. Which group provided the most active opposition to the Vietnam War?
    (A) Religious groups
    (B) Democratic Party
    (C) Supporters of funding for the Great Society
    (D) Students opposed to the draft

15. The most important mistake the U.S. government made in the Vietnam War, according to many historians, was
    (A) the failure to maintain public support for the war
    (B) the lack of Asian experts to advise the government
    (C) the restrictions it placed on the military
    (D) the weak presidential leadership by Johnson and Nixon

16. How did the Vietnam War protest movement compare with other protest movements in American history?
    (A) Like the American Indians Movement, it had roots deep in history
    (B) Like the union movements, many protesters were killed
    (C) Like the civil rights movement, it used mass marches
    (D) Like the Populist movement, it tried to form an independent party

Questions 17–19 refer to the excerpt below.

"Besides being political to the core, Clinton is notable for his intelligence, energy, and exceptional articulateness. He is also marked by a severe lack of self-discipline that leads to difficulties, and a resiliency and coolness under pressure. . . . The most damaging blow of the year for Clinton was the failure of his most ambitious policy initiative, a bill guaranteeing health care to all Americans. . . .

"Clinton's first two years in the White House were marked by such legislative successes as NAFTA, the creation of a youth volunteer corps, a major deficit-reduction measure, and a law permitting family members to take unpaid leave to attend to children and sick relatives. . . . Clinton seems certain to be recognized for moving the Democratic party to the center of the political spectrum and for many incremental policy departures."

—Fred I. Greenstein, political scientist, *The Presidential Difference*, 2000

17. According to most historians, which of the following legislative efforts from Clinton's first term had the greatest lasting impact?

    (A) Ratification of NAFTA

    (B) Creation of a youth volunteer corps

    (C) Passage of a "motor-voter" law

    (D) Reform of Social Security

18. Which is the most important reason why many Americans viewed Clinton's presidency as a success?

    (A) Clinton's personal popularity

    (B) Clinton's peacekeeping and humanitarian efforts

    (C) economic expansion

    (D) democratic control of Congress

19. Based on Clinton's actions as president, which of the following most accurately describes his political philosophy?

    (A) radical

    (B) pragmatic

    (C) conservative

    (D) progressive

Questions 20–22 refer to the cartoon below.

Source: Walter L. Fleming, "A Prospective Scene in the City of Oaks, 4th of March, 1869," *Independent Monitor,* Tuscaloosa Alabama, 1868. ClipArtETC

20. Which of the major targets of the Ku Klux Klan after the Civil War is portrayed in the above cartoon?

(A) Carpetbaggers

(B) Abolitionists

(C) Former slaves

(D) Union officers

21. Which of the following best describes how the Compromise of 1877 affected the issues addressed in this cartoon?

(A) By resolving the1876 election peacefully, it encouraged people to negotiate

(B) By making Rutherford Hayes president, the KKK became superfluous

(C) By withdrawing federal troops from the South, it reduced lynchings

(D) By ending Reconstruction, it improved race relations in the South

22. Who of the following would have been most likely to support the message of this cartoon?

(A) People who criticized the Ku Klux Klan

(B) Republicans who opposed Redeemer governments

(C) Northerners who advocated Radical Reconstruction

(D) Southerners who supported the end of Reconstruction

Questions 23–25 refer to the excerpt below.

"That evening there was a general discussion in regard to the main subject in hunters' minds. Colorado had passed stringent laws that were practically prohibitory against buffalo-hunting; the Legislature of Kansas did the same. . . .

"General Phil. Sheridan was then in command of the military department of the Southwest. . . . when he heard of the nature of the Texas bill for the protection of the buffaloes. . . . He told them that instead of stopping the hunters they ought to give them a hearty, unanimous vote of thanks. . . . 'These men . . . will do more in the next year, to settle the vexed Indian question . . . they are destroying the Indians' commissary. . . .'

"But there are two sides to the question. It is simply a case of the survival of the fittest. Too late to stop and moralize now. And sentiment must have no part in our thoughts from this time on."

> —John R. Cook, soldier, hunter, and author,
> *On Buffaloes and Indians*, 1877

23. In the 1870s, after wars with American Indians and shifts in public opinion, the government began basing its Indian policies on
    (A) establishing tribal reservations
    (B) supporting tribal culture
    (C) removing Indians to lands farther west
    (D) assimilating Indians into white culture

24. John Cook's philosophy toward buffalo hunting and the future of American Indians shows the influence of the idea of
    (A) gospel of wealth
    (B) laissez faire
    (C) Social Darwinism
    (D) protectionism

25. The efforts to protect the buffalo herds in the 1870s were directed by which of the following movements that was developing in that decade?
    (A) Grange
    (B) Conservationists
    (C) Assimilationists
    (D) National Labor Union

Questions 26–28 refer to the excerpt below.

"They were begging for workers. They didn't care whether you were black, white, young, old. . . . I got caught up in that patriotic "win the war," "help the boys." The patriotism that was so strong in everyone then. . . .

"The first paycheck I got in aircraft was more money than I'd ever seen in my life. I didn't even know what to do with it. I didn't have a bank account. You couldn't buy anything much. . . .

"Soap was rationed, butter, Kleenex, toilet paper, toothpaste, cigarettes, clothing, shoes. And you saw people making a lot of money and not doing anything for the war effort. . . .

"By 1944 a lot of people were questioning the war. . . . I think when we actually began to see boys come home in late 1943, 1944 —those that had been injured. . . .—then the rumbles grew into roars, and the young people thought maybe they were being led into this."

—Juanita Loveless, African American worker in a war plant,
Rosie the Riveter Revisited, 1988

26. One group of people whose lives improved during World War II were
    (A) Women working in factories who received equal pay with men
    (B) Mexican American farmworkers who won citizenship
    (C) American Indians who made life on reservations better
    (D) African Americans who moved to jobs in the North and West

27. How did the outbreak of the war change the country's economy?
    (A) Factory jobs paid higher wages but rationing limited spending
    (B) Taxes increased so much that people could not afford to buy much
    (C) The sale of war bonds got money circulating again
    (D) Union demands for higher wages caused prices to increase dramatically

28. During World War II, unlike in earlier wars, the U.S. government took action to
    (A) tax incomes
    (B) sell war bonds
    (C) provide equal pay for women
    (D) freeze wages and prices

"We. . . . declare that this act on our part implies no sanction of, nor promise of voluntary obedience to such of the present laws of marriage, as refuse to recognize the wife as an independent, rational being. . . .

"We believe that personal independence and equal human rights can never be forfeited, except for crime; that marriage should be an equal and permanent partnership, and so recognized by law; that until it is so recognized, married partners should provide against the radical injustice of present laws, by every means in their power.

"We believe that where domestic difficulties arise, no appeal should be made to legal tribunals under existing laws, but that all difficulties should be submitted to the equitable adjustment of arbitrators mutually chosen.

"Thus reverencing law, we enter our protest against rules and customs which are unworthy of the name, since they violate justice, the essence of law."

—Lucy Stone, abolitionist and feminist, speech at her marriage, 1855

29. Who of the following would be most likely to support the views expressed by Stone in this excerpt?
    (A) Participants in the Second Great Awakening
    (B) Members of the American party
    (C) Supporters of the Liberty party
    (D) Individuals who attended the Seneca Falls Convention

30. Women's rights advocates in the mid-19th century such as Lucy Stone were also most active in which of the following reform movements?
    (A) Public asylums
    (B) Antislavery societies
    (C) Communal experiments
    (D) Free common schools

31. At the time this statement was made, most people accepted that women could
    (A) work in factories
    (B) vote in most states
    (C) hold political office
    (D) serve on juries

Questions 32–34 refer to the map below.

MEAN CENTER of POPULATION for the UNITED STATES, 1790 to 2010

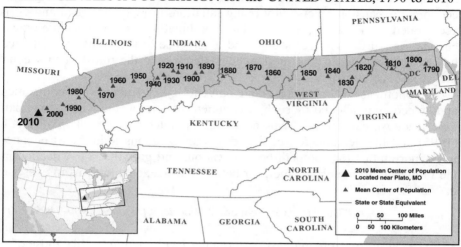

32. Which of the following contributed most to the northward movement shown between 1860 and 1880?

   (A) Start of the California gold rush

   (B) Completion of the Erie Canal

   (C) End of the Civil War

   (D) Purchase of Alaska

33. Which of the following best explains why the westward movement of the center of population slowed in the first decades of the 20th century?

   (A) The end of World War I caused people to return to rural areas

   (B) Many people were settling in the Midwest

   (C) Former slaves moved away from the South

   (D) Eastern cities grew rapidly through immigration during these decades

34. Which of the following changes in the United States during and after World War II contributed to the shift shown in the map?

   (A) Conflicts between younger and older generations caused people to move

   (B) Increasing prosperity allowed people to move to lower-wage regions

   (C) The expansion of the defense industry created jobs in certain regions

   (D) Changes in climate made some regions more liveable than they had been

Questions 35–37 refer to the excerpt below.

"**New Economy** The second half of the 1990s marked the longest sustained stretch of economic growth in U.S. history. Unlike other periods of long-term economic expansion reversed by rising inflation, growth continued and even accelerated as inflation declined. The combination of rapid technological change, rise of the services sector, and emergence of the global marketplace had experts convinced that the United States was in the midst of 'a second industrial revolution.' . . .

"Economists attributed these developments to a restructuring of companies and an economy abetted by such government policies as the North American Free Trade Agreement. . . . Many economists pointed to the breakup of AT&T (1995) and the deregulation of the telecommunications industry as enhancing opportunities for competition, innovation, and growth. . . . A decline in the influence of organized labor, for better or worse, enable firms to exercise greater flexibility."

—"The American Economy," *American Decades, 1900–1999*, 2001

35. The causes of economic prosperity in the 1990s were most like those of
    (A) the prosperity of the 1950s
    (B) the expansion in the mid-19th century
    (C) the rapid industrialization after the Civil War
    (D) the boom in the 1920s

36. The changes described in this excerpt affected politics in the 1990s by
    (A) increasing the popularity of Bill Clinton
    (B) causing many voters to vote for Republicans in 2000
    (C) expanding the political influence of conservative Christians
    (D) decreasing support for additional deregulation

37. Which of the following did not share in the economic growth of the 1990s as much as other groups did?
    (A) Large corporations
    (B) College graduates
    (C) Southern states
    (D) Labor unions

Questions 38–40 refer to the excerpt below.

"There is not among these three hundred bands of Indians one which has not suffered cruelly at the hands of either the Government or of white settlers. . . .

"It makes little difference, however, where one opens the record of the history of the Indians. . . . every page and every year has its dark stain. . . . but neither time nor place makes any difference in the main facts. Colorado is as greedy and unjust in 1880 as was Georgia in 1830, and Ohio in 1795. . . .

"President after president has appointed commission after commission to inquire into and report upon Indian affairs. . . . These reports are bound up . . . . and that is the end of them. . . .

"All judicious plans and measures for their safety and salvation must embody provisions for their becoming citizens as fast as they are fit. . . .

"Cheating, robbing, breaking promises—these three are clearly things which must cease to be done."

—Helen Hunt Jackson, writer and activist for American Indians,
A Century of Dishonor, 1881

38. The actions referred to in Georgia in 1830 are strongly associated with the policies of which of the following individuals?

(A) Henry Clay

(B) William Henry Harrison

(C) John Marshall

(D) Andrew Jackson

39. The legal status of American Indians in the 1880s could most closely be compared to that of

(A) Eastern European immigrants in the late 19th century

(B) Japanese Americans during World War II

(C) African American slaves

(D) American Tories after the Revolution

40. Partially in response to Jackson's *A Century of Dishonor,* a new federal government policy for American Indians was enacted in which of the following laws?

(A) Dawes Act

(B) Civil Rights Act of 1875

(C) Assimilationist Act

(D) Reservation Control Act

Questions 41–43 refer to the graph below.

U.S. BIRTH RATE, 1909 to 2009

Year

Source: U.S. Census Bureau

41. The graph above provides evidence of a population change following World War II, which is popularly referred to as the

(A) greatest generation

(B) population bomb

(C) baby boom

(D) generation gap

42. Which generalization about the birth rate between 1949 and 2009 is best supported by this graph?

(A) It generally increased as immigration increased

(B) It generally increased during the civil rights movement

(C) It generally decreased whenever the economy got worse

(D) It generally decreased when more women entered the workforce

43. The post-World War II population changes in the birth rate can be partially explained by government policies that

(A) contained communism around the world

(B) reduced the power of labor unions

(C) encouraged steps toward racial equality

(D) helped GIs attend college and buy homes

Questions 44–46 refer to the excerpt below.

"I like much the general idea of framing a government into Legislative, Judiciary and Executive. . . . . I will now add what I do not like. First the omission of a bill of rights . . . .

"The second feature I dislike, and greatly dislike, is the abandonment in every instance of the necessity of rotation in office and most particularly in the case of President. . . .

"I own that I am not a friend to very energetic government. . . .

"I think our governments will remain virtuous for many centuries; as long as they are chiefly agricultural; and this will be as long as there shall be vacant lands in any part of America. . . .

"Above all things I hope the education of the common people will be attended to; convinced that on their good sense we may rely with the most security for the preservation of a due degree of liberty."

—Thomas Jefferson, Letter to James Madison, December 1787

44. Jefferson's feelings about "rotation in office" were at least partially resolved by
    (A) George Washington's establishment of a two-term tradition
    (B) the Tenure of Office Act passed in 1867
    (C) the decision by FDR to seek a third term and a fourth term
    (D) a series of Supreme Court rulings written by John Marshall

45. Which action by Thomas Jefferson most clearly supported his belief that a government based on an agricultural society would be long-lasting?
    (A) agreeing to the Louisiana Purchase
    (B) passing the Embargo Act
    (C) funding internal improvements
    (D) establishing a national bank

46. Based on this excerpt, which of the following would Jefferson most likely have supported?
    (A) Expansion of voting rights to women, blacks, and 18-year-olds
    (B) Establishment of land-grant universities starting in 1862
    (C) Creation of an income tax
    (D) Prohibition of the sale of alcohol

Questions 47–49 refer to the excerpt below.

"Monday, January 3, 1983

"A tough budget meeting & how to announce the deficits we'll have—they are horrendous & yet the Dems. in Cong. are saying there is no room for budget cuts. . . . Newt Gingrich has a proposal for freezing the budget at the 1983 level. It's a tempting idea except that it would cripple our defense program. . . .

"Monday, October 24, 1983

"Opened with NSC brf. on Lebanon & Grenada. Lebanon gets worse as the death toll climb. . . . Ambas. Hartman (Russia) came by. He confirms what I believe: the Soviets won't really negotiate on arms reductions until we deploy the Pershing II's & go forward with MX. . . .

"Then at 8 P.M., Tip, Jim Wright, Bob Bryd, Howard Baker, Bob Michel & our gang met upstairs in the W.H. & told them of the Grenada operation that would take place in the next several hours."

—Ronald Reagan, *The Reagan Diaries*, 2007

47. At the end of his presidency, on which of the following topics would Ronald Reagan have said that he had the most success?

(A) "freezing the budget"

(B) "Lebanon"

(C) "the deficits"

(D) "arms reduction"

48. The increase in the federal budget deficits during the Reagan administration can be attributed largely to which of the following?

(A) Agricultural and food stamp payments

(B) Mandatory increases in Social Security

(C) Expansion of welfare benefits

(D) Military buildup in all services

49. Eventually as Speaker of the House, Newt Gingrich would be successful in reducing budget deficits with which of the following presidents?

(A) Bill Clinton

(B) Ronald Reagan

(C) George H. W. Bush

(D) George W. Bush

Questions 50–52 refer to the excerpt below.

"I have now to perform the most pleasing task of exhibiting. . . . the existing state of the unparalleled prosperity of the country. . . .

"The greatest prosperity which this people have enjoyed since the establishment of their present constitution, it would be exactly that period of seven years which immediately followed the passage of the tariff of 1824.

"This transformation of the condition of the country from gloom and distress to brightness and prosperity, has been mainly the work of American legislation, fostering American industry. . . .

"When gentlemen have succeeded in their design of an immediate or gradual destruction of the American system, what is their substitute? . . . . Free trade!

"Gentlemen are greatly deceived as to the hold which this system has. . . . They represent that it is the policy of New England. . . . and most determined in its support is Pennsylvania. . . . Maryland was against it; now the majority is for it. . . . The march of public sentiment is to the South."

—Henry Clay, "Defense of the American System," 1832

50. The most difficult part of Henry Clay's American System to implement
   (A) was the protective tariff
   (B) were the internal improvements
   (C) were the agricultural subsidies
   (D) was the national bank

51. Which of the following groups disagreed most strongly with Clay's ideas about tariffs and trade?
   (A) Owners of manufacturing companies during the Civil War
   (B) Most Republicans in the late 1800s
   (C) Populists and many Progressives
   (D) Supporters of the Hawley-Smoot Tariff

52. The most persistent opposition to Clay's American System came from which of the following groups?
   (A) Voters opposed to government debt
   (B) Politicians involved in sectional rivalries
   (C) Strong advocates of states' rights
   (D) Believers in a strict interpretation of the Constitution

Questions 53–55 refer to the excerpt below.

"I, Francis Daniel Pastorius, ... laid out and planned a new town. . . . we called Germantown. . . . in a very fine and fertile district, with plenty of springs of fresh water, being supplied with oak, walnut, and chestnut trees, and having besides excellent and abundant pasturage for the cattle. . . .

"The air is pure and serene. . . . and we are cultivating many kinds of fruits and vegetables, and our labors meet with rich reward.

"Our surplus of grain and cattle we trade to Barbados for rum, syrup, sugar, and salt. The furs, however, we export to England for other manufactured goods. We are also endeavoring to introduce the cultivation of the vine, and also the manufacture of woolen cloths and linen, so as to keep our money as much as possible in the country. . . .

"William Penn is one of the sect of Friends. . . . Still he will compel no man to belong to his particular society."

—Francis D. Pastorius, German colonist, *A Particular Geographical Description of the Lately Discovered Province of Pennsylvania,* 1700

53. By the mid-18th century the largest group of non-English people to come to America were

   (A) Germans

   (B) Scotch-Irish

   (C) African Americans

   (D) Irish

54. The development of various industries by the German settlers suggests that the English who controlled the colony rejected the commonly accepted ideas about

   (A) the structure of a joint-stock company

   (B) the role of a colony under mercantilism

   (C) how to recruit new German immigrants

   (D) how to use American Indian labor

55. Which of the following phrases from the excerpt indicates the feature of Pennsylvania that was most attractive to settlers?

   (A) "being supplied with oak, walnut, and chestnut trees"

   (B) "we trade to Barbados for rum, syrup, sugar, and salt"

   (C) "endeavoring to introduce the cultivation of the vine"

   (D) "he will compel no man to belong to his particular society"

Section 1

Part B: Short Answer—40 minutes, 3 questions

Use complete sentences; an outline or bulleted list alone is not acceptable.

Question 1 is based on the following painting.

Source: Benjamin West, *American Commissioners of the Preliminary Peace Negotiations with Great Britain,* London, England, 1783. Winterthur Museum, gift of Henry Francis du Pont, 1957.856

1. Using the painting above, answer (A), (B), and (C).

   (A) Briefly explain the implications of the peace negotiations in 1783 for American policies toward Great Britain.

   (B) Briefly explain the implications of the peace negotiations in 1783 for British policies toward the United States.

   (C) Briefly explain ONE specific policy of the American government from the period 1783–1812 that developed in response to the British view expressed by the painting.

Question 2 is based on the following excerpts.

"By the fall of 1963 the Kennedy administration, though still worried about its ability to push legislation through a recalcitrant Congress, was preparing initiatives on civil rights and economic opportunity. . . .

"John F. Kennedy cautiously eased tensions with the Soviet Union, especially after Kennedy found himself on the brink of nuclear war over the presence of Soviet weapons in Cuba in 1962.

"Although Kennedy did not rush to deal with domestic issues—in large part because he believed that foreign policy needed precedence—the press of events gradually forced his administration to use government power to confront racial discrimination and advance the cause of equality at home."

John M. Murrin, et al., historians, *Liberty, Equality and Power,* 1996

"Chopped down in his prime after only slightly more than a thousand days in the White House, Kennedy was acclaimed more for the ideals he enunciated and the spirit he had kindled than for the concrete goals he had achieved. He had laid one myth to rest forever—that a Catholic could not be trusted with the presidency of the United States.

"In later years revelation about Kennedy's womanizing and allegations about his involvement with organized crime figures tarnished his reputation. But despite those accusations, his apparent vigor, charisma, and idealism made him an inspirational figure for the generation of Americans who came of age in the 1960s."

—David M. Kennedy, et al., historians, *The American Pageant,* 2006

2. Using the excerpts above, answer (A), (B), and (C).

   (A) Briefly explain ONE major difference between Murrin and Kennedy's historical views of President John F. Kennedy.

   (B) Briefly explain how ONE development from the period 1960 to 1963 not directly mentioned in the excerpts supports Murrin's view.

   (C) Briefly explain how ONE development from the period 1960 to 1963 not directly mentioned in the excerpts supports Kennedy's view.

Choose EITHER Question 3 OR Question 4.

Question 3. Answer (A), (B), and (C).

(A) Briefly describe ONE specific historical difference between American society and culture in the mid-18th century and the mid-19th century.

(B) Briefly describe ONE specific historical similarity between American society and culture in the mid-18th century and the mid-19th century.

(C) Briefly explain ONE specific historical effect of American society and culture in either the mid-18th century or the mid-19th century

Question 4. Answer (A), (B), and (C).

(A) Briefly describe ONE specific historical similarity between the women's rights movement in the period from 1900 to the 1920s and in the period from the 1960s to the 1970s.

(B) Briefly describe ONE specific historical difference between the women's rights movement in the period from 1900 to the 1920s and in the period from the 1960s to the 1970s.

(C) Briefly explain ONE specific historical effect of the women's rights movement in either the period from 1900 to the 1920s or the period from the 1960s to the 1970s.

Section 2

Part A: Document-Based Question—60 minutes, 1 question

Directions: Question 1 is based on the accompanying documents. The documents have been edited for the purpose of this exercise. You are advised to spend 15 minutes planning and 45 minutes writing your answer.In your response you should do the following:

- **Thesis:** Make a defensible claim that establishes a line of reasoning and consists of one or more sentences found in one place.
- **Contextualization:** Relate the argument to a broader historical context.
- **Document Evidence:** Use content from at least six documents.
- **Outside Evidence:** Use one piece of evidence not in the documents.
- **Document Sourcing:** Explain how or why the point of view, purpose, situation, or intended audience is relevant for at least three documents.
- **Analysis:** Show the relationships among pieces of historical evidence and use them to support, qualify, or modify an argument.

1. To what extent were the reform efforts of the Progressive Era aimed at maintaining the existing society and to what extent did they bring about radical changes?

Document 1

The conscience of the people, in a time of grave national problems, has called into being a new party, born of the nation's sense of justice. We of the Progressive party here dedicate ourselves to the fulfillment of the duty laid upon us by our fathers to maintain the government of the people, by the people and for the people whose foundations they laid. . . .

Political parties exist to secure responsible government and to execute the will of the people. . . . Instead of instruments to promote the general welfare, they have become the tools of corrupt interests which use them impartially to serve their selfish purposes. Behind the ostensible government sits enthroned an invisible government owing no allegiance and acknowledging no responsibility to the people.

To destroy this invisible government, to dissolve the unholy alliance between corrupt business and corrupt politics is the first task of statesmanship of the day.

Document 2

Source: President Woodrow Wilson, First Inaugural Address, March 4, 1913

No one can mistake the purpose for which the Nation now seeks to use the Democratic Party. It seeks to use it to interpret a change in its own plans and point of view. Some old things. . . . as we have latterly looked critically upon them. . . . have dropped their disguises and shown themselves alien and sinister. Some new things, as we look frankly upon them. . . . have come to assume the aspect of things long believed in and familiar, stuff of our own convictions.

We have itemized. . . . the things that ought to be altered. . . . A tariff which makes the Government a facile instrument in the hands of private interests; a banking and currency system perfectly adapted to concentrating cash and restricting credits; an industrial system which restricts labor, and exploits natural resources; a body of agriculture never served through science or afforded the facilities of credit best suited to its practical needs.

Document 3

Source: Senator Elihu Root, former secretary of state and secretary of war, "Experiments in Government," lecture at Princeton University, April 1913

The recognition of shortcomings or inconveniences in government is not by itself sufficient to warrant a change of system. There should be also an effort to estimate and compare the shortcomings and inconveniences of the system to be substituted, for although they may be different they will certainly exist.

Document 4

Source: J.L. De Mar, 1903. Library of Congress

The caption on the cartoon reads: "A bear was on the engine of the President's Special, it was in a bad humor and snarled viciously at the President when he went near it. —News item of yesterday."

The caption says: "A bear was on the engine of the President's Special, it was in a bad humor and snarled viciously at the President when he went near it."

Document 5

Source: W. E. B. Du Bois, sociologist and civil rights activist, An Open Letter to Woodrow Wilson, September 1913

Sir, you have now been President of the United States for six months and what is the result? It is no exaggeration to say that every enemy of the Negro race is greatly encouraged; that every man who dreams of making the Negro race a group of menials and pariahs is alert and hopeful.

A dozen worthy Negro officials have been removed from office, and you have nominated but one black man for office, and he, such a contemptible cur, that his very nomination was an insult to every Negro. . . .

To this negative appearance of indifference has been added positive action on the part of your advisers, with or without your knowledge, which constitutes the gravest attack on the liberties of our people since emancipation. Public segregation of civil servants in government employ. . . . has for the first time in history been made the policy of the United States government.

Document 6

Source: Mary Harris "Mother" Jones, labor and community organizer, *Miners' Magazine,* April 1915

When one starts to investigate conditions the result is appalling. . . . For instance, it is a fact that although this country is in its infancy, and has gained in wealth more in fifty years than any other country has in 700 years still we have more poverty in comparison with any of those old countries.

I have always felt that no true state of civilization can ever be realized as long as we continue to have two classes of society. But that is a tremendous problem. . . . I think myself that we are bound to have a revolution here before these questions are straightened out. We were on the verge of it in the Colorado strike and the reason we did not have it then was not due to the good judgement of public officials, but to that of labor officials, who worked unceasingly to prevent it.

Document 7

Source: George Grantham Bain Collection, Library of Congress

Section 2

Part B: Long Essay Question—40 minutes, 1 question

LONG ESSAY QUESTIONS

Directions: *Choose Question 2 OR Question 3 OR Question 4.* The suggested writing time for each question is 40 minutes. In your response you should do the following:

- **Thesis:** Make a defensible claim that establishes a line of reasoning and consists of one or more sentences found in one place.
- **Contextualization:** Relate the argument to a broader historical context.
- **Evidence:** Support an argument with specific and relevant historical evidence.
- **Reasoning:** Organize an argument using the skill in the question.
- **Analysis:** Demonstrate a complex understanding of the question using historical evidence to support, qualify, or modify an argument.

2. Compare and contrast the prevailing views of the American people in the years following the Seven Years' War (French and Indian) War and the Revolutionary War.

3. Compare and contrast the prevailing views of the American people in the years following the War of 1812 and the Mexican War.

4. Compare and contrast the prevailing views of the American people in the years following World War I and World War II.

INDEX

Arts: of 1920s, 482; of antebellum period, 211; colonial achievements in, 50–51; in Era of Good Feelings, 151; of Gilded Age, 368–371
Ashburton, Lord Alexander, 232
Ashcan School, 370
Asia. *See also* specific countries: Cold War in, 566–569, 583–584; nuclear proliferation in, 670; U.S. policy toward, 670, 691
Asian Americans, 639, 671
Asiento system, 8
Assemby line, 478, 510, 532
Astor, John Jacob, 232
Asylums, 212–213
Athabaskan language, 4
Atlanta, 180
Atlanta Constitution, 347
Atlantic Charter, 530
Atlantic Seaboard, Native Americans of, 5
Atlantic world, xviii. 35–38
Atomic bombs, 537, 566
Atoms for peace plan, 585
Attlee, Clement, 538
Attucks, Crispus, 74
Auburn system, 213
Audubon Society, 347
Austin, Moses, 230–231
Austin, Stephen, 231
Australian ballots, 435
Austria, 158
Automobile industry, 510, 606, 632, 657, 686, 687
Automobiles, 478, 479
Axis of evil, 683
Azores, 6
Aztecs, 2, 8, 11

B

B-52 bombers, 569
Baby boom, 558, 592
Baby boomers, 611, 671
Bachelor subculture, 372
Back-to-Africa movement, 483
Bacon, Nathaniel, 29
Bacon's Rebellion, 29, 37
Baez, Joan, 611
Bailyn, Bernard, 77
Baja California, 236
Baker, Jim, 655
Baker, Newton D., 462
Baker v. Carr, 609–610
Balanced budget, 667
Balboa, Vasco Núñez de, 8
Balkan wars, 669–670
Ballinger, Richard, 440

Baltimore and Ohio Railroad, 320, 329
Bank of the United States, 111; rechartering of, 197, 280; Second, 152, 153
Banks, 442, 496, 503
Baptists, 50, 181, 208, 299
Barbados, 33
Barbary pirates, 136, 157
Barnes, Harry Elmer, 468
Barnum and Bailey Circus, 371
Bartholdi, Frédéric-Auguste, 362
Bartram, John, 51
Baruch, Bernard, 460
Baseball, 372, 588
Basketball, 372
Batista, Fulgencio, 587
Battle of the Atlantic, 536
Bay of Pigs, 602
Beard, Charles, 119, 143, 260, 332, 540
Bear Flag Republic, 234
Beatles, 611
Beatniks, 592
Beckwourth, James, 237
Beer-Wine Revenue Act (1933), 503
Begin, Menachem, 635
Beliefs, *see* Religion, Moral Majority
Bell, Alexander Graham, 325
Bell, John, 258
Bellamy, Edward, 364
Bellows, George, 369
Benton, Thomas Hart, 482
Bentsen, Lloyd, 662
Berkeley, Lord John, 33
Berkeley, Sir William, 29
Berlin airlift, 564–565
Berlin crisis, 586–587
Berlin Wall, 602, 663
Bernanke, Ben, 687
Bessemer, Henry, 323
Bethune, Mary McLeod, 513
Beveridge, Albert, 409
Bicentennial celebration, 633
Bicycling, 372
Biddle, Nicholas, 197
Biden, Joseph, 686
Big-stick policy, of Teddy Roosevelt, 417–420
Billion-dollar Congress, 386
Bill of Rights, 108–109
Bingham, George Caleb, 211
Bin Laden, Osama, 682, 691
Birmingham, Alabama, 347
Birney, James, 215
Birth control, 445, 481, 611
The Birth of a Nation (1915), 303, 486
Birthrates, 365
Black abolitionists, 215

Douglas, Stephen A., 255, 256, 317; Compromise of 1850 and, 249; election of 1860 and, 258–259; Kansas-Nebraska Act and, 252, 253; Lincoln-Douglas debates, 256–257

Douglass, Frederick, 215, 250, 291, 317

Doves, 615

Draft: during Civil War, 279–280; during World War I, 461–462; during World War II, 528–529

Drake, Edwin, 323

Drake, Joseph Rodman, 226

Drake, Sir Francis, 9

Dreamers, 690

Dred Scott v. Sandford, 255–256

Dreiser, Theodore, 369, 434

Dress reform, 216

Du Bois, W. E. B., 304, 350, 368, 443–444, 462, 483

Due process clause, 295–296

Dukakis, Michael, 662

Duke of York, 33

Dulaney, Daniel, 128

Dulles, John Foster, 581–582, 603

Dust Bowl farmers, 512

Dutch colonies, 33

Dutch East Indies, 582

Dutch exploration, 10

Dutch West India Company, 10

Dwight, Timothy, 207

Dylan, Bob, 611

E

Eagleton, Thomas, 629

Eakins, Thomas, 369

Earth Day, 639

East Asia, 419, 420

Eastern Europe, 562–563, 662–663, 664

East Germany, 563, 602, 663

East India Company, 75

Eastman, George, 325

Eaton, Peggy, 195

Economic bubbles, 681

An Economic Interpretation of the Constitution (Beard), 119

Economic mobility, 164

Economic nationalism, 151–153

Economic Recovery Act (1981), 656

Economics: after Civil War, 280–281; imperialism and, 424; Keynesian, 511, 656; laissez-faire, 324–325, 380; of slavery, 178; supply-side, 656–657, 659

Economic Stabilization Act (2008), 685

Economic stimulus program, 666

Economic theories, 324

Economy: of 1800s, 159–164; in 1800s, 238–239; of 1920s, 477–479; of 1970s, 633, 636; of 1980s, 658; after American Revolution, 104; under Bush, George H. W., 664–665; under Clinton, 668; colonial, 48; consumer, 478–479; growth of, 319; money supply and, 384, 387; under Nixon, 628; of North, 270, 280–281

Eddy, Mary Baker, 365

Edison, Thomas, 325–326, 401

Education. *See also* Schools: in 1920s, 481; for African Americans, 293, 299; colonial, 51–52; elementary, 51, 367; higher, 51–52, 213, 367–368; moral, 213; reforms, 213, 367–368, 681; in South, 180; Sputnik and, 586

Edwards, Jonathan, 49–50, 51

Egypt: Arab Spring, 691; Camp David Accords, 635

Ehrlichman, John, 630

Eighteenth Amendment, 212, 484–485

Eighth Amendment, 109

Eight-hour day, 387, 440, 460, 461

Eightieth Congress, 559–560

Eisenhower, Dwight D.: civil rights movement and, 589–590; Cold War and, 581–587; domestic policies of, 580–581; election of 1952 and, 579–580; election of 1956 and, 581; historical perspective on, 593; legacy of, 587; NATO and, 565; presidency of, 579–587; in World War II, 536

Eisenhower Doctrine, 584

Elected offices, 193

Election campaigns, 381

Election(s): of 1796, 115; of 1800, 117–118, 131; of 1804, 135; of 1808, 137; of 1812, 140; of 1816, 150, 153; of 1820, 153; of 1824, 153, 193–194; of 1828, 194; of 1836, 198; of 1840, 199; of 1844, 232–233; of 1848, 248; of 1852, 236, 252; of 1856, 255; of 1858, 257; of 1860, 258–259; of 1864, 278; of 1866, 296; of 1868, 297; of 1872, 301; of 1876, 302–303, 381, 382; of 1878, 385; of 1880, 381, 382; of 1884, 381, 383; of 1888, 381, 385–386; of 1890, 353, 386; of 1892, 381, 387; of 1896, 388–389, 390; of 1900, 416; of 1908, 439; of 1910, 440; of 1912, 441; of 1916, 458; of 1920, 475; of 1924, 477; of 1928, 477; of 1932, 501–502; of 1936, 507–508; of 1938, 512; of 1940, 529; of 1944, 535, 558; of 1948, 560–561; of 1952, 572, 579–580;

of 1956, 581; of 1960, 600–601; of 1964, 605; of 1968, 615, 616–617; of 1972, 629–630; of 1976, 634; of 1980, 636, 655–656; of 1984, 658; of 1988, 662; of 1992, 665–666; of 1994, 667; of 1996, 667–668; of 2000, 679–680; of 2004, 684; of 2008, 686; of 2010, 688; of 2012, 688; of president, 106

Electoral college, 106

Electricity, 477, 478, 505, 507

Electric power, 326

Elementary and Secondary Education Act, 605

Elementary education, 367; colonial, 51

Eliot, Charles W., 368

Eliot, T. S., 481

Elizabeth I (Queen of England), 9

Elkins Act (1903), 438

Ellington, Duke, 483

Ellis Island, 362

Ellsberg, Daniel, 626–627, 630

Ely, Richard T., 368

Emancipation Proclamation, 275–276, 280

Embargo Act (1807), 136, 140

Emergency Banking Relief Act (1933), 504

Emerson, Ralph Waldo, 209, 213

Empire State building, 482

Employment Act (1946), 559

Encomienda system, 8, 11

Engel v. Vitale, 610

England. *See also* Great Britain: conflicts between Spain and, 9; early settlements by, 25–26; exploration of North American by, 9; Glorious Revolution in, 37; policy toward Native Americans of, 12; Restoration in, 31

English colonies. *See* Colonies

English immigrants, 46

Enlightenment, 53, 76–77, 207

Enron, 681

Entertainment, in 1920s, 480

Environment, *See also* Conservation movement: 2, 53, 182, 239, 340, 341, 342, 360, 512, 581, 606, 639, 657, 662, 666, 680

Environment Protection Agency (EPA), 639

Episcopalians, 181

Equal Employment Opportunity Commission, 606

Equality, of opportunity, 191–192

Equal Pay Act (1963), 612

Equal protection clause, 295–296, 349

Equal Rights Amendment (ERA), 612

Era of Good Feelings, 150–153, 193

Erie Canal, 161

Ervin, Sam, 630

Escobedo v. Illinois, 609

Espionage Act (1917), 461, 476

Espionage cases, 570–571

Established churches, 49

Estonia, 663

Ethiopia, 526

Ethnic neighborhoods, 363

Europe. *See also specific countries:* Napoleonic wars in, 136; U.S. policy toward, 691

European exploration, 5–6

European Union (EU), 669, 691

Evangelists, 655

Evolution, 368, 433, 483, 484

Ewen, Stuart, 489

Exchange, *See* Trade, Tariffs, Transportation

Excise taxes, 113

Executive branch, 109, 110

Executive power, use of during Civil War, 269

Ex Parte Milligan, 279

Exploration: Dutch, 10; early, 7–8; economic motives for, 6–7; English, 9; European interest in, 5–6; French, 10

Exports, 238–239

Exxon Valdez, 639

F

Factories, 174

Factory system, 162–163, 164, 238

Factory workers, 163, 164, 174, 281–282, 327–328, 437, 467

Fair Deal, 561

Fair Employment Practices Commission, 559

Fair Employment Practices Committee, 513

Fair Labor Standards Act (1938), 511

Fall, Albert B., 476

Fallen Timbers, Battle of, 113

Falwell, Jerry, 655

Families: changes in, 214; colonial, 47; decline of traditional, 671; during Great Depression, 512; impact of industrialization on, 164; pioneer, 342; single-parent, 671; slave, 178; in urban society, 365

Family and Medical Leave Act (1994), 666

Family Assistance Plan, 628

Fannie Mae, 685

Farewell Address (Washington), 115

Farm Credit Administration, 504

Farmers. *See also* Agriculture: colonial, 53; Dust Bowl, 512; frontier, 237–238; as minority, 350; problems facing, 350–353, 479, 498; programs for, 500–501, 505,

Gun control, 666
Gunpowder, 5
Gun rights, 688, 689
Gun violence, 689–690

H

Habeas corpus, 269, 279, 280
Haiti, 422, 523, 669
Haldeman, H. R., 630
Halfbreeds, 381, 383
Halfway covenant, 31
Hallucinogenic drugs, 611
Hamilton, Alexander: at Annapolis
    Convention, 104; at Constitutional
    Convention, 104; duel with Burr, 135;
    Federalist Papers and, 106; Federalists
    and, 114, 116; Jefferson and, 110–111,
    118; as secretary of the treasury, 110–111;
    Whiskey Rebellion and, 113
Hamilton, Andrew, 52–53
Hammer v. Dagenhart, 443
Hancock, John, 105
Hancock, Winfield S., 382
Handlin, Oscar, 373
Hanna, Marcus, 389, 390
Harburg, E. Y., 496
Harding, Warren G.: election of 1920 and,
    475; presidency of, 476
Harlem Renaissance, 482–483
Harpers Ferry, 257
Harrison, Benjamin, 346, 385–386, 387
Harrison, William Henry, 381; at Battle of
    Tippecanoe, 138–139, 155; election of
    1840 and, 199; in War of 1812, 140, 142
Harte, Bret, 369
Hartford, settlement of, 30
Hartford Convention, 141
Harvard University, 51, 368
Harvey, William H., 388
Hawaii, annexation of, 414–415
Hawley-Smoot Tariff, 500
Hawthorne, Nathaniel, 210, 211
Hay, John, 416–417
Hay, Samuel P., 447
Hay-Bunau-Varilla Treaty (1903), 418
Hayden, Tom, 610
Hayek, Friedrich, 696
Hayes, Lucy, 382
Hayes, Rutherford B., 380, 382; election of
    1876 and, 302–303; Great Railroad Strike
    and, 329; vetoes by, 294
Haymarket bombing, 329–330
Hayne, Robert, 196
Haynsworth, Clement, 629

Hay-Pauncefote Treaty (1901), 236, 418
Headright system, 28
Health care reform, 666, 681, 687–688, 693
Hearst, William Randolph, 371, 413
Heller, Joseph, 592
Hell's Kitchen, 364
Helper, Hinton R., 250–251
Hemingway, Ernest, 481
Henry, Patrick, 52, 73, 105, 107; as delegate to
    First Continental Congress, 85
Henry the Navigator (Prince of Portugal), 6, 7
Henry VII (King of England), 9
Hepburn Act (1906), 438
Herberg, Will, 592
Heritage Foundation, 655
Heroes, of 1920s, 480
Herzegovina, 664
Higher education, 51–52, 213, 367–368
Higher Education Act, 605
High schools, 367, 481
Highway Act (1956), 580–581
Highway Beautification Act, 606
Highways, 161
Hill, James, 321
"Hillbillies," 180
Hippies, 611
Hirohito (Emperor of Japan), 567
Hiroshima, 537
Hispanic Americans, 643, 688
Hispanic culture, 346
Hiss, Alger, 570–571, 580
Hitler, Adolf, 521, 524–525, 526, 527–528,
    536
Hobby, Oveta Culp, 580
Ho Chi Minh, 583
Hofstadter, Richard, 143, 391, 424, 489
Hokokam, 4
Holder, Eric, 686
Holland, 90
Hollywood, 480
Holmes, Oliver Wendell, Jr., 368, 461
Holocaust, 536
Holy Roman Empire, 6, 7
Home Insurance Company Building, 363
Homeland security, 683
Homeland Security Department, 683
Homeless, 499
Homeownership, 671
Home Owners Loan Corporation (HOLC), 504
Homer, Winslow, 369
Homestead Act (1862), 281, 320, 342
Homesteaders, 342
Homestead Strike, 330
Homosexuals, 639

Hooker, Thomas, 30
Hoover, Herbert: election of 1928 and, 477; election of 1932 and, 501–502; foreign policy of, 521–523; as lame duck president, 502; policies of, 500–502; in World War I, 460
Hoover, J. Edgar, 467
Hoovervilles, 499
Hopi, 343
Hopkins, Harry, 365, 504, 506
Hopper, Edward, 482
Horatio Alger myth, 326–327
Horses, 4, 181, 343
Horseshoe Bend, Battle of, 141
House of Burgesses, 27, 28, 54, 73, 74, 127
House of Representatives. *See also* Congress, U.S.: African Americans in, 298; balance in, 155; election of 1824 and, 194
House Un-American Activities Committee (HUAC), 570–571
Housewives, 480–481, 558, 592
Housing boom, 685
Houston, Sam, 231
Howard, Oliver O., 293
Howe, Elias, 238
Howe, Louis, 503
Howe, Samuel Gridley, 213
How the Other Half Lives (Riis), 434
Hudson, Henry, 10
Hudson Fur Company, 232
Hudson River school, 211
Huerta, Victoriano, 423
Hughes, Charles Evans, 436, 458, 476, 486
Hughes, Langston, 483
Huguenots, 10, 46
Hull, Cordell, 524
Hull House, 364
Human rights diplomacy, 634
Humphrey, Hubert, 600, 605, 616
Hungarian Revolt, 586
Hungary, 663
Hurricane Katrina, 685
Hussein, Saddam, 664, 670, 683–684
Hutchinson, Anne, 29–30
Hydrogen bomb, 566, 582

I

Ickes, Harold, 504, 513
Idaho, 341
Ideas, *See also* Religion: Enlightenment, 53, 77; Transcendentalism, 209; slavery, 250–251; Progressivism, pragmatism, and scientific management; 433; New Deal, 503; the 1950s, 592.

Identify. *See* Immigrants; Religion
Illinois, 175, 192
Illinois Central Railroad, 238
Immigrants: Chinese, 321, 362; discrimination against, 362, 419; European, to colonies, 45–46; German, 46, 176, 212; hostility toward, 254; Irish, 176, 212; Mexican, 346, 462, 590, 671; new, 361; "old," 361; Roman Catholic, 365; undocumented, 637, 671, 685; westward expansion and, 155
Immigration: in 2000, 671; Chinese Exclusion Act, 341; growth of, 361, 637; historical perspective on, 373; in Northeast, 175–176; in postwar era, 590; restrictions on, 362, 485
Immigration Act, 605
Immigration Act (1965), 637
Immigration Reform and Control Act (1986), 637, 671
Impending Crisis of the South (Helper), 250–251
Imperialism: historical perspective on, 424; in Latin America, 411–412; new, 410–412; Spanish-American War and, 415–416
Imperial presidency, 625, 640
Imperial wars, 69–71
Implied powers, 154
Imports, 238–239
Impressment, 111–112
Incandescent lamp, 326
Incas, 2, 8, 11
Income inequality, 497, 672
Income tax, 271, 280, 387, 388, 439
Indentured servants, 28, 48
Indiana, 175, 192
Indian Appropriation Act (1871), 345
Indiana Territory, 155
Indian Removal Act (1830), 195–196
Indian Reorganization Act (1934), 346, 513
Indian Self-Determination Act (1975), 638
Indian wars, 344–345
Individualism, 343
Individual Retirement Accounts (IRAs), 657
Individual rights, 609–610
Indochina, 583
Industrial empires, 322–324
Industrialization, 161–164, 214, 238, 280–281; historical perspective on, 332; impact of, 326–328; regional differences in, 331; urbanization and, 362; workers and, 327–328
Industrial Revolution, 174, 433
Industrial Revolution, second, 322
Industry: growth of, 319; in North, 280–281;

oil, 323; in South, 347–348; steel, 323; during World War I, 460; during World War II, 532
Infant industries, 110
Infectious diseases, 8, 11, 363
Inflation, 384, 559, 628, 636
Initiatives, 387, 435
In re Debs, 330
Insular cases, 416
Intellectual movements, 367–372
Intercolonial committees, 74
Interest rates, 681
Intermediate-range missiles, 661
International Bank for Reconstruction and Development, 562
International Darwinism, 410–411
International Migration Society, 350
International Monetary Fund (IMF), 670
Internment, of Japanese Americans, 534
Interstate Commerce Act, 322, 352, 384, 405
Interstate Commerce Commission (ICC), 322, 352, 438, 439
Interstate highway system, 580–581
Interstate roads, 161
Intolerable Acts (1774), 75–76, 85
Inventions, 161–162, 163, 175, 238, 325–326
Iran, 683, 684; overthrow of government in, 582; agreement, 691
Iran-contra scandal, 660, 662
Iran hostage crisis, 635
Iranian revolution, 635
Iraq, 670; Persian Gulf War, 664
Iraq War, 683–684, 690
Ireland, 45, 46, 176, 456
Irish immigrants, 176, 212
Iron Curtain, 563
Iroquois Confederation, 5, 113
Irving, Washington, 211
Isabella (Queen of Castile), 5–6, 7
ISIS (ISIL), 691
Islam, 5
Islamic fundamentalism, 681–682
Isolationism, 525, 528
Israel: Camp David Accords, 635; Palestinians and, 660–661, 670; Six-Day War, 631, 635; U.S. policy toward, 660–661
Isthmus of Panama, 8
Italy, under Mussolini, 524

J

Jackson, Andrew, 155; election of 1824 and, 193–194; election of 1828 and, 194; Florida military campaign of, 158;

Indian policy of, 195–196, 343–344; nullification crisis and, 196–197; presidency of, 191, 195–199; spoils system and, 193, 199; in War of 1812, 141, 142
Jackson, Helen Hunt, 345
Jackson, Jesse, 658
Jackson, Thomas (Stonewall), 271
Jacksonian democracy, 191–193; historical perspective on, 199–200
James, William, 433
James I (King of England), 25, 26
James II (King of England), 33, 36, 37
Jamestown: early problems in, 25; founding of, 24, 25; political institutions in, 27
Japan: aggression into Manchuria, 521–523; China and, 521–523, 526; Cold War and, 566–567; "Gentlemen's Agreement," 419; militarism in, 525; opening of, 239; Pearl Harbor, 531, 537, 540; reconstruction of, 567; relations with, 419; Russo-Japanese War, 419; World War II and, 530–531, 536–537
Japanese Americans, during World War II, 534
Jay, John, 105; as delegate to First Continental Congress, 85; *Federalist Papers* and, 106; Jay Treaty and, 111–112
Jay Treaty (1794), 111–112
Jazz, 371
Jazz age, 479–480, 483
Jefferson, Thomas, 51, 105; Democratic-Republican party and, 114; election of 1800 and, 118, 131; election of 1804 and, 135; foreign policy of, 136; Hamilton and, 110–111, 118; Letter to Congressman John Holmes of Massachusetts, 228; Louisiana Purchase and, 132–134; Monroe Doctrine and, 165; presidency of, 131–136; as secretary of state, 110; as vice-president, 115; Virginia Resolution and, 117; writing of Declaration of Independence by, 88
Jenny, William Le Baron, 363
Jews, 49; Holocaust and, 536
Jim Crow laws, 349, 350, 372, 432
Jingoism, 412
Johns Hopkins University, 368
Johnson, Andrew, 278; election of 1866 and, 296; impeachment of, 297; Reconstruction under, 293–294; vetoes by, 294
Johnson, Hiram, 436
Johnson, James Weldon, 483
Johnson, Lady Bird, 606

Johnson, Lyndon B.: election of 1960 and, 601; election of 1964 and, 605; Great Society of, 605–606; presidency of, 604–606; Vietnam War and, 613–615; War on Poverty of, 604–605
Johnson, Tom L., 436
Johnston, Albert, 274
Jolliet, Louis, 10
Jones, Bobby, 480
Jones, Samuel M., 436
Jones Act (1916), 422
Joplin, Janis, 611
Joplin, Scott, 371
Josephson, Matthew, 332
Judicial branch, 109
Judicial impeachments, 135
Judicial review, 117, 134
Judiciary Act (1789), 110
The Jungle (Sinclair), 438

K

Kagan, Elena, 686
Kamikaze pilots, 537
Kansas, "Bleeding Kansas," 253–254
Kanagawa Treaty, 239
Kansas-Nebraska Act (1854), 249, 252–254
Karzai, Hamid, 682
Kavanaugh, Brett, 693
Kazin, Michael, 391
Kearney, Stephen, 234
Kelley, Florence, 437
Kelley, Oliver H., 351
Kellogg, Frank, 487
Kellogg-Briand Pact, 487
Kelly, William, 323
Kemp, Jack, 655, 668
Kennan, George F., 468, 563
Kennedy, Anthony, 658, 686
Kennedy, Edward, 655–656
Kennedy, Jacqueline, 601
Kennedy, John F.: assassination of, 603–604; civil rights and, 606–607; domestic policies of, 601–602; election of 1960 and, 600–601; foreign policy of, 602–603; inaugural address of, 600; presidency of, 600–604; Vietnam War and, 612–613
Kennedy, Robert, 616
Kent State, 626
Kentucky, 113; during Civil War, 269
Kentucky Resolution, 117
Kerouac, Jack, 592
Kerry, John, 684
Key, Francis Scott, 141
Keynes, John Maynard, 511

Keynesian economics, 511, 656
Khmer Rouge, 633
Khomeini, Ayatollah, 635
Khrushchev, Nikita, 586–587, 600, 602
Kindergarten, 367
King, Martin Luther, Jr., 589, 590, 606; assassination of, 608–609; leadership of, 607–608
King Cotton, 177–178, 274–275
King George's War, 69–70
King Philip's War, 31
King William's War, 69
Kinsey, Alfred, 611
Kissinger, Henry, 625, 627
Kitchen cabinet, of Jackson, 195
Kitchen debate, 600
Knights of Labor, 329–330, 365
Know-Nothing party, 176, 254, 255
Knox, Henry, 110
Kodak, 325
Kolko, Gabriel, 447
Korean armistice, 583
Korean War, 568–569, 579
Korematsu v. U.S., 534
Kosovo, 670
Ku Klux Klan, 302, 486, 589
Kuwait, 664
Kyoto Accord, 683

L

Labor: in 1920s, 479; child, 163, 329, 437, 443, 511; conflicts, 467; discontent, 328; factory, 163; laws, 437; organized, 174, 328–331; "Square Deal" for, 438; Taft-Hartley Act and, 560; during World War I, 460
Labor force: 1800–1860, 179; women in, 164, 281–282, 327
Ladies' Home Journal, 371
La Feber, Walter, 424
Laffer, Arthur, 655
La Follette, Robert, 435, 436, 477
Laissez-faire capitalism, 324–325, 380
Lakota Sioux, 4
Land, western, 163
Land-grant colleges, 367
Land grants, to railroads, 238, 320–321
Landon, Alf, 507
Land Ordinance (1785), 93
Laos, 583
La Salle, Robert de, 10
Las Casas, Bartolomé de, 11
Latin America: anti-American sentiment in, 582–583; dollar diplomacy in, 420; good-neighbor policy, 523–524; human rights

Novels, 592
Noyes, John Humphrey, 210
NSC-68, 566
Nuclear proliferation, 670
Nuclear Test Ban Treaty, 603
Nuclear weapons, 582
Nugent, Walter, 391
Nullification crisis, 196–197
Nursing, 282
Nye, Gerald, 525

O

Oakley, Annie, 372
Obama, Barack: election of 2008 and, 686; election of 2012 and, 690; first term of, 686–690; foreign policy of, 690–692, 691; keynote address by, 679; presidency of, 686–692; domestic policy of, 686–690
Obamacare, 687–688, 692–693
Obergefell v. Hodges, 689
Oberlin College, 213
Ocala platform, 352–353
O'Connor, Sandra Day, 658
Officeholders, rotation of, 193
Office of Equal Opportunity (OEO), 604
Office of Price Administration (OPA), 532
Office of Research and Development, 532–533
Office of War Information, 533
Office of War Mobilization (OWM), 532
Oglethorpe, James, 35, 69–70
Ohio, 175
Ohio Territory, 113
Oil embargo, 631–632
Oil industry, 323, 478, 488, 584
Okies, 512
Okinawa, Battle of, 537
Oklahoma, 340
Oklahoma City bombing, 667
Oklahoma Territory, 343
Old Lights, 50
Old Northwest, 173; agriculture in, 175; immigration to, 176
Olive Branch Petition, 87
Olmsted, Frederick Law, 364, 371
Olney, Richard, 412
Olympics (1980), 636
Omaha platform, 386–387, 391
"On Civil Disobedience" (Thoreau), 209
Oneida, 5
Oneida community, 210
O'Neill, Eugene, 481
O'Neill, William, 593
Onondaga, 5

Open Door policy, 416–417, 419, 420, 421, 487, 531
Open shops, 479
Operation Iraqi Freedom, 683–684
Operation Rolling Thunder, 613
Operation Torch, 536
Operation Wetback, 590
Opioid Epidemic, 695
Oppenheimer, J. Robert, 537
Oregon: boundary dispute in, 232, 233; settlement of, 236–238
Oregon Territory, 157
Oregon Trail, 343–344
Organization of Petroleum Exporting Countries (OPEC), 584, 631–632
Organized crime, 485
Organized labor: in Northeast, 174; struggles of, 328–331
Original sin, 207
Origin of Species (Darwin), 433
Orlando, Vittorio, 465
Ostend manifesto, 235–236
O'Sullivan, John L., 230, 313
Oswald, Lee Harvey, 604
Otis, James, 51, 52, 73, 74
Ottoman Empire, 681
Ottoman Turks, 5
Overland trails, 237
Overtime, 511
Owen, Robert, 210

P

Pacific Railway Act (1862), 281
Packaged foods, 326
Paine, Thomas, 51, 85, 87–88, 105, 129
Painting, 151; of 1920s, 482; of antebellum period, 211; colonial, 51; of Gilded Age, 369–370
Palestinian Liberation Organization (PLO), 635, 660–661
Palin, Sarah, 686
Palmer, A. Mitchell, 467
Palmer raids, 467
Panama: invasion of, 664; revolution in, 418
Panama Canal, 418, 422, 634
Pan-American conferences, 412, 523
Panics, 496; of 1819, 150, 153; of 1837, 198, 199, 693; of 1857, 239; of 1873, 302, 384; of 1893, 321, 387
Paperbacks, 591
Paper currency, 111, 384, 385
Paris, Treaty of (1783), 90–91, 103
Paris, Treaty of (1898), 415

Ringling Brothers Circus, 371
Rio Grande, 234
Ripley, George, 209
Road building, 152, 155, 161, 175
Roanoke settlement, 9
Robber Barons, 332
Roberts, John, 685
Roberts, Oral, 655
Robertson, Pat, 655
Robeson, Paul, 483
Robie House, 370
Robinson, Jackie, 588
Robinson, Jo Ann Gibson, 655
Rockefeller, John D., 323, 325, 332, 368, 403
Rock music, 591, 611
Rockwell, Norman, 533
Rocky Mountains, 181–182, 237, 339
Roe v. Wade, 629, 655, 658
Rolfe, John, 25
Rolling Stones, 611
Roman Catholics: in colonies, 49; conflict
   between Protestants and, 6, 10, 25–26;
   discrimination against, 176; election of
   1960 and, 601; England's break with, 9;
   immigrants, 365; Ottoman Turks threat
   to, 5; papal line of demarcation and, 8;
   prejudice against, 362; in Quebec, 75–76;
   slavery and, 181; victory over Moors, 5–6
Romania, 663
Romney, Mitt, 690
Roosevelt, Eleanor, 502, 512, 513
Roosevelt, Franklin D., 200, 521; background
   of, 502; death of, 535, 538; election of
   1932 and, 501–502; election of 1936
   and, 507–508; election of 1940 and, 529;
   election of 1944 and, 535; fireside chats
   of, 504; first hundred days, 503–505;
   foreign policy of, 523–527; Four
   Freedoms of, 530, 554; Native Americans
   and, 346; New Deal of, 502–512;
   quarantine speech, 526–527; reforms by,
   367; Supreme Court and, 509–510; World
   War II and, 528–533
Roosevelt, Theodore, 350; conservation and,
   439; death of, 475; election of 1912 and,
   441; election of 1916 and, 458; foreign
   policy of, 417–420; imperialism and, 411;
   on muckrakers, 434; Nobel Peace Prize
   of, 420; Panama Canal and, 418; pledge
   of loyalty, 551; presidency of, 437–439;
   progressivism and, 431; in Spanish-
   American War, 414; Square Deal of,
   437–439; trust-busting by, 438; as vice
   president, 416; on World War I, 457
Roosevelt Corollary, 418–419

Root, Elihu, 419
Root-Takahira Agreement (1908), 419
Rosenberg, Julius and Ethel, 571
Rosie the Riveter, 534
Roth, William, 655
Rough Riders, 414
Rousseau, Jean-Jacques, 77
Royal African Company, 37
Royal colonies, 24, 54
Ruggles, David, 215
Rural Electrification Administration (REA),
   507
Rush, Richard, 159
Rush-Bagot Agreement (1817), 157
Russia: 11, 158, 165, 454, 691–692
Russian Republic, 663, 669–670
Russian Revolution (1917–1922), 95, 459,
   463, 562
Russo-Japanese War, 419, 420
Rutgers University, 52
Ruth, Babe, 480

S

Sacco, Nicola, 485–486
Sadat, Anwar, 635
Saigon, fall of, 633
Salem, Peter, 89
Salinger, J. D., 592
SALT II treaty, 635, 663
Salt Lake City, Utah, 208, 238
Salvation Army, 365
Same-sex marriage, 689
Samoa, 411
Sampson, Deborah, 94
San Diego, California, 11
Sandinistas, 660
San Francisco, California, 11, 238
Sanger, Margaret, 445, 481
San Jacinto River, Battle of, 231
San Juan Hill, 414
Santa Anna, Antonio López de, 231
Saratoga, Battle of, 90
Savings and loans (S&Ls), 664–665
Scalawags, 298
Scalia, Antonin, 658, 689
The Scarlet Letter (Hawthorne), 211
Schechter v. U.S., 505
Schenck v. United States, 461
Schlesinger, Arthur M., Jr., 13, 200, 261,
   446–447, 489, 514, 625, 640
School prayer, 655
Schools. *See also* Education: for African
   Americans, 299; for blind and deaf
   persons, 213; desegregation of, 588–589;

T

Taft, Robert, 579
Taft, William Howard, 372; dollar diplomacy of, 420; election of 1912 and, 441; at National War Labor Board, 460; presidency of, 439–441; progressivism and, 431
Taft-Hartley Act (1947), 560
Taiwan, 567–568, 635, 670
Taliban, 682, 684
Tallmadge, James, 156
Tallmadge Amendment, 156
Tammany Hall, 364
Tampico incident, 423
Taney, Roger, 198, 256
Tarbell, Ida, 434
Tariffs, 153; of 1816, 151–152; in 1890s, 385; in 1920s, 498; of Abominations, 194, 196–197; Dingley, 390; Fordney-McCumber, 476, 488; Hawley-Smoot, 500; McKinley, 386, 387; Morrill, 280, 281; Payne-Aldrich, 440; protective, 110, 151–152, 385; reduction in, 442; state, 104; Underwood, 442; Wilson-Gorman, 388
Taverns, 48
Taxation without representation, 33, 74, 129
Tax cuts, 668; in 1920s, 478; by Bush, George W., 681; by Reagan, 655, 656–657, 658–659
Taxes: under Bush, George H. W., 664–665; on colonies, 71, 72–74; excise, 113; on farmers, 351; federal, 507; income, 280, 387, 388, 439
Taxpayers' revolt, 654–655
Taylor, Frederick W., 433, 478
Taylor, Zachary, 442; death of, 249; election of 1848 and, 248; in Mexican-American War, 233–234
Tea Act (1773), 75
Tea Party, 391, 688
Teapot Dome scandal, 476, 477
Technology: advances in, 5; boom, of 1990s, 668, 681; industrial, 238
Tecumseh, 138–139
Teheran Conference, 538
Telegraph, 238, 325, 387
Telephone, 325, 387
Televangelists, 655
Television, 591; election of 1960 and, 601
Teller Amendment, 414
Temperance movement, 212, 216, 367, 436–437
Tenements, 363
Ten-hour workday, 163, 437
Tennessee, 113; secession by, 269
Tennessee Valley Authority (TVA), 505

Tennis, 372
Tenochtitlán, 2
Tenth Amendment, 109
Tenure of Office Act (1867), 297
Term limits, 665
Territorial disputes, 247–248
Terrorism, domestic, 690; in Lebanon, 660; roots of, 681–682; September 11, 2001, 682; War on, 681–684
Tet offensive, 615
Texas: annexation of, 231, 232–233; cattle ranching in, 341–342; conflict over, 230–231; Republic of, 231; secession by, 259; Spanish settlement of, 10
Textile mills, 163, 174, 178, 238, 347, 479
Thames River, Battle of, 140
Thanksgiving, 26
Theaters, 371, 482
Think As a Historian, 20, 44, 62, 84, 102, 125, 149, 172, 190, 206, 223, 246, 267, 290, 310, 338, 359, 379, 397, 430, 453, 474, 495, 520, 546, 578, 599, 624, 647, 678, 700
Think tanks, 655
Third Amendment, 108
Third parties, 192
Third World, unrest in, 582–583
Thirteenth Amendment, 276, 282, 294
Thomas, Clarence, 664
Thomas, Norman, 551
Thoreau, Henry David, 209
Thorpe, Jim, 480
Three-Fifths Compromise, 105
Three Mile Island, 639
Thurmond, J. Strom, 560
Tiananmen Square, 662
Tilden, Samuel J., 302–303
Time zones, 320
Tippecanoe, Battle of, 138–139
Title IX, 628
Tobacco, 25, 28, 33
Tocqueville, Alexis de, 191
Tojo, Hideki, 567
Toland, John, 540
Tonkin Gulf Resolution, 613
Tordesillas, Treaty of (1494), 8
Tories, 89
Torture, 687
Total war, 277–278
Town meetings, 55
Townsend, Francis E., 509
Townshend, Charles, 73
Townshend Acts (1767), 73–74
Trade: Columbian Exchange, 7–8; expansion of, 6–7; foreign, 1805–1817, 137; fur, 12, 33, 232, 237; international, 238–239;

U.S. Steel Corporation, 323, 439, 467, 510
U.S. Term Limits Inc. v. Thorton, 665
U.S. v. Darby Lumber Co., 511
Utility companies, 436

V

Valentino, Rudolf, 480
Valladolid debate, 11
Vallandigham, Clement L., 279
Valley Forge, 89
Van Buren, Martin, 195; election of 1836 and,
    198; election of 1844 and, 232; election
    of 1848 and, 248; presidency of, 199
Vancouver Island, 233
Vanderbilt, Cornelius, 320
Vanderbilt, William H., 400
Vanderbilts, 326
Vanzetti, Bartolomeo, 485–486
Vasco da Gama, 6
Vaudeville, 371
Venezuela, 412
Venice, 6
Vermont, 113; War of 1812 and, 139
Verrazano, Giovanni da, 10
Versailles, Treaty of (1919), 464–466, 521
Vesey, Denmark, 179
Vespucci, Amerigo, 7, 13
Veterans: of World War I, 477, 501; of World
    War II, 557–558
Vice-president, 115
Vicksburg, Battle of, 277
Vietnam, 583; division of, 583–584
Vietnamization, 626
Vietnam War, 609; controversy over, 614–615;
    early stages of, 612–613; escalation of,
    613–614; historical perspective on, 617;
    Nixon and, 625–627; peace negotiations,
    615, 627; Tet offensive, 615; Tonkin Gulf
    Resolution, 613
Vikings, 5
Villa, Pancho, 423
Villard, Oswald Garrison, 549
Violence, against African Americans, 302,
    349, 443, 486
Virginia: House of Burgesses, 27, 28, 54,
    73, 74; Jamestown, 24, 25, 27; labor
    shortages in, 28–29; ratification of
    Constitution by, 107; as royal colony, 54;
    secession by, 269; slaves laws in, 37
Virginia City, Nevada, 341
Virginia Company, 25, 26, 27, 28
Virginia Plan, 105
Virginia Resolution, 117
Volcker, Paul, 636

Volstead Act (1919), 484–485
Voter participation, 435
Voting: after American Revolution, 91; in
    colonies, 54–55
Voting rights: for African Americans, 297,
    606, 608; for women, 366–367, 445
Voting Rights Act (1965), 606, 608

W

Wabash v. Illinois, 352
Wade, Benjamin, 295, 300
Wade, Richard C., 373
Wade-Davis Bill (1864), 292
Wage earners, 327
Wages, 164; minimum, 511, 561
Wage slaves, 251
Wagner Act (1935), 507, 508, 510
Walden (Thoreau), 209
Walesa, Lech, 662–663
Walker, David, 215
Walker, William, 236
Walker expedition, 236
Wallace, George, 391, 607, 616–617, 629
Wallace, Henry, 535, 560
Wall Street, crash of 1929, 497
Wampanoags, 31
War bonds, 461, 533
Ward, Lester F., 368
War debts: from American Revolution, 104,
    110; from World War I, 488, 500
War Democrats, 278
War hawks, 139, 140, 615
War of 1812: causes of, 138–139; division
    over, 139–140; Hartford Convention and,
    141; legacy of, 142; military defeats and
    naval victories in, 140–141; opposition
    to, 140; Treaty of Ghent, 141
War on Poverty, 604–605
War on Terrorism, 681–684
War Powers Act (1973), 631
War Production Board (WPB), 531
War profiteers, 280–281
War propaganda: in World War I, 457, 461; in
    World War II, 533
Warren, Earl, 579, 588, 604, 609–610
Warren, Joseph, 128
Warren Commission, 604
War reparations, from World War I, 488
Warsaw Pact, 565, 586
Washington, Booker T., 350, 443
Washington, D.C.: burning of, in War of 1812,
    141; establishment of, 110
Washington, George, 104; in American
    Revolution, 88–89, 90; biography of,